Volume 1

A General History of
China's Foreign Trade

Volume 1

A General History of
China's Foreign Trade

Yuqin Sun
University of International Business and Economics, China

Xu Chang
Chinese Academy of Social Sciences, China

Translated by

Rui Su
Northwest University, China

Robin Gilbank
Northwest University, China

World Scientific

NEW JERSEY · LONDON · SINGAPORE · BEIJING · SHANGHAI · HONG KONG · TAIPEI · CHENNAI · TOKYO

Published by

World Scientific Publishing Co. Pte. Ltd.

5 Toh Tuck Link, Singapore 596224

USA office: 27 Warren Street, Suite 401-402, Hackensack, NJ 07601

UK office: 57 Shelton Street, Covent Garden, London WC2H 9HE

Library of Congress Cataloging-in-Publication Data

Names: Sun, Yuqin, 1965–   author. | Chang, Xu, 1983–   author. | Su, Rui (Translator) |
    Gilbank, Robin (Translator).
Title: A General History of China's Foreign Trade / Yuqin Sun, University of International
    Business and Economics, China, Xu Chang, Chinese Academy of Social Sciences,
    China ; translated by Rui Su and Robin Gilbank, Northwest University, China.
Other titles: Zhongguo Duiwai Maoyi Tongshi (Di-Yi Juan).
Description: Hackensack, NJ: World Scientific, [2024] | Includes bibliographical references and index.
Identifiers: LCCN 2022013198 | ISBN 9789811256424 (hardcover) |
    ISBN 9789811256431 (ebook) | ISBN 9789811256448 (ebook other)
Subjects: LCSH: China—Commerce.
Classification: LCC HF3834.Z48413 2024 | DDC 380.10951--dc23/eng/20220505
LC record available at https://lccn.loc.gov/2022013198

British Library Cataloguing-in-Publication Data
A catalogue record for this book is available from the British Library.

中国对外贸易通史 (第一卷)
Originally published in Chinese by University of International Business and Economics Press
Copyright © University of International Business and Economics Press, 2018

This book is published with financial support from the Chinese Fund for the
Humanities and Social Sciences.

For any available supplementary material, please visit
https://www.worldscientific.com/worldscibooks/10.1142/12838#t=suppl

Desk Editors: Nandhakumar Krishnan/Nicole Ong

Typeset by Stallion Press
Email: enquiries@stallionpress.com

Preface

China boasts a long history of foreign trade. As early as the pre-Qin period around the early 2nd century BCE, residents of the country began to ship silk and other merchandise on outbound voyages. From the 2nd century BCE, the ancient China was connected to the outside world via the later called Overland and Maritime Silk Road initiated during the reign of the Han Emperor Wu of the western Han Dynasty (141–87 BCE). China's trade relations with foreign countries and regions began to sprout and continued to forge ahead. Trade contacts drove Sino-foreign economic and cultural communications to such an extent that the Chinese civilization benefited all mankind on the one hand, while learning from and absorbing the splendid achievements in civilization from other countries on the other hand. Communications of this sort allowed the Chinese economy and culture to prosper and progress alongside its foreign counterparts.

Constrained by socio-economic patterns, the Sino-foreign political and economic landscape, different ideology as well, the development of China's foreign trade appeared to be a tortuous process. For the sake of national defense and security, the Silk Road was created in the reign of the Han Emperor of Wu (r. 141–87 BCE). Objectively speaking, this opened up a channel for economic and cultural exchanges between China and the outside world. From then on, China engaged increasingly in extensive exchanges, politically, economically and culturally, with other countries and peoples through the ancient Overland and Maritime Silk Road. Trade during this period was characterized by a limited scale of interaction and was dominated by luxury goods, with only a small stratum of the aristocracy being its direct beneficiaries. Nevertheless, a large number of foreign vi A General History of China's Foreign Trade (Vol. 1)

plant strains were introduced into China via trade activities, thus enriching the variety of Chinese crops and improving the welfare of the general population. Meanwhile, China, as a relatively economically developed country, possessed advanced production technologies. The gradual outward transmission of these, together with trade activities, was to prove beneficial to the improvement of social productivity in countries and regions along the Silk Road.

The Wei, Jin, Southern and Northern Dynasties (220–581 CE) witnessed constant disputes between ethnic groups. Politically, China was split into two halves: the north and the south. The economy fell victim to these internal wars, with the socio-economic basis for developing foreign trade being weakened. Fortunately, however, in order to expand their habitable space, both the northern and southern regimes were committed to maintaining the smooth flow and security of the Silk Road. The situation thus facilitated the continuation and further development of foreign economic communication along the overland and maritime Silk Road.

During the Sui and Tang Dynasties (581–907 CE), China once again achieved unprecedented national unity. Under the active policy of opening up to the outside world, the trade boom along the Overland Silk Road, particularly trade with Central Asia, developed to a new peak. In the late Tang Dynasty, the Maritime Silk Road played an increasingly important role in China's foreign trade due to the shifting of China's economic center of gravity toward the south as well as improvements in shipbuilding and navigation technologies.

The Song Dynasty (960–1279) was faced with a serious internal financial crisis. Therefore, greater attention was paid to overseas trade, and regulations were issued to promote its development. The improvement in shipbuilding technology and the application of the compass to navigation provided technological guarantees for the development of overseas trade. Therefore, the number of foreign trade partners increased substantially and the range of merchandise was enriched and diversified. Many daily necessities began to enter overseas markets. For instance, coarse and heavy pottery jars and urns were exported to Southeast Asia. Meanwhile, a large number of common spices, like pepper, were imported into the country. Such trade activities directly benefited the lives of ordinary people. The introduction of Champa rice not only promoted the further development of the economy of the south, but also relieved food shortages among the masses. On the whole, people's basic survival condition was further improved.

During the Yuan Dynasty (1206–1368), impediments were removed from overland and marine transportation in the Eurasian region. The bettering of transport conditions triggered the revival of the Overland Silk Road. Meanwhile, the Maritime Silk Road came to connect the country with more foreign regions. Sino-foreign trade, particularly with Asian, African and European countries, was further enhanced to a new level.

In the early years of the Ming Dynasty, private Sino-foreign trade was prohibited since the government implemented a strict policy of curbing overseas transport. This was intended to prevent harassment from Japanese pirates and various rebellious forces along China coastal areas. In the early 15th century, the world-famous admiral Zheng He's expeditions to foreign countries largely helped to prolong the Maritime Silk Road and the development of official trade between China and foreign countries reached a new high. China's traditional trade pattern changed dramatically after the 16th century as Europeans gradually came to China. Under the threat of colonization from western powers and in the dying days of the imperial society, the Ming and Qing rulers strenuously defended the established order of governance. The highly matured political systems of the two dynasties, founded on feudalism, were their bedrock. Their foreign policy took a conservative turn, with trading activities with other nations being subject to severe restrictions. China pitifully fell into an increasingly passive and disadvantageous position in its trade with the European colonizers. Being at that time self-important, complacent and reactionary, China failed to secure the expected benefits from trading silk and tea leaves with other countries in spite of the fact that China deserved to reap greater gains by virtue of its supremacy in these commodities. Unfortunately, the nation lost its original leading position in the world economy entirely.

After the Opium War of 1839–1842, China was forced to embark on the road of opening up. This openness was induced through military invasion by western powers. China was forced to sign a swathe of unequal treaties. Consequently, the country was reduced to a semi-colonial and semi-feudal fiefdom. What had been a tradition of independent feudal foreign trade, had at that time denatured into a modern yet semi-colonial foreign trade. By virtue of their strong economic and technological might and power politics, the western countries pressurized China to accept a series of modern institutional arrangements that compelled China's economic development to conform to their own interests. Gradually, they wrested control of China's political and economic lifelines and drew

China into the orbit of western capitalist economic development. The country became a sales market and a supplier of raw materials for western industrial goods, and its foreign trade thus took on a semi-colonized character.

The development of foreign trade during 1840–1949 brought China into the global economy. Consequently, the prosperity and depression of the world economy, as well as any fluctuation in the international market, would influence profoundly the development of China's foreign trade and further impact upon its national economy. Capitalist powers competed for dominance over foreign trade with China and the control of the Chinese economy. China's semi-colonized state, in the first instance, affected its normal development of foreign trade and inhibited the capacity of foreign trade to promote the economic development in the second.

In the first half of the 20th century, China's political situation was turbulent, with constant internal disputes and external invasions by Japanese militarists. The social economy was severely damaged and its foreign trade was dealt a fatal blow.

Since the founding of the People's Republic of China in 1949, China has vanquished completely the domination of western powers, putting an end to the semi-colonial foreign trade. Nevertheless in the 30 years from the early 1950s to the end of the 1970s, China's foreign trade developed slowly and stayed outdated. This was as a result of the embargoes imposed by western countries, the deterioration of Sino–Soviet relations, the constraints of the outdated planned economy and other factors. Thanks to the Third Plenary Session of the Eleventh Central Committee of the Communist Party of China held in 1978, the national policy of Reform and Opening-up was established. China's foreign trade accelerated and her integration with the global economy was deepened. Since the beginning of the 21st century, China has become a major partner in the world arena with her foreign trade having played an increasingly important role in the development of the national economy. At the same time, international economic and trade competition continues to intensify day by day. China therefore has to confront a series of international contradictions and conflicts of different sorts.

The lived reality of today is the extension of all past history. By compiling a systematic study of more than two thousand years of China's trade with foreign countries, we can define the context of China's foreign trade development, and summarize the experiences and lessons as well. Doing so will not only enable us to better understand the past, but allow us to utilize history as a reference for understanding the situation of the present and move forward from being a major trading country to a trading power. This study will also yield historical wisdom for the construction of the Belt and Road Initiative.

The series encompasses four volumes. The first volume comprises the section on the ancient China, covering foreign trade from the pre-Qin Dynasty to the early Qing. The second volume covers the modern China section, dealing with the foreign trade from the end of the Qing dynasties to the Republic of China period (1912–1949). The third volume is the contemporary section, focusing on more than 60 years of development of China's foreign trade since 1949. The fourth volume is a picture album, illustrating the history of the development of China's foreign trade.

This series was written with the assistance of several young co-authors. Chief editor Yuqin Sun cooperated closely, from the overall structure of the book to the specific content of the series. As a professor at University of International Business and Economics, Sun wrote Chapters 1–6 (Vol. 1), part of Chapters 7 and 8 (Vol. 1), Chapters 1, 2, 5, and part of Chapter 6 (Vol. 2). Those coauthors are as follows: Jinwen Chen, a professor at Beijing Technology and Business University, wrote Chapters 3 and 4 (Vol. 2); Yun Qu, an associate researcher at the Institute of Economics of Chinese Academy of Social Sciences, did Chapters 1–5 (Vol. 3); Qinghong Jiang, an associate researcher at the Institute of Modern History of Chinese Academy of Social Sciences, part of Chapters 5 and 6 (Vol. 2); Qian Sun, an associate professor at the UIBE, part of the fourth volume; Xu Chang, an associate researcher at the Institute of Economics of Chinese Academy of Social Sciences, Chapter 7, part of Chapter 8 (Vol. 1) and part of Chapters 1 and 2 (Vol. 2); Weiwei Wang, an associate professor at the University of Chinese Academy of Social Sciences, Chapter 6 (Vol. 3); Luqing Zhang, an associate professor at Capital Normal University, Chapter 7 (Vol. 3); Chunfang Zheng, a professor at Beijing Union University, Chapters 8 and 9 (Vol. 3); and Dr. Xiaoli Su, working at the Center for Development Strategy Research of China Electronics Technology Group Co., Ltd., Chapter 10 (Vol. 3).

In addition, those who helped in providing images or taking photographs, include Ruizhe Li (an associate professor at Northwest University), Xu Chang (an associate researcher at the Institute of Economics of Chinese Academy of Social Sciences); colleagues at the UIBE include Mei Ye, Hu Wang, Yahong Cao, Haijun Liu; students at the UIBE, include Jianshu Li, Yuxuan Zhou, Yang Zhang, Enyan Xing,

Hao Luo, Mei Xie, Le Zhao, Shuo Yu, and Chang Xu; overseas students from Greece include Marianna Erotokritou and Sofia Erotokritou. And Ping Liu, a doctoral candidate at the UIBE, assisted in the proofreading. I owe my sincere thanks to all the aforementioned.

The chief editor helped closely in the preparation of the text. To ensure this series is consistent in academic style, the chief editor conducted supplementary work, made some additions and integrated all the materials. Any original academic contribution arising from this series is jointly credited to the coauthors. Factual errors and typing mistakes have been avoided wherever possible. Experts and readers are welcome to contribute their valuable opinions and criticisms.

Yuqin Sun
University of International Business and Economics

Acknowledgments

The debts incurred in completing a translation project over a three-year period are numerous. Indeed, the personal influences are too many to list on this page. I might begin with Prof. Hoover, who first discussed the application of this translation project with me, and Prof. Haitang Ren, whose encouragement and assistance in every aspect of my research is beyond words of thanks.

The publishers and contributors to this book would like to thank the Editors-in-Chief of the original volume, Professor Yuqin Sun and Xu Chang, for permission to produce an English version of their work.

I owe much to Dr. Robin Stephen Gilbank, who worked as a co-translator and proofread the English text. My sincere thanks go to my dear young assistants Jiale He (Northwest University), Yingdi Zhao (Shaanxi Institute of International Trade and Commerce) and Dr. Peng Li (Xi'an Medical University) who worked as project members and assistants helping closely in draft translation, text alignment, terminology consistency, literature mining and analysis.

Thanks are due to editors at the University of International Business and Economics Press, Ms. Dai Dong, Ms. Yuhong Guo and Mr. Peifeng Chen for their help in negotiating the contracts and handling communications between the parties involved.

The author and translators wish to thank World Scientific for bringing this publication to fruition and the Chinese Fund for the Humanities and Social Sciences for its financial support.

My special thanks are extended to Ms. Dandan Zhao and Mr. Fengqing Li in the Social Science Department at Northwest University for their support during the project application process.

About the Authors

 **Yuqin Sun** is Professor and Doctoral Supervisor in the School of International Trade and Economics at the University of International Business and Economics (UIBE). She holds a doctoral degree in Economics and has served as a visiting scholar at the University of Colorado at Boulder. She is the Vice President of the Society of Chinese Commercial History and the Director of the China Foreign Trade History UIBE branch.

Her main research areas include the history of China's foreign trade, economic history, and international trade theory and policy. She has published dozens of papers in journals including *International Business, Journal of International Trade* and *Intertrade*. She has edited several textbooks, and authored or coauthored a number of books, among which, *A General History of Chinese Business* (a collaborative work) won the 13th Sun Yefang Economic Science Award in November in 2009, the first prize in the 13th Excellent Achievement Awards in Philosophy and Social Sciences in Beijing in 2014, and the First Huozhi Award from the Society of Chinese Commercial History in 2015.

Xu Chang is associate researcher at the Institute of Economics of Chinese Academy of Social Sciences. He is mainly engaged in the study of modern Chinese economic history, and has published articles on modern Chinese foreign trade and state-owned enterprise reform, respectively, in the *Journal of Tsinghua University* (*Philosophy and Social Sciences Edition*), *Researches in Chinese Economic History* and *Contemporary China History Studies*.

About the Translators

 **Rui Su** is Associate Professor in English Literature at Northwest University (NWU). She received her PhD from Shanghai International Studies University (SISU) and MA from NWU. She was a visiting scholar at Southern Utah University and Harvard University in 2015–2016. Her major academic interests include translation studies and Chinese American English Literature studies. She is the author and translator of *Western Culture Screened: Exploring Culture through the Cinema and Television Series* (2022), *Is the Author Dead? Textual Research into Contemporary Western Literary Theories* (2022), *Ancient Chinese Theater Stages: Research and Conservation* (2022), *Translating the Bible into Chinese: Framing Readerly Perspective* (2021), *An English Guide to Shaanxi Intangible Folk Culture* (2021), *A Guidance Manual on Mental Health during the NCP Outbreak* (2020), *50 Questions and Answers about the Prevention and Control of COVID-19* (2020), *The Blood Red Sun* (2019), *The Howl of the Wolf* (2019), *How Old Dan Became a Tree* (2017), *and Old Land, New Tales* (2011).

 **Robin Gilbank** was born in North Yorkshire, UK, and is Associate Professor in English Literature at Northwest University, Xi'an. He is the author of *The Prettiest Liar* (2012), *An Englishman in the Land of Qin* (2018), *Exploring China* (2018) and *Selected Readings of the English Novel* (2022). His main interests include medieval literature, the history of foreign residents in Western China and the translation of local Shaanxi literature into English.

Contents

Chapter 1

Foreign Trade prior to the Han Dynasty

Over the years, production within human society has grown to be bifurcated into two parts, namely agriculture and manufacturing. There then emerged a situation whereby production was undertaken with the purpose of exchange. That is to say the first stage was commodity production, followed by trade within tribes, then trade along tribal boundaries, and finally trade overseas. It can therefore be concluded that foreign trade, as a social and economic activity, has been in existence since late primitive society.

China is blessed with a brilliant ancient civilization. Sharing borders with quite a few countries and nations, this vast land also possesses a wave-lapped seaboard. China's foreign trade enjoys a long history. Prior to the Han Dynasty, ancient Chinese people were seen to do business, over land and on the sea, with people in other countries and nations.

1.1 Communication between the East and West in Ancient Times

It has been confirmed by numerous literary and archaeological materials that economic and cultural exchanges have been taking place between the Central Plains, known as the cradle of Chinese civilization, and neighboring countries at least since as far back as the Xia and Shang Dynasties.

In the ancient Chinese classic *Master Zhuang: Heaven and Earth*, it is recorded how "the Yellow Emperor traveled to the areas along the northern bank of the Chishui River and climbed to the summit of the

Kunlun Mountains — the mountain of jade — in order to survey the south."
A political commentator and littérateur named Jia Yi also describes in his
work the *Political Essays of Jiayi* how "the Yellow Emperor trudged
through the desert and ascended to the summit of the Kunlun Mountains;
Emperor Yao once trekked through the desert to visit the *Xi Wangmu*
(Queen Mother of the west), a legendary matriarch. *Master Xun: The
Great Strategy* states that: "Emperor Yu once pursued his studies in the
countries ruled by the Queen Mother of the west." In addition, *Bamboo
Annals* records that "in the 9th year of his reign, Emperor Shun was
visited by the Queen Mother of the west with white jade rings being paid
as tributes." What is also mentioned here is how the Qusou people (an
ancient Central Asian country people) submitted to the rule of Emperor
Yao.

Produced during the Warring States Period, the *Tale of King Mu, Son
of Heaven* describes what happened 3,000 years ago when King Mu, the
5th monarch of the Zhou Dynasty, traveled westward in carriages pulled
by eight horses with quantities of silk products and other items.

Embarking from Haojing (present-day Xi'an), King Mu, accompanied by a retinue of about 20,000 persons, arrived in the Quanrong region,
on the south bank of the Hutuo River, by way of Henan Province. Then
they moved westward along the Yellow River, arriving in Xinjiang by way
of the Hexi Corridor and reached the Kunlun Mountains, where they purchased cartloads of raw jade and thousands of jade artifacts. Afterward,
they continued their journey westward, eventually reaching the areas in
the possession of the Queen Mother of the west. King Mu gifted her with
exquisite silk. They were received so warmly that King Mu was almost
reduced to a slave of pleasure and forgot all about going home.

Later on, King Mu and his people traveled 2,000 *li* (equivalent to
1,000 kilometers) northward along the northern bank of the Black River
to the Central Asian prairie and returned to China by way of the Yili River
Valley, north of the Tian Shan Mountains. Whenever his journey brought
him to a new part of the western regions, King Mu gave silk products,
bronze products and cowries (used as money in ancient times) to local
tribal chiefs as presents. In return they received horses, cattle and sheep
as well as various kinds of local specialties.

According to researchers, King Mu of Zhou took the following route
when traveling westward. He, together with his people, began his journey
from today's Shaanxi Province, by way of Henan Province, Shanxi
Province and as far as Inner Mongolia; they then crossed the Yellow

River, passed through Ningxia, Gansu and Qinghai. After negotiating the Kunlun Mountains and the Pamir Mountains (Mountain Range), they finally set foot on the Iranian Plateau in Central Asia.

The *Tale of King Mu, Son of Heaven* was set down in the Spring and Autumn Period (770–476 BCE) and Warring States Period (475–221 BCE). It is formed on the basis of tales, including King Mu's expedition to the Quanrong[1] tribal peoples and his romance with the Queen Mother of the west. The contents cannot therefore be treated as trustworthy. However, the book does, to some extent, reflect on situation in transportation and trade between the Central Plains and northwestern China as well as with areas in Central Asia in ancient times.

In modern times, archaeological excavations at home and abroad have continued to supply supporting evidence, providing further proof as to the truth of the past. In 1976, a quantity of jade products were unearthed from the tomb of Fu Hao[2] in Anyang, Henan Province. Scientific investigations determined that the discovered funerary items originated from Xinjiang, where seashells from the southeast coast of China and the coast of the Indian Ocean have also been found.

Investigations have further helped to reveal the connections, both direct and indirect, between the Yin and Shang cultures in China and Bronze Age culture as far afield as Siberia and Europe. For instance, along the upper reaches of the Yenisei River and the E'bi River where the Karasuk culture flourished (13th century BCE–8th century BCE), 30 items of pottery *ding*[3] *and li*[4], and many bronze wares, such as bronze knives and bow-like objects apparently conforming to the Shang Dynasty style, were found. These bore a striking resemblance to the Anyang troves. When compared with their counterparts excavated in Anyang, the only difference determined was in the number of loops on the unearthed bronze spears and copper arrowheads. The copper spears bear only one loop on one side while the specimens from Anyang possess two on both sides.

---

[1] The Quanrong or Dog Rong were an ethnic group, classified by the ancient Chinese as "Qiang," active in the northwestern part of China during and after the Zhou Dynasty.

[2] The queen of the Shang Dynasty. She was not only an outstanding administrator, but also the earliest female general who had won many battles.

[3] One of the standard vessels for food sacrificing. Generally, it has two looped handles and three or four legs.

[4] *Li* is a round-bellied food container with three hollow legs which was used from early Shang times to late Warring States.

Documents and cultural relics have confirmed that further to the land route across the northwest, economic exchanges were conducted between the Bashu areas in southwestern China and South Asian countries as early as the Shang and Zhou Dynasties. Seashells and pieces of ivory found in historic sites of the ancient Bashu culture, like the Sanxingdui and Jinsha in Sichuan Province, are generally thought to have come from the vicinity of the Indian Ocean.

When heavy bronze wares were transported westward, delicate Chinese silk products flowed unabated across mountains and along rivers into Central Asia, West Asia and even Europe.

1.2 The Ancient Trade in Silk in other Regions and Countries

China was among the first countries to begin silkworm rearing and silk reeling from very ancient times. But as to the exact time when the practice started, there is disagreement in ancient documentary sources. Some ascribe the origin to Fu Hsi,[5] some say Shennong (Divine Husbandman), and still others cite Leizu, the legendary wife of the mythical Yellow Emperor and discoverer of sericulture, and daughter of Lady Hsi-Ling-Shih, who was ascribed by Chinese legend as Goddess of Silk.

The aforesaid can be regarded as myths and legends and so should be treated with skepticism. In effect, the skills of rearing and reeling came to fruition after years of practical experience accumulated by hardworking artisans.

But it is safe to assert that China has enjoyed a long history of raw silk production. In 1958, a collection of processed silk textile fragments, silk thread and other silk remains were discovered at the Qianshanyang Archaeological Site of the Neolithic Culture in Wuxing, Zhejiang Province. Following authentication, it was established that these unearthed items dated back to about 4,700 years, thus bolstering the argument that raw silk production had been practiced since the Yin and Shang Dynasties of China.

---

[5]Fu Hsi was the first of the Three Sovereigns of ancient China who was credited with being the originator of the *I Ching* (also known as the *Yi Jing* or *Zhou Yi*). His long reign varies between sources from 115 years (2852–2737 BCE) to 116 years (2952–2836 BCE).

During the course of the continuous development of the craft in the Shang Dynasty, Chinese characters, such as *can* (silkworm) and *si* (silk) began to appear in oracle bone inscriptions. Other excavated articles include delicate embroidery and shadow-stitched satin, indicating comparatively advanced silk weaving skills.

In the Western Zhou Dynasty, the silk industry emerged in many places, including Yanzhou and Qingzhou in Shandong Province, Xuzhou and Yangzhou in Jiangsu Province, Jingzhou in Hubei Province and Yuzhou in Henan Province. There were two modes of production: the state-run and the privately owned.

The Spring and Autumn Period saw the application of iron-made tools, which further enhanced the evolution of silk-related skills. *The Book of Songs: A Simple Fellow*[6] records that "a simple fellow, all smiles/Brought cloth to exchange for thread", referring to how an idiot young man brought money (*bu* — cloth) with him to buy silk in the market. Sima Qian's *Records of the Grand Historian: Biographies of Celebrated Merchants* includes an account of a businessman named Bai Gui who earned healthy profits through his transactions in the Warring States Period. His secret was to "buy in grain at harvest when the price was low and sell off silk and paint when their price was high, whereas silkworm cocoons should be bought in the season when silkworms produced a lot of cocoons and likewise grain should be sold off then."

With the development of silk production, trade in silk fabrics gradually reached a saturation point in the Central Plains and had to push outwards. In the 1970s, pieces of silk fabric produced by residents of the Central Plains in the Warring States Period were found at the eastern entrance of Alagou at Turpan in Xinjiang Uyghur Autonomous Region. They are believed by Chinese archaeologists to have originated from the Central Plains of China.

According to *Records of the Grand Historian: Biographies of Celebrated Merchants*, a Qin Dynasty merchant named Wushiluo became rich rapidly by transporting silk from the Central Plains to western China in exchange for horses and cattle. It states that "(he was adept at) animal husbandry, selling beasts when there were too many animals on the market, then buying in rare treasures and silk products, and covertly sending them to the King of the Rong. In return, the King of the Rong rewarded him with so many animals — ten times as much as he paid in his previous purchase

---

[6] A diaspora man. Maybe a person who lost his land and wandered in the state of Wei.

of the measures — that they measured them in the way they measured grains. Meanwhile, Wushiluo was declared by Qin Shi Huang[7] to be of equal rank to a minister, having the right to meet the Emperor with other officials at the given time."

As early as the 1950s, Soviet archaeologists uncovered a batch of stone-topped tombs belonging to nobles of the 5th century BC in the Altai area of Central Asia. "Being securely sealed, those tombs served to preserve very well the Chinese silk products and other items found therein." Excavated from the tomb No. 3 in the Pazyryk area of the Ulagai River Basin were there was "very delicate satin silk, the embroidery on which consists of loop-like needlework in colorful silk thread. The subject of the embroidery is a male phoenix perching on a tree, while a female phoenix flying around it."

According to the *Behistun Inscription* in Persian found in Iran in West Asia, by the second half of the 5th century BC Chinese silk was to be found in the markets of Persia.

As for South Asia, in India, a book titled *Arthasastra* written in the 4th century BCE by Kautiliya, an Indian philosopher and economist, records how "China produces silk, some of which is transported and sold in India."

In Europe, fragments of clothing made from Chinese silk were found by German archaeologists in an ancient tomb dating back to 500 BCE in Hochdouf Village, Stuttgart, Germany.

In ancient Greece, clothes worn by figures depicted on sculptures and ceramic paintings are considered to be Chinese silk products of the 5th century BCE. These include the transparent Chinese silk-made chiton on the Parthenon Fates and on the Erechtheion Karyatids.

The above records make it clear that Chinese silk was being sold in the west at least as early as the Warring States Period, making silk the first Chinese product known to western people. China, therefore, came to be known as *Seres*, "the country of silk."

In summary, prior to Zhang Qian's being dispatched to Serindia in the Han Dynasty, the Silk Road had appeared to be operating as an international trading route, characterized mainly by the exchange of silk and silk products.

---

[7]Also known as Shihuangdi, Emperor (r. 221–210 BCE) of the Qin Dynasty (221–208 BCE) and creator of the first unified Chinese empire.

1.3 The Formation of East–West Transportation

From the 6th century BCE to the 4th century BCE, the ancient Persian Empire in West Asia possessed great national strength. In its heyday, its boundaries stretched from the east bank of the Mediterranean in the west, to the Indus River Valley in the east, and from the Syr Darya in the north to the Amu Darya in the south. Within this empire, the transportation was well-developed, with courier routes branching all over the empire to connect Central Asia with West Asia and South Asia and farther with Eurasia.

Meanwhile in the 4th century BCE, the eastward conquests of Alexander of Macedonia helped the route to expand from the Mediterranean to Pamir. In 334 BCE, troops under Alexander's command set off from Macedonia to conquer Asia Minor and Syria in the east, then Egypt in the south, followed by the acquisition of Mesopotamia — the land "between the rivers" (Tigris and Euphrates Rivers) — the ancient Persian Empire and the Indus River Valley. After decades of wars, Alexander established an empire, stretching across Europe, Asia and Africa. Following his death, the empire split into several independent smaller entities, among which the Syria-centered Seleucid Empire was vast in territory, embracing at its peak the sprawling lands between the Indus and the eastern bank of the Mediterranean. This forcefully drove the expansion of the trading route from the west of Pamir to the Mediterranean.

To the east of Pamir, within the territory of China, the State of Qin grew in might during the Spring and Autumn Period. Consequently, it persistently waged wars with and overthrew many Western Rong barbarian states located to the northwest of the Qin territory (modern-day Shaanxi, Gansu, Qinghai and Ningxia). It was not until the Warring States Period that all the Western Rong barbarian states were swallowed up by the Qin, thereby guaranteeing smooth transportation from Central Plains to the west of the Yellow River.

To the west of the Western Rong, prior to the Han Dynasty, there lived many ancient Chinese peoples, such as the Sakas, the Yuezhi people and the Wusun people. They led a nomadic existence along the Hexi Corridor, and gradually migrated to Xinjiang and the west of Pamir.

Sakas were the pre-Qin "Yunrong," one of the minorities in northwest China. They used to dwell in Dunhuang along the Hexi Corridor and were driven by the Yuezhi people to migrate to Central Asia after climbing over the Pamir Mountains. In the course of their westward migration, the Sakas brought Chinese silk with them for trade. It is inferred that the owner of the Pazyryk Cemetery in Central Asia was a Saka noble.

The Yuezhi people were at one time scattered between Dunhuang and Qilian, and were powerful enough during the Spring and Autumn Period to drive the Sakas to the west. Nevertheless, they were defeated by the Xiongnu (nomadic tribes) in the early years of the Han Dynasty and compelled to move westward to the Ili River Basin, where the Sakas lived. They then drove away the Sakas and dominated their territory. Generally, in the second half of the reign of Laoshang Chanyu[8] (the supreme tribal leader) of the Xiongnu from 174 BCE to 161 BCE, a number of the Yuezhi people were elbowed out by the Xiongnu-supported Wusun people to move southward to the Guishui area (present-day Amu Darya) and were called the Greater Yuezhi. Those who did not migrate but chose to cohabit with the Qiang people in the Qilian Mountain were named the Lesser Yuezhi in history books.

The Wusun people who formerly lived in the Hexi Corridor and Dunhuang were subject to constant harassment from the Yuezhi people. With the support of the Xiongnu, they migrated into the Ili River Basin, driving away the Yuezhi, and founding, on the land where the Yuezhi people used to live, a Wusun state centered in Tianchi (present-day Issyk-Kul Lake).

The Sakas, the Yuezhi, the Wusun and other nomadic peoples continuously migrated on a large scale to the Hexi Corridor, Xinjiang and then Central Asia. This aided directly the formation of the transportation routes from the Hexi Corridor to Xinjiang, and from China to Central Asia.

To conclude, prior to the Han Dynasty, a transportation route between the East and the West had been formed, along which silk was perpetually traded. However, foreign trade of this sort was operated without governmental intervention. Trade between China and other countries during this period was consigned to being civil, non-recurrent and border-wandering in nature, owing to the lack of forceful support and protection from governments and the partial inaccessibility of some places along the route.

---

[8]Laoshang, whose personal name was Jiyu, was a Chanyu of the Xiongnu Empire who succeeded his father Modu Chanyu in 174 BCE. Under his reign, the Xiongnu Empire continued to expand against the Yuezhi and the Xiongnu thus gained control of the Hexi Corridor.

Chapter 2

Foreign Trade in the Western and Eastern Han Dynasties

The Qin and Han Dynasties witnessed China becoming unified and further establishing a centralized feudal empire, thereby turning over a new page in China's national history. China's outbound development gradually accelerated with the development of its feudal economy and national power. The overland and seaway connections between the Chinese feudal government and foreign countries and nations became active in politics as well as economy. The gradual intervention of the feudal government in foreign trade became more extensive, thus further stimulating material exchanges.

2.1 The Socio-Economic Foundation of Foreign Trade Development

The development of agriculture, the flourishing of industry and commerce, and the improvement of transportation conditions all laid a material and technological foundation for the operation of foreign trade.

2.1.1 *The Socio-Economic Foundation*

In 206 BC, Liu Bang established the Han Dynasty. Prior to this, years of war had left the domestic economy severely damaged. The early years of the Han Dynasty saw a great depression in agriculture, industry and commerce. To solve the problem, the early Han rulers enacted the policy of "reducing taxes to alleviate the burden on the people." Meanwhile, large-scale irrigation projects were devised to popularize agricultural production technology. Following the cumulative efforts of the first Emperor Gaozu (r. 206–195 BCE) of the Han, the second Emperor Hui (r. 195–188 BCE) and then the Empress Dowager Lü Zhi (wife of the first Emperor Gaozu), and the well-known "Rule of Wen and Jing,"[1] the economy began to recover and the society headed toward prosperity, with unprecedented improvements being made in the productive capacity of agriculture and manufacturing. The commodity economy found its full vitality.

The national recovery policy implemented by the Western Han Dynasty functioned effectively insofar as deserted land was cultivated and grain yields greatly increased. Meanwhile, commercial agriculture developed rather well with more crops commercialized than in previous dynasties and industrial crop production becoming more specialized on a larger scale. Therefore, it is recorded by a history book that "(we see) thousands of date trees in Anyi; thousands of chestnut trees in Yanqin; thousands of orange trees in Shu, Han and Jiangling; thousands of pear trees in Huaibei between Changshan and Heji, dozens of acres of lacquer trees in Chen and Xia together with mulberry trees and castor-oil plants in Qi and Lu."[2] These specialized industrial crop products were partially intended for farmers' own consumption and partially utilized as materials for handicrafts. They thereby not only activated the commodity economy of the day, but drove the development of the handicraft industry.

The handicraft industry at that time was characterized by its variety. It ranged from the consumption sector, including the non-staple food processing industry and textile industry, to the manufacturing industry responsible for smelting iron and copper from which were cast the tools and implements of daily life. Of note was the remarkable progress made in silk weaving, lacquerware manufacturing, iron smelting, and ironware casting.

The silk weaving industry was improved greatly during the Han Dynasty, both in terms of its production scale and manufacturing technology.

---

[1] The "Rule of Wen and Jing" refers to the reigns of The Han Emperor Wen (r. 180–157 BCE) his son Emperor Jing (r. 157–141 BCE), a period known for the benevolence and thriftiness of the Emperors, reduction in tax and other burdens on the people, pacifism, and general stability.

[2] (The Han Dynasty) Sima Qian. *Records of the Grand Historian: Biographies of Celebrated Merchants*. Beijing: Zhonghua Book Company, 1959.

Written sources record that within the state-run silk-weaving workshop in Linzi, Shandong Province, "there are thousands of workers, whose payments amount to ten thousand per year."[3] While, for workers working in the East Weaving Room and the West Weaving Room in the then capital city Chang'an (modern day Xi'an), their payments were much more than that. The non-governmental silk weaving industry at that time developed as a household subsidiary business, with "mulberry trees planted around dwelling places and women breeding silkworms and weaving silk."

Silk production yields surpassed those in previous dynasties. The traditional courtesy of "only seniors (over 90 years old) wore silk clothes" was abandoned when ordinary people began to wear garments made from that material. Even wealthy people's "dogs and horses were seen to wear silk clothes and saddles, sometimes with embroidery on them."[4]

Further progress was made in silk weaving technology. In the Western Han Dynasty, there was a citizen in Julu City in Hebei Province named Chen Baoguang. His wife invented a precursor to the jacquard loom with 120 wire healds and 120 foot pedals. This promoted the craft of weaving to such a level that various decorative patterns could be produced.

Unearthed relics indicate that silk products in the Han Dynasty were much more diverse in variety, produced by excellent dyeing and printing technology. Dozens of patterns recorded in the literature include *wan* (fine silk fabrics), *qi* (damask on tabby), *jian* (thick cloth with doubled warps and wefts), *ti* (crepons), *chou* (rough crepe), *su* (white silk), *lian* (boiled and scoured raw silk), *ling* (twill damask), *juan* (silk tabby), *gao* (plain white silk), *jin* (polychrome woven silk), *xiu* (embroidery), *sha* (plain gauze), *luo* (silk gauze), *duan* (satin), etc., with the range of colors recorded as encompassing vermeil (vermilion; ponceau), crimson, dark reddish purple, dark green, yellow, gray, and black. All these colors could be dyed fast and distributed evenly throughout the silk cloth, reflecting high-level dip-dyeing and tinting technology.

Lacquerware manufacturing accelerated on the basis of previous development. There were two forms of workshops: the state-owned and the private.

---

[3] (The Han Dynasty) Sima Qian. *Book of Han: Biography of Gongyu*. Beijing: Zhonghua Book Company, 1962.

[4] (The Han Dynasty) Huan Kuan. *Discussions on Salt and Iron*. Shanghai: Shanghai People's Publishing House, 1974.

The state-owned kind embraced the Central Royal Workshop run by the *Shao fu* (Palace Revenues), as well as the subordinate workshops in counties, and those in the capital city. The *Book of Han: Annals of Geography*[5] records that "Counties, like Huai in the Henei[6] area, Chengdu in the Shu area and Guanghan, have official workshops, specializing in making lacquerwares."

Private workshops flourished as well. The *Records of the Grand Historian: Biographies of Celebrated Merchants* records that "owners of big workshops who sell thousands of woodblock paintings can be wealthier than those who possess thousands of chariots."

In modern times, a considerable number of lacquerwares have been excavated in northern China, southern China, southwest China, northwest China, and eastern China. The excavation of 148 pieces in a single hoard at the Mawangdui Mausoleum of Han, Changsha, Hunan Province, denotes how large the scale of production was at that time.

Division of labor was practiced in the production of lacquerware. Roles included *gong gong* (raw material supplier), *su gong* (tyre makers), *xiu gong* (lacquer painters), *shang gong* (embedding ware with decorations), *huang tu gong* (gilders for copper wares), *hua gong* (commercial painter), *diao gong* (sculptors), *zao gong* (designers), *qing gong* (polishers), and so forth.

Such refinements of division inevitably brought about improvement of technology. Lacquerwares with exquisite designs, bright colors and consummate manufacturing techniques were used by ordinary folk in Han times as vessels to meet their daily needs, whereas wares of better quality were set aside for the upper-class families as decorations and curios.

Iron puddling and forging developed to a new level in the Han Dynasty, spreading to more areas and taking place on a larger production scale with comprehensive advancements having been made in puddling and forging technology. To date, related relics have been found in provinces, regions and cities, including Henan, Hebei, Shaanxi, Shanxi,

---

[5] The first geography book in Chinese history with "*dilĭ*" (geography) appearing in the title. Written by Ban Gu, a scholar in the Eastern Han Dynasty, in 54–92 CE, it is one of the 10 volumes of *the Book of Han*.

[6] It refers to the northern reaches of the Yellow River. The south and the west areas of the Yellow River are called Hewai, "the outside of the river." During the Chu-Han Confrontation (460–220 BCE), the government began to set up *Jun* (modern day area or region) here, hence the Henei area, the headquarters of which was in Huai County.

Shandong, Inner Mongolia, Xinjing and Beijing. In Henan alone, 20 plus key relic sites have been discovered.

In addition, hydraulic driven blowers were widely employed, which helped to expand the volume of iron-forging furnaces and increase production. The burning of coal as a fuel and the employment of lime as a solvent contributed to an improvement in the quality of iron.

Advancements in Han iron-forging technology can also be witnessed in the technological innovation of decarburization of cast iron, molting pig iron into steel, and decarburization of cast iron. These expanded the application of tools made from iron, and production efficiency as well.

The development of iron puddling helped to produce a large number of affluent businessmen. For example, the Kong family, whose ancestors used to forge iron in Yuan County, became very rich. After moving to Nanyang County, the family expanded their business to a larger scale and planned to dig ponds to breed fish. The Kong family was seen paying visits to vassals on carriages seeking to secure further business opportunities. This in turn earned them a reputation for philanthropy, which, consequently allowed them to recuperate more money than they had spent in promoting their renown. The Zhuo family in Sichuan, who became rich by forging iron, employed thousands of servants, thus enjoying a lifestyle as sumptuous as that of an Emperor.[7] Cheng Zheng, a migrant from Shandong, forged iron too, selling iron products to ethnic minorities living in the southwest of the country and becoming far richer than the Zhuo family. Cao Bing, born in Shandong, became an ultra-wealthy tycoon by forging iron.

The development of agriculture and manufacturing provided a material basis for the development of commerce, while the unification of the country and the increased stability of the society facilitated the circulation of commodities. The early years of the Han Dynasty "stressed agriculture and restrained commerce." In the reign of the first Emperor Gaozu, "businessmen were not allowed to wear silk clothes, to ride a carriage. They had heavy taxes imposed upon them."[8] In the reign of

---

[7](The Han Dynasty) Sima Qian. *Records of the Grand Historian: Biographies of Celebrated Merchants*. Beijing: Zhonghua Book Company, 1959.

[8](The Han Dynasty) Ban Gu. *Book of Han: Treatise on Food and Commodities* II. Beijing: Zhonghua Book Company, 1962.

the second Emperor Hui and the Empress Dowager Lü Zhi, "in view of the fact that the country had just been united, regulations on businessmen were imposed in a loose way. Although encouraged to revitalize business, their offspring were not allowed to be promoted to be officials."[9] However, it is true that "people came hither in their droves with an eye to benefits people went thither in a bustle with an eye to benefits,"[10] which suggests a greatly endowed commodities economy. "With the unification and prosperity of the Han Dynasty, nearly all roadblocks were leveled, allowing for the better transportation and exchanges of mountain products. Merchants were seen to travel within the country to conduct their business in the way they liked and to glean whatever they wanted. Outstanding talents, like heroes, vassals, powerful clans were attracted to migrate to the then capital city."[11]

During the Eastern and Western Han Dynasties, merchants who possessed fortunes fraternized with imperial dukes and grew powerful. "They bribed nobles, bullied and oppressed lower-leveled officials and dispossessed farmers of their lands. When traveling to distant places, they were visited by successive officials, wearing silk garments and riding sturdy horse-pulled carriages."[12]

Even noble descendants were keen on pursuing commercial profits by transacting business. In the reign of the tenth Emperor Chengdi, "the younger generations of noble relatives and ministers were monopolists pursuing profits."[13] A cruel official named Ning Cheng once claimed, "how you could tell others that you are an official with your income less than 2,000; how you could tell others that you were a businessman with your wealth less than 10 million!"[14] Wang Fu, a scholar in the Eastern Han Dynasty, therefore, wrote that "most people had given up farming to engage in doing business. Roads were jammed with their horse-and-cattle-pulled

---

[9] *Ibid.*

[10] (The Han Dynasty) Sima Qian. *Records of the Grand Historian: Biographies of Celebrated Merchants* Beijing: Zhonghua Book Company, 1959.

[11] *Ibid.*

[12] (The Han Dynasty) Ban Gu. *Book of Han: Treatise on Food and Commodities.* Beijing: Zhonghua Book Company, 1962.

[13] (The Han Dynasty) Ban Gu. *Book of Han: Biography of Zhai Fangjin.* Beijing: Zhonghua Book Company, 1962.

[14] (The Han Dynasty) Ban Gu. *Book of Han: Biography of Cruel Officials.* Beijing: Zhonghua Book Company, 1962.

carriages. Idlers flocked into the cities. Farm laborers became fewer and fewer with more and more people needing to be fed."[15]

Just as the great scholar Sima Qian observed, "when the poor want to be rich, agriculture was no better than industry, and industry was no better than commerce; embroidering at home is no better than conducting business out of home, which means commerce is the way for poor people to make a fortune."[16] So it was reasonable to see countless businessmen emerge during the Eastern and Western Han Dynasties. Commerce became a trade patronized by many people.

When the renowned Emperor Wu of the Han succeeded to the throne in 141 CE, "society had been prosperous for more than 70 years, with no floods or droughts. The population enjoyed a life of abundance; the national treasury was filled with revenue; the granaries were loaded with more grain than could be eaten, and horses were to be seen everywhere in streets, alleys and fields."[17]

This economic development laid a material foundation for opening up, with the market increasingly expanding. Characteristic Han-style handicraft articles like silk products, lacquerwares, and quality iron-made farming tools were to be seen in circulation on the domestic market. In the push for huge profits, they transgressed ethnic and national boundaries to access foreign markets, hence the birth of foreign trade.

2.1.2 *The Development of Transportation Industry*

During the Spring and Autumn & Warring States Periods (770–476 BCE & 475–221 BCE), China was divided into many smaller states with the respective regimes being ruled by vassals. Wars were waged between them. Each state possessed its own currency, system of measurement, characters, and axle track and rail gauge for vehicles. The whole land was therefore fragmented and blocked by tariffs, city moats and embankments, which impeded economic connections. Ying Zheng or Qin Shihuang, the First Sovereign Emperor defeated all the rival states and established the first unified Chinese empire in

[15](The Southern Dynasty · Song) Fan Ye. *Book of the Later Han: Biography of Wang Fu.* Beijing: Zhonghua Book Company, 1982.

[16](The Han Dynasty) Sima Qian. *Records of the Grand Historian: Biographies of Celebrated Merchants.* Beijing: Zhonghua Book Company, 1959.

[17](The Han Dynasty) Sima Qian. *Records of the Grand Historian: Book of Price Control.* Beijing: Zhonghua Book Company, 1959.

221 BCE. He issued orders for almost universal standardization — from weights, measures, and the axle gauges of carriages and carts to the written language — in order to sweep away all the obstacles blocking exchanges.

To reinforce his authority over the country, Qin Shihuang ordered his people to construct roads across the nation, forming a transportation network from Central Plains to every corner of the country. Records say the roads network stretched "to the State of Yan and the State of Qi in the east, and the State of Wu and the State of Chu in the south, to lakes, rivers and seas."[18]

The Han Dynasty paid more attention to the construction of more roads, bridges and infrastructure. On the one hand, the central government was responsible for constructing cross-border roads like the Southwestern Road connecting Yunnan with Central Plains, and the Bao Gallery Road linking the central Shaanxi area (Guanzhong, "within the Passes") and Bashu (Sichuan). On the other hand, local governments were responsible for constructing and repairing roads, bridges, and postal kiosks within their respective jurisdiction, ensuring smooth regional transportation. For instance, Wei Sa, the Governor of Guiyang in the early years of the Eastern Han Dynasty, organized people in his term of office "to tunnel through mountains and construct roadways longer than 250 kilometers, along which postal kiosks and courier stations were set up."[19] Officials who made no contribution to constructing roads of any nature and postal kiosks would be deemed unqualified when their performance was assessed.

Therefore, the domestic transportation network was further improved during the Han Dynasty, facilitating commodity exchange and economic communications between different places, and creating the preconditions for the operation of foreign trading activities.

2.2 The Formation of Overland and Maritime Silk Road

Beginning from the Eastern and Western Han Dynasties, China's foreign trade was conducted via the Silk Road over land and sea. The formation of the Silk Road was the result of joint efforts made by countries and

---

[18](The Han Dynasty) Ban Gu. *Book of Han: Biography of Jia Shan*. Beijing: Zhonghua Book Company, 1962.

[19](The Southern Dynasty · Song) Fan Ye. *Book of the Later Han: Biography of Honest and Upright Officials*. Beijing: Zhonghua Book Company, 1982.

nations over an extended period of time. As the most highly developed economy in the world at that time, China played an extraordinary role in the creation and development of the Silk Road.

2.2.1 *The Overland Silk Road*

(1) Zhang Qian and the Western Regions

In order to withstand the military threat from the Xiongnu in the north, the Han Dynasty dispatched Zhang Qian to visit countries in the Western Regions. Zhang Qian's journey and the series of military and administrative strategies he employed to defeat the Xiongnu and consolidate the borderland not only helped to stabilize the country's northern border, but, more importantly, opened up a passage for communications between China and foreign countries as well. Comprehensive advancement in politics, economics, and cultural communication was therefore seen to be initiated between the then China and foreign countries.

(i) Relations between the Han and the Xiongnu

In the early years of the Han Dynasty, the Xiongnu, a nomadic nation with many tribes in northern China, grew increasingly strong after Modu Chanyu, the supreme leader of the united Xiongnu tribes, led a force of 300,000 soldiers, known to be skillful at plying bows and arrows, to expand the territory in three directions. In the east, they defeated the neighboring Eastern Hu people. The Greater Yuezhi were driven farther to the west, leaving the vast areas of land from the Liaodong Peninsula to Xinjiang under the domination of the Xiongnu people. To the southern border of the Xiongnu territory was the seat of government of the Han Dynasty. It was confined to the narrow Huanghe River Basin but still faced threats and harassment from the southbound Xiongnu troops. In 200 BCE, the 7th year of the reign of Gaozu, the Emperor led his army to attack the Xiongnu, only to find himself besieged in Baideng (present-day Yanggao County in Shanxi Province). This is recorded in history books as "Being Besieged in Baideng."

The Han Dynasty at that time was newly founded and its national power was too weak to wage any kind of sustained war against the Xiongnu. Emperor Gaozu had no choice but to follow his adviser Lou Jing's stratagem of "*heqin*," or "marriage for peace," marrying the Han princesses to the Xiongnu Chanyu, with generous dowries and yearly presents, such as silk products, choice wine, and grain.

The stratagem of a marriage alliance was continued to be practiced in the reigns of fourth and fifth Emperors Wen and Jing. Still the Xiongnu was gradually growing stronger in its comprehensive power. When Emperor Wen was on the throne (180–157 BCE), the Xiongnu conquered states in the Western Regions, thus initiating its brutal domination over that area. According to the *Book of Han: Bibliography of the Xiongnu*, "petty states like Loulan, Wusun, Hujie and 26 others were enslaved by the Xiongnu and their soldiers were integrated into the Xiongnu forces. The wars in the border area of northern China have not been put into an end." The Western Regions fell thereafter under the control of the Xiongnu. At that time, the Xiongnu began to treat the Han government in a peremptory way. They frequently harassed the border area, pillaging people, and animals as well as damaging farmland. Their mobile cavalries even once galloped close to Chang'an, the capital city, placing the Han Dynasty under extreme pressure.

With the recovery and development of the economy, the national power of the Han government gradually improved to the extent that its material abundance became sufficient to put an end to the threat of the Xiongnu.

Since the reign of the famous sixth Emperor Wu began, the Han government had been working on strategies to resist the Xiongnu. The Han troops were dispatched to attack them from the front. At the same time, the government tried its best to build up alliances with those states in the Western Region which had themselves endured vicious conflicts with the Xiongnu. In other words, both sides could attack their common adversary from its right flank, with the aim of breaking its "right arm."

The Han gleaned intelligence from the captives of the Xiongnu, and the Greater Yuezhi people who were displaced westward by the Xiongnu hated them as much as they did. Weak as they were with no allies, the Han Emperor Wu saw how they thirsted for revenge. He dispatched an envoy to seek opportunities of cooperation to defeat the Xiongnu with a united force. It was against these historic backgrounds that Zhang Qian, born in today's Chenggu County, Hanzhong, Shaanxi Province, answered the call to fulfill his role as Court Gentleman.

(ii) Zhang Qian's Diplomatic Mission to the Western Regions

Zhang Qian was twice dispatched as an envoy to the West Regions. The first time was between 138 and 126 BCE. In 138 BCE, Zhang Qian, together with more than 100 people, embarked from Chang'an, the capital city, on his journey to the Western Regions. Unfortunately, they were captured by the Xiongnu people when crossing the Hexi Corridor. In an attempt to induce Zhang Qian and his people to surrender to the Xiongnu, arrangements were made for the envoy to get married and sire children. Even so, Zhang Qian still remained unyielding to his identity and kept his warrant (tally) as an envoy. After being detained in the Gobi Desert for decades, he finally managed to escape with his companions.

They continued their westward journey across the Taklamakan Desert. Difficulties and dangers failed to prevent them from climbing over the Pamir Mountains to arrive in the country Dayuan[20] (within the present-day Republic of Kyrgyzstan). The King of the Dayuan had heard that "[t]he Han government was rich with treasures but hard to establish relations with." So upon Zhang Qian's arrival, he greeted him with a fine reception. Afterward, Zhang Qian was escorted to K'ang-chu[21] (between Lake Balkhash and the Aral Sea) where they went southward to the Greater Yuezhi.

In 129 BCE, when Zhang Qian arrived in the Greater Yuezhi, it had dominated the Kingdom of Bactria (the present-day Amu Darya Basin), where land was fertile and people were living in harmony and contentment, reluctant to engage in hostilities against the Xiongnu. Despite more than one year's efforts, Zhang Qian failed to persuade them to join the Han in their fight against the Xiongnu. He had no choice but to decide to return to his own country.

In order to avoid being intercepted by the Xiongnu, Zhang Qian and his men chose a new route back. They entered the Qaidam Basin via the south of the Tarim Basin, in an attempt to retreat along the areas controlled by the Qiang people. Unfortunately, they again fell into the hands of the Xiongnu mobile cavalries. A year later, Zhang Qian managed to escape for a second time with Gan Fu, his guide and interpreter, taking

---

[20] Dayuan is the Chinese exonym for a country that existed in Ferghana valley in Central Asia described in the Chinese historical works of *Records of the Grand Historian* and the *Book of Han*.

[21] K'ang-chu was the Chinese name of an ancient kingdom in Central Asia which became for a couple of centuries the second greatest power in Transoxiana after the Yuezhi. Its people, the K'ang, were an Indo-European semi-nomadic people probably identical to the Iranian Sogdians or other Iranian groups closely related to them, such as the Asii.

advantage of the Huns' internal strife. In 126 BCE, when they finally came back to Chang'an, the sixth Emperor Wu was still on the throne.

Zhang Qian's first visit to the Western Regions took him 13 years. He left with a retinue of hundreds, but only two came back — Gan Fu and himself. Although he failed to build an alliance with the Greater Yuezhi, he spread the reputation of the Han as a powerful country to the Western Regions. In return, he got to know the Western Regions, and, in particular, their geography, regional products, military, and so on, which served as crucial information in reading the Han troops for a war against the Xiongnu.

Thereafter, Zhang Qian worked as a guide for the Han troops on several occasions helping them to win wars with the Xiongnu based upon his knowledge about "where to find water and food to ensure sufficient military provisions." He thereby was ennobled by the Han government to be a "Vassal of Knowledge and Prestige" (see *Records of the Grand Historian: Biographies of Dayuan*). In 121 BCE, the Han troops overran the Hexi Corridor, marking a significant moment when the opening up of a passage to the Western Regions was made possible when the Xiongnu were not any longer obstacles from the Central Plains to Yanze (modern-day Lop Nur, Xinjiang).

When Zhang Qian was in the Kingdom of Bactria, he observed bamboo sticks and cloth made in Sichuan, from which he concluded that there should be a route leading to Central Asia from Sichuan and Yunnan in southwestern China via Burma and India.

In 122 BCE, a diplomatic corps was sent out by Emperor Wu in an attempt to find this so-called "southwest Silk Road," but they were impeded by ethnic tribes in the territory of Yunnan. In 111 BCE, Emperor Wu dispatched troops to Yunnan, but in vain. Despite remaining beyond the control of the Han government, this passageway exerted considerable influence on non-governmental trade between China, Burma and India.

In 119 BCE, Emperor Wu dispatched Zhang Qian as an envoy to the Western Regions for a second time. The purpose now was to seek an alliance with Wusun, a kingdom of great power, as compared with others in the Western Regions. Zhang Qian's visit, on the one hand, was meant to persuade the Wusun people to return and relocate to their homeland in the Hexi area. On the other hand, he was to try to persuade other countries within the Western Regions to join with the Han government in an onslaught on the Xiongnu.

On this trip, Zhang Qian was accompanied by his deputy envoy and a strong army of 300 generals and soldiers. Each of them was equipped with two horses. They left with thousands of heads of livestock, gold coins and silk products. After arriving in Wusun, they were received hospitably by the king, but their proposal to return to Hexi was declined. During their stay, Zhang Qian sent his deputy envoy to other kingdoms like the Dayuan, the K'ang-chu, the Greater Yuezhi, Bactria, Parthia (modern-day Iran), Sindhu[22] (modern-day India), the Kingdom of Khotan (now Hetian in Xinjiang), Yumi (now Yutian in Xinjiang) and other adjacent countries.

In 115 BCE, Zhang Qian returned to Chang'an with dozens of envoys from the Wusun. An alliance with the Wusun was thereafter built up after those Wusun envoys who came to the Han government with Zhang Qian. Back to their home country, they reported to their King the prosperity they had witnessed during their stay in Chang'an City. Meanwhile, the envoys sent out by Zhang Qian came back to Chang'an with their counterparts from those countries they had visited. From then on, concord existed between the Han government and countries in the Western Regions and the western world. Zhang Qian's extraordinary visit won him the title *Da xing* (Senior Messenger). The following year he died of illness in Chang'an.

In conclusion, the motive behind Zhang Qian's visit to the Western Regions was mainly to remove the threat the Xiongnu posed to the Han's further consolidation. Zhang Qian went to the Western Regions twice, realizing the aim of isolating the Xiongnu, and creating the conditions conducive for the Han troops to counter them. With the Xiongnu being weakened in power, the Silk Road became gradually accessible as their resistance was removed. The blockade upon the Han was breached, enabling the country, in an objective sense, to step further along the road toward opening up.

Politically, the opening-up of the Silk Road connected Xinjiang with Central Plains for the first time forging a closer relationship. In 60 BCE, the Han government set up a regulatory agency employing a Protector-General of the Western Regions, exercising its administration of the central government over Xinjiang as a subordinate.

Diplomatically, the bilateral visits between Zhang Qian and his envoys and the envoys from Central, South and West Asian countries served as a starting point from which regularized foreign relations were established between China and the countries along the Silk Road.

---

[22](Rare, obsolete) the Chinese term used to refer to India.

Economically, prosperous trade was seen to flourish increasingly along the Road, with official trade, in the form of envoy exchange, growing to dominate the market. History relates how dozens of batches of envoys, each batch containing hundreds or tens of hundreds of members, were dispatched every year by the Han government to the west. Each visit often took several years or even a decade or so before their return. They would always encounter each other either on their outward or inbound journeys.

Those who were sent out to the Western Regions as envoys were "poor persons. Taking the presents as their own possessions, they sold them at lower prices to make profits in other countries." Meanwhile, the western envoys — humble merchants by nature — attempted to initiate trade with China under the aegis of being officially dispatched envoys. In this light, the diplomatic corps was on par with official caravans of traders, being sent out for official visits. And yet they were seen to conduct business as well.

Therefore, products from Central Plains like silk, lacquerwares, iron wares, etc, were found to flood into the areas of the Tian Shan Mountains, Central Asia, South Asia and West Asia, while foreign animals and ivory-made luxurious jewelries were seen to flood into Central Plains.

Under the administration and protection of the Western Han government, trade along the Silk Road developed with unprecedented vitality to become official, frequent and far-reaching in nature. Together with the Silk Road trade, Chinese ideological culture was diffused and spread along the Silk Road to communicate with that of other countries.

To sum up, Zhang Qian being dispatched to the Western Regions and the subsequent triumph of the Han Dynasty over the Xiongnu relieved the border threat against it. It thus created a peaceful environment for the economic development of the Han and contributed directly to the opening of the Silk Road, along which Sino-foreign communication was made via economy and culture to promote the advancement of human civilization. In this light, Sima Qian praised Zhang Qian's contribution to the opening of the Silk Road as unparalleled and unprecedented.

(2) Silk Road Routes

The Silk Road was a trans-Asian trading route, stretching from the ancient Chang'an of the Han and Tang Dynasties (now to the northwest of Xi'an City in Shaanxi Province) in the east, to the eastern bank of the

Mediterranean in the west, passing along the route of the Hexi Corridor, Xinjiang, the Pamir Plateau, and areas in Central Asia, South Asia and West Asia.

Owing to the natural topography and conflicts between countries along the Road, the route was not linear, but consisted of a transportation network with interweaving stages. Though its roadways altered frequently, the trunk line remained comparatively stable, encompassing many cities and towns of political and economic importance. The trunk line stretched over 7,000 kilometers in length, with over 4,000 kilometers of that being within China proper.

(i) Silk Road Routes within China Proper

The Silk Road within China proper can be split into three respective sections, the east, the middle and the west.

The Road started from Chang'an, the capital city during the Han and Tang Dynasties, which was a terminus for foreign merchants and the departure point for their Chinese counterparts. Stretching from Chang'an in the east to the Hexi Corridor in the west was the eastern section of the Silk Road.

Within this section, there were two trade routes — one in the south and the other in the north, both of which were opened up in the Western Han Dynasty. The northern route started from Chang'an and reached Wuwei in Gansu, passing by many places like Xianyang, Xingping, Liquan, Qian County, Bin County, Changwu, Jingchuan, Pingliang, Guyuan, Haiyuan, Jingyuan, Jingtai, and Gulang. The southern route started from Chang'an to reach Zhangye via Xiangyang, Xingping, Wugong, Mei County, Baoji, Qianyang, Long County, Longcheng, Qin'an, Tongwei, Longxi, Weiyuan, Lintiao, Linxia, Minhe, Ledu, and Xining in Qinghai Province. It then advanced north, crossing the Datong River, climbing over the Qilian Mountain, passing by Biandukou and arriving at Zhangye via Minle, where the two routes converged into one.

This was the route Zhang Qian took during his first expedition. The southern route ran through the agricultural area to the south of Yellow River and was thereby endowed with better natural conditions than the northern one. Those two were the trunk routes. In addition to them, there were many branch lines which will not be enumerated here.

The middle section of the road was the Hexi Corridor. Lying to the west of the Yellow River, the corridor gained fame as a natural passage with the Qilian Mountain on the southern side and the Corridor Mountains (including Heli Mountain, Dragon Head Mountain, Red Cliff Mountain, and Alagu Mountain) on the northern side. It was more than 1,000 kilometers in length and its width varied from several hundred to several thousand meters. It was deemed to be the most ideal access route from Central Plains to the Western Regions and was therefore of massive importance to ancient transportation between China and western countries.

The Hexi Corridor extended from Wushaoling Mountain in the east to as far as Dunhuang in the west, passing by many important cities and towns on the way, such as Wuwei, Yongchang, Shandan, Zhangye, Linze, Gaotai, Yanchi, Linshui, Jiuquan, Jiayu Pass, Yumen Town, Bulongji, the Parthian Empire, and Dunhuang.

The western section of the Silk Road lay within the Xinjiang area with the special topography of the Taklimakan Desert as its central part. The snow-capped Kunlun Mountains stand on the north side of the desert and the Tian Shan Mountains on the south. Both mountain ranges are snow-covered throughout the year. Human habitation is therefore restricted to the oasis areas on the edge of the desert, which are irrigated by the melt water from the snowy mountains. Merchants and envoys had no choice but to walk along the southern side of the Tian Shan Mountains or the northern side of the Kunlun Mountains, resulting in the splitting of the western section of the Silk Road (within Xinjiang) into a southern route and a northern one.

The southern route refers to the east–west passage between the northern foothills of Kunlun Mountains and the south edge of the Taklamakan Desert. The route started from Dunhuang, passing by the Yangguan Pass (now near Gudongtan in the southwest of Dunhuang) and Shanshan (now Ruoqiang in Xinjiang). Then it advanced westward along the northern foothills of the Kunlun Mountains to reach Shache (now Shache in Xinjiang), passing by Qiemo (now Qiemo County in Xinjiang), Jingjue (now to the north of Minfeng in Xinjiang), Kingdom of Khotan (now Hetian, in Xinjiang), and Pishan (now Pishan in Xinjiang).

Between the southern edge of the Tian Shan and the northern fringes of the Taklamakan Desert lay the westward northern route. This started from Dunhuang and proceeded to the Former Jushi County (now Turpan in Xinjiang) at Dunhuang, passing by the Yumen Pass (now Xiaofangpan City in Dunhuang) and Liusha. It then advanced westward along the western foothills of the Tian Shan passing by Karasahr (now to the south-west of Yanqi in Xinjiang), Kucha (now Kuche in Xinjiang), Gumo (now Aksu in Xinjiang), and Kashgar (now Kashi in Xinjiang).

(ii) Silk Road Routes outside of China

After crossing the Pamir Mountains, the Silk Road left China proper behind bifurcating into two routes — one in the north and the other in the south.

The southern route was subdivided into two further lines — a trunk line and a branch line. The branch one started from southwest Pishan to Ki-pin (now the Kashmir area) and Sindhu via Wucha (now the upper reaches of the Qiang River). The trunk one extended from Shache to reach in Merv (now eastern Mary in Turkmenistan), passing by Puli (now Tashkurghan), Komedae (now Wakhan in Afghanistan) along the Pamir River to the City of Balkh (ancient Bactria, present-day Wazirabad in Afghanistan). This route connected China with countries like the Greater Yuezhi, the Bactria and the Parthia, thereby constituting a major trading route within Central Asia during the Western and Eastern Han Dynasties.

The northern route was subdivided into a trunk line and a branch line as well. The former one crossed the Tian Shan Mountains from Gumo and passed Tianchi (present-day Issyk-Kul Lake) and the Pamir Mountains to reach Zhizhi City in K'ang-chu (now Dzhambul in Kazakhstan). The trunk line stretched westward from Kashgar to reach the Dayuan, the K'ang-chu, and the Alan (now in Kazakhstan) via the Pamir Mountains. To the west of the Alan lay the Kingdom of Bosporus. It was established during the era of Greek colonization and fell under the control of Rome in the middle of the first millennium BC, function-ing as an intermediate station to transfer oriental goods to Rome. This route played an important role between the 1st and 2nd millennium BCE when Parthia controlled the trade route from the Iranian Plateau to the Persian Gulf.

Traveling further westward along this road was a trading route run-ning through Iran from its east to its west. That was the middle section of the Silk Road outside of China. It lay between the Alborz range and the Kavir Desert and ran straight so as to make transportation convenient. It was the principal artery of the Silk Road outside China. It proceeded west-ward from Merv, passed through Hecatompylos (now near Damghan in Iran), Lagai (now Teheran in Iran), Acbatana (now Hamadan in Iran), and reached Ctesiphon (also called Ktesiphon, the sometime winter capital of the Sasanian Empire. It was situated on the eastern bank of the Tigris in the modern-day southeastern Baghdad) and Seleucia (a Greek commercial city on the west bank of the Tigris River opposite Ctesiphon, within the Baghdad Governorate in Iraq). The two cities facing each other on the two banks of the Tigris River were taken as a whole to be where the capital city of the Persian Sassanid Empire was once located. They are recorded in Chinese historical documents as "City Sūli" or "City Sùli" or "Sucisadangna", or "Al-Madain" by the Rabic people.

Running from the Parthia to the west was a northwestward trading route or the western section of the Silk Road outside of China. This can be subdivided into three routes.

The first route started from Seleucia and ended in Nicephorium (now Al-Raqqa in Syria), running northwestward along the eastern bank of the Euphrates River, or crossing the desert area of the Arabian nomadic tribes near the Euphrates to reach Apamea City by way of the Euphrates. Then from the town of Zeugma, the route ran southwestward to Antioch City (modern-day Antakya in Turkey).

Antioch used to be the capital city of the Seleucid Kingdom, the residence of the governor administrating the Orient during the period of Roman Empire and the capital city of Daqin (Roman Empire) as recorded in Chinese historical documents. It was also a terminus where China's silk products arrived and were transported to European countries.

The route carried on running north from Antioch and turned west to Ephesus, the capital city of Asia Minor (the modern day area of Izmir in the west of Turkey) via the Toros (the present-day Taurus Mountains). This route lay in the middle part of the western section of the Silk Road. It rose and flourished with the Seleucid Kingdom during the 2nd–3rd centuries BCE.

The second route stretched northwestward from Seleucia to Dura-Euopos (present-day Salihiyya in Syria) via the Euphrates River. It continued running west to Palmyra (modern day Tadmor in Syria) first, then Antioch City (modern-day Antakya in Turkey) and Damascus where it ran southwest to several ports like Sidon, Tyre, and Beirut on the eastern bank of the Mediterranean. This represented the southern line of the western section of the Silk Road outside China. It emerged with the flourishing of commercial cities in the north of the Syria Desert and then declined in the 3rd century AD. The eastern bank of the Mediterranean is home to murex, which can secrete fluid to be used as a source of the dye Tyrian purple, i.e., the purple dye could be made from the shells of the murex shellfish. It was because of this purple dye, together with the making of silk clothes, that Port Tyre earned its fame as Phoenicians, a name from the Greeks — *Phoinikes* — which means "purple people." Silk products from China were further processed and dyed purple before being made into the fine gauze favored by the local people.

The third was the northern line of the western section of the road. It commenced at Ctesiphon, ran northward along the eastern bank of the Tigris River, passing by Nineveh, the capital city of the ancient Assyrian Empire (near present-day Mosul, Iraq) to Mosul (in present-day Mosul) across the river. Then it wen northwest to Antioch City after passing by Nisibis (present-day Nusaybin, Iraq), Adyssa (present-day Urfa, Turkey), Apamea, and Zeugma. This line was situated in the north with fine weather, sufficient rainfall, abundant water, and vegetation. As a result, many caravans of traders came and went along this route.

Spanning the vast continent of Asia, the Silk Road has witnessed the passage of thousands of years and connects a great number of ancient countries and nations. Although national and regional boundaries have changed through history, if defined from the present geographical conception, the Silk Road passes the following countries: China, India, Pakistan, Kazakhstan, Uzbekistan, Tajikistan, Turkmenistan, Afghanistan, Iran, Iraq, Syria, Lebanon, and Turkey. The ancient civilizations represented by these counties and nations exerted their influence upon each other along the Silk Road and moved on to interact with those of more countries in Europe and Africa via the eastern bank of the Mediterranean.

In addition, the Southwestern Silk Road was opened in the Han Dynasty. As mentioned above, as early as in the Qin Dynasty, the exchange of goods was conducted between the State of Shu and India. When Zhang Qian was dispatched to the Western Regions, he found bamboo sticks and cloth made in Sichuan on the market. They had been transported from India and were being retailed on the local market in Bactria (within modern day Afghanistan). He therefore deduced that a trading route must exist between Sichuan and India. After returning to Chang'an, he reported this message to Emperor Wu and suggested that the Han Dynasty should open up the passage from Southwest China to India.

Following Zhang Qian's advice, Emperor Wu dispatched four groups of envoys to search for passages to India starting from Sichuan Province.

All envoys were hindered by minorities in southwestern China, failing to fulfill the task. Later, Emperor Wu waged wars against the minorities and managed to open up a passage from Chengdu to the Er Lake area, where the Han's troops were resisted by the Kunming and other minorities.

Under the Eastern Han Dynasty, in 69 CE, the Ailao people (a minority in the southwest) paid allegiance to the Han. As a result, the Yongchang Prefecture was established. Thus, the Yunnan–Burma passage was opened up. The Han government started the process of inaugurating official relations with the Shan ethnic people in Myanmar. This started the cultural communication between China and Sindhu, representing the opening up of the Southwestern Silk Road from Sichuan to India.

2.2.2 *The Maritime Silk Road*

The Maritime Silk Road, as an East–West marine trading line in ancient times, was composed of two routes, namely the East China Sea Silk Road and the South China Sea Silk Road.

The former one, as a trading route, reached Japan from the sea coast of northeastern China via the Bohai Sea or the Yellow Sea, the East China Sea, and the Straits of Joseon. The latter trading route started from the coast of southeast China and traversed the South China Sea and the Indian Ocean to reach West Asia and Africa.

The formation of the Maritime Silk Road resulted from the joint efforts of people both in the East and the West. Those who dwelt alongside the Mediterranean were historically adept at sailing and have always been engaging in sea-based activities. As early as the 5th century BCE, Persian warships were seen navigating the Indus River Basin. In the 4th century BCE, the ancient Macedonian ruler Alexander the Great's oriental conquests brought his powerful navy and army into the Indus River Valley. The Maritime Silk Road forced to open through military conquests brought about constant contact on the sea between peoples to the west of India, prompting the development of maritime trade.

China is blessed with vast sea territories with long coastlines and numerous islands, providing convenience for developing trade over the sea. Therefore, the ancient ancestors of the Chinese made contact with foreign people not only across the land but over the sea, gradually creating comparatively regular shipping routes between China and countries overseas.

(1) Xu Fu's Eastward Voyage and the Silk Road in the East China Sea

Geographically adjacent as they were to each other, China has maintained marine contacts with Joseon and Japan since ancient times. History books record how that at the end of the Shang Dynasty, a nobleman named Ji Zi led his people to Joseon, where he established a regime called Ji's Joseon in the northern part of the region. Since the Warring States Period, people in the states of Qi and Yan engaged in contact with the people of Joseon. In the early years of the Han Dynasty, a man named Wei Man from the State of Yan led his people to reach Joseon via sea. They overthrew Ji's Joseon regime and established Wei's Joseon. The Qin Dynasty witnessed the alchemist Xu Fu and his followers voyaging eastward to Japan. All the above-mentioned historically recorded stories help to validate the fact that many Chinese visited Japan via sea in ancient times.[23]

The route taken by Xu Fu was as follows: embarking from the Shandong Peninsula, he reached Japan via the Bohai Sea, the Joseon Peninsula, and the Straits of Joseon. Even though the specific authenticity of Xu Fu's eastward voyage was in doubt, it is safe to conclude that the Silk Roads over the East China Sea to Joseon and Japan were created during the Qin and Han Dynasties. Generally speaking, the route started from Dengzhou (modern day Penglai in Shandong Province) or Laizhou to the southern end of the Liaodong Peninsula where they crossed the Bohai Straits, going northeastward to the mouth of the Yalu River. Then they voyaged south along the fringes of the Joseon Peninsula to Japan via the Straits of Joseon.

All this evidence demonstrates that the Silk Road over the East China Sea had existed as a marine transportation route between China, Joseon, and Japan as early as the Qin Dynasty, through which communication was initiated and gradually developed economically, politically, and culturally between ancient China, Joseon, and Japan.

---

[23] Researchers believe that Xu Fu was born in the Xu Fu Village in Ganyu County, Lianyungang City, Jiangsu Province. He voyaged eastward to Japan to look for the elixir of immortality for Emperor Qin Shi Huang. In the legendary place of his landing from the sea, Xingong City in Xiongye County, a memorial tomb and temple were built for him. His eastward voyage diffused China's agriculture and production technology as well as medical knowledge; therefore, he was honored as "God of Agriculture" by the Japanese people.

(2) The Silk Road between the South China Sea and the Indian Ocean

People in Southwestern China have been engaged in maritime activities since the Pre-Qin Period (2,100–221 BCE) with the gradual emergence of foreign trade. Pan Yu, in the Lingnan[24] (an area in the south of the Nanling Mountains), became well-known before the Qin Dynasty for its trading in rare foreign treasures. After the establishment of the Qin Dynasty, the first Emperor of the Qin sent military troops to the Lingnan, with the intention of obtaining rhinoceros horns, ivory, and jadeite from the Yue people (a southern minority). From the end of the Qin Dynasty to the early years of the Western Han Dynasty, the kingdom of Nanyue,[25] having ruled the Lingnan for almost a century, had established economic contacts with countries along the Indian Ocean via the South China Sea. This much can be ascertained by the foreign-imported ivories, frankincense, censers, and silver boxes recently unearthed from the cemetery of the King of Nanyue.

In the reign of Emperor Wu of the Han, the country was strong in power and people were rich in life, the ambitious Emperor tried his best to expand the borders of the country by strengthening and consolidating the unified feudal empire. In the north of the country, dispatched several expeditions against the Xiongnu, while in the south, the Shuishi (name of the ancient Chinese navy) was dispatched to conquer the Baiyue,[26] Hundred Yue, which stayed independent from the central governance in southeast China.

The shipbuilding and seafaring industry advanced rapidly in tandem with the expansion of the maritime trading route. Cargo ships built in the Han Dynasty were loaded with more goods than ever before. The *Records of the Grand Historian: Book of Price Control* mentions that "*Lou Chuan*

---

[24] Lingnan is a geographic area referring to the lands in the south of the Nanling Mountains. The region covers the modern Chinese subdivisions of Guangdong, Guangxi, Hainan, Hong Kong, and Macao, as well as modern-day northern Vietnam.

[25] Nanyue, Nam Việt or Namz Yied, was an ancient kingdom ruled by Chinese monarchs of the Triệu dynasty that covered the modern Chinese subdivisions of Guangdong, Guangxi, Hainan, Hong Kong, and Macau, as well as parts of southern Fujian and northern Vietnam.

[26] The Baiyue, Hundred Yue, or simply Yue were various ethnic groups which inhabited the regions of South China and Northern Vietnam during the 1st millennium BCE and 1st millennium CE. They were known for their short hair, body tattoos, fine swords and naval prowess.

(a multi-story warship) is more than 10 cords (*zhang*) in height." The *Imperial Readings of the Taiping Era*[27] compiled in the Song Dynasty records that "battle wagons could be loaded with hundreds of thousands of kilograms of grain." This appears to be something of an exaggeration, but archaeological documents confirm that the warships were strong in structure, installed with a transverse compartment and were self-righting. Both innovations made long-distance voyages possible.

The Western Han's naval conquest of the Baiyue minority and the opening of a maritime route not only further expanded the political influence of the Han government but helped to collect many foreign rare treasures. Emperor Wu dispatched a long-distance flotilla heading for the Indian Ocean, thereby opening up a marine route from the South China Sea to the Indian Ocean.

The *Book of Han: Annals of Geography* records that: "despite the barricades of Rinan, or Xuwen, or Hepu, traveling five months one will reach the Dungun. From there traveling further by sea for some four months, one will get to the country of Arramaniya. Again sailing for twenty-plus days, one will reach the country of Tagaung. Then, proceeding on foot for some 10 days, one will reach the country of Pagandhara. From Pagandhara, after sailing for about two months, one reaches the country of Kanchi. The customs [in these places] are somewhat similar to those in Zhuya (Hainan). Their territory is broad, their populations great, and their unusual products numerous. Since the reign of Emperor Wu of Han, they have come to the imperial court to offer tributes. There are chief interpreters, part of the eunuch service at the Yellow (palace) Gate. They will go on a voyage with those who have responded to their recruitment calls, to trade for pearls, glass, precious stones, and exotic products. They take with them gold and diverse types of silks. In all the countries they reach, they are provided with food and companions. The barbarian trading ships transfer them to where they are going ... From Kanchi, after a journey of eight months one will reach Pisang. After a further journey of two months, one will arrive at the borders of

---

[27] It was compiled during 977–983 CE by order of Emperor Taizong (r. 976–997) of the Song with the aim to provide emperors and officials with encyclopedic knowledge. Since three volumes of it would be sent to Taizong every day for his reading, the title of the book was later changed to *Taiping Yulan*. *Yulan* literally means 'the book read by the emperor', while *Taiping* is a *Nian Hao*, an era name, given to a year in Chinese culture. It is a subdivision in the reign of Emperor Taizong named *Zhao Jiong*.

Xianglin County in Nhat Nam. To the south of Kanchi, there is the country of Sihadipa. This is from where the Han interpreting envoys returned."

The above account tells us that The Han Emperor Wu sent imperial eunuchs[28] serving at the Yellow (palace) Gate as interpreters to lead recruited businessmen and sailors to voyage overseas with gold and silk on them to purchase pearls, jewelry, and other rare treasures.

The oceangoing voyage begun southward from Xuwen (present-day Xuwen County in Guangdong Province, at the south end of the Leizhou Peninsula), or Hepu (present-day Hepu County, within the Beibu Gulf, Guangxi Zhuang Autonomous Region), passing by many ancient countries. After years of research, both Chinese and foreign scholars have agreed that they were Dungun Country, which was perhaps Da Nang in Vietnam; Arramaniya Country was modern-day Ratchaburi, a province of Thailand; Tagaung Country was centered on modern-day Tenasserim in Myanmar; Pagandhara was in modern-day Prome in Myanmar; Kanchi was in modern-day Kanchipuram of Tamil Nadu in southeastern India; Sihadipa was present-day Sri Lanka; and Pisang Country was perhaps the Pulau Pisang in the Strait of Malacca.

It is, therefore, safe to deduce the general line of the outbound sailing route in the Han Dynasty: Starting from Xuwen in Guangdong or Hepu in Gunagxi, it passed along the coastline into the Gulf of Thailand after crossing the South China Sea. Then it ran through the Malay Peninsula to the Bay of Bengalalong, finally reaching the southeast end of the Indian Peninsula and Sri Lanka.

The China–India maritime route linked the Pacific Ocean and the Indian Ocean and officially initiated the transportation and trade communication between China, southeast Asia, and South Asia. Thereafter trade interactions began to take place between oriental and occidental countries, symbolizing the preliminary formation of the Maritime Silk Road.

---

[28] Eunuchs were state employees serving not only in the women's quarters, but all over the palace in a wide range of duties, from the lowest positions up to the administration of the imperial household. The terms used for eunuchs varied over time: *siren, yanren, yanren, yanhuan, huanzhe, zhongguan, neiguan, neichen, neishi,* or *neijian,* yet the most common was *huanguan,* and, when serving in a higher office during the Ming and Qing (1644–1911) periods, *taijian* "grand supervisors". Normally eunuchs had no chance to get involved in politics, but some of them actively sought access to power.

2.3 Silk Road Trade Policy

During this period, China was constrained by its limited regional economic development as well as its somewhat primitive shipbuilding and navigation technology. Consequently, the main foreign trade route during this period was via land, particularly the Silk Road across northwestern China, which served as the main channel for Sino-foreign trade. In this light, foreign trade policies of the Han Dynasty were characterized by their emphasis on maintaining this Road, taking the initiative in outbound diplomatic visits and treating inbound foreign businessmen in a preferential way. With the gradual opening of the Silk Road, the Han governments implemented a series of measures to strengthen the control and management of the Silk Road in order to guarantee safety and smoothness of the route. This promoted objectively the development of the Silk Road trade.

2.3.1 *Maintenance of the Silk Road*

(1) Military Administrative Organs help to Develop the Silk Road Economy

In 121 BCE, the Han won a great victory in the war against the Xiongnu and drove them out of the Hexi area, where "four prefectures (Wuwei, Zhangye, Jiuquan and Dunhuang) were set up and two Passes (the Yang Pass and the Jade Door Pass) thereafter garrisoned." Subsequently, the Han government focused on the economic development along this route. Troops were sent to the places along the route in order to reclaim the wasteland. Inland residents were relocated to the Hexi Corridor as a labor force. The agricultural production technology these people brought with them helped to turn the place from a traditional livestock area into a farming one. The growth of population and agriculture gave birth to towns and created conditions for the development of China's foreign trade.

Later on, the Han army continued to advance westward and fought fierce battles with the Xiongnu in the Western Regions. In 101 BCE, General Li Guangli led his troops to defeat the Dayuan nation. The Han government then set up a dedicated post there. The new Western Regions Envoy Commandant,[29] together with his army, cultivated the wasteland in

---

[29] An official position second in rank to marshall during the Han Dynasty.

Luntai (present-day Luntai in Xinjiang) and Quli (to the southwest of the present-day Korla in Xinjiang), and operated transfer stations to provide food, accommodation, and protection for envoys and merchants traveling along the Silk Road. Later, another military office, the Commandant Protecting Areas to the west of Shanshan, was designated to maintain the smooth flow of the south Silk Road.

In 60 BCE, the Xiongnu surrendered to the Han government and withdrew all their forces from the Western Regions. The Han ordered Zheng Ji, the then Commandant Protecting Areas to the west of Shanshan, to expand the area of his dominion "to the northwest of the Jushi," and appointed him to be the "Protector-in-Chief and Grand Master of Remonstrance in charge of 36 countries in the Western Regions," shortened to "Protector-in-Chief of the Western Regions." This means that he was tasked with protecting both the Northern line and the Southern line of the Silk Road within the Western Regions. His jurisdiction covered a vast area, from Dunhuang in the east to the Dayuan and the Pamir Mountains in the west, from the north foot of the Karakoram in the south to the Tian Shan Mountains in the north.

The main tasks of the Protector-in-Chief of the Western Regions were to carry out the decrees of the Han government, to prevent the Xiongnu from staging a comeback, to ensure safe and unimpeded trade along the Silk Road, and to organize and manage farming in the region. As an official title, the Protector-in-Chief of the Western Regions stood as the supreme level of officialdom in that region, equivalent, in importance, to the governor of a prefecture in Central Plains. The establishing of the position signaled how the development of the Silk Road had entered a new phase, heading toward prosperity with fewer impediments.

(2) Repairing and Extending the Great Wall to Strengthen Military Defense

In 127 BCE, the armies of the Han Dynasty regained the Hetao area, where the Han government then set up the Shuofang Commandery (now Hangjin in Inner Mongolia) and the Wuyuan Commandery (now Baotou in Inner Mongolia). Afterward, the government relocated people to the two commanderies to reclaim the wasteland and renovate the Qin's Great Wall along the Yellow River.

In 121 BCE, after the Han army had regained control of the Hexi Corridor, the Great Wall was extended westward along the Yellow River to the west of Lingju (now Yongdeng in Gansu Province), and then a

Great Wall in parallel to this corridor was built on the north side of the corridor so as to extend the fortified structure to the Jiuquan Commandery. "The Han government began to build the Great Wall to the west of Lingju, then further extended it to the Jiuquan Commandery to connect with the northwest country."[30] This indicates that the purpose of building the Great Wall and setting up prefectures and counties in the Hexi Corridor was to ensure safe and smooth traffic between China and the west and then maintain ties with regions and countries along the Silk Road.

In 108 BC, during the reign of the sixth Emperor Wu of the Han, the Great Wall was extended as far as the Yumen Pass. In 101 BC, after Li Guangli's victory over the Dayuan Country, the Great Wall was extended from Dunhuang to the west to Lop Nur. "From Dunhuang to Yanze (referring to Lop Nur) in the west, fortresses are often set up,"[31] thus establishing a complete network of fortified defense systems. During the reigns of Emperors Zhao (r. 87–74 BCE) and Xuan (r. 74–48 BCE), the Great Wall was continually built up, forming a barrier stretching for more than 20,000 *li* (approximately equivalent to 6,214 miles) from the northern banks of the Heilongjiang River in the east to Lop Nur in the west.

The Great Wall of the Han Dynasty, also known as the "Han-garrison," has one "fortress" or "beacon tower" built in every 10 *li* (approximately equivalent to 3.1 miles), and a barrier built in every several fortress or towers. Troops were stationed in the fortresses and barriers, which also provided lodging for passing messengers and merchants. The soldiers there were responsible for investigating the enemy situation, sending signals when emergencies arose and were also engaged in farming. Therefore, fortresses and barriers functioned both as outposts and as military stations. The 10,000-*li* Great Wall in the Han Dynasty effectively ensured the safety and smoothness of the Silk Road and provided convenience for envoys and merchants who used it.

Prior to the Eastern Han Dynasty, many postal kiosks had been set up at important places along the Silk Road for information transmission and accommodation for business trips. At the same time, roads were built in some places with custom passes functioning as inspection points to ensure safe traffic along the Silk Road.

---

[30] (The Han Dynasty) Sima Qian. *Records of the Grand Historian: Biographies of Dayuan.* Vol. 123. Beijing: Zhonghua Book Company, 1959.

[31] (The Han Dynasty) Ban Gu. *Book of Han: Biography of the Western Regions.* Vol. 96. Beijing: Zhonghua Book Company, 1962.

To meet the food demands of the army and travelers, the Eastern Han government encouraged farming of the wasteland in the vast areas from the Hexi Corridor to the Western Regions. A special official organization, the "Sihe Mansion," was therefore set up in Xinjiang to manage agricultural affairs.

2.3.2 *Recruiting Envoys to Undertake Official Trade Activity*

Due to the harsh natural environment, traveling to the Western Regions would have meant contending with thousands of miles of the Gobi Desert, or other wastelands, and unpredictable dangers and risks. Since the days of Emperor Wu of the Western Han Dynasty, envoys have been openly recruited to conduct official trade. Anyone from all walks of life could apply for such a position. Those recruited set off with official goods, such as gold and silk, to trade in foreign countries. On the one hand, they went westward to buy luxury goods for the Court; on the other hand, they took advantage of their status as emissaries to seek after personal gain. The envoys sent by the Han government were "seen in such large numbers in places between Jiu Quan and Bactria that the Han treasures and products began to be depreciate in value in the eyes of foreign countries."[32]

During the Eastern Han Dynasty, envoys were also sent many times to visit foreign countries. The most influential instance came in the year 97 CE, when Bang Chao, the then *Zhang shi* (Senior Subaltern) of the Western Regions, sent his subordinate Gan Ying to Daqin (the Roman Empire) as an envoy. Gan Ying arrived at the Persian Gulf on the western border of Parthia via Central Asia. Initially, Gan Ying wanted to cross the sea, but was overawed by the Parthians' exaggerated description of the perils of the maritime passage and finally retreated. The truth was that the Parthians were deliberately obstructive in this matter since they wanted to monopolize the interests of the silk trade and were loath to allow the Han to establish direct trade relations with Daqin. Therefore, they told these lies. Gan Ying and his people were gulled into retreating by the purported difficulties. As a result, a direct relationship between China and Daqin failed to be established. Nevertheless, Gan Ying's records of the then politics, geography, properties, ethnic groups, and other conditions of

---

[32] (The Han Dynasty) Sima Qian. *Records of the Grand Historian: Biographies of Dayuan.* Vol. 123. Beijing: Zhonghua Book Company, 1959.

the places played a beneficial role in the subsequent economic and cultural exchanges between China and foreign countries.

2.3.3 *Giving Preferential Treatment to inbound Foreign Merchant Envoys*

The Western Han government attached great importance to developing political and economic relations with countries along the Silk Road, so it vigorously encouraged the development of Sino-foreign trade. In the Western Han Dynasty, as soon as foreign merchants arrived in Chang'an (present-day Xi'an in Shaanxi Province), they were received and treated with dinners by the *Da hong lu*[33] (Chamberlain for Dependencies). On the Gao Street in Chang'an, there stood a hotel, reserved exclusively for catering to minorities and foreign visitors. Here foreign merchants were also treated to free accommodation. The Han Emperor Wu often laid on banquets for foreign merchants. It is recorded that they received "Han operas and gifts. Foreign merchants were also shown how full the national treasury was with wealth. The abundance of treasure and strength in national power really shocked them."[34] This, in a way, made the Han government more attractive to foreign merchants. When they returned home, the Han government also sent military men to escort them back.

Through the above measures, the security of the Silk Road and the facilitation of trade were greatly improved. Foreign merchants found themselves enticed by both the material affluence of the Han government and the preferential policies it extended.

2.4 Foreign Trade Development in the Han Dynasty

With the unification of the country during the Han Dynasty, China grew stronger in national strength, with its material civilization becoming highly developed. Via the Continental and Maritime Silk Road, it conducted extensive trade with foreign countries in an open manner. The

---

[33] The official in charge of foreign affairs and etiquette between the emperor and vassals in the Han Dynasty.

[34] (The Han Dynasty) Ban Gu. *Book of Han: Biography of Zhang Qian*. Vol. 61. Beijing: Zhonghua Book Company, 1962.

Book of the Later Han: Biography of the Western Regions records that "every month saw horses come and go. Every day saw merchants shuttling along the Silk Road and guests from foreign countries being treated hospitably at the hotels along the road." This formed such a vivid picture of the development of foreign trade. However, owing to the dominance of the Continental Silk Road via the Western Regions, China's foreign trade was concentrated mainly in the countries along this route. At the same time, the countries linked by the Maritime Silk Road came to gradually conduct trade with China.

2.4.1 *Trade Relations with Central Asian Countries*

During the Han Dynasty, the region that is now referred to as Central Asia was inhabited by many peoples who established their own regimes one after another. Those regimes would be consolidated into countries. Sometimes they were seen in fights with each other, and sometimes they lived in peace. Though boasting different characteristics, all of them were neighbors with the highly developed nation of China and were located along the Silk Road, which extended westwards from China. Under these circumstances, the ancient states of what became Central Asia developed close political and economic ties with China, with frequent bilateral trade exchanges.

From Zhang Qian's pioneering an access route to the Western Regions to the end of the Western Han Dynasty, Central Asia was peppered with tiny countries. In the north, there were the K'ang-chu (now north of the middle and lower reaches of the Syr River), the Dayuan (now the Ferghana Basin), and the Alan (or Aorsi, called Alanliao, i.e., Alani, in the Eastern Han Dynasty, located north of the K'ang-chu). In the south, there were the Yuezhi (now north of the Amu Darya River), Bactria (now to the south of the upper reaches of the Amu Darya River), the Ki-pin (now the Kashmir area) and other countries. Residents of these countries were mostly nomads. The Western Han government developed close trade relations mainly with the K'ang-chu, the Dayuan, and the Greater Yuezhi.

The K'ang-chu people in the Western Han Dynasty lived in the present-day Kyrgyzstan, with a population of more than 600,000. Of these 120,000 were soldiers, making it a populous country in the north of Central Asia. The K'ang-chu people lived as nomads with fur as their staple product. During Zhang Qian's first mission to the Western Regions, he arrived at the K'ang-chu via the Greater Yuezhi. The King of the K'ang-chu asked his people to escort Zhang Qian to the Greater Yuezhi. In 129 BCE, Zhang Qian embarked on his second mission to the Western Regions. After arriving in Wusun, he sent his deputy to the K'ang-chu. Afterward, the envoys of K'ang-chu, together with their Han counterparts, paid a return visit to Chang'an, the capital of the Han Dynasty, thereby establishing official contacts between the Han Dynasty and the K'ang-chu. The K'ang-chu was located on the hinterland of Central Asia and was an important intermediary on the route by which Chinese silk was transported westward. Through the Southern line of the Silk Road, K'ang-chu maintained a long-term trade relationship with China.

The Dayuan was located in the Ferghana Basin in the present-day Central Asia, and its capital was Guishan City (now Kasansai in Uzbekistan). During the Western Han Dynasty, it had a population of 300,000 and more than 70 cities. Its agriculture and animal husbandry were relatively well developed. The country produced rice, wheat, wine, and "renowned bloody sweat" horses. When Zhang Qian embarked on his first mission to the Western Regions, he went to the Dayuan. The King of Dayuan had heard about the munificence of the Han Dynasty and wanted to establish official contact with it, so he took the initiative to send Zhang Qian for visiting the Greater Yuezhi and other places. During Zhang Qian's second visit, the two countries established official relations. "The emissaries from the two countries often met each other on the way to their respective places." The Dayuan became one of the important distribution centers for China's silk to be transported to the west and at one time they attempted to monopolize the silk trade between China and the western countries.

The *Records of the Grand Historian: Biographies of the Dayuan* recounts that "when the Han envoys come, they shall not eat before giving money or silk, and they shall not ride horses unless they buy something. The reason should be: for one thing, the Han China is far away in distance from the Dayuan; for another, the Han, well known as a country with more wealth and treasures, can afford to buy whatever they wanted." In the reign of the Han Emperor Wu of the Han, the trade relationship between the Dayuan and the Han government was often influenced by the incursions of the Xiongnu. The *Book of Han: Biography of the Western Regions* records that the Han–Xiongnu war needs more good steeds. After Emperor Wu was told by the emissary who had been to the Western Regions that the Dayuan produced good-quality steeds named Ferghana horses (a treasured horse said to sweat blood), he sent people to buy horses in the Dayuan with thousands of gold. The King of the Dayuan, who sided the Xiongnu, thought them as a rare commodity suitable for hoarding, so he refused to sell his horses to the Han and had the Han envoy murdered, robbing him of the property he carried. This enraged Emperor Wu of Han. In 104 BCE, Emperor Wu sent General Li Guangli to lead the Han army to fight the Dayuan. In 101 BCE, the Dayuan was defeated and surrendered. After the Xiongnu's power in the Dayuan was eliminated, the Han and the Dayuan formed restored ties. Thereafter a large number of Ferghana horses were transported to the Central Plains, which helped the improvement of horse breeds in inland China.

To the southwest of the Dayuan lay the Greater Yuezhi, which straddled the Guishui River (now Amu Darya River). With a population of 400,000 civilians and 120,000 soldiers, it was a huge nomadic country. In the Western Han Dynasty, the Bactria regime established by the Tocharian people was situated to the south of the Greater Yuezhi. Chinese history books record "Bactria" as Daxia. Bactria had fertile land and rich natural resources, with a population of more than 1 million. It was adjacent to India, China, and Parthia as an important channel for exchanges between China and the west. In the 2nd century BC, the Greater Yuezhi conquered Bactria and moved its capital to Bactra (today's Balkh in Afghanistan).

From then on, the power of the Greater Yuezhi grew. When Zhang Qian went to the Western Regions, the two countries established formal trade relations. The first millennium CE, in the early years of the Eastern Han Dynasty, saw the unification of the Greater Yuezhi tribes by Kujula Kadphises and the establishment of the Kushan Empire, with its capital being located in Purusapura (now Peshawar in Afghanistan). Subsequently, it continued to expand outward, occupying successively the K'ang-chu, the Ki-pin, the Bactria (now south of the Hindu Kush Mountain), the Kophen (now Kabul), eastern Parthia, and northwestern India (around the present-day Pakistan). By the time of Kaniska's reign between 100 and 162 CE, its dominion encompassed vast areas of the present-day Amu Darya River Valley and the Indus River Valley, making it a superpower straddling Central Asia and Northwest India.

The Kushan Empire thereafter became the first stop for Chinese silk to be transported to the west. Making full use of its geographical advantages, the Yuezhi people maintained frequent exchanges of envoy visits with tributes, and private trade with China in the east. Meanwhile, it transferred Chinese goods to the west, becoming an important freight forwarder along the Silk Road, thus earning high profits. The Yuezhi people had already been engaged in silk trade for as long as 200 years and played an important role in the trade along the Silk Road. In the 2nd century AD, their gold coins became one of the common currencies circulated on the Silk Road.

According to the *Periplus Maris Erythraei (Circumnavigation of the Red Sea)* written by a Greek scholar, Northern China-produced items, such as raw silk, silk thread, and satin, were transported overland to Bactres (Bactria) and then southward to Barygaza (present-day Mumbai in India). In 1936, a large number of Chinese silk fabrics were found in a site in ancient Bactria, north of Kabul, Afghanistan, which provided strong evidence for the silk trade being conducted by the Greater Yuezhi people. The commodities that the Greater Yuezhi exchanged with China mainly included treasures re-exported from the west, Yuezhi horses, woolen textiles, etc., as well as raw silk, silk threads, and satin from China.

2.4.2 *Trade Relations with Parthia*

Parthia, during the Han Dynasty, was a large country in West Asia on the Iranian Plateau, which was known as the Parthia Kingdom in the west. It was built around 248 BCE. Its first king was Arsaces, so the period of time in which he ruled was called the dynasty of Arsaces, from which the Chinese term Anxi is derived.

In the 2nd century BCE, Parthia continuously launched wars with other countries and finally became a powerful empire. Its territory reached the Caspian Sea in the north, the Persian Gulf in the south, Bactria and India in the east, and the Tigris and Euphrates Valleys in the west. Prior to Zhang Qian's expedition to the Western Regions, it was known as "the largest country with hundreds of cities covering thousands of miles of land." The Parthians were so adept at business that "civilians and businessmen used carriages and ships to travel thousands of miles to other countries." When Zhang Qian embarked on his second mission to the Western Regions, he sent his deputy to visit Parthia. The King of Parthia especially sent 20,000 cavalries to receive him in Merv City (now Mary in Turkmenistan) on its eastern border, which stood several kilometers away from the capital city.

In 117 BCE, the King of Parthia sent an envoy of his, along with the Han envoy, to Chang'an, the capital of the Han Dynasty. The Parthian envoy "paid large bird eggs and magicians as tributes to the Han government." From then on, an official relationship between the two countries was established. Thereafter envoys and businessmen from both sides kept coming and going for visits and trade until the Eastern Han Dynasty. The *Book of Later Han: Biography of the Western Regions* states that in 84 CE, Parthia sent lions and Fu Ba (like a unicorn but with no horns) as gifts to the Han. In 101 CE, Parthia sent lions and big birds.

Parthia was located in the bottleneck of the Silk Road. When Chinese silk was transported westward to Rome, the routes would eventually converge in Parthia in the eastern section of the Silk Road. Therefore, Parthia was able to monopolize the trade between the East and the West. Induced by high trade profits, Parthia actively prevented Rome from establishing direct trade relations with China. The *Records of the Three Kingdoms: Book of the Wei Dynasty* records that Daqin (Rome) "has always wanted to send envoys to the Han. But Parthia intends to monopolize the trade between China and Daqin, so it has been blocking the two sides from being connected with each other." The *Book of Later Han: Biography of the Western Regions* also records that "Emperor of Daqin has always wanted to send envoys to the Han, but since Parthia has sought to block it and thereby monopolize the trade of colored silk with the Han, this has all been in vain." In 97 CE, during the Eastern Han Dynasty, the Western Regions Envoy Commander Ban Chao sent his deputy Gan Ying as an envoy to Daqin. When Gan Ying reached the Persian Gulf and wanted to cross the sea to Daqin, Parthian deceived him by saying that "the sea is so vast that it takes those who are lucky enough to survive three months to cross it. Sometimes, it takes two years. That's why people who plan to voyage on the sea usually take three year's food with them, just in case. There is also a Goddess living in the sea. No one can resist her temptation but dies in the deep." After hearing this, Gan Ying had to change his mind and returned to the Han.

Parthian people, on the one hand, prevented direct trade between China and Rome. On the other, they transshipped goods between the East and the West. Chinese silk and iron wares flowed continuously to West Asia, Rome, and other places, while western jewelry, colored glazes, spices, medicines, ivory, rhinoceros horns, lions, ostriches, and other exotic birds and animals were also shipped to China by Parthian merchants.

2.4.3 *Trade Relations with Sindhu*

Sindhu is now known as India. China and India are connected by land and sea, so ancient India occupied an important position on both the Continental and Maritime Silk Road. The two countries have a long history in transportation and trade. As was mentioned above, Chinese silk and ironwares were introduced to India long before Zhang Qian's first visit to the Western Regions. In Bactria, Zhang Qian also saw Chinese goods shipped from India. It can be seen that there was a certain scale of trade between China and India before the Han Dynasty. When Zhang Qian embarked on his second mission to the Western Regions, he sent his deputy to visit Sindhu. In 117 BCE, the Sindhu envoys, accompanied by their Han counterparts, came to Chang'an. Thereafter, the official relationship between China and India was established. Transit for the two sides became more convenient with obstacles along the Continental and Maritime Silk Roads being removed.

In addition to the northwest Silk Road, the southwest overland route also ran from Sichuan and Yunnan Provinces in southwest China through Myanmar. After Zhang Qian learned of this and the trade route on his visit to the Western Regions, a steady stream of foreign trade between China and other countries was undertaken here, though the official trade conducted by the Western Han government was blocked by the ethnic minorities in the Southwest. Godfrey Eric Harvey's *History of Burma* records that since the 2nd century BCE, China has used Burma as a commercial channel exchanging Indian rhinoceros horns and ivory for Chinese silk and other famous products. In the Eastern Han Dynasty, the Ailao tribe in western Yunnan was subjugated to the Han government. The Han set up Yongchang County in there, and northern Myanmar was annexed as Han's territory. Trilateral trade between China, Myanmar and India became more frequent with a greater number of merchants and envoys being seen constantly shuttling from the two countries.

The maritime route from the South China Sea to India was opened during the reign of the Han's sixth Emperor Wu. This promoted the Asian overseas trade between China and the southeastern countries of the subcontinent. As mentioned above, the state of Kanchi (Kanchipuram in

India) in southeastern India traded repeatedly with China. However, in the Western Han Dynasty, commerce between China and India was conducted mainly by land, even though the Silk Road was not impeded.

During the Eastern Han Dynasty, the political situation in various parts of the Western Regions was turbulent. Northwestern India was occupied by the Kushans. Most Indian merchants and envoys came to China by sea. The *Book of Later Han: Biography of the Western Regions* records that India "sent envoys to pay tribute many times during the reign of Emperor He (r. 88–106 CE) of the Han. Later on, when the Western Regions rebelled, this ended. During the early years of Emperor Huan (r. 146–168 CE) of the Han, it frequently offered donations." Emperor Huan sent envoys to India as well.

2.4.4 *Trade Relations with Daqin*

Daqin, or the Roman Empire, was also known as Li Xuan or Li Jin during the Han Dynasty. As powerful empires — one in the East and the other in the West — both China and Daqin were committed to developing foreign relations. Exquisite Chinese silk, which passed through many hands and places, was sought after assiduously by Romans, making their wealthy Rome the biggest market for this material and its products.

However, the Han and Rome were geographically distant from each other, with many countries standing in the way of their transportation over the land or on the sea. Among them, the main intermediary on the land route was Parthia, Rome's eastern neighbor; Arabians set up obstacles on the sea route. Before the middle of the first millennium CE, Roman merchant ships that zigzagged along the coast toward India were often blocked by Arab merchants in the Arabian Peninsula. Nevertheless, Rome conducted most of its trade with eastern countries on the sea since the resistance on the sea was less than that over the land.

In the Western Han Dynasty, Roman merchant ships sailed to the southwest coast of India every year to buy Chinese silk goods. As a result, Chinese silk was extremely expensive in price when sold in Rome. H. G. Wells wrote in his book *Outline of History* that "during the Nervan-Antonian dynasty of Rome, it takes a long and circuitous journey to ship Chinese silk to Rome, whose price is higher than gold." In order to reduce the transit shipment of Chinese silk, the Roman Empire strove to seek direct trade with China. The *Book of Later Han: Biography of the Western*

Regions records that "the Emperor of Rome has wanted to send envoys to the Han government for direct trade, but was always blocked by Parthia that tries to monopolize dyed silk trade with the Han."

In order to obtain high profits by monopoly, Parthia also obstructed the envoys sent by both China and Rome to each other. In 97 CE in the Eastern Han Dynasty, Ban Chao, the Senior Subaltern of the Western Regions, once sent his subordinate Gan Ying to Daqin as an envoy. Gan Ying arrived, via Central Asia, in the Persian Gulf on the western border of Parthia. He initially wanted to cross the sea. But the Parthians were keen to monopolize the silk trade interests and did not want China to establish direct trade relations with Daqin. Therefore, they exaggerated the dangers of crossing the sea. Gan Ying and his party retreated in fear of difficulties, and a direct relationship between China and the Daqin failed to be established. However, Gan Ying recorded the politics, geography, properties, ethnicity, and other conditions of the places he passed by, which played a beneficial role in the subsequent economic and cultural exchanges between China and foreign countries.

The *Book of Later Han: Annals of Emperor He* records that November 100 CE witnessed "envoys from Macedonia and Tyre (two countries in the Western Regions), sending to the Han government their kings' golden seals and purple silk ribbon," from which it could be inferred that the envoys actually came from Rome as merchants, and were organized by the agent entrusted by Mace, the great merchant in Macedonia. The main members of that mercantile contingent were people from Macedonia and the City of Tyre in the Roman Empire. In 99 CE, setting off from Macedonia and traveling eastward along the Silk Road, they arrived in Luoyang City, the then capital, one year later.[35]

With the development of maritime transportation and the improvement of navigation technology during the Eastern Han Dynasty, trade between China and Rome operated on the sea in a much larger scale. Roman goods were trafficked to China by Roman merchants, or West Asian merchants, or those from Central Asia, mainly included gold and silver, glass, asbestos cloth, golden-thread cloth, and so on. Among them, asbestos cloth was at that time quite a phenomenon in China by nobles to compete with each other in wealth. Meanwhile, Chinese silk continued to flow into Rome. Some Roman cities, along the east coast of the

---

[35]Lin Meicun. *The Trip of the Roman Business Corp to China in 100 CE* [J]. Social Sciences in China. 1991(4).

Mediterranean, such as Tyre and Sidon, grew to be centers for the silk industry. They would tear into proper pieces the Chinese silk items and redyed them before weaving them into *ling* (twill damask) and *qi* (damask on tabby) favored by Romans. It was quite common for Romans to wear Chinese silk clothes.

The Sino-Roman silk trade was huge in scale, but it was manipulated by multiple intermediaries. Rome paid a high price for this. According to Pliny's estimation, the amount of gold coins gushing into the Arabian Peninsula, India, and China each year was not less than 100 million sestertius or sesterce (approximately 100,000 ounces of gold). This serious trade deficit brought about an adverse impact on the finance and economy of the Roman Empire. As a result, in the early years of the Empire, Emperor Tiberius once banned men from wearing silk clothes. But the ban exerted little effect since wearing silk clothes had become a social fashion.

2.4.5 *Trade Relations with Southeast Asian Countries*

During the Han Dynasty, most Southeast Asian areas were characterized by their primitive tribal alliances, with a few embryonic countries appearing in some areas. After the Han Emperor Wu of the Han Dynasty opened the route from the South China Sea to the Indian Ocean, trade relations between various parts of Southeast Asia and China were gradually initiated. According to the *Book of Liang: Biographies of Babarians*, "all the countries in the south China sea ... have paid tributes to the Han government since the time of Emperor Wu."

Among them, the country that had most contacts with the Han was the Kingdom of Shan (now Myanmar), which borders on China, so its connection in trade enjoyed a long history. The aforementioned goods from Sichuan in China that Zhang Qian saw in Bactria during his first visit to the Western Regions entered Central Asia first via Myanmar, and then India. Foreign scholars therefore believe that Myanmar became an important commercial channel between China and India from the 2nd century BCE. Godfrey Eric Harvey's *History of Burma* records that "the merchants exchanged Chinese silk and other famous products in Myanmar for Myanmar gems, jade, kapok, Indian rhino horns, ivory, European gold, etc." During the Eastern Han Dynasty, the Ailao area in Yunnan was noted for its pearls, emeralds, colored glazes, and amber. They were not produced locally by the Ailao, but imported from Myanmar, India, and even Rome.

In addition to non-governmental trade, official contacts between the two countries were frequent during the Eastern Han Dynasty. According to historical accounts, the Kingdom of Shan sent envoys to China many times. The first time was in 97 CE when they brought with them many domestic treasures, and the Han presented silk goods in return. In 120 CE, the envoys from the Kingdom of Shan brought music and magicians, and the Han presented them with silk products, gold and silver. Later in the years 130 and 131 CE, envoys from the Kingdom of Shan came to pay tributes.

Trade relations between Yavadvīpa and China conducted on the island of Java (in present-day Indonesia) during the Han Dynasty have been recorded by Chinese history books. Both the *Book of Later Han* and the *Book of Eastern Han Compiled at Dong Guan* detail how Yavadvīpa sent envoys to the Han government with local products in 131 CE.

2.4.6 *Trade Relations with Gojoseon and Japan*

Both Gojoseon and Japan are close neighbors of China. Their ancient inhabitants started to trade with China. During the reign of the Han Emperor Wu of Han, commanderies and counties were set up in Gojoseon before the advanced production technology of Central Plains was introduced into the region, thereby promoting the development of the local society and economy. At the end of the Western Han Dynasty, the Gojoseon in the north of the Korean Peninsula rose up and sent envoys to China in 32 CE. Since then, the two countries established diplomatic relations. The economic and cultural exchanges between the Korean Peninsula and China were increasingly strengthened. Silk, silkworm rearing and silk reeling techniques, "Five Zhu" cash coins,[36] iron wares, lacquerware and bronze mirrors of the Han Dynasty were introduced to Gojoseon, while horses and animal skins from Gojoseon were also imported into China.

The Japanese archipelago was home to primitive tribes in the Han Dynasty. According to historical records, more than 30 tribes had contacts with China. The *Book of Later Han: Biographies of Eastern Barbarians*

---

[36]"Five Zhu" is a type of Chinese cash coin produced from the Han Dynasty in 118 BCE when they replaced the earlier "San Zhu" cash coins, which had replaced the *Ban Liang* cash coins a year prior, until they themselves were replaced by the *Kaiyuan Tongbao* cash coins of the Tang Dynasty in 621 CE.

records that in 57 CE, "Japan paid tributes to China, ... Emperor Guangwu (r. 25–75 CE) bestowed them with seal ribbons." In 107 CE, Japanese envoys offered 160 slaves as tributes. Researches make it clear that "Wo Guo" used to be located in present-day Fukuoka City, north of Kyushu, Japan. The gold seal given by Emperor Guangwu was unearthed on Shiga Island, Kyushu, Japan in 1784, providing evidence of Sino–Japanese contacts during this period. With the deepening development of Sino–Japanese contacts, Chinese goods, such as silk, bronze mirrors and bronze swords, were imported to Japan, and Chinese silkworm eggs were also introduced in 199 CE via the Korean Peninsula.

2.5 Economic and Cultural Communication with Foreign Countries

With the development of Sino-foreign trade, Chinese economic culture carried by Chinese commodities was spread to other countries. Meanwhile, foreign cultures were introduced into China. Thus, Chinese culture intermingled with foreign culture to a higher level.

2.5.1 *Commodity Exchanges and Commodity-Manufacturing Technology*

(1) Exporting Chinese Commodities and Manufacturing Technology
During the Han Dynasty, goods exported from China via the Silk Road covered diverse categories. They included not only silk and lacquerwares, which were luxury consumer goods in the eyes of westerners, but also production tools like iron wares. They also included plant varieties unique to China, such as cinnamon, ginger, millet, and sorghum. Among them, silk and ironwares were the most important.

The *Records of the Grand Historian: Biographies of the Dayuan* records that from the west of the Dayuan to Parthia, "no silk and lacquares are found, let alone casting iron." Along the Silk Road, Chinese silk was shipped continuously to the west. Since modern times, specimens of Chinese silk have been found and unearthed in many places along the Silk Road. Chinese silk diversified western people's clothing and purified their lives, too. For example, both the Roman general Julius Caesar and the Egyptian Queen Cleopatra felt honored to wear brocaded robes made of

Chinese silk. The exquisite quality of Chinese silk was increasingly recognized by eastern and western countries.

While great amounts of money were spent in importing Chinese silk, efforts were made to discover the secrets of sericulture technology. In the Han Dynasty, the sericulture spread from Central Plains to the Xinjiang region. In his book, the *Great Tang Records on the Western Regions*, the Buddhist scholar and translator Xuanzang recorded a story about the transmission of silkworm eggs to the west. The book says that Gostana (the ancient Kingdom of Khotan) had no sericulture industry at first. Later, it was said that its eastern neighbor (probably the State of Shanshan to the east of Kingdom of Khotan) had acquired this skill, so the King of Gostana sent envoys to ask for it. He was declined by the King of the Shanshan, who also warned his border guards to prevent any eggs from being carried abroad.

The King of Gostana came up with another idea. He sent envoys to the neighboring country to propose marriage to the Shanshan princess. The King of Shanshan consented to this request. The King of Gostana asked the marriage envoy to tell the Shanshan princess to bring some silkworm eggs with her on the wedding day to make clothes for her since there was no silk in Gostana. The princess accepted the advice and brought some in her headdress. When reaching the border, the guards checked all the belongings except her headgear since checking that was prohibited according to the rituals of the day. Silk eggs thus entered Gostana this way, which started its own sericulture. Upon the princess's request, a decree was carved onto stone steles, stating that silkworms and mulberry trees should be protected from destruction. Any violation of this edict would be severely punished. This story can also be read in the Tibetan text *Chronology of Early Khotan Kings*. In 1900, Marc Aurel Stein found in Khotan Historic Site (now Heqian in Xinjiang) a piece of colored woodblock illustration, which vividly depicts the above-mentioned story.

In the Han Dynasty, the sericulture technology of Central Plains was not only spread outwards through northwestern China along the Silk Road, but also to the present-day Korea, Japan, Vietnam, and other places along the sea route. The *Important Arts for the People's Walfare*[37]

---

[37] The *Important Arts for the People's Welfare* is the most completely preserved of the ancient Chinese agricultural texts, and was written by the Northern Wei Dynasty official Jia Sixie. The book is believed to have been completed in the second year of Wu Ding

records that "in the Han Dynasty, silkworms in the Rinan (today's northern Vietnam) were seen to break through their cocoons eight times a year."

Besides silk, products exported by the Han government included lacquerware, ironware, glazed pottery, paper, etc. In the modern era, some Han products like lacquer dowries, plates, and cups with ears have been unearthed among Buddhist relics in northern Dandanoilik, Afghanistan. Paper was a great invention of the Chinese people during the Han Dynasty. In the Eastern Han Dynasty, China began to produce paper in bulk, which was low in price, convenient to carry and easy to write on, making it a new product traded by merchants both at home and abroad. After the founding of the People's Republic of China, plant fiber paper produced in Central Plains was excavated in many places in the Xinjiang region. During that period of time, paper was transported into northwestern India via the Pamir Mountains.

Technologies transported into foreign countries also included iron smelting and irrigation methods. The metallurgical industry appeared in the Spring and Autumn and Waring States periods. Heading toward the period of the Han Dynasty, the making of ironwares developed to a new level. Nodular Cast Iron, as used nowadays, appeared at that time. Multiple-refined steel made by decarburization cast iron was invented. Therefore, it is clear that the iron products made during the Han Dynasty were well known in the world for their fine quality.

In the 2nd century BC, the Dayuan people learned from China the iron casting technology. This technology was later introduced into Parthia. In Merv, iron was forged into sharp weapons, which was called by the Roman historian Plutarch as "Merv Weapon". Towards the first millennium CE, iron products flowed into Rome. Pliny once wrote that "iron products from China are the best." Han-produced iron and steel also spread into India, therefore, in Sanskrit, Chinese steel is called *Zhi na sheng* (made in China). In addition, iron and iron casting technology was spread to Southeast Asia along the sea route. This has been proved by the ironwares unearthed in the modern era on Java Island in Indonesia.

The export of Chinese commodities and their manufacturing technology enriched the material life of the people in the East and the West. The

---

of Eastern Wei, 544 CE, while another account gives the completion between 533 and 544 CE.

spread of iron and iron smelting technology helped to improve foreign production tools, thus greatly increasing productivity and promoting social progress in local areas.

(2) Importing Western Commodities and Manufacturing Technology
With the development of foreign trade, Chang'an City, the capital of the Han Dynasty, gradually grew to be an international metropolis. The *Book of Han: Biography of the Western Regions* records that "pearls, hawksbill sea turtles, rhinoceros horns, and jewels fill the imperial harems; four varieties of fine Ferghana horses as *Pu Shao, Long Wen, Yu Mu,* "bloody-sweat," "heavenly" horses,[38] are ridden by imperial guards; elephants, lions, fierce dogs, ostriches are seen in the imperial zoo. Various foreign things have been gathered from four directions." Oriental and occidental artifacts inundated China.

The northern countries in Central Asia, such as K'ang-chu and Alan, produced more fur than in other places. These furs were imported in great quantity into China during the Han Dynasty. Therefore, many furriers appeared in big cities, such as Chang'an, the capital. The rich merchants among those furriers were thought to be as rich as vassals to "possess thousands of chariots." In addition, woolen textiles produced in Central Asia, West Asia, and Daqin entered China continuously, too. The *Book of Later Han: Biography of the Western Regions* records that the Yuezhi, the Ki-pin and Sindhu produced a kind of woolen blanket, among which the Yuezhi-made type was the most well known. The woolen textiles traded from Rome were various in category and excellent in quality, being said in history books to be "of good quality, and brighter in color than those produced by other countries." With the import of woolen textiles, the relevant manufacturing technology was gradually accepted by the people of Xinjiang in the Han Dynasty. This played a beneficial role in the development of the woolen textile industry in Xinjiang.

Among the goods imported from Central Asia in the Han Dynasty, the largest in terms of quantity were horses. China had made its with living by traditional farming techniques with horses relatively inferior in quality

---

[38]A Turkmen Akhal-Teke horse. In China this breed of horse is also known as Ferghana horse or "heavenly horse." It is believed to be the mount of the legendary Genghis Khan, Alexander's famous horse Bucephalus was also an Akhal-Teke. The steed is depicted in Chinese literature as "being able to gallop about 1,000 *li* a day and another 800 at night."

and few in quantity. These couldn't meet the needs of fighting against the Xiongnu. Therefore, the Han government kept introducing excellent horses from abroad. During Zhang Qian's second mission to the Western Regions, he brought back from the Wusun dozens of fine steeds, which were praised as "heavenly horses" by the Han Emperor Wu of Han. Later on, the Ferghana horses of the Dayuan entered China and earned a fame as "heavenly horses." The Wusun horse was renamed the "westernmost horse." Not until the Eastern Han Dynasty, Yuezhi horses and Parthian horses were exported into China. In Ban Gu's letter to Ban Chao, he said that "300 bolts (approximately 3,900 meters in length) of white raw silk was given to you, with which you could trade for Yuezhi horses, Styrax, etc." The importing of fine horses in large quantity from Central Asia helped to a great extent the improvement of Chinese horse breeds and was therefore beneficial too for the development of China's animal husbandry. In the later years of Emperor Wu of Han, the central government were directly in charge of more than 400,000 war horses. While in people's daily lives, "horses were used in farming and transportation" as important tools.

Some varieties of plants were also introduced to China from Central Asia and West Asia, including grapes, alfalfa, pomegranates, benne, vicia faba, juglans, *hugua* melon, coriander, rocambole, etc. Grapes, also known as *putao*, were grown originally in West Asia, later being introduced to areas of Central Asia during the Han Dynasty. It was from the Dayuan that the Han envoys obtained their seeds. The *Book of Han: Biography of the Western Regions* records that ancient countries like the Dayuan, the K'ang-chu, the Greater Yuezhi, the Ki-pin, Kucha, and the Jushi produced grapes and wine. Particularly in the Quici, rich households could store up to 50,000 kilograms of grapes, while in the Dayuan, rich people could store 500,000 kilograms of wine. "Some even stored wine for as long as ten years without any deterioration. Wine drinking was quite popular among people." When the grape was introduced into Central Plains, it was firstly planted in the palace. The *Records of the Grand Historian: Biographies of Dayuan* notes that around Emperor Wudi's summer and winter palaces, grapes and alfalfa were planted, which were then cultivated gradually by ordinary people.

Alfalfa was also introduced from the Dayuan. As the fodder for Ferghana horses, it came along with the horses into China. Pomegranates originated from Parthia or Central Asia. Benne is actually sesame, which is said to have come from the Dayuan. Juglans refers to walnuts, coming from Parthia. Vicia faba is known in the culinary sense as the broad bean or peas coming from Central Asia and Parthia. The *Hugua* melon is the cucumber, originating in Egypt. It was planted in the Han Dynasty both in the Wusun and the Greater Yuezhi, from where it was introduced into China. Coriander is Chinese parsley, and rocambole is garlic, both of which came from Central Asia or West Asia. The introduction of such new varieties of plants greatly enriched the variety of Chinese crops and further perfected the Han agricultural production system.

In addition, large quantities of luxury goods and exotic birds and animals were imported into China during the Han Dynasty. During the reign of Emperor Wu, "various foreign things gathered from different directions in China."[39] Among them were luminous jades, pearls, amber, coral, asbestos cloth, fine cloth, and colored glazes from Daqin; elephants, rhinoceros, peacocks, hawksbill from the Sindhu; and lions, ostriches from Parthia. The import of those exotic things and animals, though mainly for the pleasure of the ruling class, did exert a salutary effect on the development of Chinese handicrafts by expanding people's horizons.

2.5.2 *Foreign Trade and Regional Economic Development*

The central Shaanxi area (Guangzhong, "within the Passes") and the Hexi Corridor were two important hubs on the Silk Road. Driven by foreign trade, the towns along the Road prospered economically. Chang'an and Luoyang were not only the national commercial centers, but also international metropolises due to the development of foreign trade. During the Han Dynasty, Chang'an was the country's political, economic, and cultural center as well as a trade center. The city was divided into the Eastern District and the Western District. Within the two districts, there were nine markets with eight main streets. Shops stood on both sides and goods gathered there from both home and abroad. Ban Gu wrote in his *Rhapsody of the Western Capital* about the spectacle of the then prosperous markets in Chang'an, where "three wide roads and 12 gates were built up to make streets and markets within the two districts well connected with each other

---

[39](The Han Dynasty) Ban Gu. *Book of Han: Biography of the Western Regions*. Beijing: Zhonghua Book Company, 1962.

and commodities were categorized. (The two districts were too crowded for) people to turn around and for carriages to take U turns." Gathered in Chang'an were not only merchants from within China, but also foreign businessmen coming via the Silk Road. Some of them resided in Chang'an and established their businesses by running shops. A poem, written by Xin Yannian in the Eastern Han Dynasty, titled the *Captain of the Guard*, mentions the lodging business run by the ethnic "Hu people," living in the north and west of China. It says that "the Huo family had a slave, Feng Zidou by name; relying on the power of the High Marshal, he ogled a Xiongnu maid serving in a tavern. This girl had just turned fifteen and was alone in the tavern one spring day. She wore a long gown with double girdle, wide sleeves and a jacket with a mimosa design. She wore jade from Lantian[40] in her hair. Behind her ears were pearls from Byzantine; and so charming were her two tresses that the likes could nowhere be found. For one tress alone was worth five million cash, the two of them more than ten."

The Western Han Dynasty witnessed that Luoyang had been very energetic in its economy. The *Records of the Grand Historian: Biographies of Celebrated Merchants* states that "Luoyang traded with the Qi and the Lu in the east, as well as with the Liang and the Chu in the south." The Eastern Han Dynasty chose Luoyang as the capital, which further promoted the prosperity of its development. Lu Ji's *On Luoyang* said that there were three markets in Luoyang, "with one in the west of the city, one in the south, and one in the east." Merchants and commodities from home and abroad converged in Luoyang; Hu merchants dressed in Hu-styled hats and clothes could be seen everywhere in the city. The trade between China and foreign countries was unprecedentedly prosperous.

During Wang Mang's reign (8–23 CE), Chang'an, Luoyang, Linzi, the Yuan, and Chengdu were known as the "five capitals," i.e., economic centers of the region where they were located. The economic prosperity of the "five capitals" drove the development of the regional economy in their surrounding areas. For instance, residents in the areas surrounding Chang'an mainly lived on industry and commerce thanks to the urban economy of the metropolis. "The city attracts people to flow in from different directions, making it too crowded in population.

---

[40]A county in Shaanxi Province where jade of quality was produced.

As a result, the residents became more crafty and more willing to run businesses."[41]

As a strategic passage on the Silk Road, the Hexi area could not be avoided by merchants traveling along the road no matter which route they took. Pushed by the Sino-foreign trade, the economy of the Hexi developed in a rapid manner. By the time of the Eastern Han Dynasty, the "four commanderies" in the Hexi enjoyed great economic prosperity. The *Book of the Later Han: Biography of Kong Fen* records that "Guzang could be regarded as a rich county, trading with the Qiang people and the Hu people. The economy of Guzang was the most active one in the whole country that its shops in the market had to open doors four times a day." In addition, Dunhuang also thrived with the development of the Sino-foreign trade at that time to be "a metropolis where trade took place between China and foreign people."[42]

After passing the Hexi area, the Silk Road entered the Western Regions. Driven by the trade between China and western countries, many cities, prosperous economically and culturally, sprang up in the oases along the northern and southern edges of the Taklamakan Desert, such as Loulan, Karasahr, Kucha, Kingdom of Khotan, and Kashgar. In these cities, the Hu and the Han cultures integrated with each other with accelerated progress in civilization.

2.5.3 *Cultural Communication with Foreign Countries*

Commodity exchange is itself a kind of cultural exchange. Material exchanges promote pure cultural exchanges. The Han culture spread westward along the Silk Road, entering the Xinjiang region, Central Asia, West Asia, and Europe. The Chinese language, music, and philosophy had at various times exerted a positive influence upon Eastern and Western countries. For instance, ancient countries like the Wusun, Kucha, the Shache in the Western Regions were deeply influenced by the Han culture in terms of clothing, etiquette, and architectural art. Confucianism and its classics had been continuously introduced into Korea and Japan along the maritime Silk

---

[41](The Han Dynasty) Sima Qian. *Records of the Grand Historian: Biographies of Celebrated Merchants*. Beijing: Zhonghua Book Company, 1959.

[42](The Southern Dynasty · Song) Fan Ye. *Book of the Later Han: Annals of Commanderies and Countries*. Vol. 113. Beijing: Zhonghua Book Company, 1982.

Road in East China since the Han Dynasty. The two countries have been using Chinese characters for a long time. The Indo–China Peninsula had also been deeply influenced by Chinese culture.

At the same time, the Han Dynasty also saw China's adoption and acceptance of a large number of aspects of foreign culture. Due to the introduction of exotic birds and animals from abroad, lions and giraffes appeared in Chinese works of carved stone. The import of plants from the outside world resulted in the appearance of grape ornamentation among the patterns of bronze mirrors and silk fabrics. During the reign of Emperor Wu of the Han, conjuring was introduced from Daqin via Parthia. By the time of the Eastern Han Dynasty, acrobatic art was introduced from Daqin via the Kingdom of Shan (now Myanmar), helping the traditional Chinese acrobatics to develop into "Bai Xi" (acrobatics) with a variety of performance patterns.

Music also came from Central Asia, Sindhu, and the Dan Country. Together with music came music instruments, such as *pipa*,[43] *konghou*,[44] *hujia*,[45] and bamboo flute. Chinese culture was dyed profoundly by the influx of foreign objects, the import of foreign culture and the mobility of its people.

The *Book of the Later Han*[46]: *Annals of Five Elements* records that "Emperor Ling (r. 168–189 CE) preferred many things from the Hu people, including their clothes, bed curtains, beds, food, *Konghou*, flutes, and dancing, while people living in the capital city followed his example as fashions." It was clear that Emperors' preferences influenced common people's lives in a great way.

The book *Imperial Readings of the Taiping Era* also mentions that "people living in the capital city loved eating the Hu pancake due to the Emperor's favoring it." The most important thing imported during the Han Dynasty was Buddhism from India. Generally speaking, in about 80 BCE, Indian monks followed merchants to the Kingdom of Khotan in Xinjiang and spread Buddhism there. In the Eastern Han Dynasty, the Greater Yuezhi occupied northwestern India and its king Kanishka ordered that pagodas and temples be built there since he advocated

---

[43] A plucked string instrument with a fretted fingerboard.

[44] Harp, an ancient plucked stringed instrument.

[45] Nomad flute.

[46] A Chinese document covering the history of the Han dynasty from 6–189 CE, compiled by Fan Ye in the 5th century.

Buddhism, which enabled Buddhism to thrive to a great extent. The monks of the Greater Yuezhi continuously came to China to translate Buddhist texts and spread Buddhism. With the introduction of Buddhism, Gandhara art deeply influenced by Greek culture was introduced into China from the Gandhara area in India. This added some special features to Buddhist sutra, painting, and architectural art. The translation of Buddhist classics had a far-reaching influence on both Chinese literature and history studies. All in all, the development of cultural exchanges based upon economic exchanges contributed to the brilliance of Chinese culture during the Han Dynasty.

Chapter 3

Foreign Trade in the Wei, Jin, Southern and Northern Dynasties*

From the end of the 2nd century to the end of the 6th century CE, political instability was witnessed in ancient civilizations. On the one hand, the feudal system was about to take shape while the classical European slavery system still lingered on. In the year 395 CE, the Roman Empire split into an eastern portion and a western one. The Western Roman Empire fell

---

*The Wei, Jin, Southern and Northern Dynasties (420–589 CE) were a period of long-standing disunion and hostility between various rival regimes within China. Altogether over thirty regimes claimed the founding of a certain "empire," and one dynasty succeeded another based on various regions of China.

It can be mainly divided into three periods as follows: (1) From 220 to 280 CE, the country was divided into three parts, Wei, Shu, and Wu, termed as the Three Kingdoms; (2) From 265 to 420 CE, the Western Jin and Eastern Jin; (3) the Southern and Northern Dynasties.

The Southern Dynasties (420–589 CE) refer to the Liu Song Dynasty (420–479), the Southern Qi Dynasty (479–502 CE), the Liang Dynasty (502–557 CE), and the Chen Dynasty (557–589 CE); at the same time, the North was ruled by a succession of kingdoms founded by invaders from Central Asia. Important among these were the Bei (northern) Wei (386–534/535 CE), with its capital at Datong (later Luoyang); the Dong (eastern) Wei (534–550 CE), at Ye (now Anyang); the Xi (western) Wei (535–556/557 CE), at Chang'an (now Xi'an); the Bei Qi (550–577 CE), also at Ye; and the Bei Zhou (557–581 CE), also at Chang'an.

This period can also be termed as the Six Dynasties period. The name is derived from the six successive dynasties of South China that had their capitals at Jianye (later Jiankang; present-day Nanjing) during this time: the Wu (222–280 CE), the Dong (eastern) Jin (317–420 CE), the Liu Song (420–479 CE), the Nan (southern) Qi (479–502 CE), the Nan Liang (502–557 CE), and the Nan Chen (557–589 CE).

into decline from 476 CE after invasion by the Germanic people. At the beginning of the 3rd century, the Sasanian Persian Dynasty, established after the overthrow of the last Parthian ruler, began its outbound expansion. Under the attack of the Persians, the Kushan Empire of Central Asia gradually waned and eventually split. At that time, small states sprouted up in ancient India. In the 4th century, the Hephthalites began to invade the Sassanid Empire. From the 5th century to the 6th century CE, the Sassanid Empire was gradually on the wane amid attacks from the Hephthalites and Arabians.

Even under the powerful oriental regime of the Han Empire, a peasant revolt, known as the Yellow Turban Rebellion since all insurgents wore yellow turbans, broke out in 184 CE owing to the intensification of the social contradictions. After it was suppressed by force, China entered into a period of convoluted warfare among warlords. In 220 CE, Cao Pi, the son of Cao Cao, proclaimed himself Emperor and named his regime the Wei. This signaled the end of Eastern Han Dynasty in Chinese history and the start of the Wei, Jin, Southern and Northern Dynasties.

Thereafter, China's north–south division lasted for nearly four hundred years with relentless ethnic conflicts and wars. As a result, the social economy, particularly the economy of the north, incurred severe damage. Nevertheless, the economy of the south developed to such a great extent that the silk industry, as a traditional commodity manufactured for export, experienced remarkable progress. Meanwhile, in order to fortify themselves, both the south and the north directed their efforts at developing foreign relationships. Consequently, foreign trade, both overland and overseas, was established with a greater range of countries.

3.1 The Socio-Economic Foundation for Foreign Trade Development

3.1.1 *The Socio-Economic Recovery and Development in Northern China*

The late period of the Eastern Han Dynasty witnessed vassals trying to establish their own separate regimes, continuous wars waging and the social economy being severely damaged. Central China suffered more from this social turbulence than other regions to such an extent that historical records depicted how "sun-blanched bones lie bare in fields abandoned, while not a cock-crow was heard for a thousand *li.*"[1] After the Cao-Wei Regime united northern China, the government committed itself to rebuilding up the social order. Homeless people were organized to work on state farms with civilian and military families. Irrigation facilities were reconditioned. More wasteland was cultivated. Agricultural production was recovered step by step.

By the end of the Cao-Wei Regime, agriculture was revitalized "with land cultivated and cock-crows heard from Shouchun (present-day the Shou County in Anhui Province) to the metropolitan area."[2] A brief unification period appeared in the Western Jin Dynasty, during which great leaps were made in the development of agricultural production in northern China. After the "Disaster of Yongjia"[3] in 311 CE, northern China fell back into intractable ethnic conflicts and endless wars once again. Its agricultural production was unavoidably damaged. Then followed a comparatively stable social environment during the Southern and Northern Dynasties after the Northern Wei Dynasty unified northern China.

The Northern Wei recovered and developed the agricultural production of northern China in a rapid way by encouraging, supervising and promoting agriculture and manufacturing with its implementation of the San Zhang (three elders[4]) System and the Equal-Field System. Therefore,

---

[1] *Hao Li Xing* written by Cao Cao, one of the greatest generals at the end of the Han Dynasty (206 BCE–220 CE) of China. It is a Yue Fu (Music Bureau) tune, sung as an elegy for ordinary deceased people. *Hao li*, also known as *Xia li*, is believed superstitiously by ancient Chinese people to be the place where a person's soul will go after his or her death.

[2] (The Tang Dynasty) Fang Xuanling *et al. Book of Jin: Treatise on Food and Commodities.* Beijing: Zhonghua Book Company, 1974.

[3] Events in Chinese history that occurred in 311 CE, when Han Zhao forces, mostly from non-Han ethnic groups, sacked Luoyang, and captured Emperor Huai. This was seen as the event that led to the fall of the unified Western Jin Dynasty and the reestablishment of the Eastern Jin Dynasty, as well as the loss of northern China to a series of short-lived dynasties known as the Sixteen Kingdoms.

[4] The Northern Wei Court in 486, in accordance with statements in the venerable *Zhouli*, began the establishment of the three-elders (*sanzhang*) system below the district administration. Five households were to make up one neighborhood (*lin*), headed by one neighborhood elder (*linzhang*). Over five neighborhoods, there was one village elder (*lizhang*). In five villages, there was one ward elder (*dangzhang*). The neighborhood elder, the village elder, and the ward elder were collectively termed the three elders.

"people were diligent in harvesting their crops every year with animal husbandry flourishing. Both the people and the country were wealthy enough to stand up to disasters, like floods or droughts."[5] The Cao-Wei policy of encouraging agriculture was inherited by the Eastern and Western Wei Dynasties, the Northern Qi Dynasty and the Northern Zhou Dynasty. For example, the Eastern Wei in the periods of Yuanxiang and Xinghe (538–542 CE) were affluent in grain, as is recorded by the *Book of Sui: Treatise on Food and Commodities*. This work states that "years of harvest have filled people's granaries and, as a result, the price of grain saw a sharp decline."

Manufacturing restored itself on the premise of agricultural development and began to prosper. The silk industry developed fast. The Chinese feudal society was characterized by a combination of farming and weaving, which formed the basic economic pattern, so the feudal regimes in Chinese history gave equal priority to agriculture and the silk industry. For instance, in the Cao-Wei period "in cultivating state farms, people were required to take agriculture and silk industry as their livelihood."[6]

The implementation of the bipartite "*Zu Diao* System"[7] (field tax and household tax system) accelerated the development of the household textile industry. During the Cao-Wei Period, an inventor named Ma Jun, born in Fufeng (present-day Xingping, Shaanxi Province), pioneered the twill weaving machine, further promoting the development of the textile industry in northern China. Zuo Si[8] (250–305 CE) wrote in his *Rhapsody of the Three Capitals*[9] about the well-known silk products with different characteristics and fine qualities in different places, like Xiangyi (present-day Xiangyi in Sui County, Henan Province), Zhaoge (present-day Qi County in Henan Province), Fangzi (present-day Lincheng County in Xingtai

---

[5](The Northern Qi Dynasty) Wei Shou. *Book of Wei: Treatise on Food and Commodities*. Vol. 110. Beijing: Zhonghua Book Company, 2003.

[6](The Jin Dynasty) Chen Shou. *Records of the Three Kingdoms: Biography of Sima Zhi* in the *Book of Wei*. Beijing: Zhonghua Book Company, 1959.

[7]The bipartite Zu Diao Tax System consisted of two components, namely the field tax (*zu*), and household tax (*diao*). In the Tang Dynasty (618–907 CE), it was changed into the *Zu Yong Diao* System, the Tripartite Tax System, which consisted of three components, namely the field tax, household tax, and labor corvée (*yong*).

[8]A poet in the Western Jin (265–316 CE).

[9]One of his *San Du fu* (*Rhapsody of the Three Capitals*). "Three Capitals" refer to the capitals of the states Shu, Wu, and Wei.

City, Hebei Province) and Qinghe (present-day Qinghe County in Xingtai City, Hebei Province).

During the Sixteen States Period (304–439 CE), the social economy was subjected to devastation, but gradually recovered in the time leading up to the Northern Dynasty. As a result, silk was produced in such a great quantity in the northern area of the Huaihe River that the price continually decreased from 1,000 bolts of silk to 300 from the Northern Wei (386–534 CE) to the Eastern Wei (534–550 CE). A large number of silk weaving workshops appeared in the Northern Qi Dynasty, some even being run illegally by officials. For instance, one official, in Yanzhou (in present-day Jining City, Shandong Province), named Bi Yiyun "employed craftsmen privately and possessed dozens of weaving looms."[10]

As a necessity in producing agricultural implements and weaponry, iron casting industry redeveloped quickly after the restoration of the social order due to the increased public and private demand. The Cao-Wei Regime set up official posts, such as the Court Gentleman of Metals and Commandant of Metals, to supervise the iron casting industry. Meanwhile, the development of the private iron casting industry encouraged professional iron-casting workshops to emerge. For instance, at the end of the Cao-Wei Regime, Ji Kang (224–263 CE), a man of letters, was seen to "work as a blacksmith under a big tree to make a living."[11] During the Northern Dynasty, this industry became popular with "agricultural implements, weapons and many other things made of iron."[12]

In addition, the wine-brewing industry and the salt-boiling industry were quite advanced, while the chinaware industry was about to blossom.

On the basis of the development of agriculture and manufacturing, the commodity economy gradually picked up the pace to become dynamic. Trade was transacted at home in places within northern China, between southern and northern China and abroad as well.

---

[10](The Tang Dynasty) Li Baiyao. *Book of Northern Qi: Biography of Bi Yiyun*. Vol. 7. Beijing: Zhonghua Book Company, 1974.

[11](The Tang Dynasty) Fang Xuanling *et al. Book of Jin: Biography of Ji Kang*. Vol. 47. Beijing: Zhonghua Book Company, 1974.

[12](The Northern Qi Dynasty) Wei Shou. *Book of Wei: Treatise on Food and Commodities*. Vol. 110. Beijing: Zhonghua Book Company, 2003.

3.1.2 *The Economic Development and Advancement in Southern China*

During the Han Dynasty, the economy in Jiangnan[13] was quite backward. Sima Qian's *Records of the Grand Historian: Biographies of Celebrated Merchants* records that "southern China covers a vast territory but is less populated. People there feed themselves with rice and fish. Though farming is largely dependent on cultivation and irrigation, life is abundant with no need to trade for materials. They don't accumulate wealth, so they neither suffer from hunger, nor are wealthy." This confirms that the middle and lower reaches of the Yangtze River were in the process of exploitation. From the late period of the Han Dynasty, the northern people witnessed strife among warlords, while the southern society enjoyed a relatively stable social environment, which attracted a continuous influx of people from the north to the south. These migrants brought with them advanced production technology and a good workforce. Under the management of the Six Dynasties, the southern economy was exploited and developed in a comprehensive way with great progress being gained in agriculture, industry and commerce.

During the Three Kingdoms Period (220–280 CE), Sun Quan, the Emperor of the State of Wu established in the Jiangnan, realized the importance of people and agriculture, as was recorded that "people are fundamental for states, just as food is for people; a monarch won't be a ruler without his people's support, just as agriculture is for people's life." In this light, he attached great importance to the development of agriculture. The Wu Regime reduced labor corvee and taxation so as to encourage agriculture and the silk industry. Sun Quan and his heir improved farming tools so that "eight heads of oxen could [be used to] pull four turnplows (*li*)."[14] The "Disaster of Yongjia" at the end of the Western Jin Dynasty triggered the second wave of migration from the north to the south. As a result, the economic development zone was further expanded in the Jiangnan.

---

[13] One of the two sections of the Yangtze River (Chang Jiang): Jiangnan, literally, "South of the River," and Subei, "North (Jiang) Su." The Jiangnan is fertile and well watered, famed for its silk and handicrafts, and very densely populated and industrialized.

[14] (The Jin Dynasty) Chen Shou. *Records of the Three Kingdoms: Biography of Sun Quan* in *Book of Wu*. Beijing: Zhonghua Book Company, 1959.

Apart from encouraging agriculture and the silk industry, the Six Dynasties also paid great attention to constructing farmland irrigation systems. The Qu'e Xinfeng Pool (or Xinfeng Lake in Qu'e, to the modern-day southeast of Zhenjiang, Zhejiang Province), constructed in the Eastern Jin Dynasty, could irrigate over 800 hectares of farmland. This allowed a vast but sparcely populated and barren land to be greatly and rapidly improved. From 420 to 479 CE, the Liu-Song Regime repaired some existent irrigation facilitates, new projects for stagnant water drainage were constructed and watercourses were dredged. By the time of the Southern Dynasty, the agriculture in Jiangnan had assumed a thriving appearance, so that it was said that "vast good farmlands stand side by side with stretched ditches; houses with high ridges and blue tiles are connected with each other; farm tracks expand into the far distance across fields as beautifully as embroidery."[15]

The Six Dynasties also set up prefectures and commanderies to settle the influx of northerners so as to develop the Minjiang River Basin and the Pearl River Basin. Most areas in the Lingnan were under-exploited wilderness during the Han Dynasties. From the Six Dynasties on, large-scale waves of northerners began to migrate to the Lingnan, which brought labor force and production technology there. With the setting up of more prefectures and commanderies there, great leaps had been made in the socio-economic development of the Lingnan area. In 226 CE, Sun Quan split Lingnan into the prefectures of Jiao Zhou and Guang Zhou so as to strengthen the control and development of the region. In the Han Dynasty, Panyu, a port for foreign trade, was renamed Guangzhou. Its rapid economic development laid a foundation for becoming China's center for foreign trade. In the later years of the State of Wu, the Pearl River Delta area boomed with "commerce and tourism operating safely; people becoming wealthy and healthy; and agriculture enjoying a good harvest."[16] The former wasteland had been converted into an emerging economic zone.

The development of agriculture laid the basis for manufacturing and commerce. The leader of the Eastern Wu State in Jiangnan, attached great importance to developing the silk industry in order to meet the fashion

---

[15](The Tang Dynasty) Yao Silian. *Book of Chen: Annals of Emperor Xuan.* Beijing: Zhonghua Book Company, 1972.

[16](The Jin Dynasty) Chen Shou. *Records of the Three Kingdoms: Biography of Lu Yin* in *Book of Wu.* Beijing: Zhonghua Book Company, 1959.

requirements of the upper class. Sun Quan, King of the State of Wu, decreed that officials at different levels should encourage the development of agriculture and silk production. He even asked his wife Madame Zhao to spin and weave in the palace in order to set a fashion for the subjects to follow.

In the capital city of Jianye (present-day Nanjing in Jiangsu Province), the *Cantang* (silkworm room, i.e., weaving room) as a state-owned silk industry organ was set up exclusively for silk production. According to records, there were hundreds of weavers in the palace during the reign of the Wu's King Sun Quan (r. 229–252 CE). The number grew to several hundred in the reign of the Wu's Emperor Jing (r. 258–264 CE), which indicated the large scale of production at that time.

The civilian silk production was booming as well. Historical records describe women in the State of Wu "competing to make gorgeous and extravagant clothes instead of making coarse cloth. It would be a shame if they failed to follow suit." Those who were among the lowest social classes, like soldiers and civilians, "might not have extra grain in their granaries, but would dress in silks and satin when going out."[17] According to the *Book of Song* written by Liang Shenyue, Jinzhou and Yangzhou produced so large a quantity of "silk cloth that it could provide clothing material for the whole population (of the whole country)."

From the Western Jin Dynasty to the Southern and Northern Dynasties (265–589 CE), Emperors continued to advocate the development of agriculture and silk industry, issuing the bipartite *Hu Diao* System whereby apart from a land tax a contribution of light silk cloth and silk floss was required from each household. This objectively expanded the scale of silk production in the Jiangnan areas, south of the Yangtze River. In the late period of the Eastern Jin Dynasty when Liu Yu defeated the Later Qin, hundreds of manufacturers from the central Shaanxi area (*Guan zhong*, "within the Passes") migrated to the Jiangnan. Meanwhile, a state-owned silk bureau named *Douchang* was set up in the capital city Jiankang (present-day Nanjing in Jiangsu Province). Thereafter, silk production began to blossom in the Jiangnan. In the Southern Qi Dynasty, even the Rouran Khaganate, located on the northern side of the Great Wall, sent envoys to central China to ask for

---

[17] *Ibid.*

more weavers. This indicated how well-developed the silk industry was in southern China.

The demand for weapons and arms and agricultural implements pushed the development of the iron industry. During the Eastern Wu Dynasty, the corresponding government agency supervising the iron industry was set up in Jiangnan. The *Book of Song: Annals of Officials* clarified that nearly every commandery in Jiangnan had an iron industry and set up relevant government agencies, most of which are set up by the State of Wu." This system of the State of Wu was inherited by the Eastern Jin and the Southern Dynasties to develop the state-owned iron industry. Well-known centers of iron industry were Yangzhou and Danyang along the lower reaches of the Yangtze River, Jiangxia (now Wuhan, Hubei) and Wuchang along the middle reaches, Linqiong (now Qionglai, Sichuan) and Guangdu (now southern Shuangliu, Sichuan) along the upper reaches.

Meanwhile, many noblemen competed to control mountains and labor forces to commence a private iron-casting units for profiteering. Progress was made in iron smelting technology, too. The invention of the "Steel-Perfusion Method" lifted metal-casting industry to a new level. Its widespread application to casting farming tools improved production efficiency to a great extent.

The ceramics industry was also upgraded in the Jiangnan during the Six Dynasties. In particular, glazed porcelain wares in Zhejiang could boast a superb manufacturing technique.

In the period of the Three Kingdoms (220–280 CE), the State of Shu (221–263 CE) attached importance to production. Further advancements were made in agriculture and manufacturing with "land cultivated, granaries full, tools appropriate and the exchequer abundant."[18]

The silk products in the Ba Shu area gained nationwide renown during the Han Dynasty. Among the Three Kingdoms, the State of Shu paid greater attention to mulberry planting, silkworm breeding and silk weaving, which promoted the advancement of both the state-owned and civilian silk industry. The *Rhapsody on the Capital of the Wei State* written by Zuo Si, depicts such spectacular scenes as "high officials and noble lords being seen in the market; skillful weavers working in their own homes with weaving looms clacking in harmony; once flowery satin is to be

---

[18] (The Jin Dynasty) Chen Shou. *Records of the Three Kingdoms: Biography of Zhuge Liang* in *Book of Shu*. Beijing: Zhonghua Book Company, 1959.

rinsed for brighter colors in the river when it is done." As a silk product of high quality, the Shu Jin sold well at home and abroad as the main fiscal resource of the State of Wei. Hence, Zhuge Liang, the then noble states-man and strategist once said, "at the time when our people are poor and the country are scarce in materials, military expense can only rely on Shu Jin."[19]

Under such a relatively stable social environment, the handicraft industry in the Six Dynasties saw remarkable development in silk weav-ing, the metallurgical industry, the chinaware industry, paper making, etc. The *Book of Song: Treatise on Food and Commodities* records that "the Jiangnan is so prosperous with its vast land, fertile soil, diligent and law-abiding people; a year's harvest will ensure the whole county's basic needs; the advanced fishing industry, the salt industry and the mining industry can meet the demands of people in every corner. The abundance of silk, clothing and cotton can provide clothes-making materials for the whole population." The advancement of agriculture and handicrafts made it possible to develop the domestic and foreign commodity economy; the economic development of Southern China laid a material foundation for the maritime trade to blossom.

3.2 Silk Road Trade Policy

China was split into the south and the north during this period. During the North–South Division, keen to acquire more living space, both the southern and northern regimes made great efforts to develop foreign exchanges in politics, economy and culture by implementing a series of affirmative measures, which accelerated the development of foreign trade.

3.2.1 *Silk Road Trade Policy in the Northern Dynasty*

During the Wei, Jin, Southern and Northern Dynasties, the Xiongnu, the biggest threat along the Silk Road, became enervated and had to move westward. Thus, the traffic, between central China and the Western

---

[19](The Song Dynasty) Li Fang *et al. Imperial Readings of the Taiping Era.* Vol. 815.

Regions, between China and Central Asia, basically became unobstructed. The productivity development made countries and regions along the Silk Road sufficient in materials, ready to initiate trade activities along the road. To expand living space, the northern regimes that controlled the Silk Road within China devoted their efforts to maintaining the transportation along the Road to vouchsafe, to a large extent, trade along the route. Trade, although temporarily interrupted by wars, never paused since that time and progressed to some degree.

A series of measures aimed at promoting the development of the Silk Road trade were taken by the following northern regimes: the Wei, the Western Jin, the Former Qin, the Five Liang and the Northern Wei, which ruled northern China successively.

(1) Restoring Military Agency and Administration

In 220 CE, after the Cao-Wei Regime destroyed the separatist regimes in the Hexi area, a Regional Inspector was appointed to be stationed in Liangzhou (present-day Wuwei in Gansu province), who was also in charge of overseeing political and economic affairs between Central China and the Western Regions. Two years later in 222 CE, the Cao-Wei Regime gave the Governor of Dunhuang an additional post as Commandant of the Western Regions and established in the Western Regions the post of Commandant of the Center in Gaochang. This was the strategic pivot, where troops were sent to cultivate farmland. Another post of Commander of the Western Regions was restored in order to attend to the affairs of the Western Regions. This official was stationed in Haitou (to the northwest present-day Lop Nur). As the two highest ranking officials in the Western Region, the Self-protection Commandant and Administrator of the Western Regions were in charge of ensuring the safety and smoothness of the Silk Road, as a means of strengthening the relationship between Central China and the Western Regions.

In 265 CE, the Sima family replaced the Cao-Wei Regime and founded the Western Jin. In 280 CE, the Jin defeated the Wu, after which there was a short period of unification in the Chinese history. The Jin went on to establish such organs as the Self-protection Commandant and the Administrator of the Western Regions, compelling almost all states in the territory including the Shanshan, the Karasahr, Kucha and the Kashgar, to submit to them. Even the Dayuan, far away in Central Asia, had its monarchical title "the King of the Dayuan" conferred by the Jin. During this period, the Jin dynasty in Central China maintained a very close relationship with the Western Regions to keep the Silk Road open. This is recorded thus: "the Western Regions are unimpeded with no warning signs sent out from beacon towers."[20] The society assumed a peaceful and stable complexion.

In the early period of the 4th century, the northern minorities moved southward into Central China, forcing the Royal families of the Jin to retreat to the Jiangnan area. Northern China was caught up in chaos again. This period is known as the period of the Sixteen Dynasties, with regimes emerging in the northwestern China, including the Former Liang, the Former Qin, the Later Qin, the Southern Liang, the Western Liang, the Northern Liang, etc. Difficult to move southward to Central China, they therefore maintained close contact with the Western Regions in the west. There they appointed officials, sent troops and maintained the safe operation of the Silk Road. Measures taken by the Former Liang included inheriting the system of the Jin, setting up the posts of Self-protection Commandant in Gaochang and Administrator of the Western Regions in Haitou.

When striving to achieve and maintain social stability, local governments in different places also took active measures to restore the social economy in the Hexi area. For instance, during the reign of Cao Rui (226–239 CE) of Wei, when Xu Miao was the Regional Inspector of Liangzhou, he, considering how the locality suffered from shortages of rainfall and grain, encouraged the "cultivation of paddy fields by hiring more poor people." As a result, "households became wealthy and granaries got full even to the brim."[21] The revival of the agricultural economy laid the foundation for commercial activities. Therefore, the transportation between the Hexi area and the Western Regions proceeded so well that goods from Central China and western countries could be exchanged in the Hexi area.

---

[20](The Song Dynasty) Wang Qinruo *et al. Primary Tortoise of the Records Office*. Vol. 696. Beijing: Zhonghua Book Company, 1960.

[21](The Jin Dynasty) Chen Shou. *Records of the Three Kingdoms: Biography of Xu Miao* in the *Book of Wei*. Vol. 27. Beijing: Zhonghua Book Company, 1950.

(2) Implementing the Guosuo System

Since the later years of the Eastern Han Dynasty, Central China had been embroiled in endless wars. Merchants and commodities, from home and abroad, had to instead move westward to conduct transactions in the Hexi area, where Dunhuang emerged to become the most prosperous commercial area. Geographically, Dunhuang was situated at the key junction of the Silk Road, where most of the non-Han merchants sold the western goods they brought with them and purchased products from Central China.

However, they were often bullied, oppressed and deprived by the powerful local clans, who, on the one hand, stopped the non-Han merchants from moving eastward; on the other, the local clans purchased the non-Han merchants' commodities at a lower price. Such transactions damaged severely the non-Han merchants' interest, leaving them exasperated. After the Cao-Wei Regime took over the Hexi area, Cang Ci, the Governor of Dunhuang, enacted a series of measures against the powerful local clans in order to protect Chinese and foreign merchants and the healthy development of Silk Road trade. As is recorded, non-Han merchants' coming with tributes from the Western Regions were always declined by the powerful local clans in the Hexi area who refused to have contact with them. Trade between them was seen as non-Han merchants being bullied, cheated. Fortunately, their complaint about the unfair trade in business later got compensated by Cang Ci in that he helped them in many ways to facilitate their trade conducted in Central China. For example, he helped non-Han merchants with documents necessary to go through passes of examination along their way to Luoyang; when some merchants wanted to stop doing business to go back to their hometown, their goods were taken over by the government at a fair price and they got paid immediately afterward. Armed soldiers were then sent to escort them home. What Cang Ci had done for the people in the Hexi area was highly praised by the local people.[22]

(i) The implementation of *Guosuo* Pass system. Issued by the Dunhuang Commandery for merchants traveling along the Silk Road as traffic permits, which state the holders' age, facial appearance, dress style, goods and nationality. The Cao-Wei authority provided protection and support for *Guosuo* Pass holders along the Silk Road.

---

[22] *Ibid.*, 1959.

(ii) Parity-price commodity transaction. According to the will of the non-Han merchants, free trading was allowed if they preferred to conduct trade in Dunhuang; or they could sell goods to the Dunhuang government at parity.

(iii) Assisting the purchase of domestic commodities. The Dunhuang government would assist merchants to make purchases if they wanted to buy silk products and other items from Central China.

The implementation of the above-mentioned measures restrained the local powerful clans. Therefore, the Chinese and foreign trade were allowed to move forward smoothly. Cang Ci developed a good reputation and became respected by non-Han merchants. After his death, non-Han merchants gathered at the stations of the Self-protection Commandant and Administrator of the Western Regions to express their condolences; some of them even scratched a scar with a knife on their faces to express their grief according to their own ethnic custom; others built memorial temples for him to hold commemorative ceremonies. The *Guosuo* Pass system continued to be operational after Cang Ci's death. During the Western Jin Dynasty, a constant stream of Chinese and foreign merchants trod on the unimpeded Silk Road, and the system began to be practiced nationwide.

In the early 20th century, a batch of *Guosuo*-related documents issued by the Western Jin Dynasty were unearthed in the Niya River Drainage Basin in Minfeng County, Xinjiang. One of them records that "today 319 service men bought 4,326 bolts (*pi*) of silk for the non-Han merchants," from which it could be concluded that silk trade was conducted on a large scale.

Since Emperor Wu of the Western Han Dynasty sent envoys to visit and connect foreign countries, successive dynasties had inherited this tradition as a positive and active dimension in opening-up. Even during the turbulent period of the Sixteen Dynasties, some relatively powerful regimes still exerted efforts to developing relationships with the Western Regions. According to historical records, during the reign of Emperor Fu Jian of the Former Qin Dynasty (351–394 CE), "Liang Xi was sent as the envoy to the Western Regions. He acclaimed Fu Jian's morality and gave the kings he visited colorful silk products as gifts. Afterward, dozens of foreign countries paid tributes to the Former Qin with 500 plus gifts, including the Thousand-*li* Dayuan Horse, known as "Heavenly Horse," which are of precious varieties as *hanxie* (bloody sweat), scarlet neck hair, five colored hair, phoenix chest, unicorn body."[23]

During the early years of the Northern Wei, Emperors paid little attention to opening up, with only loose connections being maintained with the countries of the Western Regions. Some officials petitioned the Emperors that the government should "learn from the Han Dynasty to establish connections with the Western Regions with the purpose of spreading its reputation and attracting foreign goods to be traded within the country."[24] This was refused by the first Emperor Taizu (r. 386–409 CE) of the Northern Wei. After the third Emperor Taiwu succeeded to the throne, some officials once again petitioned him to have envoys dispatched to the Western Regions. Therefore, "Wang Ensheng and Xu Gang as well as others were sent westward as envoys. Unfortunately, they were captured by the Rouran Khaganate after they went out of the desert area. Dong Wan and Gao Ming were then sent to visit nine countries by way of the Shanshan with copious quantities of silk products and jewelry as presents."[25] The visit of Dong Wan and Gao Ming achieved such fruitful results that it made the rulers of the Northern Wei further realize the significance of active opening-up politically and the economically. As a result, the government grew more forthcoming at dealing with foreign relationships.

The Northern Zhou Dynasty took the initiative to send envoys and actively opened up to the outside world, trying to achieve economic prosperity. History records that "(since) the country was economically weak with empty stables and granaries, it had to seek alliance with the West Rong State. In social governance, the dynasty attached importance to moral education and severe criminal penalties as well to gradually establish a good reputation nationwide. Clothes made from different materials were sold within the country; non-Han merchants were to be seen everywhere."[26]

---

[23] (The Tang Dynasty) Fang Xuanling *et al. Book of Jin: Biography of Fu Jian.* Beijing: Zhonghua Book Company, 1974.

[24] (The Northern Qi) Wei Shou. *Book of Wei: Biography of the Western Regions.* Beijing: Zhonghua Book Company, 2003.

[25] *Ibid.*

[26] (The Tang Dynasty) Linghu Defen *et al. Book of Zhou: Preface to the Biography of Foreign Countries* Beijing: Zhonghua Book Company, 1971.

(3) Lü Guang's Conquest of the Western Regions

Breaking through the Silk Road became an important military strategy. In 376 CE, the Former Qin Regime, established by northern non-Han tribes named the Di, defeated the Former Liang and the Dai Regime in Shanxi, and unified northern China. At that time, many countries in the Western Regions expected to expand their exchanges with Central China. In 382 CE, the King of the Former Jushi and the King of the Shanshan together with their officials and merchants came to visit Chang'an, capital of the Former Qin, demanding the setting up of the regulatory Protector-in-Chief to lead the countries in the Western Regions. Nevertheless, some countries in the Western Regions were hostile toward the Former Qin. Such countries included the Karasahr, Kucha, etc. They controlled the petty countries bordering them, which severely hampered transportation along the Silk Road.

In the same year, by the order of the Former Qin's Emperor Fu Jian, Lü Guang was appointed to embark on a conquering mission westward with 70,000 soldiers. With the assistance of the King of the Shanshan and the King of the Former Jushi, the countries in the Western Regions surrendered in the end. The Silk Road was therefore unimpeded. In 385 CE, the non-Han merchants advanced eastward under the protection of Lü Guang. The *Book of Jin: Biography of Lü Guang* records how Lü Guang's troops "used over 20,000 camels to bring back with them precious foreign treasures, performing troops, birds, animals, horses, etc."

However, in 383 CE, shortly after Lü Guang's departure, the Former Qin was defeated by the Northern Jin in the "Battle of Feishui" and soon perished. Consequently, Central China plunged into chaos again. When Lü Guang returned to the Hexi area and was told the news, he crowned himself king and established a regime of his own known as the Later Liang. Thus he maintained a close connection with the Western Regions, where he set up official agencies. His son, Lü Fu was appointed governor and Great Protector-in-Chief of the Western Regions, stationed in Gaochang, taking charge of affairs in the regions and safeguarding the transportation and safety of the Silk Road.

(4) The Northern Wei Defeat of the Northern Liang

In the early years of the 5th century, the Northern Wei Regime established by the Tuoba (also known as the Taugast or Tabgach), a Xianbei clan gradually reunified northern China. The Northern Liang in the Hexi area vowed its allegiance to this government. In 437 CE, (the 3rd reigning year of the Northern Wei's third Emperor Taiwu, r. 423–452 CE), countries in the Western Regions, including Kucha, Kashgar, Wusun, Yueban, Kebantuo, Shanshan, Karasahr, Jushi, Sogdia, or Sogdiana, dispatched envoys with tributes, seeking to strengthen bilateral political and economic ties.

Consequently, the Northern Wei sent envoys westward with gold, silver and silk products as gifts. Among those envoys, Dong Wan and Gao Ming had previously visited the Polona (i.e., the Dayuan) and Chach (i.e., Tashkent in Central Asia). "On their return journey, they were accompanied by the envoys of Wusun and Dayuan. Most of them came with tributes. From then on, envoys came every successive year for more than ten years in a row."[27] Envoys and merchants continued to visit Central China thereafter.

To weaken the Northern Wei, the Northern Liang tried to cut off the connection between the Northern Wei and the Western Regions, so it imposed a heavier tax on the non-Han merchants who were bound for Central China. In 439 CE, the Northern Wei annihilated the Northern Liang in a war and thereafter commanded the Hexi area, the choke point leading to the Western Regions. The Northern Wei governed the Western Regions with moral kindness and severe penalty, thereby gaining submission. The Silk Road thus opened up as a smooth passageway. As a result, domestic and foreign trade along the road developed and blossomed to an unprecedented level.

(5) Measures Facilitate Foreign Trade

After the Northern Wei reunified northern China, unprecedentely few of obstacles were met on the Silk Road. Foreign envoys and merchants arrived in droves. The Northern Wei built reception points to accommodate them, namely the "Four Hostels" (*Si Guan*), for foreign envoys and merchants, including *Jinling Guan, Yanran Guan, Fusang Guan, Yanzi Guan* to the east of the imperial road between the Yihe River and the Luohe River outside the city of Luoyang, the then capital. Among them, the *Yanzi Guan* was designated exclusively for the envoys and merchants from the Western Regions.

---

[27](The Tang Dynasty) Li Yanshou. *History of the Northern Dynasty: Biography of the Western Regions.* Vol. 97. Beijing: Zhonghua Book Company, 1974.

Those foreign merchants coming to Luoyang "enjoyed Chinese customs so much that multitudes of them choose to stay and live there."[28] For this reason, the Northern Wei set up the *Si Li* residence community to the west of the imperial road for foreign merchants to live in. Among them, the *Mu Yi Li* residence community was exclusively for merchants from the Western Regions.

In addition, the Northern Wei provided foreign merchants venues named *Si Tong Shi* (markets for trading with countries in four directions). Such venues greatly facilitated those merchants' lives and commercial activities and helped to further promote the development of China's foreign trade. Historical records state that the "*Mu Yi li* was lined with ordered shops ... with commodities gathered together which are otherwise hard to find in other places."[29]

In addition, foreign currency was allowed to circulate in order to facilitate foreign trade. It is recorded by the *Book of Sui: Treatise on Food and Commodities* that during the Northern Zhou, "commanderies in the Hexi area used the gold and silver currency issued by countries in the Western Regions, which was not forbidden by the host."

The policy toward encouraging foreign trade adopted by the regimes in northern China made it possible for foreign merchants to trade freely with the regimes that were hostile to each other. History records that in 574 CE, Queen Hu of the Northern Qi planned to have split skirts made out of precious beads after her existing one was accidentally burned by fire. She asked a non-Han merchant to go to the Northern Zhou to buy pearls with 30,000 bolts (*pi*) of colorful silk products she gave. That this important mission was entrusted to a non-Han indicated the privilege that foreign merchants enjoyed in Central China.

To conclude, despite the turbulence in the North, the regimes of all ages which enjoyed comparative peace directed their utmost efforts into safeguarding the Silk Road and providing protection and preference to foreign merchants by means of military actions and administrative approaches. All of these factors proved useful in easing the continuous transit of foreign trade along the road.

---

[28] (The Northern Wei) Yang Xuanzhi. *Luoyang Garland*. Vol. 3. Beijing: Zhonghua Book Company, 1959.
[29] *Ibid.*

3.2.2 Maritime Trade Policy in the Six Dynasties Period

During the Six Dynasties period, the ruling class consisted of the aristocratic families who enjoyed privileges in politics and the economy. Politically they could be promoted to be higher-level officials and enjoyed high salaries by virtue of their family status or pedigree. Economically, they seized land according to their own will and deprived laborers of their rights. Hence, societal wealth accumulated in the hands of the ruling class.

The social turmoil as from the later years of the Han Dynasty compelled the elite to realize how uncertain the world was. As a result, most of them lacked the enterprising spirit in politics and were excessively self-indulgent with material goods but led dissipated lives. They only wished to compete in the pursuit of precious treasures imported from overseas, triggering an intensive demand for maritime trade. Meanwhile, the Six Dynasties were intent upon expanding their political reputation. Therefore, they had to develop foreign relationships. However, the overland Silk Road, as a traditional channel for foreign trade was only confined to Northern China. Under these circumstances, the only way out for them was to quest for treasures across the seas.

(1) Dispatching Envoys to Foreign Countries
In 226 CE, Sun Quan, King of the Wu, dispatched a diplomatic mission led by Zhu Ying, a retainer, and Kang Tai, a leader of Court Gentlemen, to visit countries in Southeast Asia. History records that during their visit in more than ten years, "they passed or heard of more than one hundred countries and have written gazetteers of those places."[30] Their visit helped to understand those countries in terms of politics, the economy, and in particular trade and local products. After they returned, Zhu Ying and Kang Tai wrote, respectively, *A History of Foreign Things in the Funan* and *Biographies of Foreign Countries in the Wu Regime*. This diplomatic activity not only consolidated Chinese people's understanding of Southeast Asia but also directly promoted their bilateral trade development. History recorded that after their visit, "Emperors of the Funan, Champa and the Tangming, respectively, dispatched envoys to pay

---

[30] The two books are nowhere to be found, but their contents can be referred to in the following books: the *Commentary to the River Classic*; the *Classified Anthology of Literary Works*, a Chinese *leishu* encyclopedia; the *Comprehensive Statutes*; the *Imperial Readings of the Taiping Era*.

tributes to China." The Eastern Jin and the Southern Dynasty sent envoys to foreign countries as well, which was recorded in the literature.

(2) Organizing Large-Scale Official Trade

Diplomatic activities, during the Six Dynasties, were to some extent economic in nature. In order to get more materials that were rare in the South and for more revenue, the governments of the Six Dynasties sent large-scale fleets overseas for trade activities. In 232 CE, King Sun Quan of the Wu dispatched General Zhou He and the military officer Pei Qian to lead a fleet carrying tradable commodities. They advanced northward, via the East China Sea and the Yellow Ocean, to trade with the people around the coastline of the Liaodong. Even Gongsun Yuan, who set up a separatist regime in the Liaodong, used the well-known Liaodong horse to exchange with them. In 233 CE, Sun Qun's envoy Xie Hong was sent to visit the Goguryeo with "clothing and precious treasures as gifts," while he returned with "80 famous horses."[31]

(3) Canvassing Foreign Merchants

To attract more merchants to China, the governments of the Six Dynasties warmly received such men and tried every means to protect their profits. According to the *Book of Liang: Biography of Central Sindhu,* in 226 CE, Qin Lun, a merchant from the Cippus Dynasty, came to Cochin (a commandery built originally by the Han Emperor Wu in present Northern Vietnam). "The then governor Wu Miao introduced him to the King Sun Quan. When asked by Sun Quan of his local customs, he answered in a detailed way." When he went back to his country, dozens of male and female slaves were given to him as gifts and officials were appointed to escort him to the border area. The fact that Sun Quan, the King of the Wu, received ordinary foreign merchants in person and gave them generous gifts demonstrated the regime's emphasis on developing overseas trade.

(4) Safeguarding the Maritime Silk Road

In the early years of the Southern Dynasties, Champa on the Indo-Chinese Peninsula (in the present-day southern part of central Vietnam) frequently

---

[31](The Jin Dynasty) Chen Shou. *Records of the Three Kingdoms: Biography of Jiang Biao* in the *Book of the Wu.* Beijing: Zhonghua Book Company, 1959.

paid tributes. And yet they also plundered merchants and envoys on the sea, impeding overseas exchanges between China and other foreign countries. In 445 CE, Emperor Wen of the Southern Dynasty sent troops and defeated Champa in the battle of Xiangpu Village, about which it was recorded that "the battle at Xiangfu spread the reputation of the Song Dynasty across the seas." Countries in the South China Sea came to visit afterward. During the Qi and Liang Dynasties, Champa relapsed, threatening the trade along the Maritime Silk Road. In 484 CE, the King of the Funan Kingdom dispatched envoys to the Qi Dynasty, requesting that the Qi conquer Champa to clear the maritime channel for the development of commerce and trade. Emperor Wu of the Qi then ordered the Regional Inspector of Jiaozhou, assisted by the King of Funan, to declare war against Champa. After Champa surrendered, the maritime channel resumed its prior track.

3.3 Changes in the Route of the Silk Road

During the Wei, Jin, Southern and Northern Dynasties, China's opening up continued to proceed along the continental and maritime Silk Roads, the routes of which changed according to internecine conflicts and technological developments in shipbuilding and seafaring.

3.3.1 *The Extension and Expansion of the Silk Road*

During the Wei, Jin, the Southern and Northern Dynasties, the trading routes between China and western countries continued to increase on the foundations laid out by the Han Dynasty. Among these changes, the most prominent lay in how two routes grew to three within Xinjiang proper, namely the Southern Route, the Northern Route and the New Route.

The New Route, also known as the New North Route, refers to the track to the north of Tian Shan Mountains. During the Han Dynasties, roads to the north of the mountain were connected with each other but later were obstructed by the Xiongnu. Not until the Three Kingdoms when the Later Jushi (*Jushi Houbu*) subordinated itself to the Wei Regime, the route was made smooth with no obstructions.

To differentiate from the former North Route, it was named New North Route. Generally speaking, it ran north from the Yumen Pass, passing through Yiwu (present-day Kumul in Xinjiang), Gaochang and Karasahr, to converge as one with the Middle Route in Kucha.

From there, it ran north, negotiating the Tian Shan Mountains. Then it ran west to the Later Jushi (present-day Urumqi in Xinjiang), where it could run southwestward to Gongyue City (present-day Yining in Xinjiang), then reached the Wusun, after crossing the Ili River. After it conquered the Beiliu River (present-day Chu River or the Xi'er River), it reached the K'ang-chu. In the northwest of the K'ang-chu, it connected with the North Route of the Han, which led, via the Alan, to the Polin, the Eastern Roman Empire territory along the Caspian Sea. From the Polin, it ran westward to the east bank of the Mediterranean.

This route was of significantly economic importance for the Eastern Roman Empire. The Roman Empire had competed with the Parthia and the Sasanid Empire (present-day Iran) for the upper and middle reaches of the Tigris and Euphrates during the 1st to the 3rd centuries CE. To usurp Parthia's control over the silk trade, the Roman Empire channeled its efforts into starting a new route for the Silk Road. On the one hand, it established overseas trade with the East by taking advantage of the Indian Ocean monsoon; on the other hand, it managed to obtain silk from the Black Sea. This met the Roman Empire's needs for silk from the continental route and thereby helped the opening and the formation of the New North route.

The Silk Road extended not only northward but also southward. During that period, the Tuyuhun[32] living on the present-day Qinghai Plateau grew stronger and moved eastward and westward as well. As a result, a new route formed, from Central China to Qinghai, passing through the north of the Qaidam Basin (in Qinghai Province), Shaqi, the Altun Mountains, to Qiemo (present Qiemo County in Xinjiang), where it converged with the Southern Route of the Silk Road to form a new trade route. History records that it was this new route that Song Yun, an eminent monk from the Northern Wei, took on his pilgrimage to India.

In addition, the establishment of the State of the Shu in Southwestern China helped to improve the regional economy there. The road from Chengdu to Kunming was so unimpeded that it became an important channel for the foreign exchanges of the Shu. According to the *Rhapsody on the Capital of the Shu State* written by Zuo Si, "bamboo sticks produced by Lin Qiong are seen to be traded in the capital of Bactria." It can be observed that the trade route starting from Sichuan or Yunnan, passing

---

[32] Tuyuhun, a special pronunciation instead of Tuguhun, were a nomad people of proto-Mongolian stock living in the region of modern Qinghai, Gansu, and northwest Sichuan between the 4th and the 7th centuries CE.

through Myanmar and India, to Central Asia had been prosperous in terms of transactions.

In summary, in the Wei, Jin, Southern and Northern Dynasties, the channels for China's foreign exchanges widened with the expansion of the northwestern and southwestern Silk Road, serving as a premise for the advancement of the trade between China and foreign countries.

3.3.2 *The Development of the Maritime Silk Road*

(1) The Development of the Shipbuilding and Seafaring Industries
Jiangnan is crisscrossed with rivers and lakes, so transportation there was mainly reliant upon the waterways. This laid a sound foundation for its shipbuilding and seafaring industries. To meet the demands of the transportation and seafaring industry, as well as to utilize the Yangtze River as a natural watershed against the northern powers moving southward, the Six Dynasties attached great importance to the shipbuilding and seafaring industries.

During the period of the Wu, many shipbuilding bases were set up in Jiangnan, such as the Ship Depot established as an exclusive shipbuilding workshop in Yongning (present-day Wenzhou in Zhejiang), Hengyang (present-day Pingyang in Zhejiang) and Wenma (present-day Lianjiang in Fujian). In Houguan (now Minhou, Fujian) of Jian'an (now Fuzhou, Fujian), a shipbuilding administrator was appointed as Commandant of Shipbuilding to be responsible for organizing craftsmen and apprentices to build ships. The ships they built surpassed those of the previous dynasties in terms of scale and quality. History records that up to 5,000 ships were captured in the battle when the Jin defeated the Wu. At that time, huge ships, over 20 cords (*zhang*) in length, 2 or 3 cords above seawater, could be built to be loaded with 600–700 people and hundreds of thousands of piculs (*dan*) of goods. Those ships were also equipped with rudders to control the heading and sails to be adjusted flexibly according to the direction in which the wind was blowing. Some ships were even equipped with seven sails.[33]

---

[33](The Han Dynasty) Liu Xi. *Explaining Terms*. Vol. 7. Beijing: Zhonghua Book Company, 1985. The book is a glossary dictionary compiled at the end of the Later Han period (25–220 CE) by Liu Xi. With the Confucian concept of rectifying names and terms (*zhengming*), Liu tried to write a dictionary providing the correct designation of all items humans deal with.

The Eastern Jin and the Southern Dynasties saw the further development of the shipbuilding industry. There was a remarkable growth in the scale and quantity of ships being produced then. During the reign of the Eastern Jin's last but one Emperor, a gale destroyed over 10,000 state-owned and private ships which were moored along the Yangtze River. Moreover, the deadweight capacity of the ships improved so that by the Southern Dynasty they could be loaded with 20,000 *hu*[34] (equal to 1,500,000 kilograms) in weight. This is recorded in the *Family Instructions of the Yan Clan*.[35]

With the accumulation of navigation experience and the improvement of seamanship, Wu's seafarers were able to calculate navigational speed and cruising range.[36] By the time of the Eastern Jin, they could tell the course of a long-distance voyage as well as take advantage of the monsoon, as was recorded that "they sail forward by observing the sun, the moon and the stars."

Based on the improvements in the shipbuilding and seafaring industries, the Six Dynasties adopted proactive active policies to develop overseas relations, which further enhanced the development of the Maritime Silk Road.

(2) The Expansion of the Maritime Silk Road
(i) The Expansion of the Maritime Silk Road in the South China Sea

During this period, the development of the Silk Road in the South China Sea could be seen in two main aspects. For one thing, Guangzhou, replacing Xuwen and Hepu of the Han Dynasty, rose to be a primary port for foreign trade. For another, the maritime Silk Road proceeded to expand to western countries on the basis of that of the Han Dynasty.

As was previously mentioned, the Maritime Silk Road of the Western Han Dynasty commenced from Xuwen and Hepu. During the Three Kingdoms Period, after the Wu set up Guangzhou as a prefecture in the

---

[34] *Hu* as a dry measure in ancient China equal to some ten *dou,* approximately 75 kilograms.

[35] Written by Yan Zhitui (531–590 CE), who was a courtier and cultural luminary who served the Southern Liang Court and several northern dynasties. Today he remains one of the best-known medieval writers for his book-length "family instructions" (*jia xun*), the earliest surviving and the most influential of its kind.

[36] (The Wu of the Three Kingdoms) Wan Zhen. *History of Foreign Things in Southern China.*

Lingnan area, the economy along the Pearl River developed rapidly. Together with its advancement in shipbuilding and the seafaring industries, Guangzhou replaced Xuwen and Hepu owing to its geographical advantages.

Compared with Xuwen and Hepu, Guangzhou was advantageous in the following aspects. Neither Xuwen nor Hepu had inland waterways to connect them with landlocked places, thus preventing waterborne transit to the interior of China. The conditions there were unsuitable for taking in and sending out commodities in large quantities. But Guangzhou, as the economic center of the Lingnan area, had far more convenient connections with inland places, such as Hunan, Jiangxi and Fujian, via the Pearl River network.

The reason why the two places became harbors for foreign trade in the Han Dynasty was the limitations of ship sizes back then. Smaller vessels could not sail far from the shore. Added to that, the skills of seamanship were underdeveloped. Meanwhile, ships from Panyu, the then economic center of the Lingnan area, couldn't sail through the Qi Yang Zhou, the dangerous waters to the east of Hainan. Under these circumstances, Xuwen and Hepu, well known for their convenient sailing, became the main harbors for foreign trade in the Han Dynasty.

During the early years of the Six Dynasties, with the improvement in ships' sizes and the advancement of seamanship, it was relatively safe for vessels to sail further away from the shore. Starting from Guangzhou, ships could directly reach Southeast Asia and South Asia via the sea to the east of Hainan and the Xisha Islands. By so doing, they bypassed the Qiongzhou Strait. Guangzhou, therefore, became the center for China's overseas trade. The starting point of the Maritime Silk Road thus shifted to Guangzhou.

With the development of the shipbuilding and seafaring industries, foreign and Chinese merchants set sail across the South China Sea and the Indian Ocean, which helped the Maritime Silk Road to extend westward on the route of the Han. An Arab historian wrote that "since the middle period of the 3rd century, the Chinese merchant ships, departing from Guangzhou, sailed westward to Penang Island, to Ceylon in the 4th century, and to Aden in the 5th century. They finally monopolized the business rights in Persia and Mesopotamia." Another Arab scholar named Masudi also wrote in his book *The Meadow of Gold* (the Arabic title is *Muruj al — Dhahab wa Ma'adin al-Jawhar*) that "in the 5th century Chinese ships reached Hillah of the Euphrates to do business with the Arabs." The *Book*

of Song: Biographies on Barbarians also records that "ships sailed to connect China, the Roman Empire and Sindhu." Obviously, the destination of
the Maritime Silk Road had moved westward from the southeastern India
Peninsula to the Persian Gulf, via the Arabian Sea, though this route has
not been specified by scholars.

(ii) The Extension of the Maritime Silk Road in the East China Sea

This period also saw the further development of the routes from China to
North Korea and Japan. As was mentioned above, during the Qin and Han
Dynasties, the outbound maritime routes from China to North Korea were
mainly situated in the Bohai Gulf of the Shandong Peninsula. This was
where frequent exchanges between China, North Korea and Japan were
seen to have taken place until the time of the Six Dynasties.

The Eastern Jin and the Southern Dynasties witnessed rivalry between
the Koguryo and the Wo Country (now Japan), which impeded the traditional route from the coastal area of the Liaodong Peninsula to Japan, via
the Korean Peninsula. Therefore, ships voyaging from Japan to China had
to cross the Yellow Sea from the Korean Peninsula, which, as a result,
prolonged this oriental route southward, especially after Jiankang (now
Nanjing) became the political and economic center of southern China.
This was recorded in Vol. 324 of the *Comprehensive Investigations Based
on Literary and Documentary Sources*[37]. It relates how "in the early years
of Japan–China transportation, *Wajin*[38] (Japanese people) came from the
Liaodong Peninsula, whereas, during the Six Dynasties and the Song, they
were re-channeled to China by the south route, to pay tributes or do business with China, since the Liaodong, at that time, was not included in
China's territory."

The Southern Dynasties saw the oriental route run thus: it passed
eastward along the Yangtze River from Jiankang to the Yangtze Estuary.
Then it moved northward to the Chengshan Cape of the Shandong
Peninsula. Afterward it moved along the coast to the northern Korean

---

[37] The *Comprehensive Investigations Based on Literary and Documentary Sources* is an
administrative history written during the Yuan period (1279–1368) by the historian Ma
Duanlin (1254–1324), whose courtesy name was Guiyu and style Zhuzhou.

[38] In general the "*Wajin*" that established themselves on the Japanese archipelago became
the Yayoi people, the ancestors of the Yamato people. The word "*Wajin*" also refers to
related groups outside of Japan.

Peninsula. Alternatively, it could advance eastward from the Chengshan Cape to the southeastern Korean Peninsula by way of the Yellow Sea. Finally, it ran southward down the coast to Japan via Straits of Joseon. The opening of this route greatly shortened the cruising range between China and Japan, facilitating their bilateral exchanges.

3.4 Foreign Trade Development

Between the 3rd century and the 6th century CE, China, though carved up by separatist regimes and turbulence, remained at the summit of the world in terms of its economic and cultural development. Meanwhile, its economic and cultural exchanges with foreign countries grew deeper thanks to the continued advancement of material and spiritual civilization.

The number of countries trading with China significantly increased during this period. According to related records, during the Northern Wei, "hundreds of cities in countries from the western Pamir Mountains to the Roman Empire submitted to China, with the non-Han merchants being received everyday in border areas."[39] Official trade undertaken in the name of "paying tributes (*jingong*)" was quite considerable in scale, with envoys sent to trade with both oriental and western countries. Quantities of rare and foreign treasures flooded into China so that there even were no enough state-owned warehouses to hold them.

China has always been a country that observes the rule of "giving more for fewer returns." This resulted in a situation whereby the Northern Wei government couldn't bear any more the burden of giving gifts back to those countries which came to pay tributes. Some officials suggested that tribute trading be curbed. When tributes were no longer crucial to the development of foreign trade, whether officially or privately, the government had no choice but to restrain the official exchange as such to lessen the fiscal burden.

An endless stream of envoy merchants were also seen to come to the south of China over the sea. Jiankang (present-day Nanjing in Jiangsu) as the capital of the Eastern Jin Dynasty was "filled with envoy merchants who came by the thousands on ships." What was more, Guangzhou, as the

---

[39] (The Northern Wei) Yang Xuanzhi. *Luoyang Garland.* Vol. 3. Beijing: Zhonghua Book Company, 1959.

well-known port for foreign trades, gathered an abundance of merchants from home and abroad. The *Book of Southern Qi: Biography of Wang Kun* records that the prosperous foreign trade during the Southern Dynasty made the Regional Inspector of Guangzhou a remunerative post as "30,000 of money would be given to him as bribery when he passes by the city gate."

3.4.1 *Trade Relations with Central Asian Countries*

As was previously mentioned, during the 3rd century CE, a sharp turnaround in politics and economy occurred in Central Asia. The Kushan Empire, once powerful during the Han Dynasties, was on the wane. It only possessed the narrow areas along the Kabul River in the 4th century. Although its once-dominant position along the Silk Road was lost to history, it sustained business relations with China. According to historical records, in 229 CE, during the reign of the second Emperor Ming of the Wei, the King of the Greater Yuezhi dispatched envoys to pay tributes. In the reign of Emperor Shizong (r. 499–515 CE) of the Northern Wei, merchants from the Greater Yuezhi taught the western techniques of producing glass in Luoyang. Other countries of Central Asia which kept a close trading relationship with China included the Dayuan, the Sogdiana and the Yanda, etc.

The Dayuan was also known as Poluona during the Northern Wei Dynasty. The King of the Dayuan dispatched envoys as early as 265 CE to present famous horses to the Wei. In 285 CE, the first Emperor Wu of the Western Jin, sent Yang Hao as an envoy to the Dayuan to enthrone Lan Geng as King of the Dayuan, thereby further enhancing bilateral relationships. Later, in 331 CE, the Dayuan sent envoys to China with coral, glazes, blankets, white cloth, etc. as gifts. In 378 CE, envoys were sent from the Dayuan to Chang'an City with Ferghana horses as tributes. By the time of the Northern Wei, bilateral tributary trade had become so frequent that the Dayuan sent envoys with tributes to China five times during the period from 437 to 465 CE.

The envoy merchants made profits as well. Apart from purchasing large quantities of silk, they earned much more gold and silver by trading other commodities from other countries. The *Book of Jin: Biography of the Dayuan* records that the Dayuan people were "good at doing business, even bargaining for very small profits. The gold and silver they earned from trade were forged into vessels, instead of being used as currency." This indicated just how considerable the amount of gold and silver they earned from China was and how large the trading scale was.

The Sogdiana, also known as the Alan in the Han Dynasty, resided between the Aral Sea and the Caspian Sea. During the reign of Emperor Wu of the Northern Wei, the Sogdiana people paid tributes four times. Civilian trade was practiced even more closely with a great many Sogdian merchants coming to the Northern Wei. In 439 CE, hundreds of Sogdian merchants joined the Northern Liang to fight against the Northern Wei and were captured by the Northern Wei when the Northern Liang was defeated. When the Sogdian King sent an envoy to negotiate for those captives, the Northern Wei set them free in order to develop a friendly trading relationship with Sogdiana. In modern times, large quantities of Sogdian documents were unearthed from northwestern China, which showed us how active those Sogdian merchants were along the Silk Road.

The Yanda, also known as the Hua State during the Southern Dynasties, rose from the area of the River Amu Darya to become a powerful state in Central Asia in the early years of the 5th century, with Bactria City (present-day Wazirabad in Afghanistan) as its capital. The Yanda expanded across almost the whole of Central Asia and controlled the Silk Road, monopolizing trade along it. Attracted by the prospect of high profits, the Yanda maintained a close bilateral relationship with both southern China and northern China. History records the Yanda paid frequent tributary visits to China. According to statistics, from 456 to 558 CE, the Yanda dispatched waves of envoys to cities in northern China for tributary trade, such as Ping City (now Datong, Shanxi), and Luoyang. The Yanda also paid tributes three times during the Liang Dynasty.

3.4.2 *Trade Relations with Persia*

In 226 CE, the Parthian Empire was overthrown and the Sassanid Empire was established. It continually waged wars of conquest with the Roman Empire to its west and later with the Eastern Roman Empire. As a result, it expanded its territory to Mesopotamia and the outfall of the Persian Gulf. To its east, it conquered the Kushan Empire and incorporated the areas of northwestern India and the south of the Caspian Sea into its territory. Consequently, Persia controlled not only "the artery for the trade caravans from China to Central Asia, West Asia and Byzantine" but also "the maritime trade between China, the Near East and India."[40]

After Persia took control of the continental and maritime Silk Roads, it became active in dispatching envoys to develop trade relationships with China, wishing to acquire adequate sources of goods for intermediary trade. According to Chinese historical records, Persia had sent more than ten rounds of envoys to pay visits to the Northern Wei from 455 to 553 CE. The Northern Wei also paid more attention to developing a trade relationship with Persia. In 525 CE, after Persian envoys presented a lion to China, the Northern Wei built a lion garden in Luoyang. Emperor Wen of the Northern Wei sent envoys to visit Persia with blue embroidered brocades as gifts to King Khosrow I.

The civilian trade between the Northern Dynasty and Persia proceeded on a relatively large scale. When Wang Chen, born in Hejian (in present-day Hebei Province), served as Regional Inspector of Qinzhou, he once authorized merchants to purchase dozens of horses from Persia. At that time, it was the merchants who helped the government purchase horses from Persia, sometimes even ten heads at a time. So the trade was well developing between the two countries.

Besides the overland connection with northern China, Persia also led itself to southern China relying solely on its maritime strength. Chinese historical materials claimed that among the foreign ships "the Persian ship is the biggest." In 530 CE, Persian envoys came to China with ivory as tributes.[41]

Meanwhile, Persia imported from China more and more paper in addition to traditional silk and ironwares. From the 3rd century onward, the clerks of the Sassanid Empire can be seen to have written on paper.

In modern times, many Sassanid coins were unearthed in Yingde and Qujiang in Guangdong. These must be related to the continental and maritime Silk Road. Most of the coins were found to have been circulated from the 3rd century to the 6th century, serving to confirm or justify the booming trade between China and Persia during this period.

---

[40] (Soviet Union) M. S. Ivanov. *A Brief History of Iran*. Beijing: SDX Bookstore, 1973. *Also see* Иванов М. С. Очерк истории Ирана. DjVu, Russia, 1952.

[41] (The Tang Dynasty) *Book of Liang: Biographies of Countries in Ancient Hainan*. Beijing: Zhonghua Book Company, 1973.

3.4.3 *Trade Relations with South Asian Countries*

In this period, India was separated into dozens of small states, and was generally called Sindhu in Chinese historical records. In the 4th century CE, the Gupta Dynasty rose in northern India and made frequent contacts with China along the Silk Road. History records that Vikramaditya, the king of the Gupta Dynasty, dispatched envoys in 381 CE to Chang'an, the capital of the Former Qin Dynasty, to present tributes of "fire-washed cloth"[42] (asbestos cloth) and other articles. In the Northern Wei for the Gupta Dynasty sent envoys to Luoyang, the capital of Wei Dynasty five times, paying tributes in the form of horses, gold, silver and statues of Buddha, etc. In 425 CE, the Gupta Dynasty sent envoys to Jiankang, the capital of Southern Dynasties. They came along the maritime Silk Road to present diamond rings and other tributes.

According to the *History of Song: Biographies on Barbarians*, in 428 CE, the Gupta Dynasty dispatched envoys to China once again, presenting precious diamond rings, gold rings, a red parrot and a white one, as well as correspondence, which said that "the Gupta King is willing to present any precious things that the Emperor of China desires ... May our two countries keep in touch with each other forever." This expressed the strong wish of the Gupta Dynasty to maintain a commercial relationship with China.

In addition, other small states within the Sindhu, such as Gandhara and Uddiyana in northwestern India and Kosala in central India, also dispatched envoys to China, for tributary exchanges. Both the *Book of Song: Biography of the Kapilacastu* and the *Book of Liang* record that during the reign of the Ha Emperor Wu, envoys from Sindhu presented a variety of spices, and requested "the two countries to keep in touch by envoys and via letters."

The Simhalauipa (present-day Sri Lanka), an island nation in South Asia, also enjoyed a close relationship with China. The *History of Southern Dynasties* records that from the early years of the Eastern Jin Dynasty (405–418 CE), the Simhalauipa "started to dispatch envoys to present jade statues," and "pay tributes", respectively, in 428, 435 and 527 CE to express its demand for "constant communication, despite being

---

[42]Researchers agree that it might refer to the fireproof textile called asbestos in the *Natural History*. However, even Pliny is vague as to whether this could be identified as a kind of textile or a mineral.

separated by mountains and rivers." It showed how close the relationship between the two countries had become.

More prosperous than official trade was civilian trade. As early as the Three Kingdoms Period, the State of Wu already received foreign merchants from Sindhu, some of whom settled down in China. History related the particulars of Kang Senghui, a renowned monk, "whose family lived in Sindhu from generation to generation. He moved to Cochin since his parents are merchants there."[43]

By the time of the Eastern Jin Dynasty, the merchant ships from Sindhu were seen not only in coastal ports but also in inland rivers and on the hinterland. The *Memoirs of Eminent Monks* recorded that during the Eastern Jin Dynasty, five Sindhu merchant ships once sailed upward along the Yangtze River to Jiangling (present-day Jinzhou in Hubei Province) for commercial trading.

Unobstructed transportation between China and Sindhu by merchant ships made it possible for Buddhist monks to journey westward to gather scriptures or eastward to spread the Buddhist Sutras. For instance, Fa Xian, a monk in the Eastern Jin Dynasty, went westward to India to research on the Buddhist doctrines. He returned on a merchant ship which carried on it hundreds of merchants commuting between China and Sindhu for trade. This bears testimony to how prosperous the maritime trade between the two was.

3.4.4 *Trade Relations with Daqin*[44]

In the 4th century, the Roman Empire was on the wane since its internal contradictions grew increasingly acute. In 395 CE, it was divided into the Eastern Roman Empire and the Western Roman Empire. Thereafter, Daqin in Chinese historical books only refers to the Eastern Roman Empire. Nevertheless, both the Roman Empire prior to the 4th century CE and the Eastern Empire afterward kept frequent trade contacts with China. In the *A Brief History of Wei: Biography of the West Rong Commented by*

---

[43] (The Liang of the Southern Dynasties) Shi Huijiao. *Memoirs of Eminent Monks: Kang Senghui*. Beijing: Zhonghua Bookstore, 1992.

[44] Daqin (literally, "Great Qin"), the Roman Empire in the Ancient Chinese Sources. Through a careful examination of the accounts of Daqin, presumably the Roman Empire, Fulin and Byzantine. The use of such a name for a foreign state probably reflects the comon process of mythologizing distant and unfamiliar cultures.

Pei Songzhi, it states that "compared with Cochin and other places in the South China Sea, Daqin enjoys better transportation, which can be connected to northern China via overland route, and to Yi Zhou and Yongchang over the sea. Therefore, many foreign things are to be seen in Yongchang." It could be inferred that the Romans traded with China via both the continental and maritime routes of the Silk Road. Moreover, they entered southwestern China from Myanmar by way of the southwestern Silk Road.

The official tributary trade between China and Daqin was recorded in literature during the Wei, Jin, Southern and Northern Dynasties. In 281 CE, Daqin envoys came to China with various precious treasures and "fire-washed cloth" as tributes. From 343 to 361 CE, Roman envoys visited Jiankang, the capital of the Eastern Jin. In 363 CE, the Eastern Jin court once dispatched envoys to Byzantium.

Meanwhile, civilian trade became more active than official trade. Waves of Roman merchants traded in China. The *Yanzi Guan* in Luoyang, the capital of the Northern Wei, accommodated many Roman merchants. Roman merchants were also seen living in Guangzhou and other places in southern China. The British scholar Joseph Needham recorded in his book *History of Chinese Science and Technology* that during the Six Dynasties, Roman merchants who lived in Guangzhou cultivated land to grow western plants, which they would then sell for a profit.

With the channels of transportation and trade between China and the Romans growing in number, particularly the further development of maritime trade, the scale of trade between China and Rome greatly exceeded that of the former dynasties. In the 4th century CE, the Greek historian Ammianus Marcellinus mentioned Chinese silk in his book *Res Gestae*. He wrote that "in our country (the Roman Empire) during ancient times, only nobles could wear silk clothes. But now, people at all levels of classes, even as humble as pedlars and servants, can wear them."

In the meantime, the commodities China imported from the Roman Empire increased to such an extent that colored glaze had become a thing of daily necessity for the nobles at that time. During the reign of Emperor Wu (265–290 CE) of the Western Jin Dynasty, noble families used colored glaze to make common vessels for food and drink. As was mentioned above Wang Chen, the Regional Inspector of the Qinzhou in the Northern Wei owned crystal vessels, agate cups and colored glazed bowls, all of which were displayed at his home. After 1949, the tombs of the Six Dynasties were excavated and many-colored glazed vessels of the Daqin were discovered there. Recently, some Byzantine golden coins and Roman copper coins were unearthed in tombs in Xinjiang, Shaanxi and Shanxi. Without doubt, the trade between China and Daqin was carried out both on the continental and maritime Silk Roads, with a large number of commodities transferred to China from other countries.

3.4.5 *Trade Relations with Southeast Asian Countries*

By the time of the Wei, Jin, Southern and Northern Dynasties, the relationship between China and Southeast Asia had grown closer. As was already stated, Sun Quan of the Wu State dispatched envoys to visit Southeast Asian countries, which enhanced the bilateral understanding to such an extent that the Southeast Asian countries frequently paid tributes to China afterward.

(1) Champa
Situated in the south of what is the present-day central Vietnam, Champa belonged to Xianglin County, Rinan Commandery in the Han Dynasties, and then was established as an independent state during the last years of the Han. It was connected to China both overland and across the sea. Therefore, constant streams of merchant envoys traveled back and forth between the two countries. During the Three Kingdoms Period, the King of Champa dispatched envoys to the State of Wu, bearing golden rings to be presented to the Wu's emperor Sun Quan. During the Southern Dynasties (420–589 CE), the King of Champa sent envoys to present tributes to the State of Song. Champa, on the one hand, continued its tributary trade with China; and on the other, it sent troops to invade the Rinan, the Jiude and the Jiaozhou (in present-day northern Vietnam, Guangxi and Guangdong). For this reason, in 446 CE, during the reign of Emperor Wen, the Southern Dynasty waged a war. Champa was defeated and subjugated to the Song Dynasty, with the trade relationship then being recovered.

Thereafter, Champa sent envoys several times to pay tributes to China. By the time of the Southern Qi Dynasty, such a close communication had been formed that the traditional Chinese architectural culture was introduced to Champa. In 498 CE, the King of Champa, Fan Zhunong, unfortunately "died in a maritime calamity" on his way to China. By the Liang Dynasty, the relationship between China and Champa had reached its peak with envoys of Champa paying tributes to China every year. They brought to China aromatic drugs, treasures, rhinoceros horns and ivory as well as cotton and cotton cloth.

(2) Funan

Funan refers to present-day Cambodia, lying in the traffic artery between the East and the West. In the 3rd century, the Funan pursued an active foreign trade policy. The Funan merchant fleet was so renowned over the Indian Ocean as to be nicknamed "the giant ships of Funan." During the Three Kingdoms period, Zhu Ying and Kang Tai were sent as envoys to the Funan, which further strengthened the bilateral trade relationship. Regular bilateral tributary trade proceeded during the Wu Period (222–280 CE). The Funan also dispatched envoys to China three times during the Liu-Song period (420–479 CE).

The *Book of Southern Qi: Biography of Funan* records that in 484 CE, the King of Funan dispatched envoys to present tributes, such as a golden statue of the seated Dragon King, a white sandalwood statue, a hawksbill shell, betel nuts, etc. In return, Emperor Wu of the Qi gave them colorful silk products as gifts, such as 5 bolts (*pi*) in dark reddish purple, 5 bolts in ginger yellow and 5 bolts in dark green. Apart from the tributary official trade as such, the Funan also developed its direct official trade. *The Book of Southern Qi: Biographies of Barbarians in Southeast Asia* records that "the family name of the king of the Funan is Kaundinya and his given name is Jayavarman. Once he sent envoy merchants with commodities to Guangzhou. On their way to China, they were met with a Sindhu monk named Nagasena, who asked for a lift. When caught in a big wind, they had to retreat to Champa, where their commodities were stolen." There were many such instances of civilian trade.

During the Liang Dynasty, the Funan paid tributes every year. From 503–548 CE, its envoy merchants came to China more than a dozen times with coral, Buddha statues, etc. to be presented to Emperor Wu, himself a Buddhist disciple. An army of envoy merchants from the Funan came to China, so the Liang Regime had a *Funan Guan* (hostel especially built in the capital city Jiankang) to accommodate and receive the merchants and envoys from the Funan.

(3) Countries on the Malay Peninsula and Archipelago

During the Wei, Jin, Southern and Northern Dynasties, there were many small countries scattered along the Malay Peninsula and the Malay Archipelago. They traded with southern China via the maritime route.

Dunson on the Malay Peninsula (an ancient country of southern Thailand) lay on the East–West traffic artery. Specifically, since navigation skills were backward in ancient times, the Kra Isthmus (the narrow neck of the Malay Peninsula) was the only place where passing ships had to stop there and their goods would be transported. It was not until the 6th century that such a mode was displaced by the Malacca Strait. It was for this reason that Dunson gathered merchants from both the Oriental and Occidental worlds.

To the south of the Dunson were the Lankasuka (now Pattani, Thailand), the Bandon and the Kelantan (likely located on the east coast of the Malay Peninsula). These countries had traded with China since the early years of the Southern Dynasties. Historical materials record that "the Pranpuri dispatched envoys several times to pay tributes." By the Liang Dynasty, mutual contact became more frequent so that "in May of 529, the Bandon envoys came with dozens of tributes. In June of the same year, they came again with towers, bodhi tree leaves, Lindera erythrocarpa Makino, etc."[45] In 531 CE, Kelantan sent envoys with "towers, pearls, shells, etc." In 535 CE, Kelantan envoys came with tributes, such as gold, silver, colored glaze, treasures and fragrant medicines.[46] The Kandari on the island of Sumatra "paid tributes of gold, silver, precious vessels in the reign of Emperor Xiaowu of the Song Dynasty." The Kandari envoys visited China again in the Liang period with tributes such as fragrant medicines, rare treasures and local produce.

Countries like the Yavadvīpa and the Karitan on Java Island had been dispatching envoys to China since the Southern Song Dynasty. During this period, civilian trade advanced on a rather large scale. In the Eastern Jin Dynasty during Fa Xian's homeward trip, he took a merchant ship from India to Java Island, where he joined another merchant ship loaded with over 200 merchants to return home. Besides, people at that time already knew that it would take more than 50 days to sail from Java Island to Guangzhou. People even knew very precisely that they should expect to encounter storms and rocks during the voyage. This indicated that bilateral trade between countries on Java Island and China at that time had proceeded in a very frequent and routinized way.

---

[45] (The Tang Dynasty) Yao Silian. *Book of Liang*: *Biography of Bandon*. Vol. 54. Beijing: Zhonghua Book Company, 1973.
[46] *Ibid.*

3.4.6 *Trade Relations with Gojoseon and Japan*

During the Wei, Jin, Southern and Northern Dynasties, both Gojoseon and Japan, as China's neighbors to its east, achieved greater leaps in development than China. In both of them, the establishment of slave regimes improved productivity.

This period of time witnessed two regimes in Gojoseon, with the Goguryeo Regime in the north and Baekje and Silla in the south. Since the Three Kingdoms Period, countries on the Korean Peninsula started to develop official contacts with China. In the *Book of Wu: Selected Translations from Records* of the *Three Kingdoms with Pei Songzhi's Commentary*, "envoys of the Wu reached Gojoseon in 233." The King of the Goguryeo presented them with martens and other gifts. By the Wei, Jin, Southern and Northern Dynasties, bilateral contact had entered a new period with a closer mutual trade relationship being established. During the Liu Song Period (424–453 CE), the Goguryeo presented 800 fine horses to China. The Baekje also dispatched envoys with tributes to Jiankang, the then capital city. During the Liang Chen Period, the Baekje and the Silla frequently sent envoys to China. The Southern Dynasties gave a great many gifts to Gojoseon envoys during every visit.

Cultural exportation occurred during this period. History records that the King of Baekje dispatched envoys several times in 534 CE and 541 CE to present local specialties. In return, they requested *Nirvana* and other Buddhist scriptures, teachers who could teach the *Mao Shi*[47] (now known as the *Book of Songs*). "Emperor Wu of the Liang gave them all that they required."[48]

During the Three Kingdoms Period, there appeared a relatively larger country named Yamatai-koku[49] in the Japanese Islands. The *Book of Wei: Biographies of the Wuwan, Xianbei and Dongyi* in *History of the Three Kingdoms* records that in 238 CE, Himiko, the Queen of the Yamatai-koku, also known as Shingi Waō, sent envoys to the Wei. They brought with them

---

[47]Its original name was *Shi* (Poems). It was so titled due to the fact that it was compiled and commented by the "two Maos," that is, Mao Heng and Mao Chang in the Western Han.

[48](The Tang Dynasty) Li Yanshou. *History of Southern Dynasties: Biography of Yimo.* Beijing: Zhonghua Book Company, 1975.

[49]Yamatai-koku was an ancient country somewhere in what is now Japan, described in the ancient Chinese chronicle *History of the Kingdom of Wei*, written in 297 CE.

"4 male slaves, 6 female slaves, and 2 bolts (*pi*) of mock main cloth in 2 cords (*zhang*)." The Cao-Wei Regime conferred on her the moniker of the "Pro-Wei Japanese Queen, and presented her with a golden signet and purple ribbon," together with 50 bolts of white tough silk (*juan*), 8 taels (*liang*) of gold, 2 knives 5 ells (*chi*) in length, 100 copper mirrors, 50 catties of pearls and Lead Oxide."

In 240 CE, the Wei Regime initially dispatched envoys to Yamatai-koki to strengthen the diplomatic relationship. The envoys with them gave tributes, like gold, silver, silk products, copper and iron, etc. In 243 CE, the envoys of the Yamatai came with tributes, such as "slaves, Japanese cloth, blue silk products," etc. The presence of silk products among the tributes indicated that Japan had developed its own silk industry after silk weaving technology was introduced there from China. During the Southern Dynasties, the Japanese managed to cultivate a southern route to China without passing the Korean Peninsula. This made the bilateral trade relationship with China more convenient.

In the early years of the 3rd century, Japanese costumes were as simple in style as "pullovers." In the central part of the cloth, a hole was made, through which one could insert his head so that the garment could act as clothing. *The Kojiki*[50] (*Record of Ancient Things*) has it that from 270 CE to 309 CE, the Baekje of the Korean Peninsula once contributed two outstanding craftsmen in weaving and sewing, with "one named Zhuo Su, the other Xi Su." In addition, the *Nihon Shoki* (*Chronicle of Japan*)[51] records that in 308 CE, the King "dispatched envoys to the Wu Regime for women weavers ... Emperor of the Wu sent four women weavers, respectively, named Xiongyuan, Diyuan, Wuzhi, and Yuezhi, to Japan." At the time of the Southern Dynasties, another Japanese emperor sent envoys to China again for recruiting technically brilliant women weavers and needlewomen. In 469 CE, the weavers, like Hanzhi and Wuzhi, went to Japan with Japanese envoys from Zhejiang.

Moreover, wars and turmoil at the end of the 3rd century forced many Chinese people to emigrate to the Japanese islands. Most of them were

---

[50] Also sometimes read as Furukotofumi, this is an early Japanese chronicle of myths, legends, songs, genealogies, oral traditions, and semi-historical accounts down to 641 concerning the origin of the Japanese archipelago, the kami, and the Japanese imperial line.

[51] *Nihon Shoki* (Chronicle of Japan) is the first official Japanese history book, edited by Imperial Prince Toneri and others and completed in 720.

professional craftsmen. By this means, China's advanced technologies were introduced to Japan. Some Japanese scholars admit that "remarkably, they made contributions to Japan's silkworm breeding and silk industry."[52]

3.5 Economic and Cultural Communication with Foreign Countries

Regimes during the Wei, Jin, Southern and Northern Dynasties pursued the policy of opening up, allowing the Continental and Maritime Silk Road to become further developed, with more material and cultural products being exported and imported, thereby pushing the economic and cultural communications between China and foreign countries to a new level.

3.5.1 *Economic Communication with Foreign Countries*

The Wei, Jin, Southern and Northern Dynasties witnessed economic exchanges between China and foreign countries advance to a higher level both in their breadth and depth. Exchanges took place not only in commodities, such as handicrafts and local specialties, but also in technology, which shifted from the "one-way output" of the Han Dynasty to the "two-way output and input." The most important export was silkworm rearing and silk reeling techniques, while the most important import was western glass-making technology.

(1) Spreading Silkworm Rearing and Silk-Reeling Techniques to the West

During the Wei, Jin, Southern and Northern Dynasties, among China's exported commodities, silk was the largest in quantity. As was mentioned previously, the silk export exceeded in scale that of the former dynasties. China's silkworm rearing and silk reeling technology were introduced to Xinjiang, from where it was further spread to foreign countries, albeit slowly. By the time of the Jin Dynasty, Guo Pu recorded in his novel

---

[52] (Japan) Yasuhiko Kimiya. *Nikka bunka kōryūshi*. Fuzanbō, 1955. Reprint 1977.

Records from Within the Recondite[53] that "in our country there are silk-worms, as small as one's little finger. They eat mulberry leaves and produce silk, but foreign people don't believe it." The 4th century saw the technique was introduced from Xinjiang to Central Asia, where it was introduced from Persia. The geographical position of the ancient Persia was extremely critical compared with other places along the Silk Road. Chinese silk was imported there a long time ago. After Zhang Qian visited the Western Regions, diplomatic relations were established between the Western Han Court and Parthia (another name of Persia). Thereafter, Chinese silk flowed in large quantities into Parthia together with envoys and merchants.

With the influx of silk into Persia came the silkworm rearing and silk reeling technology. Prior to it, the well-known Persian brocade was woven out of golden and silver thread. The advent of Chinese technology started Persian's brocade in its real sense with silk as the main material. The *Book of Wei: Biography of the Western Regions* records that the King of Persia "wears silk brocade." Ever since then, Persian brocades had begun to be widely sold in China. Its commonly used designs of pearls, pairs of birds, pairs of animals were gradually adopted in places like Kucha, Gaochang, etc. At roughly the same time, this Chinese technology was introduced to India.

It was not until the 6th century that Chinese silkworm rearing and silk reeling technology was exported to the western countries. As was mentioned previously, it was only after much effort that Chinese silk could be transported to the Roman Empire. The Persian monopoly over silk trading forced the Romans to pay a higher price for it. Therefore, both the Roman Empire and the Byzantine Empire made efforts to overthrow the Persian monopoly. In the middle of the 6th century, in the reign of Justinian the Great, the Roman Empire finally obtained this Chinese technology.

A historian in the Byzantine Empire named Procopius wrote in his book *The Gothic War* that "an Indian monk arrived in Constantinople. He got to know that Emperor Justinian had hoped his people would no longer buy silk products from the Persians. So he went to see the Emperor with his suggestion. He told the Emperor that he had been living in China, to

---

[53] Originally, the Chinese title was *Xuan Zhong Ji*. However, in the Qing Dynasty, "xuan" was changed into "yuan" since "xuan" the first character in the Emperor Kangxi's name "Xuanye". The social norm at that time was to avoid using any character which was a part of the Emperor's name.

the north of India, for many years, and he knew the way to raise silk-worms and could introduce it to Byzantium. When Justinian heard of this, he asked him how it could be done successfully. The Indian monk said that it was the silkworm, not man, that produces silk from its mouth. Though it was impossible to bring silkworms to Rome, there were ways to get some silkworm eggs. A silkworm, if put in a greenhouse, can pro-duce numerous eggs, and rear far more young silkworms. Justinian prom-ised him a handsome reward if he succeeded. Then people were sent to China to bring back silkworm eggs. According to the method given by the monk, many young silkworms were hatched and fed on mulberry tree leaves. Gradually, Roman people got to know the method of making silk."

At the end of the 6th century, a Byzantine historian named Theophanes set down a similar record. He wrote that "during the reign of Justinian, a Persian taught how to rear silkworms in Byzantine. The Persian once lived in Sinae. Upon departure, he hid silkworm eggs in his crotch and brought them to Byzantine. In early spring, those eggs were put on mul-berry leaves, the best food for the silkworms. Later, silkworms crawled out from the eggs and grew up to fly with two wings."

The above records show us how the technology was introduced to the Byzantine Empire by Persians or Indian monks who once lived in China and knew the relevant techniques. Since the Byzantines obtained the methods of producing silk, large imperial silk workshops appeared in Byzantium with pools of women workers. Their silk products were not only consumed at home but also shipped and sold in other European coun-tries. The Byzantine Empire also monopolized the techniques of silkworm rearing and silk reeling, right up until the 12th century when the technol-ogy was introduced to southern Italy. It took another one hundred years to spread to Western European countries.

The spreading of the techniques not only enriched the people's cloth-ing around the world but also promoted the advancement of civilization in some backward regions. For instance, with the development of the China–Funan relationship, the men of Funan began to wear clothes. The *Book of Liang* records that "during the Wu Period, Zhu Ying and Kang Tai were dispatched to visit the Funan, where they saw people naked, with only women wearing something on the head. They said that the country was good, but it was so strange to see people naked. From then on, the Funan people were ordered to wear clothes, with men wearing barrel skirts, noblemen silk clothes, and poor men coarse cloth."

(2) Importing Glass and Glass-Making Technology from the West

Glass was called "glaze" in Chinese historical materials. China was among the earliest countries to begin producing glass. Based on the archeological materials, China began to produce clear glass at least from the Western Zhou Dynasty. Nevertheless, the glass produced in China was not as good as that in the west in transparency and hardness. The reason lay in the fact that the materials westerners used were different in chemical composition, with the Chinese variety including lead and barium, whereas western glass contains sodium and calcium. This led to glasswares mainly produced in Alexandria, North Africa, a province of Rome, being transported as precious treasures into China with the development of China's foreign trade.

Daqin glass was called "luminous jade" by the Han people. Egyptian glass was not imported in great quantity to China both along the maritime and overland routes until the Wei, Jin, Southern and Northern Dynasties. The technique of producing glass came along with the product. The alchemist Ge Hong (281–341CE) of the Jin Dynasty mentioned in his monumental work, the *Master Who Embraces Simplicity: Inner Chapters*[54], that "a foreign-made crystal bowl was actually made from five kinds of ashes. Some people in Jiaozhou and Guangzhou have learned the method and made them by themselves." A crystal bowl was in fact a transparent glass bowl. It could be seen that the Egyptian glass-making technique had spread, via the maritime route, to Jiaozhou and Guangzhou, the then foreign trade centers in southern China in the 4th century.

In northern China, the 5th century saw the Greater Yuezhi merchants introduce the western glass-making technique to China. The *Book of Wei: Biography of the Greater Yuezhi* records that "from 424 to 452 CE, the Greater Yuezhi merchants came to the capital, saying that they were able to make five-colored glaze. Then ores were gathered from mountains as materials to be used in the capital. Glazes were produced, which shone more beautifully than those produced by western countries. When some 100 people were allowed to watch them in a resort palace, they were shocked to see glaze with such transparent brightness and colors and commended them as creatures of deity. Ever since then glaze had become less

---

[54] It is a key source for exploring early Chinese alchemical theories. In this work, Ge makes it abundantly clear that ingesting elixirs is the best way to prolong life and the only way to transcend death. "Bao Pu" means "to hold to simplicity," as stated by ancient Chinese philosopher Laozi, who touts the key virtues of "simplicity and humility."

precious, descending to being a common daily item. People cherished it no more."

It could be concluded that the division of China into two parts, the southern part and the northern part, under different regimes resulted in the fact that the import of glass-making technique followed two routes: to northern China overland and to southern China overseas.

3.5.2 *Spreading of Buddhism and Cultural & Artistic Communications*

Indian Buddhism was introduced into China by the Han Dynasty. During the Wei, Jin, Southern and Northern Dynasties, the Chinese society was caught up in turmoil and disturbance. Under these circumstances, people bore a strong desire for spiritual consolation. This provided the soil for further growth and development of Buddhism in China. Meanwhile, the unimpeded outbound maritime route saw constant streams of merchant ships, which provided convenient transportation for Chinese monks heading westward to seek out authentic Buddhist Sutras and for foreign monks coming eastward to spread Buddhism.

According to historical records, there were quite a few well-known monks who shuttled to and from China by merchant ships. In 339 CE, Fa Xian of the Eastern Jin set off from Chang'an, via the Western Regions, to Sindhu and the Simhalauipa (present-day Sri Lanka), where he took, in 412 CE, a merchant ship to Java, then took a merchant ship in Yebo to the homeland. Another monk named Tan Wujie went, with other 25 Buddhists, on pilgrimage to Sindhu in 420 CE, and later took a merchant ship from southern Sindhu back to Guangzhou. An Indian monk named Gunarata came to Guangzhou in 546 CE via Lankasuka and Funan. Moreover, Dharmayas, a monk of the Kophen, together with an Indian monk named Bodhidharma, took a merchant ship to China during the Southern Dynasties. All those monks with a fine command of the Buddhist Sutras helped to promote the development of Buddhism in China.

The blossoming of Buddhism in China proceeded with more and more scholar bureaucrats getting to know the religion and gradually becoming disciples. Buddhism influenced Chinese thought and culture in such an extensive way that it began to be displayed in architecture, painting and sculpture. For instance, the concave–convex painting method and the halation method of Sindhu were introduced to China with Buddhism, influencing the style of Chinese painting to a striking degree. Indian Buddhism gradually became localized after coming into contact, conflict and integrated with traditional Chinese culture. Korea and Japan kept close contact with China and imported many Chinese Buddhism Classics, which made Chinese Confucian culture gradually and deeply infiltrate Korean and Japanese societies.

Chapter 4

Foreign Trade in the Sui and Tang Dynasties

The Sui and Tang Dynasties witnessed the Chinese feudal economy and culture climb in a vigorous way to a new high. After the previous 400 years of national assimilation and fusion during the Wei, Jin, Southern and Northern Dynasties, China experienced a new infusion of blood. The joint efforts of all nationalities created the advanced material and spiritual civilizations in the history of Chinese feudal society. This in turn laid a solid foundation for her opening-up to the world.

The Sui and Tang Dynasties, which were established after this national fusion, were receptive and welcoming to people from all nationalities together with their cultures. The second Emperor Taizong (r. 626– 649) of the Tang Dynasty once said that "the former Emperors thought highly of the Han people and looked down upon minorities, but I treat them as equal."[1] The awareness of national equality constituted the ideological and cultural basis for opening up in the Tang Dynasty. Therefore, the Tang Dynasty implemented the most emancipated policy ever seen in the feudal era in the fields of industry, commerce and the service industry, as well as in the selection of officials. An unprecedentedly sound premise was created for exchange with foreign countries, politically, economically and culturally, as well as for foreign trades.

---

[1](The Song Dynasty) Sima Guang. *Comprehensive Mirror to Aid in Government.* Vol. 198. Beijing: Zhonghua Book Store, 1976.

4.1 The Socio-Economic Foundation of Foreign Trade Development

The extent and level of a country's foreign trade is circumscribed by its economic development. The socioeconomic prosperity during the Sui and Tang Dynasties, particularly in the Tang, laid a material foundation for the advancement of foreign trade.

4.1.1 *Twists and Turns in Socio-Economic Development*

The Sui Dynasty was founded in 581 and united the whole country thereafter, putting an end to the South–North divisions and wars. This provided conditions conducive for socioeconomic development.

To consolidate the new-born regime, the first Emperor Wen (r. 581–604) of the Sui reformed the "Equal Field System" to enable more farmers to have cultivatable land. This policy, together with tax relief, aroused farmers' enthusiasm for production. Both the central and local governments also paid much attention to the construction of irrigation facilities, creating advantageous conditions for agricultural production. Consequently, the entire country could bear witness to thriving scenes in which "men help each other in farming, and women in weaving." With the extension of farmland and the increase in grain yields, the national treasury was filled to abundance.

Agricultural development was followed by prosperity in industry and commerce. For instance, in the central Shaanxi area, "many farmers left their farmland to go into business for daily or hourly profits; idlers have increased; more people compete for minor profits."[2] This implies that both manufacturing and commerce developed in a prosperous way.

On the basis of comprehensive national strength, the second Emperor Yang (r. 604–618) of the Sui Dynasty waged reckless wars with other countries. Large-scale construction projects all called for the recruitment of labor to build canals and the Eastern Capital of Luoyang. To meet this demand, heavy military service was needed and the burden of imposed labor corvee on the people separated farmers from their lands. Consequently, the agricultural economy of the Sui Dynasty gradually waned, disrupting the basis of living for the feudal regime.

---

[2](The Tang Dynasty) Wei Zheng *et al. Book of Sui: Geography* I. Vol. 29. Beijing: Zhonghua Book Company, 1973.

The Sui Dynasty proved to be a short-lived regime and was soon replaced.

4.1.2 *Economic Development and Economic Center Migration in the Tang Dynasty*

Li Yuan and his son Li Shimin who rose to power through the peasant revolts in the later Sui Dynasty, established the Tang Dynasty. The infrastructures of the Sui Dynasty, particularly the Great Canals, provided a premise for South–North economic connections and the integrated development of the south and north as a whole. Meanwhile, the early Tang Emperors learned lessons from the collapse of the Sui, making efforts to avoid extravagance and waste as well as the burdens of tax and labor corvee. The social economy was revitalized within a short span of time, giving rise to the lengthy and prosperous regnal periods such as the "Prosperity of Zhenguan"[3] and the "Heyday of Kaiyuan."[4] Undoubtedly, agricultural development formed the basis for the prosperous feudal economy. The Tang Dynasty saw an improvement of land use efficiency with the employment of advanced tools, like Curved Shaft Plows and Chinese Noria as well as the production method of multiple crop rotation. During the regnal years of the Kaiyuan (Opening the Origin, 713–741) and Tianbao (Heavenly Treasure, 713–756), the grain was so abundant that Du Fu, the well-known Tang poet, wrote in his poem *Recalling the Past* that "during the heyday of the Kaiyuan, a small city would have been populated with tens of thousands of households. They produced more rice and maize with both private and national granaries remaining full."

On the basis of agricultural development, the handicraft industry also rose to a new level with more varieties of craft and more complex division of labor. Remarkable advancements could be seen in the textile industry, the iron smelting industry, the porcelain-making industry, the papermaking industry, as well as the printing industry.

---

[3] The Tang Dynasty (618–907) witnessed the first period of efflorescence in the reign (627–649) of Emperor Taizong, which was called the Prosperity of Zhenguan, an era of peace and prosperity.

[4] During the Kaiyuan period (713–741) of Emperor Xuanzong, the Tang Empire justifiably became the largest, richest, most sophisticated state in the world at that time.

In the early Tang period, the Chinese textile industry, particularly the silk production industry, was centered on the middle and lower reaches of the Yellow River. For example, Dingzhou in Hebei Province was renowned for its silk products in terms of yield, varieties and quality. Those silk products of high quality were offered up as tributes to the Imperial Court. By contrast, the silk production industry was quite backward in the south. Li Zhao, a scholar in the mid-Tang Dynasty recorded in his writing *Supplement to the History of the Tang Dynasty*[5] that "from the outset, southern people didn't produce silk products."

In 767, the Military Commissioner[6] of Zhedong (eastern Zhejiang) named Xue Jianxun "issued a secret order to recruit unmarried soldiers who would be sent, with much money on them, to the north to look for girl weavers to be taken as their brides. After their return, the southern people were taught to weave, and the silk industry was seen to boom in southern China." Since the middle Tang Dynasty, the southern silk industry made a great leap forward, exceeding the northern silk products. Advanced silk products of high quality were mainly produced in Wuyue[7] area, notably in Yuezhou. During the thirteenth Emperor Dezong's reign (780–805), silk products from Yuezhou were said to be more diversified in range. Among the silk items contributed to the Imperial Court, there were "dozens of different kinds, such as texturing damask silk, monofilament damask silk, cinnabar silk, etc."[8] In the reign of the twelfth Emperor Daizong (762–779), the Saaya Irie of the East Circuit of Zhejiang was a well-known product in the Jiangzuo area, south of the lower reaches of the Yangtze River.

Porcelain manufacturing reached its maturity in the Tang Dynasty with kilns spread nationwide. To date, remains of these have been found in Hebei, Shanxi, Shandong, Henan, Shaanxi, Jiangsu, Zhejiang, Anhui, Hunan, Jiangxi, Fujian, Guangdong, Guangxi and Sichuan. They produced fine porcelain wares, among which the snow-like or silver-like white porcelain, produced in Xingzhou (present-day Xingtian, Hebei Province), and

---

[5] This is a collection of stories from the history of the early Tang period (618–907 CE).

[6] Military commissioners were high officials nominally controlling the military affairs of one circuit (*dao*). The office was created during the Tang period (618–907) and played a major role in the disintegration of the Tang Empire.

[7] In the modern day, it covers the following areas: the south of Jiangsu Province, Shanghai, Zhejiang Province, and the south of Jiangxi Province.

[8] The *Illustrated Annals of Prefectures and Countries*. Vol. 26.

the jade-like glazed porcelains of Yuezhou were well-known for their delicacy and refinement.

The metal casting industry was also developed in the Tang Dynasty. The Directorate for Imperial Manufacturers was set up by the central government as a state organ with relevant Metal Casting Offices in local governments to administer and supervise the official-run metal casting industry. Civilians were allowed to run private metal casting businesses, but were required to pay taxes.[9]

The paper-making industry of the Tang Dynasty continued to move forward on the basis of that of the Wei, Jin, Southern and Northern Dynasties. According to "On the Refined Paper Produced in Different Places" in the *Supplement to the History of the Tang Dynasty* written by Li Zhao, "varieties of renowned paper were produced in places, like Yuezhou, Sichuan, Yangzhou, Shaozhou (near present-day Shaoguan in Guangdong Province), the Pu (present-day Changyuan County in Henan Province), and Linchuan, etc; in Songhao (near present-day Shangqiu city), some paper was made with fine lines in red ink and black ink; cocoon paper also appeared" This demonstrated the prosperous growth of the paper-making industry in the Tang Dynasty.

The developments in agriculture and the handicraft industry in the Tang Dynasty laid a foundation for the booming of the commodity economy. Many goods were seen in circulation not only at home but abroad as well, including silk products, porcelain, ironware, paper, etc., which functioned as material carriers for the opening up of the Tang Dynasty.

Although the political center of the country lay in northern China, the south, particularly the area to the South of the Yangtze River (*Jiangnan*[10]) came to enjoy more important status in the national economy. This was facilitated via accelerated development in commerce and greater convenience in south–north material circulation via the Sui Canal originating from the Six Dynasties. The Tang further improved the economic exploitation and development of the south by strengthening the construction of irrigation systems and encouraging people to move southward. As a result, the Jiangnan area gradually ascended to be the most important economic zone in China.

---

[9] *Six Codes of the Grand Tang.* Vol. 22. Directorate for Imperial Manufactories.

[10] *Jiangnan* refers to the section of the alluvial plains divided by the estuary of the Yangtze River (Chang Jiang). Literally, it means "South of the River" (while the north is called *Subei*, namely, northern Jiangsu).

After the "Rebellion of An and Shi,"[11] the economy in the central Shaanxi area was severely damaged. The economy of the south demonstrated its overwhelming superiority and came to exceed that of the north in the middle Tang period. History records that "after the Tianbao period (742–756) the tenth, people in the Central Plains of China put down their implements, with some moving to Yuezhou for clothing and some to Wu for food."[12] Han Yu, a well-known poet, said that "nine tenths of the country's revenue comes from the Jiangnan area."[13] It could be seen that the Jiangzhe area (Jiangsu and Zhejiang) occupied a premier position in agriculture and manufacturing. Owing to the development of the south, the center of the Chinese economy shifted from the north to the south. This provided the material premise for China's opening up via the maritime route while the economy was rooted in the Jiangnan area.

4.2 Foreign Trade Policy

The opening-up policy in the Sui and Tang Dynasties involved diverse fields. The country was economically open to encouraging external trade, with foreigners running businesses in China; it was culturally open, for foreigners were allowed to further their studies, undertake missionary jobs and participate in cultural and artistic activities; it was politically open, for foreigners could sit for the Imperial Chinese Civil Service Examination[14] and be recruited to work in China. With regards to the openness, the economic opening-up laid in the core status, accompanied by the transfer of the nation's economic center to the south. The early years of the opening-up in the Sui and Tang Dynasties placed more emphasis on continental trade, while the late period mainly focused on the maritime route trade.

---

[11] The rebellion of An Lushan (703–757), known as the "rebellion of An [Lushan] and Shi [Siming]," was an 8-year long disturbance of the Tang Empire (618–907).

[12] *Finest Blossoms in the Garden of Literature.* Vol. 901.

[13] Han Yu. *Preface to Poems for Lu's Departure to She Zhou.*

[14] The Imperial Chinese Civil Service Examination allowed the state to find the best candidates to staff the vast bureaucracy that governed China from the Han Dynasty onwards (206 BC–220 CE). The exams were a means for a young male of any class to enter that bureaucracy and so become a part of the gentry class of scholar-officials.

4.2.1 *Silk Road Trade Policy in the Sui Dynasty*

Despite the short duration of the Sui Dynasty, many policies it implemented came to fruition in its successor, the Tang Dynasty. The opening-up policy in the Sui Dynasty laid a foundation for the prosperity of the Silk Road in the Tang Dynasty. The related measures were as follows:

(1) Tempering Justice with Mercy to Clear the Silk Road

In the early years of the Sui Dynasty, the Tuyuhun people of Qinghai often invaded the Hexi Corridor area. In 609, the second Emperor Yang sent troops to defeat the Tuyuhun, relieving the threat to the Hexi Corridor.

At the end of the 6th century, the Türks (Chinese rendering Tujue), a nationality in ancient China, were split into Eastern and Western groups. The Eastern Türks affiliated themselves to the Sui Dynasty, while the Western Türks controlled the Western Regions. The Sui government tempered justice with mercy for the Western Türks by setting up "mutual markets." Trade communications between them lifted the impediments to the Silk Road. The opening-up along the northwestern continental road proceeded smoothly.

(2) Establishing Prefectures to Administer State Farm Cultivation

Prior to the Sui Dynasty, regimes established on the Central Plains of China set up loose administrative organs in Xinjiang. The Sui strengthened its administration by setting up subordinated commanderies in the Silk Road hubs, such as Shanshan, Qiemo and Yiwu. Garrison troops or peasants were to work on state-owned tracts called State Farms (*Tuntian*). This was enacted in each commandery and county, ensuring supplies to travelers along the Silk Road.

(3) Dispatching Envoys to Develop Official Trade

In the early years of the Sui Dynasty, the second Emperor Yang dispatched the Regional Inspector Du Xingman to pay a visit to countries in Western Regions. The envoys he led successively arrived in countries in the Central Asia, like Boukhara, Shi, Ki-pin (now Kashmir) and Rajgir (now the south of Patna in Bihar, India). They returned with many artifacts as gifts, such as "five-colored salt from the An, agate cups from the Ki-pin, Buddhist Sutras from the Rajgir, 10 dancing girls, a lion leather and

Huoshu (literally fire rat) furs from the Kesh."[15] In addition, the second Emperor Yang once "dispatched Commandant of Fleet-as-clouds Cavalry Li Yu to Persia with gifts."[16]

Besides the countries along the continental Silk Road, envoys were also sent to countries along the maritime route in the Sui Dynasty. The "Scarlet Earth" in the *Book of Sui: Biographies of the Southern Babarians* observes that "Emperor Yang recruited talents who were capable of communicating with foreigners." In 607, Chang Jun and Wang Junzheng, together with recruited men, embarked on their voyage, along the maritime route, to visit the country Chitu on the Malay Peninsula.

(4) Appointing Supervisory Officers to Govern Silk Road Trade
Prior to the Sui Dynasty, Silk Road trade came under the jurisdiction of local administrations or military organs. After the Sui Dynasty united the whole country, non-Han merchants went to trade in the Hexi Corridor area as usual. The second Emperor Yang specially designated Pei Ju, the Vice Minister of the Ministry of Personnel, as the Directorate of the Mutual Market in Zhangye to manage the foreign trade there.

(5) Canvassing Foreign Merchants
Pei Ju implemented a series of policies and measures to attract and ensure the fair treatment of foreign merchants in the Hexi Corridor area, such as providing board and lodging along the Silk Road and shipping goods for free, as well as actively encouraging foreign merchants to trade in inland China. In addition, Pei Ju often paid visits to non-Han merchants, getting to know about the transportation, products, politics, economy, etc., in the countries and regions where they lived. All the information he collected was edited into a book titled the *Western Regions Illustrated*. The book introduced the topography and local products of the places to the west of Dunhuang with detailed maps. The book was presented to Emperor Yang, thus his understanding of the Western Regions was deepened and he paid more attention to the development of the Silk Road.

In 609, Emperor Yang of the Sui paid a visit to Zhangye in person. Guided by Pei Ju, the kings and envoys of 27 countries in the Western Regions paid their respects to the Emperor in Zhangye. To demonstrate

---

[15] (The Tang Dynasty) Wei Zheng *et al. Book of Sui: Biography of the Western Regions.* Vol. 83. Beijing: Zhonghua Book Company, 1973.
[16] *Ibid.*

the prosperity and abundance of the Sui Court, the Emperor ordered people in Wuwei and Zhangye to attend the event in splendid attire and with magnificent carriages pulled by horses. If their carriages failed to be magnificent, commanderies and counties were required to help them meet the standard. As a result, the spectacle was so marvelous that horses and carriages of the attendees swarmed on the road, stretching hundreds of kilometers.

In 610, at the request of the non-Han merchants in the Western Regions, a trade fair in Luoyang was approved by Emperor Yang for Chinese and foreign commodities to be traded. The Emperor, who liked grandiose things, ordered the redecoration of Luoyang City. Abundant commodities were prepared to receive merchants from the Western Regions. From January 15 in the first lunar month to the end of it, a fortnight long trade fair of foreign and western commodities was launched in the Fengdu market at Luoyang. It was observed that "all tribal chiefs gathered in Luoyang ... at a cost of tens of thousands ... as an annual event."[17] From then on, constant streams of non-Han merchants from the Western Regions swarmed into Luoyang, Chang'an and other places in inland China. A booming foreign trade was gradually taking shape.

4.2.2 *Silk Road Trade Policy in the Tang Dynasty*

Generally, the opening-up in the Tang Dynasty was more active with diverse fields involved. Under the general guideline of sustaining a high degree of opening up, a series of effective promotion measures were implemented both with regard to the continental and maritime Silk routes. The essence of implementing these measures lay in: first, strengthening the political and economic relationships with foreign countries through foreign trade activities to safeguard the international prestige of the Tang Empire as the Heavenly Court and Celestial Empire; secondly, to meet the imperial need for extravagant overseas commodities; and thirdly, to increase the national revenue by developing overseas trades.

Zhang Jiuling of the Tang wrote in his *On the Opening of the Dayu Mountain Range Road* that during the Tang Dynasty, "trade in foreign goods is to be seen on a daily basis. The traded commodities range from all kinds of leather and feather to fish, salt and clams, which would not

---

[17] *Ibid.*

only fill the state treasury but meet the needs of everyone in the Jianghuai area." After the Huang Chao Rebellion, "the trade in the South China Sea was said to make outlaws super rich with the central government running short of revenue." Nevertheless, the first measure taken had always been the number one guideline in foreign policy-making and implementation.

(1) Envoys to and from Foreign Countries for Tributary Trade

To strengthen political and economic contacts with foreign countries, the Tang Dynasty, on the one hand, actively dispatched envoys to visit foreign countries, and on the other hand, bestowed lavish gifts to visiting diplomatic corps. The Tang envoys successively visited many countries and regions, such as India, the Korean Peninsula and Japan. To be specific, Shen Shu'an, Zhu Zishe, Zhangsun Shi, Chen Dade, Xiangli, Xuanjiang, Yuan Jifang, Cui Ting and Deng Su were sent to Goguryeo; Jin Enlan, Gai Sun and Gui Chongjing were sent to Silla; Gao Biaoren, Liu Degao, Guo Wucong, Sima Decong, Yuan Jinqing, Huangfu Dongchao, Shen Weiyue, Sun Xingjin, Zhao Baoying and Jiang Renshi were sent to Japan.

The Tang bestowed lavish gifts to those diplomatic corps coming for tributary trade as well. The government provided the visitors' board and lodging as well as transportation fees for them to come over. Upon their departure, farewell banquets would be held and quantities of gifts bestowed. According to the *Old Poetry of Tang Dynasty*, in 625 during the reign of the Tang Emperor Gaozu (r. 618–626), Champa sent envoys to China with its local specialties. Emperor Gaozu "treated them with an imperial band playing nine types of music and with silk products." In 628 CE during the reign of the second Emperor Taizong (r. 626–649), when Khmer (now Cambodia) dispatched envoys to China, Emperor Taizong "gave them many presents in return in consideration of their being travel-worn." The official communication between China and foreign countries was a part of the opening-up policy in the Tang Dynasty, which created a friendly diplomatic atmosphere for further opening-up.

(2) Improving Military and Political Administration in the Western Regions

There were many natural and man-made obstacles along the sprawling Silk Road. Therefore, maintaining the smoothness of this route hinged on ensuring the safety of traveling merchants. In the early years of the Tang Dynasty, the Western Türks blocked trade along the Silk Road but were then defeated by the Tang troops. The Silk Road was then unimpeded. Emperor Taizong of the Tang Dynasty told the envoys of the Tashkend: "the Western Türks have surrendered and merchants can pass along the road," hearing which "all those non-Han merchants were overjoyed."[18] Afterward Emperor Taizong established the Protectorate of the Parthian Empire in Gaochang, where troops were stationed to garrison the Western Regions. Emperor Taizong also set up military and administrative agencies, such as the *Du du fu* (Area Command), *Zhou* (Prefectures) and *Xian* (Counties) in the Western Regions. In 702, the Tang set up the Beiting Protectorate in Tingzhou (now Jimsar in Xinjiang), supervising the vast areas to the north of the Tian Shan Mountains. All the above measures contributed effectively to a safer and unimpeded Silk Road.

(3) Improving Convenience and Freedom of Foreign Trade
In the vast areas from Chang'an to the Western Regions via the Hexi Corridor, the Tang set up many courier stations to provide board and lodging for merchants and envoys and feed for livestock as well. A Tang poet named Cen Sen recorded the conditions of the courier stations and the smooth going along the Silk Road in his poem *Bumping into Mr Yuwen when Passing by the Longshan Mountain*: "a station is followed by another station; courier horses run like flow of stars; (we) depart Xianyang early in the morning; reaching at the top of the Longshan Mountain at dusk."

The laws of the Tang clearly regulated that: foreign merchants "were allowed to trade freely in China,"[19] without regional restrictions. The tenth Emperor Xuanzong (r. 847–859) of the Tang once attempted to send envoys to purchase foreign treasures in Southeast Asia, but was rebuffed by some ministers who stated that "it is inappropriate for the heavenly court to trade with merchants who chase after profits."[20] This implies that the Tang government provided a relatively unrestricted environment for the development of civilian trade between China and foreign countries.

---

[18](The Song Dynasty) Ouyang Xiu, Song Qi. *New Poetry of the Tang: Biography of the Western Regions* II. Vol. 221. Beijing: Zhonghua Book Company, 1975.

[19]Ma Zhenshu. *The Calligraphy of the Tang: Regular Script of the Tang People.* Lanzhou: Gansu People's Publishing House, 1988.

[20](The Song Dynasty) Sima Guang. *Comprehensive Mirror to Aid in Government.* Vol. 211. Beijing: Zhonghua Book Company, 1973.

(4) Preferential Reception of Inbound Foreign Merchants

The Tang Dynasty even offered treatment to foreign merchants in preference to its own native people. This could be discerned from the following four aspects:

First of all, foreign merchants and envoys were received freely. The Foreign Guest Yard (attached to the Dependencies) was set up in Chang'an, dedicated to receiving foreign guests. The annual expenditures of boarding and lodging, daily items and transportation spent on foreign guests could reach as high as 13,000 *hu* (1,560,000 catties) of silver.[21]

Secondly, in order to attract talents, the Tang Court permitted foreigners to settle in China, a policy known as "Entering the Court to Inhabit." Countless foreigners, including monks, scholars, painters, craftsmen, artists and merchants, swarmed into China, to participate in society, the economy and other fields of life in the Tang. Foreign merchants were allowed not only to trade commodities in China, but also to run their own luxury goods stores, hotels, food stores, etc. These policies ensured a high degree of opening-up in the commodity trade and service industries.

Thirdly, the Tang government reduced tax on foreign merchants' businesses. As early as in the reign of the first Emperor Gaozu (r. 618–626), the Tang stipulated that "for those non-Han people who come to live in China a preferential tax policy will be practiced: rich families are to pay ten *wen*, middle-income families five, and tax will be exempted for those of lower income."[22]

Fourthly, trading with foreign merchants enjoyed a preferential price. The Arabian merchant Abu Zuid Hassan recorded in his book *Accounts of China and India*[23] that "merchants come to China via the sea. Their commodities are to be stocked at state-owned commodities stations for 6 months. Then 3 out of 10 commodities are required to be purchased by the government before the remaining 70% is returned to those merchants. It is true that the government purchases at the highest price. Each *mana* of

---

[21] A measure of weight in China, corresponding to a bushel (*dan*), equivalent to 120 catties (*jin*), say 60 kilograms.

[22] (The Later Jin Dynasty) Liu Xu. *Old Book of Tang: Treatise on Food and Commodities* I. Vol. 48. Beijing: Zhonghua Book Company, 1975.

[23] It is believed to be the earliest (four and a half centuries earlier than *The Travels of Marco Polo*) travel notes about China by Arabic people, compiled in 851 based upon the experience in China of an Arabic merchant named Sulaymān.

camphor is sold at the price of 50 *Fakkouj*, equivalent to 1,000 copper coins at that time. It will be otherwise sold at a half price without the government purchase. The Chinese people act fairly and squarely in trading and handling debts." The government purchased commodities at a higher price than that of the market, providing foreign merchants with more profits.

(5) Respecting and Protecting Foreign Customs, Religions and Legal Interests

Given the large number of foreign merchants in China with many taking up residency here, a Foreign Quarter (*Fan Fang*), dedicated for foreigners to live, was set up in ports with a large foreign population, such as Guangzhou. The head of the *Fan Fang* was chosen by foreign merchants and ratified by the Tang government. On the premise of obeying Chinese law he administrated the *Fan Fang* in accordance with the residents' national customs and religious beliefs. According to the Tang law, "disputes between foreign merchants should be resolved by their own laws, while the conflicts between merchants of different nationalities should be treated according to the laws of the Tang."[24] Then the foreign customs and laws were respected and Chinese judicial supremacy was safeguarded.

The Tang protected foreign merchants' interests by way of laws and regulations, which could be seen from the following three aspects:

Firstly, heavy taxation upon foreign merchants was forbidden. In 834, Emperor Wenzong (r. 826–840) issued an order that: "foreign ships come to China for the foreigners admire China, so we should treat them with preference, make them feel welcome ... As for foreigners in the Lingnan area, Fujian and Yangzhou, it's better to have a Military Commissioner as an observer for supervision. Foreign merchants were encouraged to do business according to their wishes but with no heavy tax burdens on them except for keelage, market taxes and tribute taxes.[25] Government-purchased commodities and tributes could be traded freely without heavy taxation imposed on." It could be seen that the major responsibility of the coastal magistrates was to encourage foreign trade and implement

---

[24] *The Tang Code with Comments*. Vol. 6. It is the penal law code of the Tang Dynasty (618–907 CE), enlarged by commentaries. It is the oldest preserved complete law code in Chinese history.

[25] *Anthology of the Tang*. Vol. 75.

the normative taxation system to protect the legal interests of foreign merchants.

Secondly, severe punishment was enforced on corrupt officials among the coastal magistrates. During the reign of the tenth Emperor Xuanzong (r. 847–859), several magistrates were executed or exiled for they extorted foreign merchants. The Arabian merchant Abu Zuid Hassan recorded in his book *Accounts of China and India* that an Arabian merchant came to Guangzhou with a large amount of goods which were forcefully bought away by eunuchs who purchased them as luxuries for the Emperor. The Arabian merchant went to distant Chang'an to appeal directly to the Emperor. After an investigation, the Emperor "confiscated the minister's property ... and sent him to guard the imperial mausoleum."

Thirdly, protection regulation for foreign merchants was observed. According to the Tang regulations, the legacies of foreign merchants left after their death in China should be safeguarded by the local government until their relatives could claim it. If no one showed up within a scheduled time, the legacy would be confiscated.

(6) Strengthening Administration of Overland and Maritime Silk Road Trade

Where overland trade was concerned, the Directorate of Tributary Trade (headed by a Director) was set up in border areas to supervise trade carried on by tributary delegations.[26] The *Guosuo* Pass System of the former dynasty continued to be implemented. Both Chinese and foreign merchants along the Silk Road were required to apply for a Travel Pass from the government. On the *Guosuo* Pass was the pass holders' information, such as their name, age, and commodities they brought. When passing the main gateways, Travel Passes were examined. Anybody without a pass was forbidden his admittance.

To protect safety and food supplies along the Silk Road, commercial tax was collected in places along the southern route of the Silk Road, such as Karasahr, Kucha, Kashgar, Kingdom of Khotan and Luntai on the northern route of the road.

---

[26] The early Tang continued to use the Sui *jiao shi jian* before 632 when the Emperor Taizong (r. 626–649) changed the name to *hu shi jian*. In 685 during the reign of Wu Zetian, it was changed to *tong shi jian* for a while and then was renamed *hu shi jian*. No matter what name was given to it, *jiao shi*, *hu shi*, and *tong shi* all refer to the tributary trade. *Jian (Director)* means the head of the organ who supervises the operation of it.

As for maritime Silk Road trade, the *Shibo*[27] System ("Maritime Trade") was implemented in the Tang Dynasty. To meet the need for developing overseas trade, the *Shibo* System managing the overseas trade was operated from the Tang Dynasty. In 714 during the reign of the tenth Emperor Xuanzong, the "Maritime Trade Commissioner" (some say it was established as early as in the reign of Emperor Xuanzong), a minister for overseas trade, was appointed in Guangzhou, the largest port for foreign trade, which marked the birth of the *Shibo* system. During the early years of its development, the system was simple in organizational structure, with only the Maritime Trade Commissioner as the head, but with no exclusive organization.

The Maritime Trade Commissioner was also known as the "goodwill envoy" or the "Envoy Supervising Foreign Ships". The post was generally undertaken by eunuchs trusted by the Emperor. The position was not very lofty in hierarchy but wielded much power.

Besides Guangzhou, the Tang also had Maritime Trade Commissioners in Mingzhou, Jiaozhou and Yangzhou.

The Maritime Trade Commissioner was sent to coastal ports to manage foreign trade. His responsibility incorporated the following five specific aspects:

Firstly, imported commodities were recorded and classified. When ships entered the harbor, information about the commodities onboard were to be recorded and classified by municipal ship officials into coarse cargo (ordinary goods) and refined cargo (luxurious goods) for the convenience of collecting taxes.

Secondly, there was tax collection. China began to collect foreign trade tax from the Tang Dynasty onwards. Maritime Trade officials were in charge of collecting taxes on incoming ships. The "Principal Tax" was called *ship feet*, i. e., tonnage tax, though no record existed to testify to the tax rate. In addition to the "Principal Tax," taxes on luxury cargoes were sometimes paid by means of material objects.

Thirdly, free trading of luxury cargo was forbidden. As for precious imported commodities, no merchants were allowed to trade with others by themselves. The central and local governments maintained a monopoly on purchases and sales.

---

[27]Literally, it means the overseas ships traveling back and forth to China for trade. It was later used to mean overseas trade.

Fourthly, warehouses were set up to keep foreign commodities under custody. Due to the relatively small deadweight capacity of ships, foreign commodities were often shipped to China in separate batches. The Tang government therefore set up warehouses in Guangzhou for foreign merchants to store commodities that arrived ahead of other batches.

Fifthly, there was the matter of managing foreign merchants' trade in China. When initiating trade activities within inland China, foreign merchants needed to apply for credentials from the local government and the Maritime Trade Commissioner. The local government was in charge of issuing identification cards indicating the holder's name, age, nationality, etc. It was the Maritime Trade Commissioner who issued official letters to indicate the commodities and silver amount they brought with them. The official letter needed to be shown for examination when passing any checkpoint.

To sum up, under the general guideline of comprehensive opening-up, the trade policy of the Tang was more systematic and mature than that of the former dynasties both in the continental and maritime Silk Road routes. Following the unprecedented development of foreign trade over land and sea, significant improvements were made in terms of safety and convenience for foreign merchants wishing to trade in China. Nevertheless, the foreign trade policy during this period retained numerous limitations. Policies encouraging trade applied mainly to foreign merchants instead of to Chinese merchants. Consequently, the opening-up of the Tang was mainly one way and pertained to imports, rather than concerning the two-way traffic of imports and exports. This accounted for the fact that foreign merchants were more active in the international trading activities of the Tang.

4.3 Changes in the Route of the Silk Road

In the Sui and Tang Dynasties, opening-up extended along both the continental and maritime roads. With the shift of the economic center from the north to the south, together with technological advances, the opening-up of the Tang gradually hinged more on the Maritime Silk Road. Therefore, the Maritime Silk Road assumed the leading position in the opening-up.

4.3.1 *The Development and Variation of the Silk Road Route*

On the basis of the former dynasties, the Silk Road moved forward in the early period of the Tang Dynasty. To the east of the Pamirs, the government built up a *Tubo* road, forming a route from the hexi corridor to Nepal and India via Qinghai and Tibet.

To the west of the Pamirs, the development of the Silk Road could be seen in the following three aspects:

(1) The extension of the branch line of the northern road. After it crossed the Ili River to Jiangbu'er, the route ran to the Aral Sea along the Syr Darya. Then it ran northwestward, via the Emba River, the Ural, the Volga, and the Kuban to Kerch (now in Ukraine) on the Crimean peninsula, opposite to the estuary of the Kuban. This may be attributable to the trade between the Eastern Roman Empire and the Western Türks, which further promoted the prosperity of the northern Silk Road.

(2) The variation of the trunk line of the northern road. It ran from Kashgar, after climbing over the Pamirs, to Bukhara in Uzbekistan. Then, instead of running northwestward, it crossed the Amu Darya, running southwestward to Merv in Turkmenistan to be integrated into the southern trunk line of the Han Silk Road.

(3) The variation of the trunk line of the southern road. In the Sui and Tang, after the road passed Komedae (now Wakhan), it no longer ran westward to Wazirabad in Afghanistan. Rather, it stretched southward to northern India via Bamian (in central Afghanistan) and Ghaznin (in southern Afghanistan).

4.3.2 *The Expansion of Route for Maritime Trade and Transportation*

The coastal economy of southeastern China achieved a great leap forward in shipbuilding and marine technologies in the Tang Dynasty. In the field of shipbuilding, the fleet grew great in number with significant improvements to shipbuilding technology. Shipyards spread all over the country, including, according to records, to Yi (now Yicheng, Hubei), Run (now Zhenjiang, Jiangsu), Chang (now Changzhou, Jiangsu), Su (now Suzhou, Jiangsu), Hu (now Huzhou, Zhejiang), Yue (now Shaoxing, Zhejiang), Tai (now Linhai, Zhejiang), Wu (now Jinhua, Zhejiang), Jiang (Jiujiang, Jiangxi), Hong (now Nanchang, Jiangxi) and the coastal area of the Jiannan Circuit (now in Sichuan).

Many places in coastal areas gained fame for their shipbuilding industry, notably Dengzhou (now Penglai, Shandong) and Laizhou (now

Laizhou, Shandong) in northern China, Hangzhou, Yangzhou, Fuzhou, Quanzhou, Guangzhou and Jiaozhou in southeastern China. For instance, there were more than 10 shipyards in Yangzi (now Yizheng, Jiangsu) alone. The technological advancement in shipbuilding was evidenced mainly in the solidness and utility of ships. History records that Tang ships adopted a watertight compartment design. The compartments were jointed with iron nails and tung oil lime to ensure they were sealed.[28]

Considerable progress was also made in seafaring skills, especially with more comprehensive knowledge being upon the causes and rules governing the rise and fall of ocean tides. Therefore, China's shipbuilding and seafaring technologies assumed the pole position in the world during the Tang Dynasty. At that time, many foreign merchants took Chinese ships for long voyages. Du You, as the prime minister of the Tang, wrote in his book *Encyclopedic History of Institutions*[29] that "currently ships sailing on the sea are big "vessels," boarded by the Kunlun (now countries on Malay Peninsula) people and Goguryeo people." J. Sauvaget, the French translator of the book *Accounts of China and India* claimed that "Chinese contribution in leading the Arabian seafaring to the Far East should be admitted. It was by the Chinese ship that merchants of the Persian Gulf succeed in the first several voyages across the South China Sea."

The advancements made in shipbuilding and seafaring technologies improved the navigational capacity of the Sui and Tang Dynasties. Therefore, the Silk Roads were further expanded on the Eastern Sea and the Southern Sea.

(1) The Expansion of the Maritime Silk Road in the South China Sea

During the Six Dynasties period, the starting point of the maritime Silk Road shifted to Guangzhou from Xuwen and Hepu of the Han Dynasty with only few ships sailing to the Persian Gulf. The route, from Guangzhou to the Persian Gulf, became fixed and normalized in the Tang Dynasty. The *New Book of Tang: Annals of Geography* recorded in detail about "the

---

[28] At the same time, other overseas countries still used materials like Arenga pinnata silk, coconut bark and olive sugar.

[29] This is a Chinese institutional history and encyclopedic text. It covers a panoply of topics from high antiquity through the year 756, whereas one quarter of the book focuses on the Tang Dynasty. The book was written by Du You from 766 to 801, and is regarded as one of the most representative contemporary texts of the Tang Dynasty.

route from Guangzhou (Canton) to the sea," that is, the route to the Persian Gulf.

The sea route started from Guangzhou. Ships began to sail from the north of Lantau Island of Hong Kong. After passing the northeastern corner of the Hainan Island and the Duzhu Mountain in the southeast of the island, it went by the Linggaparvata (known more commonly as Cu Lao Cham), Swallow Gorge, Qui Nhan, Nha Trang, Phan Rang and the Kunlun Island. Then it stretched southward to Sumatra Island via the Singapore Strait, or eastward to Java Island; or northwestward to the Nicobar Islands, via the Strait of Malacca, the southern Brouwers Island, Medan in the eastern coast of northern Sumatra Island and the Poros Island. It then sailed westward to Sri Lanka. A northwestward passage proceeded from Sri Lanka, along the east coast of Arabian Sea, to Kollam in western India, Broach and Karachi. It continued westward to Abadan in the Persian Gulf, and Obollah at the estuary of the Euphrates River. Sailing along the river, it arrived at Basra (a port city in southern Iraq), from which the journey could be continued on road as far as the capital of the Arab Empire, Baghdad.

The sea route from the Indian Peninsula to the Persian Gulf in the Tang Dynasty was the extension of that which had already been opened ever since the Han Dynasty. The route was also connected to the passage to East Africa. As is recorded in the *New Book of Tang: Annals of Geography*, "starting from Malé Country in the south of Braham (near present-day Manipur in India), it can lead to the Ubullah Country (now Basra in Iraq) along the eastern seaboard. To the west of the sea was Dayi Country, to the southwest of which was Sanlan Country (now Yemen). A ten-day northward voyage from the Sanlan led to the Shahr-iKalhat (now Kalat in Oman), reached after passing by 6 or 7 smaller countries. Another one-day voyage brought ships to the Ubullah, where this route met with the east coast route."

This record described the route from East Africa to the Persian Gulf. Generally speaking, it ran northeastward, along the coast, from the Dar-es-Salaam of Tanzania in East Africa to Ash Shihr of Yemen, and Muscat and Sohar in Oman. Along the Strait of Hormuz, it ran west to Manama of Bahrain island. Then it went northwestward from the shore of the Persian Gulf to Obollah at the estuary of Euphrates to be connected to the route from Guangzhou to the Persian Gulf.

The maritime route from Guangzhou connected southern China with other countries in East Asia, Southeast Asia, South Asia, the Persian Gulf, the northeastern coast of Arabian Peninsula and the coastal areas of East Africa, making it the longest route to have been regularly used before the 16th century. At that time, the Tang ships sailed back and forth over the waters between the Western Pacific Ocean and the northern Indian Ocean, having promoted the prosperity of the Tang maritime trade.

(2) The Extension of the Maritime Silk Road in the East China Sea
With the increasing communications with countries during the Korean Peninsula and Japan, the trade routes also extended further during the Sui and Tang Dynasties.

During the Sui Dynasty, there were two routes leading to the Korean Peninsula. One crossed the coasts of the Bohai and the Yellow Sea; the other crossed the Yellow Sea. In the Tang Dynasty, China established a close relationship with Silla on the Korean Peninsula. They communicated with each other frequently through two routes. One route was recorded by Jia Dan, a geographer of the Tang, in his book the *Records of Roads*. He wrote that by "sailing from Dengzhou (now Penglai, Shandong) one can reach Goguryeo and the Bohai Circuit (in modern-day Tianjin), Hebei and Shandong." This route was to start from Dengzhou to the south coast of the Liaodong Peninsula via the Bohai Strait. Then it moved northeastward along the coast to the mouth of the Yalu River. Then it ran southward along the west coast of the Korean Peninsula to the mouth of the Asanman, via the Sinmi-do, the estuary of the Taedong Port, the Cho-do, Changming town in Changyuan County, the outer archipelagos of the Ongjin Peninsula, the Kanghwa-do and the Taebu-do. Then, one could travel by road along the overland route to Qingzhou, the southeastern part of the Korean Peninsula. The route was quite long but proved safer.

The second route commenced from Dengzhou and Laizhou on the Shandong Peninsula, crossed the Yellow Sea to the mouth of the Taedong Port or the Ganghaw-man on the west coast of the Korean Peninsula.

As for the route to Japan, there were four alternatives in the Sui and Tang Dynasties.

(i) Northern Route of the Northern Road
This could be embarked on by a sailboat from the coast of the Shandong Peninsula, traveling to the west coast of the Korean Peninsula, then ran southward to the south end of the Peninsula, or crossed the Jeju Strait to

Hakata in Fukuoka, the northern Kyushu of Japan; or sailed eastward along the south coast of the Korean Peninsula to Geoje Island and Busan, then crossed the Tsushima Island and the Iki Island to Fukuoka. The voyage continued eastward to Seto Naikai, and finally ended in Mitoteramachi in Osaka, the starting port for Japanese mission ships bound for Tang China and the destination to which they would return.

(ii) Southern Route of the Northern Road

This could be embarked on by a sailboat from Dengzhou on the Shandong Peninsula, ran eastward to the Ongjin Peninsula, then to the west coast of the Korean Peninsula after crossing the Yellow Sea. Subsequently, it sailed southward to join the northern route of the northern road to Japan. The envoy Pei Qing sailed along this route when he was sent to Japan during the Sui Dynasty and returned with the Japanese monk Ennin.

(iii) Southern Route of the Southern Road

In the 8th century, after Silla united the Korean Peninsula, the trade route was caught in a tense situation between Silla and Japan, which made the former Sino–Japanese northern route no longer viable. Under these circumstances, a new route was opened. It started from Mingzhou (now Ningbo) and Yuezhou (now Shaoxing), crossed the East Sea to the Amami Great Island. Then it ran northward to the port of Hakata in Fukuoka and Osaka, via Osumi-kaikyo, Kagoshima and several other islands. It was along this route that Jian Zhen, an eminent monk, sailed eastward to Japan.

(iv) Northern Route of the Southern Road

Since the southern route of the southern road was too long, the fourth batch of the Japanese missions to the Tang sailed to China by way of the northern route of the southern road. The route started from the ports along Jiangsu and Zhejiang Provinces, such as Chuzhou (modern-day Huai'an), Yangzhou, Mingzhou, and Wenzhou, running northeastward across the East Sea, northeastward to Fukuoka and Osaka via Zhijia Island, which belonged to Japan (now located between the Gotō Islands and the Hirado Islands), and then reached the port of Hakata and Namba.

The above four routes clearly demonstrated the active maritime communications between China and Japan, which could be accounted for by the constant streams of Japanese missions to the Sui and Tang Dynasties.

4.3.3 *Foreign Trade Center Migration*

In 751, a fierce battle took place in Dalus in Central Asia (now Taraz in Kazakhstan, formerly called Zhambyl) between the Tang and Arabia. This was known in history as the Battle of Dalus. The Tang troops were disastrously defeated owing to the Karluks of Central Asia suddenly changing sides in the war. Many Tang soldiers, some of whom were skilled craftsmen, were caught as prisoners of war. Their being sent to the Arabian region brought about, to some extent, a large-scale exportation of Chinese technology.

After the Battle of Dalus, the advantages once enjoyed by the Tang in Central Asia gradually waned. Soon after this war, the "Rebellion of An and Shi" broke out back in China. Tang soldiers stationed in Central Asia had to retreat to the Central Plains of China, thereby relinquishing control over this region. Subsequently, Central Asia was embroiled in internecine disputes, which led to the Silk Road becoming blocked. Therefore, China began to shift its focus of foreign trade from overland to overseas.

This shift resulted not only from the impeded overland Silk Road, but more importantly from China's economic center shifting southwards. Having been under cultivation since the later period of the Eastern Han Dynasty, the Jiangnan area grew to be the most important economic zone in the late Tang period, and the Chinese economic center shifted from central Shaanxi to the middle and lower reaches of the Yangtze River. This eventuated after the joint efforts of previous dynasties, which continued through the early period of the Tang. In the article *Preface to Poems for Lu's Departure to She Zhou*, Han Yu wrote that "nine-tenths of the country's revenue comes from the Jiangnan area." In the late Tang Dynasty, southern China produced more silk (China's traditional exported commodity) than northern China, providing abundant commodities for foreign trade.

The varied patterns of import and export goods called for new means of transportation. The porcelain making industry developed remarkably in the Tang Dynasty. The glazed porcelain produced in the south was "like jade and ice"; the white porcelain produced by the north was "like silver and snow." Chinese porcelain, when exported, was welcomed enthusiastically by foreigners, making it a new high quality product exported in large quantities. However, porcelain was fragile, delicate yet heavy, inappropriate to be transported along the traditional northwestward Silk Road with ridges and mountains to negotiate. The camel, as a traditional pack animal, was not suitable for carrying excessively heavy loads, too. Compared with overland transportation, maritime transportation was more smooth and steady. Ships could sail with a larger capacity, and were therefore better suitable for porcelain exports.

At the same time, with the economic development of the Tang, its need for foreign spices was gradually increasing. Even so, foreign spices were mainly produced in countries around the South China Sea and countries which enjoyed convenient transportation, like Dayi.[30]

The remarkable improvements in shipbuilding and seafaring skills provided a technological guarantee for the rise and boom of the Maritime Silk Road. With accumulated knowledge and advancements in technology, mankind was better able to conquer the ocean. At the same time, the Tang Dynasty made new progress in building ships with greater deadweight tonnage and sturdiness. This made them suitable for oceangoing voyages. Some foreign merchants also took Chinese ships to trade. In the *Zilin* (*Forest of Words*) compiled by Lü Chen in the Western Jin Dynasty, "*bo*" is an ocean-going ship. All ships currently sailing in the Jiangnan area were called "*bo*" (vessels), and they were so large that the merchants of Kunlun and Goguryeo could take them to sail on the sea. The largest "vessel" can "carry hundreds of thousands of *hu* in weight."[31]

Meanwhile, the people of the Tang Dynasty had already grasped the knowledge to understand the laws of seasonal monsoons and tides. Their awareness of marine geomorphy increased also. The advancement in shipbuilding and seafaring technology greatly reduced the risk of seafaring on the open ocean, enabling the Chinese to initiate foreign trade activity via maritime transportation. With improvements in seafaring and shipbuilding, the southeastern coastal areas gradually demonstrated their advantages when it comes to foreign communications. Outbound travel via the Silk Road in northwestern China, though prevalent in former foreign exchanges, was no longer advantageous in terms of geography.

With the decline of the continental Silk Road, regions which lay along the Silk Road but far away from the sea in location gradually transformed from frontier zones to closed areas with their economic development rate slowing down. In "the 12th Year (753) of the Regnal Period of Tianbao"

---

[30]"Dayi" was used in the Tang Dynasty to refer to Arabia in ancient times. It was transliterated into Chinese directly from Persian language "Tay" used by Persian to mean Arabic tribes.

[31](The Tang Dynasty) Xuan Ying. *All Scriptures in Pronunciation and Meaning.* Vol. 1.

in the *Comprehensive Mirror to Aid in Government*, it says that "at that time China was powerful covering a territory of 12,000 *li*[32] from the Anyuan Gate[33] to the west, where alleys stood with mulberry trees and hemp trees covering the land. No place is richer than places to the east of the Longshan Mountain." With the Continental Silk Road on the wane, the economy of the northwest decreased in prosperity. The center of opening-up duly shifted from the northwest to the southeast of China.

4.4 The Development of Foreign Trade

The material and spiritual civilization which emerged during the Tang Dynasty attracted foreign merchants, politicians, and artists. The opening-up policy of the Tang pushed economic and cultural exchanges with foreign countries to a new high. Many countries established official relationships with the Tang. Foreign merchants were seen to come to China in an endless stream. The scale of commodity exchanges with foreign countries extended to an unprecedented scope. The Second Emperor Taizong's poem *A Normal Day at the Imperial Court* recorded this prosperity by recounting how "hundreds of foreign peoples and countries have come to the court with tributes." The prosperity during the reign of Tang's Emperor Xuanzong was once recorded by poet Li Gong in his poem *On the Melody on Splendid Fairy Costumes during the Provincial Examination* that "hundreds of countries come to celebrate the peace and abundance of the Tang," as recorded in the Tang poet Wang Zhenbai's poem the *Chang'an Circuit*[34]. He wrote that "foreigners travel long distances to the Tang with gold and silk as tributes." The effect of the opening-up could be seen in the development of foreign trade.

4.4.1 *The Development of Overland Trade*

(1) The Advancement of Trade Relations with Foreign Countries

Under the policy of opening-up, overland trade with foreign countries boomed in the Sui and Tang Dynasties. According to historical records, "the Emperor has to set up a Commandant of the Western Regions to deal

---

[32] 6,000 kilometers.

[33] The north gate of the Chang'an City at that time.

[34] *Complete Tang Poems*. Vols. 1, 542 and 701.

with relevant business when over 30 countries of the Western Regions paid tributes to China during the reign of the Sui's second Emperor Yang,"[35] such as Gaochang, the Samarqand, the Boukhara, the Chach, Karasahr, Kucha, Kashgar, Kingdom of Khotan, Ferghana, Tokharistan, Ephthalies, the Maimargh, the Kesh, the Khebud, the Koshana, the Balkh, the Maru, and the Zabul. And the Emperor sent the Commandant of the western Regions to receive them. After that, Pei Ju, the Vice Minister of Personnel during the Sui Dynasty, was sent to the Hexi Corridor area to implement and develop Silk Road trade, which attracted more western merchants to come and trade with the Sui. "Since then those non-Han merchants in the Western Regions came to China constantly."[36]

In the early period of the Tang Dynasty, the continental Silk Road enjoyed unprecedented prosperity and entered a golden time of development.

During that period, merchants came to China along the Silk Road mainly from Central Asia and West Asia.

During the Sui Dynasty, countries in Central Asia maintained close political and cultural contact with China. According to the *Book of Sui: The Western Regions*, during the reign of the Sui's Emperor Yang (r. 604–618), countries that "frequently paid tributes" to China were Ferghana, Tokharistan, Ephthalies, Maimargh, Kesh, Khebud, Koshana, Balkh, Maru, Boukhara, and Chach.

After the 7th century, countries in Central Asia came under threat from the Arabs. Some of them turned to the Tang for protection since they, including the Maimargh, the Kesh, the Chach, the Big Boukhara, the Small Boukhara, the Khebud, the Samarqand, the Koshana, and the Maru, were convinced by the legend that their ancestors used to be the Nine Barbarian Tribes from Zhaowu (now Gaotai in Gansu). The Tang sent troops to be stationed in Central Asia, removing all impediments along the Silk Road between Central Asia and Central China. Trade between them grew unprecedentedly prosperous.

---

[35] (The Tang Dynasty) Wei Zheng. *Book of Sui: Biography of the Western Regions*. Vol. 83. Beijing: Zhonghua Book Company, 1973.

[36] (The Song Dynasty) Sima Guang. *Comprehensive Mirror to Aid in Government*. Vol. 180. Beijing: Zhonghua Book Company, 1976.

During this period, Persia and the Fulin were among the West Asian countries that had a close trade relationship with China along the continental road.

In 651, Persia was annexed by the Arab Empire but retained some residual elements of power and maintained the official relationship with China. Meanwhile, many Persians migrated to China. The Tang government helped them settle down. Persian Temples were established for their convenience in Chang'an, the capital of Tang. Some Persian royals were seen in serving the Tang Court. For instance, Narsieh,[37] a King of Persia, who took refuge in the Chinese imperial Court, was granted the elevated courtly title of Great General of the Left Flank Imperial Guards. Moreover, An Yuanliang were appointed to be Military Commissioner of Longyou, and Abraham ("Bahram" in Arabic) as Suppression and Pacification Commissioner of the Fulin. More Persians began their own commercial businesses by investing in stores as Persian Residence in the West Market of Chang'an and Fengdu in Luoyang. Many of them sold treasures to make their living. The *Extensive Records of the Taiping Period*[38] reveal anecdotes about Persian merchants (*Bosi hu*[39]) who were adept at evaluating treasures.

Polin was also known as the Eastern Roman Empire, which maintained both direct official trade with China, as well as indirect transit trade. The direct official trade referred to the exchanges of a variety of luxuries carried with them by emissaries sent to each side. For instance, in 643, Pope Theodorus I of Polin dispatched envoys to Chang'an with red glass and lapis lazuli. The second Emperor Taizong (r. 626–649) of the Tang Dynasty returned them quantities of silk as gifts. Indirect transit trade was mainly undertaken through the Western Türks. Under the policy of conciliation, the two countries opened Mutual Markets, from which the Türks attained a large amount of silk. To avoid Dayi, the Western Türks transported Chinese silk and other commodities to the Mediterranean Sea

---

[37] Narsieh was a Persian general who fled to the Tang Dynasty with his father Peroz III, son of Yazdegerd III, the last Sassanid emperor of Persia, after the Muslim conquest of Persia.

[38] It is a collection of stories compiled in the early Song Dynasty under imperial direction by Li Fang. Completed in 981 CE, it was compiled from informal, unofficial sources, such as histories written by private scholars and even accounts, which we would regard as fairy tales. It is now the most important source for early Chinese fiction.

[39] Old-fashioned word referring to Persians. Also used as a metaphor for a person who is adept in evaluating treasures.

and to the Eastern Roman Empire by way of the Northern Tian Mountain, the Aral Sea, the Caspian Sea and the northern Black Sea.

(2) Trade Flourishes among Civilians

In addition to official trade, non-governmental trade between civilians proceeded more actively. In the *Collection of Imperial Edicts and Orders of the Tang Dynasty* compiled by Song Minqiu, a Northern Song geographical historian, it is reported that during Tang times "trade caravans with tributes were to be seen shuttling constantly through the areas stretching westward from Yiwu to the east of Persia." The Tang poem *Words for Liangzhou* by Zhang Ji captured the scene of the silk being shipped across the land that "with countless tinkling of bells passing the dunes, the camel trains carry white silk to the Parthian Empire."

The *Old Book of Tang: Biography of Western Regions*[40] records that the people of the Samarqand (now Uzbekistan) "were adept at trade. Young men aged 20 left for Central Plains of China at 20 to do business. They actually went anywhere profits could be found." In the early period of the Tang Dynasty, merchants of the Samarqand would bring with them more than 4,000 horses at a time. In addition to war horses and fur products, merchants from Central Asia also transported to China treasures and rare animals, etc. from western countries. Documents of the Tang recorded that merchants from Central Asia transported lions, leopards and ostriches to China, and purchased back substantial commodities such as silk, ironware and lacquerwares.

This period saw constant commercial communications between Chinese and foreign merchants, but many foreign merchants also took up their residence for a long term in China. The *Old Book of Tang: Biography of Western Regions* records that "foreigners from western countries were to be seen in Gaojie (where foreign diplomatic missions stay) during the regnal periods of Zhenguan and Kaiyuan." Most foreign merchants were engaged in all kinds of industries. For instance, in the then capital cities of Chang'an and Luoyang, there were jewelry shops, food shops, taverns and *Di* shops (as warehouses and hotels) run by merchants from Central Asia

---

[40] The *Old Book of Tang*, or simply the *Book of Tang*, is the first classic historical work about the Tang Dynasty, comprising 200 chapters, and is one of the Twenty-Four Histories. Originally compiled during the Five Dynasties and Ten Kingdoms period, it was superseded by the *New Book of Tang*, which was compiled in the Song Dynasty, but later regained acceptance.

and Persia. Tang documents record how non-Han merchants ran taverns in Chang'an and Luoyang. In the North Market of Luoyang, foreign merchants learned from Chinese people to set up similar merchant organizations as *hang* and *she*. To date, the shrine built by the "Xiangxing Merchant She in the North Market"[41] was still well preserved in the north of Guyang Cave, the Longmen Grottoes, Luoyang. Terracotta figures of "merchant leading camels" among Tang tri-color glazed ceramics reflected the prosperous scene of the Silk Road trade between China and foreign countries.

Apart from merchants in Chang'an and Luoyang, foreign merchants were also active in some medium-sized and small inland cities. For instance, Shangrao, Raozhou, "kept quite a close trade relationship with foreign merchants, with commodities imported from Persia and Parthia and transacted with domestic merchants"[42]; during the "Rebellion of An and Shi" (755–763), some non-Han merchants "were willing to offer donations"[43] to help the Tang to suppress the revolt in Hongzhou (now Nanchang, Jiangxi); in Chenliu (in Henan Province) the Tang people could hear "one evening how non-Han merchants argued over the evaluation of jewelry"[44]; within Jiangling City in Hubei Province there was the Goguryeo Residence (mansion) built by long-term-resided Goguryeo merchants. All these records suggested that foreign merchants were widespread across Tang China, exerting a degree of influence over the dynamism of the local commodity economy.

After the "Rebellion of An and Shi," the northwestern Silk Road was basically cut off by the Tibetan Regime (*Tu bo*). The Tang Dynasty had now to conduct foreign trade with the Tibetan Regime and the Uighurs through Mutual Markets. Continental trade, though not abandoned, no longer held a dominant position in China's opening-up.

4.4.2 *The Development of Maritime Trade*

The maritime Silk Road of the Tang Dynasty gradually became prosperous on the basis of the Six Dynasties. The center of China's foreign trade shifted from land to sea in the late period of the Tang under the influence

---

[41] Merchant organization for spice business.

[42] (The Song Dynasty) Li Fang. *Finest Blossoms in the Garden of Literature*. Vol. 371. Beijing: Zhonghua Book Company, 1996.

[43] (The Song Dynasty) Li Fang. *Extensive Records of the Taiping Period*. Vol. 403. Beijing: Zhonghua Book Company, 1981.

[44] *Ibid.*

of multiple factors. China's opening-up was more reliant on the maritime Silk Road. A further development occurred in the trade relationship with countries along the maritime Silk Road. Namely, more coastal ports opened to foreign countries.

(1) The Development of Trade Relations Overseas

In the Tang Dynasty, the maritime Silk Road was not only used by merchants coming to trade in China from West Asia, Northeast Asia and Southeast Asia, but by merchants from China looking to trade overseas with the rest of the world.

(i) West Asian Countries

China established a long-term trade relationship with Arabic States in the Western Regions and Persia through the maritime Silk Road. From the late 6th century to 7th century, the Arabian Empire grew to a gigantic scale, spanning Europe, Asia and Africa. In 651, the 2nd year of the reign of the Tang's third Emperor Gaozong (r. 649–683), the third Caliph Osman dispatched envoys to the Tang, initially establishing official relationship with China. From then on, unceasing streams of envoys undertook official bilateral trade. Nevertheless, the Arabian Empire constantly extended eastward, so conflicts with China broke out in Central Asia. Persistent tensions hanging over them in the early period of the Tang hindered the full development of their trade relationship.

After the mid-8th century, China's opening-up focused more on the southeastern coast. And the conflicts between China and the Arabs were put to an end. Under the opening-up policy of the Tang, many Arabian merchants came to trade in China. The trade relationship between them gradually improved and occupied an important position in China's foreign trade. Joseph Needham, the English scholar of the history of science wrote in his book the *Science and Civilization in China* that "from the 8th to the 13th centuries was the great Chinese-Arab period."

In the late period of the Tang Dynasty, many Arabian merchants gathered in Guangzhou, the preeminent port for Chinese foreign trade. According to Arabian historical accounts, in around 870 CE, there were more than 120,000 foreign people in Guangzhou, including Dayi people, Persians, Jews, and others. Obviously, the records contained a degree of flourish. But they did reflect how there were at least numerous Arabian merchants in Guangzhou. This accounted for construction of *Fan Fang* in the city, built exclusively for Arabs, and the Huaisheng Mosque.

However, the "Huangchao Rebellion" (875–884) in the late Tang Dynasty severely damaged the trade between China and Arabia. According to Arabian records, "the rebellion in China even influenced the merchants at Xilafu Port (now Theili, Iran) and Wengman (now Oman) so badly that numerous merchants who used to trade with China have now gone bankrupt." The stories in the *One Thousand and One Nights* also record trade between China and Arabia. One story told the experience of a merchant named Xinde Bade who sailed to China to trade. Meanwhile, many Chinese merchants sailed westward to Arabia as well. Hundreds of foreign ships moored in the docks of the capital city Baghdad, which measured only a few miles long. Many of these were Chinese vessels. In the streets, there were also markets exclusively selling Chinese silk products, porcelains, papers, musk, etc.

(ii) Northeast Asian Countries

The trade relationships between China and the Korean Peninsula and Japan were extremely close in the Tang Dynasty.

In the early period of the Tang Dynasty, there were three great countries on the Korean Peninsula, namely, Goguryeo, Baekje and Silla. They all maintained tributary trade with the Tang. In 668, Silla successively defeated Baekje and Goguryeo and united the Korean Peninsula. Trade between Silla and China proceeded via both the continental and maritime roads. So large quantity of Silla people traveled along the maritime road, gathering mainly on the Shandong Peninsula and the lower reaches of the Huaihe River. Silla Residences, Silla Squares and Silla Temples were especially built for receiving the merchant envoys of Silla in Wendeng, Dengzhou and Chuzhou as well. At that time, abundant varieties of goods were exchanged between them. China-exported silk, clothing, porcelain, tea, ironware, books and cultural items to Korea and imported ginseng, copper and handicrafts from Korea. The seeds of the tea bush were introduced to Korea in around 828, initiating the history of tea plantation on the Korean Peninsula.

At that time, the official trade activities between China and Japan were mainly undertaken by "Japanese missions to Tang China." Japan had sent many parties of envoys to China since the Sui Dynasty to learn advanced Chinese culture, regulations and systems, and advanced production technologies,. After "Taika Era Reforms," the Japanese paid much attention to learning from China, and the Japanese envoy groups were unprecedentedly huge in size. In the late period of the Tang Dynasty, when Japan ceased to dispatch envoys to China, civilian trade between China and Japan started to develop, with more Chinese merchants going to Japan. For instance, the Mingzhou business groups led by Li Linde, Zhang Youxin and Li Yanlao were frequently to be seen sailing between Mingzhou and Hakata in Japan. In 862, "the Tang's Li Yanxiao and other 43 retinues came to Japan and were received well in the residence of the Grand Steward."[45] Japan also especially appointed an official as "Commissioner in Charge of Trading with the Tang" to manage trade between their nation and China.

Major commodities exchanged between the two sides were Chinese silk, porcelain, tea, copper coins, while the classics of Confucianism and Buddhism were exported to Japan, and alluvial gold, pearls, woods and ox horns imported from Japan.

(iii) Southeast Asian Countries

Countries in Southeast Asia which maintained a close trade relationship with China were distributed principally through present-day Cambodia, Myanmar and Indonesia.

Cambodia, also known as Khmer (modern-day Kampuchea), traded frequently with China since the Sui Dynasty. In the early years of the 8th century, it split into the Overland Khmer and Maritime Khmer, both sustaining close relationships with China. In 753 during the reign of the Tang Emperor Xuanzong, the prince of Overland Khmer visited China in the company of 26 royals. This was the first senior ranking visit between China and Cambodia. The Tang Emperor Xuanzong (r. 848–859) conferred upon the prince the title of Commander-in-Chief for Resoluteness and Persistence. During the reign of the Tang Emperor Daizong (762–779), the under king of Khmer visited China, bringing with him 11 elephants as tributes.

Myanmar was called the Kingdom of Pyu in the Tang Dynasty. Besides the exchanges with the Tang Dynasty along the maritime road, Myanmar also kept up a trade relationship with the Nanzhao Regime of Yunnan along the continental road.

---

[45] Zudasinnnou nyutou ryakki (Toujikanntiinn). Also see Lin Shimin. *A Comparison of the Tang Port of Mingzhou and Japanese Port of Hakata.* Sanjiang Forum, 2009 (6).

Close trade relationships were also established between China and Srivijaya on Sumatra Island and Yavadvipa on the Java Island. Most foreign merchants came to China from Indonesia, and mainly gathered in Guangzhou. A Foreign Community (*Fan Fang*) was specially set up for Indonesian merchants to stay. Pu Gaosu, an Indonesian merchant, once took on the role of head. Majorly exchanged commodities were Chinese silk products, porcelain, copper coins, ironware and farming tools, as well as Indonesian spices, precious woods, jewelries, Hawkbill turtles and rhinoceros horns.

(iv) Southeast Asian Countries
China sustained close trade relationships with India and Sri Lanka in Southern Asia as well.

Further development was made in the maritime trade between China and India in the Tang Dynasty. The *Supplementary History of Tang Dynasty* records that "every year sees foreign ships sailing to Annam and Guangzhou, among which the biggest one comes from Simhala, being more than ten cords (*zhang*) high and full of treasures." Chinese ships also constantly traveled outbound to the west. For instance, Wang E, a corrupt official of the Tang Dynasty, violated the prohibition on conducting business in Sindhu and hid his commodities in civilian ships. More than 10 ships were "seen to sail out each day." This demonstrated a rather considerable scale on which Chinese merchants traded in South Asia. In *the Great Tang Records on the Western Regions*, Xuanzang wrote that he met in central Sindhu merchant ships from Guangzhou, as tall as 20 cords (*zhang*), and carrying 600 or 700 people.

The main imported commodities from Sindhu and the Simhalauipa were rhinoceros horns, Hawkbill turtles, peppers, pearls, jade figurines of the Buddha and the Buddhist sutras; while China's main exported commodities were silk products, porcelain and Chinese medical materials.

(2) Ports Flourish through Maritime Trade
With frequent maritime communications between China and foreign countries, the number of coastal ports for foreign trade increased in the Sui and Tang Dynasties. When traditional foreign trade ports further developed, some new coastal ports emerged and were opened to foreign trade. According to historical records, the ports boasting prosperous

overseas trade in the Tang Dynasty were Guangzhou, Mingzhou (now Ningbo), Yangzhou, Jiaozhou, Yuezhou (now Shaoxing), Chuzhou (now Huai'an), Suzhou, Hangzhou, Fuzhou, Quanzhou, Dengzhou, etc., among which Guangzhou, Mingzhou, Yangzhou and Jiaozhou were of the greatest importance. They were therefore known as the "Four Great Trade Ports of the Tang."

(i) Guangzhou Port

The Tang Dynasty was the golden time for maritime trade development in Guangzhou. Jia Dan (730–805), a Chinese scholar and geographer of the Tang Dynasty, wrote a book titled the *Records of Roads*, including a description that "Guangzhou possesses the major maritime trade route from China right through to the sea, i.e. Persian Gulf." Obviously, it was from Guangzhou that Tang ships found their way to the Persian Gulf and East Africa. Along the route, merchants ships disembarked from Guangzhou, sailed via the Indochina Peninsula, the Malay Peninsula and the Malay Archipelago, and the Indian Subcontinent, to arrive in the Persian Gulf, then sailed southward to the Arabian Peninsula and Eastern Africa.

In the late period of the Tang Dynasty, with the decline of the continental Silk Road, China paid far greater attention to international trade via the maritime Silk Road. Thereafter, Guangzhou became the largest foreign trade port by virtue of its favorable geographical location and long maritime trading tradition. In particular, the rapid development in foreign trade with Arabia further improved the prosperity of Guangzhou port. According to the Arabian text *Accounts of China and India*, "Guangzhou was a commercial port with foreign ships, a collection and distribution center for Arabian and Chinese commodities," as well as "a place with a constellation of Arabian merchants."

A ceaseless torrent of merchant ships arrived in Guangzhou along the maritime Silk Road. The Japanese scholar Ōmi no Mihune recorded in his book *Todaiwajo Toseiden* that there were "countless foreign ships from Brahmin, Persia and Kunlun Park in Guangzhou, carrying aromatic drugs from the mountains and treasures." Also, "numerous ships carrying spices made Guangzhou one of the biggest spice markets in the world at that time." Han Yu also recorded in his *Preface* to the *Seeing off Minister Zheng* that "foreign ships arrive in Guangzhou everyday overflowing with more foreign commodities than China can consume, including pearls, spices, ox horns, rhinoceros horns and Hawkbill turtles."

The development of overseas trade promoted the prosperity of markets in Guangzhou. "Foreign ships moor in the South China Sea. Every year sees foreign ships sailing to Annam and Guangzhou, where the biggest ship comes from the Simhalauipa, rising more than ten cords (*zhang*) high and full of treasure. The arrival of these commodities was reported by the local government, exciting people in prefectures and counties."[46]

Foreign merchants assembled in crowds in Guangzhou, with a considerable number living there, most of them were Arabian merchants.

To adapt to the rapid development of maritime trade in Guangzhou, the official "Maritime Trade Commissioner" was set up by the Tang Dynasty to manage maritime trade for the first time, starting the trade management system in ancient China.

(ii) Mingzhou Port

Mingzhou Port (now Ningbo) lies on the coast of the East China Sea, neighboring the Western Pacific Ocean. Mingzhou boasts a flat topography, favorable climate, clear maritime routes and a prosperous economy. Since ancient times, it had been the political, economic and cultural center of eastern Zhejiang area for many dynasties.

Mingzhou in the Tang Dynasty was one of the four biggest trade ports in China. Ships sailing from Wanghai town in the Yongjiang Estuary, over 70 miles away from Mingzhou, frequently reached Silla and Japan. From the 8th century, ships carrying Japanese envoys came back and forth to China along the South Island Road (the southern route of the south road) or the Nan Road (the Northern route of the South Road), and berthed in Mingzhou or departed from Mingzhou. Since Japanese envoys ceased voyaging, Japanese civilian ships often sailed from Mingzhou to Tsukushi. Therefore, the port of Mingzhou could be considered as the gateway for trade between Japan and Korea. At the same time, many foreign and Chinese ships sailed southward from Mingzhou to Guangzhou and Jiaozhou and passed the western Route to Southeast Asia and West Asia. Obviously, the port Mingzhou connected the eastern and western routes, therefore it enjoyed an important position in the history of China's foreign trade.

(iii) Yangzhou Port

Yangzhou was a riverside settlement during the period of the Sui and Tang Dynasties. The excavation of the Grand Canal in the Sui Dynasty further

---

[46] (The Tang Dynasty) Li Zhao. *Supplementary History of the Tang Dynasty*. Vol. II.

demonstrated the advantageous geographical location of Yangzhou, making it a pivot of transportation, over the land and on the sea as well as a collection and distribution point for commodities, with an increasingly dynamic goods economy. Yangzhou had become the most prosperous commercial city in China by the time of the Tang Dynasty. Xu Ning, a middle Tang poet, thought highly of the scenery of Yangzhou in his poem *Recalling Yangzhou*, observing that "among all those bright moon nights, two-thirds are in Yangzhou." Apart from Chinese merchants, a succession of foreign merchants was also to be seen in Yangzhou. From the poem written by Du Fu, one could tell that Yanghzhou was an international metropolis at that time. In the second of his *Twelve Poems for Relieving Boredom* he relates that "when a non-Han merchant is leaving for Yangzhou, he recalls a hostel building on his way to Xiling; in order to know the price that the rice sold in the Jiangnan area, I am, on an impulse, trying to travel to that place." This illustrated how Yangzhou had become a cosmopolitan city.

Situated in the middle of the eastern coast, Yangzhou was positioned advantageously for connecting the south and the north, which made reaching overseas convenient via the East China Sea Silk Road Route or the South China Sea Silk Road Route.

During the Sui and Tang Dynasties, China was connected with Korea and Japan by the southern route and the northern route. The northern route sailed from Jiuzhou in Japan to the southern tip of the Korean Peninsula. The voyage went firstly northward and then westward along the western coast, landing at Dengzhou on the Shandong Peninsula (now Penglai). From Dengzhou, ships entered the Huaihe River from Jishui, and arrived in Yangzhou along the Grand Canal within the Huainan. Alternatively, they berthed at Chuzhou in northern Jiangsu or on the neighboring coast, then arrived in Yangzhou by the Grand Canal within the Huainan. This route was often used to sail from Yangzhou to Korea. Therefore, it was the main sailing route between China and Japan in the period prior to the flourishing period of the Tang.

The southern route led directly to Yangzhou from Jiuzhou Island, specifically from the Satsuma Peninsula in its south or port of Hakata in its north. Then it reached Xiangyang, Hubei along the Yangtze River or to the capital city Luoyang along the Grand Canal. This route was taken by the former visitors of the Japanese Mission to the Tang and the eminent monk Jianzhen (Ganjin in Japanese), who sailed eastward to Japan several times along this route.

The connections between Yangzhou and Southeast Asia, West Asia and Northern Africa were made along the Silk Road, starting from Luoyang to Yangzhou by way of the Bianshui River and the Huaihe River. Ships then sailed from Yangzhou to Hunan, Hubei, Fujian or Guangdong.

The outbound connection of Yangzhou was also made by the Maritime Silk Road to Guangzhou or the ships sailed along the coast of Fujian. The route ran through Meiling, Hongzhou (now Nanchang), Jiangzhou (now Jiujiang) and reached Yangzhou along the Yangtze River; or took the maritime Silk Road directly to Yangzhou.

Merchants, both domestic and those from abroad, shuttled frequently for trade in Yangzhou. Some chose to take up long-term residence and started trade activities in Yangzhou. The *Extensive Records of the Taiping Period* described how foreign merchants ran jewelry shops in Yangzhou. For instance, Vol. 402 titled the *Ship Keeper* recorded that during the early years of Yuanhe period (806–820), a "salt ship keeper" obtained a pearl and "sold it in a foreign shop in Yangzhou." Vol. 33 *Wei Yan* also recorded that during the Kaiyuan Era (713–741), Wei Yan acquired three treasures in Sichuan, "he then traveled eastward to at Yangzhou. The non-Han merchants there liked to purchase the treasures with 100,000 gold." Most of those merchants came from West Asia, such as Persia and Arabia. During the reign of the Tang's eleventh Emperor Suzong (756–762 CE), there were as many as thousands of foreign merchants in Yangzhou. The *Old Book of Tang: Biography of Deng Jingshan* recorded the "Rebellion of Tian Shengong" that "when Tian Shengong led his followers to reach Yangzhou, they robbed almost all of the residents' properties right away, causing the death of thousands of non-Han merchants from Da Yi and Persia."

Prior to the Tang Dynasty, Korean and Japanese merchants were greater in number in Yangzhou. They included not only envoys, merchants, but many overseas students and scholar monks. For instance, Japan sent nine missions to the Tang. The scholar monk Rong Rui spent 18 years in China, during which time he went to Yangzhou four times. Pu Zhao was also a scholar monk. During his 21 years of staying in China, he traveled eight times to Yangzhou.

Driven by the trade between China and foreign countries, the economy of Yangzhou was extremely prosperous in the Tang Dynasty, especially in its late period. It assumed the leading position in China's economy, and therefore was prized as the number one port in China, followed by Yizhou.

The period of Kaicheng (836–840) saw constant deposits from the Yangtze River, causing its mouth to migrate gradually eastwards, and Yangzhou was left far away from the sea. From the Song and Yuan Dynasties, the mouth shifted southeastward to Jiangyin and Huating (now in the Songjiang District, Shanghai). This caused Yangzhou's position as an international trade port to be superseded by a single-functioned domestic inland river port.

(iv) Jiaozhou Port

There were two seaports in Jiaozhou in the Tang, respectively, the "North Scene" in the south, and the "Longbian" in the north. The latter used to be the site of Jiaozhou government. The *Old Book of Tang: Annals of Geography* recorded that "after the Sui controlled the Chen, Jiaozhou was set up there. Its name was changed to Cochin with Prefectural Governor heading the Longbian." The "North Scene" was an inescapable port when the Tang's ships wanted to sail to the South China Sea. The route from the north scene to Guangzhou (Canton) was easy and convenient. It became a seaport lying at the very southern end of China in the Tang Dynasty as well as the first gateway among the ports along the southeastern coast in the Tang Dynasty.

In the middle and late periods of the Tang Dynasty, due to the severe exploitation by officials at the port of Guangzhou, many foreign merchant ships moved to trade in Jiaozhou, facilitating the prosperity of that port. The *Supplementary History of Tang Dynasty* recorded in *Oceangoing ships in the Simhalauipa* (name of ancient Sri Lanka) that "the South Sea ships are foreign ships and sail to Annam and Guangzhou." The "Annam" referred to the "North Scene," port of Jiaozhou.

4.5 Foreign Trade and Economic & Cultural Communication with other Countries

Under the comprehensive opening-up policy of the Tang Dynasty, frequent trade communications promoted political, economic and cultural exchanges between China and foreign countries. Achievements in Chinese civilization were absorbed by foreign countries to promote the advancement of their social economy. The Tang also was positive in learning and absorbing excellent foreign culture.

4.5.1 *Exporting Major Commodities and Manufacturing Techniques*

(1) Exporting Silk and Silk-Weaving Techniques

The Tang silk still continued to be exported to eastern and western countries along the continental and maritime Silk Roads. In the official trade of the Tang with other countries, silk was not only taken as gifts to other countries, but as gifts given in return by other countries. It was an important commodity in civilian trade as well.

Before the Tang Dynasty, Persian silk products had already been resold to China. It didn't take very long before artificial silk fabric appeared on the market. The situation continued to exist in the Tang and Five Dynasties, which could be confirmed by the unearthed artifacts. The tombs in the Sui and Tang Dynasties contained Chinese silk products with typical silk patterns of the Sassanid Empire.[47] Some brocades from the Tang Empire collected and kept in Shaosoin of Japan were obviously affected in their pattern by the Sassanid style. At the same time, Chinese weaving craft began to feature horizontal patterns akin to those in Central Asia and West Asia.

Japanese silk products were seen to swarm into China. The "Ministry of Finance" in *Engishiki* records that the Japanese government would confer parting gifts of coarse silk, silk floss and cloth to missions to bring with them to the Tang. In the first place, those gifts were taken as "tuition" for Japanese students and monks to study in China. Meanwhile, they could also be traded with Chinese merchants. A considerable quantity of Japanese silk products flowed into China, and they were praised by the Tang Chinese. The Japan-made style "pearl silk" was particularly favorably received by the Tang Chinese.

The 8th century was considered the Golden Age for the communications between the Tang Dynasty and Arabia, which happened when the Chinese silk weaving techniques were introduced there. After the Battle of Talas between Arab Muslim forces and the army of the Chinese Empire in 751, Chinese prisoners of war, some of whom were trained weavers, were sent to Mesopotamia — the land "between the rivers (Tigris and Euphrates Rivers)." Thereafter, West Asia was seen to develop rapidly in manufacturing advanced silk products, with imperial workshops and

---

[47]Xia Ding. *The Ancient Silk Products — Damask, Silk floss and Embroideries Excavated in Xinjiang*. Acta Archaeologica Sinica, 1963 (1).

state-run workshops established to produce silk products known as *Dui la zi* exclusively for the royalty and the upper class. *Dui la zi* referred to the silk products with names of the caliph (Arabic khalifah, "successor") or sultan (ruler of some Muslim states) weaved or embroidered into them. These were tailored as materials for embroidering the emperor's gowns or as gifts to award ministers who rendered meritorious service. Later, a considerable quantity of silk of different varieties was purchased from the Arabs to meet the demand in Europe.

(2) Exporting Porcelainware and Porcelain-Making Techniques

There were more than 20 kilns in the Tang Dynasty, among which the most famous ones were the Xingyao kiln (Neiqiu county, Hebei), the Yueyao kiln (Yuyao, Zhejiang), the Changnan kiln (Jingde county, Jiangxi), the Qiongyao kiln (Qionglai, Sichuan), the Ding kiln (Quyang, Hebei) and the Chaozhou kiln (Chaozhou, Guangdong). They produced more porcelain than other kilns in the country. In the 8th century, Yueyao porcelain (blue porcelain) began to be sold to foreign countries. This marked a new stage for Chinese porcelain exportation. By virtue of its delicate shapes, bright colors and distinct styles, Chinese porcelain won great attention from the world. China became internationally known as "China," that is "the country of porcelain." The porcelain of the Tang Dynasty was exported to eastern and western countries along the continental and maritime Silk Roads. Transmitted together with it were Chinese culture, technology and aesthetics.

As early as the Southern and Northern Dynasties, Chinese porcelain which was in its embryonic stage was introduced into the Korean Peninsula. With the great development of Tang porcelain manufacturing techniques, a large quantity of porcelain products were exported to the Korean Peninsula along the maritime Silk Road in the Tang Dynasty. In modern times, many specimens of porcelain from the Tang Dynasty were unearthed on the Korean Peninsula. In the Chaoyang Cave, near Qingzhou in Korea, an intact Tang tri-color glazed ceramic "three-foot snake" was uncovered. Its shape and palette were extremely similar to the ceramics unearthed in Yangzhou.[48] Moreover, a considerable quantity of glazed porcelain from Yuezhou were unearthed in Cheongju and Jeollanam-do, etc., as well. "Silla Tri-Color Glazed Ceramics" were made based on Tang

---

[48] Feng Xianming. *A Survey of China's Porcelain Sales in Asia prior to the Yuan Dynasty.* Cultural Relics. 1986 (6).

prototypes. Kilns were built in Jeollanam-do in 918 to counterfeit China's Yueyao celadon. Silla produced celadon was named "Silla-fired" porcelain or "emerald color" porcelain.[49]

The Sui and Tang Dynasties were the periods when Sino–Japanese communications were infused with dynamism. The Sui Dynasty saw much Chinese porcelain exported to Japan. The Tang began to export porcelains to Japan in quantity. To date, a large amount of Tang porcelain, including the Tang tri-color glazed ceramics, glazed porcelains of Yueyao, white porcelain of Xingyao kiln and porcelain of Changsha, have been uncovered in Japan. Tang tri-color glazed ceramics were introduced into Japan in the flourishing Tang period, and found in Nara and Fukuoka. The blue porcelain of Yueyao was successively found in almost 50 Japanese relic sites. Many examples of porcelain from Tongguan and Changsha were exported to Japan in the middle and late periods of the Tang, which were found in temples in Nara, Kyoto, port of Hakata and Jiuliumi of Kyushu, Kagoshima and Iriomote-jima, as well as in residential relics and old tombs. The Changnan porcelains of the Tang were excavated from official sites, temples and tombs in Nara, Kyoto and Fukuoka.[50]

Once introduced into Japan, Chinese porcelain of the Tang and Five Dynasties deeply influenced the development of the local porcelain industry. The Japanese highly praised Tang tri-color glazed ceramics when they encountered it for the first time. When the supply fell short of the demand, the Japanese government ordered that it be replicated. And their imitations were so similar to the Tang tri-color glazed ceramics in design, glaze color, pattern and style that they were known as "Nara Tri-Color Glazed Ceramics." Since a great number of imitations had been preserved in Shosoin (the treasure house of Tōdai-ji Temple in Nara), the name "Shosoin Tri-Color Glazed Ceramics" came into being. With a large number of porcelains exported to Japan from the Yueyao, the Changsha kiln and the white porcelains produced by both southern and northern kilns, the kiln techniques were also introduced into Japan. At the end of 9th century, the Japanese redesigned the structure of the kiln by taking advantage of the kiln techniques of Yueyao. They even imitated the shapes and styles of the kiln tools of the Tang and Five Dynasties. The sham Yueyao style glazed porcelains made by the Yuantou[51] of Aichi County (a

---

[49] Japan Shogakukan. *Ceramic Works in the World: The Sui and Tang.*

[50] Mikami Tsugio. *A Study on the Sino-Japanese Cultural Communication from the Perspective of Ceramic Trade.* Social Science Front, 1980 (1).

[51] The kiln located in the southeast of Seto City.

famous Japanese kiln) resembled very closely the wares from the Yueyao in terms of shape, glaze color and decoration skills.

Moreover, porcelain from the Tang Dynasty was also exported to South Asia. Some was unearthed in present-day India, Pakistan and Sri Lanka. The blue porcelain of the Yueyao and porcelain of Changsha of the late Tang and Five Dynasties were collected in the Mysore State Museum (present-day Karnataka State) in southern India;[52] some blue porcelain plate fragment of the Yueyao kiln from the late Tang and Five Dynasties were excavated from the relics of ancient ports along the Coromandel Coast in southern India; some water-holder fragments and glazed porcelain bowl pieces from the Yueyao of the late Tang Dynasty and Five Dynasties were unearthed from the relics of the ancient port of Banbhore to the southeast of Karachi, Pakistan.[53]

Tang porcelain was exported to West Asian countries, like Persia and Arabia, along the overland and maritime routes. A large quantity of Chinese porcelain was unearthed from the Port of Siraf (now Tahiri, Iran) in the Persian Gulf, among which the very earliest were glazed porcelain from the Yueyao and white porcelain from the Xingyao of the middle and late Tang Dynasties. In the relics of Nashapu in Huolasan Province, northern Iran, a pivotal location along the old Silk Road, late Tang Dynasty deep bowls from the Yueyao, colored jars from the Changsha kiln and white porcelain from the Xingyao were uncovered.[54] The blue porcelain from the Yueyao and the colored decorated plates from the Changsha kiln of the Tang and Five Dynasties were unearthed in the relics of Rayy to the south of Tehran.[55] Moreover, Tang tri-color glazed ceramics were also unearthed in Iran. Iranians were adept at absorbing foreign culture and produced their own "Persian Tri-Color Glazed Ceramics" and white porcelains. Imitations of Tang tri-color glazed ceramics have been found in Nashapu'er, Liyi, Amole and Agehan.[56]

The Lebanese-American scholar Philip K. Hitti recorded in his book the *History of the Arabs* that, from the middle 8th century to the middle 9th

---

[52] *Shixu Qingbao*, Trial Edition, p. 159.

[53] Mikami Tsugio. *A Study of Sino-Japanese Cultural Communication from the Perspective of the Ceramics Trade*. Social Science Front, 1980 (1).

[54] *Ibid.*

[55] Feng Xianming. *A Survey of China's Porcelain Sales in Asia prior to the Yuan Dynasty*. Cultural Relics. 1986 (6).

[56] Ou Zhipei. *Ancient Chinese Porcelain in West Asia*. Cultural Relics Information Series II, 1978.

century was the flourishing period of the Abbasid Dynasty of Arab. In its capital city Baghdad, "commodities of china, silk and musk were sold in the market," and "there were markets exclusively selling Chinese commodities."

Chinese porcelain was also exported to Africa. In the relics of the Old City Fustat, in the south outskirts of Cairo, Egypt, up to 12,000 pieces among a total of 600,000 or 700,000 unearthed porcelainware were Chinese products. The earliest by date were Tang and Five Dynasties tricolor glazed ceramics, glazed porcelain of the Yueyao kiln and the white porcelain of the Xingyao kiln.

Egypt not only imported Chinese porcelains, but also produced their imitations. According to statistics, among the Egyptian and local porcelains unearthed in the Fustat relics, imitations of Chinese porcelain accounted for about 70% or 80%. Moreover, porcelain from the Tang and Five Dynasties were uncovered in the Aizhabu relics of Sudan along the coast of the Red Sea as well, and on Kilwa island belonging to Tanzania along the eastern coast of Africa, etc.[57] Almost all households in Cairo used fine Chinese porcelain in the Middle Ages. They called porcelain "Ceramic" (خزف), meaning "Chinese."

(3) Exporting Tea Leaves, Tea-bush Planting and Tea-Making Techniques

The Tang Dynasty saw the Chinese tea industry start to thrive. Chinese tea, tea seeds and the techniques of tea bushes planting and tea-making started to spread to neighboring countries and regions. Related historical documents recorded that the monks of Silla had brought Chinese tea seeds in the early Tang back to Silla, but their distribution was limited. During the later reign of Emperor Wenzong (r. 826–840) in the early 9th century, envoys came to the Tang from Silla and received tea seeds given by Emperor Wenzong as awards. The tea bushes planting industry started in Korea. The Korean document *Dongguk Tonggam* records that "during the reign of King Heungdeok of Silla, an envoy whose surname was Jin was sent to the Tang and returned with tea seeds given by Emperor Wenzong of the Tang, which were planted in the Jirisan of Jeolla-do.[58] The 10th history book titled *Annals of Silla* in the *Annals of the Three Kingdoms of*

---

[57] Mikami Tsugio. *A Study of Sino-Japanese Cultural Communication from the Perspective of the Ceramics Trade*, Social Science Front, 1980 (1).

[58] Chen Qikun, Zhuang Xuelan. *A Centennial History of the World Tea Industry*. Shanghai Scientific and Technical Publishers, 1995.

Korea recorded that in the third year of the reign of King Heungdeok of Silla, "*Huilian*, the envoy sent to the Tang, came back with tea seeds. The king ordered them to be planted in the Jirisan. Tea began to flourish since it appeared in the reign of Queen Seondeok of Silla."

Tea seeds of the Tang were introduced to Japan mainly by Japanese monks. In the late Tang Dynasty, the Japanese monk Saichō came to Zhejiang and studied in succession in the Tiantai School and Tantric School in the Tiantai Mountain and Longxing Temple of Yuezhou. In 805 AD, during the reign of Emperor Shunzong (r. 805–806), Zui Deng carried tea seeds from Tiantai Mountain in Zhejiang to Japan. According to the *Secret Records on Japanese Shinto*, the tea seeds that Zui Deng brought back to Japan were planted in Hiyoshi Shrine (now Hiyoshi tea plantation in Kyoto). Another Japanese monk named Kūkai also studied in the Tantric School in the Qinglong Temple, Chang'an in the Tang. He returned to Japan in 806 CE, with not only Chinese tea seeds, but with the tools for tea-making and techniques for tea drinking.

(4) Exporting Paper and Paper-Making Technology
As early as in the late Eastern Han Dynasty, Chinese paper had been introduced to the Korean Peninsula. During the Wei, Jin, Southern and Northern Dynasties, many Chinese books had spread over the Korean Peninsula, before its paper-making industry started. During the Sui and Tang, the Korean paper-making industry had advanced enough to make mulberry paper, renowned in the world for being made from mulberry bark.

The Sui and Tang also saw the Goguryeo monk Damjing introduce Chinese paper-making technology into Japan, which helped the Japanese to start their paper-making industry. The main materials for this were broken flax and paper mulberry bark. The pulping technology was identical to that of China. After the 8th century, the Japanese paper-making industry became further advanced with paper-making factories scattered all over the country. So the Japanese could produce a greater variety of paper. While Chinese paper was introduced into Japan, Japanese paper also flowed into China and won praise from the Chinese people.

Chinese paper was introduced into India along the Silk Road after its being widely used and circulated as a commodity. At the end of the 7th century, the paper-making industry was introduced into South Asian countries, including India. From the mid-7th century to the early 8th century, Chinese paper, as an export commodity, was also introduced to the Arabs. After the Battle of Talas in 751, the Chinese captives included craftsmen and among them paper makers. They introduced the technique to Samarkand, and the first paper-making factory was founded in Arabia. Thereafter, "Samarkand paper" spread to the Asian areas under the control of Halifa. Within a short period of time, a second paper-making factory was built in the Arabian capital of Baghdad. In the 10th century, the paper-making factories were established, respectively, in the places on the southeast bank of Arabia and Damascus. In the centuries thereafter, Damascus became the major source of supply for paper in Europe, so paper was generally called "Samarkand paper" across that continent. In the early 10th century, the paper-making technology was introduced from Arabia to Egypt, and then to Morocco in the early 12th century.

(5) Exporting Printing
Printing has been considered as one of the greatest inventions in ancient China. Engraved type was invented in the Tang Dynasty, and was introduced to neighboring countries soon after. It was the Korean Peninsula that imported this technology. Great quantities of books printed in the Tang Dynasty flowed into the Korean Peninsula in the form of gifts or commodities, directly spurring the Korean need for a printing industry and encouraging the mastery of Chinese printing technology. When dispatching Japanese envoys, students and monks to study Tang culture, Japan introduced Chinese engraved type, too. It was not until the Song Dynasty that Japan started its own book printing industry.

After the 10th century, printing technology, following the paper-making technology, was introduced into Arabia, Egypt, etc.

Besides the above-mentioned exports of commodities and technologies, China also exported spices, like agilawood, camphor, cinnamon and musk.[59]

4.5.2 *Importing Foreign Material Civilization*

Research shows that the Tang imported more than 170 kinds of commodities, among which the major ones were various spices, herbs and jewels. The Japanese Ōmi no Mifune recorded in his book *Todaiwajo Toseiden* that in Guangzhou "countless foreign ships from Brahmin, Persia and the

---

[59](Arab) Ibn Khordadbeh. *Book of Roads and Kingdoms*. Trans. by Song Xian. Zhonghua Book Company, Beijing, 1991.

Kunlun moored in rivers with spices, herbs and jewels heaped like mountains; ships were as much as 6–7 cords (*zhang*) in length."

(1) Importing Aromatic Drugs

Spices and herbs formed major commodities that the ancient China imported from foreign countries, with the Tang and Song Dynasties as the heydays of that trade. China mainly imported spices from the Indochina Peninsula, the Malay Peninsula, the Indian Peninsula, the coast of the Arabian Sea and some countries and regions of East Africa, among which Arabia was not only the Tang's major trading partner but the principal spice-exporting area. According to history records, "in March 724, Dayi dispatched envoys to present ... and kapor," and "in the lunar January of 731, the Persian prince paid tributes to China, presenting spices and rhinoceros, etc."[60] "In 824, during the reign of the Tang's Emperor Muzong (r. 821–824), the Persian merchant Li Susha presented aquilaria agallocha woods used for constructing pavilions."[61]

These imports greatly influenced Chinese people's lives, both materially and spiritually, as well as fulfilling the feudal emperor's desire for luxury. Imported medicines and herbs were mainly used in medications, environment sanitation, food, religious activities, etc.

(2) Importing New Species of Crops

The major foreign crops imported along the continental and maritime roads into the Tang included the Persian date (*Phoenix dactylifera*), the almond produced in Persia, the ponasuo (jackfruit) and the olive (*olea europaea*) produced in Persia and Polin (also known as the Eastern Roman Empire), peppers from the Kingdom of Magadha (now in northeastern India), figs (*ficus carica*) produced in Persia and Polin; spinach (*Spinacia oleracea*) of Nepal, dill (also known as Fennel) of Srivijaya (now Sumatra Island). The introduction of foreign strains widened the variety of Chinese crops, particularly of fruit trees and vegetables, with direct benefits for people's lives.

---

[60](The Song Dynasty) Wang Qinruo. *Primary Tortoise of the Records Office*. Vol. 971. Beijing: Zhonghua Book Company, 1960.

[61](The Later Jin Dynasty) Liu Xu. *Old Book of Tang: Emperor Jingzong*. Beijing: Zhonghua Book Company, 1975.

(3) Importing Fine-Breed Horses
In the Sui and Tang Dynasties, war horses from Central plains of China mainly came from the Western Regions. During the reign of the Sui's Emperor Yang (r. 604–618), "the Dayuan Kingdom presented *thousand-li* horses."[62] The *Compendium Manuscript of the Tang*, a 10th-century institutional history of the Tang, recorded that "in the early Tang Dynasty, the Samarqand presented 4,000 horses. The now official horses were of this breed." The famous "Six Steeds of Zhao Mausoleum," according to research, were all from the northern Xinjiang, Central Asia and Iran in West Asia.

(4) Importing Indian Sugar Extraction Techniques
The sugar extraction technique was practiced very early in China. During the period from the late 5th century to the early 6th century, sugarcane juice was used to make granulated sugar in Jiangnan. Owing to extensive communications with India, the sugar extraction technique was introduced from India to Tang China. In 647, Magadha (now in northeastern India) on the Indian Peninsula dispatched envoys to establish an official relationship with the Tang, and flaunted their tasteful granulated sugar. The Tang's Emperor Taizong (r. 626–649) appraised it highly and sent people to learn the method. When returned, they chose Yangzhou sugarcane to make sugar, and were successful, which even surpassed the Indian sugar in both color and taste.

4.5.3 *Importing Foreign Culture*

With the establishment of the trade relationship between China and foreign countries in the Tang Dynasty, a large quantity of foreigners came to China, together with many commodities, foreign science and technology, culture and religious customs. In the Tang Dynasty, the opening-up of politics and the economy and the emancipated environment for development were quite enticing. Many foreign scholars, artists and merchants coming to China were attracted by this reputation. Those foreign residents and immigrants played key roles in many fields.

In the Tang Dynasty, there were many foreign residents in Chang'an, Luoyang, Guangzhou, and Yangzhou, with more than 100,000 foreigners

---

[62] The horse is believed to able to run a thousand *li* (500 kilometers) a day.

in Chang'an and more than 100,000 foreigners settling down in Guangzhou during the late Tang period. These foreigners included merchants, monks, scholars, painters, craftsmen and artists. They were engaged in cultural and artistic activities with distinct national features in China, which greatly influenced Chinese people's social lives. In 714, "as the Inner Gentleman of the Right Flank Imperial Guards, Zhou Qingli was appointed as Maritime Trade Commissioner. He tried every means to locate a Persian monk, whom he planned to recommend to the Emperor."[63]

Apart from big cities and coastal ports, foreign trade activities proceeded in inland cities and towns, providing that there was convenient transportation. According to the *Records of Deities* in the *Extensive Records of the Taiping Period*, a man from Linchuan with the family name Cen obtained two precious stones. He then went to Yuzhang (now Nanchang in Jiangxi), "and a Persian merchant requested to buy them at a price of 30,000." In addition, non-Han merchants also ran *Di* Hostels in Hongzhou (now Jiujiang, Jiangxi), Yixing (now Yixing, Jiangsu), Chenliu (now Chenliu in Kaifeng, Henan) and Weijun (now Linzhang, Hebei). Nationwide, non-Han merchants exerted an extensive influence on the customs of the communities where they stayed.

Knowledge about astronomy, the calendar and the medical classics of Sindhu, Byzantine, Persia and Arabia was also introduced into China. Many foreign medical prescriptions were included in the medical classics of the Tang Dynasty, such as the *Essential Prescriptions Worth a Thousand Emergencies*, the *Supplement to the Essential Prescriptions Worth a Thousand Gold* and the *Medical Secrets of an Official*. Li Xun, the author of the book *Materia Medica of Foreign Medicine*, was a descendant of a Persian merchant who traded spices and herbs. Due to the lack of legislation governing foreigners' economic and cultural activities in the Tang Dynasty, many foreign merchants practiced medicine all over China, further enhancing its spread.

Moreover, some foreign astronomers served in the Administrative Division of Astronomy in the Tang Dynasty. For instance, three generations of Qu Tan's family from Sindhu served, after Qu Tan's term was for as long as 110 years in China successively as Grand Astrologer, Directorate of Astrology and Directorate of Astronomy to lead and charge the official

---

[63] (The Later Jin Dynasty) Liu Xu. *Old Book of Tang: Primary Chronicle of* Emperor Xuanzong. Vol. 8. Beijing: Zhonghua Book Company, 1975.

astronomical institution of the Tang Dynasty. They combined the Indian astronomical calendar and China's traditional astronomy to compile books, like the *Latitude and Longitude*, the *Lighthouse Calendar* and the *Ganzhi Calendar*, making significant contributions to the advancement of China's astronomy and calendar system.[64]

Buddhism, which was introduced to China in the Han Dynasty, thrived in the Tang Dynasty. Moreover, some new religions, like Zoroastrianism, were introduced by Persians, and the Nestorianism (a sect of Christianity) also was introduced into Chang'an from the Western Regions. "Xian Ci" as temples of Zoroastrianism were established in Buzheng Lane, Liquan Lane, Puning Lane, and Jinggong Lane in Chang'an. There were four "Xian Ci" found in Huijie Lane, Lide Lane and Nanshixi Lane in the eastern capital city Luoyang. Persian temples were seen in Yining Lane and Liquan Lane in Chang'an and in other places but with different names. So in 745, during the reign of the Tang's Emperor Xuanzong, all temples of Nestorianism in the two capitals, Chang'an and Luoyang, and other prefectures were renamed as "Daqin Temples." Manichaeism and Islam were also introduced by Persian and Dayi people and grew prevalent in the Tang.

Many dancers, singers and painters gathered in Chang'an and Luoyang as well. Dances and songs from the Western Regions also achieved popularity here. According to historical accounts, Emperor Zhongzong of Tang once "descended the south gate tower to watch non-Han operas."[65] The dance moves, known at the time as "*Hu*[66]-*teng*" (jumping dance) and "*Hu-xuan*" (swirling dance), were received rapturously by the Tang people, officials and civilians. The Tang's Emperor Xuanzong also created the renowned *Melody on Splendid Fairy Costumes* on the basis of the music of the Western Regions. Acrobats and conjurers from India and the Eastern Roman Empire could frequently be seen in the streets of Chang'an.

With the opening-up of the service industry, non-Han merchants also ran taverns and food stores in Chang'an, making the catering culture of the Western Regions prevail in the Tang Dynasty. During the reign

---

[64] Zhang Huimin. *The Qu's Activities and Achievements in Astronomy in the Tang Dynasty*. Journal of Shaanxi Normal University (Natural Science Edition), 1994 (2).

[65] (The Later Jin Dynasty) Liu Xu. *The Old Book of Tang: Emperor Zhongzong* (Primary Chronicle). Vol. 7. Beijing: Zhonghua Book Company, 1975.

[66] The word "*Hu*" was a concept subject to change throughout the history of ancient China.

(826–840) of the Tang's Emperor Wenzong, "non-Han cakes and porridge were served in imperial families and in civilian families alike."[67] Obviously, non-Han cakes and other foods were widely consumed by people. Non-Han people living in China popularized their own costumes among the Han people. During the reign (r. 683–684; 705–710) of the Tang's Emperor Zhongzong, Lü Yuantai, the Defender of Qingyuan appealed for "people to follow non-Han people to wear non-Han cos-tumes, ride non-Han horses and dance Sumozhe (samudra in Sanskrit) in Chang'an."[68] In the early years of the Kaiyuan period (713–741), "eunuchs who rode horses to guard beside the imperial chariot wore non-Han hats; the Ceremonial Chamber valued non-Han music; high-ranking officials and even the Emperor were served with non-Han food; young women were dressed in non-Han clothes."[69]

Introducing foreign material and spiritual civilizations into the Tang enriched people's lives and improved their well-being.

4.5.4 *Foreign Trade and Economic Development in the Tang Dynasty*

With the frequent international communications, the cities boasting many foreign merchants gradually came to demonstrate some of the characteristics of the international metropolis in the Sui and Tang Dynasties. Their industries and commerce became more prosperous under the stimulus of foreign trade. Meanwhile, the Jiangnan area, as China's economic center, obtained far greater profits from the opening up to accelerate its economic development.

(1) The Urban Economy Thrives

In Luoyang, where domestic and foreign trade prospered in the Sui and Tang Dynasties, there were three markets, respectively, Fengdu market in the east, Tongyuan market in the north and Datong market in the south. Among these, the Fengdu market was the largest in scale; "situated within two communities, it had three gates, respectively, in four sides of the

---

[67] (Japan) Ennin. *Ennin's Diary: The Record of a Pilgrimage to China in Search of the Law*. Vol. 3.

[68] (The Song Dynasty) Ouyang Xiu, Song Qi. *New Book of Tang: Biography of Song Wuguang*. Vol. 118. Beijing: Zhonghua Book Company, 1975.

[69] (The Later Jin Dynasty) Liu Xu. *Old Book of Tang: Record of Vehicle, Clothing and Guard of Honor*. Vol. 45. Beijing: Zhonghua Book Company, 1975.

market; hostels were scattered in all 312 districts; 100 trades were practiced;"[70] while in Datong, "the market covered an area of 4 *li* (2 kilometers) with 4 doors in four directions; hostels were seen in 141 districts; 66 trades were practiced."[71] After Luoyang became a commercial city, the opening-up of the Sui Dynasty raised the city's position to a new high. Many foreign merchants came eastward to China and they were designated to trade in the "three markets" of the city, so that "Luoyang swarmed with foreign merchants." The foreign merchants brought with them the religions they believed in so that many temples appeared in the non-Han inhabited areas. Four of these were Zoroastrian temples.

As the political and economic center of the Tang, Chang'an was the biggest city at that time with millions of inhabitants. Under the opening-up policy of the Tang Dynasty, Chang'an became a pioneering and international metropolis. The prosperity lay directly in its flourishing commerce. Chang'an boasted the large-scale east and west markets with a vast numbers of foreign merchants and commodities. Those merchants not only did business, but ran shops in the two markets.

History has recorded that in the East Market "there were 220 trades, with hostels and rare treasures gathered there"; in the West Market "shops within were running according to the overall arrangement in the east one".[72] Shops within the markets were arranged in rows. According to records in *Ennin's Diary, Record of a Pilgrimage to China in Search of the Law,* "at 3 a.m. on June 27, 843, the East Market in Chang'an caught fire and more than 4,000 shops were burned." Then some scholars estimated that there were probably more than 80,000 shops in total in the East Market.[73]

Apart from local merchants, Chang'an also gathered together rich merchants from other places within the country, minority merchants from border areas and foreign merchants, who mainly inhabited the West

---

[70] (The Tang Dynasty) Wei Shu, Du Bao. *New Records of the Two Capitals.* Edited by Xin Deyong. Xi'an: Sanqin Press, 2006.

[71] (The Qing Dynasty) Xu Song, Zhang Mu. *A Study of the Cheng and Fang in the Two Capitals.* Commented by Fang Yan. Beijing: Zhonghua Book Company, 1985.

[72] (The Song Dynasty) Song Minqiu. *Annals of Chang'an.* Vols. 8, and 10.

[73] Yang Dequan. "*A Study of the Guild System in the Tang and Song*" in *Collected Papers of the Tang and Song Studies.* Deng Guangming ed. Shanghai: Shanghai Classics Publishing House, 1982.

Market, doing business or running shops of different trades. The foreign merchants proceeded in a very thriving manner.

The *New Book of Tang: Biography of Uigur* recorded that Persian merchants who believed in Manichaeism "came to the West Market in the capital city every year." The taverns, foreign cake shops and jewelers that foreigners ran were widespread in Chang'an. Li Bai, the famous Tang poet, wrote in the second poem of the poem series *"A Young Man's Trip,"* "with nowhere to visit after investigating falling flowers? Entering a tavern run by non-Han singers."

A Tang novelist named Duan Chengshi wrote in his *Miscellaneous Morsels from Youyang* that a monk of Chang'an obtained a "precious bone" as long as several *cun* (one *cun* is equal to 0.762 inches) which looked like a rusty nail. He "then brought it with him to the West Market and showed it to a non-Han merchants." Some of them offered to purchase the stone at a price of ten million *qian* (one *qian* is equal to 60–70 *yuan*), which illustrated the operation scale of the business run by foreign merchants in the West Market.

Included were not only items pertaining to the basic necessities of life, but luxury goods such as pearls, agates, crystals, Hawkbill turtles and all kinds of gold, silver and jade vessels and spices, many of which were imported goods, were found in these shops. Among the silk products, there were traditional Chinese silk and hemp textiles, as well as white cloth (cotton fabric) and many kinds of woolen fabrics.

In effect, the commercial activities of Chang'an were not confined to these two markets. Instead, shops and stores were scattered over the streets and communities of the whole city. For instance, foreign cake shops, branded as "non-Han cake stores," were found within the Shengping community, *biluo* (like present-day steamed dumplings) shops were found within the Changxing community, and jewelers in the Yanshou community. The most thriving community was Chongren, since it "was close in distance to Personnel-Recruiting Archive Bureau of the department of State Affairs, and connected with the East Market, so that many officials who were recruited to the capital but had no house there could have somewhere to stay. Therefore, industries and commerce gathered in the two markets, where there was the hustle and bustle around the clock; lights blazed from dawn to dusk. No other communities could compete with it."[74]

---

[74](The Song Dynasty) Song Minqiu. *Annals of Chang'an*. Vol. 8.

The commercial activities in Chang'an also broke the limitations of operations to serve at night. During the reign (840–846) of the Tang's Emperor Wuzong, when Wang Shi was the Junior Metropolitan Governor "night-market restaurants were run in the middle of the streets until midnight. Wang paused to watch on horseback. The owner of the food stand was happy so that he knelt down in front of the horse, offering a cupful of drink in his hand to Wang, who took it and drank."[75] This story illustrated a scene of singing and dancing around the clock.

The development of foreign trade and foreign merchants running shops of various trades fueled the dynamism and prosperity of the industry and commerce in Chang'an. Moreover, the popularity of various foreign fashions and customs made the urban culture of Chang'an more diverse, gradually endowing the capital city with the flavor of an international metropolis.

After the "Rebellion of An and Shi," "thousands of Uighur people stayed at Chang'an, with several times this number of foreign people dressed like the Han people." Those foreign merchant residents in Chang'an "invested in their own businesses, competed to build houses, earned huge profits and gained considerable profits."[76] Moreover, some foreign merchants started to offer usurious loans in Chang'an. This occurred on an increasingly large scale so that "within the capital city, people, including noble descendants, soldiers, envoys, merchants and civilians, were all indebted to them."[77]

Besides Chang'an and Luoyang, some towns along the Silk Road also thrived under the opening-up policy. For instance, Liangzhou (now Wuwei in Gansu) "a pivotal city in the Hexi Corridor area, was connected with the Western Regions, and marked a key terminus before reaching other foreign countries to the west of the Pamir Mountains. Processions of foreign merchants were also seen shuttling in and out of it."[78]

---

[75] (The Song Dynasty) Wang Dang. *Tang Yu Lin*. Vol. 2. Shanghai: Shanghai Classics Publishing House, 1982.

[76] (The Song Dynasty). Sima Guang. *Comprehensive Mirror to Aid in Government*. Vol. 225. Beijing: Zhonghua Book Company, 1976.

[77] (The Song Dynasty). Wang Qinruo. *Primary Tortoise of the Records Office*. Vol. 999. Beijing: Zhonghua Book Company, 1960.

[78] (The Tang Dynasty) Hui Li, Yan Zong. *Biography of Mage Sanzang of the Daci'en Temple*. Vol. 1. Beijing: Zhonghua Book Company, 1983.

(2) The Economic Development Accelerates in the South

Prior to the mid-Tang period, China's economic center lay in the north. The prosperity of the continental Silk Road further enhanced the advantageous position of the northern economy. During the reign (847–859) of the Tang's Emperor Xuanzong, "the areas of over 10,000 *li* (5,000 kilometers) of distance westward from the Kaiyuan Gate paid quantities of taxes so that the national treasury was filled with numerous treasures piled like a mountain."[79]

During the Tang's Tianbao period (742–755), "China boasted a strong national power, covering a territory of 12,000 *li* (6,000 kilometers) from the Anyuan Gate[80] to the west, where alleys stood within alleys and mulberry trees and hemp trees covered the land. Nowhere was richer than the places to the east of the Longshan Mountain."[81] This illustrated the reciprocal relationship between the opening-up of the northwestern overland trade and the regional economic development.

As mentioned previously, the advanced silk industry of Dingzhou, Hebei attracted foreign merchants to do business. The development of foreign trade greatly promoted the production and sale of Dingzhou silk, further improving the development of the local silk industry. For instance, the famous merchant named He Mingyuan "ran three public station hostels ... exclusively tailored for non-Han merchants. He possessed immense assets counting to tens of thousands. 500 weaving machines were under his name."[82]

The maritime Silk Road had begun thriving gradually since the Tang Dynasty. In the early Tang Dynasty, the continental and maritime Silk Roads were almost united as one. Some non-Han merchants came to the Tang along the continental Silk Road and started to do business in port cities by sailing southward from Luoyang to Yangzhou and Guangzhou along the Grand Canal, realizing the integrated development of the continental and maritime Silk Roads. The Tang poet Du Fu wrote in his poem that "when a non-Han merchant was leaving for Yangzhou, he recalled a hostel building on his way to Xiling," which told an anecdote that a foreign merchant came to the Tang Dynasty via the northwestern road, then

---

[79](The Tang Dynasty) Zheng Fan. *Records of the Kaiyuan and Tianbao Eras.*
[80]The north gate of the Chang'an City at that time.
[81](The Song Dynasty) Sima Guang. *Comprehensive Mirror to Aid in Government.* Vol. 216. Beijing: Zhonghua Book Company, 1976.
[82](The Song Dynasty) Li Fang. *Extensive Records of the Taiping Period.* Vol. 243. Beijing: Zhonghua Book Company, 1981.

sailed along the canal to trade in Yangzhou. Arabic literature also embraced the records that merchants from Samarkand in Central Asia entered China from the northwestern road and passed by many towns to arrive in the capital city of Guang Fu (Guangzhou).[83]

After the mid-Tang period, the Chinese economic center gradually moved to the south, especially to the southeastern coast with eminent position in the national economy. History recorded that "after the Tianbao Era (742–755) of Emperor Xuanzong, people in Central Plains of China put down their implements, with some moving to the Yuezhou for clothes and some to the Wu for food."[84] Undoubtedly, developed regions were the major sources of national taxation. Han Yu once said in his poem that "nine-tenths of the country's revenue comes from the Jiangnan area."[85] The development of overseas trade directly pushed the prosperity of the economy of the southeastern coast. "Trade with foreign countries was seen to be transacted on a daily basis … and could not only fill the state treasury but meet Jianghuai people's needs."[86] By virtue of their advantageous geographical locations, Yangzhou, Mingzhou and Guangzhou on the east and southeastern coast gradually ascended to be flourishing port cities on the basis of the development of overseas trade. History records that the development of foreign trade in Guangzhou made "Guangzhou people inhabited with foreign merchants, engaging in commerce, which resulted in so less production from agriculture that Guangzhou resorted to Sichuan for help."[87]

Compared with the overland trade, the transportation cost via the maritime road decreased sharply. Therefore, more commodities circulated on the overseas market, and extended the structure of the tradable goods with luxuries as leading commodities. Some ordinary products and handicrafts also were traded with foreign countries, following the fast development of related industries under the stimulus of such a great demand.

---

[83] Abu Zuid Hassan. *Accounts of China and India*. Trans. by Mu Genlai. Beijing: Zhonghua Book Company, 1983.

[84] (The Song Dynasty) Li Fang. *Finest Blossoms in the Garden of Literature*. Vol. 901.

[85] (The Tang Dynasty) Han Yu. *Collected Works of Han Changli*. Collated and annotated by Ma Qichang. Shanghai: Shanghai Classics Publishing House, 1987.

[86] (The Tang Dynasty) Zhang Jiuling. *Qujiang Collections*. Vol. 17 in the Complete Library in the Four Branches of Literature. Photocopy of the Imperial Library.

[87] (The Later Jin Dynasty) Liu Xu. *Old Book of Tang: Biography of Wang'e* Vol. 151. Beijing: Zhonghua Book Company, 1975.

Spurred by the development of overseas trades, the porcelain, weaving and shipbuilding industry in the southeastern coast proceeded with more dynamism. Foreign trade developed more prosperously in port cities. The *Book of Tang: Records of Astrology* claimed that "the Wuyue, a state by the sea, was a port suitable for commerce." The development of the foreign trade endowed some coastal areas with outward-looking characteristics. Craftsmen custom-made their products to suit foreign cultural characteristics in consideration of sales abroad. For instance, brocades bearing coupled birds and animals were specially tailored for selling to West Asia; foreign silk gowns were produced in Yangzhou exclusively for exportation; Tang porcelain bearing the Arabic inscription "Allahu Akbar" has been unearthed in Yangzhou; some Islamic merchants even customized their own products in the kilns near Guangzhou.

To sum up, the unprecedented opening-up policy carried out in the Tang Dynasty encouraged all things beneficial to its own development. It embraced foreign civilizations and pioneered wide communication exchanges in the economy and technology with more foreign countries and nationalities. In so doing, it developed trade both by continental and maritime roads. In the process of exporting its outstanding products in civilization, China also absorbed advanced parts of foreign cultures. Nevertheless, the feudal small-scale peasant economy still dominated the Tang's social structure. The closed and conservative pattern of the wider economy saddled it with great limitations in the opening-up to the world. In essence, the Tang's foreign trade activities aimed at obtaining political interests so as to create feudal prosperous scenes with "countries being subjected to its leading." Thus, economic profits had to retreat to being of secondary consideration, thus weakening the benefits obtained by trade.

Chapter 5

Foreign Trade in the Song Dynasty

With the rapid development of ethnic minorities in northern China, during the Southern and Northern Song Dynasties, severe conflicts arose between the Song government and minorities as well as between minorities themselves. National conflicts and struggles were complicated and intense. During the Northern Song Dynasty, the Central Plains of China were relatively unified, with the north under the rule of the Liao, the Tangut, the Jin and other minorities, which blocked the outbound continental route, discontinuing Silk Road trade. The Song Dynasty retreated to the south as the Southern Song regime. Conflicts between Song and Jin, Song with the Jin and Mongolia still existed, leading to a gradual decline of northwest Silk Road trade as well.

Progress in shipbuilding and seafaring industry provided important premises for the development of overseas trade. On the basis of previous dynasties, the Maritime Silk Road extended further and reached more nations and countries.

The Song faced unprecedented huge financial pressures owing to its engagement in protracted wars. Hence, overseas trade assumed a high priority. It took a series of policies to encourage overseas trade, pushing the opening-up of ancient China into a new phase.

Under the general policy of opening-up, businessmen from Southeast Asia, South Asia, the Arabian Peninsula and East African countries came to trade in China, allowing the overseas commerce in this period to develop rapidly, and economic and cultural exchanges between China and overseas countries to reach an unprecedented level of prosperity.

5.1 Socio-Economic Development

For any country, development of the social economy is the foundation of overseas trade. This is influenced by the level of the commercial economy and the conditions of its marketing and transportation technology. The political and economic needs of overseas trade determine the policy trend within different periods. In the Song Dynasty, these conditions of supply and demand changed greatly, determining the trend of overseas trade policy and the level to which overseas trade developed.

5.1.1 *Socio-Economic Development: an Overview*

From the late Tang Dynasty, the economic center of China started to gradually shift southward. During the Song period, its political and economic center further moved from the Yellow River area to the Yangtze River region.

Compared with those in the previous dynasties, agricultural tools in the Song improved remarkably. The usage of farm implements was greatly expanded accordingly. For instance, the curved plough, which appeared in the Tang Dynasty came to be seen both on the southern banks of the Yangtze River and in today's Zhejiang Province. The "scoop water-wheel" for irrigation was also in widespread use.

New farming systems improved the multiple crop index. In Jiangsu, Zhejiang, Anhui, Jiangxi, Fujian, Sichuan and other important agricultural areas of the south, the extensive application of the double cropping farming system saw a concomitant increase in grain output with more grain entering the market as commodity. For example, in the Song Dynasty, "the cities of Suzhou, Huzhou and Xiuzhou in the Yangtze River delta were known for rice planting. Carts of rice were transported to all parts of the country in years of plenty."[1] Grain production by large landowners of Jizhou, Jiangxi for the market was huge. For example, a rich family of Fuzhou sold as much as 34,617 bushels (*dan*) or hectoliter of grain and another family, 31,217 bushels.

With the progress of agricultural production techniques, agricultural productivity improved markedly and the surplus increased sharply. Improvement in the rate of commercialization for agricultural products promoted specialization in commodity production. The development of

---

[1](The Song Dynasty) Wang Yan. *Shuangxi Classical Draft to the Prime Minister Zhao.* Vol. 21. Complete Library in the Four Branches of Literature Collection 4.

the commodity economy in the Song Dynasty conspicuously exceeded that in the previous dynasties.

The increase in grain output also resulted in distributing more farmland for cultivating of cash crops and provided commodity grain to the cultivator, thus creating specialization within agriculture. The limited amount of farmland in densely populated southeastern areas also forced local farmers to seek higher-profit cash crops, facilitating commercial farming. Commercial cropping characterized by tea, sugarcane, mulberries, bamboo, fruit, vegetables, flowers and other cash crops accelerated, with the Taihu Lake area, the Chengdu Plain, and the coastal areas of Fujian all serving as commodity production bases. Professional tea farmers, fruit farmers, sugarcane farmers and vegetable growers sprang up in large numbers. Their market-oriented production boosted the prosperity of the commodity economy.

While providing grain for the development of industry and commerce, commercial agriculture also produced raw materials and labor. The increase in commercially specialized households promoted the rise of industry and commerce as well as the commodity economy. Silk weaving, ceramics and other handcrafts in the southeastern coastal areas burgeoned, particularly the market-oriented private manual workshops, which produced varieties of goods that were continuously improving in quality. This greatly expanded the circulation of domestic commodities and supplied sufficient commodities for overseas trade.

In this period, the production of Chinese silk and porcelain exported in large quantities developed rapidly via a big leap forward. The textile industry continued to develop as an artisan household sideline, but with large numbers of professional silkworm breeding households appearing in Huzhou, Yanzhou, Lin'an and other places in Jiangnan, where "they were engaged in raising silkworms," and "depended upon other places to provide them with grain." Chen Fu in the Song Dynasty wrote in his *Book of Agriculture* that the people of Anji "fed themselves through breeding silkworms. A family would raise ten *bo* (boxes) of silkworms. Each *bo* produced twelve catties (*jin*) of cocoons. Each catty of cocoon yielded 1.3 taels[2] in weight of thread. Every five taels of thread could be woven into one bolt[3] (*pi*) of silk, which can be exchanged as one bushel

---

[2] 1 *liang*, as a dry measure in ancient China, is equal to 0.05 kilogram.
[3] 1 *pi* is equal to 13 meters.

(*dan*)[4] and four pecks (*dou*)[5] in volume. They counted everything in such an accurate way to ensure that their life was provided with sufficient food and clothes. People living on silk industry were found to be busy for a whole month in rearing and taking care of silkworms. However, they earned more than some people who worked for a whole year. What's more, silk rearing and silk production were operated at home, with no worries of droughts or floods. What an affluent life they led."

At the same time, mulberry growing, silkworm raising, silk reeling, spinning, dyeing and other divisions of work in the textile industry were further refined and the degree of specialization was improved. For example, in the Huzhou area, "most people earned their living by raising silkworms. Rich households even raised hundreds of *bo* of silkworms as well as providing workers for weaving."[6] It could be seen that in the Song Dynasty households specializing in silk weaving, also known as *Jihu* (household weavers), emerged in large quantities. It was estimated that there were about 100,000 *Jihu* in different parts of the Northern Song, accounting for 0.5–0.7% of the total population, which was a considerable number.[7]

Jihu were independent commodity producers, normally with family members acting as the weavers. Few *Jihu* hired professional operatives for production so as to become domestic workshops specializing in weaving. A few *Jihu* were located in cities, like Jinhua, Zhejiang Province. Most citizens "were engaged in weaving and their products could meet the needs of the whole country. Therefore they became super rich."[8] Most *Jihu* were to be found in the countryside and became households specializing in silk weaving. For example, in Yiwu in Wuzhou (Jinhua, Zhejiang) "mountain people made their living by weaving,"[9] while "in Jurong County in Jiankang (Nanjing) weaving was very popular among the people."[10]

---

[4] 1 *dan*, is equal to 50 kilograms.

[5] 1 *dou* is equal to 75 kilograms.

[6] (The Song Dynasty) Tan Yao. *Records of Wuxing in the Jiatai Period*. Vol. 20.

[7] Qi Xia. *Truth Seeking*. Tianjin: Tianjin People's Publishing House, 1982.

[8] (The Song Dynasty) Liu Chang. *Gongshi Collection*. Vol. 51. Shanghai: The Commercial Press, 1937.

[9] (The Qing Dynasty) Xu Song. *Compiled Manuscripts of Song Dynasty: Food and Commodities*. Beijing: Zhonghua Book Company, 1981.

[10] (The Yuan Dynasty) Fang Hui. *A Sequel to the Tongjiang Collection*. Vol. 14. Complete Library in the Four Branches of Literature.

Their products were collected by middlemen and transported incessantly to the market, so transacted silk products were available in great quantities. Higher levels of professionalism lifted greatly the productivity of the textile industry in the Jiangnan area, making it surpass the north as a developed region with the most extensive silk industry.

In the Song period, ceramic production also reached its maturation. Besides traditional famous kilns, new kilns also emerged, like the Longquan kiln, the Geyao kiln and the Diyao kiln in Longquan, Zhejiang; the Ruyao kiln in Linru, Henan; the Junyao kiln in Yu County, the Cizhou kiln in Ci County, Hebei; and the Yaozhou kiln in Tongchuan, Shaanxi.

During the Southern Song, most northern kiln operatives moved southward, so massive progress was made in porcelain technology in the south. Day by day advances were seen in Zhejiang, Fujian, and other provinces. To date, unearthed Song kilns have been found in over 17 provinces and 130 counties, most of which were civilian-owned, particularly the Dehua kiln in Fujian, kilns in Jinjiang, Xiamen; the Ciyao kiln in Quanzhou, kilns in the Parthian Empire, Nanan, and Tong'an. All of them were production bases for commercial wares exported from Caiton Port, Quanzhou City.

In the Northern Song Dynasty, the prosperity of porcelain in Guangdong Province created a ceramics production network, thus making Guangzhou its center, stretching eastward to Chaoshan and Mei County, westward to Zhaoqing, northward to Shaoguan and southward to Huiyang. In the Song Dynasty, the porcelain-making industry expanded to a larger scale with better quality wares, which not only met the needs of domestic market, but also made porcelain the leading commodity exported in bulk.

Urban economic development also gradually picked up pace. The number of towns grew quickly with a booming urban population, and more people were engaged in industry and commerce. Cities as regional economic centers emerged one after another, transforming the traditional political-oriented cities into economical commercial ones. The trend of urbanization was self-evident day by day.

At the same time, the layout of cities underwent significant changes owing to the collapse of the traditional community (*fang*) and market (*shi*) system. Urban commerce challenged the limits of space and time so that shops appeared along ordinary streets, anticipating the layout of the modern city. Great changes also occurred in the commodity structure. More and more staple materials (like grain, cloth, tea, etc.) and production materials (like land, cattle, wood, coal, and farm implements) came into circulation. The traditional commerce serving the upper class with luxury and local products began to serve ordinary people with products for production and daily use.

In the economically developed or densely populated countryside, as well as in ferry terminals and along the traffic channels, *Caoshi* (ancient business districts) sprang up in batches, forming a three-layered local market system with *Caoshi* organized in villages, *Zhenshi* in towns, and the regional economic center.

With the expansion of trade in terms of scale and region, currency as the medium of exchange was faced with higher requirements. Traditionally, Chinese coins were cast from copper. They were carried in large quantities, but the value of the denomination was low, making them no longer suitable for larger transactions. This hastened the birth of the earliest paper money in the world as well as the monetization of silver. *Jiaozi*, as the earliest paper money, took the lead to be taken as currency, in commodity exchange in Sichuan Province in the early Northern Song Dynasty. Later, currency cast from precious metals, notably silver, came into circulation too, thereby forming a transitional monetary system with copper coins, iron coins, paper money and silver used as currency. "Gold, Silver, Salt and Securities Transaction Shops" spread over Bianjing (the capital of the Song) and Lin'an, as the place of exchange for different currencies, with Lin'an City alone boasting more than 100 such establishments.

The developed trade and the rising status of trade in national economy promoted the rising of the merchant class as a group. Meanwhile, the benefit-chasing concept (as "market rule") of businessman posed a growing anathema to traditional norms. The rise of utilitarianism in eastern Zhejiang Province, represented by Ye Shi and Chen Liang, showed that the traditional Confucian theory of justice and benefit was no longer unified as one. The prevalence of the benefit-chasing concept attracted an increasing number of bureaucrats, landlords, scholars and farmers to be engaged in business. Coastal farmers even raised funds to invest in overseas trade. The expanding merchant teams and the solid business capital raised the actual status of merchants who began to exert more influence on the society.

In the Song Dynasty, overseas trade consistently expanded. The Han and Tang continental silk road was replaced by the "Spice Route" and "the

Porcelain Road," which were of such a large scale that no land route between China and the west could compare. More than 60 countries and regions had established trade relations with the Song. Meanwhile, the material exchange and economic relations between the Song and the Liao, the Xia, the Jin, the Tubo, the Dali and other surrounding regimes never ceased even for a moment, whereas the scale kept on expanding and the forms varied gradually to encompass the market trade, the smuggling trade, the tea-horse trade, the tribute trade and other forms. For this reason, millions of bunches of copper cash minted by the Song every year flowed into surrounding areas to become an "international currency".

At this moment, China's commodity economy flourished and prospered far ahead of any country and region in the world in terms of scale or level.

5.1.2 *The Advancement of the Shipbuilding and Seafaring Technology*

Based on the developing social economy, especially the rapid progress made in the south, the shipbuilding industry of the Song Dynasty reached a stage of prosperous development. On the one hand, China-built ships grew in number with a greater capacity for deadweight capacity. Shipyards were scattered widely across Jiangsu, Zhejiang, Fujian, Guangdong and other coastal areas, with Suzhou, Yangzhou, Hangzhou, Ningbo, Wenzhou, Quanzhou and Guangzhou in particular being vital and productive centers for this industry. For example, in 997, "the number of ships built per annum by the entire country ... reached 3,237".[11]

The deadweight capacity of China-built ships at that time was the greatest in the world. According to the 12th volume "Vessels on the River and Sea" of the *Records of Linan* written by Wu Zimu in the Southern Song, "maritime vessels were different in size. Sizable vessels could carry 5,000 *liao* and four or five hundred people; the medium could carry 1,000–2,000 *liao* and two or three thousand people." One *liao* was equal to one bushel (*dan*), which was 60 kg in weight. Thus, 5,000 *liao* was equivalent to 300 tons and 2,000 *liao*[12] to 120 tons. This showed that

---

[11](The Yuan Dynasty) Tuotuo. *History of Song Treatise on Food and Commodities Grain Transport*. Beijing: Zhonghua Book Company, 1977.

[12]Approximately equal to 0.28–0.33 tons.

capacity of the ships at that time was impressively large. The vessel that Emperor Huizong (r. 1100–1125) of the Song took to visit Goguryeo was called the "10,000-*hu*[13] ship," which caused a stir when it reached Goguryeo. Beside, the manufacturing technology also improved. Maquettes were used in ship building, as were dry docks, water-tight compartments, balanced rudders, etc. to prevent capsizing and enhance stability.

At the same time, rapid progress was made in navigation technology. On the one hand, people of the Song had a sophisticated understanding of the nature of marine monsoons, and used this knowledge in making voyages to South Asia, Southeast Asia, West Asia and other places. In winter, they set out with the help of the north wind and in summer they came back on the south wind. On the other hand, the application of compass in navigation was another huge technological breakthrough. In the book the *Stories of Pingzhou*, Zhu Yu of the Song Dynasty wrote that "navigators were equipped with a knowledge of geography, observing stars in the night, the sun in the day and using the compass on gloomy days." With the improvement of the compass, it was widely used in oceangoing voyages and took the place of the traditional method of navigation by the stars in the Southern Song Dynasty. Zhao Rushi of the Southern Song wrote in his book the *Records of Foreign Counties* that "on foggy days when the water and the sky merge into one color, the compass is the only guide for navigating on the sea." The British scholar Joseph Needham argued that the use of the compass ended the primitive navigation times and indicated the coming of metering navigation times." At the same time, the method of oceanic astronomy location (star observing) which used a ruler as a tool to measure the dimensions of a ship also appeared. The compass, together with observing the stars, improved the accuracy of oceangoing to such an extent that ships could not only sail along the shoreline, but could also cross the ocean, thus shortening voyage time and lowering possible risks.

On the basis of such technological progress, voyage speeds were greatly improved. For example, traveling from Guangzhou to Java used to take about 50 days in the Eastern Jin Dynasty, while in the Song it was shortened to 30 days; traveling from Guangzhou to Sumatra formerly took 30 days and was also shortened to 20 days. With the lowering of voyage risks and transportation costs, areas for overseas trading further expanded

---

[13] *Hu* as a dry measure in ancient China was equal to a bushel (*dan*), but equivalent to 120 (*jin*), say 60 kilograms.

and, as foreign trade ports, Guangzhou and Quanzhou enjoyed consider-able prosperity. The Maritime Silk Road extended to the west. According to the British scholar Basil Davidson, "around the 12th century, in terms of technology, Chinese vessels could travel to any place could be reached." In this period, it was common for Song vessels to voyage as far as Aden on the western end of the Arabian Peninsula and the coast of East Africa.

The route taken by Song vessels was as follows: they started sailing from Guangzhou or Quanzhou, heading to the Zanzibar coast area, pass-ing by in succession Ramree (today's Banda Aceh, Sumatra) and Malabar (in the south of Arabian Peninsula), the Aden, Somalia. Alternatively, they started their sailing from Guangzhou or Quanzhou, directly heading to the East Africa Coast, passing by Ramree, Quilon (today's Kollam, India); or by way of the Maldive Islands, they crossed over the Northern India Ocean to the East Africa Coast.

5.1.3 *National Contradictions and Fiscal Crisis*

During the Song Dynasty, the northern ethnic minorities grew rapidly in population. Contradictions and struggles among the ethnic groups were quite sharp. At the same time, owing to the consolidation of the central authority of the feudal autocracy and the national policy of "preventing abuse" and "guarding the inside," the Song Dynasty was always caught in a plight of enduring impoverishment and long-standing inability.

"Enduring impoverishment" referred to the financial difficulties of the Song. Ye Shi once summarized the financial conditions during the period (960–1022) thus: "during the reign of Emperor Taizu (960–976), in order to govern the vassals, he controlled their property, so that the vassals would follow commands and fear the stateliness of the Emperor. While during the reigning period (960–1022), when the two monarchs, Emperor Taizong (r. 976–997) and Emperor Zhenzong (r. 997–1022), did not care about the budget, after 1021 the national treasury was exhausted."[14]

Emperor Taizu weakened the power of local separatist regimes and strengthened central control over local finance. From the reign of Emperor

---

[14](The Song and Yuan Dynasties) Ma Duanlin. *Comprehensive Investigations based on Literary and Documentary Sources.* Vol. 24. Complete Library in the Four Branches of Literature the *Chi Zao Tang* version.

Taizong to the early years of the reign of Emperor Zhenzong, there were no fiscal problems. However, in the middle and later periods of Zhenzong's reign, a fiscal deficit began to appear. By the time of Emperor Renzhong (1022–1063), financial difficulties were more acute. Although "the year 1063, the last year of the Song Emperor of Renzong, was known as the most prosperous and peaceful year in the Song Dynasty," "the nation was in great need of money so that the whole country was concerned about it."[15] In a document handed to Emperor Renzong in his later reigning years, stateman and historian Sima Guang of the Northern Song also expressed concerns about this situation thus: "in peaceful years, efforts should be paid to solve the budget deficit"[16] since "the present expenditure was far more enough. Neither public nor private needs can be satisfied."[17] The reason for the crisis lay in the fact that the expenditure grew faster than that of revenue.

As to the fundamental reasons for this, Su Zhe once surmised that "the Xixia suddenly attacked the north before the garrisons on the border heard of this. Stationed soldiers were ordered to fight. More soldiers were recruited. Expenditure was meager and urgently needed to be paid by the people. With other borders under attack, the disturbance aroused the people. After the Xirong were pacified, there was temporarily no need for soldiers, but troops would still be paid. In addition, there was a surplus of officials in every level of the government. All these brought about the long-term budget deficit."[18] Although Su Zhe's observations were far from comprehensive, he pointed to two major areas of "superfluous expenditure," namely "superfluous troops," and "superfluous officials."

The Song Dynasty was the first dynasty in China that made a more comprehensive implement of the mercenary system and the maintaining of an army which basically relied on government fiscal resources. And out of the requirements of the centralization of authority and war, the Song Dynasty maintained an unprecedentedly huge and redundant army, which undoubtedly brought huge fiscal burdens.

---

[15] *Ibid.*

[16] (The Song Dynasty) Sima Guang. *Collection of Sima Wenzheng's Heirlooms.* Vol. 25. Wanyou Library. Shanghai: Commercial Press, 1937.

[17] *Ibid.*

[18] (The Song Dynasty) Su Zhe. *The Later Anthology of Luancheng.* Vol. 15 Wanyou Library. Shanghai: Commercial Press, 1937.

During the regnal period of Kaibao (968–976) of the reign of Emperor Taizu, there were 193,000 imperial guards and 185,000 *wing* forces. By the time of Emperor Renzong (r. 1022–1063), the number ballooned to 800,000, and in 1049, the total number rose to 1.4 million, four times of that in the early Song. Scholars once estimated that if the annual expenditure for one imperial guard was 70 *guan* and one *wing* force 37 *guan*,[19] the average annual expenditure for one soldier was 50 *guan*, then 1.4 million soldiers would consume 70 million *guan* a year. Therefore, at that time, the fact was that "of the whole year's expenditure, the amount for maintaining the soldiers reached 60 or 70% of the total, and there was very little left for the country."[20]

The same happened to the bureaucratic apparatus of the Song Dynasty. During the regnal era of Jingde in the reign of Emperor Zhenzong (r. 997–1022), there were more than 9,700 civil and military officials, a bit fewer than 10,000. In 1088, the number of officials surged to more than 34,000, and in 1119 over 51,000, not including candidate officials, like capital officials, military officers who had not been assigned positions.

The Song saw an important phase for the development and perfecting of the ancient imperial examination system, and an unprecedentedly huge number of people passed the examination. Besides this route of recruiting officials, there were various means for the people of Song to be selected as officials, such as to be endowed titles by their parents, to be promoted from being petty officials, to be promoted owing to military exploits and to gain titles by purchase. On average, 360 people gained positions via the imperial examination every year, but more than 500 people were promoted through nepotism. If other types were added, the number of the latter was twice as many as the former. In 1213, there were 38,870 people in the Ministry of Official Personnel Affairs, of which 10,925, or 28% of the total, were selected through examination and 22,116, or 57%, through nepotism — twice as many as that chosen via examination. The Song government was destined to bear a heavy fiscal burden for such a huge bureaucratic apparatus.

A Chinese historian named Ma Duanlin also pointed out that the serious fiscal problems in the Song were caused by "four factors: maintaining the soldiers, maintaining patriarchal clan salaries, covering redundant

---

[19]Approximately equal to 1,000 copper coins.

[20](The Song Dynasty) Cai Xiang. *Anthology of Cai Xiang.* Vol. 22. Punctuated and collated by Wu Yining. Shanghai: Shanghai Classics Publishing House, 1996.

officials, and sacrifice rewards, among which the last two were especially costly." This showed that the expenditure on sacrifices was also enormous.[21] The total amount of strings of copper coins, gold, silks rewarded by Emperor Zhenzong in the regnal period of Jingde (1004–1007) during one journey to the south even reached 600,000 strings. Moreover, the expenditure on sacrifices increased constantly. During the reign of Emperor Yingzong (r. 1063–1067) this item grew to twice as much as that of the Jingde Era.[22] Although many expenses were cut in Emperor Renzong's reign (r. 1022–1063), it was still noted that "Taoist rituals that lasted for 7 days, one month or 79 days were all held in the name of the Emperor and never ceased. And the expenditure on wax, vegetable, oil, flour, wine, rice, coins, silks, fees for officials of all ranks, reached a hundred million."[23]

Besides, in order to avoid the disaster caused by imperial clans, the government adopted the policy of providing them with rich material conditions though they were not assigned to actual official positions. With an increase in the number of imperial clans, the expense on their supporting as well as the imperial household also became a huge fiscal burden.

Consequently, the Song government could not eliminate the intractable financial crisis. After 1048, it was hard to make ends meet with a deficit exceeding three million strings of copper coins. In 1064, the deficit was over 15,700,000 strings. The Summer tax, Autumn tax and feudal land tax could no longer meet such enormous expenditure.

In order to cover the high fiscal deficit, the Song government adopted different methods to squeeze farmers with many titles besides the normal tax. These included grain requisition, silk collecting and taxation variation. On the one hand, the government sought profits through the monopoly of major consumer goods like salt, tea, alcohol and alum. On the other hand, the government increased tax revenues and tax bases by a series of incentives, of which developing overseas trade and border trade were also the important measures for releasing fiscal pressure. These measures

---

[21] (The Song and Yuan Dynasties) Ma Duanlin. Comprehensive Investigations based on Literary and Documentary Sources. Vol. 24. Beijing: Zhonghua Book Company, 1986.

[22] (The Song Dynasty) Zeng Gong. *A Classificatory Compilation of Yuanfeng*. Vol. 30. The photocopy of the Imperial Library version of the Complete Library in the Four Branches of Literature.

[23] (The Song Dynasty) Song Qi. *Anthology of Song Jingwen*. Vol. 26. Beijing: Zhonghua Book Company, 1985.

massively increased the fiscal revenue of the Song government. For example, during the almost 40 years (1004–1041) of the Northern Song, taxes from various kinds of channels increased from 12.33 million *guan* to 44 million *guan*.

In conclusion, the economic development in the Jiangnan area, especially the rapid progress of porcelain manufacturing and the advance of shipbuilding and navigation technology, provided the economic base and technological support to the opening of the maritime route. Great financial pressures lifted overseas trade tax to an unprecedented high position of great importance. Under those circumstances, the government had to rethink about its opening-up to develop overseas trade.

5.2 Foreign Trade Policy

The huge financial pressures became even worse when the Song was threatened by the invasion and territorial occupation of the northern ethnic minorities, which made it harder for the Song to keep the traditional agricultural taxes as stable as before. In this light, the Song had to pioneer new finances to alleviate the financial crisis. Considering the fact that the economy of the south proceeded with dynamism in line with the improvement of shipbuilding and navigation technology, the opening-up to the oceans with the Southeastern coastal areas as its center became a realistic choice for the Song, especially when the north was threatened by enemies on the border.

5.2.1 *Enacting Foreign Trade Policy*

The Song government had a clear understanding of the status of overseas trade in fiscal revenue. For example, Emperor Shenzong of Song (1067–1085) fully recognized the role of overseas trade in national finance from historical experiences. He once pointed out clearly that "overseas trade, especially ship merchants, was an important part of the lucrative southeastern coastal areas. In the past, Liu and Qian, who once monopolized the foreign trade in Zhejiang and Guangdong provinces, became affluent enough to counter the central government." That is to say, overseas trade revenue also provided important support for separatist regimes, like the Wuyue regime and the Nanhan regime in the Jiangnan area. In view of this, he requested that ministers "engage in overseas trade, make annual substantial profits and attract foreign countries, which would create a spectacle."[24] It could be seen that Emperor Shenzong (r. 1067–1085) laid great expectations on overseas trade to acquire more fiscal revenue. Although "foreign countries coming to China" was indeed "a spectacular thing", it was at most just a by-product of "annual substantial profits", That is to say, developing the economic function of overseas trade was the theme of the opening-up at that time, while the political function took a back seat as the second consideration. All these determined the basic direction of overseas trade policy in this period. To be specific, the Song government encouraged the development of civilian overseas trade, restricted official tributary trade and interfered in the process of trading in profitable luxuries.

The Southern Song government was geographically located in the corner of southeast China. When threatened by the northern army approaching the border, the government had more trouble in fiscal expenditure and relied more on overseas trade. Emperor Gaozong of the Song (r. 1127–1162) claimed explicitly that "overseas trade was the most profitable. Millions in revenue would be garnered if it was dealt with appropriately," and "it has been a great benefit to the country, so it is best to use the traditional ways to attract people from afar for business."[25] The Emperor placed foreign trade in an unparalleled high position.

In order to increase fiscal revenue rapidly in a short time, foreign trade was prioritized and encouraged. The policy was in essence orientated by financial interests therefore attracting foreign merchants for maritime commerce had become the basic principle of foreign trade during the Song Dynasty.

5.2.2 *Foreign Trade Policy and its Evolution*

Foreign trade policy of the Song Dynasty consisted mainly of three aspects: restricting the development of defective official tributary trade, endeavoring to lower the financial losses of the government; strengthening the national monopoly over the trade in luxuries and gathering excess

---

[24](The Qing Dynasty) Huang Yizhou *et al. Supplements to the Long Draft Continuation of the Comprehensive Mirror that Aids Administration.* Vol. 5. Punctuated and Collated by Gu Jichen. Beijing: Zhonghua Book Company, 2004.

[25](The Qing Dynasty) Xu Song. *Compendium Manuscript of Song: Officials.* Beijing: Zhonghua Book Company, 1981.

profits from foreign trade directly through government monopoly; motivating businessman to trade overseas to attract foreign businessman to China, and increasing revenue by expanding overseas trade.

(1) Restricting Tributary Trade

The official barter trade conducted in the name of paying tributes, namely the tributary trade, had long taken a leading role in China's foreign trade since the Han Dynasty. As the feudal dynasties of the past ages considered themselves as the "Celestial Empire" and upheld the traditional idea of "not contending with foreigners for profits," they did not seek commercial benefits for tributary trade, so the government "gave more gifts but received less" during the official visits. At that time, the tributary trade was made for the political outcome of having "ambassadors of numerous countries coming to China with admiration" at the expense of sacrificing economic benefits.

However, during the Song Dynasty, it was another story. In fighting the northern ethnic minorities, the Song had been placed in a disadvantageous position. The signing of a series of humiliating treaties made it impossible to maintain the dignity of the "Celestial Empire." The Song's prime objective was to seek more chances for survival. The development of the tributary trade, if continued, was bound to intensify the embarrassing financial situation in which the Song was already caught. That was completely contradictory to its prime objective.

The failure of the early Song to restrict the tributary trade yielded bitter fruit, as was pointed out by Su Shi. He wrote of how "every ambassador could easily lay his hands on more than 50,000 bolts (*pi*) of silk during their visit. The envoy and the delegates could receive at least 200,000 strings of copper coins."[26] When the Song Dynasty paid high costs to tributary trade, "the cost in board and lodging was incalculable, ... the trade as such did no good to the Court. Only the distant minorities gained interests from it."[27] The huge financial pressure made it hard to continue this trade. Moreover, progress in the tributary trade was bound to

---

[26](The Song Dynasty) Lü Zulian. *Anthology of the Song Literature*. Vol. 55. Punctuated and collated by Qi Zhiping. Beijing: Zhonghua Book Company, 1992.

[27](The Song Dynasty) Li Tao. *Supplements to the Long Draft Continuation of the Comprehensive Mirror that Aids Administration*. Vol. 435. Beijing: Zhonghua Book Company, 1980.

restrict civilian trade development, thus reducing the tax revenue of Song's overseas trade and making it suffer dual losses in finance.

Therefore, from 1016, the Song government began to restrict tributary trade, making a regulation that "those tributes that landed from Guangzhou, rhinoceroses, elephants, pearl, chinaberry and rare treasures, were free of tax. Other tributes should be taxed according to their value."[28] At the same time, restrictions were imposed on the number of people who could come to China to pay tributes. Those who could not prove their bonafides were rejected. As for fake missions, which came without authorization, once investigated, members were "sentenced to three years of imprisonment and had their property confiscated."[29]

The restrictions on the tributary trade not only reduced the fiscal expenditure of the Song government, but left space for the development of civilian trade to earn more fiscal revenue for the government.

(2) Easing Foreign Trade Restrictions

Due to the continued threat from the northern ethnic minorities, the Song Dynasty endeavored to increase state revenue through foreign trade. At the same time, in order to weaken the hostile forces in the north, it strove to prevent information, people and supplies from flowing out to the Liao, the Jin and other territories at the cost of restricting foreign trade activities in a certain period and range. The restrictions on foreign trade in the Song Dynasty were manifested in three aspects: conducting a state monopoly over profitable luxuries; banning the export of certain commodities; and restricting the trade with certain countries. As time passed by, some restrictive methods proved ineffective and were gradually tended to be lax.

In order to increase state revenue through developing overseas trade, since the setting up of the "Maritime Trade Commission" in Guangzhou in 971, the Song government gradually strengthened the regulations on foreign trade, and even issued the imperial edict of "forbidding foreign trade,"[30] strictly prohibiting outbound civilian maritime voyages or private deals with overseas businessmen. For example, in

---

[28] *Ibid.*, Vol. 87.

[29] (The Song Dynasty) Li Xinzhuan. *Miscellaneous Notes on the Court since the Jian Yan.* Vol. 29. Beijing: Zhonghua Book Company, 2013.

[30] (The Yuan Dynasty) Tuotuo. *History of the Song: Annals of Emperor Taizong.* Vol. 5. Beijing: Zhonghua Book Company.

976, there existed an order that "for those who dared to trade with foreign businessman, if the value of the transaction exceeded 100 *wen*,[31] the culprit would be convicted; if the value was over 15,000 *wen*, they would be tattooed on the face and exiled to an island; and if the amount was too large, men would be sent to the Court (central government in the capital city), and women would be sent to serve as seamstresses."[32]

In 977, the officials Gao Tang and Zhang Xun, who managed the spices and herbs warehouse, recommended the court to "please set up a Monopoly Exchange Bureau to sell spices, medicines and treasures at higher prices to increase revenue and allow businessmen to buy them with gold and silk, then 500,000 *guan* (approximately equal to 1,000 copper coins) of money could be earned in a year. It could also limit the accumulation of foreign goods. The Emperor agreed on his idea. Not surprisingly, the country obtained 300,000 *guan* in one year and the amount increased yearly, soon reaching 500,000 *guan* a year."[33]

Thereafter, foreign trade policies began to be relaxed. In 982, imported goods were divided into two categories: prohibited transactions and permitted transactions. The former comprised only eight goods, including pearls, the woolly rhinoceros, and frankincense, which were constrained by government monopoly. All other goods were permitted transactions and traded freely by civilians. In 989, "trade caravans that went abroad to conduct overseas trade were required to present permission certificates issued by the Maritime Trade Commission of Zhejiang"[34], and the policy of soliciting overseas tributes and permitting countrymen to trade with overseas countries was gradually established.

---

[31] *Wen* are round coins with square center holes, ranging in diameter from approximately 19 mm to 28 mm. The *wen* had an approximate average value of about 1/1,000 of a silver dollar in China during the 17th through the 19th centuries (see Marjorie Kleiger Akin). The Noncurrency Functions of Chinese *Wen* in America[J]. *Historical Archaeology*, Vol. 26, No. 2. 1992: 59.

[32] (The Qing Dynasty) Xu Song. *Compendium Manuscript of Song: Officials*. Vol. 44. Beijing: Zhonghua Book Company, 1981.

[33] (The Song Dynasty) Li Tao. *Supplements to the Long Draft Continuation of the Comprehensive Mirror that Aids Administration*. Vol. 18. Beijing: Zhonghua Book Company, 1980.

[34] (The Qing Dynasty) Xu Song. *Compendium Manuscript of Song: Officials*. Vol. 44. Beijing: Zhonghua Book Company, 1981.

Actually, in the early Song Dynasty, the government tried to gain monopoly benefits through prohibiting import of luxuries by private operators. But the injunction was not strictly enforced. Prior to 1025, two or three ships came to trade near Fuzhou every year and the local officers and people used "money, gold and silver to buy pearls, rhinoceros, elephants, spices, medicines and other prohibited treasures." After receiving the report, the Court only "ordered the province to carry out the injunction in a stricter way" and gave no punishment. Besides, in some ports with more developed trade, the monopoly of the Maritime Trade Commission seemed to be ignored. Before Emperor Shenzong ascended the throne (1067), in Quanzhou "merchants came with twenty ships with exotic goods being piled high like a mountain." Local officials didn't try to curb the trade, and most of them in fact participated in such activities.

The Song boasted a developed monetary economy. With the development of foreign trade, copper coins gradually flowed out to other countries. In some Southeast Asian countries, due to the backward smelting and casting technology and the lack of credit instruments, Chinese copper coins were widely taken as a medium for exchange as they was stable in value. Some even kept Song's copper coins as treasures. When they "obtained Chinese coins, they stored them in several warehouses as heirlooms of the state. Therefore, people went abroad only with copper coins and foreign goods were sold only for copper coins."

But the Song itself had limited reserves of copper, so the outflow of copper coins led to currency shortages, which threatened the monetary base of the Dynasty. Therefore, the government banned the export of copper coins. Emperor Taizu (960–976) of the Song issued an imperial edict that "those who exported copper coins out of Jiangnan, beyond the Great Wall and to other countries to the South of China, according to the law, would be sentenced to one year's imprisonment if the amount exceeded two *guan*; they would be subject to public execution if the amount exceeded five *guan*; people who reported such a case to the government would be rewarded."[35] In the first year of the Qingli period (1041), the ban was even more rigorous: "for those who exported copper coins out of the boundaries, if the amount exceeded one *guan*, the leader would be sentenced to death; as to the followers, if the amount was not exceeding one *guan*, those, who lived in the east and north of the Yellow River, the Jingxi

---

[35] (The Yuan Dynasty) Tuotuo. *History of Song: Treatise on Food and Commodities*. Vol. 180. Beijing: Zhonghua Book Company, 1977.

area, and Shaanxi, would be exiled to the southern Guangdong; while those, who lived in Zhejiang and Fujian would be exiled to Shaanxi."

By the reign of Emperor Shenzong (r. 1067–1085) of the Song, the issue of numerous types of paper money had relieved the "monetary shortage" to a certain degree. In order to increase fiscal revenue through overseas trade, in 1074 Emperor Shenzong even broke the convention of previous dynasties which prohibited copper coins from flowing out. He permitted copper coins to be exported. He "issued new imperial orders, abrogated old ordinances and removed the ban on currency. Since then, carriages loaded with goods were seen moving to other countries and foreign vessels returned with full loads of merchandise. ... the currency of copper coins was originally created by China, but was used now by other countries."[36] The ban on exporting copper coins was abolished for a while. The direct intention of this policy was to promote the prosperity of foreign trade and to increase foreign trade revenue.

In the stalemate between the Song and the Liao, the Song implemented many restrictive measures on trade between civilian sea merchants and countries related with the Liao. For instance, sea traders were prohibited from trading in countries and regions bordering the Khitan and exporting copper cash overseas. According to the *Qingli Edited Edict*, "traders who traveled by sea were not allowed to go to Korea, Silla and Laizhou boundaries. If the trade was necessary, then applications should be made for necessary official documents with details of the goods' information on them. No forbidden items and military weapons should be loaded. Violators would be convicted and goods confiscated." The Song issued a stipulation that people were not allowed to trade in Korea and its bordering regions and had to provide others' guaranteeing certification. If they broke the treaty, the goods would be confiscated and they would be condemned as guilty based on the law.

In 1085, the ban on sea merchants trading in Korea was removed and it was stipulated that "merchants who came to trade in foreign countries by sea were not allowed to approach the Great Liao, Tengchow and Lai

---

[36](The Song Dynasty) Li Tao. *Supplements to the Long Draft Continuation of the Comprehensive Mirror that Aids Administration.* Vol. 269. Beijing: Zhonghua Book Company, 1980.

Chau."[37] The restriction of this regulation was only aimed at the Liao regime, while the trade with other countries including Korea was not limited. Meanwhile, overseas countries were welcomed to conduct government and private trade in China, thus promoting the liberalization of Sino-foreign trade.

(3) Legalizing Foreign Trade Management

With the expansion of the scale of overseas trade, the Song gradually enforced its management of this trade. The Song government set up Maritime Trade Commissions in major ports, assumed special charge of overseas trade matters and "set up the Laiyuan Station equipped with furniture, and other everyday items. The post was taken by one envoy who supervised the commission and served as the receptionist of the Laiyuan Station," responsible for receiving foreign merchants.

From the early Song on, overseas trade scale constantly expanded, but there were no regulated laws to manage overseas trade. As a result, most managerial measures were temporarily taken according to individual situations. As trade developed, related edicts became more complicated and inconsistent, even contradictory, which led to many malpractices. Some officers even indulged in favoritism, committed irregularities and practiced fraud, harming the progress of overseas trade. In view of this, Emperor Shenzong of the Song felt that there was a necessity of setting up regulations and unifying laws to govern it. He emphasized repeatedly that the rule of overseas trade should commence with "creating laws." This accorded with the guiding financing thoughts of Wang Anshi's political reform, for "what gathered the people was the wealth, what governed the wealth was the law and who enforced the law was the officials,"[38] which meant that financing must adhere to the rules of law and prompting the rule of law must depend on a batch of officials who were adept at finance. After many years of planning and discussion, the Song finally enacted the *Maritime Trade Decrees* ("Overseas Trade Treaty and Law") in 1080 of in the reign of Emperor Shenzong of the Song.

---

[37] (The Song Dynasty) Su Shi. *Complete Works of Su Dongpo*. Vol. 58. Photocopy of the Imperial Library Version of Complete Library in the Four Branches of Literature.
[38] (The Song Dynasty) Wang Anshi. *Anthology of Wang Anshi*. Vol. 10. Shanghai: Shanghai People's Publishing House, 1974.

Afterwards, the Song revised its overseas trade treaties and laws many times. According to the *Overseas Trade Decrees*, the Song issued a series of overseas trade control regulations, constantly regulating overseas trade management.

With the rising status of overseas trade in national fiscal revenue, the overseas trade policy was further adjusted.

In 1076, Cheng Shimeng, who once served as Prefect of Guangzhou for 6 years there, submitted memorials to the throne, pleading for the abolition of the Hangzhou and Mingzhou Maritime Trade Commission and recommending directing all the taxation from overseas trade ships to the Maritime Trade Commission in Guangzhou, in the hope that an individual Maritime Trade Commission would control the whole foreign trade, thus streamlining the management. The central government asked Cheng Shimeng and other three officials to discuss this issue. But Emperor Shenzong didn't adopt the "taxation treaty" they agreed with. He pointed out that "if the treaty is accepted, something may happen in Zhuzhou, so reconsider it in more detail before putting it into practice." In 1080, after several rounds of revision, foreign trade control regulations based on Cheng Shimeng's proposal were finally approved by Emperor Shenzong and were called the "Yuanfeng Foreign Trade Regulations" or the "Yuanfeng Guangzhou Foreign Trade Regulations." After scholarly research, it was recommended that the regulations be composed of six articles:

(i) Only ports in Guangzhou, Mingzhou and Hangzhou could release foreign trade ships. Foreign trade ships departing from other ports would be found guilty for violating the Emperor's order.

(ii) All merchant ships bound for Southeast Asia and territories west of the country could only be sanctioned by the Maritime Trade Commission of Guangzhou; all merchant ships bound for Japan and Korea could only be sanctioned by the Maritime Trade Commission of Mingzhou. Merchant ships which sailed south without being sanctioned by the Maritime Trade Commission of Guangzhou, as well as the merchant ships bound for Japan and Korea without being sanctioned by the Maritime Trade Commission of Mingzhou, would be found guilty of violating the Emperor's order. Charges would not be mitigated even in the case of amnesty of the convict leaving the post.

(iii) Upon returning, merchant ships for foreign trade must pay in the first place trade taxes in the Maritime Trade Commission where they were permitted to sail abroad for trade.

(iv) Each Maritime Trade Commission should be responsible for governing foreign tributary ships, tribute missions and their activities within its operational zone. The imperial envoy of each Maritime Trade Commission was required to land and depart from the work post to which he was assigned.

(v) Tributes paid by foreign countries would not be sent to the capital. Instead, they should be just sold in the place where they were paid.

(vi) Ships that went to Hainan Island from the coastal areas of Guangdong and Guangxi Provinces should apply for a sailing voucher from the Maritime Trade Commission of Guangzhou.[39]

The implementation of the "Yuanfeng Foreign Trade Regulations" further strengthened the power of the Maritime Trade Commission Overseas Trade and made it manage Sino-foreign trade activities according to the laws, which enhanced the ordered process of the overseas trade development.

(4) Incentives for Maritime Trade Officials and Oceangoing Merchants

In the Song Dynasty, the Maritime Trade Commission was set up in major coastal ports to govern overseas trade. The scale of overseas trade and tax revenues generated by it were taken as the performance evaluation index for the officials governing overseas trade in the commission. During 1131–1162 in the reign of Emperor Gaozong (r. 1127–1162), the Song issued an imperial edict that "Fujian and Guangdong officials who were in charge of frankincense transaction would be promoted to a higher position if the amount of the revenue from the transaction reached millions of taels."[40]

In 1119, well-behaved Quanzhou Overseas Trade officials, like "officials Cai Bai and Zhao Shi in Fujian were commended and reappointed to a higher position." In the Southern Song Dynasty, the "Maritime Trade

---

[39](The Qing Dynasty) Xu Song. *Compendium Manuscript of Song: Officials.* Vol. 44. Beijing: Zhonghua Book Company, 1981.

[40](The Yuan Dynasty) Tuotuo. *History of Song: Treatise on Food and Commodities.* Vol. 185. Beijing: Zhonghua Book Company, 1977.

Commission of Guangnan earned for the country more money from foreign trade. If the amount reached a certain degree, a higher official position would be assured."[41] At the same time, those who committed malfeasance, embezzled money or engaged in corrupt practices in the management of overseas trade were severely punished. For example, an imperial edict stated that "supervising officials or other officials who used aliases to buy in the Maritime Trade Commission or bought foreign traders' goods by force would be convicted of breaking the rules and no amnesty and demotion could mitigate their crime. The informant would be rewarded a hundred *guan* of money."

All merchants conducting business abroad, including native maritime merchants with outstanding contributions in the overseas trade, would be rewarded or even granted official posts. To meet the idea proposed by the Quanzhou magistrate Lian Nanfu, it was regulated that "as for the head of the commission who had ways to attract ships and collect taxes from goods, if the accumulated amount he earned for the country reached 50,000 *guan* or 100,000 *guan*, they could get promoted accordingly."[42] Cai Jingfang, head of the commission of Fujian, was given the position of Gentleman of Trust[43] by the Song Court for his "charging of 980,000 strings of copper coins." All these were used to stimulate the head of the commission to actively organize overseas trade so as to increase maritime revenue. It also set up an example for civilian sea traders, thus benefiting the further development of overseas trade.

Some overseas trade merchants were entrusted with trade or diplomatic duties by the government from time to time. For example, in 1084, Emperor Shenzong of the Song once issued a decree of "recruiting merchants to purchase 500,000 *catties* of sulphur in Japan." Meanwhile, the Song Dynasty often entrusted merchants to act as envoys to handle diplomatic matters for the government. In 1075, the government once "recruited several merchants to serve as envoys to persuade the Emperor

---

[41](The Qing Dynasty) Xu Song. *Compendium Manuscript of Song: Officials*. Vol. 44. Beijing: Zhonghua Book Company, 1981.

[42](The Yuan Dynasty) Tuotuo. *History of Song: Treatise on Food and Commodities*. Vol. 180. Beijing: Zhonghua Book Company, 1977.

[43](The Qing Dynasty) Xu Song. *Compendium Manuscript of Song: Officials*. Vol. 44. Beijing: Zhonghua Book Company, 1981.

of Champa."[44] In the Southern Song, "envoys, regardless of whether they were virtuous or not, were mostly the sons of rich merchants in this period,[45] and were dispatched to other countries." The Song government delivered many documents, letters and communications to overseas countries via merchants. The fact that the government did not send official envoys but entrusted merchants to purchase overseas goods and deal with diplomatic affairs was related to the financial constraints of the Song government, which could reduce costs, and highlighted the role of businessmen simultaneously, and enhanced their status at sea. Objectively, it became the policy of the Song Dynasty to encourage maritime merchants.

With more merchants in southeastern coastal areas sailing overseas for trade activities in the Song, because of possible risks arising from the oceangoing voyages there appeared the custom of praying for wind and offering sacrifices to the sea in coastal areas of Zhejiang, Fujian and Guangdong. In the Southern Song, this custom was institutionalized. In the winter and summer of each year, when sea traders disembarked and returned to port, the Maritime Trade Commission was responsible for hosting large-scale activities praying for winds in ports such as Guangzhou and Quanzhou. That the government presided over this religious activity reflected the policy orientation of the Song Dynasty towards the development of overseas trade.

(5) Preferential Policies for Foreign Merchants

To attract foreign merchants to China, the Song Dynasty adopted a series of proactive policies and measures:

(i) Dispatching Envoys

Attracting foreign merchants to China was one of the key principles in opening the continental Silk Road and the Maritime Silk Road in the Han and Tang Dynasties. But prior to the Song, the strong national power made previous dynasties basically committed to creating a favorable domestic environment in attracting foreign merchants to China. In the

---

[44](The Song Dynasty) Li Tao. Supplements to the Long Draft Continuation of the Comprehensive Mirror that Aids Administration. Vol. 271. Beijing: Zhonghua Book Company, 1980.

[45](The Song Dynasty) Li Xinzhuan. *Miscellaneous Notes on the Court since the Jian Yan*. Vol. 271. Beijing: Zhonghua Book Company, 2013.

Song Dynasty, due to national power being on the wane, policies of attracting foreign merchants were more proactive than before, and one of the important measures was to send people directly to overseas countries to attract foreign businessmen.

In 987, the Song dispatched official missions to Southeast Asian regions to attract foreign investors, which was an unprecedented move in the history of China's overseas trade. Historical records show that "in May of 987, eight eunuchs formed into four groups were dispatched with imperial decrees, gold and silk to foreign countries to attract tributes and buy spices, herbs, rhinoceros, ivory, pearl and borneol."[46] In 1028, few ships arrived in Guangzhou, and Emperor Renzong of Song issued a decree "to order the department in charge of transshipment to attract foreign merchants and keep them". In 1115, the Fujian Maritime Trade Commission once specially sent people to Champa and Lavo to persuade the local government and businessmen to trade in China.

Foreign merchants who had been in trade with China sailed, by order of the Song government to other countries to attract more merchants to China. Their ships "were not specially operated for tax, but intended to attract and appease foreign merchants." Since the head was not only the officially dispatched merchant, but also the special diplomatic envoy of the government, he performed both economic and political functions. But one of the main tasks was to persuade foreign businessmen to conduct transactions in China. For instance, the Maritime Trade Commission of Quanzhou once "issued an official invitation to Liu Zhu and others who were sent to Lavo and Champa to persuade and attract merchants to come to trade in China with their treasures."

(ii) Tax Exemption and Profit Surrendering

Most Japanese businessmen who came to China in the Song Dynasty were only merchants with small and middle-sized businesses. They were employed by the wealthy or by aristocrats to transport Japanese timber and sulfur to China. They usually carried a small amount of gold and earned low profits. In order to expand Sino-Japanese trade, the Song government exempted Japanese merchants from gold import taxes. "Japanese ships were free of gold import tax. If taxation was inevitable,

---

[46](The Qing Dynasty) Xu Song. *Compendium Manuscript of Song: Officials*. Vol. 44. Beijing: Zhonghua Book Company, 1981.

the department would pay for them with the taxation in the latest year."[47] As a result, the practice of "exempting Japanese from gold taxation made merchants suffer no losses but, instead, gain profits" attracted more Japanese merchants to China and increased the government's revenue from overseas trade.

(iii) Rewarding Foreign Trade Contributions
In the Song Dynasty, foreign businessmen who engaged in large-scale import trade and thus brought a large amount of tax revenue were rewarded with official posts or a noble title. For example, in 1131, a Dayi merchant named Pu Luoxin "built a vessel and loaded it with frankincense for the Maritime Trade Commission of Quanzhou, which brought in 300,000 *guan* of tax."[48] Considering that transacting this relatively large scale of trade was meritorious, so awarded him the honorific title of Gentleman of Trust and an "official costume with shoe and scepter." At the same time, the Song requested that he carry out extensive publicity to encourage more foreign merchants to trade in the Song.[49]

(iv) Appointing Foreign Merchants and their Descendants to be Officials
The *Compendium Manuscript of Song* recorded that during the reign of Emperor Gaozong (1127–1162) of the Southern Song, there was an Arab businessman named Puyari (transliterated from Arabic Abu Ali) came to trade in Guangzhou. "To gain his wealth, the Right Grand Master of Military Zeng Na married his younger sister to Puyari, who therefore stayed behind and didn't return." After knowing this, Emperor Gaozong of the Song ordered his men to talk him into returning and continuing the trade.

During the reign of Emperor Lizong of the Southern Song (1228–1233), the overseas trade of Quanzhou stagnated owing to improper management. The Southern Song government appointed Pu Shougeng (transliterated from Arabic Abdallah), who was of Arab descent, as the Maritime Trade Supervisorate to manage Quanzhou foreign trade. Pu

---

[47] (The Song Dynsty) Mei Yingfa *et al. A Sequel to the Annals of Mingzhou in the Kaiqing Period*. Vol. 8. Beijing: Zhonghua Book Company, 1990.
[48] (The Qing Dynasty) Xu Song. *Compendium Manuscript of Song: Fan yi*. Vol. 4. Beijing: Zhonghua Book Company, 1981.
[49] *Ibid.*

Shougeng "ran the overseas trade well for thirty years," so that trade made great progress. Many Arab merchants flocked to Quanzhou so that it was called the "Half-Hui City".

(v) Protecting Foreign Merchants' Lawful Rights

To ensure the implementation of the opening-up policy, the Song severely punished officials who violated laws and regulations or harmed the benefits of foreign merchants. In 1135, "supervisorates who used aliases to buy in the Maritime Trade Commission or bought the goods of foreign traders by force would be convicted of breaking the rules and no amnesty or demotion would be given in lieu of the crime. Any informant would be rewarded 100 *guan* of money. If the Supervisorate himself knew the crime but didn't report or make an impeachment, he would be demoted to a lower official position."[50] Both Yuan Fuyi, who had "cut the prices of foreign merchants" in 1146, and Zhao Buxi who had "overtaxed foreign merchants" in 1213, were demoted to a lower official position of official post. In 1203, Cao Ge, who "violated the law" and "transferred frankincense"[51] was deposed. In 1146, the prime minister reported that "frankincense merchants had suffered great deficits in recent years." Emperor Gaozong of the Song attached great importance to this and immediately assigned an official to investigate whether "the former Maritime Trade Commissioner of Guangnan cut the price of overseas trade."[52]

The Song government stipulated that foreign businessmen had the right to appeal to higher level officials in case of exorbitant taxes or the forcible purchase of goods by the Maritime Trade Commission or local officials; the Song could provide assistance, accommodation and repatriation convenience for foreign merchants who drifted off to the coast of China after being struck by wind and waves; foreign merchants who suffered ship damage on the sea were exempted from import duties. If the shipowner died, the overseas trade institutions were responsible for taking custody of the goods and waiting for their relatives to reclaim and return them; as for the foreign merchants who resided in the Song, if they had no partner, heir, or will, their estate would be managed and disposed of by the Maritime Trade

---

[50] (The Qing Dynasty) Xu Song. *Compendium Manuscript of Song: Officials.* Vol. 44. Beijing: Zhonghua Book Company, 1981.

[51] *Ibid.*, Vols. 74, 75. Beijing: Zhonghua Book Company, 1981.

[52] *Ibid.*, Vol. 44. Beijing: Zhonghua Book Company, 1981.

Commission in accordance with the "household exclusion law" after his death.

Piracy was a phenomenon along with maritime trade, which constituted a major risk. There were many pirate activities along the coast of China in the Song Dynasty. The pirate "specially waited for the foreign merchant ships and conducted interception and robbery ... and their activities became more frequent."[53] During the Yuanfeng period (1078–1085) of the Northern Song, the government set up shipping inspection departments in Guangzhou, Quanzhou and other ports and military stockades in coastal areas, deploying troops to ensure the safety of merchants who entered the port. For example, in Guangzhou, "within the 700 *li* of distance between Xiaohai and Ruzhou, there were shipping inspection departments in Ruzhou. The first one in the very south was called the first Wang. Slightly northward were the second and third ... If merchants reached Ruzhou, they would celebrate with each other. They treated the stockade soldiers with wine and meat and would protect them to as far as Guangzhou with wine and meat."[54] The establishment of inspection departments and stockade soldiers cracked down on pirate activities and improved the safety of maritime trade on the one hand; it also performed the function of eliminating smuggling and ensuring the standardized development of overseas trade on the other.

(vi) Preferential Reception of Foreign Merchants

When foreign merchants departed from their port, the Maritime Trade Commission would hold a "reward banquet" to see them off and the Court would also send a special envoy to participate. For example, in 1009, "when foreign merchants in Guangzhou gathered together, the Court would send the chamberlain Zhao Dunxin to ride to the post and treat them to banquet as a reward."[55] During the banquet, "foreign and Chinese leaders of merchants, craftsmen and helmsman were treated. They sat next to each other and felt overjoyed." This move showed the strong willingness of the Song Dynasty to develop overseas trade and enhanced

---

[53] (The Song Dynasty) Zhen Dexiu. *Anthology of Mr. Xishan.* Vol. 15.

[54] (The Song Dynasty) Zhu Yu. *Stories of Pingzhou.* Vol. 2. Beijing: Zhonghua Book Company, 2007.

[55] (The Song Dynasty) Li Tao. *Supplements to the Long Draft Continuation of the Comprehensive Mirror that Aids Administration.* Vol. 72. Beijing: Zhonghua Book Company, 1980.

foreign investors' understanding of China's policies to encourage overseas trade.

As more and more foreign businessmen came to China, the Song Dynasty adopted more substantive measures to provide them with convenience in trade and life. For example, to inherit and develop the practices of the Tang Dynasty, Foreign Communities were set up in the ports of Guangzhou and Quanzhou for foreign businessmen. The heads of these were prestigious foreign businessmen selected by the Song government and they were granted corresponding official titles, and they were mainly responsible for managing the internal affairs of the *Fan Fang*, assisting the Song government to deal with foreign businessmen who had committed crimes in China and to attract more foreign businessmen to trade in China. In order to show respect for the customs of foreign merchants, the Song government stipulated that in addition to major events, the patriarch of the *Fan Fang* could deal with internal disputes according to their own national customs. In Vol. 88 of the *Anthology of Mr. Gongkui* written by the Song writer Lou Yao whose style name was Mr. Gongkui, it was recorded that "foreigners lived together with local civilians. According to the old law, if they fought with others and didn't cause severe injury, they would be punished according to their own customs."

In order to facilitate the trade activities of foreign merchants in China, the Song government also set up *Fan* markets in areas where foreigners proliferated, like Guangzhou, Quanzhou and other places. In addition, the Song government also allowed foreigners to enter various schools in China to receive education. From the Directorate of Education in the capital to schools in local prefectures, there were often foreign students. In Guangzhou and other places where lived foreigners, the Song government even set up *Fan* schools for their children.

The implementation of a series of policies to solicit and favor foreign businessmen in the Song Dynasty not only made foreign businessmen who traded in China enjoy higher than expected profit margins, but also provided them with trade and convenience for life, and improved the levels of safety for them and their property. The trade environment between China and foreign countries was developed to an optimum.

(6) Ensuring Affluent Financial Support of Maritime Trade Commission

As the management organ of overseas trade, the Maritime Trade Commission also retained certain operational functions. To maintain the prosperity of overseas trade, sufficient funds were needed to buy imported goods and attract foreign businessmen to China. In the Southern Song Dynasty, the funds of the Maritime Trade Commission were misappropriated by the transshipment department, which adversely affected overseas trade, thus leading to the "reduction of foreign merchants there." Therefore, in 1133, Emperor Gaozong of the Song issued the decree that "except for the collection and payment designated by the Court, any other officials or departments, even those with special decrees, were not allowed to use the funds of Guangnan Maritime Trade Commission." In 1144, Emperor Gaozong also permitted the Fujian Maritime Trade Commission to change the old rules of "drawing cash every year to let overseas trade officials hold the banquet" to attract foreign merchants and allowed the "Guangnan Maritime Trade Commission to draw three hundred *guan* of money by rule to hold banquets at the time of sending off foreign ships every year. Besides, the Supervisorate and governor were responsible for rewarding merchants from foreign countries."[56]

(7) Improving Infrastructures at Foreign Trade Ports

In addition to the official incentives, the development of overseas trade also required the government to invest a certain amount of labor, financial and material resources in the maintenance of port facilities, river channels and other public infrastructures. The Song Dynasty attached great importance to the construction of infrastructure in main trade ports. For example, Qinglong Town, Huating County, Xiuzhou, "which converged Zhejiang and Huaihe River, connected Fujian and Chu by sea" once occupied an important position in foreign trade of the Song Dynasty. In order to ensure the smooth development of overseas trade, the Song government ordered that the Wusong River be dredged many times.[57]

During 1008–1016, foreign merchants who came to trade in Guangzhou were struck by hurricane damage at the port. The Maritime Trade Supervisorate named Shao Ye organized the masses to excavate a new entrance waterway, thus releasing the imported merchant ships from the hurricane. "When Shao Ye fell sick, officials, people and foreign

---

[56](The Qing Dynasty) Xu Song. *Compendium Manuscript of Song: Officials*. Vol. 44. Beijing: Zhonghua Book Company, 1981.

[57](The Ming Dynasty) Zheng Luoshu. *Shanghai County Gazetteer: Landscape*. Vol. 1.

merchants gathered in the temples to pray for him. After he died, many people wept for him."[58]

However, Quanzhou boasted the largest scale of infrastructure construction. To facilitate the development of trade between China and foreign countries, the local Quanzhou government and the Maritime Trade Commission of Song carried out large-scale port construction. More than ten ports were built and navigational equipment, such as lighthouses, were improved at the same time. In addition, dozens of bridges were built, such as the Luoyang Bridge and the Anping Bridge, which played an important role in overseas trade for a long time.

The Song government took overseas trade as the key to the opening-up. Meanwhile, it also implemented emancipated policies in politics and culture. For example, in politics, foreign students were not only welcomed to study the political system of the Song, but were allowed to take part in Chinese imperial examinations with the prospect of serving as officials in the Chinese Court. In terms of culture, the active exchange of various classics promoted the communications between China and the neighboring countries in Northeast Asia and Southeast Asia to a new height.

To sum up, through a series of systematic measures, the Song Dynasty created a good environment for the development of Sino-foreign trade. Merchants who engaged in overseas trade activities gained higher social and political status, and the convenience and security of trade activities were greatly improved, thus creating a new stage in China's opening-up.

Nevertheless, the opening up in this period was still carried out under the feudal political and economic system, the main motive of which was focused on increasing fiscal revenue. Consequently, the government continued to monopolize the lucrative luxuries trade and encouraged the import of high value items. However, insufficient encouragement was given to the export of Chinese merchandise so it did not gain such great advantages on the overseas market. Thus, the role of exports in promoting economic development was not exerted to the fullest effect. Besides, in order to maintain political stability, foreign trade tended to be more important than domestic trade. In this period, although some policies were introduced to encourage domestic merchants to trade abroad, more advantageous policies were still given to foreign merchants. At the same time,

---

[58](The Song Dynasty) Li Tao. Supplements to the Long Draft Continuation of the Comprehensive Mirror that Aids Administration. Vol. 83. Beijing: Zhonghua Book Company, 1980.

owing to the government restrictions on the sailing of merchant ships based on the political turmoil at home and abroad, Chinese merchants were discouraged from exploiting overseas markets by virtue of their superior products and advanced marine technology. The limitations of the opening-up policy of the Song Dynasty embodied the natural restriction of feudal economic form on overseas trade.

5.2.3 Changes in the Route of the Silk Road

From the late Tang Dynasty, on the continental Silk Road began to decline and China's route of opening-up was transferred from the land to the sea. In the Song Dynasty, as the conflict between the empire of the Central Plains and northern minorities intensified, the opening-up became more dependent on the sea route. But in order to alleviate conflicts with the northern ethnic minorities and increase fiscal revenue at the same time, the opening-up of the Song via the northern land route was not completely abandoned and foreign trade in the Song also developed along the continental route and the maritime route. Overland trade with neighboring minority regimes such as the Khitan, the Tangut and the Jurchen functioned well as economic and commercial communications between the Central Plains of China and the Western Regions, Central Asia and West Asia. The vast sea route covered North Korea in Northeast Asia, Japan and countries in regions, such as Southeast Asia, the Indian Peninsula, the Red Sea and East Africa.

(1) Route Changes in the Overland Silk Road

The overland Silk Route, which had been blocked since the Tang Dynasty, not only failed to reopen until the Song Dynasty, but was even more sluggish. After the Liao and the Tangut were founded, they controlled the north and northwest of China and blocked the traffic road between the Song Empire and the Western Regions. Although western ethnic minorities such as the Uighur, Kingdom of Khotan, and Kucha continued to maintain diplomatic ties and trade with Song, nevertheless the scale declined compared to that of their former generation.

Due to the diplomatic and political situation in the long-term confrontation between the Song and the Liao, the Tangut, the Jin and other northern minority regimes, the Song and the northern regimes were at peace and war alternatively from time to time, and this tumultuous situation was changeable. Therefore, the Song government inherited the previous regime's policies of restraining and finding conciliation with frontier nationalities. During the war, the two sides ceased to trade and the Silk Road was interrupted; during the armistice period, the two sides conducted market trading with each other at the border, thereby occasionally reviving trade between China and the Western Regions.

Due to the backwardness of the economy and the weak foundations of foreign trade, although there were business management institutions in the Tangut to solicit foreign businessmen, the lack of attractive export products and undeveloped currency economy limited foreign trade to an extreme extent. Hence, imported goods, such as spices were sometimes obtained from the Song Dynasty. From 1007 onwards, the Northern Song had set up in Bao'anjun (now Zhidan County, Shaanxi Province) trading markets, where the Tangut people traded with their local products, such as camels, horses, wax, and bupleurum falcatum for spices, porcelain, and silk from the Northern Song.[59] Merchants from the Western Regions also sometimes went to trade in the Song via the Liao and Tangut. Businessmen from Dayi and other countries reached the Northern Song via the Tangut along the northwestern Silk Road.[60] The Liao and Tangut regimes adopted an encouraging attitude toward this. Historically, the Tangut even actively invited foreign businessmen to pass through its territory to trade in the Song. "When Dayi paid tributes, they would pass the west side of Shazhou to reach Qingting. In 1022, Zhao Deming requested to visit Dayi."[61] The Tangut Dynasty gained large benefits from it, "with the ratio of one to ten. They were destined to get the best goods ... and the amount was immeasurable."[62] Apart from Dayi, countries in the Western Regions, such as Sindhu and ancient Rome, there were also merchants who went to trade in the Song via the Liao and the Tangut.

---

[59] (The Yuan Dynasty) Tuotuo. *History of Song: Treatise on Food and Commodities · Maritime Trade Law*. Vol. 186. Beijing: Zhonghua Book Company, 1977.

[60] (The Yuan Dynasty) Tuotuo. *History of Song: Biography of the State of Xia*. Vols. 485, 486. Beijing: Zhonghua Book Company, 1977.

[61] (The Song Dynasty) Li Tao. *Supplements to the Long Draft Continuation of the Comprehensive Mirror that Aids Administration*. Vol. 101. Beijing: Zhonghua Book Company, 1980.

[62] (The Song Dynasty) Hong Hao. *Travel Records of the Pine and Desert Lands*, Vol. 1.

The Hexi Corridor had always been a must-stop for Sino-foreign trade on land. The confrontation between the Song and the Tangut obstructed the Silk Road, especially in the Southern Song Dynasty. As well as the barrier posed by the Tangut, the Western Liao established by the imperial clansman of the Liao Dynasty, Yelü Dashi, appeared. In 1141, when the Southern Song and the Jin signed the "Shaoxing Peace Treaty," the area north of the Huaihe River, including the part of what is now Shaanxi, fell under the jurisdiction of the Jin. After the Mongolians who emerged in Mobei destroyed the Western Liao, the Tangut, and the Jin successively, the above areas were transferred to the Mongolian Empire, and the northwestern overland trade between the Song Dynasty and the Western Regions declined gradually.

At the same time, the past Central Asia and West Asia regions along the Silk Road were also in turmoil and the Arab Empire was divided. At the end of the 10th century, the Samanid dynasty in Central Asia declined, and was destroyed by the Ghaznavid Dynasty in 999. From then on, continuous fighting together with the Crusades from the 11th century to the early 13th century caused astonishing devastation to the lives, property and economy of the people in the region. The century-long disputes and wars in West Asia greatly weakened its ability to make foreign economic exchanges, and the Silk Road was thus blocked.

Owing to the political and military turmoil in the areas along the Silk Road and the obstruction of the Silk Road, China's traditional outbound route along the northwest lost its former prosperity. Although the Song still conducted overland trade with foreign countries and ethnic groups, the development of the trade failed to be manipulated by the Song government due to the disadvantageous position of the Song in the military context. This passive state of the Song, together with the political and military risks of overland trade, made the Song government incorporate all the opening-up activities into the seaway. Emperor Taizong of Song once decreed that "envoys from the Western Regions, such as Dayi, could come by the sea route." In 1023, Emperor Renzong ordered again that envoys of various countries "take the sea route from and to the capital."[63]

---

[63](The Song Dynasty) Li Tao. *Supplements to the Long Draft Continuation of the Comprehensive Mirror that Aids Administration.* Vol. 101. Beijing: Zhonghua Book Company, 1980.

(2) Route Changes in the Maritime Silk Road

The southward shift of the economic center of gravity provided the material foundation for the sea route trade based on the southeastern coastal ports, and the development of shipbuilding and navigation technology, particularly the widespread use of the compass, provided technical support for the development of overseas trade. Advances in shipbuilding and navigation technology, especially the reduction in risks associated with ocean navigation, made it possible for China's foreign trade to turn to the sea route. Compared with land transportation, the cost of overseas transportation was much lower, which enabled a lot of heavy and valuable goods to circulate on the international market.

On account of the disputes among the northern minorities, there was no guarantee that the continental Silk Road could be kept safe. The great efficiency of the overseas routes during the Song Dynasty ensured that the Maritime Silk Road became the mainstream during this period. Southeastern coastal areas enjoyed the highest degree of opening-up anywhere in China with major coastal ports as their center.

In 971, after the Song had wrested control of Guangzhou, an overseas trade management agency was set up there, which promoted the development of Guangdong coastal overseas trade centered in Guangzhou. With the submission of the Wuyue regime and the expansion of the overseas trade activities area, in 989 Emperor Taizong established the Maritime Trade Commission of Hangzhou in Zhejiang Province. Ten years later, in 999, Emperor Zhenzong set up the Maritime Trade Commission of Mingzhou (present-day Ningbo). Due to its superior geographical position, Mingzhou became an important port for trade with Korea and Japan, and in 1080, it even became the only legal port for issuing trade certificates to Korea and Japan. Hangzhou, Guangzhou and Mingzhou were collectively referred to as the "Three Departments." In the late Northern Song Dynasty, the port of Hangzhou gradually ceded its premier position to Mingzhou.

In the early years of the period of 976–984, after the submission of Quanzhou, Fujian Province, which was ruled by Chen Hongjin, the Song government implemented an imported goods monopoly on overseas trade in this region. In 1087, the Maritime Trade Commission was set up in Quanzhou. As Quanzhou was located geographically between Mingzhou and Guangzhou, during the downturn of the port of Guangzhou in the middle of the Northern Song it became a center for trade between the

Song and the merchants from the South China Sea, also serving as a starting point for maritime trade with Korea.

As the opening-up area extended from the coast of Guangdong to the coast of Zhejiang and Fujian, it also expanded to the north. In 1113, an overseas trade market was established in Huating County, Xiuzhou (present-day Sungkiang in Shanghai). The "Mutual Trade Law" item in the 168 volume *Treatise on Food and Commodities* in the *History of Song* recorded that "in 1119, Xiuzhou began to repair the Qinglong River mouth. When ships converged there, the local government in Xiuzhou pleaded the Court to reset a post as Supervisorate. There used to be a Supervisorate in Huating County, where later, ships were was seldom anchored when rivers were blocked up with sand. That's why the post of Supervisorate was revoked and was taken over as additional post by the county magistrate." In 1088, Emperor Zhezong of the Song approved the proposal of Fan E and set up the Overseas Trade Development in Banqiao Town, Mizhou.

The development of overseas trade at each coastal port was the basis of the establishment of the institutions, which formally incorporated each port into the opening-up system of the Song Dynasty, thereby accelerating the development of foreign trade in these regions and further improved the overall opening-up.

By the Southern Song Dynasty, Mizhou had been occupied by the Jin regime. The Southern Song set up the Maritime Trade Commission in Jiangyin and Wenzhou as well as an overseas trade market in Xupu (present Haiyan City, Zhejiang). The number of ports under the jurisdiction of Quanzhou and Guangzhou increased and the development of overseas trade depended increasingly on the southern coastal areas.

The overseas trade routes of the Song Dynasty could be divided into the East China Sea routes and the South China Sea routes. The East route was mainly for transportation with Japan and Korea; the South route mainly dealt with countries in the western South Pacific and the Indian Ocean regions, such as Cochin in Southeast Asia (now northern Vietnam), Champa (now southern Vietnam), Khmer (now Cambodia), Tchen-li-fou (now in Malaysia), Lavo (now southern Thailand), Yavadvipa (now Java in Indonesia), Srivijaya (now eastern Sumatra, Indonesia), Borneo (now Kalimantan, Indonesia), Dayi of West Asia (the collective name of the entire Arab region) and East African countries.

5.3 Overseas Trade Flourishes in the Song Dynasty

Under the active policy of opening-up spearheaded by the Song Dynasty, the volume of overseas trade reached an unprecedented level, with the regional expansion of foreign trade, an increase in trade commodity types, the diversification of trade operators, the expansion of the scale of trade and an increase in the number of trading countries and regions.

5.3.1 *The Development and Prosperity of Trading Ports*

The overseas trading ports of the Tang Dynasty were mainly concentrated in Guangzhou, Jiaozhou, Mingzhou, and Yangzhou, and the Maritime Trade Commission was mainly centered in Guangzhou, indicating that the area where the overseas trade activities were conducted at that time was geographically narrow. In the Song Dynasty, the number of foreign trade ports governed by the Maritime Trade Commission system increased significantly. From Quang Nam, Fujian to Zhejiang and the Shandong Peninsula, the vast coastal areas were basically involved in the tide of overseas trade development. The expansion of trade scale also urged the Song government to continuously improve the trade management of each port. This helped to change the overseas trade system of the Tang with only specific officials assigned to a special agency called the Maritime Trade Commission, the management scope of which encompassed the entire southeast coast. The Commission had long been established in Guangzhou, Quanzhou, Hangzhou, Mingzhou, Huating County in Xiuzhou, Jiangyin, Ganpu, Wenzhou and other ports, also Mizhou in the north. Among them, Guangzhou, Quanzhou and Mingzhou enjoyed particularly important status and were known as the "three-route Maritime Trade Commissions."

The Song Dynasty saw Guangzhou Port continue to develop on the basis of its predecessors. In 971, the Song took the lead in setting up the Maritime Trade Commission in Guangzhou to manage trade along the coast of Guangdong and Guangxi. Owing to the convenient geographical location and the long tradition of overseas trade, Guangzhou enjoyed clear advantages in the opening-up. Merchants from Southeast Asia, South Asia and the Arabian Peninsula congregated mainly in Guangzhou. During the period of Xining (1068–1077), the "Maritime Trade Commissions in Mingzhou, Hangzhou and Guangzhou collectively bought 354,449 catties of frankincense in total, of which 348,673 catties were bought in Guangzhou.[64] In other words, for that commodity Guangzhou accounted for almost 98% of the whole foreign purchase volume of major Maritime Trade Commissions. This showed that it played an important role in the country's foreign trade. By the end of the Northern Song Dynasty, the overseas trade of Fujian and Zhejiang had been developing rapidly, and the premier position of Guangzhou in the foreign trade of the nation had declined relatively. Even so, it still retained an absolute advantage. According to historical accounts, among these three trade departments of Fujian, Zhejiang and Guangzhou, "Guangzhou was the most prosperous."[65]

In the early Southern Song Dynasty, as overseas trade continued to flourish, Guangzhou was still the largest port in China. It was said that "the harbor received vast amounts of treasures, goods and money every day." In 1132, overseas trade officials stated that "revenues from Guangzhou totaled several times those of other ports since it was established as an overseas trade institution from ancient times."[66] In order to receive foreign businessmen and envoys, Guangzhou even converted the Fengzhen Temple into the Laiyuan Station. A considerable number of foreign businessmen came to trade in numerous foreign goods. According to records, "a great many merchants from Champa, Khmer, Srivijaya and Yavadvipa came by sea every year. They brought with them numerous treasures and items from countries in the southwest and articles like rhinoceroses, elephants, beads, incense, and glaze, the names of which had not been known by the Chinese before."[67] In addition, the ports affiliated to the Maritime Trade Commission included Leizhou and Xuwen in Leizhou Peninsula, Qinzhou Port in Beibu Gulf as well as Qiongzhou, Jiyangjun, and Wananjun on Hainan Island. Among them, Qiongzhou Port enjoyed a certain scale of overseas trade since it was a must stop before ships arrived in Guangzhou. In close proximity to Cochin, the scale of trade through Qinzhou Port was also considerable in size. Historically, Cochin merchants came to Qinzhou Port every year with "thousands of

---

[64] *Records of Guangzhou Customs*. Vol. 3. Shanghai Classics Publishing House, 2002.

[65] (The Song Dynasty) Zhu Yu. *Stories of Pingzhou*. Vol. 2. Beijing: Zhonghua Book Company, 2007.

[66] (The Qing Dynasty) Xu Song. *Compendium Manuscript of Song: Officials*. Vol. 44. Beijing: Zhonghua Book Company, 1981.

[67] (The Song Dynasty) Hong Shi. *Anthology of Panzhou*. Vol. 31.

strings of copper coins in trade volume."[68] In the late Southern Song, as Arab merchants gathered in Quanzhou Port, the overseas trade there gradually surpassed that of Guangzhou, whose status in the overseas trade of the whole country declined relatively.

In the early Northern Song Dynasty, Quanzhou occupied an important position in the country's overseas trade. Emperor Taizong (r. 976–997) of the Song once issued a decree in the period of 976–984 dictating that "spices, perfumes and treasure from foreign countries that reached, Cochin, Quanzhou, Zhejiang couldn't be exchanged privately unless they came from the official treasury."[69] By the middle of the Northern Song Dynasty, at Quanzhou port were moored "numerous foreign ships loaded with mountains of groceries," suggesting a thriving overseas trade. With the improvement of navigation, Chinese and foreign merchants no longer needed to sail along the coast. Originally, trade vessels sailing in and out of Fujian coastal ports had to travel around Zhejiang or Guangdong when sailing north or south. Now, they could sail directly to Korea, Japan, or countries in the Indian Ocean in the most economical way. Therefore, the former system of governing Fujian trade by the Zhejiang and Guangzhou Maritime Trade Commission became increasingly unsuitable. For this reason, the Song government set up the Maritime Trade Commission in Quanzhou in 1087 to manage overseas trade along the coast of Fujian, and the overseas trade of Quanzhou Port further developed with many foreign countries. According to written records, "precious and exotic things from seven cities and millions of families were gathered here; dozens of overseas countries were influenced by this trade."[70] The poet Li Bing of the Northern Song once praised the prosperity of Quanzhou port by observing that "a gray-haired official lingered on the Sanzhou Road; the merchant ships of thousands nations came with the tide."[71] In order to receive foreign businessmen, the Laiyuan Station was specially set up in Quanzhou in the late Northern Song. In 1125, the Song government issued certificates to these three Maritime Trade Commissions, including 300 to

---

[68] (The Song Dynasty) Zhou Qufei. *Representative Answers from the Region beyond the Mountains.* Vol. 5.

[69] (The Qing Dynasty) Xu Song. *Compendium Manuscript of Song: Officials.* Vol. 44. Beijing: Zhonghua Book Company, 1981.

[70] (The Song Dynasty) Zhen Dexiu. *Anthology of Mr. Xishan.* Vol. 49. Photocopy of the Imperial Library Version of Complete Library in the Four Branches of Literature.

[71] (The Song Dynasty) Zhu Mu. *The Overall Survey of Geography.* Vol. 12.

Mingzhou, and up to 500 to Quanzhou and Guangzhou, indicating that Quanzhou had surpassed Mingzhou in the overseas trade of the whole country and kept abreast with Guangzhou.

The overseas trade of Quanzhou developed more rapidly during the Southern Song Dynasty. The reasons were as follows: first, unlike the ports in the Liangzhe area, Quanzhou was not damaged by wars. In 1130, when the ports of the Liangzhe area were damaged in the fires of war, Quanzhou even "bought more than 1,386,780 catties of foreign frankincense."[72] Second, the Southern Song government set up in Hangzhou "the temporary imperial abode", the functioning capital of the Southern Song Dynasty. Nevertheless, all the ports in the Liangzhe area (now Zhejiang Province), including Hangzhou Port, were in a decline for various reasons at that time. The imported cargoes couldn't satisfy the demands of the Court and the ruling class, and offered only limited benefits in fiscal revenue.

Under the circumstances, Quanzhou Port became the primary market for Zhejiang merchants to resell their cargoes, and also the port from which Zhejiang merchant ships sailed out to conduct ocean-going trade with foreign countries since that port was geographically advantageous. It was located at the center of the coastline of the Southern Song, with "Liangguang" (Guangdong and Guangxi) in the south, while Jiangsu and Zhejiang in the north. Therefore, during the Southern Song, the overseas trade of Quanzhou flourished and it quickly caught up with Guangzhou, the country's largest port at the time. Just as, Zhen Dexiu wrote that "prior to 1195, no residents lived in poverty. At the time, Quanzhou boasted hefty feudal land taxes and plenteous cargoes, and was called the 'Rich District'."[73]

In the early Southern Song Dynasty, merchants from up to 31 countries and regions frequently came to trade in Quanzhou,[74] and then the number increased to 50,[75] including such places as Japan, the South Sea, Persia, Arabia and East Africa and others. Moreover, the volume of

---

[72](The Yuan Dynasty) Tuotuo. *History of Song: Treatise on Food and Commodities.* Vol. 185. Beijing: Zhonghua Book Company, 1977.

[73](The Song Dynasty) Zhen Dexiu. *Anthology of Mr. Xishan.* Vol. 15. Photocopy of the Imperial Library Version of Complete Library in the Four Branches of Literature.

[74](The Song Dynasty) Zhao Yanwei. *Anecdotes of the Southern Song Dynasty.* Vol. 5.

[75](The Song Dynasty) Zhao Rushi. *Records of Barbarians.*

transactions was also very considerable. For example, during the 7 years from 1127 to 1134, the profit gained from the cargoes attracted by a group of government-sent ships to lure foreign merchants to Quanzhou was more than 980,000 *guan* of money.[76] In 1167, the goods that the envoy of Champa shipped to Quanzhou included more than 100,000 catties of frankincense, thousands of catties of spices and more than 7,000 elephant tusks.[77] Because of the prosperity of the trade, the annual income of the Quanzhou Maritime Trade Commission also increased sharply. In the later part of the Shaoxing period (1131–1162), "through taxation and silk collecting, the Maritime Trade Commissions of Guangzhou and Quanzhou obtained two million strings of coins in interest in a single year." By the end of the Southern Song Dynasty, the scale of Quanzhou overseas trade had surpassed that of Guangzhou, and it had become the largest overseas trade port in China and was even praised by foreign businessmen as "the largest trade port in the world."

In addition to Quanzhou, the development of foreign trade in coastal areas of Fujian also expanded to ports, such as Fuzhou and Zhangzhou. Among them, as the political center of the Southeast, Fuzhou possessed a great consumption capacity and well-developed industry and commerce. Historically, it was known as "the best in Fujian with the prosperity of the aristocracy exceeding that of the southeast and there were rich industry and commerce even in its remote places."[78] As a result, Fuzhou became an important market for Chinese and foreign businessmen. "Thousands of ships with waves on the sea" vividly described the importance of overseas trade in this region's economy. In 982, Zhangzhou was mentioned in the decree on coastal trade, indicating that the overseas trade of Zhangzhou had reached a certain scale in the early Song Dynasty. In the Southern Song Dynasty, Zhen Dexiu once said that "in the Quanzhou and Zhangzhou areas, robbers disappeared and foreign ships passed safely through them." The joint naming of Zhangzhou and Quanzhou highlights the important status of Zhangzhou to the Fujian coastal overseas trade.

---

[76](The Qing Dynasty) Xu Song. *Compendium Manuscript of Song: Officials*. Vol. 44. Beijing: Zhonghua Book Company, 1981.

[77] *Ibid.*, Vol. 7.

[78](The Song Dynasty) Su Zhe. *Anthology of Luan Cheng*. Vol. 30. Photocopy of the Imperial Library Version of Complete Library in the Four Branches of Literature.

Foreign trade along the coast of Jiangsu and Zhejiang developed to a remarkable extent during the reign of Qian Liu in the Five Dynasties and Ten Countries Era. According to historical records, "the thirteen states of Zhejiang Province covering an area of thousands of miles and garrisoned by ten thousands of soldiers made efforts in exploiting the copper ore in mountains and developed foreign trade over the sea. The wealth they owned, such as elephants, rhinoceros, beads, jades, made the area the richest in the country ... During the period from 923–926, overseas merchants came frequently to pay tributes ... the annual income from voyages exceeded millions in cash."[79] As the economic center moved southward in the Song Dynasty, the overseas trade in Jiangsu and Zhejiang developed rapidly. In the reign of Emperor Zhenzong of the Song (998–1021) the Maritime Trade Commission was set up in Mingzhou in 999, which further promoted the development of overseas trade in the coastal areas of Jiangsu and Zhejiang. The *Records of Mingzhou* stated that Minzhou "was on the southeast coast facing the sea, with links to linking many countries. When the wind and tide were favorable, merchant ships would come." The volume of goods traded in Mingzhou was so large that overseas trade warehouses had to be expanded in the reign of Emperor Lizong (r. 1224–1264) of the Southern Song. The size of the new storage units was quite considerable, for "there were four warehouses, respectively, in the east, west, north, and south, which could be divided into 28 parts."[80]

Geographically, the overseas trading partners of Minzhou Port included the countries of Southeast Asia, South Asia and West Asia, as well as Japan and North Korea in East Asia, among which the latter was the major player. Owing to geographical proximity, most Sino-Japanese and Sino-Korean trade in the Song was concentrated in Minzhou Port. The Song government even stipulated in 1080 that merchant ships traveling to Korea and Japan must stop off at Mingzhou to go through the relevant procedures. The ban was lifted later, but Mingzhou had always been the main gateway for China's trade with Japan and Korea. In the early Southern Song Dynasty, Mingzhou had been plundered by the southward army of the Jin, and foreign trade was depressed for a time, but the recovery was relatively rapid in pace. The first volume of the *Illustrated Mingzhou in the Qiandao Period* stated that geographically, Mingzhou

---

[79](The Song Dynasty) Xue Juzheng *et al. Old History of the Five Dynasties: Biography of Qian Liu.* Vol. 133. Beijing: Zhonghua Book Company, 1976.
[80]*General Annals of Yin County: Treatise on Food and Commodities.*

"had Fujian and Guangdong in the south, Japan in the east, Goguryeo in the north and foreign ships sailed to and from with abundant goods." Xupu, which was only a salt flat, was regarded as the outer port of the Hangzhou Port in the Southern Song, which also quickly developed into a port of considerable scale.

5.3.2 *The Expansion of the Song's Trading Areas*

Under the opening-up policy of actively encouraging foreign trade in the Song Dynasty, envoys and businessmen from countries to the east and west came in droves along the east–west route. According to the *Records of Foreign Countries*, there were 53 countries and regions in the South China Sea trading with the Southern Song and Southern Song merchants traded with more than 20 overseas countries. In addition to the traditional East Asia, Southeast Asia, South Asia, and West Asia markets, the territories covered by these countries also extended to Africa.

(1) East Asian Countries
(i) Goguryeo
This period was the era of the Goguryeo in Korean history, which had a close trading relationship, both official and non-governmental, with the Song Dynasty.

In the Song Dynasty, diplomatic envoys of the two countries maintained frequent contact. During the more than 200 years from 962 to 1170, the Goguryeo sent envoys to develop friendly relations with the Song 57 times and the Song envoys also went to Goguryeo more than 30 times.[81] Among them, the most illustrious was the journey of Xujing to Goguryeo. Through official trade channels, Goguryeo exchanged with the Song gold, silver, goldwares, silverwares, bronzewares, swords, famous horses, ginseng, fine cloth and sulfur for various silk fabrics, clothing, gold belts, gold and silver vessels, pommel horses, various books and Buddhist scriptures.

At the same time, civilian businessmen increased their contact. Most Korean businessmen who came to the Song stayed in Mingzhou. Even if they went to Quanzhou and Guangzhou, or Southeast Asia, they arrived in

---

[81] Chen Taixia. "On the Tributary Routes between Goguryeo and the Song Government" in the *Study of the Ancient Relation between China, Korea and Japan*.

Mingzhou first. In 1117, the Song government specially set up the "Goguryeo Department" (also called "Laiyuan Department") in Mingzhou to receive merchants from Gorye. It also built "Goguryeo Travel Accommodations" for their sojourn; two large cruise ships and hundreds of gaily-painted pleasure-boats were moored under Zhaobao Mountain for them to go on tour.

Merchants of the Song also went to Goguryeo. For example, in 1035, 147 individuals including the Mingzhou merchant Chen Liang and the Taizhou merchant Chen Weiji went to Goguryeo. In 1103, 38 people traveled to Goguryeo, including the Mingzhou official coach Zhang Zongmin, Xu Cong, *et al.*, and the transport leader Yang Zhao; in 1124, the Mingzhou merchants Du Daoji and Zhu Yanzuo went to Goguryeo and stayed there.[82] According to the *History of Goguryeo*, merchants of the Song sailed to Goguryeo about 129 times and their number ranged from dozens to hundreds each time, reaching a total of more than 5,000. Some Song merchants also lived in Goguryeo for a long time. The *History of Song: Goguryeo* noted that Goguryeo had "hundreds of Chinese in its kingdom, most of them being from Fujian Province who came with maritime trade."

(ii) Japan

During the Northern Song Dynasty, Japan adopted a policy of seclusion, but for much of that time merchant ships from the Song still arrived in Japan. During the Southern Song Dynasty, on the one hand, the environment for economic and trade development remained stable at least as far as the central government was concerned, and they broke peace with the Jin regime; on the other hand, with the establishment of Kamakura Bakufu regime in Japan, the policy of seclusion was replaced with an opening-up policy and Japanese merchant ships began to sail to China, forming a situation of mutual trade between the merchant ships of the two countries. According to Japanese statistics, in the more than 160 years of the Northern Song alone, Chinese merchant ships sailed to Japan as many as 60 or 70 times. "Exchanges between merchant ships of Japan and the Song were extremely frequent, which took place almost annually."[83]

---

[82] (North Korea) Jeong In-ji. *History of the Goryeo*. Vols. 6, 12, 15.

[83] (Japan) Yasuhiko Kimiya. *Nikka bunka kōryūshi*. Fuzanbō, 1955.

According to another Japanese author, during the Song Dynasty, Chinese merchant ships sailed to Japan as many as 114 or 115 times.[84]

The goods that Chinese and Japanese ships transported from Japan were divided by type into general merchandise and valuable merchandise. The *Records of Mingzhou* stated that "valuable merchandise included gold, gulch-gold, beads, medicine beads, mercury, pilose antler, poria cocos; while general merchandise embraced sulfur, screw head, pine board, fir board and so on." Among these, the main commodities were sulfur and wood. The Song Dynasty had a huge demand for Japanese sulfur. In the Northern Song, merchants sailed to Japan to traffic some commodities into China. The Northern Song government also funded businessmen for this purchase.

The geographical and climatic conditions of Japan were suitable for growing trees, so many valuable types of timber became major exports to the Song Dynasty. Among them, Chamaecyparis obtusa was the most precious and was once used in Emperor Gaozong's reign of the Southern Song (r. 1127–1162) to build the Cui Han Hall.

The price of gold in China and Japan in the Song Dynasty differed greatly. Motivated by this disparity, the Song merchants transported vast quantities of placer gold to China. At the same time, placer gold was used as a payment method in the trade between Daizafu (a Japanese city located in Fukuoka Prefecture) and the Song merchants, as well as in the trade between private merchants between the two countries. This made Japanese placer gold flow into the Song in volume, and it was not only carried by the Song merchants, but by Japanese vessels. The *Study of Bullion from the Tang and Song Dynasty* written by a Japanese author named Katō Shigeshi indicated that the quantity of gold exported by Japanese merchant ships to China reached 4,000 or 5,000 taels per year. Added to the gold brought back by the Chinese merchant ships, the final amount of gold far exceeded this figure. The gold outflow to China made Mutsu, Japan's major gold producing area, fail to pay the annual tax of gold to the Court of Japan several times,[85] which led to a sharp rise in the value of Japanese gold. At the beginning of the 11th century, the official value of gold in Kyoto was that 1 tael of gold was equal to 1 bushel (*dan*) of rice.[86] By the beginning of the 12th century, 1 tael of

---

[84] (Japan) Mori Katsumi. 続日宋貿易の研究 [M]. 勉誠出版, 2009. p. 12.

[85] *Xiao you ji*. June 14, 1024.

[86] *Quan ji*. July 13, 1000.

gold equaled 3 bushels of rice.[87] Japanese refined handicrafts were also targeted by the Song merchants. Various handicrafts, such as Japanese pearls, crystals, fine folding fans, and sharp swords, were important commodities and were deeply loved and appreciated by the people of the Song.

Many kinds of goods were also exported to Japan from the Song, including a variety of silk fabrics, various spices, various books, and such new commercial products as pigments, clay, medicines, and handicrafts. Although Japan already had a silk weaving industry at this time, and some silk fabrics were also imported into China, the Japanese still craved the fine silk textiles of China, especially the high-end kind, and they regarded them as treasures.

Spices were a necessity for Japanese religious rituals and daily life, and were in great demand. Of the spices transported by Song merchants, only a portion was produced in China, and most of the rest were imported from Arabia, Southeast Asian, and East African countries and then transferred to Japan.

The volume of books transported during the Song Dynasty was so large that no previous generations could compare with it. Specifically, through the exchange of books between the two countries, Song merchants brought back from Japan many Chinese books which couldn't be found within China, which was of far-reaching significance.

It is worth noting that from the middle of the 12th century, with the development of the Japanese monetary economy, the demand for money increased, leading to huge quantities of copper coins flowing into Japan. Although the Song government banned the export of copper coins repeatedly, plenty of copper coins still entered Japan through smuggling.

(2) Countries on the Indochina Peninsula

Important in the Song Dynasty were the states of Cochin in northern Vietnam and Champa in the south-central part. Both countries "paid tribute every year" and the scale of trade with the Song Dynasty was also considerable.

---

[87] *Konjaku Monogatari.*

(i) Cochin

This country was close to China and traded with the Song Dynasty by land and sea. The *History of Song* recorded that during the Song, Cochin sent envoys to develop friendly relations with China as many as 46 times. The envoys from Cochin came with rhino horns, ivory, various spices, gold and silver, gold beads, gold, silver and seven treasure-decorated chairs, seven treasure-decorated gold bottles, silver basins, silk cloth, rhinoceros, elephants, pedigree horses, green feathers, etc., and returned with coins, silk, utensils, clothes, gold belts, and pommel horses.

(ii) Champa

According to the *History of Song*, from 961 to 1167, Champa dispatched envoys with local products to develop friendly relations with China 43 times in succession. They carried such goods as ivory, rhino horns, hawks-bill turtles, various spices, textiles, elephants, lions, rhinoceros, peacocks, chickens, peacock feather umbrellas, betel nuts, glass, coral, drinking vessels, *Dayi* bottles (fire oil imported from Dayi). The quantity was considerable. Once, they carried 1,000 catties of frankincense. At another time, they even brought 72 elephant tusks, 86 rhino horns, and 1,000 catties of hawksbill turtles. The gifts that envoys brought back included silver, white horses, post horses, pommel horses, coins, warriors and crown belts. Once the silk totaled as much as 4,700 taels. Continuous mercantile contact was recorded in historical literature.

(iii) Khmer

The *History of Song* stated that the Khmer sent envoys with local products to develop friendly relations with China in 1116 and in 1120 during the reign of Emperor Huizong (r. 1100–1125) of the Song. The merchants of the two countries also maintained constant contact. History recorded that the great merchants of Khmer once came to China to trade in four vessels.[88]

(3) Countries on the Malay Archipelago

During this period, there were many countries on the Malay Archipelago which maintained trade relations with the Song Dynasty. Among them, the most closely related were the Kingdom of Srivijaya, Yavadvipa, and Borneo.

---

[88](The Song Dynasty) Lou Yao. *Anthology of Mr. Gongkui.* Vol. 88.

(i) Srivijaya

Srivijaya was the main target destination of maritime trade during the Song Dynasty. Holding the policy of actively developing overseas trade, it rose to become a maritime power, occupying an important position in Chinese and western maritime transportation. Its capital was what is now Jambi in Sumatra, Indonesia.

The *History of Song* recorded that during the 218 years from 960 to 1178, the Kingdom of Srivijaya sent envoys to develop friendly relations 25 times. The merchant ships sailed to the Song Empire more frequently with frankincense. The *Stories of Pingzhou* written by Zhu Yu of the Song records that "of the nations of Hainan, ... Srivijaya was the largest.... It boasted much sandalwood and frankincense shipped by Srivijaya to be traded for Chinese products." At the same time, many Chinese merchants also went to Srivijaya. At the beginning of the 12th century, Quanzhou merchants traded in the Kingdom of Srivijaya. "Years of trading back and forth between China and Srivijaya gained hundred times of profits." As well as directly conducting trade with China, Srivijaya also re-exported a large amount of Indian and Arab goods.

(ii) Yavadvipa

Yavadvipa, located in the central part of present-day Java Island, was one of the major countries that traded with the Song Dynasty. According to the *History of Song*, in 992 and in 1109, Java, respectively, sent envoys to develop friendly relations. The tributes it carried included: ivory, pearls, hawksbill, borneol, sandalwood, clove, embroidered gold and silk skeins, variegated silk skeins, silk cotton woven variegated cloth, hawksbill betel nut dishes, seven treasure-decorated sandalwood pavilions, vine-woven flower mats, rhinoceros swords, gold and silver swords, and white parrots. The Song Court presented them with gold coins, pedigree horses, and warriors, in return.

Javanese merchant ships often sailed to Guangzhou for trading. Merchant ships that sold pepper, especially, often proved themselves to be very profitable. The *History of Song* recorded that: "in this time, pepper was traded and merchants' gains multiplied." Ships from the Song also voyaged to Java. Mao Xu from Jianxi, Fujian Province traded in Yavadvipa (now Java in Indonesia) many times and became a tycoon merchant engaged in maritime commerce at that time. He was simultaneously employed by Java as a guide for the "tribute ship."

(iii) Borneo

Borneo, currently located on the Kalimantan Island, sent envoys carrying local products to the Song Empire in 997. Besides various kinds of borneol, envoys also brought sandalwood, hawksbill, ivory and so on. In 1082, the King of Borneo sent envoys to the Song again. Upon their return, they requested to set out for home from Quanzhou port.

(4) Countries on the Indian Peninsula

In this period, there were many countries on the Indian Peninsula, among which Chola and Kulam in Southern India had particularly close trade relations with the Song Dynasty.

(i) Chola

The Chola kingdom was located in the northeast of Cape Comorin, southeastern India. According to the *History of Song*, in 1015, 1020, 1033 and 1077, the Chola, respectively, sent envoys to build good relations with China. In addition to various kinds of fragrant medicines, they also brought treasures, such as pearl shirts and hats, pearls, rhino horns, and ivory, the number of which was strikingly huge. In 1015, the Chola kingdom sent a mission of 52 people to China, bringing 60 elephant tusks, 27,700 taels of pearls and 3,300 catties of fragrant medicines. In 1033, an envoy even brought up to 100 elephant tusks. Chola ships which came to the Song always landed at Guangzhou port or Quanzhou port. The number of Chinese merchants who traded in India was so large in number that there were pagodas built by them at the mouth of Gavuli, India.

(ii) Kulam

Kulam, located in Kollam area in the southwestern part of present-day India, was a country with developed commerce and gold and silver as coined money.

During this period, limited by navigation technique, the trade ships sailing between China and Dayi always needed underway replenishment in order to reach their destinations; besides, seaworthy ships were needed to pass through the shallow Persian Gulf during the round trips. Geographically, Kulam was the communications hub between the East and West where merchants, whether bound eastward or westward, needed to stay there, so it played an important intermediary role in the ancient trade between China and the west, especially China and Dayi.

(5) Dayi[89]

Sino-Arab trade in the Song Dynasty further developed based on the achievements of the previous Tang Dynasty. Both official and non-governmental trade was greatly improved, and bilateral trade reached unprecedented prosperity. Especially after the 11th century, when the European economy recovered with the improvement of market development degree, there was even more demand for Eastern commodities and Arab merchants who were active in the Mediterranean region became a bridge connecting the East and West trade. "Speaking of foreign countries that were prosperous and rich in treasuries, Dayi was the first name which sprang to mind" wrote Zhou Qufei of Song in his *Representative Answers from the Region beyond the Mountains*. This indicates the prosperity of China–Arabia trade, which made Arabia China's largest trading partner during the Song Dynasty.

In the Song Dynasty, Arab envoys came to China more than 50 times, ranking first among foreign countries.

In addition to official trade, the overseas trade between the Song and Dayi flourished. The merchant ships of the Song bound for Dayi mostly set out from Quanzhou, and sailed along the South China Sea Silk Road to Basra, Siraf, Bahrain and other ports in the Persian Gulf to trade with Dayi merchants. Basra was the largest port in the Persian Gulf at that time, with canals connecting it to Obollah (the mouth of the Euphrates). Through those channels, many goods were transported to the Dayi capital, Baghdad.

The largest consignment imported to ancient China via the sea was spices, which were abundant in the Arabian Peninsula and all over East Africa. Many Arab merchants gained high profits by coming to China to engage in the spice trade. Chinese historical books record a large number of exploits of Arab merchants. For example, Yue Ke (the grandson of Yue Fei) recorded how the home of a wealthy Arab merchant appeared in his *Ting History*. He wrote that "the house was … wonderful and magnificent," "in the main hall there were four pillars made of agalloch eaglewood … Spending gold like dung, … fragrant pearls scattered in the seat." The family of the aforementioned Pu Shougeng traded in China for generations and he was once the most affluent foreign businessman in Guangzhou.

Of the Dayi merchants who came to the Song, some even lived in Southeast Asian countries and trafficked in large amounts of incense to

---

[89]The Chinese name for the Arabs and the Muslims in Persia and Central Asia in general.

China. Others lived in China for a long time, being mostly concentrated in Guangzhou Port in the Northern Song and in Quanzhou Port in the Southern Song. These two ports have still kept the records of Dayi merchants doing business in China in ancient times. The Huaisheng Mosque (Lighthouse Mosque) in Guangzhou was one of the earliest mosques in China. In the Southern Song, there were so many Arab merchants in Quanzhou that it was nicknamed the "half-Hui city." There were as many as six or seven ancient mosques in Quanzhou, among which only the Aishabha Temple and the mosque presided over by Najib Mudhhiru al-Din still remain as historical relics and can be dated back to the Song Dynasty.

The Song Dynasty set up *Fan Fang* in settlements with a high concentration of Arab merchants. To facilitate their children's schooling, *Fan* schools were also established for them.

(6) African Countries

The people of Song blazed a direct route across the Indian Ocean to Africa, establishing regular trade ties between their country and that continent. The African countries traded their special ivory, rhino horns and spices in exchange for the silk, porcelain, and copper coins of the Song Dynasty.

Ancient countries along the coast of East Africa, such as the Berbera (now Canberra in northern Somalia), the Central State (now the northeast coast of Somalia), the nation of Zanzibar (now in the south of Somalia on the east coast of Africa) and the nation of Komr Zangī (now on the coast of East Africa and Madagascar) were areas where merchant ships of the Song Dynasty often arrived and traded.

At the end of the 10th century, Egypt was conquered by the Fatimid Dynasty (called the Green Dayi in Chinese historical records), which relocated its capital to Cairo, and Egypt became the center of the Arab world. In the mid-11th century, trade on the west bank of the Indian Ocean was diverted to Aden and the Red Sea port, Olzum of Egypt, and Egypt gradually became an important hub for transferring eastern goods from the Red Sea to the Mediterranean. There were many Egyptians among Dayi merchants of the Song who transported Chinese silk and porcelain to all parts of Africa and then to countries such as Italy, Spain and Morocco, thereby contributing to trade between Asia and Europe.

5.3.3 *The Diversification of Foreign Trade Business Entities*

Relying on the progress in shipbuilding and navigation technology and the trade policies of the Song Dynasty, the risks associated with overseas trade activities during this period were reduced and the profits were lucrative, thus inducing more and more people in the coastal areas to participate in this field. In addition to rich merchants, some small and intermediate merchants went to sea together on large merchant ships. According to historical accounts, "large vessels could hold hundreds of people and small ships about one hundred ... merchants shared their space with the goods on the ships. Everyone got a square inches to themselves, with goods stored below and people sleeping above."[90] There were also many coastal households whose funds were too limited to be able to set out to sea on their own. They engaged in import activities by asking people to buy on their behalf, "giving money to people on the merchant ships and entrusting them to buy foreign goods."[91]

During the Song Dynasty, there were many instances of bureaucrats and wealthy officials participating in overseas trade. As early as 995, Emperor Taizong (r. 976–997) warned Guangzhou officials against dabbling in overseas trade activities, stating "Internal and external civil and military bureaucrats who dare to send trusted followers to trade will be punished."[92] At the same time, the Emperor reminded officials at all levels in the area where the Maritime Trade Commission was located that "governors, magistrate officials and Maritime Trade Commissioners were not allowed to obtain fragrant medicines and embargoed goods from local foreign merchants." But the ban was implemented in vain, and officials from across the whole country still indulged in overseas trade. For example, during the reign of Emperor Zhenzong (r. 997–1022), the Guangzhou overseas trade official and prefect Zhang Jian used to "pay to sea traders and trade on the market."[93] Su Shi also publicly "bought several shiploads of logwood to resell in Sichuan." In the Southern Song Dynasty, it was

---

[90](The Song Dynasty) Zhu Yu. *Stories of Pingzhou*. Vol. 2.

[91](The Song Dynasty) Bao Hui. *Draft of the Broomstick*. Vol. 1. Photocopy of of the Imperial Library Version of Complete Library in the Four Branches of Literature.

[92](The Qing Dynasty) Xu Song. *Compendium Manuscript of Song: Officials*. Vol. 44. Beijing: Zhonghua Book Company, 1981.

[93](The Yuan Dynasty) Tuotuo. *History of Song: Biography of Zhang Jian*. Vol. 277. Biography 36. Beijing: Zhonghua Book Company, 1977.

more common for officials at all levels to send people as their proxies or entrust maritime businesses to conduct foreign trade in their stead. Therefore, in 1171, the Court imposed a ban to the effect that "officials who paid to the leader to buy goods in overseas countries will be punished."[94] Although the Song Court repeatedly issued injunctions afterwards, officials and dignitaries still participated in overseas trade activities by various means, and even coastal soldiers were engaged in overseas trade activities. It was recorded that "generals didn't govern the army but did business affairs ... countless soldiers who were well armed with armor and weapons were converted to being merchants."[95] Besides, in the prefectures adjacent to the coastal areas between Guangxi and Cochin "the accumulated salaries of officials below the level of guardsmen were directed into trade."[96]

Some monks also participated in overseas trade activities. "There was a monk named Jingyuan in Hangzhou who once lived on the seashore and traded with foreigners to gain profits."[97]

The increasingly diversified and numerous operating entities of overseas trade brought about the expansion of the overall scale of foreign trade. "Carts loaded with heavy goods were seen moving across the border and ships returned with full loads." [98] Such descriptions vividly reflected the trade boom of this period.

5.3.4 *The Expansion of Trade Scale*

With the improvement of shipbuilding and navigation skill, the scale of Chinese and foreign maritime transportation enlarged, and it was common for individual maritime merchants to trade hundreds of thousands of

---

[94](The Yuan Dynasty) Tuotuo. *History of Song: Treatise on Food and Commodities.* Vol. 186. Beijing: Zhonghua Book Company, 1977.

[95](The Song Dynasty) Li Xinzhuan. Vol. 189. Photocopy of Siku Quanshu (the Imperial Library Version).

[96]Chen Zhichao. *Supplement to Compendium Manuscript of Song.* p. 661. National Library Document Microfilming Center, 1988.

[97](The Song Dynasty) Li Tao. Supplements to the Long Draft Continuation of the Comprehensive Mirror that Aids Administration. Vol. 435. Beijing: Zhonghua Book Company, 1980.

[98]*Ibid.*, Vol. 269.

catties of spices at one time. For example, the above-mentioned merchant of Dayi, Pu Luoxin, once transported 300,000 *guan* of frankincense. The transport chief Cai Jingfang promoted foreign businessmen and then told them to trade in the Song; on one occasion he brought back with him fiscal revenue of 980,000 strings of coins of money. The *Eastern Capital: A Dream of Splendor* recorded that the transactions between Chinese and foreign merchants "easily exceeded ten million strings of cash."

Owing to a dearth of corresponding statistics, it was difficult to know the total volume of overseas trade in the Song Dynasty, but the amount could be roughly inferred from the overseas trade tax. The *History of Song: Treatise on Food and Commodities* recorded that "at about one tenth rate foreign goods would be collected." The 10% tax rate was not a uniform and stable tax rate, and the government would generally make corresponding adjustments according to fluctuations in trade. Sometimes it was as high as 30% or as low as 6%. At the same time, taxes on luxury goods were slightly different from those on ordinary goods, the former usually being higher than the latter. In 1159, the Guangzhou and Quanzhou Maritime Trade Commissions "got two million strings of coins of money as the interest in a year through taxation and silk collecting," which meant the Song government gained a profit of 2 million strings of coins of cash from taxation and the sales of government collected goods. According to the regulations, "the interest rate should not exceed two tenth," i.e., the profit margin on government sales of imported goods was generally 20%, and the proportion the government collected from the Southern Song was generally about 40% of imported goods. Based on this calculation, the scale of imports during this period was about 16.67 million strings of coins. In the long run, a country's foreign trade should be roughly in balance, so the export and import trade scale remained in virtual equilibrium. The total import and export trade amount in this period was about 33 million strings of cash.

5.3.5 *The Increase in the Variety of Import and Export Commodities*

The increase in the types of goods in international trade was largely based on advances in maritime transport technology. Progress in shipbuilding and marine technology in the Song greatly improved the speed and safety of Chinese and foreign maritime navigation. The shortening of voyage time and the increase in the carrying capacity of ships reduced the cost of shipping, thus making it possible for more goods of relatively low value to enter the international trade market.

Compared with the previous generation, the range of import and export commodities surged in the Song. According to the statistics found in the *Compendium Manuscript of Song* and the *History of Song: Records of Foreign Countries*, there were more than 330 kinds of imported goods in the Fujian overseas trade in the Song Dynasty. The records of the Maritime Trade Commission in the Qingyuan period of the Southern Song explained in detail that there was a total of more than 220 kinds of imported goods, including over 130 kinds of valuable merchandise and about 90 kinds of general merchandise. In addition to traditional luxury consumer goods such as spices and treasures there was a myriad of imported production materials like minerals and dyes as well as many ordinary perishables and daily necessities. The recorded bulk imports included spices, such as frankincense, cloves, aloe and sandalwood; treasures, such as pearls, ivory, rhino horns, and agate; medicinal materials, such as myrrh, poria, lingshu, and storax oil; mineral products, such as mercury, sulfur, gold and silver, and iron; dyes, like purple ore, and sappanwood; food, like white sugar, and Wansui jujube; raw animal and plant products, such as beef tendons, and rattan mats; wool cotton products, such as white folded cloth, camel hair, plain thin silk, Yuenuo cloth, kapok yarn, and so on. Only the first two categories were luxury goods, with the rest being basically ordinary ones.

The types of goods exported during the Song Dynasty also increased significantly. In addition to traditional silk and porcelain, copper coins, books, food, and daily necessities were also exported to overseas markets. More types of silk and porcelain were exported compared with in the past. For example, silk products included spun silk, silks, brocade, satin, five-color velvet or silk thread and other various kinds; ceramics included bowls, altars, urns, pots, boxes, earthen bowls and so forth; metal products included copper coins, various types of bronzes, various iron tools and gold and silver jewelry; daily necessities embraced lacquerwares, silk fans, wooden combs, umbrellas, and mats. Cultural products included paper, ink, and books; food covered rice, salt, tea, sugar, and wine; and dried or fresh fruits, such as lychees and longans also entered the overseas market. Among these, silk, ceramics, iron wares, copper wares and other manufactured goods occupied the leading position in export.

5.4 The Influence of Foreign Trade on Socio-Economic Development

5.4.1 *The Economic Influence of Foreign Trade*

Under the guidance of an active policy, the opening-up of the Song Dynasty surpassed its predecessors in terms of breadth and depth. Among these, great achievements were made in overseas trade, with increased varieties of commodities, an expanded scale of trade, and extensive range of exchanged objects. In the Song Dynasty, as in all pre-capitalist eras, foreign trade did not occupy a dominant position in the economy of various countries, but its commodity and technology exchanges in a wider area had a profound impact on the economy of all countries in trade. First, the development of trade enriched the material lives of the Chinese people and foreigners alike, and improved the general welfare situation; secondly, trade promoted the further development of handicraft industries, such as silk weaving, lacquer making and porcelain manufacturing in China, accelerating the economic development in the southeast coastal areas of China; thirdly, trade led to the spread of handicraft technologies, such as silk weaving, porcelain making, smelting and casting, and the outward spread of advanced science and technology, including shipbuilding, and compass design and navigation, providing technical support for the development of foreign trade of countries along the Maritime Silk Road; and fourthly, the vigorous development of Sino-foreign trade further promoted economic and cultural exchanges between the Song and overseas countries, and played a beneficial role in the economic development and burgeoning civilization of both.

(1) The Influence of Foreign Trade on China's Economic Development
(i) Accelerating Economic Development

The development of foreign trade expanded overseas markets for domestic commodity production, and became an important driving force for the development of the commodity economy. Facing huge financial pressure, the Song government adopted the opening-up policy, employing various means to stimulate the development of foreign trade so that the Chinese feudal economy reached its peak in the Song.

The rapid development of the commodity economy in southeastern coastal areas provided a solid material basis for overseas trade activities in the Song. At the same time, the development of foreign trade, in turn, promoted the economic development of coastal areas, making the commodity economy in this area proceed with more dynamism than in the interior. Export-oriented economy appeared in some industries, thus greatly accelerating economic development.

As was mentioned previously, since China's economic and cultural development level was higher than that of most trading partners in the Song Dynasty, the differences in productivity, especially in technology, were also reflected in the type of import and export goods. In general, the export commodities of the Song were mainly handmade products with high technological features and high added value, and the export of these products became a channel for spreading Chinese production technology abroad. Also, with the expansion of the export scale, the positive effect of exports on the industry appeared, the production of related industries increased, and the economy of the southeastern coast developed rapidly. For example, as overseas trade via Quanzhou developed and the export of silk fabrics increased, the Fujian silk reeling industry received a great stimulus. In the Tang Dynasty, the Fujian silk reeling industry was relatively backward, and the its silk and ramie production only ranked eighth in the country. Driven by overseas trade, it made remarkable progress in the Song Dynasty. For instance, Quanzhou became known for "silk fabrics comparable to that of Sichuan and regions south of the Yangtze River." A myriad of locally produced Fujian silk products was exported to overseas countries so that "the number of Fuzhou silks, Zhangzhou spun yarns and Quanzhou ... that was exported overseas was countless."[99] The porcelain kilns in Guangdong, Fujian and Zhejiang were mostly distributed along the coast. Many of them produced wares exclusively for export. Studies showed that porcelain produced in kilns of Dehua, the Parthian Empire and Nanan in Fujian were rarely found in China, while many were found in Southeast Asia, indicating that these porcelain kilns mainly produced for overseas markets. The *Jinjiang County Gazetteer* also records that "as for the porcelain-making in Cizao County, kilns were made out of earth to fire ceramics, like large and small bowls, crocks and urns in large quantities to be exported overseas." Overseas market-oriented production promoted the diversification of product categories and the improvement of craftsmanship, which was conducive to the progress of the porcelain industry.

---

[99](The Ming Dynasty) Wang Shimao. *History of Fujian Province*. Beijing: Zhonghua Book Company, 1985.

In terms of imported goods, in addition to perfumes and treasures intended as luxury goods exclusively for the upper ruling classes, other commodities such as dyes, minerals, beef tendons and woods were raw materials, whose import drove the development of related artisanal processing industries. Food, medicinal materials and wool cotton fabrics fell into the category of daily necessities. The import of the above products promoted the sustainable development of the export-oriented economy in the southeastern coastal areas of the Song. More people were accommodated in places where they served. For example, the economy of Quanzhou in Fujian was more dependent on overseas trade. The great poet Su Shi once observed in his *On the Goguryeo Tribute* that "people in Fujian and its surroundings were all engaged in maritime commerce." Residents in all coastal areas scrambled to sell goods on their ships. "In Zhangzhou, Quanzhou, Fuzhou and Xinghua, all ships built by people in coastal areas were their own property and were used to trade for profit."[100] As a result, the region was known as "taking foreign ships as life." In the Southern Song, "at least half a million of people live free of worries about their livelihood."[101] During the Southern Song Dynasty, the prefect of Quanzhou named Zhen Dexiu also said that "in Quanzhou, what can be depended on to meet both official and private needs is foreign ships."

Excess profits existed in overseas trade. Therefore, it was very profitable to be engaged in foreign trade. The people of the Song believed that the profit rate of conducting business overseas could be as high as nearly 10 times. "Every one *guan* of Chinese goods could be exchanged for one hundred *guan* of foreign goods, and one hundred of *guan* of Chinese goods could be exchanged for one thousand *guan* of foreign goods."[102] Capitalizing on the geographical and traditional advantages, the masses of merchants in coastal areas participated in overseas trade activities and obtained huge wealth. For example, "Yang Ke in Quanzhou had been a maritime merchant for more than ten years and earned 20 million in

---

[100](The Qing Dynasty) Xu Song. *Compendium Manuscript of Song: Penal Law*. Vol. 2. Beijing: Zhonghua Book Company, 1981.

[101](The Song Dynasty) Wang Xiangzhi. *Records of Scenic Spots across the Country*. Vol. 13. The article was quoted from Lu Yu. *Repair of the City*.

[102](The Song Dynasty) Bao Hui. *Draft of the Broomstick: Prohibition of Copper Coin Application*. Vol. 1. The Copy of *Siku Quanshu* in Wenyuan Pavilion.

cash."[103] The prefect of Quanzhou Lian Nanfu also said that "Maritime merchants went to foreign countries and attracted many people to do business."[104] The "Jiankang (Nanjing) merchant Yang Erlang, ... traded in the South China Sea for more than 10 years and accumulated tens of millions in wealth."[105] It was recorded in *The Steles of Auspicious and Efficacious Temple* that "before the Quanzhou foreign trade leader named Zhu Fang sailed to Srivijaya, he burned incense before the God he worshiped for good luck. The ship traveled fast and met with no resistance. He came back many years later with hundred times of profits."[106] Since many people acquired wealth through conducting foreign trade, the whole region enjoyed huge affluence and became known as the "rich state in the south."[107]

Under the policy of rewarding foreign merchants with official positions in the Song, a group of wealthy traders received high posts and titles. For example, due to the large scale of foreign trade, the foreign trade leader Cai Jingfang was ennobled as Gentleman of Trust; the Quanzhou businessman Wang Yuanzhang was appointed as *Gentleman for Trustworthy Service*; and Pu Yanxiu was titled Court Gentleman of Trust for their attracting foreign merchants into China. A Dayi merchant named Pu Shougeng was appointed as the Supervisorate of the Quanzhou Maritime Trade Commission. The opportunity to become officials through overseas trade greatly improved the political status of maritime merchants, which shook the traditional ideology of constraining trade. The *Comprehensive Investigations based on Literary and Documentary Sources* stated that "when making the laws, our ancestors hated merchants seeking after profits and tried to restrain their activities, while descendants envied the profits gained by merchants and wanted to share them." This revealed how the state policy no longer restricted the development of commerce and

---

[103] (The Song Dynasty) Hong Mai. *Ghost Stories Recorded by Erudite Scholars: Mr. Yang in Yangzhou* Vol. 6.

[104] (The Yuan Dynasty) Tuotuo. *History of Song: Treatise on Food and Commodities* Vol. 185. Beijing: Zhonghua Book Company, 1977.

[105] (The Song Dynasty) Hong Mai. *Supplements to Ghost Stories Recorded by Erudite Scholars.* Vol. 21.

[106] Compiled by China Overseas Transportation History Research Association. Compilation of Quanzhou Overseas Transportation Historical Materials (Internal Journal), 1975.

[107] (The Song Dynasty) Zhen Dexiu. *Anthology of Zhen Dexiu.* Vol. 49. The copy of Complete Library in the Four Branches of Literature in Wenyuan Pavilion.

merchants, and the tradition of "merchants being kept outside of official posts" gave way to a situation in which "even the sons of merchants can be appointed officials." The improvement of the political and economic status of merchants lured more people to participate in commodity exchange activities.

It could be seen that the boom in overseas trade trained a large number of specialized merchants who were engaged in overseas trade in the coastal areas, and the flourish of trade promoted the prosperity of the regional econ-omy, thus altering to some extent the social and economic structure of the southeastern coastal areas. Although the closed natural economy always occupied the leading position, commodity production oriented by sectors, industries and markets closely related to foreign trade to a certain extent, became increasingly active and took on slightly more export-oriented econ-omy features. According to the *Ganshui Record* written by Chang Tang in the Southern Song, the residents of Gan Pu, Zhejiang "did no farming, but earned a living by receiving Southeast Asian goods and then transported them to the counties of western Zhejiang for sale." This reflected the improvement in the degree of opening-up during this period.

A group of coastal towns relying on overseas trade emerged. Huating in the lower reaches of the Yangtze River was known as "the No. 1 large county in southeast China"[108] with "wealthy families and rich merchants being busy over the sea and land route." Shanghai also rose due to the pros-perity of foreign trade. History recorded that "at the end of the Song, Shanghai as a town was populous, with ships on the sea. The Maritime Trade Commission was set up and a trading market proceeded well."[109] With the convenient marine transportation, Ganpu Town of Haiyan County in Zhejiang Province developed to be a hinterland of porcelain and silk produc-tion. Meanwhile, it was geographically advantageous since it was adjacent to the consumer metropolis of Hangzhou. Gradually, it grew to be a huge overseas trade port where "merchants traveled in from all directions." During the Southern Song, Zhenjiang Port was anchored with "foreign ships coming by seaway from Fujian, Guangdong and Hainan," thus forming a propitious situation whereby "merchants gathered and rich goods traded smoothly."[110]

---

[108] (The Song Dyansty) Sun Go. *Anthology of Sun Di*. Vol. 34.

[109] Jiajing. *Shanghai County Gazetteer*. Vol. 1. a photocopy of the 21st Republic of China.

[110] (The Qing Dyansty) Xu Song. *Compendium Manuscript of Song*: *Food and Commodity*. Beijing: Zhonghua Book Company, 1981.

Under the impetus of overseas trade, Guangzhou, Quanzhou, Mingzhou and other traditional foreign trade ports became more prosperous. For example, in Quanzhou, "what can be held to meet both official and private needs were foreign ships." The *Records of Quanzhou Prefecture* stated that "the salt marshes in Quanzhou made the land barren. Therefore it obtained food from overseas, clothes from the Wuyue, and utensils from Jiaozhou and Guangzhou. The goods produced here were very few." The Northern Song poet Xie Lu stated in his book *Ode to Sothern Quanzhou* that "Quanzhou boasted a dense population but only had barren valleys with no land for cultivation. However, there were vast seas to the south of Quanzhou and every year people sailed their ships overseas."[111] This showed that the economy of Quanzhou was very far from being self-sufficient and depended on domestic and foreign markets was quite high. The simultaneous development of domestic and foreign trade promoted the prosperity of the regional economy, while the role of overseas trade was particularly prominent.

The economy of Mingzhou also relied on overseas trade to prosper. The first volume of the *Illustrated Mingzhou in the Qiandao Era* described how Mingzhou was "a secluded area, though not a metropolis, the sea routes converged there, ... and foreign ships came and went loaded with abundant goods."

Guangzhou was more dependent on overseas trade for sustained prosperity. Hong Shi of the Song mentioned in his *Anthology of Panzhou* that Guangzhou, "in south of the ridge, was widely known as a metropolis. Big merchants from Champa, Khmer, Srivijaya and Yavadvipa came by seaway with dozens of ships every year." It was a collection and distribution center for various luxury goods, such as spices, herbs, and pearl jade, so that the fiscal revenue of Guangzhou from overseas trade exceeded the total sum of military and commercial taxes in the prefectures of Quangnan.

Import trade promoted the rise of the processing industry of imported goods. In the Song, China's imports were mainly raw materials, which had to be processed before they were converted into direct consumer goods. With the large-scale import of spices, rhinoceros horns and ivory, corresponding processing industries were developed. In the Northern Song, the Wensi Courtyard and Manufacturing Bureau were established in capital Kaifeng as the processing institution of palace imports, the production

---

[111](The Song Dynasty) Wang Xiangzhi. *Records of Scenic Spots across the Country.* Vol. 130. Beijing: Zhonghua Book Company, 2012.

scale of which was so large that "thousands of craftsmen of various types worked everyday."[112] Corresponding developments also occurred in the associated private sector, leading to the emergence of a group of skilled artisans. One of the most important items of luxury goods imported from overseas was ivory, which played a beneficial role in the development of handicrafts, particularly ivory carving. The people of Song not only used ivory to make a variety of utensils, but also used it to create their world-famous ivory-carved goods.

Overseas trade directly drove the development of the import and export commodity processing industry and the prosperity of the regional coastal economy. The active domestic and foreign trade activities, the expansion of the scale of trade and the rise of ports and cities injected new vitality into the coastal economy, and changed the inherent economic structure to some extent.

(ii) Improving People's Welfare

With the development of overseas trade, fine varieties of overseas crops were introduced to China. The most important plant species introduced along the Maritime Silk Road during this period were Champa rice and cotton. The Vietnamese were known for being adept at growing rice. In ancient Chinese literature, there were records of rice originating in the Jiaozhi. During the reign of Emperor Zhenzong of the Song (r. 997–1022), drought-tolerant Champa rice seeds were introduced from the Quang Nam region of central Vietnam and planted in Fujian. In the period from 1008 to 1016, droughts occurred in the Yangtze and Huaihe river areas and Zhejiang, and the Champa rice seeds were introduced into these places. From then on, Champa rice was not only cultivated in the Fujian, the Yangtze and Huaihe river areas and Zhejiang, but also spread to northern China. The introduction of new rice seeds not only expanded the variety of Chinese crops, but more importantly, improved land utilization and greatly increased grain yields, thereby solving the food supply needs for more people. This was directly beneficial to people's lives on the one hand and provided a basis for the development of the commodity economy on the other.

As early as the Han Dynasty, cotton had been introduced into China's borderlands. From the Song Dynasty, cotton was introduced into the

---

[112](The Song Dynasty) Chen Jun. *Song Nine Dynasties Chronicles*. Vol. 29. The Copy of Complete Library in the Four Branches of Literature in Wenyuan Pavilion.

Central Plains from the bordering areas in the north and in the south. Since cotton was superior in production and processing to other raw materials of fabric, it gradually replaced silk and hemp and ascended to the leading position, thereby breaking the position where silk was the only raw material.

The introduction of rice and cotton from Champa alleviated the shortage of food and clothing for the people, and improved their basic living conditions.

Among the imported commercial goods of the Song, spices took up the biggest share. The influx of large quantities of spices was said to have perfumed the Chinese nobility. At the same time, the arrival of masses of fragrant medicines with practical value also contributed to the development of Chinese medicine and health, and the beverage and food industry, thus enriching and facilitating people's daily lives. Among them, aucklandia lappa and frankincense could be formulated into a secret recipe for treating hemiplegia and headache.[113] Plum-blossom borneol (a type of borneol) could be used to treat "excessively long tongue" syndrome.[114] Storax pills made from various aromatic drugs, such as storax, frankincense, long pepper, benzoin, and borneol, "could tonify the *qi*[115] and tranquilize blood as well as remove exogenous evil."[116] The medicinal functions of some spices were explored and utilized. This promoted the development of traditional Chinese medicine and helped to improve the health level of the people.

The increase in food and clothing together with the improvements in medication helped to lower the mortality rate among the population and

[113](The Song Dynasty) Shen Kuo, Su Shi. *Su and Shen Neihan Effective Prescription.* Vol. 2. Commented and Proofread by Song Zhenmin, Li Enjun. Beijing: Ancient Books Publishing House of Traditional Chinese Medicine, 2009.

[114](The Song Dynasty) Hong Mai. *Ghost Stories Recorded by Erudite Scholars.* Vol. 13.

[115]In traditional Chinese culture, *qi*, also ki or ch'i in Wade–Giles romanization, is believed to be a vital force forming part of any living entity. Literally meaning "vapor," "air," or "breath," the word *qi* is often translated as "vital energy," "vital force," "material energy," or simply as "energy." *qi* is the central underlying principle in Chinese traditional medicine and in Chinese martial arts. The practice of cultivating and balancing *qi* is called Qigong.

[116](The Song Dynasty) Shen Kuo, *Su Shi. Su and Shen Neihan Effective Prescription.* Vol. 2. Commented and Proofread by Song Zhenmin, Li Enjun. Beijing: Ancient Books Publishing House of Traditional Chinese Medicine, 2009.

promote an increase in the number of laborers, on the one hand;[117] and on the other, it improved the health condition of the existing population and the quality of the labor force, which contributed to the expansion of total social output.

(iii) Increasing Fiscal Revenue

With the expanding scale of overseas trade, the Song government's overseas trade income increased significantly, thus enriching the state finances. The Song Dynasty acquired the revenue through collecting import and export taxes, on the one hand, and the monopolization of luxury goods, on the other.

One of the main functions of the Maritime Trade Commission in the Song was to seize a large amount of imported goods through the *choujie*, *jinque* and *bomai*, and directly participate in marketing, so that the government could obtain profits, which was different from only imposing limited commercial tax on imported goods. *Choujie* (produce levies) meant that import duties were levied in the form of practical items; while *jinque* (monopoly) stipulated that some highly profitable commodities were prohibited from private trading and owned exclusively by the government; *bomai* (governmental purchase) meant that goods that the government required should be prioritized in purchase.

Through the above measures, the Song government benefited greatly from overseas trade every year. The *History of Song: Treatise on Food and Commodities* records that in 991, Guangzhou alone gained more than 500,000 catties[118] of fragrant medicines and treasures through the overseas trade, while the income in the Huangyou period (1049–1054) of Song was more than 530,000 thousands catties and it increased by 100,000 in the Zhiping period (1064–1067) to 630,000.[119] The second volume of the *Records of Guangzhou Customs* also features similar accounts, outlining how "the number of annually imported items, like rhinoceroses, jewelry, and fragrant medicines derived from overseas

---

[117]The population in Yuanfeng period of Emperor Song Shenzong exceeded 100 million.

[118]Catty was the counting unit of Song, reflecting that this number was the calculation result of the sum of different articles, but it is not clear whether it was the calculation of quantity or value.

[119](The Yuan Dyansty) Tuotuo. *History of Song: Treatise on Food and Commodities. Mutual Trade Shipping Law.* Vol. 186. Beijing: Zhonghua Book Company, 1977.

trade exceeded 530,000 in the Huangyou period, increased by 100,000 in the Zhiping period, and reached 2,000,000 strings in the Zhongxing period."[120] The *Comprehensive Investigations based on Literary and Documentary Sources* recorded that "in 1076, Hangzhou, Mingzhou and Guangzhou, the three Maritime Trade Commissions, collected 540,173 strings, bolts, catties, taels, sectors, bars, grains, and fragrant medicines, etc.; by the reign of Zhezong (r. 1085–1100) of the Song the income from overseas trade totaled 5 million min in the space of 12 years, or about 420,000 min per year. In the early Northern Song Dynasty, the trading department (also known as the Fragrant Medicine Department or the Fragrant Medicine Court) was set up in the capital Kaifeng. In the year 997, also the inaugural year of the trading department, the Northern Song government gained 300,000 strings in sales revenue, and the figure continued to increase subsequent to that.[121] By the time of Emperor Huizong (r. 1100–1125) of the Song government "reached 10 million in 9 years," with an average annual income of more than 1.2 million strings.

In the Southern Song Dynasty, the dependence on overseas trade taxation further increased. "When the new regime was established in the south, governmental funds were so inadequate that the government had to depend on overseas trade, which produced much revenue every year."[122] Under the more active overseas trade policy, the income from overseas trade further increased in the Southern Song. In 1159, Emperor Gaozong of the Song mentioned that "I once asked Zhang Chan the annual income of the Maritime Trade Commission. Chan told me if *choujie* (produce levies) and *bomai* were calculated by year, it would be around two million strings. So the revenue of these three departments were more than double that of the normal tax."[123] The *Miscellaneous Notes on the Court since the Jian Yan* also recorded that "at the end of Shaoxing period (1131–1162), through extraction and collection, the two

---

[120] (The Song Dynasty) Wang Yinglin. *Jade Sea: Tang Overseas Trade Envoy.* Vol. 186. The Copy of Complete Library in the Four Branches of Literature in Wenyuan Pavilion.

[121] (The Song and Yuan Dynasties) Ma Duanlin. *Comprehensive Investigations based on Literary and Documentary Sources: Official Purchase.* Vol. 20.

[122] (The Qing Dynasty) Gu Yanwu. *Benefits and Faults of Prefectorial China.* Vol. 120.

[123] (The Qing Dynasty) Xu Song. *Compendium Manuscript of Song · Officials.* Vol. 44. Beijing: Zhonghua Book Company, 1981.

Maritime Trade Commissions received annual interests of two million string of coins."[124] It could be seen that the income from overseas trade at that time was as high as two million, more than double the maximum amount obtained by the Northern Song. At the same time, the foreign trade income obtained by the government monopoly during the Southern Song was also considerable. In 1154, the total amount of taxes from alum collected from "three tax-payer places" — Hangzhou, Jiankang, and Zhenjiang — reached 109 million strings of copper coins, which mainly came from the income of imported spices.

The increase in overseas trade tax revenue could reduce the burden of farmers who were the dominant tax payers, to a certain extent, which was conducive to political stability and sustaining the people's livelihoods. Emperor Gaozong (r. 1127–1162) of the Song once pointed out clearly that "overseas trade was the most profitable. If the measures were appropriate, the income would be millions, which could win the hearts and minds of the people. Besides, in order to show his so-called benevolence and love for the people, Emperor Gaozong described his interest in the income from overseas trade, thus "I, the Emperor, paid attention to this just because it could release people's burden."[125]

(iv) Promoting Economic Exchanges between the North and South

The territory of the Northern Song was mainly confined to the south of the Yellow River. In the Southern Song Dynasty, it further retreated to the Huaihe River and even to the south of the Yangtze River. In the north, there were the Liao regime established by the Khitan and the Jin established by the Jurchen. In the northwest, there was the Western Xia founded by the Tanguts. Fierce conflicts between the Song and those northern minority regimes led to the division of China, and intermittent battles between them also destroyed the economic ties between the north and the south. But at the same time, in order to make up the shortfall in goods urgently needed by the north and the south, the two sides set up trade markets in the border area.

---

[124](The Song Dynasty) Li Xinzhuan. *Miscellaneous Notes on the Court since the Jian Yan.* Vol. 15. The Copy of Complete Library in the Four Branches of Literature in Wenyuan Pavilion.

[125](The Qing Dynasty) Xu Song. *Compendium Manuscript of Song: Officials.* Vol. 44. Beijing: Zhonghua Book Company, 1981.

In addition to the southern products, such as silk, lacquerwares and grain, the Song also traded with the Liao, the Jin, and the Western Xia with a large number of goods imported by the sea route. Right at the beginning of the Song Dynasty, the Liao set up mutual markets in Zhuozhou, Zhenwu Jun (now Huangyuan County in Qinghai Province), and Shuozhou to trade with the Song. After the Treaty of Chanyuan was signed in 1005, more markets were set up in the above-mentioned places and in Xiongzhou, Bazhou, Ansu Jun (now Xushui County in Hebei Province) and Guangxin Jun (now near Xushui County in Hebei Province) as well. The transaction amount was considerably huge. For instance, when market was resumed in 1005, the Song "exported 200,000 *guan* of spices stored in the state treasury."[126] "In 1006, the Emperor ordered that officials were allowed to conduct commercial trade as some of them did before. Traded goods expanded to silk fabrics, lacquers and japonica rices. Imported goods included silver, money, cloth, sheep, horses, and camels, so that the annual gain was more than 400,000. ... after the reign of Emperor Renzong (r. 1022–1063) and Yingzong (1063–1067) died ... the bordering trade still continued."[127]

In 1055, the Song "exported 200,000 *guan* of spices stored in the state treasury." to "trade"[128] with the Khitan in Hebei. In 1075, the Song also conducted market trade with the Liao in ivory, rhino horn, and pearls to the value of 200,000 strings of cash.[129] According to written records, the items exported by the Song to the Liao were mainly fragrant medicines, rhinoceroses, elephants and tea, and later on silks, lacquerwares, japonica and others were added. The items traded by the Liao with the Song were silver, currency, cloth, sheep, horses, camels, pearls, iron knives, lake salt and others. Among them, sheep were the major exports of the Khitan.

The market trade between the Song and the Tangut began from the setting up of trading markets in Bao'an Jun (now Zhidan County of

---

[126](The Qing Dynasty) Xu Song. *Compiled Manuscripts of Song: Economy.* 5 of No. 36. Beijing: Zhonghua Book Company, 1981.

[127](The Yuan Dynasty) Tuotuo. *History of Song: Treatise on Food and Commodities. Mutual Trade Shipping Law.* Vol. 186. Beijing: Zhonghua Book Company, 1977.

[128](The Qing Dynasty) Xu Song. *Compiled Manuscripts of the Song Dynasty: Economy.* 5 of No. 36. Beijing: Zhonghua Book Company, 1981.

[129](The Song and Yuan Dynasties) Ma Duanlin. *Comprehensive Investigations based on Literary and Documentary Sources.* Vol. 20.

Shaanxi Province) in 1007. In 1044, after the Song signed a peace treaty with the Tangut, besides restoring the Bao'an Jun trading market, the Gaoping village trading market in Zhenrong Jun (now Guyuan of Ningxia Hui Autonomous Region) was also set up. In order to seize the initiative in trade, the Song always set up marketplaces within its own territory, and unilaterally undertook the management of these institutions. In the market trade, the main official trade sphere in the Song was "exchanging silks and silk fabrics for camel, horses, cattle, sheep, jade, carpet, hay; and exchanging spices, porcelain, lacquerwares, ginger and other items for wax, musk, hairy cloth, saiga horns, sal ammoniac, bupleurum, desert cistanche, safflower, and feathers."[130]

While the South and the North coexisted in relative peace and the Northern Song traded with the Liao and the Tangut, also a number of countries in the Western Regions sometimes passed through many places to trade in the Song, "western ethnic minorities, such as Sindhu, Kingdom of Khotan, Uighurs, Huihu, Dayi, Gaochang, Kucha, Polin, despite occupying territories between the Liao and the Tangut, came frequently with loads of goods and were treated with to receptions many times."[131] The development of trade between the two sides strengthened the ties between Xinjiang and the mainland, which was beneficial to the economic development of both.

In 1115, the Jurchen established the Jin regime under the leadership of Aguda and destroyed the Liao in the same year. In 1126, the Jin waged a war of aggression against the Song. In 1127, the Northern Song perished. That same year, Zhao Gou declared himself Emperor in Yingtian Prefecture, Nanjing and rebuilt the Song Dynasty, which was known in history as the Southern Song. From then on the Jurchen waged numerous wars, trying to destroy the Southern Song. In 1141, the Song and the Jin signed a peace treaty. The Southern Song gave in and bowed to the Jin. The boundary ran from the Huaihe River midstream in the east to the Greater *San-kuan Pass* in the west. In addition, the Southern Song would send 350,000 taels of silver and 250,000 bolts (*pi*) of silk to the Jin every year as tributes, which became known as the Shaoxing Peace Treaty.

---

[130](The Yuan Dynasty) Tuotuo. *History of the Song: Treatise on Economy·Mutual Trade Shipping Law*. Vol. 186. Beijing: Zhonghua Book Company, 1977.

[131](The Yuan Yuan) Tuotuo. *History of the Song*. Vol. 485. Beijing: Zhonghua Book Company, 1977.

After the signing of the Shaoxing Peace Treaty, although the North–South peace was not really achieved, the two sides began to trade, with the main trading form being taken conducted on the trading market. The trading markets of the Southern Song were mainly located in Xuyi, Beishen Town in Chuzhou; Yangjia Village of Mopan in Huaiyin; Shuizhai Town and Huayan Town in Anfeng Jun (now the Shou County of An Hui Province); Fengjiadu in Huoqiu County; Qimao Town in Xinyang Jun (now Xinyang in Henan Province) and other places. Among them, Xuyi boasted the central market. In the mean time, the Jin regime set up trading markets in Si, Shou, Ying, Cai, Tang, Deng, Fengxiang County, Qinzhou, Gongzhou, Taozhou and Jiaoxi County of Mizhou, with Sizhou as the central locus.[132]

Although battles continued and trading markets operated sporadically, in the two centers in Xuyi and Sizhou, markets never ceased their service. Among the goods exchanged by the two parties, the main products exported by the Southern Song included tea, rice, wheat, spun silk, *qian* cloth (produced by Qianhua town, Ningdu County, Jiangxi province), silk, flex, books, cows, sappanwood and various types of fruit grown in the south, such as lychees, kumquats, and longans. In addition, imported goods, such as rhinoceroses, elephants and fragrant medicines were also shipped overseas for trading. The Jin regime mainly exported sea salt, silk, spun silk, wool, herbs, sheep and pigs to the Southern Song.

In addition, during the Northern Song Dynasty, the establishment of the Maritime Trade Commission in Banqiao Town in Mizhou also greatly facilitated economic exchanges between the North and the South. In his proposal to set up the Maritime Trade Commission in Banqiao, Fan E stated clearly that "both Mingzhou and Hangzhou traded with southern merchants, but Banqiao traded with, apart from southern merchants, merchants from northwest for silk products like silk, silk floss, thick waterproof silk, and so on."

The market trade of the Song with the northern minority regimes not only made the Song obtain the corresponding short-handed important materials, but helped in the establishment of the North–South economic ties. This, to some extent, maintained the North–South peace, and created

---

[132](The Song Dynasty) Li Xinzhuan. *Miscellaneous Notes on the Court since the Jian Yan.* Vol. 145. Beijing: Zhonghua Book Company, 1956. *Also see* (The Yuan Dynasty) Tuotuo. *History of Jin: Treatise on Food and Commodities.* Vol. 50. Beijing: Zhonghua Book Company, 1975.

a relatively stable social environment for economic development and maintaining people's livelihoods.

To sum up, the development of overseas trade during the Song had a relatively comprehensive impact on the social economy of the coastal areas of China. The expansion in the scale of import and export trade caused more people in the coastal areas to be involved in commodity exchange activities. The enlargement of the handicraft industry and commercial activities bolstered the role of non-agricultural industry in the economic structure of coastal areas, and the commodity economy tended to proceed with dynamism. Industries related to import and export trade accelerated their pace of moving forward. Therefore, an export-oriented economy emerged in some regions and industries, reflecting the leading impact of import and export trade on economic growth.

(2) The Influence of the Song Export Merchandise on Foreign Countries

In the Song Dynasty, the Chinese economy and culture occupied the leading position in the world. With the development of Sino-foreign trade, Chinese industrial products and manufacturing technologies were exported to neighboring countries and regions, which promoted the progress of their productivity.

(i) Silk

During the Song Dynasty, China's silk as the traditional export commodity was still the bulk export cargo. With the export of silk, sericulture and silk reeling technology were further spread to more distant regions. As a high-end textile, Chinese silk was very popular with people all over the world for its exquisite patterns and comfort of wearing. However, its costliness inspired other countries to master the sericulture and silkworm reeling technology and to find their own substitutes. The development of the Chinese silk trade in the Song Dynasty further accelerated the export of manufacturing technology, and silk manufacturing technology was spread to the Malay Islands in the Song. The Javanese people on the island began "sericulture and silk weaving with thin silk and silk skeins."[133] The brocading technique was introduced to the Jiaozhi during the Song Dynasty.

---

[133] (The Yuan Dynasty) Tuotuo. *History of the Song: Java*. Vol. 489. Beijing: Zhonghua Book Company, 1977.

The advances in Chinese textile satin technology in the Song Dynasty once again attracted Japanese craftsmen over for their study, through which they mastered the technique of weaving Guangdong silk and satin, and devised their own "Hakata weaving"[134] after their return to Japan.

(ii) Porcelainware

The Song Dynasty was a period of rapid development in the Chinese porcelain manufacturing industry. As porcelainware were exported to eastern and western countries, the ever-improving porcelain technology gradually spread outward. In the middle of the 11th century, Goguryeo fired Goguryeo-style glazed porcelain on the basis of imported Chinese porcelain technology. According to the *Illustrated Records of the Visit to Goguryeo during the Xuanhe Period* (1122–1123), porcelains made there "were in jadeite color and exquisitely crafted with extraordinary hues." Goguryeo-style blue porcelain was mainly influenced by the technology of the Yueyao kiln in the Song and fired in reducing flame, also known as carburizing flame. In the early 12th century, inspired by the inlaid lacquerware, Goguryeo fired the inlaid blue porcelain and made its own innovation based on imported technology.

Chinese porcelain manufacturing technology was also exported to Japan in the Song Dynasty. The Japanese Kato Shiro Saemon came to the Song with the Japanese monk Dogen in the late Southern Song era and went to the Tianmu Mountains to study pottery making for 6 years. After his returning to China, he built a kiln in Seto, Owari, specializing in the manufacture of "Seto-yaki," dark brown and yellow-glazed porcelain with the Song style, thus opening a new era[135] of Japanese ceramics technology.

During the excavations of the Angkor Palace ruins in the modern-day Cambodia, many pieces of Chinese porcelain from the Song, Yuan, and early Ming Dynasties were found. At the same time, the porcelain discovered at Phnom Kulen bore the characteristics of Guangxi's Xicun kiln.

---

[134] Yan Yong. *The Ancient Sino-Japanese Silk Culture Exchange and the Development of Japanese Fabrics.* Archaeology and Cultural Relics, 2004 (1).

[135] (Japan) Yasuhiko Kimiya. *Nikka bunka kōryūshi* 日華文化交流史. Fuzanbō, 1955.

In the Song Dynasty, Myanmar was called Bagan, and among the cultural relics unearthed there, there were a pair of duck-shaped ceramic water holders[136] used by the Chinese literati.

The products of the Jingdezhen kiln and the Cizhou kiln were also unearthed in Quang Yen, Bac Ninh and Thanh Hoa in the modern-day Vietnam. Vietnam introduced Chinese porcelain manufacturing technology, and its monochrome porcelain was deeply influenced by the Song porcelain.

The delicate and unique porcelain of the Song Dynasty, especially its daily ware, also flowed into the ancient countries of the Malay Islands and played an important role in changing their humble dining habits. At that time, owing to the backward economy and a shortage in daily utensils, no tableware was available in this region. The *Records of Foreign Countries* written by the Southern Song geographer Zhao Rushi observed that in the Lamuri Kingdom (presently Banda Aceh, Sumatra), people "grab rice by hand"; in Sugitan State (in present central Java), "people didn't use utensils but leaves to eat and drink and discard them afterwards." So they had a very urgent demand for the daily porcelain of the Song, which were not only imported in large numbers as tableware, but also taken as wine sets, components of a dowry, funeral utensils, and signs of wealth at the same time. The quantity of Chinese porcelain unearthed in the Philippines ranked first in Southeast Asia, and many native households also treasured ancient Chinese ceramics.

Many different kinds of Song porcelain were unearthed in the ruined port of Bampol, not far from Karachi, Pakistan. Among them, there were fragments of wire-engraved Yueyao kiln porcelain dating from the early Song, pieces of southern China white porcelain covered with lotus petals, and also fragments of Longquan glazed porcelain from the late Song and the early Yuan. In the ruins of Blaf Minabad, northeast of Hyderabad, capital of the Sindh Province, blue porcelain, white porcelain and brown-glazed ceramic pieces of the early Song Dynasty were unearthed.

At the Mysore Museum in India blue porcelain pieces from the Longquan kiln and white porcelain pieces from Fujian and Guangdong were discovered. In the remains of Arika Meidu Village, south of Pondicherry City, South India, there were complete and exquisite

---

[136] Du Shenggao. *Chinese Antiquities in Pugan* [J]. Journal of Myanmar.1912, 1 (2); Zhou Yiliang. *History of Sino-foreign Cultural Exchanges* [M]. Zhengzhou: Henan People's Publishing House, 1987.

high-end glazed porcelain bowls produced by the Longquan kiln of the Southern Song; and ceramic pieces of the Song were unearthed in Pondicherry, India.

Around the *stupa* in Dekama Village, south of Kagora Town, Sri Lanka, many pieces of the Song porcelain were found, including pieces of fine glazed porcelain bowls from the Longquan kiln in the Southern Song.

Glazed porcelain and greenish white porcelain of the Song Dynasty were also found in the Shari Daknus ruins near the Harilu Valley in the interior of Iran.

Buried specimens of the Song porcelain were found on the Southern, Eastern and Northern shores of the Arabian Peninsula as well.

The Song's Longquan kiln blue porcelain was excavated in northern Zaharan, near the border with Saudi Arabia. In the ruins of Abyan, not far from the port of Aden, Song porcelain relics were also uncovered.

In addition, remnants of the Longquan kiln glazed porcelain bowls and the Dehua kiln white porcelain of the Song were found in the ruins of Baalbek in Lebanon and Hama in Syria.

Glazed porcelain, greenish white porcelain and white porcelain of the Song Dynasty were also unearthed at the Samara ruins north of Baghdad, Iraq.

Ancient Egypt originally had its own ceramics industry. In the Song Dynasty, with the rapid development of trade between China and the Arabian region, Egypt introduced Chinese porcelain-making technology, which made its porcelain manufacturing industry develop rapidly. The famous blue porcelain from the Longquan kiln, glazed porcelain, white porcelain and greenish white porcelain fired in the Fujian and Guangdong kilns, greenish white porcelain and white porcelain from the Jingdezhen kiln, white porcelain from the Dehua kiln and white porcelain from the Ding kiln school of northern China all dating from the Song Dynasty were found in Egypt. After the 11th century, myriad imitations of blue porcelain, greenish white porcelain and blue and white porcelain appeared in Egypt.

(iii) Coins

Since the foreign trade revenue and the government monopoly income mainly came from imports during the Song Dynasty, encouraging overseas trade served to develop imports. With the import of myriad spices and herbs, not only a large number of Chinese silks and porcelains were exported to foreign lands, but Chinese copper coins also flowed to many trading partners as a global hard currency. The outward flow of copper coins was different from the international payments deficit caused by trade deficit. During the Song, since the currency economies of neighboring Japan and Southeast Asian countries were underdeveloped and their technology for coinage was backward, Chinese copper coins with their defined casting, high credit ratings, and relatively stable value which could serve as both general equivalents and important commodities were "wanted by all overseas Southeast Asian countries." The Japanese scholar Fujisuke Nosuke thought that Japan at that time was "drawn into the vortex of the vast sea of the Song's monetary economy" for "the reliable coins of the Song were used as an effective currency, and finally developed into an indispensable currency to be reused."[137]

However, China had no absolute advantage in copper coin casting resources. The enlargement in import scale led to the shortage of copper coins in the domestic market, so the Song government had to restrict the export of copper coins. However, the strong overseas demand for copper coins made their export hugely profitable, so Chinese and foreign merchants often ignored the ban of the Song and "secretly carried coins for the purpose of exchange." "People who went abroad only traded with copper coins and foreign goods only sold for copper coins."[138] As a result, the smuggling of copper coins reached an acute situation. In July, 1242, the number of Japanese coins exported to the Song in one sailing reached up to 100,000 strings or *guan*.

Through envoys, trade and merchant smuggling, Chinese coins poured into Japan, Southeast Asia, South Asia, West Asia and Africa. At the Archaeological Museum of Mysore, India, the "Yuanfeng Tongbao" coins minted during the period 1068–1085 were unearthed from the Chandravalli ruins.

The "Xuanhe Tongbao" coins made during the period of 1119–1125 were unearthed in the ruins of Arika Medu village, south of Pondicherry, South India.

As many as 1,352 Song bronze coins were found in the ruins of the city of Yapahuwa, south of Anuradhapura in northern Sri Lanka.

Copper coins were also unearthed in Kalatun, on the other side of the Hormuz Island in the Persian Gulf; in Katif, near the Dhahran in Saudi Arabia, the "Xianping Tongbao" coins minted during the period

---

[137](Japan) Fujiie Reinosuke. *Two Thousand Years of Exchanges between Japan and China* [M]. Beijing: Peking University Press, 1982.

[138](The Qing Dynasty) Xu Song. *Compiled Manuscripts of Song Dynasty: Criminal Law* [M]. 144 of No. 2. Beijing: Zhonghua Book Company, 1981.

998–1003 and the "Shaoxing Tongbao" coins minted during the period 1094–1098 were also unearthed.

"Qingyuan Tongbao" coins minted during the period 1195–1200 and "Shaoding Tongbao" coins minted during the period 1228–1233 were excavated among the ruins of Godi Town in northern Mombasa, Kenya, along the east African coast. Song coins were also found in Mogadishu in Somalia and Zanzibar in Tanzania.[139]

The influx of Chinese coins promoted the development of the local currency economy, and Chinese coin casting technology was gradually exported. For example, when Chinese copper coins were discovered in Java and other places, many local copper coins and tin coins from the 9th to 16th centuries (mainly during the Majapahit era) were also discovered. Most of these ancient coins were round in shape with square holes in the center, apparently influenced by Chinese coinage technology. Korea produced copper, but was not adept at casting. During the Song Dynasty, the country imported a large number of Chinese copper coins, then imitated them and made "Haidong Tongbao" coins and "Sanhan Chongbao" coins of the Korean Style.

(iv) Books
During the Song Dynasty, the popularization of woodblock printing technique and the invention of movable type printing technology made the Chinese book printing industry develop significantly. Among them, Hangzhou in Zhejiang, Chengdu in Sichuan, and Fujian became the centers of the printing industry. As important cultural products, books not only circulated domestically, but also entered overseas markets through envoys and merchants. Countries, such as North Korea, Japan, and Cochin, which had long been influenced by Chinese culture were in great need of various Chinese classics. For example, when the Song government sent envoys to Goguryeo, they went with various books as tributes. These included the *Finest Blossoms in the Garden of Literature*, the *Imperial Readings of the Taiping Era*, the *Divine Medicine Remedy*, and the *Buddhist Sutras*. Envoys from various countries also often asked for Chinese books. For example, the King of Goguryeo once asked for "bestowing Nine Classics."[140]

---

[139] (Japan) Mikami Tsugio. *Porcelain Road* [M]. Trans. Li Xijing, Gao Ximei. Beijing: Cultural Relics Publishing House. 1984.

[140] (The Song Dynasty) Jiang Shaoyu. *The Categorical List of Historical Facts in Song Dynasty*. Vol. 77. Shanghai: Shanghai Ancient Books Publishing House, 1981.

It was also normal for merchants to ship in books. For example, in 1027, the Song merchant named Li Wentong shipped 597 volumes of books to Goguryeo. It is recorded that the King of Goguryeo "would clean clothes and burn incense before merchants came with books."[141] Merchants in the Song not only transported a large number of books in outbound maritime trade, but even directly carried the carved versions. Su Shi once mentioned that there was a merchant named Xu Jian who shipped to Goguryeo "books carved on more than 2,900 pieces of plates."[142] The exchange of numerous books played a positive role in the cultural development of countries.

Chinese books also flowed into Japan in huge quantities. In 1029, merchants of Song publicly sold the *Collections of Poems*, the *Anthology of Bai* and other books in Japanese markets. Among all the books imported from China to Japan during the Song Dynasty, Buddhist Sutras occupied an important share, which was recorded in many documents. For instance, in 984, a Japanese monk "asked for a photo copy of the *Tripitaka* and the Emperor decreed to meet the demand."[143]

Since the export in books was so large in the Tang Dynasty when Chinese books continued to enter countries such as North Korea and Japan, in the Song, some versions of books that had been lost in China flowed back into China from these two countries, thereby promoting the continued inheritance of Chinese culture.

(v) Medicine

In the Song Dynasty, rich knowledge and practical techniques of Traditional Chinese Medicine were accumulated. Owing to frequent trade contacts, countries like Korea, Japan and Cochin introduced Traditional Chinese Medicine to their countries through various channels. The *History of Song: Goguryeo* stated that Goguryeo "originally had no knowledge of herbs. Since King Wang Yu (1079–1122) came to seek medical treatment, there have been masters of it." The Song constantly

---

[141] (The Yuan Dynasty) Tuotuo. *History of the Song: The History Biography of Goguryeo.* Vol. 487. Beijing: Zhonghua Book Company, 1977.

[142] *The Complete Works of Su Tungpo.* Vol. 58. The Copy of Complete Library in the Four Branches of Literature in Wenyuan Pavilion.

[143] (The Yuan Dynasty) Tuotuo. *History of the Song: The History of Japan.* Vol. 491. Beijing: Zhonghua Book Company, 1977.

sent doctors to Goguryeo for medical treatment and medical teaching. In 1072, the medical officers Wang Yu and Xu Xian were sent to Goguryeo; in 1074, another eight people, including the Yangzhou medical assistant Ma Shi'an, were dispatched to Korea, where they were all respected and warmly received by the King of Goguryeo. In 1080, the Song sent Ma Shi'an to Korea again, and the King of Goguryeo not only treated him with banquets, but also gave him gifts. At the invitation of the King of Goguryeo, the Song also dispatched a medical delegation, including medical officials of the Imperial Academy, to Goguryeo with Chinese medicines to treat the king who was very sick. Japanese monks who entered the Song on merchant ships also brought Chinese medical technologies back to Japan.

5.4.2 *The Influence of Foreign Trade on Cultural Communication*

(1) Overseas Trade and China's Science and Technology Transmission
(i) Paper-Making Technology
Prior to the Song Dynasty, Chinese paper and paper-making technology had been widely spread. In the Song Dynasty, some countries that had mastered Chinese paper making in the early days made their own innovations in technology, and their products began to be sold back to China. For example, paper imported to China from Goguryeo was highly praised by the people of Song. A Southern Song subject named Chen You stated in the *Anthology of Chen You* that "Goguryeo paper was like Sichuan gold-dusted paper, solid and lustrous." Scholars in the Song often used Korean paper as gifts to each other, especially Korean paper fans, which were superior to Chinese round silk fans and feather fans, and were loved by the people of Song. Japanese paper was also imported into China during this period and was well reputed.

During the Song Dynasty, Morocco in North Africa became the paper-making center of the Arab world, from which paper-making technology was further introduced into Spain, thus initiating the history of European paper making. Subsequently, paper-making technology was gradually introduced from Spain to Western European countries, such as France. During the late Southern Song Dynasty, paper-making technology passed from Egypt to Italy via the Mediterranean.

(ii) Printing

In the 11th century, in the middle of the Northern Song Dynasty, there was a fresh leap forward in Chinese printing. During the period of 1041–1048, Bi Sheng invented the movable-type printing, which became the starting point of typographic printing, 400 years earlier than the time the German Gutenberg printed the *Bible* with movable type. In the Southern Song Dynasty, on the basis of Bi Sheng's movable clay type printing, Korea invented movable metal type printing during the period of 1234–1241.

In the Southern Song Dynasty, Chinese printing promoted the development of the printing industry in Vietnam. Probably during the years of 1241–1258, the first printed work in Vietnamese history, the Hukou Post, came out. From the late Southern Song to the early Yuan, the block printing invented in the Tang was spread to Iran. Later, it was passed on from Iran to Europe.

The spread of printing drove the cultural dissemination and progress of civilization in the countries and regions concerned, with mutual influence encouraging constant innovation.

(iii) The Compass

As early as the Warring States Period, the "Si Nan compass" employing natural magnets was invented in China. In 1044, the "compass fish" produced by artificial magnetization appeared. In 1063, the Northern Song scientist Shen Kuo also expounded the steel needle magnetization method in the *Dream Pool Essays*. It stated that "the Fang's ground the blade of a knife with a magnet and then the knife could point to south, though always pointing slightly to east, not totally south."[144] Shen Kuo also introduced four ways to install a compass. From the perspective of navigation, the water float needle was the most simple and practical method. At the beginning of the 12th century, the end of the Southern Song Dynasty, the people of the Song had already used the compass for navigation. By the time of the Southern Song, the water float needle had evolved into the floating magnetic compass, or the dial indicator. At the end of the 12th century and the beginning of the 13th century, the use of the compass needle was introduced to Persia and Arabia by sea, and then to Europe. The application of the compass to navigation not only promoted the progress of sea exploration in China and the world, but also

---

[144](The Song Dynasty) Shen Kuo. *Dream Pool Essays*. Vol. 24. The Copy of *Siku Quanshu* in Wenyuan Pavilion.

propelled Columbus's discovery of the American continent and the completion of Magellan's voyage around the world, which greatly accelerated the course of world history.

(2) Foreign Trade and the Introduction of Islam to China
Foreign trade ports, such as Guangzhou and Quanzhou, were the windows of opening-up during the Song. With the influx of foreign merchants and Chinese merchants going abroad, especially many foreign merchants residing in China, Islam was brought into China by Arab merchants and took root in China under the Song's policy of respecting and protecting foreign customs and interests.

In the Song Dynasty, large numbers of Arab merchants who engaged in Sino-Arab trade made vast profits and accumulated great wealth. Many people moved to coastal areas of China, such as Guangzhou and Quanzhou. They successively built mosques in their residences. For example, in 1009, Arab merchants built the first mosque, "Masjid al-Ashab" in Quanzhou. And in 1131, they also built the Qingjing Mosque, and later the Yemen Mosque. As more and more Arab Muslims traded in and migrated to China, they constructed more monasteries with more religious practices, which promoted the spread and development of Islam in China.

To sum up, on the one hand, the Song Dynasty witnessed rapid social and economic development, advanced science and technology, unprecedented improvement in shipbuilding and navigation, and strong material foundations for developing foreign trade, especially overseas trade; on the other hand, the northern ethnic disputes exerted a heavy financial burden on the Song government, and the broad financial resources became the foundation of regime consolidation. Overseas trade could alleviate the financial crisis to a certain extent, thus gaining unprecedented attention. In the early Northern Song, the governor once sent envoys to engage in overseas trade, and took the opportunity to attract foreign countries to trade in China. At the same time, various channels, such as politics and economy were also used, and the preference for foreign merchants was much stronger than that of the Han and Tang Dynasties, thereby bringing the opening-up of China to a new height in this period.

However, the opening-up in this period still had its limitations. Based on the fiscal and luxury consumption demands of the upper society, the Song pursued a policy of opening-up and developing overseas trade.

While under the natural economy, the degree of social and economic development dependence on the outside was very low. Therefore, it was only limited openness. Foreign trade could not develop freely and had to be practiced under the control of the government. When the free development of private foreign trade failed to meet the goal of maximizing the government's interests, the government often adopted various methods of intervention, such as implementing state monopoly or preferential procurement of high-profit commodities. In order to prevent smuggling and ensure taxation, the Song restricted private overseas trade in ports with the setting up of the Maritime Trade Commission. Meanwhile, foreign trade was used as a political diplomacy from time to time. For instance, the northern minority regimes had greater dependence on the advanced agricultural economy of the Song Dynasty, so the Song government often resorted to stopping and banning trade with ethnic minority regimes and punishment for their constant border plundering. This was its method of bringing the rebels to heel.

Chapter 6

Foreign Trade in the Yuan Dynasty

From the 11th to the 12th century, the Mongol tribes, who wandered as nomads to the north of the Yinshan Mountains, the west of the Xing'an Mountains and the east of the Altai Mountains gradually grew in power. At the beginning of the 13th century, Temujin of the tribe of Borjigin unified all the Mongol tribes and established the Grand Mongol Empire in 1206, so he was honored with the title Genghis Khan or Strong Ruler.

After the founding of the Grand Mongol Empire, Genghis Khan pioneered a series of measures to construct a regime, including establishing the authority of the autocratic Khanate, setting up administrative organizations from the Khanate Court to local areas, reforming the standing army, and the formulation of laws and so on. From Genghis Khan to Cuy kaan and to Mongon kaan, all parties were open to recruiting talents from every ethnic group to carry out regime construction, develop the economy, and improve and consolidate the Mongol regime. At the same time, wars of conquest and expansion were waged constantly with the outside world in the hope of expanding the area ruled by the Grand Mongol Empire.

In 1260, Kublai Khan, also known as Emperor Shizu of the Yuan, ascended to the throne. He changed the name of his Empire from the "Grand Mongol Empire" to the "Yuan" in 1271. In 1279, as the Southern Song Dynasty was perished, a unified, multi-ethnic new feudal dynasty with an unprecedentedly vast territory was finally established.

Created by dint of military conquest, the Yuan was much stronger than the Song in terms of comprehensive national strength. The Mongolian army's missions from Mobei (the vast area of the desert and Gobi in northern China) to Jiangnan, and from China proper to Central Asia,

West Asia and Europe, created an empire on a scale that had never been seen before, and with smooth logistical links, and it also broadened the horizons of the Mongolian nobility and sharply roused their appetite for all kinds of exotic foreign goods.

With the disintegration of the Grand Mongol Empire, the rulers of the Yuan realized that the stability of the Empire could not be maintained and the foundations of its rule couldn't be consolidated by force. Rather it could only achieve those feats by virtue of accepting an advanced culture and developing its economy. With the development of the transportation between China and foreign countries, foreign trade in the Yuan Dynasty, especially of the maritime kind, flourished to a high level, and the economic and cultural exchanges between China and foreign countries reached a new height.

6.1 The Economic Development and Advancement in the Shipbuilding and Seafaring Industries

During the Yuan Dynasty, China's economy was further developed. The creation of traffic roads, the upgrading of service facilities, and the advancement of shipbuilding and seafaring further improved transportation conditions and laid a more solid material foundation for the development of foreign trade.

6.1.1 *Socio-Economic Recovery and Development*

At the beginning of the 13th century, Genghis Khan launched an expedition westward and southward from the Mobei. In the decades before and after the war, people suffered grievously as farmland was destroyed, craftsmen were kidnapped, and the population was displaced. Meanwhile, the Mongolians with their nomadic tradition also occupied a large area of cultivated land as pasturage, bringing about serious damage to agriculture and the handicraft industry.

In 1260, Kublai Khan ascended to the throne. The economy at that time was extremely depressed, especially in Henan, Hebei, Shandong and other places in the Yellow River Basin. Here were seen scenes of devastation with vast tracts of deserted land and a sparse population. This left the

Yuan Dynasty with no choice but to restore and develop social productivity as a means of consolidating its rule.

Therefore, Kublai Khan issued an edict stating that "a country is based on its civilians while civilians live on food grown through agriculture," and adopted the advanced political and economic system of the Central Plains to restore and develop the economy.

The top priority was to restore and further agriculture at that time. Therefore, the Court of the Yuan Dynasty adopted a series of measures which emphasized farming. The first one was to set up a National Granary as an agricultural management organization in 1270 to encourage people to engage in agriculture. The National Granary would send an Agricultural Development Commissioner all over the country to pacify and unite refugees and rectify the household registration system.

The second step was promulgating laws and regulations via several rounds to protect and develop agricultural production. For example, Kublai Khan issued multiple edicts to prohibit people's cultivated land being seized as pasturage, and to ban marquesses and nobles from trampling fields for hunting. In 1307, he "reiterated the prohibition, and that those who worked hard at agriculture would be rewarded while those who were lazy would be punished"; in 1271, the Emperor "ordered the Department of State Affairs to carry out a national census, promulgate regulations and notify the whole nation about them."[1] He rectified the household registration system on a large scale, and helped those who were illegally held as slaves by the families of marquesses, nobles and powerful clans to escape bondage and gave them the status of being ordinary citizens with proper household registration.

The third step was to build State Farms and encourage the reclamation of wasteland. In 1288, the new rule stipulated that "hands should be recruited to cultivate wasteland and the government's public land in Jiangnan. Those laborers will be exempted from three years' corvee and one-third of their taxes will be remitted."[2]

The fourth step was to establish the Directorates of Waterways and the Office of Rivers and Canals, to build water conservancy systems and repair and construct plenty of irrigation projects to expand the irrigated areas.

---

[1](The Ming Dynasty) Song Lian *et al. History of Yuan: Emperor Shizu*. Vol. 7. Beijing: Zhonghua Book Company, 1976.
[2]*Ibid.*, Vol. 15.

The fifth step was to actively promote advanced agricultural production technology. The Yuan government assigned people to collect ancient and modern agricultural books and edited together many practical measures into a new compendium titled The *Fundamentals of Agriculture and Sericulture*, which was promoted all over the country. In addition, a relatively loose tax policy and a series of agricultural policies were implemented, which created favorable objective conditions for the rapid recovery and development of agriculture.

In the reign of Kublai Khan, the social economy gradually recovered, and the situation of "burgeoning population and wasteland being cultivated" appeared. The economic development of border areas yielded remarkable fruits. For example, in the area around Helin in Mongolia, land reclamation brought about a large increase in grain output, making "grains cheap in price, administration in the bordering areas in order," the society became so stable that "no land was idle; everyone worked hard; and the land was fertile" in areas of today's Yunnan Province.

The cotton textile industry was an emerging handicraft in the Yuan Dynasty. Cotton cloth was remarkably advantageous as a material for clothing because of its simple production process and relatively low cost. Wang Zhen, an agronomist of the Yuan Dynasty, wrote in his *Book of Agriculture* that "compared with silk, cotton cloth requires no leaves from mulberry trees to be picked, no silkworms to be bred, no reeling and weaving, but still serves the purpose of keeping people warm." Therefore, the planted area of cotton expanded constantly from its introduction in the Song Dynasty. In 1289, the Yuan government set up Cotton Supervisorates in today's eastern Zhejiang, Jiangnan, Jiangdong, Hunan, Hubei, Guangdong, Guangxi, Fujian and other places to promote cotton production, and make cotton tax an official item of levy for the Yuan Dynasty. Later, the Yuan government added a stipulation saying that local tax should be paid in the form of cotton cloth in some southern areas.

During 1295–1296, Huang Daopo, who was proficient in making cotton textiles, returned from Yazhou (present-day Hainan) to Wunijing, Songjiang (to the southwest of Shanghai's old urban district), and brought back cotton textile technology from Hainan. Her skills included how to assemble the cotton gin (an old-fashioned Chinese cotton seed rolling mill), and how to make a pedal spinning wheel with three spindles and a cotton fluffer. She "span and wove 'Yazhou Bedding' for her family. She also taught other housewives the method of conducting the trade tirelessly. Before long, the fame of 'Wunijing Bedding' spread far and wide so that over thousands of households made a living from the trade."[3] "Songjiang Cloth" was sold all over the world. Songjiang thus became the center for the national cotton textile industry, which boosted the development of the national cotton textile industry.

The silk industry remained important in the Yuan Dynasty. In the wars of conquest, the Mongolian army captured and plundered a large number of silk weavers. Mongolian rulers set up many bureaus and institutes related to the handicraft industry in their occupied areas and ordered craftsmen to engage in weaving. After the unification of the whole country, the state-owned handicraft bureaus and factories, which existed on an unprecedentedly large scale, spread almost all over the bigger and medium-sized cities nationwide. Excellent craftsmen working together at the same venues accelerated the advancement of technology. Silk fabric produced in the bureaus and factories were characterized by their high yield, rich varieties of colors, and exquisite textures.

The civilian silk weaving industry developed widely in places, too. In addition to being a household sideline, specialized handicraft workshops gradually emerged. For example, in Chengdu City, "thousands of households lit up at night with the sound of looms filling the whole city."[4] In the late Yuan Dynasty, Xu Yikui described the production status of the silk workshop in Xianganli of Hangzhou in his book the *Antithesis Poem on Weavers*. He wrote of how "four or five looms were arranged from north to south; over ten weavers were at work, swift at hand-lifting and foot-pedaling, but retaining their composure." When Marco Polo was in China, he witnessed the grand scene of producing silk in central and southern China. For instance, in the villages near Chengdu, "a variety of silk fabrics were produced." Shaanxi residents wove "all kinds of brocade and silk." In Dongping, Shandong, "the yield of silk was incredible." Most of the residents in Kaifeng, Henan and Baoying, Suzhou, Wuxing and Wujiang and other places in Jiangsu "owned plenty of silk and made a living from the silk business," and were engaged in producing all kinds of

---

[3](The Ming Dynasty) Tao Zongyi. *Retirement to the Countryside*. Vol. 24. The third edition of Collectanea of the Four Categories; (The Yuan Dynasty) Wang Feng. *Wuxi Collection*.

[4](The Yuan Dynasty) Dai Liang. *Singing Praising Song to Send Prefect Ma off.*

brocade and silk. In the Yuan Dynasty, professional weaving households continued to develop, with silk production centers to be found especially in areas of Jiangnan, like Suzhou, Huzhou, Hangzhou, Changzhou and Songjiang. Numerous weaving households were engaged in the trade, among which over 300 were found in Dantu County (in today's Zhenjiang, Jiangsu Province) alone.

The development of the silk industry increased the supply of products. Simultaneous with the development of the cotton textile industry, the consumption of silk fabrics was superseded by cotton fabrics and domestic demand for them declined, thus enabling more silk fabrics to enter the overseas market.

The porcelain industry of the Yuan Dynasty continued to develop on the basis of the Song Dynasty. The migration of a large number of craftsmen transformed Jingdezhen in Jiangxi into a major porcelain manufacturing center. At the same time, the Yuan government set up the Fuliang Porcelain Bureau in Jingdezhen to manage the production of the porcelain. Volume 88 of the *History of Yuan* records that "the Fuliang Porcelain Bureau, headed by officials ranked ninth in the administrative hierarchy, was set up in 1275 to take charge of porcelain production." During the Taiding period (1324–1327), the Fuliang Porcelain Bureau was replaced by the Taxation Bureau, an organization set up by the central government of the Yuan to collect taxes on porcelain kilns in Jingdezhen. This shows that the development of the porcelain production had reached a fairly high level, that government supervision was not absolutely crucial to promoting production, and that the government could gain more benefits from the trade. The porcelain of Jingdezhen also represented the summit of the ceramics manufacturing industry in this period. On the one hand, in this small town which covered an area of barely ten square miles, there were about 200 or 300 porcelain kilns on a considerable scale and hundreds of thousands of craftsmen. The concentration of porcelain kilns produced a significant agglomeration effect and accelerated the development of the technology. In this period, the porcelain made in Jingdezhen was rich in variety, especially the blue and white porcelain, and the technology for refining and firing its glazes gained in maturation.

The smelting industry developed afresh on the basis of the Song Dynasty. The mushrooming of the handicraft industry extricated some farmers from agriculture, and a number of them flowed into the cities, resulting in a decrease in the agricultural population and an increase in the non-agricultural population, thereby fueling the demand for grain in commodities and stimulating the development of commercial agriculture.

Beginning from the Tang and Song Dynasties, China's economic center gradually migrated towards the South. After the Yuan Dynasty overthrew the Southern Song Dynasty and unified the whole country, economic exchanges between the North and the South were further expanded. As the political center of the whole country, Dadu (known in the west as Khanbaliq, present-day Beijing) of the Yuan Dynasty "was extremely far away from the southern regions of the Yangtze River, but numerous government officials, guards and people here were reliant on regions south of the Yangtze River for supplies."[5] The Yuan government decided to dig through the Grand Canal that connected the North and the South, so Guo Shoujing was appointed as an officer of Directorates of Waterways to build the Tonghui River from Tongzhou to the capital Dadu, which would connect the four major basins of the Yellow River, the Huaihe River, the Yangtze River and the Qiantang River, creating favorable conditions for the development of North–South transportation and national material exchange, and promoting the vitality of the domestic commodity economy.

6.1.2 *The Development of the Shipbuilding and Seafaring Industries*

The shipbuilding industry in the Yuan Dynasty continued to develop with shipbuilding bases scattered all over Zhigu, Linqing, Dengzhou, Jiankang (Nanjing), Yangzhou, Hangzhou, Quanzhou, Fuzhou, Ganzhou, Longxing (Nanchang), Chaozhou and Guangzhou, etc. A considerable number of ships were built, for example, in 1273, "Liu Zheng requested that the Court recruit 50,000 or 60,000 sailors to build 2,000 ships in Guangzhou, Yangzhou, Bianliang, etc."[6] In September, 1282, Kublai Khan ordered the construction of "3,000 ships in Pingluan … Yangzhou, Longxing and Quanzhou."[7]

---

[5](The Yuan Dynasty) Wei Su. *Records of Maritime Transport of the Yuan Dynasty.*
[6](The Ming Dynasty) Song Lian *et al. History of Yuan: Annals of Emperor Shizu.* Vol. 8. Beijing: Zhonghua Book Company, 1976.
[7](The Qing Dynasty) Bi Yuan. A *Sequel to Comprehensive Mirror to Aid in Government.* Vol. 186.

Ships built in this period were not only large in number, but also had a great deadweight capacity. *The Travels of Marco Polo* recorded that "Khan ordered the fitting out of 14 ships, each with four masts and nine sails." "At least 4 or 5 of them could accommodate a crew of up to 250 or 260." Ibn Battuta, a Moroccan who traveled to the East from the 1420s to the 1440s, gave a detailed description of Quanzhou's shipbuilding industry, stating that "a large ship had ten or at least three sails, woven with mat-shaped rattan scales. The sails would not be hung down no matter when the sails were arranged to suit the wind or when the ships were anchoring. Every big ship can be loaded with a thousand men... Such huge ships were only built in China's Caiton (present-day Quanzhou), or in Guangzhou. Those ships were equipped with four layers of decks, and room cabins, official cabins and merchant cabins inside."[8] Generally, the deadweight capacity of oceangoing merchant ships reached hundreds of tons.

The Yuan Dynasty also actively supported the Quanzhou shipbuilding industry through its policies. Quanzhou, known as the largest port in the Eastern China, was connected inextricably to the advanced shipbuilding industry at that time. Shipbuilding was the main economic industry in Quanzhou. In 1283, the Yuan Dynasty issued extraordinarily favorable regulations on stevedores, which greatly stimulated the development of shipbuilding industry in Quanzhou. Quanzhou port took the lead globally in terms of shipbuilding technology, shipping equipment and voyage performance. In its heyday, there were as many as 15,000 ships. The huge fleet was unmatched by other ports at home and abroad. Ibn Battuta witnessed that some Chinese owned many ships, so he felt that there was nobody richer in the world than the Chinese.

The compass, which was invented in the Song Dynasty, became a necessary piece of equipment for ocean-faring merchants in the Yuan Dynasty. *A Record of Cambodia: The Land and Its People* written by Zhou Daguan of the Yuan Dynasty recorded his use of a 48-position mariner compass in his ocean trip from Wenzhou to Angkor Thom in detail. When his ship set sail from Wenzhou, the mariner took a phonograph needle management of Ding-wei placement, which is equivalent to 22.5 degree SW. After they arrived at Baria, the mariner took "Kun-shen needle," or 52.5 degree SW.

In the Yuan Dynasty, people were more adept at making use of the variations in monsoons. They "set sail southward by the north wind in the

---

[8] [Morocco] Ibn Battuta. *The Travels of Ibn Battutah* [M]. Pantianos Classics, 1929.

winter" to the South China Sea, and then "sailed back by the north wind in the next summer." Traveling to the Koryo in the north they would set sail in summer by the south wind, and return in winter by the north wind, which took only three or five days if sailing downwind. Traveling to Japan they usually set sail in summer by the southwest monsoon, and returned in the spring and autumn by the northeast monsoon. The voyage would take about 10 days if sailing downwind.

After the reunification of the whole county, the recovery and development of agriculture and the handicraft industry laid an economic foundation for foreign trade, and the advancement of shipbuilding and seafaring technologies provided technical support for the development of overseas trade.

6.1.3 *The Recovery and Development of Overland Transportation*

The importance of the Maritime Silk Road declined from the late Tang Dynasty period. In the Song Dynasty, ethnic disputes in the North made it far weaker. In the first half of the 13th century, the Mongols rose in the Mobei. Under the leadership of Genghis Khan, the Mongolian army launched several large-scale wars in Asia and Europe, especially the three western expeditions which opened the road connecting with Asia and Europe and established four khanates in there.

Among them, the Chagatai Khanate boasted a territory extending east to west from Turpan and Lop Nur to the Amu Darya River and south to north from the Hindu Kush Mountains to Tarbagatai Mountains when it was at its peak.

The territory of the Kipchak Khanate stretched from the Irtysh River in the east to the River Danube in the west, from the Balkhash Lake in the south to the Caspian Sea and the Black Sea to the Arctic in the north, setting up its capital Sarai near Astrakhan in Russia.

The Ilkhanate ruled from the Amu Darya and Indus River in the east to Asia Minor in the west, and from Persian Gulf in the south to the Caucasuses in the north.

The territory of the Ogodai Khanate was mainly located in the upper reaches of the Irtysh River and the east area of the Balkhash Lake, with its capital set in the Omyl (now Emin County, Xinjiang). The Mongolian army not only conquered numerous regions in vast areas of Asia and

Europe, but also initiated a new phase of communication between China and the west.

After the establishment of the Yuan Dynasty, the Yuan armies took control of Lin'an (now Hangzhou), the capital of the Southern Song Dynasty, in 1276, achieving another great historical unification of China since the Five Dynasties and Ten States period (907–960). Thus, a unified country ruled by the ethnic minorities was established.

The Yuan Dynasty and the four khanates constituted the Great Mongol Empire, extending from Asia to Europe. On account of the vast territory of the Empire, Genghis Khan began to build post stations to ease communications between the local and central government. The post station was not only responsible for transmitting information, but also served as the artery for business transportation providing convenient accommodation and supplies for merchants owing to the prosperity of East–West trade. After the establishment of the Yuan Dynasty, the construction of transportation facilities along the Silk Road was continuously strengthened with post stations set up along with the services of post horses, food and accommodation increasingly improved.

The post stations of the Yuan Dynasty came in great variety, including water post stations, horse stations, overland post stations, seaway stations and dog stations. Among these, the overland post stations played an important role in protecting and promoting the development of overland trade. Post stations could ensure the security of personnel and property, and provided accommodation and supplies for merchants. The Yuan authorities stipulated that "the government provided food and drink, and sent soldiers to protect them" wherever merchants arrived. Local officials should assign archers on patrol to safeguard the main business routes and lodging places.

As early as the reign of the Yuan's first Emperor Genghis Khan, the prototype of the post stations was built. For the sake of ensuring the safety of merchants, he also "assigned guards on the main roads" and "set up clean white felt tents"[9] to "ensure various businessmen travel unimpeded in cities and roads."[10] After the Yuan Dynasty was established, the

---

[9](Iran) Juvaini. *The History of the World-Conqueror*. Vol. 1. Trans. He Gaoji. Hohhot: Inner Mongolia People's Publishing House, 1980. *Also see* Juvaini, Ata-Malik. *The History of the World-conqueror* [M]. Manchester University Press, 1958.

[10]Berezin. *The Code of Genghis Khan*. Materials of Mongolian History Research, 1981 (18).

construction of transportation facilities along the Silk Roads was constantly strengthened with more post stations and better services for post horses, and improved standard of food and accommodation. The garrisons along the East–West transportation lines provided security for merchants, and the numerous post stations also provided convenient accommodation for business travelers. According to historical records, "the Yuan Dynasty set up post stations in all places where people lived, so that merchants from all over the world came as if they were in their own country."[11] And so, a huge crisscrossed transportation network connecting Europe and Asia was created, which linked East Asia, Central Asia, West Asia and Europe together. Consequently, the traffic between the East and the West was greatly facilitated. The ancient Silk Road, though silent for a long time, radiated vitality once again and further developed.

In this period, there were three main land transportation routes, namely, the North Route, the Central Route and the Southern Route. The North Route ran from Bechbaliq (now Jimusar, Xinjiang) and Almalik (now Huocheng, Xinjiang) to the north of the Tian Shan Mountains passing through the Chuhe River Basin, the Talas (now Dzhambul, Kazakhstan) to the north of the Syr Darya River, and the north bank of the Aral Sea and the Caspian Sea, crossing the Kipchak grassland. Then it went on to Sarai (now the region near Astrakhan, the East Bank of the Volga River in Russia), from which the merchants could reach the Danube Basin. Alternatively, the route could reach Constantinople after going along the Crimea Peninsula and crossing the Black Sea. Among those cities, Sarai and Bechbaliq, serving as the collecting and distribution centers of goods from the East and the West, became international cities.

The Middle Route also started from Almalik, passing through the region between the "Two Rivers" (Tigris & Euphrates) in Central Asia, then went on to the Asia Minor via Samarkand and Bukhara.

The South Route, namely the Southern Route of the Silk Road in the Han and Tang Dynasties, was restored at this time. It also went west from the Hexi Corridor to the south of Lop Nur, running along the northern foothills of the Kunlun Mountains, climbing over the Pamir Mountains and passing through Central Asia. Then this route entered Iran and the region between the "Two Rivers" (Tigris & Euphrates) via the south banks

---

[11](The Ming Dynasty) Song Lian *et al. History of Yuan: Geography*. Vol. 63. Beijing: Zhonghua Book Company, 1976.

of the Amu Darya River and the Caspian Sea, before finally reaching the Eastern Bank of the Mediterranean Sea.

Among those three routes, the North Route was known as "the Road of the Eurasian Grassland" for it passed through Central Asia and Eastern Europe and connected Europe and Asia. It became an important economic and cultural channel between Asia and Europe from the mid-13th century to the mid-14th century. European merchants came to China along this road enabling trade between China and the west to flourish for some time. Foreign caravans who came to China by land went eastward from the Hexi Corridor to Shangdu or Dadu in the Yuan Dynasty via Suzhou and Ganzhou along the Great Wall. Otherwise, caravans went along the northern foothills of the Mountains out of Almalik, Bechbaliq, climbing over the Altai Mountains, passing through the present Uliastai and the source area of the Orkhon River, then arrived in Helin. It could be seen that the land transportation between China and other countries in the Yuan Dynasty was more extensive than that in the Han and Tang Dynasties.

Apart from the Silk Road in northwestern China, the transportation of southwestern Silk Road was also valued. In 1276, the Yuan Dynasty set up post stations along both land and water routes from Wumeng (now Zhaotong, Yunnan) to Sichuan, which played an important role in keeping the transportation between Yunnan and the mainland smooth. In the Yuan Dynasty, trade activities on the southwestern Silk Road never ceased. For example, Yunnan horses also became export commodities in this period. The *Travels of Marco Polo* described how Dali horses "were big in size and beautiful in appearance were sold to India."

6.2 Foreign Trade Policy

6.2.1 *Enacting Foreign Trade Policy*

The Mongol army enlarged its ruling area rapidly as it expanded from Mobei to Central Plains of China, and from East Asia to Eastern Europe. Although this great empire established by military conquest did not last long, the Yuan Dynasty was still a regime commanding a vast territory, stretching "from the Yinshan Mountain (now the central part of Inner Mongolia Autonomous Region) in the north, the Taklamakan Desert in the west, the Liao Zuo (now in the eastern part of Liaoning Province) in the east, and sea surface (now the Xisha Islands) in the south." Compared with the territories of the Han or Tang Dynasty, the Yuan "extended its territory as far as southeast China, and farther into northwestern China. And some of its territories stretched beyond the measurement of miles."[12]

The direct contact between and the collision with various civilizations in the process of its southward and westward march enabled the rulers of the Yuan Dynasty to deepen their understanding of the world, cultivate a broad vision and an open mind, thus forming the opening-up conscious-ness of "all over the world as a home" and "building good relationships." Emperor Kublai Khan (r. 1260–1294) once proposed that "the saints regard the whole world as their home and if there was no connection, how can it be a family?" Therefore, "it is a good thing for the country to be close to and friendly with its neighbors," and the principle of diplomatic equality regardless of the size of the country should be adhered to in for-eign relations. He also claimed that "since I took the throne, the whole country has been as united as a family." Although his words were rich in rhetoric, and foreign conquests were not averted, those sentiments reflected the open-mindedness of Kublai Khan to foreign relations. He not only sent envoys to neighboring countries, such as Japan, Korea, Annan, and Myanmar, to carry out active diplomatic activities, but also to the Holy See in Europe, together with Marco Polo's father and the Sonico brothers when they returned home, to establish contact with the Pope. Although not all of those ideas were put into practice, they revealed the openness of the ruler during this period, which became the ideological basis for the Yuan Dynasty to actively develop foreign trade.

The rulers of the Yuan Dynasty realized that through the development of overseas trade they could "exchange 'useless items' (those which can be easily made domestically) from China for difficult-to-obtain items from distant places," so as to "be assisted by foreign countries by provid-ing things that were not produced in China."[13] A Yuan subject named Chen Dazhen further pointed out in the *History of the South China Sea in the Dade Period* that "seas and mountains were the storehouses of the world which produced treasures that China lacked. Exchanging what we owned for what we lacked was a good method of conducting ancient trade." In the preface to the Foreign Trade Regulations formulated in 1293 was mentioned that "a proposal was presented on August 26th in 1291 by a

---

[12] *Ibid.*, Vol. 58.

[13] *Record on the Renovation of the Seaway Transportation in Jiangsu and Zhejiang.* See *Seaway Scripture:* Appendix.

southern man named Yan Shen." This described how overseas trade was a means by which a country could gain great benefits from ... items "useless" within our country, like umbrellas, millstone, porcelains, utensils and curtains. These could be exchanged for items from other countries which would prove useful for us."[14] It could be seen that the purpose of developing foreign trade in this period was quite lucid, namely to stimulate the mutual exchange of products which were needed in order to realize the conversion of products' use value. This could then meet the demands of the upper class for overseas luxury goods. For this reason, the Yuan Dynasty attached great importance to the development of overseas trade and adopted a succession of encouraging measures.

6.2.2 *The Evolution of Foreign Trade Policy*

The Mongolian nomads who emerged from the Mobei not only controlled the Central Plains through wars of conquest, but established a vast empire via territorial expansion. In the process of conquest, the transfer of materials by merchants from various places played an important role in ensuring the supplies of the Mongolian army. Commercial trade and wars became important factors in the establishment of the Yuan Dynasty, which also shaped the tradition of mercantilism and martialism in the country. But the huge profits of overseas trade induced powerful officials and monks to be engaged in Sino-foreign trade. The imbalance in interests between the government and the elites, and between the government and wealthy merchants led to the seesawing trade policy of the Yuan. When the elites manipulated overseas trade interests to an extreme degree, it would undoubtedly trigger restrictive policies from the government and laissez-faire, and vice versa. In general, the Yuan Dynasty pursued a policy of positively developing foreign trade.

(1) Four Times of Prohibitions on Overseas Trade
From 1292 to 1322, due to the conquest of Java and the suppression of powerful forces, the Yuan Dynasty imposed four rounds of maritime bans, which lasted for 11 years. The first maritime ban started from 1292 to 1294.

---

[14] *Statutes of the Yuan Dynasty: Overseas Trade: Ministry of Revenue · Laws on Maritime Trade*. Vol. 22.

In the year of the conquest of Java, merchants and sailors of Zhejiang, Guangdong, and Fujian were temporarily banned from sailing before the military troops disembarked for Java. They could sail anywhere they wanted after their departure." The ban was mainly aimed at preventing maritime merchants from leaking information, and stipulated that they were prohibited from going to sea when the Yuan army went out on an expedition.

The second maritime ban began in 1303, when Emperor Chengzong (r. 1294–1307) of the Yuan "banned merchants from going to sea" and canceled the Maritime Trade Commission. In 1308, the "Quanfuyuan" was set up to renovate "Maritime Trade Commission matters," and the maritime prohibition was removed.

When Wokou (literally "Japanese pirates" or "dwarf pirates") began to invade the Quanzhou area of Fujian, the Yuan sent troops to fight against them. From 1311 to 1314, the Yuan Dynasty implemented the 3rd maritime prohibition, "banning ships from entering the seas of China."

The final maritime prohibition started in 1320. In order to prevent large-scale export of contraband goods, such as gold and silver, "the Supervisory Office of the Maritime Trade Commission was closed and merchants were prohibited from importing foreign goods."[15] It was not until 1322 that three Supervisory Offices of the Maritime Trade Commission were reestablished in Quanzhou, Qingyuan, and Guangdong, thus ending the maritime prohibition.

The maritime prohibition mainly targeted at those domestic private merchants who went to sea for trading, but official merchants and foreign merchants were not restricted. Lamuri Kingdom (presently Banda Aceh, Sumatra) and other countries came to China to engage tribute trade during the 1st maritime prohibition. During the 2nd maritime prohibition, the merchant Yang Shu voyaged to Krumos (Hormuz, near Minab in southeast Iran) in the Persian Gulf on an "official ship" for trade. Meanwhile, a Japanese merchant came to Qingyuan and Quanzhou for trade during this period.[16]

---

[15](The Ming Dynasty) Wang Qi. *A Sequel to the Comprehensive Investigations based on Literary and Documentary Sources*. Beijing: Modern Publishing House, 1986.

[16](The Ming Dynasty) Song Lian *et al. History of Yuan: Annals of Chengzong*. Vol. 21. Beijing: Zhonghua Book Company, 1976.

(2) Encouraging Foreign Merchants to Trade in China

In order to attract more foreign merchants to China, the Yuan Dynasty adopted a series of effective policies.

First, the Yuan actively promoted basic policies to develop overseas trade with foreign merchants. In 1278, the Yuan government announced that "foreign countries in the southeast islands admired China. Officials who are in charge of foreign trade can tell them that if they have come to pay tributes, they will be treated well by the Emperor and be allowed to conduct free mutual trade."[17] This meant that foreign merchants were treated with courtesy and their trade wouldn't be interfered with in China, and they would be allowed to proceed freely. Pu Shougeng was appointed as the Palace Secretary Left Aide, together with others, and acted under orders to "sail with ten Imperial Edits to inform foreign countries about China's foreign trade policy" to initiate tributary trade.

Second, the Yuan inherited various incentive measures for overseas trade from the Song Dynasty to create convenient conditions for foreign merchants to trade in China. For example, courier stations were set up at major trade ports to receive merchants from various countries; in Guangzhou, Quanzhou and other places where foreign merchants gathered, *Fan Fang* of the previous generation continued to be established.

Third, the Yuan Dynasty paid attention to the appointment of officials at overseas trade ports. Wars during the Song and Yuan caused tremendous damage to overseas trade in the southeast coastal ports, and also harmed the enthusiasm of foreign merchants to come to trade at the same time. Moreover, the new regime was just established, so merchants tended to wait and see. The development of overseas trade needed Pu Shougeng's participation. He had served the former Song Dynasty and was then a capitulant of the Yuan. Pu was assigned as Assistant Administrator, Palace Secretary Left Aide, and so on. Pu took advantage of his influence among the foreign merchants and overseas trade to "attract foreign countries" to trade with the Yuan China. From then on, all the officials who served at the Maritime Trade Commission of Quanzhou were Muslims, like Pu Shougeng's son Pu Shiwen and others.

Fourth, the Yuan implemented a more liberal trade policy, which was mainly reflected in the taxation on overseas trade. The overseas trade of the previous dynasty (the Song) not only imposed taxes, but was run exclusively by the government through *jinque* (monopoly) and *bomai* (governmental purchase). It therefore bore the obvious character of a state monopoly.

---

[17] *Ibid.*, Vol. 10.

Emperor Shizu (r. 1260–1294) of the Yuan abolished *jinque* and *bomai* and stipulated in 1277 that "foreign trade ships returning from abroad needed to pay *choujie* (produce levies). This referred to import duties levied in the form of practical items. Having paid these fees, they were free to conduct their trade." Later, in order to compensate for the financial losses of the government, a vessel tax was imposed in addition to the *choujie*. It was not until 1293 that a total of 21 items were stipulated on the list of commodities to be taxed. The stipulation was made to be observed at all ports engaged in foreign trade. Specifically, it said that "among the seven Maritime Trade Commissions in Quanzhou, Shanghai, Ganpu, Wenzhou, Guangdong, Hangzhou Qingyuan, a new taxation would begin to be imposed on the first trial place Quanzhou stipulating that was "apart from the tax paid by *choujie*," another 1 in every 30 of cargoes would be charged as tax. The other six ports would be taxed later on according to the example of Quanzhou. At the same time, the Maritime Trade Commission in Wenzhou was merged with that in Qingyuan and the Maritime Trade Commission in Hangzhou was incorporated into the Taxation Department."

Compared with the government monopoly, foreign trade taxation mainly increased government revenue through economic means rather than by purely administrative means. With the increase of government revenue, merchants competed in a more intense way, which resulted in the lifting of the market liberalization level, which was conducive to the healthy development of overseas trade, while the government monopolized operations restricted competition, resulting in low efficiency.

Fifth, certain trade restrictions were somewhat relaxed for foreign merchants. For example, the Yuan Dynasty restricted the export of some commodities, but with relatively loose regulations on foreign merchants' activities. In 1277, Japanese merchants brought gold to China to be exchanged for China's copper coins. Although copper coins were historically prohibited from being exported out of China, Emperor Shizu of the Yuan still granted permission, which obviously was a special measure to attract Japanese merchants. In the same year, Emperor Shizu ordered "coastal official departments to trade with Japanese merchants." These measures were quite effective. In the next year, four Japanese merchant ships with merchants and sailors went to Qingyuan in eastern Zhejiang for trade.[18]

---

[18](The Ming Dynasty) Song Lian *et al. History of Yuan: Annals of Emperor Shizu of the Yuan.* Vol. 10. Beijing: Zhonghua Book Company, 1976.

Lastly, the Yuan government also provided convenience for cargo shipments and strengthened coastal security. Historical accounts recorded that "(concurrently engaged in overseas trade) the Xingquan prefecture governed 15,000 vessels ... from Quanzhou to Hangzhou, and fifteen maritime stations were set up along the seaway. These were equipped with five vessels and 200 seamen, specializing in transporting foreign tributes and exotic goods, and guarding the safety of the seaway."[19]

The Yuan Dynasty actively promoted its opening-up policy through the above-mentioned measures, and provided convenient conditions and a safe and free trade environment for foreign merchants to trade in China.

(3) Allowing Bureaucrats and Officials to Engage in Overseas Trade

In the Song Dynasty, bureaucratic dignitaries were banned from engaging in overseas trade, but the lure of high profits rendered these statutes impotent. The ruling class of the Yuan Dynasty rose from being nomads and had a long-term commercial tradition. After entering the Central Plains, many of them continued to do business though they had been appointed as officials. The Yuan government adopted laissez-faire and even encouraging policies. In 1314, the Yuan government stipulated that "marquises, emperor's sons-in-law, powerful persons, monks, Taoist priests, Erkehün, Danishmand, etc., were all allowed to sail overseas for foreign goods trading and should be taxed accordingly."[20] This showed that the government explicitly allowed bureaucrats and dignitaries to act overseas trade, but needed them to conduct according to relevant guidelines. In 1317, Emperor Renzong of the Yuan even gave a ship as a gift to the noble named Tieshi.[21] In addition to allowing dignitaries to engage in overseas trade activities, the Yuan also actively organized official-run trade and official-merchant-run joint trade in various forms. Apart from the traditional tributary trade, the Imperial Court also sent envoys directly to purchase overseas, and at the same time carried out official-merchant joint trade as "Ortoq[22] trade" and "official ship trade."

---

[19] *Ibid.*, Vol. 15.

[20] (The Yuan Dynasty) Wanyan Nadan. *Legislative Articles from the Comprehensive Regulations: Overseas Trade.* Vol. 18.

[21] (The Ming Dynasty) Song Lian *et al. History of Yuan: Biography of Jia Xilai.* Vol. 169. Beijing: Zhonghua Book Company, 1976.

[22] "The ortoq" (merchant partners), referred to the joint-ventures of empire-merchant, who carried out commercial activities with the capital provided and shared profit with the principal at a pre-determined ratio. They were especially encouraged to trade afar in distant

(4) Regulating the Scale of Overseas Trade

Due to the backward social and economic development of neighboring countries and their limited capacity for market consumption, China's import and export trade developed with large numbers of Chinese products engulfing the markets of Southeast Asia. Market demand was rapidly becoming saturated. As a result, the prices of Chinese goods fell sharply. "At that time, rich people who went to trade in foreign countries made huge profits, so more and more people went into business," which led to the phenomenon whereby "Chinese goods were cheap in price while foreign goods were expensive." Their profits fell sharply. For this reason, the Yuan government imposed temporary restrictions on the scale of exports, stipulating that "the government sent ten *gang* (groups) of ships with official documents as passes. On their return, they would pay taxes according to regulations. As for ships sailing overseas with no permission, the cargoes on them would be confiscated."[23] It was not until 1323 when the overseas market returned to a normal situation that the restrictive regulations of the Yuan government were rescinded.

(5) Encouraging Non-governmental Trade

Although the Yuan Dynasty initiated prohibitions on civilian overseas trade on several occasions, those restrictions lasted for only 11 out of the nearly 100 years of the Yuan regime. For most of the rest of the period, merchants were encouraged to engage in overseas trade and many supporting measures were implemented. For example, powerful officials were strictly forbidden from infringing upon the interests of maritime merchants. Those who did so to a severe degree would be punished seriously. In 1281, it was stipulated that "prefectures and counties where merchants were engaged in foreign trade were exempted from miscellaneous duties." *The Law on Maritime Trade* revised in 1314 stipulated that no *Yamen* (the name of a government office in feudal China) should "use merchant ships in the name of the government" and "this rule was inviolable." When merchant ships reached port, "powerful, dignitaries and others were not allowed to buy goods using fake names"; it was

---

lands, in return, the Imperial treasury would receive part of the profit, luxury goods and information.

[23] (The Ming Dynasty) Song Lian *et al. History of Yuan: Biographies*. Vol. 250. Beijing: Zhonghua Book Company, 1976.

also required that "maritime merchants and sailors whose wives and children were poor should always be given preference by the local prefectures and counties" and would be "exempted from miscellaneous labor."[24]

In addition to direct incentives, the political rehabilitation of successful maritime merchants in the Yuan Dynasty also indirectly encouraged non-governmental overseas trade activities. For example, Zhu Qing and Zhang Xua, who used to be pirates, gained fame as bona fide maritime merchants in the Yuan Dynasty. Their successful overseas trade operations helped Taicang Port in Jiangsu Province achieve prosperity. Therefore, they were promoted by the government and enjoyed extremely high social status. It was recorded that "both father and son were elevated to posts as high as prime ministers; their brothers, uncles and nephews were all high-ranking officials; mansions under their name spread all over the country; their treasure houses and warehouses stood at very close distance."[25] In Ganpu, Zhejiang, three generations of the Yang family — from Yang Fa, to Yang Zi, to Yang Shu — were engaged in overseas trade with a huge private fleet for business. They dominated the trade in Ganpu for decades. During the Southern Song Dynasty, Yang Fa had already obtained an official position. When the Yuan armies conquered the south, Yang Fa surrendered. He was appointed as Military Commissioner of Fujian and was responsible for the management of the overseas trade of eastern Zhejiang. In 1277, Yang Fa's power was further expanded to include the management of the three Maritime Trade Commissions of Qingyuan, Shanghai and Ganpu. His family "settled down in Ganpu and made investments there and gained profits and power for generations," and thus "generations of descendants lived in what appeared to be a golden mansion and became the richest household in eastern Zhejiang."[26] "People all competed to imitate" the Yang family, and a large number of people in Ganpu rode the tide of overseas trade.

---

[24] *Statutes of the Yuan Dynasty: Overseas Trade: Ministry of Revenue.* Vol. 22.

[25] (The Yuan Dynasty) Tao Zongyi. *Retirement to the Countryside: Zhu Zhang.* Vol. 5.

[26] (The Ming Dynasty) Fan Weicheng, Hu Zhenheng. *Haiyan County in Illustration: Foreign Countries.* Vol. 3.

(6) Worshiping the Sea Goddess

From the Southern Song Dynasty, activities for offering sacrifices to Tian Fei[27] gradually appeared along the southeast coast. After the Yuan unified regions in the south of the Yangtze River in 1278, Emperor Kublai Khan officially named the sea goddess worshiped by the locals as Tian Fei, and continuously added titles to her. Moreover, the official ceremony of worshiping the sea goddess was presided over by the Maritime Trade Commissioner every year. This demonstrated the importance the Yuan Dynasty attached to the sea trade.

6.2.3 *Improving the Overseas Trade Management System*

The Yuan Dynasty inherited the Maritime Trade System of the Tang and Song Dynasties, and further improved it in terms of regulations, institutions and functions to form the Maritime Trade Commission.

(1) Amending Overseas Trade Regulations

After the establishment of the Yuan Dynasty, it adopted the overseas trade regulations of the Song Dynasty at the beginning, but owing to the different systems in various regions, much malpractice arose. In 1293, based on the laws and regulations of the Song's overseas trade, the Yuan Dynasty formulated 23 articles for "renovating overseas trade activities." In 1314, the *Law on Maritime Trade* was revised and a 22-article *Law on Maritime Trade* was promulgated, which became the first relatively systematic and complete foreign trade law in Chinese history. The law clearly stipulated the types of tax and tax rates for foreign trade in the Yuan Dynasty, the qualifications of merchants engaged in overseas trade, the specific procedures for entering and leaving the port, and the rights and interests of merchants, restrictions on the types of imports and exports, penalties for smuggling, and so on. Compared with the Song Dynasty, the *Law on Maritime Trade* in the Yuan Dynasty involved more content and more detailed regulations.

---

[27]"Tian Fei" was the sea goddess Mazu. It was said that she was originally a woman whose surname was Lin in Putian, Fujian, and could predict whether the sea would bring good or ill luck. After her death, she was revered as the goddess of the sea. Coastal merchants and fishermen built up temples for her worship and prayed she would bless them to go to sea safely.

(2) Establishing a Maritime Trade Commission

After Guangzhou was conquered in 1275, a Maritime Trade Commission was immediately established there, which also branched out to Quanzhou, Qingyuan (namely Mingzhou, now Ningbo), Shanghai, and Ganpu after the Yuan army took over Zhejiang and the Fujian province in 1277. In 1284, a Maritime Trade Commission was set up in Hangzhou and Wenzhou. In addition to the seven aforementioned Maritime Trade Commissions, in 1293, the Wenzhou Maritime Trade Commission was merged into the Qingyuan Maritime Trade Commission, and the Hangzhou Maritime Trade Commission was merged with the local taxation department. In the same year, the Yuan government also set up a "Supervisorate of Transaction in Haibei and Hainan which implemented the same taxation policy as the Maritime Trade Commission" to manage overseas trade along the coasts of Guangxi and Hainan Island. The scope of overseas trade management covered the majority of the coastal areas, including Jiangsu, Zhejiang, Fujian, Guangdong and Guangxi. In 1297, the Yuan government also merged the Ganpu and the Shanghai Maritime Trade Commissions into the Qingyuan Maritime Trade Commission, thus forming a structure with the Maritime Trade Commissions in Quanzhou, Guangzhou, and Qingyuan as the three major departments managing coastal foreign trade affairs.

(3) The Functions of the Maritime Trade Commission
(i) Inspecting Import and Export Ships and Cargoes

According to the regulations of the *Law on Maritime Trade*, merchants who intended to go to sea must apply for approval from the Maritime Trade Commission and provide a guarantor. After granting approval, the Maritime Trade Commission would issue a sea trade license as public proof. There were two types of public proofs: the public inspection and the public certificate, with the former given to large ships and the latter to small ships. The public proof recorded crew numbers, together with the type and quantity of cargoes loaded, and the countries of destination. Foreign merchant ships also needed to specify the cargo they carried for public inspection to prevent the export of illegal cargoes. At the same time, the *Law on Maritime Trade* stipulated that no ship, Chinese or foreign, was allowed to export gold, silver, copper, iron wares, weapons, grains, population, etc., and the Maritime Trade Commission strictly inspected outbound cargo according to regulations.

(ii) Levying Taxes

In the Yuan Dynasty, the ban on monopolies and purchasing were no longer implemented. Instead, import taxes were imposed in addition to the *choujie* (produce levies). Generally, the rate of *choujie* was 1/10, while the import tax rate was 1/30. Taxes were also levied according to regulations on imported goods (non-gifts) carried by officials who returned from overseas trade. In order to ensure that taxes were levied in accordance with the law, coastal provinces also sent officials to supervise the tax collection work of the Maritime Trade Commission.

(iii) Investigating Smuggling

With the development of overseas trade and the regulation of foreign trade taxation in the Yuan Dynasty, smuggling along the coast became a rather serious problem. There appeared merchants who either concealed goods without reporting them or made a false declaration of the quantity, or transferred or sold them midway. For this reason, the Yuan government ordered that coastal states and counties strengthen precautions on the one hand, and on the other, the Yuan required the Maritime Trade Commissions to block off smuggling on the sea. Once the smuggler was found, the goods would be confiscated in accordance with the *Law on Foreign Trade Tax Evasion* and the merchants would be convicted. At the same time, rewards would be given to informants who reported smuggling.

In summary, under the active development of overseas trade policy, the overseas trade management system of the Yuan Dynasty was gradually improved with the management level being lifted and management regulations being better-observed.

6.3 The Recovery and Decline of Overland Trade

In the early Yuan Dynasty, with the relatively stable political situation of the four Khanates in Central Asia and West Asia and the smooth East-West traffic, overland trade and maritime trade advanced hand in hand. In earlier times, overland trade was more important. In the late Yuan, owing to the rebellion of marquises in the northwest, there were frequent wars among the khanates, which caused difficulties and threats to trade and travel and hindered the development of overland trade.

6.3.1 *Major Geographical Directions of Overland Trade*

The restoration of overland transportation revived the continental trade between China and the west. Wei Su of the Yuan said that "People from all directions, with some from thousands of miles away, others with only hundreds of miles away, came here by seaway or overland routes with no obstacles."[28]

Before their unification, the Mongol tribes already boasted trade contacts with the Liao, the Jin and other regimes, mainly exchanging livestock and fur for ironware. At that time, the market trade between the two sides was very healthy, and the advanced production implements obtained through the trade effectively promoted the social and economic development of the Mongol tribes.

After the establishment of the Yuan, owing to the special political relations, the Yuan government maintained frequent trade exchanges with the Four Khanates, keeping an especially close relationship with the Kipchak Khanate due to its geographical proximity.

Salai, the capital of the Kipchark Khanate, was also an international city and hub of the East–West trade, in which a large number of merchants form every direction gathered with a variety of goods. Some western merchants could purchase Chinese silks and other goods without even going to China. So many Chinese merchants came here to do business, with a number of them even settling in Salai. Together with them came China's handicraft production technologies, like the manufacture of bronze mirrors, which was introduced to Salai.

The Ilkhanate Khanate was located between Central and West Asia, and it could control the Persian Gulf. It maintained exchanges with the Yuan Dynasty particularly by land. Merchants of the Yuan brought silk and porcelain to the Ilkhanate Khanate hoping for various luxury goods, such as pearls and gemstones, with a considerable quantity of "hundreds of thousands of ingots." Persian traders along the Silk Road brought jewelry, medicinal herbs and camels to China.

In addition to countries in Central Asia and West Asia, countries and regions that came to trade in China by land also included those in

---

[28](Late Yuan and Early Ming) Wei Su. *Antology of Wei Su.* Vol. 1.

Southern Europe, Eastern Europe and Northern Europe. There were streams of Chinese and foreign merchants active on the east and west land routes, with not only a large number of Chinese *Semu* merchants (merchants of the Western Regions hired by the Yuan government to run business) heading west to Central Asia and West Asia, but also with merchants of West and Central Asia controlled by Mongol Khanates and their descendants as well as merchants from Constantinople of the Byzantine Empire, Poland of the Europe, Austria, Czechia, Russia, Venice and Genoa in Italy and the early Nordic Hanseatic League who traveled eastward to China.

Merchants from Europe and Central Asia generally brought gold, silver, jewelry, medicine, exotic birds and animals, spices, bamboo cloth and other commodities to China or sold them halfway. In China, they mainly purchased silk fabrics, such as satin, embroidery, golden brocades and silk, as well as tea leaves, porcelain and medicinal materials.

6.3.2 *Major Trade Modes of Overland Trade*

The overland trade in the Yuan Dynasty chiefly included tributary trade in the traditional official sense and caravan trade organized by official and private merchants.

(1) Tributary Trade

Although the Mongol Empire lasted for only a short period in history, the four Khanate regimes in Central Asia and West Asia were long ruled by the descendants of Genghis Khan, so they maintained close tributary exchanges with the Yuan Dynasty. Through the international courier road that ran across Europe and Asia, the four Khanates sent envoys to the Yuan with their local products, such as large beads, jade articles, crystals, sabers, camels, famous horses, leopards, ligers and various medicinal materials as tributes. In turn, the Yuan government repaid them with currency coins, satin, embroidery, the northeast falcon and so on. Envoys from various countries often brought to China large amounts of gold. In addition to receiving gifts from the Yuan, they also purchased various goods for their governments and other individuals. For example, King Ghazan of the Ilkhanate sent his envoys to the Yuan with "100,000 gold to buy goods in China."[29]

(2) Caravan Trade

Due to the harsh natural conditions along the land routes, thieves were rife along them. "But if sixty people gathered together in a group, it would be as safe as at home even under the most dangerous situation."[30] Therefore, merchants traveling from east to west often journeyed in groups. With the smooth land transport between China and the west, caravans from various countries were increasingly active along the route, transporting commercial goods for sale from different countries.

As nomadic peoples, the Mongols enjoyed a long tradition of relying on trade. Genghis Khan sent caravans many times to Central Asia for trade, each on a considerable scale. For example, in 1218, the Mongol Empire organized a Khwarazmian trade caravan of up to 450 people to trade in Central Asia, which carried large amounts of fur, silk, gold and silver-made products.

In addition to official caravans, private caravans were more active. The caravans that came to China by land included merchants from Central Asia and West Asia who traded local products from various countries, such as gold, silver, jewelry, medicinal materials, exotic animals, spices, as well as many from Byzantium, Poland, Austria, Czechia, Russia, Venice, Genoa, and even as far as the Hanseatic League in northern Europe. They mainly exchanged gold and silver for goods from different countries. The principal items purchased by caravans from foreign countries in China were silk fabrics, tea leaves, porcelains and medicinal materials.

6.3.3 *Impact and Decline of Overland Trade*

The prosperous overland trade between the East and the West elevated some cities along the route to the status of Eurasian international trade centers. For instance, there was Tauris (present Tabriz in northwestern Iran),

---

[29] (Sweden) C. D'Ohsson. *Histoire des mongols, depuis tchinguis-khan jusqu a timour bey ou tamerlan* [M]. Les feres Van Cleef, 1834.

[30] Zhang Xinglang. Collection of Historical Sources on the Communication between China and the West [M]. Vol. 1. Beijing: Zhonghua Book Company, 1978.

which was connected to Asia Minor with the Byzantine Empire in the west, the traditional Silk Road to China in the east, the city of Salai in the north, and the Hormuz port of the Central and West Asia in the south. By virtue of its superior geographical location, it became the junction for Eurasian trade.

Urgench (present-day Kunya-Urgench of Turkmenistan), once the ancient capital of Khwarezmian Empire, was the hub of the commodity exchange and transit shipment between the Muslim caravan in Central Asia and the caravan of Europe and West Asia.

Meanwhile the capital of the Yuan Dynasty, Dadu was prominent among the international trade centers in terms of city scale, the number of households and commercial prosperity. According to the *Travels of Marco Polo*, "it should be known that there were many households inside and outside Khanbaliq, with several gates and outlying communities. Within the 12 major outlying communities, the number of households was larger than that inside the city. People who lived in them were foreigners from various places who came to pay tributes or sell goods into the palace." Moreover, "the foreign objects and general merchandises of high price imported into this city were incomparable in the world."[31] Imported goods included not only luxury goods but daily necessities, indicating that the impact of foreign trade on domestic consumption was gradually expanded from the upper class to ordinary people. The *La Praika Della Mercatura* written by Francesco Pegolotti also said that "... the capital Khanbaliq boasted the most prosperous business, and merchants across the world gathered together here with numerous merchandises."[32]

The revival of overland trade between China and the west drove the economic development along the route, together with the rise of towns. For example, in Ganzhou and Suzhou in the Hexi Corridor area, local specialties, such as white camel hair and cashmere woven fabrics and medicinal herbs attracted a large number of Chinese and foreign merchants wishing to exchange. Thus, it actually became a major trade center for East–West transportation. In addition, Gongchang and Hezhou to the

---

[31] (Italy) Marco Polo. *The Travels of Marco Polo.* Vol. 2. Revised from Marsden's Translation and Edited with Introduction by Manuel Komroff. New York: W. W. Norton & Company, 1926.

[32] Zhang Xinglang. *Collection of Historical Sources on the Communication between China and the West* [M]. Vol. 1. Beijing: Zhonghua Book Company, 1978.

west of Longshan Mountain were also the trade centers for foreign and Chinese merchants at that time. The commodities exchanged included grain, livestock, fur, iron, medicinal materials, saddles and some simple production and living tools.

As for the overland trade in the Yuan Dynasty, in addition to the contact with Central Asia, West Asia and Europe through the northwestern route, there was also trade with Koryo through the Northeast route, and trade with Burma and other countries through the southwest route.

The Yuan government provided certain support and protection for overland trade by setting up post stations and garrisons, and such trade was also very popular at that time. However, the overland trade was inevitably affected by the changes in political and diplomatic situations between different regimes. In the late Yuan Dynasty, the northwest marquises rebelled frequently, and wars were often waged among the Khanates, which caused difficulties and threats to trade and travel. Therefore, the foreign trade of the Yuan Dynasty became increasingly reliant upon sea routes.

6.4 Overseas Trade Flourishes in the Yuan Dynasty

Under the policy of opening-to the outside world, the overseas trade of the Yuan Dynasty achieved great progress and exceeded the level of the previous generation in terms of operational modes, geographical scope, the scale of trade as well as the range of goods traded.

6.4.1 *Diversified Operation Modes of Maritime Trade Management*

Under the highly open policy toward foreign trade, the modes of operating maritime trade in the Yuan Dynasty increased greatly compared with previous dynasties. In addition to the traditional official-run trade and civilian-run trade, there was also the official-merchant joint trade.

(1) State-Run Trade
The forms of official trade in the Yuan Dynasty were diverse. Apart from the traditional tributary trade, there was also the envoy trade.

(i) Tributary Trade

The traditional tributary trade continued to develop in the Yuan Dynasty, and the Yuan government actively promoted official-run trade with overseas countries. After the Yuan troops took over Zhejiang and Fujian to pacify the Jiangnan area, the fifth Emperor Shizhu of the Yuan Dynasty announced the policy of "free mutual trade" with overseas countries through Fujian Province. Many foreign countries sent their envoys to the Yuan to develop friendly relations with gifts that often outnumbered those to the Tang and Song Dynasties.

According to the *History of Yuan*, during the 15 years from 1279 to 1294, more than 90 rounds of envoys were sent to establish good relations with the Yuan. Their countries of origin ranged from East Asia, Southeast Asia, South Asia to West Asia, together with some countries in North Africa, East Africa and Europe.

In order to treat well the envoys from foreign countries, the Yuan government set up "Laiyuan Yi" or "Huaiyuan Yi" as hotels at some ports. After landing, the envoys would be received by the Maritime Trade Commissioners and the provincial governors according to diplomatic etiquette. They were accompanied to hotels, and then were arranged trips to the capital via the stipulated routes, along which were set up courier stations, known as Postal Relay Stations, responsible for escorting envoys and delivering gifts.

Among them, Quanzhou was one of the main ports where envoys landed, and there a great number of envoys and gifts were to be shipped. The official trade in the Yuan Dynasty was different from that of the Song in that it paid more attention to the collection of rare overseas treasures for the rich and powerful, while the earning of profits and the increase in state fiscal revenue were placed on the back burner.

(ii) Mission Trade

In order to obtain more rare overseas treasures, the rulers of the Yuan were no longer satisfied with official tributary trade and private-run trade, but directly managed large-scale maritime trade enterprises, which led to the unprecedented development of the official-merchant trade with its forms being quite diversified.

On more than one occasion, the Yuan government used large sums of money to send special envoys to overseas countries to purchase goods for the imperial family. The imperial edicts given by the Emperor to the envoys were called "Courier Horse-delivered Imperial Edicts" or "Imperial Edicts Bearing the Emperor's Seal Delivered by Postal Relay Stations." They were used exclusively for recruiting courier horses and the attaining allocations (the food and salaries given by the local government along the route to passing officials who left the places where they held officially appointed posts but to be sent out as envoys).

At the same time, envoys also wore badges issued by the Emperor to indicate their identities and ranks. In addition to supplying horses, ships and farm workers, the Manager of Postal Relay Stations along the route also helped the envoys with imperial edicts and badges to carry goods directly to the sea port where they would disembark. The envoy trade was handled entirely by the government, which strengthened the monopoly of the government over maritime trade.

(2) Official-Merchant Joint Trade
(i) Trade Operated by Ortaq Merchants

The Ortaq was a special kind of merchant who was engaged in seaway trade and money lending for officials and nobles of the Yuan Dynasty. They were called *Semu* people (merchants coming from different places for different trade purposes). As merchants hired by the imperial family and the government, they enjoyed various privileges and often made colossal profits from trafficking in prohibited goods. In the Yuan Dynasty, the government set up a special agency to manage the Ortaq, which was called the Ortaq General Administration Department, and its branches were called the "Ortaq Office." The main responsibility of the Ortaq General Administration Department was to ask for principal interest from the Ortaq merchants, and issue official debts. A large part of the capital money used by the Ortaqs to engage maritime trade were derived from the official debts issued by the Yuan government, and the interest rate of the capital invested by the government to Ortaq merchants was three-quarters lower than that of private usury, so the merchants actually received great discounts. The capital issued by the Ortaq General Administration Department to Ortaq merchants for maritime trade amounted to hundreds of thousands of ingots each year, and the Yuan government could collect millions of *guan* of interest each year, which showed the considerable scale of the maritime trade conducted by the Ortaq merchants.

In accordance with the *Law on Maritime Trade*, Ortaq trade was also subject to taxation. But Ortaq merchants often refused to comply by virtue of their power. In nature, Ortaq trade was a kind of merchant-run official trade. There was a great contradiction between the Ortaq merchants and the Yuan government in the distribution of sea trade profits. Some Ortaq merchants even went overseas and didn't return after receiving the official capital, causing great losses to the Yuan government.

(ii) Government — Invested Trade

The official ship trade was a kind of official-merchant joint trade, with the government investing in start-up capital and ships and merchants entrusted to manage the trade. Similar to the Ortaq trade, it was managed by merchants but with government investment. However, there were differences between them in that the Ortaq trade was managed by the *Semu* merchants, while the official ship trade was operated mainly by merchants from southeast coast of China.

Since Emperor Shizu of the Yuan attached great importance to and supported overseas trade, the government specially created the Ortaq General Administration Department to subsidize overseas trade and the Xingquan Office to take charge of lending for those seaway merchants with insufficient financial resources, providing government loans to them and harvesting interests. Later, due to successive years of waging wars on other countries, as well as the extreme extravagance of the wealthy and powerful, fiscal expenditures increased sharply, making it hard to make ends meet.

In order to alleviate the increasingly serious fiscal scarcities, "the Minister of Finance," the junior councilor Lu Shirong proposed the implementation of an official ship trade system to return the huge profits from overseas trade to the government. In January, 1285, he suggested to the Emperor that he "set up the Transshipment Department in Quanzhou and Hangzhou and build ships and provide start-up capital to encourage people to engage in foreign trade. 70 percent of profits would be given to the government and 30 percent to the merchants. For those who conducted private overseas trade, their previous treasures would be detained and purchased by the government. As for those who operated trade without telling their names, their property should be confiscated with half of it given to the informant."[33] Emperor Shizu of the Yuan appreciated this blueprint and ordered "its implementation as soon as possible." That was the origin of the official ship system.

---

[33](The Ming Dynasty) Song Lian *et al. History of Yuan: Biography of Lu Shirong.* Vol. 205. Beijing: Zhonghua Book Company, 1976.

According to this system, the ships were built and the capital was provided by the government. In other words, the government provided not only the capital but also the vessels for navigation, and the government chose merchants as its agents to conduct trade activities at sea. Upon their return, the two parties shared the profits with the officials taking 70% and merchants 30%. The official ship trade was also subject to the restrictions of the shipping system, which required taxation according to regulations. "All foreigners who traded on official ships would be taxed by *choujie* (produce levies)."

The objective of the Yuan government in carrying out the official ship system was not only to obtain financial revenue, but also to divide the profit from the maritime trade with the powerful merchants, thus enhancing the economic strength of the Yuan government and restraining the reach of the influential merchants. During the implementation of the official ship system, the Yuan government prohibited officials from trading overseas.

The implementation of the official ship system did enable the Yuan government to earn a huge profit of "hundreds of millions of treasures," but it also encountered a lot of obstacles in its implementation. The first was the malpractices of officials at all levels; the second was the inflation in the late Yuan Dynasty: the devaluation of the official capital made it difficult to make profits, which affected the enthusiasm of the operators; and the third was the fierce resistance of the officials and rich merchants. The official ship trade system seriously harmed the interests of officials and the rich merchants engaged in overseas trade, who finally killed the junior councilor Lu Shirong through laying accusations. In view of this, in 1323, the Yuan government finally promulgated the policy of "Free maritime trade and taxation."[34] The official ship system lasted for nearly four decades from 1285 to 1323.

The official ship trade, like other official-commercial trade, had the crowding-out effect on the private maritime trade and restrained the development of civilian overseas trade. At the same time, it should be noted that the official ship trade also involved small and medium-sized maritime merchants from the southeastern coast of China in overseas trade, which prepared certain preconditions for the development of private maritime trade in the late Yuan. But the official overseas trade didn't last for long. Its cessation eventually gave way to private-run overseas trade.

---

[34](The Ming Dynasty) Song Lian *et al. History of Yuan: Treatise on Food and Commodities.* Vol. 94. Beijing: Zhonghua Book Company, 1976.

(3) Private Merchant Trade
(i) Elite Merchants

The Yuan Dynasty changed the policy of the Song that prohibited officials from trading overseas. As long as "tax was paid according to regulations," high-ranking officials were allowed to engage in maritime trade. Powerful marquises and the Emperor's son-in-laws were engaged in such trade. They usually sent people overseas to buy foreign goods for them. The less powerful officials may have taken the opportunity to go overseas to transact their own business and make profits; or falsely claim official money and conduct private transactions.

Monks and priests often hired laity to do business for them secretly and thereby avoid being taxed. Officials at all levels in the coastal areas either used their own ships to trade overseas, or used their own capital to entrust other merchants to do business on their behalf. Among them, the most prominent were Zhu Qing and Zhang Xuan from Taicang, who made their fortunes through sea transportation and possessed quantities of assets and oceangoing ships. When they were convicted and sentenced to death, many of their ships hadn't yet returned.

(ii) *Semu* Merchants

In the Yuan Dynasty, with the implementation of the national hierarchical system, *Semu* people received strong support from the government and their power was not insignificant at coastal ports. They fell into two categories. One included the descendants of the Arabs who came to China from the Tang and Song Dynasties, like Pu Shougeng *et al.*; the other included those from the Western Regions and foreign merchants who went to Jiangnan from the Yuan Dynasty onwards, such as Ispahan in Quanzhou.

Pu Shougeng used to be an official in the Quanzhou Maritime Trade Commission in the Song Dynasty. After surrendering to the Yuan, he still served as the overseas trade official in Quanzhou, and was appointed as the Imperial Secretariat Senior councilor of Fujian Province. Awarded the golden tiger badge by Emperor Shizhu of the Yuan, he became very powerful and had an important influence over the Quanzhou maritime trade. In essence, he was a *Semu* magnate who was simultaneously an official and a merchant. After the middle of the Yuan Dynasty, Pu's family was gradually weakened in power and was replaced by *Semu* merchants from the west. At that time, there were tens of thousands of *Semu* merchants coming to Quanzhou, many of whom became merchants on a grand scale and manipulated the maritime trade of Quanzhou.

(iii) Maritime Merchants

Merchants of the Yuan were specialized in maritime trade. Among them, a number were big merchants with strong capital and ships of their own. Most of them operated trade independently, and some entrusted others to manage business affairs on their behalf. In addition, there were a considerable number of small and medium-scale merchants without sufficient money and power. They rarely operated independently, but by either borrowing capital or in partnership. The *History of Yuan: Biography of Ashabuhua* recorded that "when the Bo Jiana was the local administrator, a man named Mei Dong'er was instigated to falsely accuse 116 overseas merchants of stealing and plundering their money. After interrogation, he was sent to the Ministry of Penalty. Bo Jiana examined the case and found that all of them were innocent. The Prime Minister Bai set them free and returned money to them." One false accusation involved 116 merchants, suggesting how many were then engaged in maritime trade.

(iv) Individual Merchants

Individual traders of the Yuan Dynasty used to be bankrupt peasants in the coastal areas. They began to conduct business with the development of commodity economy. With neither vessels nor enough capital, they had to rely on big merchants to share space on the ships and bring their own goods to trade overseas. Merchants of this type were known as "companions" or "hitch hikers," who indulged in business to make a living, some of them even being reduced to pirates after becoming bankrupt.

6.4.2 *The Development of Major Foreign Trade Ports*

The prosperity of overseas trade in the Yuan Dynasty was accompanied by the development of foreign trade ports. As the frontier of Sino-foreign exchange, the ports became the focus of China's opening- to the outside world in the Yuan Dynasty. Of these Quanzhou Port, Guangzhou Port and Qingyuan Port were more celebrated.

(1) Quanzhou Port

In the later years of the Southern Song Dynasty, Quanzhou became the largest overseas trade port of China. During the Song and Yuan Dynasties, Quanzhou, unaffected by warfare, received strong support from the rulers of the Yuan, thus creating its prosperity.

Taking Quanzhou as the center, the Yuan Dynasty implemented a national policy of opening- to the outside world and encouraged foreign merchants to trade in China. In 1277, the Yuan government set up the Maritime Trade Commission at Quanzhou Port and quickly resumed overseas trade activities there. According to the *History of Yuan: Biography of Sügetü*, in 1278, "Emperor Kublai Khan ... developed overseas trade. He promoted Sügetü to the position of senior councilor of Quanzhou, ordering him to attract foreign countries, and announced the opening-up policy of "free mutual trade." In 1281, it was also stipulated that "foreign goods that had been taxed by Quanzhou were forbidden from being taxed in other trade places."[35]

In order to strengthen seaway and overland management, the Yuan Dynasty set up the Postal Relay Stations to improve the courier system. In 1288, the number of decrees of the "Courier Horse-delivered Imperial Edict" issued to Quanzhou increased to 24. In 1289, maritime courier stations were set up between Quanzhou and Hangzhou, "which were used to receive vessels from Quanzhou to Hangzhou."[36] This not only made transportation between Quanzhou and China's export goods bases in Jiangsu and Zhejiang areas more convenient, but allowed imported goods, transported via the Grand Canal, to directly reach the consumer center of the capital Dadu. In the 30th year after the Yuan was established as an empire, preferential tax rates were also applied in Quanzhou so that imports from other ports were subject to a tax rate of "one-fifteenth," while Quanzhou enjoyed a lower tax rate of "one-thirtieth." Such a large-scale tax preference further strengthened the advantageous status of Quanzhou Port in overseas trade.

The solid overseas trade foundation and the special preferential policies enabled overseas trade at Quanzhou Port to achieve unprecedented

---

[35] (The Ming Dynasty) Song Lian *et al. History of Yuan*. Vol. 11. Beijing: Zhonghua Book Company, 1976.
[36] (The Ming Dynasty) Xie Jin *et al. Yongle Canon*. Vol. 19419.

prosperity during the Yuan Dynasty, making it not only the largest port in China, but also one of the largest ports in the world.

The Venetian traveler Marco Polo wrote that "Citong was one of the largest ports in the world, where a lot of merchants gathered, and the goods were piled up like mountains, which was really unimaginable." The Moroccan traveler Ibn Battuta who personally saw hundreds of vessels and countless small boats in the harbor "called it the first commercial port in the world."[37] In a letter to the Italian explorer Christopher Columbus in the mid-15th century, the Florentine physician Paul Tosgarri extolled how "the number of goods trafficked by the merchants in the whole world was so large, but it was inferior to that of the giant port of Citong!" Wang Dayuan, a native of Jiangxi in the Yuan Dynasty, who sailed twice from Quanzhou Port and traveled to more than 90 ancient countries and regions in the world, took 27 years to write his book *A Brief Record of the Barbarians of the Isles*, in which he confirmed that Quanzhou was the largest commercial port in the world.

As the hub of the Maritime Silk Road, Quanzhou was connected with the main East–West economic artery. At this time, the number of countries and regions maintaining trade relations with Quanzhou increased to nearly 100, and the scope of trade was still dominated by overseas trade.

(2) Guangzhou Port

The rise of Quanzhou Port during the Southern Song Dynasty caused Guangzhou, traditionally the largest trading port, to decline in status. At the end of the Southern Song, Guangzhou was finally surpassed by Quanzhou. At the turn of the Song and Yuan Dynasties, Guangzhou was devastated repeatedly by warfare. Its infrastructure and social economy were damaged severely and its overseas trade was left sluggish.

During the Yuan Dynasty, the overseas trade of Guangzhou gradually prospered. Under the policy of developing overseas trade, it experienced economic recovery and thus continued to serve as a place where "foreign vessels gathered." Compared with the situation under previous dynasties, the scale of its import and export trade grew with considerable income coming from overseas trade. It was recorded at the time that "the annual crop of

[37] Zhang Xingwang. *Records of Ancient Quanzhou.*

gold, pearls, rhinoceros, spices, herbs and other products filled people's eyes and ears, and the taxation it yielded totaled at least one million."[38]

The overseas trading partners of the Yuan were various. According to the records of the *History of the South China Sea in the Dade Period* (formerly known as the *History of the South China Sea*)[39] written by Chen Dazhen in the Yuan Dynasty, traders in Guangzhou came from more than 140 countries and regions, ranging from the Philippine Archipelago, the Indonesian Archipelago, and the Indian Peninsula in the east to the coast of the Persian Gulf, the Arabian Peninsula and the coastal areas of Africa in the west.

The development of overseas trade promoted the prosperity of Guangzhou. The European traveler Friar Odoric came to China in the middle of the Yuan Dynasty, and described Guangzhou (Sincalan) as a city three times bigger than Venice. "There were too many ships in the city to be believed," he said. "Indeed, there were more ships here than those in Italy." However, as was mentioned previously, Quanzhou Port was comprehensively supported by the Yuan Dynasty, resulting in the detriment of the overseas trade of Guangzhou. This made Guangzhou lag behind Quanzhou in the Yuan Dynasty and so it ranked as the second largest port, after Quanzhou, in terms of China's foreign trade.

(3) Qingyuan Port

During the Yuan Dynasty, Zhejiang still took the lead in the silk reeling and porcelain-making industries with a solid foundation for developing overseas trade. What's more, the Yuan government attached great importance to the development of overseas trade in Zhejiang. Four Maritime Trade Commissions were set up, in Qingyuan, Hangzhou, Wenzhou and Ganpu respectively, making overseas trade activities along the coast of Zhejiang proceed with more dynamism. For example, the Maritime Trade Commission was set up in Hangzhou in 1284; maritime courier stations were set up in Quanzhou and Hanzhou in 1289, so that the imported goods of Quanzhou could reach Dadu, directly from Hangzhou via the Grand Canal.

---

[38] (The Yuan Dynasty) Wu Lai. *The History of Nanhai Landscape Figures*. Vol. 1. *Also see* Chen Gaohua, Wu Tai. *Overseas Trade in the Song and Yuan Dynasties*. Tianjin: Tianjin People's Publishing House, 1981.

[39] Published and printed in the eighth year of Dade Period of Emperor Chengzong of Yuan (1304).

Ganpu Port at the mouth of the Qiantang River became an even more important post in the Yuan's foreign trade, which was once regarded by the government as "a communication center" for "merchants from foreign countries afar and Fujian and Guangzhou nearby."[40] In 1293, the Maritime Trade Commission was established in Ganpu and it became an important overseas trade port during the Yuan Dynasty.

Later on in 1293, in order to promote the status of the Qingyuan Port, the Yuan government merged the Maritime Trade Commission in Wenzhou into the one at Qingyuan. In 1298, the Maritime Trade Commissions in Shanghai and Ganpu were merged into the one at Qingyuan. The status of Qingyuan was lifted to such a new level as to be the first port in the overseas trade of Zhejiang along coastal areas.

At the same time, Qingyuan became the main port for trade with Japan and Korea during the Yuan Dynasty. As was recorded in the first volume of *Folk Customs* of the *Continued Records of the Siming Port*, "(the Qingyuan port) linked Fujian and Guangdong in the south, Japan in the east, and Goguryeo in the north. Merchant vessels came and went overflowing with goods."

In addition to Japan and Goguryeo, Qingyuan Port also maintained trade relations with countries in Southeast Asia, South Asia, the Arab regions and even East Africa. As is recorded in *A Record of Cambodia: The Land and Its People* written by Zhou Guanda, "straw mats produced in Mingzhou (Qingyuan)" were very popular in Khmer (present-day Cambodia). In 1296, merchant ships of the Yuan departed from Qingyuan to countries such as Champa and Khmer for trade. History recorded that more than 220 varieties of goods were imported into this port in the Yuan Dynasty — 50 varieties more than those during the Southern Song Dynasty. Those included various luxury goods and native products from Southeast Asia, as well as spices from Africa. With the expansion of overseas trade, the Yuan government also set up at Qingyuan Port Maritime Trade Warehouses, which housed 28 granaries to store taxed goods.

---

[40] *Statutes of the Sacredly-governed State of the Great Yuan Dynasty: Manufacture.* Beijing: China Radio and Television Press, 1998.

6.4.3 *Import and Export Merchandise in Maritime Trade*

During the Yuan Dynasty, Sino-foreign trade was vibrant, with more types of import and export goods traded compared with those in previous dynasties. According to the records of westerners at that time, "Chinese goods outnumbered those in Rome and Paris. Foreign merchants often brought gold, silver, gemstones to China to buy silk, satin, gold dress, spices and other items, with each sold in large quantities."[41]

At the same time, in order to stabilize the domestic economic order, some goods were banned from exports. In 1286, it was stipulated that "those who were banned from overseas trade could not use copper coin as money." In 1283, "Meng Gudai pointed out that when merchants used money to trade incense wood, a prohibition was issued, with the exception of iron." In 1288, "Guangzhou officials and people were prohibited from transporting rice to the Champa and other countries for sale." In 1293, it was stipulated that "all gold, silver, copper and iron was forbidden from being sold to anybody, male or female."

(1) Export Commodities

According to *A Brief Record of the Barbarians of the Isles*, more than 150 kinds of commodities were exported to overseas countries during the Yuan Dynasty. They could be mainly divided into three categories: agricultural products, resource products and handicraft products, with handicraft products as the main kind.

(i) Agricultural Products

Agricultural products were mainly grain and fruit. It was stated in an official document issued in 1288 that "Canton officials and people bought hundreds of bushels (*dan*), thousands of bushels, even tens of thousands of bushels of rice in the countryside and shipped them to Champa and other countries for sale, making huge profits."[42] Due to the large population of China, the grain issue was listed as an important national strategic resource. Therefore, the Yuan government repeatedly banned grain

---

[41] Henry Yule: Cathay and the Way Thither. Vol. 3. New York: Cambridge University Press, 2009: 98.

[42] *Legislative Articles from the Comprehensive Regulations*. Vol. 18. It is a collection of jurisdictional edicts and laws from the Yuan Dynasty (1279–1368).

exports. Generally speaking, grain exports did not occupy an important position in foreign trade. In addition to food, a certain amount of lychees and other fruit in Fujian and Guangdong were also exported, mainly to the markets in Southeast Asia.

(ii) Resource Products

China's diverse climate and soils created rich natural resources of flora and fauna, as well as minerals. With the progress of civilization, the functions of various resources were gradually developed and recognized. Among them, the development of Traditional Chinese Medicine made medicinal materials an important commodity on the market. In the process of the opening-up, there appeared in overseas countries a demand for such substances as rhubarb, ligusticum wallichii, angelica dahurica and camphor, which were mainly exported to markets in Japan, Goguryeo and Southeast Asia. Cinnabar, which as a pigment was available for "women to dye their fingernails and clothes," was rather popular in Sugitan State (in present-day central Java).

(iii) Handicraft Products

Handicraft products fell into the following categories:

(a) Textiles

Silk of various colors was a traditional export commodity of China through the ages. It was still a bulk export good sold overseas during the Yuan Dynasty. Particularly, the five-color satin and silk produced in Suzhou and Hangzhou were widely sold in overseas markets. Cotton textile technology spread rapidly after its being introduced from abroad, and cotton textiles not only sold well on the domestic market, but also were exported overseas in the late Yuan Dynasty, becoming a new bulk export product for China. According to the data found in *A Brief Record of the Barbarians of the Isles* written by Wang Dayuan, more than 30 kinds of cotton textiles were exported overseas in the Yuan.

(b) Porcelainware

Porcelainware of the Yuan Dynasty sold well in Asian and African countries, especially in Southeast Asia, which imported a large number of Chinese porcelains, such as under-glazed blue-white bowls, tile urns, thick bowls, water jars, and pots. In modern times, a large number of Yuan ceramics produced in Chuzhou in Zhejiang, Quanzhou and Dehua in

Fujian have been unearthed in Indonesia, the Philippines and other countries. Even West Asia and Africa also imported a lot of Chinese porcelains, as was recorded by Ibn Battuta, a 14th-century Moroccan traveler. In his travel notes he related how Chinese porcelain of the best variety were sold to India and other countries, including his homeland of Morocco. To date, blue and white porcelain of the Yuan Dynasty have been preserved in the national museums of West Asian countries like Iran and Turkey. Many porcelain relics of the Yuan were unearthed in many parts of Africa. More than 10 varieties of porcelain, including glazed porcelain, white porcelain and blue and white porcelain, were sold to dozens of countries and regions abroad.

(c) Metals and Metal Products

In the Yuan Dynasty, a specialized state-run iron making industry was initiated. The government recruited craftsmen to produce iron products in fixed venues, resulting in a considerable output of iron products. Some production and living tools, such as iron pots, iron cauldrons and iron ploughs, were shipped overseas,[43] together with semi-finished products, such as iron bars, iron blocks, as well as tinware and bronzeware. Among the Chinese export commodities recorded in *A Brief Record of the Barbarians of the Isles*, Chinese copper and ironware were exported to more than 80 countries and regions. For example, Khmer (present-day Cambodia) imported many Chinese iron pots, copper plates and tin wares. Although the export of those goods was forbidden, gold and silver were still smuggled to other countries.

(d) Daily Utensils

With the expansion of Sino-foreign trade and the reduction of shipping costs, traded items increasingly shifted away from luxury goods to ordinary consumer goods. In the trade with Southeast Asia, some daily utensils, high in quality and inexpensive in price, such as wooden combs, lacquerwares, umbrellas, mats, needles, curtains, etc. were exported. The *Statutes of the Yuan Dynasty: Overseas Trade* recorded that "we could exchange our 'useless' items, like umbrellas, millstones, porcelains, utensils, curtains, for their useful objects." In addition to daily necessities, toys

---

[43] In 1993, archaeologists salvaged a Yuan Dynasty overseas trading ship in Suizhong, Liaoning, full of porcelain and iron.

begun to be exported overseas, such as Mahorage,[44] ceramic animals, which were so popular in Southeast Asia that "groups of children competed to purchase them."

(e) Cultural Items
The export of various classics and stationery continued to develop on the basis of the previous generation, and their export market was still concentrated in Goguryeo and Japan. In addition, there was a significant increase in the export records of various musical instruments, such as the *Guqin*, the *Ruanqin*, drums, and the *Ban* in the literature during this period.

(f) Processed Food
Food exports in the Yuan Dynasty mainly consisted of wine, salt, sugar, tea leaves, etc. These foodstuffs had been exported before the Yuan Dynasty, but their quality and quantity were improved during the Yuan. The demand for tea leaves was driven by the increasing number of Chinese who migrated to Southeast Asia at the end of the Southern Song Dynasty.

(2) Imported Commodities
There was also a great variety of goods imported from overseas countries in the Yuan Dynasty. According to the *History of the South China Sea in the Dade Period* in the early Yuan, "more people came here than in the past. The number of treasures were several times greater than that recorded in the previous records."[45] Among them, more than 70 kinds of cargo were imported from the east and the west via Guangzhou Port. The late Yuan Dynasty saw imported foreign goods soar in number.

According to the *Continued Records of the Siming Port* written by a subject of Yuan named Wang Yuangong during the Zhizheng period, 227 kinds of imported goods came into China from Siming (also known as Qingyuan, present-day Ningbo) port, including those from the west and

---

[44] A special ceramic product, transliterated from Sanskrit, originally meant "son of Buddha." When introduced to central China, its meaning was extended to denote a "boy." *Mahorage* therefore refers to a fired terracotta figure of a boy. Generally, it is sold around Chinese Valentine's Day on 7 July, to people who pray for a son or blessing, or to children as a toy.

[45] (The Yuan Dynasty) Chen Dazhen. *The History of the South China Sea in the Dade Period*. Vol. 7.

those from Japan and Goguryeo. A total of 352 kinds of overseas products and commodities were recorded by Wang Dayuan in *A Brief Record of the Barbarians of the Isles*. Based on the above literature, if items mentioned repeatedly were eliminated, the types of commodities imported from the southeastern coastal ports of the Yuan would number around 300. According to the *Compendium Manuscript of Song* written by Xu Song in the Qing Dynasty, more than 230 types of goods were imported by the Maritime Trade Commission in the Song Dynasty, indicating a significant increase in the types of imported goods in the Yuan.

Imported goods could be divided into the following four categories:

(i) Luxuries

Luxury goods mainly included ivory, rhino horns, crane tops, pearls, corals, turquoises, kingfisher feathers, loggerhead turtle shells and hawksbills from Southeast Asia, the Indian Peninsula, the Arabian Peninsula or Africa, which were imported principally to meet the luxurious demands of feudal aristocrats.

(ii) Spices and Medicines

Fragrant medicines included a variety of spices and medicinal materials, mainly from Southeast Asia, Arabia and East Africa, with a few from Goguryeo. Imported precious spices were mainly agarwood, instant incense, sandalwood, rose water, frankincense, and dalbergia wood. There were also some ordinary spices, that could be used as condiments or medicines. Those so-called "spice medicines" included Poria cocos, pepper, cloves, and cardamom. Meanwhile, myrrh, ferula and dragon's blood (daemonorops draco) were mainly imported as medicinal materials.

(iii) Cloth, Vessels and Leather Goods

There were white cloth, flower cloth and camel cloth; Goguryeo-made copperware, various leather goods and rattan mats, coconut palms from the East and the West.

(iv) Raw Material Products

Imported wood, mainly from Japan, was very popular among the Yuan people as a high-quality material for construction and shipbuilding. The new lacquer produced by Goguryeo was excellent in texture and suitable for wax decoration. In the production of blue and white porcelain of the Yuan, blue glaze (cobalt oxide), also known as Samarraused, were imported as glaze.

6.4.4 *Modes of Transaction in Maritime Trade*

With the development of Sino-foreign trade and the expansion of trade scale, trading modes became diversified. Prior to the Yuan, most Sino-foreign trade was conducted by foreign merchants in China, and their transactions were also completed within the Chinese territory. The typical mode of trade was that foreign merchants brought goods to China for sale, obtaining silver or copper as money, and then purchased commodities in China for export. In the Yuan Dynasty, under the government policy of encouraging maritime trade, more Chinese merchants went abroad and gradually occupied a dominant position in the Indian Ocean. Therefore, western travelers saw a large number of Chinese merchant ships in the Arabian Sea, and ports of India and Southeast Asian countries, with absolute advantage in number and scale. Ibn Battuta, the Moroccan traveler, observed that "all traffic between India and China was overseen by the Chinese."[46]

In the Sino-foreign trade communications of "introducing in" and "sailing out" of China, the trade between the Yuan and other overseas countries was sometimes conducted in the form of barter. For instance, one *peck* of tin could be bartered in exchange for a walking stick made of rattan *produced* in the Soul Mountain (present-day Swallow Cape, Vietnam) or three sticks, there were "rough and with sparse textures." "Merchants bartered with tin for the cambric produced in Vanavāsi (now on the west coast of the Indian peninsula).

Some traded with currency, like gold and silver. For example, the spices produced on Ambergris Island (now Balas Island, northwest of Sumatra) were "obtained with gold and silver." In particular, it is worth mentioning that due to the frequent trade between overseas countries and the Yuan, foreign currencies established certain exchange ratios with the Yuan banknotes. To take as an example, the copper coins of Cochin in Southeast Asia, "on the civilian market, 67 coins could be exchanged for one tael of silver, while on the official market the ratio was 70:1."

---

[46] Zhang Xinglang. *Collection of Historical Sources on the Communication between China and the West* [M]. Vol. 2. Beijing: Zhonghua Book Company, 1978.

Lavo (present-day southern Thailand) used the Pazai as currency. It was recorded that "every 10,000 Pazai could be exchanged for a certain amount of Zhongtong Banknotes made out of silk (issued in 1260, the 1st year of the Zhongtong period). The exchange rate was equal to 24 taels of silver (banned from being used directly in foreign trade at that time), which was quite convenient for exchange." Both silver and Pazai were used as currencies in Udra and other places, where every silver piece "could be exchanged into ten taels of Zhongtong banknotes, equal to more than 11,520 Pazai."[47]

6.4.5 *Major Countries and Regions as Maritime Trade Partners*

With the implementation of the policy of opening-up, the Yuan government enhanced its national power with more countries and regions conducted overseas trade with China. It was recorded that "after the Yuan was established, the whole country began to speak the same language and abide by the same rituals, the territory became unprecedentedly large, the size of which had never been heard before. Thousands of foreign countries came to establish official contact with tributes of jade and jewels. Ships loaded with mountains of cargoes were seen sailing on the sea. Mutual markets were set up. Chinese merchants sailing westward were found to engage in trade actively in foreign countries."[48] Wang Dayuan, the traveler from the Yuan Dynasty, twice "sailed on the sea by ship" and recorded his experiences in his book *A Brief Record of the Barbarians of the Isles* after his returning to China. As was recorded in the book, there were more than 90 countries and regions mentioned in the book he had visited."

It could be seen that during the Yuan Dynasty, Chinese merchant ships spread all over the East and West. Places, such as Basra (in present-day Iraq) and Zanzibar (in present-day Tanzania) in the Persian Gulf were visited frequently by Chinese merchant ships. In the Song Dynasty, merchant travelers from China to Quilon (Kaulam in the Yuan Dynasty, located in southwestern India) sailed by Chinese ships, and then they would change to Dayi ships on the westward journey. This indicated

---

[47](The Yuan Dynasty) Wang Dayuan. *A Brief Record of the Barbarians of the Isles.* Beijing: Zhonghua Book Company, 1981.

[48](The Yuan Dynasty) Wang Dayuan. *A Brief Record of the Barbarians of the Isles: Epilogue.*

that the number of Chinese merchant ships reaching the west of the Indian peninsula was quite small. It was not until the Yuan Dynasty that Chinese merchant ships often sailed directly to the Persian Gulf and various large ports in Africa. This showed that the geographical scope of China's overseas trade was extended farther and farther away in more areas.

The number of countries and regions that engaged in overseas trade with the Yuan increased greatly compared with in previous dynasties. According to the *History of the South China Sea in the Dade Period* mentioned earlier, 143 overseas countries and regions traded with Guangzhou. The names of more than 200 overseas places were mentioned as trading partners in the book *A Brief Record of the Barbarians of the Isles* mentioned earlier.

(1) Countries Connected via the Eastern Seaway
(i) Goguryeo

The Yuan Dynasty traded with Goguryeo overland and via sea. Official and non-governmental trade between the two countries occurred on a considerably large scale. Tributary trade was the main form of official trade. According to statistics, in the Yuan Dynasty, Goguryeo came to pay tribute as many as 138 times, ranking first among foreign countries. Those countries that paid tributes to China gained high profits, but the gifts given back by China were not subject to their own discretion, so the other's disappointment often ensued. Thus, the Goguryeo government sent people to conduct direct trade. For example, in March 1342, the King of Goguryeo sent Nan-kung Xin with 20,000 *pi* of cloth as well as gold and silver to trade in Youyan (northern Hebei and Liaoning). Volume 31 of the *History of Goguryeo* recorded that in 1295, the King of Goguryeo sent people to "sail to the Yidufu to trade with 14,000 bolts (*pi*) of sackcloth in exchange for Chinese paper money." The Goguryeo merchants then used the paper money they exchanged to buy goods from the Yuan. Later, the King of Goguryeo sent people to Hangzhou to discuss trade matters with the local government.

Non-governmental trade between the two sides was conducted on a more frequent basis. As early as 1222, a mutual market was set up for bilateral trade on the border between the Yuan and Goguryeo. The Yuan government sent officials to manage and collect taxes. Bilateral trade developed via sea was even more impressive. According to Vol. 30 of the

History of Goguryeo, in 1293, the Yuan government dispatched Chen Yong, the Cheonho of Jiangnan, who led 20 ships loaded with rice to trade with the imperial family of Goguryeo.

In the season when the north wind blew, Goguryeo merchant ships often sailed to Qingyuan (now known as Ningbo) and Quanzhou for trading activities; while in the season when the south wind was dominant, Yuan Dynasty merchant ships sailed north to Goguryeo for trade. Endless streams of merchants traveled from the Yuan to Goguryeo via sea. In addition to merchants from coastal ports, there were also merchants from Dadu, who perhaps sailed from the northern port of Zhigu (present Tanggu in Tianjin).

There were many merchants from Goguryeo who came to trade in the Yuan Dynasty. For instance, in the Chinese textbook of Goguryeo, a story titled *Old Qita* related how a Goguryeo merchant went to the Yuan to conduct trade.

In the Yuan Dynasty, significant progress was made in the silk production technology of Goguryeo and its textiles formed its own characteristics. Some Goguryeo merchants imported raw silk from China and then exported it back to China after the material had been processed into "flower damask silk and tight-silk brocade."[49]

In the Yuan Dynasty, China and Goguryeo exchanged a wide variety of goods. In addition to various native products, such as animal skins, seafood, and ginseng, the goods imported into China from Goguryeo also included a variety of handicraft products, such as paper, ramie, and gold and silver utensils. This showed that with the socioeconomic development of Goguryeo, more varieties of goods were considered tradable. At the same time, silk fabrics were still the main goods exported from China to Goguryeo. In addition, the export of porcelain, grain, wine, and paper money was conducted on a certain scale, too.

(ii) Japan
The Yuan Dynasty attached great importance to the development of Sino-Japanese trade. As early as 1278, Emperor Shizhu of the Yuan "issued a decree that all coastal departments and offices should develop

---

[49](The Song Dynasty) Xu Jing. *Illustrated Text of the Hsüan-ho Emissary to Korea.* Vol. 23. Complete Library in the Four Branches of Literature.

trade with Japan."[50] Although the Sino-Japanese trade was temporarily interrupted due to Kublai Khan's crackdown on the intrusion of the Wokou into China's coastal areas, in general, both governments adopted active policies and the bilateral trade relations developed quite well. During 1341–1369, more than 100 Japanese merchants who went overseas to trade were caught in a storm and drifted to Goguryeo, and unfortunately, "their goods fell into Goguryeo people's hands, and were confiscated with the consent of the Goguryeo government. Those Japanese merchants were made slaves." They were declined by the Yuan on the premise that "the Emperor equally treated Goguryeo and Japan. How could they take advantage of others when they were in difficulty? They had better return what was confiscated in the form of money." Later, the King of Japan expressed his gratitude and kept closer bilateral relations with China.[51] Based on the records found in the *History of Yuan* alone, during the 64 years from 1277 to 1341, Japanese merchant ships went dozens of times to the coastal areas of Jiangsu and Zhejiang provinces for trade.

In addition, according to the *History of Cultural Exchanges between Japan and China* (*Nikka bunka kōryūshi*) written by Yoshihiko Kinomiya, "Japanese merchant ships that sailed to the Yuan, except for the Tenryuji ship dispatched in 1342, were private merchant ships with extremely frequent visits to China almost every year. The last 60 to 70 years of the Yuan was the period when more Japanese merchant ships visited China than in previous dynasties … Monks who visited the Yuan and whose names have been passed down to the present exceed 220 in number. As for the unknown monks, nobody knew how many of them there in the Yuan. They all took merchant ships to and from China in twos and threes. This showed a the profusion of merchant ships in the Yuan Dynasty."

Most of those merchant ships were the private ships belonging to adventurous merchants from western Japan. Among them, there were also official merchant ships dispatched to complete certain tasks under the protection of the Shogunate. The most typical example was the Tenryuji ship, an official Japanese merchant ship protected by the Shogunate, whose leader was recommended by the temple and appointed by the Shogunate. The number of ships and the duration of voyages were

---

[50] (The Ming Dynasty) Song Lian *et al. History of Yuan*. Vol. 10. Beijing: Zhonghua Book Company, 1976.

[51] *Ibid.*, Vol. 140.

also determined by the Shogunate. After returning, regardless of profit or loss, a certain amount of money was to be paid to the temple. Merchant ships, both private and official, gained handsome profits from the trade.

Japanese merchants who took the initiative to trade were encouraged in the Yuan and the Yuan government took a positive attitude toward Sino-Japanese trade. The Yuan government made an exception to allow Japanese merchants to trade with gold for copper coins, and demanded that coastal governments at all levels should conduct trade with Japan.

Yuan's merchant ships went to trade in Japan as well. For example, in 1350, it was by a Yuan merchant ship that the Japanese monks Ryusan Tokuken and Wumeng Yiqing returned to Japan. Another example was how Deng Kai, a native of Jishui in Jiangxi in the late Yuan Dynasty, "once sailed eastward to Japan."

Commodities traded between the two countries were of great variety and quantity. The goods exported to Japan from the Yuan fell into three categories: (a) textiles, including silk products, such as the brocade and damask silk of the Tang, special craft fabrics, like gold gowns (woven with gold silk into patterns), gold yarn and wool-based fabrics, like felt; (b) ceramics; (c) various cultural goods, like books, stationery, paintings of the Tang, etc.; (d) a variety of spices and medicines. China has always banned the export of copper coins, but Japanese merchants were allowed to come with gold to be traded for copper coins, which was a special measure taken by the Yuan government to attract Japanese merchants. Spices and medicines were traditional commodities exported to Japan. In the middle and late periods of the Yuan Dynasty, trade between China and Japan was dominated by spices and medicines, and their export scale exceeded that in the Tang and Song Dynasties.

With the construction of Zen temples in Kyoto, Kamakura and other places in Japan, the scriptures and utensils used in Zen temples were exported continuously from China to Japan. The books of Confucianism, Taoism, philosophers, historical records, and others required by Japan were all imported from the Yuan. Main imports of the Yuan from Japan were gold, knives, swords, fans, *miaojin* (paintings using gold powder), and *luodian* (decorations made from seashells).

In the Yuan Dynasty, Qingyuan and Hakata were the principal ports for merchant ships sailing between China and Japan. During the Song and Yuan Dynasties, Qingyuan had always been a port for trade with Japan, and most Japanese merchant ships entered the Yuan from this place. There were also Japanese ships sailing in and out of the coastal areas of Shandong and Fujian. Yuan's merchant ships would sail to into Hakata Port of Chikuzen, where Japanese monks gathered to wait for the merchant ships sailing to China.

(2) Countries Connected via the Western Seaway
(i) Maritime Trade with Countries on the Indochina Peninsula

The Yuan government developed close trade relations with many countries on the Indochina Peninsula, specifically Jiaozhi, Champa, Khmer, Siam, Myanmar and others.

Cochin (in present northern Viernam) was close to China in terms of distance. The two parties maintained close trade ties for a long time. However, from the Chen Dynasty of Cochin (1010–1385), the King restricted Yuan's merchants from trading in Cochin. Regardless of this prohibition, the smuggling trade of "private ships" continued.[52] The two parties conducted mutual trade in the bordering areas, with "Cochin people exchanging fragrant incense, rhinoceros, gold, silver, salt, and money for China's damask silk, brocade, leno, and cloth every day." "Those things considered good for longevity in Cochin were imported from Qinzhou (in Guangxi). Ships were seen shuttle between the two countries."[53]

Yuntun in Cochin was the main port visited by merchants in the Yuan Dynasty. According to the Vietnamese history book written by Chen Qingyu, "they conducted trade for a living with their food and clothes dependent on imports from northern tourists, so they followed northern people's customs in life."[54] With the expansion of the trade scale, Yuan Zhongtong banknotes also flooded into Cochin. The commodities that were exported from China to Cochin were mainly silk fabrics, paper and iron wares, and the commodities imported from Cochin to China mainly included alluvial gold, silver, tin, lead, ivory, and kingfisher feathers.

---

[52] (The Yuan Dynasty) Wang Dayuan. *A Brief Record of the Barbarians of the Isle*. Beijing: Zhonghua Book Company, 1981.

[53] (The Song Dynasty) Zhou Qufei. *Representative Answers from the Region beyond the Mountains*. Vol. 5. Yang Wuquan, *Collation*. Beijing: Zhonghua Book Company, 1999.

[54] Ngô Sĩ Liên. Đại Việt sử kí toàn thư. Vol. 7.

At the beginning of the Yuan Dynasty, Champa (now southern Vietnam) fought a war with the Yuan, but later the two sides resumed friendly exchanges and trade relations afterwards. Located on the hub along the sea route, Champa occupied a critical position in sea transportation and became a supply center for Chinese merchant ships to the Indian Ocean. It was recorded that "Chinese merchant ships sailing to and fro all gathered here for supplies. It became the premiere dock in the south."[55] Merchants of the Yuan also went to Champa for trade activities. Some merchants even settled in Champa and intermarried with local women.[56] Officials also maintained the tributary trade. In 1264, Champa envoys came to China to report that had obstructed their tribute to the Yuan.

The official and non-governmental trade relations between the Yuan and Khmer (now Cambodia) were also relatively close. The two sides sent envoys to each other to develop official trade. History recorded that in 1285, "Khmer and Champa paid tributes in the form of musicians, medicinal materials, crocodile skins and others."[57] From 1281 to 1295, the Yuan government sent three batches of envoys to Khmer. The Yuan also saw merchant ships trade actively between China and Zhenla. At the end of the Song and the beginning of the Yuan, many merchants from Fujian, Zhejiang, and Guangdong lodged in Khmer to conduct trade activities and were welcomed by the locals. A Yuan subject named Zhou Daguan once went to Khmer on a mission from the empire. After returning to China, he wrote *A Record of Cambodia: The Land and Its People* based on his personal experience, which also contained records of the trade situation between the two sides. He noted that "some sailors of the Tang liked this country where people did not wear clothes, and there was more rice, more women, cheap housing, abundant utensils and easy trade, so they often escaped to Khmer." Hence, many Chinese merchants settled in Khmer because of trade. The main commodities imported from Khmer were kingfisher feathers, ivories, rhino horns, and spices. In addition to traditional bulk commodities of silk, porcelain, and lacquer, the commodities

---

[55] *Lê Tắc An Nam chí lược: Border Service*. Vol. 1. *Complete Library in the Four Branches of Literature*.

[56] (The Yuan Dynasty) Wang Dayuan. *A Brief Record of the Barbarians of the Isles*. Beijing: Zhonghua Book Company, 1981.

[57] (The Ming Dynasty) Song Lian *et al. History of Yuan: Annals of Emperor Shizu of the Yuan*. Vol. 13. Beijing: Zhonghua Book Company, 1976.

exported to Khmer from China also included daily necessities of umbrellas, iron pots, copper plates, wooden combs, needles, etc.

During the Song and Yuan Dynasties, there ruled contemporaneously the Sukhothai Dynasty established by the Thai people (now central Thailand) and the Lopburi Kingdom established by the Mon people in the lower Chao Phraya River in Thailand. Both of them conducted official exchanges and trade activities with the Yuan. In 1293, the Yuan's first Emperor Shizu "sent envoys to Siam," and official exchanges begun between the two sides. During the period 1293–1300, the Yuan government sent three batches of envoys to Sukhothai. Meanwhile, Sukhothai envoys came to the Yuan for as many as 12 times. The Yuan treated the Sukhothai envoys as distinguished guests and rewarded them with generous gifts. In 1289, 1291 and years thereafter, Lavo also sent envoys to the Yuan government. Siam was merged into Lavo in 1349, and the new regime was called Siam.

The commodities exported by the Kingdom of Siam to the Yuan mainly included lavo incense, sappanwood, rhino horns, ivory, kingfisher feathers, banca tin, chaulmoogra, beeswax and so on. The commodities imported into Siam from the Yuan mainly included mercury, blue and white porcelain, black cloth, calico, copper, iron, gold, tin, nitrate bead, and Hainan betel nuts.

At the beginning of the Yuan Dynasty, the Myanmar Pagan Dynasty collapsed and regional authorities were established one after another. Most of them submitted to the rule of the Yuan as "Fan" (vassal states). The Yuan government set up the Pacification Department there as an organ of administration. Therefore, the relationship between the two parties was closer than that in the previous dynasties. In 1289, the Burmese King of Pagan sent envoys to China. In 1296, he also sent his son Sanghapashu Sabangpa to develop friendly relations with the Yuan. The Yuan government responded with many parties of envoys going to Myanmar for return visits.

The sea route trade between the Yuan and Myanmar was relatively well developed. *A Brief Record of the Barbarians of the Isles* by Wang Dayuan gave a special description of places such as Tavoy and Martaban in Lower Burma, all of which were seaport cities in the Mon area. The Yuan merchant ships often sailed to those ports and exchanged silk, cloth, porcelain, musical instruments, gold and silver, copper and iron for special products of Burma, such as ivory, pepper, kingfisher feathers, beeswax, and kapok bush.

With the frequent trade exchanges between the two sides, the Yuan Zhongtong banknotes were found circulating in Myanmar and a certain price ratio was formed with the local currency and silver coins. At the same time, the Pazai circulating in Myanmar was also very popular in Yunnan, China. Because it was relatively convenient in traffic to trade in Myanmar, at least in the Yuan Dynasty, quantities of merchants in Quanzhou, Fujian and other places went to trade in the coastal areas in Lower Myanmar. "Nine out of ten did not return" to China. Many got married and sired children in local places, becoming the early overseas Chinese in Myanmar.

During the Yuan and Ming Dynasties, the jade trade between China and Myanmar was very prosperous. In Mengmi, northern Myanmar, there was a "treasure well" producing precious jade. In the 13th century, Yunnan people had mined jade in northern Myanmar, and the annual output reached about 1000 piculs (*dan*). More than 100 Chinese jade merchants sailed to, generally speaking, Bhamo, Myanmar. They transported jade back to Tengchong, Yunnan, where the jade were processed into trinkets, and then sold back to Myanmar and the Yuan.

(ii) Maritime Trade Countries on the Malay Peninsula
The main countries on the Malay Peninsula to trade with Yuan China were Tambralinga, Panang, Kelantan, etc.

Tambralinga, also known as Damalingam (Tambeiling River Basin in Pahang, Malaysia), was located at the main maritime route where merchant ships often passed by in the Yuan Dynasty. Batu Berlayar as a port in Tambralinga had a prosperous trade "with Quanzhou."[58] There were some Chinese people who settled here in the Yuan Dynasty. Tambralinga traded with high-end white tin, tin bar, rice brain, loggerhead turtle shell, crane top, tanarius major, yellow ripe scent for China's Ganli cloth, red cloth, blue and white flower bowl, drum, pure gold, azure satin, figured cloth, Chuzhou porcelain, iron cauldron and others of the Yuan.

Panang, also known as Pahang, located in Pahang, Malaysia, sent envoys to build good relations with China in the early Yuan Dynasty and traded China's products like thin tough silk, copper and iron wares, lacquerwares, porcelains, drums and other items of the Yuan with alluvial

---

[58](The Yuan Dyansty) Wang Dayuan. *A Brief Record of the Barbarians of the Isles: Batu Berlayar*. Beijing: Zhonghua Book Company, 1981.

gold, ranjatai, agilawood, karpura (dipterocarpus), banca tin, and acronychia pedunculata.

Kelantan, located in Kelantan of Malaysia, had a port named Kota Bharu on the lower reaches of the Kelantan River. It exchanged high-end agilawood, crude dalbergia wood, beeswax, loggerhead turtle shell, crane top, betel nut, banca tin, etc. for the Yuan's Tangtou cloth, Champa cloth, blue plates, flower bowls, red and green octopus beads, *Guqin, Ruanqin*, drum, the *Ban*, etc. of the Yuan China.

(iii) Maritime Trade with Countries on the Malay Archipelago

The Yuan Dynasty maintained close trade relations with countries on the Malay Peninsula, such as Java, Srivijaya, Samudra, Burni and Maluku.

Java used to be Yavadvipa on the island of Java, Indonesia. The war with Java in the early Yuan Dynasty affected the exchanges between the two countries. After the establishment of the Majapahit Empire, it sent envoys to rebuild friendly relations with the Yuan. In the middle period (1295–1333) of the Yuan Dynasty, Java sent more than ten waves of envoys. There were also streams of Chinese merchants sailing to Java. At the port of Manjapahit, various goods brought by Chinese merchants were traded. The local markets were crowded with people and the goods there piled up like mountains. Chinese copper coins could be used here. A Yuan subject named Zhou Zhizhong noted in his *Records on Foreign Lands: Java* that "this country had constant exchanges with China."

At the time of the Yuan Dynasty, Srivijaya (the area around Palembang and Jambi in Sumatra) declined in national power. The relationship between the Yuan government and Srivijaya was not as close as in the period of the Song Dynasty, but there were still trade contacts between the two countries. The commodities that Srivijaya exported to the Yuan were mainly plum blossom borneol, dalbergia wood, betel coconut cotton cloth, fine flower wood, etc. The goods exported to Srivijaya from the Yuan were mainly colored silk, red bead silk cloth, figured cloth, copper iron pot, and the Chu kiln-made porcelain. Palembang, the old capital of Srivijaya, was a city where merchants gathered in the Yuan Dynasty. In the late Yuan and the early Ming, Chinese people from Guangzhou, Zhangzhou, and Quanzhou who met there called Palembang the "Old Port."

Sumudura, also known as Samudra, located in the north of Sumatra, sent many batches of envoys to build good relations with the Yuan and conduct official trade. Maritime trade between the two sides proceeded with some dynamism. In the late Yuan, when Ibn Battuta departed from China, he simply had to board a Sumudura merchant ship from Quanzhou Port. The merchants of Sumudura traded with Karpura acronychia pedunculata and tin bar in exchange for western silk cloth, camphor, rose water, butter umbrellas, black cloth, five-color satin and other commodities of the Yuan.

Burni, also known as Borneo, is situated on the Kalimantan. Its trade with the Yuan China was further developed as many merchants from the Yuan Empire went to trade in Burni. Wang Dayuan once went to Burni and saw that the local people there "respected 'people of the Tang' (Chinese) very much. When they were drunk, local people would escort them back to the place where they stayed."[59] Merchants of the Yuan traded with pure gold, colored satin, and ironware, etc. in exchange for Burni-produced acronychia pedunculata, borneol, chrismatite, and hawksbill, etc.

Maluku refers to the Maluku Islands in Indonesia. With the development of sea transportation, the Yuan developed trade with Maluku in the eastern part of the Malay Archipelago. Maluku people warmly welcomed the arrival of the Yuan merchant ships and "looked forward to the vessels of Tang coming to trade here every year."[60] Merchants of the Yuan used to trade with silver, iron, damask silk, silk cloth, local printed cloth, elephant's teeth, burnt beads, glazed porcelainware, and wine jars for various spices found in abundance in Maluku.

(iv) Maritime Trade with South Asian Countries

The southern part of the Indian peninsula was a hub for East-West maritime traffic. At that time, many merchant ships from the Yuan sailed to the Indian peninsula. At the same time, most envoys and merchants traveling between China and India took Chinese ships. The principal trading partners with the Yuan in this region were Maabar (Pamban), Kaulam, Simhala, and Calicut, etc.

Maabar, located on the coast of Malabar in the southwest of the Indian peninsula, was a must-stop for ships from east to west, and also a hub and

---

[59](The Yuan Dynasty) Wang Dayuan. *A Brief Record of the Barbarians of the Isles: Borneo.* Beijing: Zhonghua Book Company, 1981.

[60](The Yuan Dynasty) Wang Dayuan. *A Brief Record of the Barbarians of the Isles: Maluku.* Beijing: Zhonghua Book Company, 1981.

transfer station for Chinese and Arab traffic. History recorded that "among overseas countries, only Maabar and Kaulam were able to lead other foreign countries, with Kaulam a backup for Maabar."[61] The Yuan and Maabar sent envoys to each other to develop friendly relations. During the nearly 60 years from 1279 to 1337, Maabar sent envoys to the Yuan as many as 11 times. In the same period, the Yuan successively sent 8 batches of envoys to build good relations with Maabar. Merchant ships of the Yuan sought kingfisher feathers, percale, and a large amount of Maabar-grown spices in exchange for alluvial gold, azure satin, alum, and red and green beads. Marco Polo recorded that most of the spices and other goods exported from Maabar were destined for the "barbarian state" (southern China), and the commercial goods shipped westward were "less than one-tenth of those shipped to the extreme east."[62]

Known as Quilon in the Song Dynasty, Kaulam, or present-day Quilon on the southwestern coast of India, was an important point for the East-West sea traffic with frequent exchanges with the Yuan. During the period of 1279–1291, the Yuan government sent 4 batches of envoys to Kaulam, while Kaulam came to develop good relations for three times. Ibn Battuta recorded that "it was the first city in the Malabar area that developed contacts with China. Many Chinese visited this place."[63] At the end of the 13th century, when Marco Polo returned from China, he described the situation of Kaulam in his book, writing that "barbarian (resident of southern China) merchant ships went to trade in this place and gained great profits."[64] The Yuan merchants traded for peppers, coconuts, betel nuts, and *liu yu* (dried fish) rich in Kaulam with gold, silver, blue and white porcelain, Padang cloth, five-color satin, and ironware.

Simhala, also known as the Lion Country (now Sri Lanka), was also one of the centers of transportation between the East and the West. The Yuan government dispatched envoys to Simhala in 1284 and 1293.

---

[61] (The Ming Dynasty) Song Lian *et al. History of Yuan*. Vol. 210. Beijing: Zhonghua Book Company, 1976.

[62] [Italy] Marco Polo. *The Travels of Marco Polo*. Revised from Marsden's Translation and Edited with introduction by Manuel Komroff. New York: W. W. Norton & Company, Inc., 1926. *Also see* Marco Polo. *Le livre de Marco polo* [M]. Nachbaur. 1924.

[63] [Morocco] Ibn Battuta. *The Travels of Ibn Battutah* [M]. Pantianos Classics, 1929.

[64] [Italy] Marco Polo. *The Travels of Marco Polo*. Revised from Marsden's Translation and Edited with introduction by Manuel Komroff. New York: W. W. Norton & Company, Inc., 1926. *Also see* Marco Polo. *Le livre de Marco polo* [M]. Nachbaur. 1924.

In 1292, Simhala too sent envoys to develop friendly relations with the Yuan. The overseas trade between the two countries was conducted in a very prosperous manner. The Yuan merchants often went to the port of Gaolangbu (now Colombo) of Simhala for trading activities. The coins of the Tang, Song and Yuan Dynasties and porcelain of the Song and Yuan Dynasties unearthed at the Saibabu Amajo Fortress in Sri Lanka were important proofs of the trade between China and Sri Lanka at that time.

(v) Maritime Trade with West Asian Countries
The overseas trade between the Yuan and West Asia was principally with Arab countries and the Iraqi Khanate.

In the Yuan Dynasty, official documents often mentioned that ships went to the "Huihui field,"[65] which was roughly equivalent to "Dayi regimes" of the previous dynasties situated in the present-day Arab regions. Many merchants sailed directly to the Arab regions. Wang Dayuan recorded in *A Brief Record of the Barbarians of the Isles* that Basrah (present-day Basra, Iraq), the Paradise (present-day Mekka, Saudi Arabia), Ligata (present-day Port of Aden, Yemen), etc., belonged to the Arab region. Yuan merchants who went to Basrah traded with carpets, five-color satin, Yunnan gold leaf, silver, Japanese iron, Chaulmoogra seed, ivory comb and ironware for the local amber, soft brocade, camel hair, walrus (testiset penis phocae), myrrh, khurma (a 1,000-year jujube), etc. Ligata was the main trade port of the Arabian Peninsula. Merchants of the Yuan often traded for the country's malachite (lapis lazuli) using gold, silver, five-color satin, and Wulun cloth.

The Yuan Dynasty boasted developed outbound transportation. The *Semu* people from Central Asia and West Asia were trusted and employed repeatedly by the Mongolian rulers, which caused a large number of Western Regions and Dayi people to emigrate to China. Quanzhou Port entered its heyday in the late years of the Song and in the years of the Yuan, and Dayi people living in Quanzhou were greatly trusted by the Yuan government. Many Arabs who came to the Yuan became wealthy merchants and were active in major ports along the coast of China. In addition to merchants, soldiers, craftsmen, upper-class people, experts and scholars. were conscripted and recruited to work in Quanzhou. Some of

---

[65](The Yuan Dynasty) Wanyan Nadan. *Legislative Articles from the Comprehensive Regulations.* Vol. 27.

them even settled in China, intermarried with women of the Han ethnicity, and gave birth to children, who gradually became a new group in China as the Hui minority.

The area controlled by the Ilkhanate included present-day Iran, Iraq and other places. It was one of the four Mongolian Khanates that had close relations with the Yuan. Official trade exchanges between the two sides were constantly conducted with non-governmental trade also being very active. In 1290 and 1299, the Yuan government sent envoys to the Ilkhanate. In 1298, the Ilkhanate sent envoys to the Yuan not only with pearls, gems, cheetahs and other gifts, but with 100,000 in cash to purchase Chinese goods.[66] Persian and Arab merchants from the Ilkhanate often went to Quanzhou and Guangzhou for trading activities. Merchants of the Yuan also went to various parts of the Ilkhanate to do business, and many of them settled down in places like Ispahan (present Isfahan).

Al-Hammer (now on the Hols island in the Strait of Hormuz) was a maritime transportation hub between the East and the West, as well as the main port for trade between the Ilkhanate and the Yuan. Most merchant ships of the Yuan landed here. They brought with them cloves, cardamom, black satin, musk, red burnt beads, Suzhou-Hangzhou colored satin, sappanwood, blue and white porcelains, porcelain bottles, iron bars, and returned to China with pepper.

(vi) Maritime Trade with African Countries

With the prosperity of the overseas trade, trade between the Yuan and African countries was further developed. Countries in North Africa and East Africa forged direct trade relations with the Yuan. Among them, larger scale trade was mainly conducted with Misr, Megarian, and Zanzibar (in present Tanzania).

Misr was present-day Egypt. At the time of the Yuan, Egypt was ruled by the Mamluk Dynasty, with developed transportation and prosperous commerce. In 1260, the Egyptian Sultan Baybars of the Mamluk Dynasty defeated the Mongolian army near Damascus and occupied Syria. As a result, the Yuan government communicated more smoothly with Egypt via Central Asia by land or via the Persian Gulf by the sea route. After Baghdad, the trading center of West Asia, was destroyed by the Mongolian army of Hulagu Khan in 1258, Egypt became even more important in

---

[66] *New History of Yuan: The 2nd Year of the Dade Period.* Vol. 109.

East–West trade, maintaining trade relations with both Europe in the west and India and China in the east. It was the communications center of East–West trade. In the Yuan period, merchant ships continued to voyage to Egypt, while many Egyptian merchants went to Hangzhou and Quanzhou to do business, and some even stayed there for the rest of their lives. For example, Osman Ibn Anfani, the leader of the Egyptians living in the Yuan, was a great merchant in Hangzhou.[67]

Megarian was what is present-day Morocco. Both the Yuan Dynasty and Megarian sent envoys to build up good relations with each other. Known as *Diao Jier* in Yuan literature, the port of Tangier in Morocco was a famous international trading port in the Mediterranean and had frequent trade exchanges with the Yuan. It was also the birthplace of the famous Moroccan traveler Ibn Battuta in the 14th century. He once met a Moroccan in the Yuan, who had been engaged in eastern trade for a long time and become rich in China.[68] These records reflected how frequently non-governmental trade was conducted between the two countries.

Tiara was what is present-day Zanzibar island in East Africa. Its merchant ships sailed to the Yuan to trade "with rice, and gained great profit."[69] Merchants of the Yuan traded for locally produced red sandalwood, elephas dentine, ambergris, and raw gold in exchange for silver money, and five-colored satin.

(vii) Maritime Trade with European Countries

The literature of the Yuan Dynasty usually referred to European countries as "Falang," "Fulang," or "Folang" and so on. With the smooth flow of land and sea transportation between China and the west, some European merchants also came to the Yuan for trade. Literature recorded that in addition to Italy's Marco Polo and his son, in May 1261, "Falang State sent people to offer flowers, clothes and other things, and it has been more than three years since they arrived at Shangdu (Dadu)"; "Falang" people said that their "women were pretty and men had blue eyes and yellow hair"; they crossed "two seas, with one voyage spending over a

---

[67] [Morocco] Ibn Battuta. *The Travels of Ibn Battuta* [M]. Pantianos Classics, 1929.
[68] *Ibid.*
[69] (The Yuan Dynasty) Wang Dayuan. *A Brief Record of the Barbarians of the Isles: Tiara*. Beijing: Zhonghua Book Company, 1981.

month, and the other several months. The ships they sailed on could carry five or six hundred people; the Zhanhu vessel they paid as tribute was half in size of a seabird egg, and could warm up cold wine instantly"; "in order to reward them for visiting from afar, the Yuan's Emperor gave back a lot of gold and silk." In the late years of the Yuan Dynasty, there was a "Fulang country offering horses."[70]

Emperor Shunzong (r. 1333–1368) of the Yuan once sent a mission to Europe to establish ties with the Holy See. In July 1342, in order to express appreciation for the kindness of the Yuan Court, the European missions led by Marignolli arrived at Shangdu of the Yuan with credentials and gifts. Among the gifts presented by the mission to Emperor Shunzong of the Yuan was a horse, which was as long as 1.13 cords (*zhang*) and as tall as 6.4 ells (*chi*), with a pure black body and white back hoofs."

6.5 The Influence of Foreign Trade on Socio-Economic Development

Under the opening-up policy of the Yuan Dynasty, foreign trade was conducted extensively and profoundly, with its material and spiritual civilization communicated with Asian and African countries, even European countries, which promoted the economic development and cultural communication of those countries and regions participating in the commercial activities. The Yuan, the leading civilization in the world, promoted its economic and cultural development through import and export trade. With the exportation of commodities and technologies, China's advanced technology spread to more countries and regions and pushed forward the course of world civilization.

6.5.1 *The Influence of Foreign Trade on China's Economy*

(1) Promoting the Advancement of Handicraft Technology

As was mentioned previously, most of the commodities exported in the Yuan Dynasty were handicrafts made from silk and porcelain. On the one hand, demand for the foreign markets led to export-oriented economies emerging in certain coastal regions. To meet the demand for the

---

[70](The Yuan Dynasty) Wang Yun. *Complete Collection of Mr. Qiu Jian's Works*. Vol. 81. Complete Library in the Four Branches of Literature.

foreign markets, products had to be augmented continuously in terms of variety, color, size, and quality. This entailed new requirements for technological innovation. On the other, China could obtain through import some commodities that were scarce domestically. Together with imported commodities came the production technology for certain products. The introduction of technology as such made the country no longer dependent on imports for some products, and realized the innovation in technology as well.

The development of exportation in foreign trade helped China's traditional silk industry innovate continually in its production technology. For example, it introduced from Persia the technology of Nasich, allowing for the production of gold brocade, and from Central Asia the technology of Zandanas, facilitating the production of silk fabric. Both were major achievements in the silk industry at that time.

According to *A Brief Record of the Barbarians of the Isles*, in the Yuan Dynasty, porcelain was exported to at least 50 countries and regions. Huge overseas demand not only expanded the scale of porcelain production, but stimulated technological progress as well. To meet the requirements of large-scale exportation, some regions produced commodities specifically for foreign trade. Archaeological excavations have confirmed that a group of porcelain kilns in Dehua in Fujian targeted their porcelain production at the foreign market. In modern times, the Yuan porcelainware unearthed in East Asian and Northeast Asian countries were quite different from those produced for domestic market in terms of size and color. The difference in size and increase in variety were facilitated by technological advances. Therefore, Yuan porcelain featured diverse technologies of production. For instance, the painting of patterns of birds and animals or scenery and figures on the white plain ground of the blue and white porcelains fired in Jingdezhen in Jiangxi resulted from the absorption of Persian Islamic porcelain art. The blue and white porcelain of the Yuan Dynasty was bright in color with black spots on the glaze because of the application of imported cobalt blue pigment. It was also low in manganese content and rich in iron.

The introduction of cotton promoted the development of China's cotton textile industry, and further accelerated the printing and dyeing industry. According to the *Records of Yuan in the Zhizheng Period* written by Kong Qi, people in Songjiang could dye a kind of blue and white cloth. From Japan they learned the method of dyeing kapok cloth so that its blue pigment wouldn't fade after washing. The book also mentioned that the blue and white cloth was painted with reeds, wild geese, flowers and grass, just like a picture of a garden.

The technology for refining sugar was originally introduced to China from India during the Zhenguan period (627–649) of the Tang Dynasty and was applied for centuries afterwards. In the Yuan Dynasty, the development of Sino-African trade brought to China more advanced sugar refinery technology from Egypt into China. Egyptians, who came to do business in the coastal areas of Fujian, instructed the residents in Wengan City (present-day Yongchun County) of Quanzhou on how to clean sugar by using tree ashes. The sugar refinery technology in local areas was elevated to a remarkable new level, and spread to other areas.

After the Tang and Song Dynasties, large amounts of Persian and Arabic medicinal materials were imported into China, followed by lots of drug merchants, some of which even ran pharmacies in China. Some Persian prescriptions, like "Beisan Soup" (made with milk and long pepper to cure dysentery), were quite popular in China. The Yuan government also set up two "Hui Medicine Academies" in Dadu and Shangdu (in the present-day, Inner Mongolia) in order to "manage the affairs concerning Hui medicine.[71] Affiliated to the Guanghui Department, the academy "was dedicated to researching and producing Hui medicine exclusively for royalty". It was, in effect, the institution specializing in practicing Persian and Arabian medication.

(2) Promoting Economic Development and the Emergence of Cosmopolitan Cities

Some towns specializing in commercial trade or handicraft industry emerged in the Yuan Dynasty. Taicang in Jiangsu "used to be a small village with few residents. Since Zhu Qing, the then Customs Officer in the Yuan, relocated there, he organized local people to cultivate wasteland and build mansions to attract maritime trade. More and more big vessels were seen coming and goling from here. It took only a few years before Taicang grew to be a prosperous city. Foreigners and Han Chinese from Fujian and Guangdong lived in the same communities, observing their own local customs being various and different." "Citizens and sailors as well as their families gathered here as thickly as fog, so were hard to

---

[71](The Ming Dynasty) Song Lian *et al. History of Yuan*. Vol. 88. Beijing: Zhonghua Book Company, 1976.

count; smoke from their kitchen chimneys drifted miles away. As time went by, varieties of precious foreign commodities were piled up all over like stars in the sky; over ten thousand people came to reside here."

During the Southern Song Dynasty (1127–1279), Shanghai as a town was administered by Xiuzhou Prefecture. In the Yuan Dynasty, a Maritime Trade Commission was set up in Shanghai on account of its rapid development in overseas trade. The local population increased so fast that it grew to be a county with its own administration established in 1292, and a new commercial port. After making a fortune as the Director of Grain Transport, Zhu Qing, in the Yuan Dynasty, built mansions in Kunshan, Jiangsu to solicit trade in overseas spices. Grain vessels were seen moored at the port. Within several years, Kunshan developed from a small village to an emerging commercial city, with merchants from afar living here.[72]

Quanzhou, the largest port for overseas trade, became the southeast commercial center driven by foreign exchange. It was recorded by historical documents that "Quanzhou was the metropolis in Fujian. Countless foreign commodities and precious rare treasures converged here. The mansions of merchants and rich tycoons outnumbered those anywhere else in the world."[73] With foreign merchants living in port cities in China, unique architectural styles were introduced to local places. Some religious temples and exotic buildings were constructed in the port cities of Hangzhou, Guangzhou, Quanzhou and so on. In the Yuan Dynasty, there were a considerable number of Muslim buildings in Quanzhou There were even six or seven mosques, all of which were in the Arabic religious style. Marco Polo wrote in his travel notes that the noble and handsome city of "Citong, which was a port on the sea coast celebrated for the shipping resort, full of merchandise, which is afterwards distributed to every part of the province of Manji (the Southern Song regime)... . It is indeed impossible to convey an idea of the number of merchants and the accumulation of goods in this place, which is held to be one of the largest ports in the world."

Dadu the capital city of the Yuan, grew into an international metropolis under the push of foreign trade. In his *Rhapsody on Dadu*, Li Weisun described vividly that "foreigners from the east came across the vast seas

---

[72] (The Yuan Dynasty) Yang Hui. *Kunshan County Gazetteer*. Vol. 1. Continued *Complete Works of Chinese Classics* (Complete Library in the Four Branches of Literature).
[73] (The Yuan Dynasty) Wu Cheng. *Collections of Wu Wenzheng*. Vol. 16.

to pay tributes; travelers from the west went to present their gifts after crossing countless forests and mountains; the aliens from the east arrived to offer their treasures after passing through hot and uncultivated regions; representatives from northern nomadic areas reached here and devoted themselves after striding out of the boundless desert ..." In *The Travels of Marco Polo*, there were more detailed descriptions concerning the prosperous commercial surroundings of Dadu. He stated how "in the public streets there are, on each side, booths and shops of every description .... In this manner the whole interior of the city is disposed in squares so as to resemble a chess-board, and is planned out with a degree of precision and beauty that is impossible to describe." "... the multitude of inhabitants, and the number of houses in the city of Kanbalu, as also in the suburbs on the outskirts of the city of which there are twelve, corresponding to the twelve gates, is greater than the mind can comprehend. The suburbs are even more populous than the city, and it is there that the merchants and others whose business leads them to the capital, take up their abode .... In the suburbs there are also as handsome houses and stately buildings as in the city ... a vast concourse of merchants and other strangers, who, drawn there by the Court, are continually arriving and departing .... To this city everything that is most rare and valuable in all parts of the world finds its way; and more especially does this apply to India, which furnishes precious stones, pearls, and various drugs and spices. From the provinces of Cathay itself, as well as from the other provinces of the Empire, whatever there is of value is brought here, to supply the demands of those multitudes who are induced to establish their residence in the vicinity of the court. The quantity of merchandise sold exceeds also the traffic of any other place; for no fewer than a thousand carriages and pack-horses, loaded with raw silk, make their daily entry; and gold tissues and silks of various kinds are manufactured to an immense extent .... In the vicinity of the capital are many walled and other towns, whose inhabitants live chiefly by the Court, selling the articles which they produce in return for such as their own occasions require."[74]

It also mentioned that the Yuan Emperor imposed heavy salt tax and commercial tax on sugar, rice, liquor, and silk in Hangzhou. There were

---

[74] [Italy] Marco Polo. *The Travels of Marco Polo*. Revised from Marsden's Translation and Edited with introduction by Manuel Komroff. New York: W. W. Norton & Company, Inc., 1926. *Also see* Marco Polo. *Le livre de Marco polo*. Nachbaur. 1924.

12 guilds in Hangzhou, from which the government conducted its extraction of tax. It continued to say that "the Ocean Sea comes within 25 miles of the city at a place called Ganpu, where there is a town and an excellent haven, with a vast amount of shipping which is engaged in the traffic to and from India and other foreign parts, exporting and importing many kinds of wares, by which the city benefits. And a great river flows from the city of Kinsay to that sea-haven, by which vessels can come up to the city itself. This river extends also to other places further inland."[75]

(3) Increasing Fiscal Revenue
The prosperity of foreign trade increased the revenue of the Yuan government, which was described as "the assets of the country." It was demonstrated that foreign trade revenues accounted for an important portion in the total financial revenue. In 1289, Sha Buding, the Administrator of the Branch Secretariat of the Jianghuai, "handed in 400 catties of pearls and 3400 taels of golds to the Maritime Trade Commission." While in 1298, the financial revenue increased to 19,000 taels of gold, 60,000 taels of silver, whose value was 3,600,000 ingots of paper money. With the development of the economy, the tax revenues increased accordingly. Thus, the income from tax in the Dade period (1297–1307) should be higher than that in the Zhiyuan period (1264–1294). Among the revenue from foreign trade, gold alone accounted for around 20% of the total. During the period of 1314–1320, it was recorded that overseas trade tax amounted to "hundreds of thousands of ingots," accounting for 10% of the annual revenue. This indicated the important effect exerted by overseas trade on the financial revenue of the Yuan.

6.5.2 *The Influence of the Yuan Export Merchandise and Sci-tech on Foreign Countries*

With the development of the export trade, the Yuan not only exported a large number of commodities, but spread China's advanced production technology overseas.

---

[75] *Ibid.*

(1) Silk Fabrics and Silk-Weaving Technology

During the Yuan Dynasty, silk fabrics remained the main exported commodities. However, as the scope of foreign trade activities in the Yuan surpassed that in the previous dynasties, the areas to which silk goods were exported widened unprecedentedly with all countries trading with China importing Chinese silk fabrics. At the same time, those exports were impressively large in quantity and silk weaving technology was further diffused. The exportation of silk fabrics and technology not only directly benefited the lives of people in the countries concerned, but promoted their silk weaving industry. For example, the development of trade between China and Java in the Yuan Dynasty brought Chinese sericulture, silk reeling and brocade-weaving technologies to Java, enabling its domestic silk industry to no longer be dependent on foreign imports.

(2) Porcelainware and Porcelain-Making Technology

With the large-scale export of porcelain and the urgent demand from overseas countries in the Yuan Dynasty, the advanced porcelainware and porcelain-making technology spread to more countries. Goguryeo originally imported glazed tiles from China, and then fired them on its own. "The quality and color were better than those sold by Southern Merchants (referring to merchants from southern China who traveled to Goguryeo by sea)."[76]

The Vietnamese first learned the pottery-making technique from China, and then the porcelain-firing technique. In the 13th century, porcelain began to be included among the tributes Vietnam paid to Yuan China. The underglazed blue porcelain (or the blue-and-white porcelain) produced in Vietnam was also influenced by that of the Yuan.

In Khmer, Zhou Daguan of the Yuan Dynasty observed how locals "used Chinese ceramic or copper plates for food."[77]

As early as the Sukhothai Era, King Ram Khamhaeng of Siam (now Thailand) visited China, in 1294 and 1300. On his second return, Ram Khamhaeng took away a group of Chinese porcelain craftsmen, and thus the Sukhothai porcelains created in Siam resembled those produced in the Cizhou kiln in Hebei Province. Decades later, another group of

---

[76](The Ming Dynasty) Zheng Linzhi. *Goguryeosa*. Vol. 28.

[77](The Yuan Dynasty) Zhou Daguan. *A Record of Cambodia: The land and Its People*. Beijing: Zhonghua Book Company, 1981.

Chinese craftsmen were invited to Siam, bringing with them the glazed porcelain technique of Longquan, Zhejiang Province. They helped to produce the celebrated Sangkhalok ceramics in Siam, which were well sold all over Southeast Asia as an important export of Siam at that time.[78]

The porcelainware of the Yuan Dynasty were not only exported to East and Southeast Asia, but also to South Asia, West Asia, and even North Africa and East Africa. The Yuan porcelainware unearthed in those areas served as powerful evidence of this.

In South Asia, the Gauhati State Museum in the capital of Assam in the east end of India displayed several specimens of big flat glazed porcelain bowls from the Longquan kiln of the Yuan Dynasty. Exquisite Chinese ceramics from the Song and Yuan Dynasties were also found at the Yapahuwa site in northern Sri Lanka.

In addition, many porcelainware of the Yuan Dynasty were also found in West Asia. Fragments of simple blue and white bowls from the early Yuan Dynasty were unearthed in Nishapur in northeastern Iran. At the Hama site in Syria, fired imitations of the Yuan's blue and white porcelains were also found, indicating that both Yuan's blue and white porcelain and the techniques for making it were exported to West Asia.

Glazed porcelainware of the Southern Song Dynasty and the greenish white porcelainware of the early Yuan Dynasty were excavated at the Samara site in the north of Baghdad. These were later housed in the Abbasid Palace Museum. Fragments of special Yuan Dynasty celadon bowls with a biscuit-shaped chrysanthemum pattern inside were found on the island of Bahrain on the coast of the Persian Gulf.

Many celadonware and blue and white porcelainware from the Southern Song, Yuan and Ming Dynasties were unearthed from the Abuyan site and other places on the southern coast of the Arabian Peninsula.

Much of the Chinese porcelain of the Yuan Dynasty or their imitations were unearthed in the coastal areas of East Africa and North Africa. All the above evidence helps to draw the conclusion that the export of porcelain in the Yuan Dynasty promoted the emergence and development of porcelain manufacturing in foreign countries.

---

[78] [Britan] W.A.R. Wood. *A History of Siam*. Beijing: The Commercial Press, 1947; Zhu Jieqin. *The Spread of Chinese Porcelain and Porcelain-making Technology to Southeast Asia* [J]. World History, 1979 (2).

(3) Coins and Coin — Minting Technology

With the development of trade between China and foreign countries, China's currency acted as a hard currency for transactions. Coins and banknotes of the Yuan have been found in many countries along the Maritime Silk Road. For example, the introduction of Zhongtong banknotes in the Yuan Dynasty had a great influence on Myanmar. In the first half of the 20th century, many of the Chinese copper coins unearthed in Java and Bali were from the Yuan Dynasty. At the same time, in Java and other places, many copper and tin coins, were locally cast from the 9th to 16th centuries. This indicated that Chinese minting technology had spread overseas. The Yuan's technology for printing banknotes spread as far as North Africa.

(4) Medicine

In the history of medicine, Vietnamese medicine as well as Korean and Japanese medicine were offshoots of Chinese medicine. The Vietnamese termed this "Eastern medicine." During the Song and Yuan Dynasties, traditional Chinese medicine became the major export to Vietnam. Chinese acupuncture was practiced widely by Vietnamese doctors.

In the Northern Song Dynasty, the introduction of Chinese pulse reading exerted great influence on Persia. In the Yuan Dynasty, Rashīdu ad-Dīn Fadl al-Lāh, a celebrated Persian doctor and historian, compiled the *Encyclopedia of Chinese Medicine* in 1313, with discussions on the pulse theory, anatomy, embryology, obstetrics and pharmacology. The Persian medical scientist Avicenna also referred to Chinese pulse theory in his book *Canon of Medicine* (*Al-Qanun Fi Al-Tibb*). At the same time, many Chinese medicines were also introduced to Persia.

(5) Plants and Poultry

Cotton planting was introduced to Goguryeo in the Yuan Dynasty. In 1363, an envoy from Goguryeo named Mun Ik-chom visited China. Upon his return, he gathered more than ten cotton bolls from roadside cotton fields in China and brought them back to Goguryeo. In 1364, he arrived at Jinju, his hometown and gave half of the cotton bolls to his uncle Chong Ch'on-ik for planting. In the autumn of that year, Chong Ch'on-ik harvested more than 100 cotton bolls. After that, Chong Ch'on-ik planted cotton every year. In

1367, Chong Ch'on-ik distributed cotton seeds to villagers and persuaded them to plant the crop, which started the history of cotton planting in Goguryeo.

When Zhou Daguan of the Yuan visited Khmer (now Cambodia), he brought Chinese lychee seeds and planted them on a mountain there. Legend has it that it was only on that one mountain that lychee could survive, though a variety of tropical fruits could thrive in Cambodia. Therefore, people called that mountain "Chinese Lychee Mountain." Originally, there were no geese in Khmer until they were brought into the country by those Khmer traders who visited and returned from their trade in China. This increased the range of poultry in the country.[79]

(6) Books and Musical Instruments

During the Song and Yuan Dynasties, merchants and envoys from foreign countries did not merely conduct trade activities in China, but brought back various stationery and books from China. In 1314 alone, Emperor Renzong (r. 1311–1320) of the Yuan gave 4,371 books as gifts to Goguryeo. These totaled 17,000 volumes. It was during this period that Chinese musical instruments, including drums, the *Ban*, *Guqin*, and *Ruanqin* were sold to the Malay Peninsula and some countries on the Malay Islands via merchant ships, thus promoting the development of culture and art in overseas countries.

(7) Printing and Gunpowder

After the Tang and Song Dynasties, China's Four Great Inventions contin- ued to spread overseas through trade and other channels.

On the basis of the engraving printing in the Tang Dynasty and glue- clay movable type printing in the Song, the Yuan's printing developed into wooden movable type, tin movable type and even copper movable type. Color overprinting was invented in the Yuan. Printing not only promoted the development of Yuan's culture, but contributed to the development of world civilization by the introduction of this technology to foreign countries.

---

[79](The Yuan Dynasty) Zhou Daguan. *A Record of Cambodia: The Land and Its People* [M]. Beijing: Zhonghua Book Company, 1981.

During the Yuan and Ming Dynasties, many Chinese engravers went to Japan to teach Chinese printing and pushed the development of the Japanese printing industry.

Engraving printing, invented in the Tang, was introduced to Iran before the end of the 13th century at the very latest. In the Il-Khanid Dynasty of Iran, during the reign of Gaykhatu, banknotes made through engraving printing's were issued in Tabriz, the capital city. They were imitations of the banknotes of "Zhiyuan Tongbao" of the Yuan Dynasty. On the course of Chinese printing's spreading to the west, Persia was a transit station, a portal to Africa and Europe.

Gunpowder was brought to Goguryeo in the late years of the Yuan Dynasty. It was recorded that the first person who was credited with the introduction of gunpowder technology to Goguryeo was a Chinese merchant from the Jiangnan. When the Yuan army conquered Java, Chinese gunpowder and firearms were brought into what is now Indonesia. After getting the firearms of the Yuan army, the Indonesians soon learned to make gunpowder and firearms for themselves.

As early as the 8th and 9th centuries, Chinese saltpeter was brought to Iran, but the technology of making gunpowder with saltpeter was passed on when the Mongolians ruled Iran. In a battle in Damascus, Sultan Baybars of the Mamluk Sultanate in Egypt defeated the Mongolian Western Expeditionary Army and captured the gunpowder makers and a large number of firearms. From then on, gunpowder entered Egypt. It was first introduced to Europe through Arab merchants who were engaged in trade with the Yuan Dynasty.

6.5.3 *The Influence of Maritime Trade and Immigration*

The opening-up to the outside world promoted the international flow of merchandise personnel as well. Personnel, moving as human capital, enabled the science and technology and cultures of different countries to be communicated in a broader sense.

(1) The Influence of Foreigners in the Yuan

Thanks to the unimpeded transportation between the Yuan China and foreign countries and the opening-up policy, a great number of foreign people came to China. Among them were mainly merchants, envoys, travelers, monks, scholars, and artists.

(i) Policy on Foreign Residents

The Yuan Dynasty not only provided convenience for foreign merchants within China, but adopted an inclusive policy for their cultural and religious beliefs.

The civilization of the Yuan China attracted many foreigners to settle there. It was recorded in historical accounts that "foreigners from the Western Regions served in the Court; some studied in Southern China. Many enjoyed themselves in China so that they even forgot their home countries."[80] *The Rihla of Ibn Battuta* recounted that "in every city of China, there were Muslim residential communities and mosques built as places of worship." The *History of Yuan* also recorded that, in 1286, immigrants from the Kipchak Khanate lived in 19 establishments of "1,000 households" (*Qian hu suo*). In 1330, "10,000 ancient Russian people were recruited to cultivate State Farms.[81]

The management of foreigners who settled in China in the Yuan was different from that in the Tang and Song. The Tang and Song Dynasties enjoyed booming overseas trade, and there were foreigners living in coastal ports in China. The *Fan Fang* system was implemented at that time. Under the premise of complying with Chinese laws, foreigners lived in separate residential areas and selected their heads from among themselves to implement autonomous management. Their customs and religious beliefs were fully respected by the government. But they couldn't enjoy fully naturalized treatment as the Chinese did, and were restricted in the assets purchase and employment.

The Mongolians were, the dominant ethnic group in the Yuan Dynasty, and they occupied the Central Plains as a nomadic ethnic group rising from the Mobei (the region north of the Gobi Desert). During their large-scale western expedition, the Mongolians came into close contact with various ethnic groups in Asia and Europe, and their ethnic policies were different from those in the previous dynasties. As early as in 1235, an imperial edict was promulgated that "anybody captured by the army, regardless of being Tatars (Mongols), Muslims, Kitans, Jurchens, Hans, etc., would, if near their homes, be reduced to servitude. If they were captured in a place far away from their homes, they would be registered as a household in the place where they were

---

[80](The Yuan Dynasty) Wang Li. *Anthology of Wang Li.* Vol. 6.
[81](The Ming Dynasty) Song Lian *et al. History of Yuan: Military Records · Palace Guards.* Vol. 99. Beijing: Zhonghua Book Company, 1976.

captured to be the Emperor's subjects."[82] All ethnic groups living in the areas ruled by the Yuan were managed under a unified household registration system.

In 1289, the Yuan government clearly decreed that "any household in the Jiangnan which accommodated people coming from northern China should have them registered." Therefore, regardless of the birthplace, the system of naturalization of other ethnic groups was practiced in the Jiangnan meant that foreign settlers could become Chinese residents in a formal manner. For foreign residents, their political and economic status was ratified in China.

(ii) The Influence of Foreign Immigrants on Yuan's Science and Technology

The Yuan government showed respect and tolerance for various religious cultures, and implemented statewide treatment for foreigners, which made the foreign residents able to carry out their economic and cultural activities in a free manner. For example, in the naturally formed "Muslim Community" in Guangzhou, mosques, hotels, markets and other places were constructed for religious practices and business activities, where judges and religious leaders were appointed for their administration.

Quanzhou, as the largest port for foreign trade, drew many foreigners from all over the world. A poet of the Yuan wrote about Quanzhou in his poem, observing that "half of the people at the port were foreign merchants with turbaned heads and bare feet; sea treasures were piled up on large ships with high masts." Among these merchants, most were Arabs. There were as many as six or seven mosques in Quanzhou. In addition, Christian churches and Brahma temples were also built there. Malinoli said of Quanzhou that "this was a fascinating sea port and an amazing city. The Franciscan friars had three gorgeous churches in this city, which were very rich in resources with a bathhouse and a storehouse for merchants to safeguard their merchandise."[83] A large number of Arabs, Persians and Muslims from Central Asia lived freely in all parts of China under the unified management of the Yuan government. They dwelt in the same

---

[82] *Statutes of the Yuan Dynasty*. Vol. 57.

[83] [Britain] Arthur Christopher Moule. *Christians in China before the Year 1550* [M]. Beijing: Zhonghua Book Company, 1984.

communities with the Hans, intermarried with the Hans to have descendants in China, thus forming a new community as "Moslems".

Under the opening-up policy of the Yuan, foreigners who settled in China became Chinese residents so they could freely engage in business, official careers and various cultural activities. Some of them made remarkable achievements and became notable merchants, politicians, scholars and artists in Yuan China, which increased the stock of human capital for social and economic development and promoted the technological progress in some fields of China. Among them, there were foreign astronomers and medical experts who even served in the government. They played a vital role in the spread of foreign science and technology in China.

The astronomical calendar, originating from overseas science and technology influenced the Yuan most. The Yuan's Emperor Kublai Khan once recruited the famous Persian astronomer, Jamal al-Din to his mansion. He ordered Jamal al-Din to be responsible for the compilation of the perpetual calendar and the establishment of an observatory in Dadu. Jamal al-Din devised seven astronomical instruments, namely the armillary sphere, the azimuth telescope, the oblique theodolite, the altazimuth, the celestial globe, globe and the astrolabe. Later, the Yuan government set up the Directorate of Muslim Astronomy, with Jamal al-Din appointed as the Superintendent. Those instruments were kept for use in the Directorate of Muslim Astronomy, of which he was in charge. In addition, some astronomical achievements of Egypt were also introduced to China, such as the *Almagest* written by the Alexandrian scholar Ptolemy, and the *Hakimi Zij* (Muslim lunar calendar) designed by the Egyptian astronomer Ibn Yunus. These were of considerable assistance to the Yuan's astronomer Guo Shoujing in revising the Chinese calendar. After the Yuan Dynasty, the trend whereby Chinese astronomical instruments became larger and larger in size was eminently influenced by Egypt.

As flocks of Arabs came to the East, Arab medicine was introduced to China. Emperor Kublai Khan once set up the Office of Medicine (later changed to Muslim Medical Office) to be responsible for the revision of Muslim medical prescriptions and provided medical services for the court and the Arabs in China during the Yuan Dynasty. The famous Arab doctor Ngai-Sie headed the Muslim Medical Office. He also founded the Arab hospital and the Capital Medical Institute in Dadu, where all the staff were Muslim doctors. With the increase in the number of Arab immigrants, the demand for Hui medicine in some coastal ports was on the rise. Muslim hospitals were built to meet the demand. For example, Ottoman, an Egyptian businessman, ran an Arab hospital in Hangzhou.

In the Yuan Dynasty, many Arab merchants sold drugs for a living, a fact which was incorporated by Wang Yi into his poem *A Song of Old Hu Selling Medicine*. He wrote that "A foreign merchant from the Western Regions was 80 years old, boasting unrivalled skills so that he was compared to "God peasant" (a mythical sage healer) living in the Jiangnan for quite a long time as if it were his hometown. He sold medicine to the north of the street at dawn and moved to the east at dusk. Crowds vied to buy his medicine on hearing him tap a copper bell." This poem vividly described the influence of the Muslim doctor on Chinese people. Besides Arabian medicine, Indian medicine was also introduced to China, thereby promoting the enrichment and development of Traditional Chinese Medicine.

With the increase in foreign immigrants and the prosperity of religions, in Guangzhou, Quanzhou and other places where immigrants gathered, some foreign buildings were found being Arab Islamic, Indian Brahman and Buddhist architectural influences. In 1260, Emperor Shizu of the Yuan, invited the architect Anigo from ancient Nepal to come to China with 80 skillful craftsmen to build pagodas and temples. They successively built up many temples and pagodas in Tibet and Dadu, bringing Indian pagoda architectural art into China.

Under the opening-up policy of the Yuan, various foreign cultures were able to survive and develop in China and continue to blend with Chinese culture, which injected fresh blood into Chinese culture to make it more vibrant and diversified.

(2) The Influence of Chinese Overseas

Since the Tang Dynasty, merchants from China who went overseas to trade settled in various regions of Southeast Asia. In the Yuan Dynasty, a large number of merchants traded overseas across vast areas to facilitate greater closeness in Sino-foreign trade relations. Owing to various reasons, the number of Chinese merchants, who stayed and then settled overseas, increased. *A Record of Cambodia: The Land and Its People* by Zhou Daguan recorded that in the Kingdom of Khmer "all trades were done by women, so the people of Tang had to marry a local woman, which could help them to trade there." Many Chinese settled in Khmer and became the earliest overseas Chinese in Cambodia. Some overseas Chinese who settled in Southeast Asia took advantage of the locally abundant natural resources to carry out agricultural production, thus spreading China's advanced agricultural production technology to Southeast Asia and advancing the progress of local agriculture.

The development of Sino-foreign trade also deepened foreign countries' understanding of the advanced technologies of China, and stimulated their strong desire to import Chinese technology. Some countries came directly to China to recruit technical craftsmen, thus making batches of Chinese craftsmen emigrate overseas. As was mentioned previously, Ram Khamhaeng, the King of Siam, came to China in person to pay tributes to the Yuan and recruit ceramic craftsmen. He thereby inaugurated ceramic manufacturing in Thailand. In order to stimulate its woodblock printing industry, Japan recruited Chinese engraving printing craftsmen, many of whom later settled in Japan, making essential contributions to the cultural development of Japan.

In summary, China's opening-up to the outside world reached a new level in the Yuan with smooth overland and sea transportation between Europe and Asia, the improvement of transportation conditions, and the support of government policies. More extensive areas and more fields were opened to the outside world. Through opening-up policy, exchanges were made in commodities, personnel, technologies and cultures, which promoted the development of the commodity economy in China's coastal areas. Some industries developed to being slightly export oriented. The technological and cultural exchanges driven by trade allowed Chinese civilization to make considerable strides and radiate more colorfully.

Admittedly, the opening-up of the Yuan still occurred within the context of the feudal economic system. Its political and cultural opening-up was reflected in a manner of tolerance toward foreign civilizations. The main purpose of its economic opening-up was to obtain scarce materials and increase their use value. This, to some extent, confined the opening-up in terms of degree, scale and level. For example, owing to military and political factors, the Yuan Dynasty at one stage implemented a maritime embargo policy, prohibiting merchants from trading overseas. Even in the period when overseas trade was permitted, restrictions were still enforced on commodities for export trade and on port entry and exit. As a result, while striving to open up to the outside world, it was difficult for the Yuan Dynasty to make high profits on account of its monopolistic products and technologies, or to greatly improve its social welfare.

Chapter 7

Foreign Trade in the Ming Dynasty

The Ming Dynasty and the early Qing marked the late period of the traditional Chinese society. During this period, the population grew and social productivity increased. Centralization and the authority of the monarchy developed to such an unprecedented degree that the feudal regime was facing a multifaceted situation characterized by both prosperity and decline. Meanwhile, simultaneously, the world was advancing from separation to integration, initiating the process of modernization. China, at this point, was increasingly faced with major challenges from the outside world.

In 1368, the Ming's first Emperor Zhu Yuanzhang claimed the throne in Nanjing and established the Ming Dynasty. During the reign of the Ming, China's social productive force was further developed. On the basis of the prosperous state of agriculture and the handicraft industry in the Jiangnan area, the commodity economy proceeded with more dynamism so that sprouts of capitalism even emerged sporadically in parts of southern China.

China's traditional exports were further commoditized, laying a strong material foundation for conducting overseas trade. Nevertheless, civilian trade ties with other countries were relentlessly and deliberately stifled in consideration of consolidating the feudal regime. The early Ming Dynasty even practiced a policy of strict maritime embargo. The groundbreaking overseas expeditions by the prominent navigator Zheng He — though initiated by the government itself — proved to be only a flash in the pan. Maritime trade was inevitably on the wane.

Meanwhile, in the late 15th and early 16th centuries, Europeans discovered the sea passage to India and Americas. From then on, the political and economic landscape of the whole world underwent significant changes. Regions in Asia, Africa, and America were claimed as European colonies. Traditional Sino-foreign relations came under attack with Sino–European trade continued, but the tributary trade with Asian and African countries on the decline. Nevertheless, private trade surged forward vigorously.

The Ming regime was forced to partially open up its overseas trade, finally legalizing civilian overseas trade. However, this business was still restricted by the feudal government and at a great disadvantage in competing with European colonizers. With governmental support, Europeans gradually dominated trade in the western Pacific and the northern Indian Ocean, and China increasingly lost its dominance over maritime trade in the East.

7.1 Socio-Economic Development

The Ming Dynasty spanned almost four centuries from 1368 to 1644. Its history can be roughly divided into three periods: the early Ming period (from the mid-14th century to the early 15th century), the middle Ming (from the early 15th century to the late 16th century), and the late Ming (from the late 16th century to the early 17th century).

During the early and middle periods of the Ming Dynasties, social production forces were developing in general and improving gradually. The economic boom was seen to occur in the first two periods. In the late Ming, the productive forces got so destroyed that the social economy decline. On the whole, great development was made during the Ming period in agriculture, commerce and handicraft industry, laying the social and economic foundation for the development of foreign trade.

7.1.1 *The Improvement in Social Productivity*

During the early Ming Dynasty the government adopted the policy of recuperation. This encouraged farmers to bring wasteland back under cultivation, so agriculture recovered and developed rapidly. The land was seriously barren during this period, so the first Emperor Taizu (r. 1368–1398, reign motto Hongwu) repeatedly ordered to recruit manpower and allowed those sentenced to exile to instead cultivate the wasteland. Farmers who reclaimed wasteland would be taxed at a preferential rate, and some would even be exempted from taxation altogether. During the reign of the third Emperor Chengzu (r. 1403–1424, reign motto Yongle), measures for reclaiming wasteland continued to be implemented. By the late years of Emperor Chengzu, most of the wasteland had been restored to cultivation. The increase in size of cultivated land made it possible to boost the yields of agricultural products.

The Ming government, meanwhile, attached importance to farmland irrigation and water conservancy. During the reign of the first Emperor Taizu, the Yellow River was tamed, and the Huaihe River and the Grand Canal were subject to regulation. During the reign of Emperor Chengzu, seawalls were built in Jiangsu and Zhejiang to protect farmland along the coast from being damaged by sea tides. The Ming government also sent water conservancy officials to take charge of river management. They constructed many major projects in succession, pacifying the risk of flood disasters to some extent. Both the Yellow River and the Huaihe River ran again without breaching their courses. The Grand Canal ran smoothly from the north to the south. Once-flooded farmland returned to cultivation.

More than 70 years of great efforts saw the revival of the Ming society with a growing labor force, an increase in the area of farmland and the construction of water conservancy facilities. Grain yields per unit acre duly burgeoned. The handicraft industry developed quickly in terms of scale and technology. Commerce, cities and transportation picked up in development apace. The rejuvenation was such that records state that "during the period from 1368 to 1435, ordinary people lived in abundance with domestic food stores and clothes aplenty. The government encouraged agricultural production and farmland cultivation with no farmland left wasted. Farmers were engaged in agriculture; more state farms were in operation; grain and salt were provided to garrisons, without the need for troops to depend on the local government for their salaries. Therefore, both the army and ordinary people lived in clover."[1]

In such an agriculture-dominated society, the size of the labor force and the area of farmland cultivated symbolized the development of social productive forces. In 1393, a total of 1,600 households were registered with a population of 60 million, exceeding the highest total in the Yuan Dynasty. This number was also much higher than that in the early Northern Song. The total area of farmland was over 8.5 million *qing*,[2]

---

[1] *The History of Ming Dynasty: Treatise on Food and Commodities.*
[2] Unit of area equal to 6.67 hectares.

being much more than the 5.24 million *qing* in the early Song (997–1022).[3]

During the Yongle period (1403–1424) of the Ming Dynasty, the development of productivity helped to facilitate social and economic prosperity. This was duly manifested in the overseas trade expeditions of the greater navigator Zheng He, the construction of Beijing as the capital and the navigation of the Grand Canal connecting the north with the south. All these phenomena reflected the great economic strength of the nation and the economy of the society.

In particular, the seven overseas expeditions of Zheng He represented the first and the last heroic undertaking of its kind in China's feudal society. This showcased the brilliance of the shipbuilding technology and capability, advanced seafaring knowledge, abundant resources, varieties of merchandise and powerful military strength, all of which required overall advanced science and technology and social productivity as their basis.

7.1.2 *The Prosperity of the Commodity Economy*

With the improvement in agricultural productivity, commodity production also developed gradually out of the agricultural economy. During the early Ming Dynasty, improvement in agricultural productivity was mainly reflected in the increase of quantity and expansion of scale. The middle Ming saw improvements in labor productivity as well.

Improvements were also made in farming implements, the cultivation and popularization of fine crop strains, soil improvement through fertilizers, the construction of water conservancy, and the extension of double cropping for rice. Rice began to be planted in Northern China, while coarse cereals were promoted in Southern China. Advances were made in agricultural technology and managerial experience. In particular, the introduction and promotion of high-yield food crops, like corn and sweet potatoes, stimulated agricultural productivity in the early Ming era, which provided a prerequisite for the development of commercial agriculture.

In the first instance, the improvement of agricultural productivity increased grain yields, and helped the commercialization of grain, which became one of the most important commodities in the commercial

---

[3] Wang Yuquan. *A General History of the Chinese Economy*. Vol. 1. Economic Daily Press, 2000.

trade of the middle Ming. Second, the improvement of agricultural productivity made it possible for more farmland to be made available for cash crops.

In the middle Ming, the division between agriculture and the handicraft industry expanded. In agricultural production, the division of labor in society and the regional division of work were also strengthened, as some areas were formed exclusively for growing cash crops. The cash crops in the Ming were mainly time-honored mulberry, sugarcane, tea leaves, forests and fruit. The introduction and promotion of peanuts, tobacco and cotton occurred at this time, too.

During the Jiajing period (1522–1566) and the Wanli period (1573–1620) of the Ming, cotton was seen planted in the Yangtze River Basin, the Yellow River Basin and the Northern China Plain, with some professional planting bases taking shape. The popularization of cash crops not only promoted the development of commercial agriculture, but provided quantities of raw materials for the development of the handicraft industry.

And lastly, the improvement in agricultural productivity made it possible for more of the labor force to break away from agriculture and move into business. After the middle Ming, more and more people were "abandoning farming and sericulture for industry and commerce." This trend provided sufficient labor force for the development of the handicraft industry and promoted the rise of industry and commerce. Signs of such a trend indicated that China's traditional economic structure and economic operation mechanism had experienced profound changes during the middle Ming.

Compared with the former dynasties, the handicraft industry underwent further development during the middle Ming. In general, different degrees of advances and improvements were made in terms of scale, capability, implements, technology, design, division, labor organization and managerial experience. New developments took place in the traditional handicraft industry, such as textiles, ceramics, mining and metallurgy, paper-making, printing, forestry, refined sugar, oil manufacturing, brewing, tea and salt making, and in the military. The Ming, particularly in the periods of Jiajing (1522–1566) and Wanli (1573–1620), began to assume a prosperous appearance. The handicraft industry in the middle Ming was revived with more vitality, and especially that in the Jiangnan area was proceeding vigorously. The improvements in silk production could be witnessed in terms of quantity and quality as well.

At that time, weaving machines which were popular in the Jiangnan area included the twill loom, the creping loom, the spinning loom, the poplin loom, and the satin loom. This indicated an improvement in production tools, the strengthened division of labor, and a plentiful variety of products. Ceramics began to thrive as production technology increasingly improved.

Jingdezhen, as the center of the ceramics industry, "vibrated with the sound of pestles pounding porcelain clay and was illuminated by kiln fires when their operators continued to work at night. Residents of the town found it hard to fall asleep." It was thus celebrated as "a town of thunderbolt." Besides Jingdezhen, the ceramics industry was also highly developed in places like Chuzhou (Zhejiang), Dehua (Fujian), Yuzhou (Henan), Quyang (Hebei) and Yixing (Jiangsu). Generally, the white glazed, blue and white porcelain of the Ming was characterized as being handsome and practical to use. It was available in all markets, being particularly well received as a major commodity from China in foreign trade.

The development of the mining industry took on some altered characteristics. The iron smelting and steel-making industries expanded on sites of large-scale production and there was greater division in the manual smelting factory. The silver mining industry was well-patronized and coal was already widely used as a fuel. The paper-making industry and printing industry in the Ming Dynasty were also highly developed. In particular, some new techniques like lead and bronze movable-type printing, color overprinting, short editing and arching techniques were invented and popularized, becoming pioneering advents in the history of Chinese printing.

In addition to the traditional handicraft industry, some new fields of manufacturing sprang up. The most prominent was the rapid development of the cotton textile industry. The Chinese cotton textile industry emerged during the Yuan Dynasty, and gradually surpassed the traditional silk and hemp industries during the reigns of Jiajing (1521–1566) and Wanli (1572–1620) of Ming. Cotton became a commonly used cloth for ordinary people and was seen across "every inch of the land." Simultaneously, "looms were also common in people's homes." Some centers for the cotton textile industry mushroomed. Songjiang, a suburb of Shanghai, with developed cotton fabric production, gained the fame that "(near) all the clothes of the country were made in Songjiang." In the north, cotton cloth made in Suning (Hebei) was relatively cheap and competitive.

On the basis of agriculture and the handicraft industry, commerce developed with unprecedented prosperity during the middle Ming. Grain, cotton, silk, salt, tea, porcelain, and iron became bulk merchandise in circulation. The commodity trade was unprecedentedly active. Regional markets and national markets developed to a larger scale. "Carriages from southern Yunnan (southwestern China) were seen trading in Liaoyang (northeast China). Merchants from the Five Ridges areas (Lingnan in Southern China) traveled in Hebei."[4] "Merchandise of Yan (Hebei), Zhao (Shanxi), Qin (Shaanxi), Jin (Shanxi), Qi (Shandong), and the Jianghuai (the Yangze River Basin and the Huaihe River Basin) was shipped to the south day and night; and the merchandise of Yunnan, Fujian, Guangdong and Guangxi, Yuzhang (Jiangxi), Nanchu (Henan), Ouyue (Zhejiang) and Xin'an was shipped to the north."[5]

Together with commerce came a prosperous urban economy. During the early Ming Dynasty there were 33 famous cities, including the two capitals, Beijing and Nanjing respectively. The number rose to 56 during the later Ming. Those cities were scattered throughout the country. The number of citizens who engaged in industry and commerce increased, becoming, in some cities, a major part of the nationa's economy.[6] It could be seen that domestic trade was conducted in an active manner, and foreign trade further developed as well. During the middle Ming period, the import and export trade — either government's tribute trade or non-governmental overseas trade, increased significantly in trade value.

Specifically, government-imposed restrictions on non-governmental overseas trade loosened and the volume of non-governmental foreign trade was increasing day by day. Especially in Fujian, various forms of merchandise "were shipped out of the seaports in numerous quantities."[7] During the middle Ming, especially after the Jiajing period (1521–1566), conducting business became a fashion.

With the rise of merchants as a powerful class, merchant groups which centered in certain regions gradually emerged as "Merchant Guilds". The best-known guilds were the Huizhou (present-day Anhui) Guild, the Shanxi Guild, the Shaanxi Guild, the Ningbo Guild,

---

[4] See the *Exploitation of the Works of Nature*, an important Chinese book covering a wide range of traditional Chinese technologies. Written by Song Yingxing, it was published in 1637 in Ming China.

[5] Li Ding. *Anthology of Li Changqing.*

[6] Wu Hui. *A General History of Chinese Commerce.* Vol. 3. China Financial & Economic Publishing House, 2005.

[7] (The Ming Dynasty) Wang Shimao. *An Introduction to Fujian.*

the Shandong Guild, the Guangdong Guild, the Fujian Guild, the Dongting (of Hunan) Guild and the Jiangyou (South of the Yangze River) Guild.

To draw a conclusion, from the perspective of historical evolution, the early Ming government implemented a series of policies unfavorable to commercial development. For example, there was a rigid categorization of households such as farming households, military households, craftsmen's households, salt-producing households; the government emphasized agriculture but restricted commerce, strictly controlled the activities of merchants, set up a system of business tax, banned maritime trade, and stringently restricted merchants from trading overseas.

In the middle Ming Dynasty, with the great changes in the production structure in many places, progress was made in commerce with the range of commodities increasing, and the circulation scope of commodities expanding. Commercial towns sprang up across the nation.

In the late Ming Dynasty, due to the improvements in social productivity, the number of farmers who became landlords increased dramatically. A capitalistic factor was springing up in the handicraft industry. Commodities were actively exchanged between the major regions within the country. Merchants accumulated capital to such a considerable extent that the late Ming ushered in a superlatively prosperous era for commerce in the traditional China.

7.2 Maritime Trade Policy

7.2.1 *The Maritime Embargo Policy in the Early Ming Period*

1. The Maritime Embargo Policy

The policy of the Ming government on overseas trade was issued in 1367, one year before Zhu Yuanzhang came to the throne as the first Emperor. In the late years of the Yuan Dynasty, the peasant uprising leader Zhang Shicheng from the west of Zhejiang Province and Fang Guozhen from eastern Zhejiang both attached great importance to the development of foreign trade. At that time, Taicang in Jiangsu was an important port for overseas trade. After Zhu Yuanzhang defeated Zhang and Fang, he immediately set up the Maritime Trade Management Commission in the seaport of Liuhe, to manage and develop foreign trade.

The Law of the Ming Dynasty or Da Ming Law was formulated in the early Ming Dynasty on the basis of the "Law on Maritime Trade" in the Yuan. A clause in the "Law of the Grand Ming" devoted to the "Tax Evasion of Sea Merchants" stipulated that "all sea merchants should report the actual number of goods and pay taxes of 'extraction' accordingly as soon as they reached the port; anyone who docked at a private port and did not report their goods and pay taxes would be punished with one hundred lashes; those who did report but still kept some goods unreported would be punished with one hundred lashes and have their goods confiscated. Private merchants who helped them to evade taxes were to be sentenced to the same punishment. Informants were rewarded with 20 taels of silver."[8] It could be seen that merchants were permitted to trade at sea in the early Ming. The fifth Emperor Taizu adopted a positive policy toward overseas trade.

However, owing to the harassment by *Wokou*[9] and the residual forces of Zhang and Fang as well as piracy in coastal areas, it didn't take long for Emperor Taizu to adopt the Maritime Embargo Policy. During the late Yuan and early Ming Dynasties, China's coast was constantly being invaded by those Japanese pirates. The scourge they brought grew increasingly serious.

In March 1369, the first Emperor Taizu dispatched envoys to Japan with an imperial letter demanding the reasons for its invasion. Similar reports were being presented constantly by the authorities of Shandong. Japanese pirates were harassing the coastal areas of that province, abducting wives, damaging domestic properties, and even killing people. Many were left homeless.[10] But Japan totally ignored those complaints and its pillaging became even more severe. The Japanese attacked and invaded Shandong, and "went on to attack fishermen near Wenzhou, Taizhou and Mingzhou and coastal areas in Fujian."[11] To make matters worse, the remnants of Zhang and Fang's forces colluded with *Wokou* and staged armed

---

[8] *Law of the Ming Dynasty: The Law of Household*. Vol. 8.

[9] *Wokou* is a general term for the Japanese pirates. They invaded coastal areas of Korea, China and Southeast Asia between the 13th and 16th centuries. Besides piracy, they were also involved in smuggling between China and Japan. These Japanese pirates were called *Wokou* since Japan was referred to as Woguo in ancient Chinese books.

[10] *The Veritable Records of Emperor Taizu*. Vol. 39.

[11] *History of Ming: Biography of Japan*. Vol. 322.

rebellions. In such a situation of attacks from both within and without, Emperor Taizu issued a decree of maritime embargo policy.

The so-called "Maritime Embargo Policy" was aimed at prohibiting non-governmental overseas trade so that no Chinese subjects could sail for the purpose of transacting business and no foreign merchants on their own behalf could enter China for trade activities.

In 1371, Emperor Taizu issued an order that "no coastal residents were allowed to sail out for overseas trade."[12] In December of the same year, the Emperor observed that "the sea route could lead directly to other countries, I therefore ban people from trading overseas." Since the Ming government had banned coastal residents from conducting overseas trade, the Maritime Trade Commission was revoked as the administrative organ. The Maritime Trade Commission of Taicang was closed down in 1370 "due to overseas barbarians being considered to be too duplicitous; they were not even allowed to come close to the capital (Nanjing)." In 1381, the Sino-Japanese relationship deteriorated further. In view of the unceasing invasions of the *Wokou*, the Ming Court reiterated that "no coastal residents were allowed to connect privately with other countries." In 1390, the Court issued an imperial edict again "prohibiting any communication with foreign countries."

The Maritime Embargo Policy by Emperor Taizu was designed mainly to prevent Chinese people from sailing on outbound journeys. As for foreigners coming to China by the sea route, the Ming government also implemented restrictions. After his death, his grandson Emperor Huizong (r. 1399–1402) succeeded the throne and the status quo in foreign affairs was maintained.

In 1402, the Marquis of Yan, Zhu Di, ascended to the throne to become Emperor Chengzu (r. 1402–1424). He continued the Maritime Embargo Policy and declared at the beginning of his reign that "there are still soldiers and people along the coastal areas who are found to be sailing abroad without permission. From now on, no one is allowed to do so. Offices and departments should curb and manage the practice according to the former order."[13]

In 1404, Emperor Huizong ordered again that "civilian ships were forbidden to sail. All existing civilian ships should be refitted as

---

[12] *The Veritable Records of Emperor Taizu.* Vol. 76.
[13] *Ibid.*, Vol. 10.

flat-prowed ships, and relevant departments would be tasked with preventing them from sailing outbound."[14] The measures to refit ships and prohibit home-built ships from sailing overseas were taken to fundamentally prohibit ships from engaging in oceangoing trade.

In a word, the early Ming witnessed the implementation of the Maritime Embargo Policy as an unswerving rule "being customized by ancestors," though that policy was sometimes strict and sometimes slack. When it was carried out in a strict manner, even "planks were not allowed to enter the sea," and "no foreign spices and goods were allowed to be used by civilians." Meanwhile, the Ming government stipulated "no tributes and no markets." That is to say, "tributary trade" was taken as the only legal means of conducting foreign trade.

2. Reasons for Implementing the Maritime Embargo Policy

The fundamental reason why the Ming Dynasty adopted the Maritime Embargo Policy was essentially the feudal nature of the Chinese economy. Foreign trade played an insignificant role in the natural economic system. When the external environment was stable, and China was not threatened with foreign incursion, rulers were content to enjoy exotic treasures and proud of the grand scene of numerous foreign envoys coming to pay tributes. In this light, the government was inclined to implement policies conducive to encouraging overseas trade. However, when the external environment deteriorated, and foreign countries appeared likely to undermine the feudal regime, foreign trade, private trade in particular, would be restricted or even strictly prohibited.

In the early Ming Dynasty, the north was subject to internal threats from the recalcitrant remnants of the Yuan Dynasty; in the southeast the residual forces loyal to the rebellious Zhang and Fang posed a counterweight to the authority of the first Emperor Taizu. Externally, *Wokou* continued to harass the southeast coast.

To consolidate the new regime of the Ming and create a stable external environment favorable to social and economic recovery and development, Emperor Taizu (r. 1368–1398), on the one hand, sent envoys to overseas countries to publicize how the Ming was pursuing a foreign policy of detente. He did so in the hope that more countries would sever ties with the remnants of the Yuan Mongols and recognize the

---

[14] *Ibid.*, Vol. 27.

legitimacy of the Ming. On the other hand, the Ming managed to stymie the collusion of domestic and foreign resistance forces. To this end, the Ming government implemented a comprehensive Maritime Embargo Policy.

7.2.2 *Tributary Trade and Expeditions by Zheng He*

To some extent, the implementation of the Maritime Embargo Policy weakened anti-Ming forces abroad and maintained domestic peace and stability, but it also ruined the established economic ties between China and foreign countries. In order to meet the demand of priceless exotic treasures and spices for the ruling class, and restore the relationship with"numerous foreign countries coming to China to pay tributes," the Ming government actively practiced the tributary trade policy while banning private overseas trade.

1. The Evolution of Tributary Trade Policy
The tributary trade policy meant that foreign countries presented their own or other foreign treasures to the Chinese Emperor in the name of paying tribute, and China gave the donors silk, gold, silver and porcelain in the name of giving reward. Alternatively, China took the initiative to send envoys to foreign countries to "bestow" them with treasures. The gifts returned by foreign countries were considered as tributes. Such ostensible diplomatic exchanges were actually a form of barter trade conducted in an official manner, which was taken as the main channel for China's official trade for a long time.

To showcase the grandeur of the Ming as a "celestial Court and a magnificent country," as well as being a land with comprehensive national power and an affluent population, where the tributary trade was concerned the Ming government adopted a principle of "giving more and receiving less." They surpassed any previous dynasty inasmuch as it was stipulated that the reciprocal gifts returned in tributary exchanges must be of much higher value than the tributes they paid. Meanwhile, free accommodation and transportation should be provided for "tribute envoys" coming to China. As for the private goods brought to China by the envoys, they should be exempt from tax. Even those envoys who violated China's law would be punished only in a mild manner or even have their punishment waived.

In this case, any "tribute envoy" coming to China could potentially gain fat profits from the trip so that some countries with no special products to present as tributes were even willing to travel by sea to purchase rare treasures and then transfer them to China for gain. Some countries even regarded the tributary trade with China as an important source of fiscal revenue. Overseas countries took "several times a year" to pay tributes to China, thus giving rise to the scene of "one country presents multiple tributes each year" and "visitors arrive incessantly."

The frequent tributary trade did create the propitious scene of "numerous foreign countries coming to China to pay tributes" and "barbarians from all directions pledging allegiance to China." However, official trade as such indeed entailed exchanges of unequal value with no consideration of economic efficiency, thus creating a heavy financial burden on the Ming government. At that time, the central government was responsible for determining what gift should be given in return, while local authorities in the area along the route they passed were responsible for the transportation, accommodation and transshipment of cargoes brought with visitors. Besides, some "tribute envoys" often recklessly blackmailed local people and local governments to the extent that irate officials kept on submitting letters to the Court demanding that the tributary trade be restricted.

In 1372, the Ming government announced the proscription that most countries should limit their visits to "three times a year."[15] The "tribute route," i.e. the port where envoys landed in China, was also specified; envoys of Japan should dock their ships at the port of Ningbo; Ryukyu in Min County in Fujian; AnNam (now Vietnam) in Pingxiang of Guangxi; Khmer, Siam, Champa and Malacca in Guangdong; Luzon in Fujian.

In 1383, in response to the phenomenon of some foreign merchants disguising themselves as envoys, the Ming government further implemented the policy of *Kanhe*. *Kanhe* referred to the license of tributary trade. A license had two identical copies. Each copy was made up of two halves, one half being the *Kanhe*, the other being the office copy. Between them was a paginating seal. Tributary counties should fill in the names of

---

[15] Huang Zhangjian. *The Veritable Records of Ming Dynasty*. Vol. 76. The Institute of History and Philology, Academia Sinica in Taiwan, 1962.

envoys and attendants, together with the names and quantities of tribute articles on the *Kanhe* before they paid their tributes.

After entering the port, the Provincial Administration Commission and the Maritime Trade Commission would jointly verify whether the *Kanhe* was genuine or not and whether the seal on the license was identical with that of the relevant office copy. In the Ming Dynasty, envoys who traveled to other countries also needed to carry the *Kanhe* retained by the Ministry of Rites to be verified with the office copy kept in the countries of destination. When returning to China, the returned gifts should be specified on the *Kanhe* and brought back together with it from that country.

According to *A Collection of Official Statutes of the Ming Dynasty*, the following countries held *Kanhe* issued by the Ming China: Siam (now Thailand), Japan, Champa (now South-South Vietnam), Java Island, Sumatra Island, Borneo (now Indonesia), Ceylon (now Sri Lanka), the Sultanate of Sulu (now in the Philippines), Calicut, Cochin (now in the southwest of the Indian Peninsula), and Melaka (now the Malacca Peninsula). Those countries represented almost all the trading partners of the early Ming.

The restrictions of the Ming government on the "tributary trade" damaged the economic interests of the "tribute" countries, resulting in a sharp decline in official trade between China and foreign countries. In 1397, only AnNam, Champa, Khmer, Siam and Ryukyu came to pay tributes. The economic ties between China and foreign countries were further damaged, and overseas countries were extremely dissatisfied with the policies of the Ming. By the late years of the Hongwu period (1368–1398) in the reign of Emperor Taizu, Sino-foreign relations deteriorated significantly.

2. Expeditions by Zheng He

The foreign policy adopted during the reign of the third Emperor Chengzu (r. 1402–1424) was to ban maritime trade and civilian trade, on the one hand, and to promote tributary trade and expand the exchanges between the Ming and overseas countries, on the other. From 1405 to 1433, under the Emperor's order, Zheng He sailed his huge fleet overseas seven times. There were more than 200 ships, with over 20,000 crew and tens of thousands of treasures in each expedition. Zheng He carried out extensive political, economic and cultural exchanges with Asian and African countries, pushingh the official trade ("tributary trade") of the Ming Dynasty and even the whole ancient China to its pinnacle.

(i) The Purpose of Zheng He's Expeditions to the Western Oceans[16]
Opinions vary as to the purpose of Zheng He's expeditions. The following four statements seem to hold a measure of veracity:

(a) To manhunt for Emperor Huizong (r. 1398-1402), who was over-thrown and disappeared after Zhu Di launched the "Jingnan Rebellion"[17] and captured Nanjing. Therefore, it was argued that "the primary purpose of Zheng He's expeditions was to look for traces of Emperor Huizong."

(b) To open up to the outside world by developing overseas trade in a proactive way.

(c) To restore and develop diplomatic relations between the Ming and overseas countries in order to enhance the international prestige of the Ming regime.

(d) To strengthen the coastal defense of the Ming. This viewpoint con-cerned the perspectives of politics, economy, diplomacy and military affairs, so no singular agreement had been reached. Any investigation of this problem should be closely related to domestic and international environments during the early years after Emperor Chengzu ascended the throne.

After Emperor Chengzu (r. 1402–1424) of the Ming succeeded the throne through a military coup, the main problem he was faced with was that a significant number of people expressed dissatisfaction at his

---

[16]"The Western Oceans" as a geographical term embraced indefinite scope in different historical periods. During the early Ming, it roughly referred to the waters, countries and regions from the west of the South China Sea to eastern Africa; in the middle Ming, it was to the west of Brunei of Kalimantan Island; waters to the east of Brunei were called the "The Eastern Oceans"; in the late Ming and early Qing, it referred to Occidental countries.

[17]Also known as Jingnan Campaign. It was a civil war in the early years of the Ming Dynasty between Zhu Di, the Prince of Yan and Emperor HUizong. It started in 1399 and lasted 3 years. The campaign ended after the forces of Zhu Di captured the imperial capital Nanjing. The fall of Nanjing was followed by the demise of Emperor Huizong, and Zhu Di was crowned Emperor Chengzu.

usurpation of the throne. Due to the restrictions on overseas tributary trade during the Hongwu period (1368–1398), Sino-foreign relations became strained and tense. The political prestige of the Ming slumped in the eyes of other countries.

To establish his status as "the chosen one" and have his legitimacy recognized by people at home and abroad, Emperor Chengzu sustained the ban on maritime trade carried out since the reign of Emperor Taizu. Meanwhile, he actively encouraged overseas countries to pay tributes to the Ming. At the beginning of his reign, he declared that he welcomed overseas countries to develop tributary relationships with the Ming Dynasty. In 1403, Emperor Chengzu sent envoys to countries like Korea, Ryukyu, Japan, AnNam, Java Island, Sumatra Island, Siam, Champa, Melaka, Cochin, and Calicut, thus restoring the diplomatic relations between the Ming Dynasty and Asian countries.

At the same time, in order to adopt the foreign policy of peace and friendship, the Ming government resumed the establishment of the Maritime Trade Commissions in Zhejiang, Fujian and Guangdong. Afterward, two Maritime Trade Commissions were set up in Jianzhi and Yunnan and took the responsibility of managing the tributary affairs of countries on the Indochina Peninsula. To further develop Sino-foreign relations, in 1405, by order of Zhu Di, Zheng He launched his massive overseas expeditions, thereby opening a glorious chapter in Chinese maritime history, Sino-foreign relations and Chinese foreign trade.

It could be concluded that the direct aim of Zheng He's expeditions was to showcase the superiority of the Ming Dynasty and to enhance its international reputation, thus ushering in a flourishing age in terms of global politics. It was true that the economic base determined the superstructure and foreign trade ought to serve foreign affairs. Ancient China combined foreign trade with diplomacy so that the means of restoring diplomatic relations depended largely on foreign trade. Therefore, Sino-foreign relations could be restored and developed when active trade exchanges had been conducted. The purpose of Zheng He's overseas expeditions was to achieve political goals through economic activities. In this sense, it was also the continuation of tributary trade in the Ming Dynasty.

(ii) The Seven Expeditions by Zheng He

From 1405 to 1433, Zheng He sailed his vast fleet to the Western Oceans seven times. He commanded more than 200 ships and 20,000 sailors and tens of thousands of items of treasure in each expedition. Through such an unprecedented endeavor, the ancient, China had carried out its extensive political, economic and cultural exchanges with a great many Asian and African countries.

According to historical records, the first expedition lasted from June 1405 to September 1407. Zheng He and his assistant minister, Wang Jinghong, led a fleet of 62 treasure ships loaded with gold, silver and silk and 27,800 crew to depart from Liujiagang port in Taicang, Jiangsu, to Fuzhou, then sailed all the way south, arriving successively at Champa (now the southern part of Vietnam), Java, Sumatra, Melaka, the Great Nicobar (now the Nicobar Islands), Ceylon (now Sri Lanka) and Calicut on the west coast of India. The most distant place they reached was Gambari (now Kambe) on the west coast of India. When Zheng He's fleet returned, it passed through Vieux Po (now Palembang), where they eliminated a group of Chinese pirates led by Chen Zuyi, thereby removing every impediment on the route from China to Southeast Asia.

The second expedition lasted from September 1407 to August 1409. This time the route was exactly the same as that of the first, with the exception that it passed through Siam (now Thailand). When Zheng He's fleet returned to China, envoys from six countries, including Guri and Siam, came to China with Zheng He's fleet. The tributary relationship between China and Southeast Asian countries became frequent.

The third expedition began in September 1409. It was essentially the same as the second. The difference was that when they entered the Gulf of Siam, they did not go directly from Siam to Java, but for first time they arrived at Palembang. From there, the fleet sailed eastward to Java, and westward to the countries on the west coast of India, and finally to Ahmedabad. In Ceylon, Zheng He captured the local King alive.

According to history books, Alagakkonara, the King of Ceylon, exploited the geographical advantages of his country to plunder envoys. When Zheng He arrived there, the King dispatched 50,000 troops to rob the treasure ships, but Zheng He successfully defeated and captured him as well as some of his officials. In 1411, Alagakkonara was escorted to Nanjing by Zheng He, but was later released by the Ming's Emperor Chengzu and returned to his own country. This example may well have served as a great deterrent to swashbuckling countries which attempted to hinder Sino-foreign exchanges.

The fourth expedition lasted from November 1413 to July 1415. The route of this journey was as follows: after arriving at Calicut (now Kozhikode) on the west coast of India, the fleet sailed bypassed the Arabian Sea to Hormuz in the Persian Gulf (near Minab in the southeast of Iran), then across the Arabian Peninsula to the east coast of Africa. From then on, African seafarers started to visit China frequently.

The fifth expedition lasted from December 1416 to July 1419. The purpose of this mission was mainly to escort envoys from Asian and African countries back home. The expedition was different from the previous ones insofar as when the fleet arrived at Champa, it neither sailed south from Java nor entered the Gulf of Siam, but arrived at the Pahang (now Kuantan) on the Malay Peninsula, and sailed southeast to Java. The fleet then sailed westward. It passed through the Malacca Strait, the Great Nicobar (now the Nicobar Islands), and past Ceylon Island to reach the countries on the west coast of India. From there, it sailed northwestward to Hormoz, and then sailed along the southeast coast of the Arabian Peninsula to Zeila (now Zula) in north Africa via Dhofar and Adan (now Aden). There the fleet sailed out of the Gulf of Aden to countries along the East African coast.

The sixth expedition lasted from January 1421 to August 1422. The mission was still to escort foreign envoys home. After the fleet arrived at Champa, it passed through the Kunlun (Kunlun island in the south of Vietnam today) and the Gulf of Siam. There the fleet sailed southward to the strait of Melaka along the Malay Peninsula. After crossing the strait, it sailed northward from the Great Nicobar (now the Nicobar Islands) to the Chittagong (now Chittagong). Passing along the southeast coast of India, it arrived at Zori. Around the south coast of India, it reached Kuri (now Kozhikode). The fleet crossed the Arabian Sea to Dhofar of Arabian Peninsula and Adan (now Aden). Along the coast of East Africa, the fleet reached various local countries.

After the sixth expedition, more and more people grew opposed to his westward expedition. In addition, in 1417, three main halls of the imperial palace were engulfed in fire. The third Emperor Chengzu (1402–1424) was forced to suspend the sea exploration. For many years thereafter, the Ming Court no longer sent envoys abroad, so the Dynasty no longer had much influence among foreign countries. In 1430, the fifth Emperor Xuanzong (r. 1425–1435) sent Zheng He and Wang Jinghong to the west again. Zheng He's fleet thus made its last or, the seventh. When the fleet loaded with treasures arrived at Hormoz, they did not advance further to the west. His detachment crossed the Arabian Sea from Kuri (now Kozhikode) to Zufar, Adam and Arab (now Mecca). This expedition visited more than 20 countries before the fleet returned China in July 1433.

In conclusion, the route of Zheng He's expeditions first took him southward and then westward to Java, and then gradually extended to East Africa. There were basically four routes.

(a) The fleet crossed the South China Sea, passed through Champa, Khmer (now Cambodia), and entered the Gulf of Siam. From there it sailed southward along the Malay Peninsula to Melaka (now Malacca).

(b) The route from Sumatra to the Java islands. The fleet sailed from Melaka through Keppel Harbor (now Lingga) to the Kingdom of Srivijaya (now East Sumatra), and then to Java by way of the Karimata Straits and Billiton. Then it sailed westward through the Malacca Straits to the north coast of Sumatra and the western states of the Malay Peninsula.

(c) The Bay of Bengal route. The fleet took the Great Nicobar (now the Nicobar Islands) as the confluence point, sailed northward to Bengala (now Bangladesh) and reached Ceylon in the west. Then it sailed westward to the Maldives Archipelago and countries on the west coast of India.

(d) The Arabian Sea Route. The fleet sailed from the west coast of India northwest to Hormuz at the mouth of the Persian Gulf. Along the southeast coast of the Arabian Peninsula, it reached Adan (now Aden) by way of Dhofar. After crossing the Gulf of Aden, it sailed along the east coast of Africa, passing successively by Mogadishu, Brava, Juba, Malindi and the Mozambique Channel. Then it took a U-turn to sail northward from the southern tip of Madagascar. Or, it sailed from Adam to the Red Sea. There it sailed northwestward to Arabia.

Zheng He's fleet visited upwards of 30 countries. Three countries — Champa, Khmer and Siam — belonged to the Indochina Peninsula; three countries — Pahang, Kelantan and Melaka — belonged to the Malay Peninsula; eight countries — including Sumatra, Burni, Lambri, Aru, Palembang, Java, Nagur and Litai — belonged to the Malay Archipelago; eleven countries — including Cochin, Soli, Cail, Lambri,

Cape Comorin, Ahmedabad, Kollam, Quilon, Calicut and Sharwayn, Bengala — belonged to the India Peninsula; three countries — Dhofar, Adam and Arabia — belonged to the Arabian Peninsula; five countries — including Mogadishu, Brava, Jumbo, Malindi and Zeila — belonged to Africa. One country — Ceylon — was on the Ceylon Island; one country — Liushan (now Maldives) — was in the India Ocean; one country — the Kingdom of Ormus — was in the Persian Gulf; as to Mozambique and Sofala, it was hard to define which country they used to be. The last one was Western Oceans Zori or Zori.

(iii) The Historical Significance of Zheng He's Expeditions
(a) Reflecting China's Advanced Shipbuilding and Navigation Capability.

Zheng He's fleet contained hundreds of vessels of different sizes, among which the biggest ones acted as the command center of the fleet and were responsible for storing the treasure, thus known as "treasure ships". The largest treasure ship was nearly 150 meters long and about 50 meters wide, and its deadweight capacity was estimated to be about 2,500 tons. The ships in Zheng He's fleet were much more advanced in terms of weight and structure than the ships used in the age of Europe's great geographical exploration half a century later.

In 1492, Italian navigator Christopher Columbus (1451–1506) sailed to the Americas with only three relatively small sailboats and 90 sailors. The deadweight capacity of the largest ship was less than 100 tons. His ships were so small that the 40-ton "Pinta" was damaged during a storm after just one month's sailing. In 1497, the fleet of Vasco da Gama sailed to India. It was made up of four of Europe's finest seagoing vessels, whose length was no more than 25 meters with a deadweight capacity of only about 120 tones. Therefore, the famous British historian of science and technology Joseph Needham pointed out that throughout the Middle Ages the tonnage of Chinese ships was much larger than that of Europian ships. Zheng He's biggest "treasure ships" were the global pinnacle of the wooden junk before the 19th century.

The navigation technology of the Ming also reached a very high level. When compass was invented in China, it began to be used for maritime navigation in the Song Dynasty. By the time Zheng He's expeditions to the Western Oceans in the Ming Dynasty, compass had been developed into a water gyrocompass that could point in 48 distinct directions. At the same time, the water gyrocompass combined the astronomical and physiographical orientation that made position determining extremely accurate.

The comprehensive use of object navigation, logs and the Star-Drawing Board[18] made the navigation routes accurate and effectively ensured the speed and safety of navigation. *Zheng He's Navigation Map* (also known as *Mao Kun Map*) included detailed and accurate records of the distance, berths, reefs and shoals of his fleet, indicating how advanced the Chinese sailing technology was.

(b) The Formation of an Afro-Asian Maritime Transportation Network

China began to conduct economic and trade exchanges with African countries prior to the Ming Dynasty, but those examples were not infrequent. Chinese merchants traded along the maritime Silk Route in the Song and Yuan Dynasties, but they reached no farther than the Arabian Peninsula. In the Ming Dynasty, Zheng He made seven ocean-bound expeditions, lasting for a total of 28 years and traversing more than 30 countries scattered across Asia and Africa. Zheng He's expeditions, based on the voyages made in the Tang, Song and Yuan Dynasties, greatly expanded the navigation scope in the world.

Zheng He's expeditions crisscrossed the routes in Asia and Africa, creating an unimpeded maritime traffic network between the Western Pacific Ocean and the northern Indian Ocean.

Firstly, He's expeditions to the Western Oceans not only opened the sea routes as far as East Africa, but many new short-distance routes and multi-point crossed routes, and established regular communications between China and East Africa. To be specific, Zheng He's fleet determined the fixed transportation routes from China to Calicut (now Kozhikode), Ceylon (now Sri Lanka) and the Maldives. Zheng He's first expedition reached Ceylon and finally returned from Calicut. Thereafter, those two places were visited by Zheng He in his later expeditions. From his fourth expedition onwards, Maldives became the starting point for Zheng He's fleet to sail across the Indian Ocean to East Africa.

Secondly, China built a condensed transport network with Southeast Asia. *Zheng He's Navigation Map* recorded the distance between China and Southeast Asian countries, such as Champa, Java, Sumatra, Palembang, Lambri, Siam, Melaka, Aru, Pahang, Kelantan, Khmer and other places. Besides, it also detailed the position of the navigation route, and the topography of shoals, reefs and ports along the route. It greatly facilitated

---

[18]An ancient navigational astronomical instruments.

the safe and convenient maritime communication between southeast Asian countries and China.

Thirdly, Zheng He's fleet opened the sea route to crossing the Indian Ocean to the Persian Gulf, the Arabian Sea, the Red Sea, and as far as eastern and southern Africa. From Zheng He's fourth expedition on, his ships sailed directly from Calicut to Hormoz (now near Minab, southeast Iran), thus opening the route from China to the Persian Gulf. At the same time, some of the ships sailed from Ceylon to the Maldives, whereupon they headed westward to cross the Indian Ocean to Mogadishu, Brawa (now Brava in Somali), and Malindi on the east coast of Africa. During his fifth expedition, Zheng He's fleet departed from Calicut, crossed the Arabian Sea and arrived at Dhofar, Adam and Zeila on the Arabian Peninsula.

Zheng He's seven expeditions were unprecedented in the history of human navigation in terms of the size of his fleet, and the length and the complexity of the routes. The ocean-going transportation network he established became the forerunner to the great geographical discoveries of the Europeans. It was not until half a century later that the Europeans bypassed the Cape of Good Hope and arrived in India along the route between Asia and Africa opened by Zheng He.

(c) Strengthening Exchanges with Afro-asian Countries

During a period of 28 years, Zheng He led his large fleet laden with Chinese gold, silver, coins, silk and porcelain and other handicrafts, sailing to more than 30 countries in Asia and Africa. Every time he arrived in a country, he immediately proclaimed an imperial edict to give gifts to all the kings and local leaders. Such peaceful and friendly diplomatic activities were amenable to promoting the interests of all countries. Therefore, Zheng He and his delegation were often welcomed warmly by all countries, which then sent envoys to China together with Zheng He's fleet on its return. At that time, envoys from overseas countries came in droves. The scale of the tributary countries was unprecedented in world history.

According to statistics, in 1415, envoys from eight countries came to China. They included Calicut, Cochin, Lambri, Cambay, Malindi, Hormoz, Sumatra and Champa. In 1416, the number of envoys coming to China increased to 19 Asian and African countries, including Calicut, Java, Melaka, Ceylon, Mogadishu, Adan and Malindi. In 1419, envoys from another 17 Asian and African countries came to China. In 1421 and 1423, envoys from 16 countries came to China. Those diplomatic corps were composed of as many as 1,200 delegates, as was the case in 1423.

In addition to sending envoys to China, the kings of some foreign countries like Borneo, Melaka, the Sultanate of Sulu and Kumalarang (Basilan), are recorded to have visited China personally, marking the culmination of their nation's official trade with China.

(d) Promoting Southeast Asian Countries' Socio-Economic Development

In the early 15th century, the countries and regions that Zheng He passed on his expeditions to the Western Oceans, especially Southeast Asia, were still relatively backward in their social economy. People in some areas even subsisted in the primitive state of fishing, hunting or picking. Zheng He's voyages pursued the principle of "giving more and receiving less," thereby enabling those countries to obtain larger economic profits. Zheng He's fleet actively spread Chinese civilization wherever it made its landfall allowing the highly developed feudal culture of China to be absorbed by those countries and greatly promoting the progress of their society.

The new situation of economic and trade exchanges between China and Southeast Asia created by Zheng He's expeditions did not end with the voyages themselves. Many Chinese followed Zheng He's footsteps to various parts of Southeast Asia and disseminated advanced Chinese material and spiritual civilization. A large number of Chinese settled in Southeast Asia. They worked hard for generations and contributed to the construction and social development of Southeast Asia, strengthening the friendship between those respective countries and China.

(iv) The End of Zheng He's Expeditions

Several of Zheng He's vigorous expeditions to the Western Oceans were made during the Yongle period (1402–1424) of the Yuan, but these terminated suddenly in 1429. During the reign of the ninth Emperor Xianzong (r. 1465–1487) of Ming, some officials proposed to follow the example of Zheng He again, but were met with strong opposition. Literary records relating to Zheng He's expeditions were even burned to ashes. The strongest argument about this was that "during Zheng He's expeditions to the Western Oceans, countless money and things were wasted and tens of thousands of soldiers and civilians lost their lives. Although they came back with treasures, what were the real benefits for the country?"[19]

---

[19] Yan Congjian. *Informative Records on Countries Far Away*. Vol. 8.

As was mentioned previously, Zheng He's expeditions to the Western Oceans aimed to achieve the political goals of the third Emperor Chengzu by means of official trade activities. The exchange principle of "giving more and receiving less" was implemented to showcase the grandeur of the empire. Whether it was a case of China's rewarding foreign countries voluntarily, or giving incoming envoys with treasures, the gifts given out by China were anyone many times more valuable than those tributes paid out. Apart from increasing the variety of consumer goods available to the Ming, these exchanges were thereby characterized by extreme inequity. They did not increase the Ming's material wealth, but caused great economic losses to the Ming. Such practices, of course, could not last for long, and were only sustainable in the early Ming "when people were wealthy and the granaries full." When the national power gradually weakened because of domestic problems and foreign invasions, the Dynasty was caught up in an increasingly severe financial crisis. In particular, the scale of the government-run handicraft industry was depleted to such an extent that the oceangoing voyage had lost its rich material basis.

Zheng He's expeditions to the Western Oceans, as a heroic undertaking, were difficult to continue without the impetus of a long-term economic motivation. However, the new situation in maritime transportation between China and foreign countries he created failed to result in considerable progress in China's overseas trade owing to the maritime prohibition policy of the Ming Dynasty. Half a century later, in order to pursue wealth, Europeans sailed to India and the Americas with a few boats and opened so-called "new passages." From then on, with the active support of their respective national governments, Europeans set sail for Asia, Africa, Europe and the Americas, ushering in an era of overseas exploration and colonization. Large-scale colonial plunder and colonial trade greatly accelerated the process of primitive capital accumulation in Europe. Thus, European capitalist civilization quickly grew to world dominance.

Under the severe Maritime Embargo Policy, tributary trade was the only sanctioned foreign trade. However, such trade activity was undertaken without consideration of economic efficiency and caused heavy financial burdens for the Ming Dynasty. In 1449, the Mongol Wala army invaded the south, and the Ming's sixth Emperor Yingzong (r. 1435–1449; 1457–1464) was captured in the "Tumu Crisis." The Mongol army besieged Beijing for a time. The power of the Ming Dynasty was weakened thereafter. The hefty military expenditure increased the tax burden on the people, and thus aroused public opposition. The government suppression of the ensuing peasant uprising further aggravated the financial deficit of the Ming. At last, regardless — of — cost and unrestrained tributary trade proved unsustainable. At the same time, however, non-governmental overseas trade in the form of smuggling became increasingly remunerative.

7.2.3 *Reasons for Removing Prohibition in the Middle and Late Ming Periods*

In the early period of the Ming Dynasty, the Maritime Embargo Policy did not allow the people to conduct maritime trade without permission, only sanctioning tributary trade to be practiced under official control. The treasures from tributary trade were mainly required to meet the needs of the imperial household and bureaucratic groups. As for foreign spices and foreign goods that were generally consumed by society, it proved difficult to satisfy public demand. Foreign countries were generally keen to more Chinese silk, porcelain and other Chinese goods. However, the coastal areas of Fujian and Guangdong were too populous and with too little farmland, so people placed their expectations on the sea. Seeking to make a living and secure a fortune to boot, they started to smuggle on the sea. For example, in Fujian Province, "all the farmland in the coastal region was saline and alkaline, thus the farmers could not expect any harvest and had to count on smuggling to earn their livings. Years of practice made it their habit. The rich households gathered lots of goods to smuggle and came back from foreign countries with amounts of rare cargoes. The poor worked for them; though as servants, they had to be self-sufficient as well."[20] Therefore, although the government in the early Ming period repeatedly issued orders to forbid smuggling, such activities still couldn't stopped.

In fact, sometimes there was prevailing tacit consent and connivance toward smuggling on the part of local officials. During the period of 1488–1505, "because of Maritime Embargo Policy, the number of private vessels engaged in black market trading increased, while foreign vessels could not come to China."[21] In this case, the Ming government had to

---

[20](The Ming Dynasty) Zhang Xie. *On the Countries in the Eastern and Western Oceans* [M]. Vol. 7. Chinese Publishing house, 1981.
[21] *The Veritable Records of the Ming Emperor Xiaozong.* Vol. 73.

make some reforms. Previously, only foreign tribute ships with *Kanhe* documents were allowed to enter China's ports, but in March 1509, "a Siamese ship drifted to Guangdong with the wind. After a meeting between the inspectors and a constable, they agreed to tax the ship and keep the tax revenue for military expenditures. But the superintendent of the Maritime Trade Commission, the eunuch Xiong Xuan, planned to levy tax on this ship, too, with the intention of gaining benefits for his department. He presented a proposal to ask for permission. The Ministry of Rites discussed the matter and rejected this. The Emperor decreed that Xiong Xuan had schemed to gain more power and transferred him to serve in Nanjing. His position in Guangdong was now filled by the eunuch Bi Zhen."[22] The local government imposed a tax on ships "drifting" to China by chance without *Kanhe* documents, meaning that such ships were now allowed to enter the port for trading activities.

Although the "strict — slack execution of the overseas trade prohibition" stimulated the development of non-governmental trade, it brought about new social problems and was opposed by many officials. The government once again limited overseas trade to the scope of tributary trade. Later, a series of events happened. In 1517, a Portuguese fleet entered the Pearl River by force; in 1523, two Japanese "fought for the right to operate tributary trade with China at Ningbo Port." The proposal to strengthen the implementation of the prohibition on overseas trade gained the upper hand in the Ming government. Strict implementation was resumed from the later years of the reign of Emperor Wuzong (r. 1505–1521) to the early reign of Emperor Shizong (r. 1521–1566), leading to the following consequences:

Firstly, there was a scarcity of foreign goods and foreign spices. Ambergris, for instance, was the intestinal secretion of the sperm whale, peculiar in fragrance with strong fixative qualities where scent was concerned. It was used as an effective perfume stabilizer and medicine. By the Tang Dynasty, ambergris had been imported to China and had become popular among the upper class. It therefore became an important commodity purchased by Zheng He during his expeditions. Although those foreign spices and foreign goods were mainly luxury goods, there were among them many daily essentials. Therefore, the prohibition in overseas trade brought inconvenience to all classes of the society.

---

[22] *Ibid.*, Vol. 48.

Secondly, there was the decrease in local fiscal revenue. With a limited number of foreign vessels entering Chinese ports, the local fiscal revenue from customs duties was also very low and had to depend on the tributary trade, which dealt a very heavy blow to the finances of Guangdong and other regions which had been embroiled in fighting against pirates for many years.

Thirdly, there was rampant maritime smuggling. The strict implementation of the prohibition policy in Emperor Shizhong not only failed to achieve its goal, but proved a catalyst to a new height of smuggling In the two years from December 1544 to March 1547, more than 1,000 residents of Fujian were escorted back to their home country for smuggling goods to Japan or being blown offcourse to North Korea.[23]

During this period, several smuggling centers formed along the coast. They included Yuezhou Port in Zhangzhou, Shuangyu Port in Dinghai, Zhejiang and Nan'ao Port in Guangdong. Among them, Yuegang was located fifty *li* east of Zhangzhou City. The adjacent waters were a traditional sea route for international transportation with many islands nearby, making it convenient for private business activities. Smuggling began to rise during the reigns of Emperor Xuande (r. 1425–1435) and Emperor Yingzong (1436–1449), and became rampant during the reigns of Emperor Wuzong (r. 1505–1521) and Emperor Shizong (r. 1521–1566). Located on the north-south route, Portuguese vessels were to be seen moored along the Shuangyu Portin Putuo in Zhejiang during the reign of Emperor Wuzong. Thereafter, the harbor gradually boomed.

In the early years of the Jiajing period, the issue of the two Japanese battling for the right to develop tributary trade with China led to the closing down of Ningbo Port temporarily. Shuangyu Port instead rose to be an international smuggling trade port.

Nan'ao was a relatively large island adjacent to Guangdong and Fujian, and it was, convenient for private business activities. Among the smugglers, in addition to the poor, there were also rich merchants and wealthy households. In other words, there were a mixture of businessmen and thieves. To resist being arrested by the government, they gradually developed into some armed smuggling bands and engaged in looting as well as black market trading.[24]

---

[23] *Ibid.,* Vol. 321.
[24] Chen Gaohua, Chen Shangsheng. *Chinese Maritime History* [M]. China Social Science Press, 2017.

In other words, the prohibition on overseas trade and tributary trade in the early years of the reign of Emperor Shizong failed to achieve the intended effect. In the face of this complicated situation, the Ming government was divided two internal camps: the prohibition one and the reform one. In 1567, the first year of the Longqing period in the reign of Emperor Muzong (r. 1567–1572), "Tu Zemin, Censor-in-chief of the Grand Coordinators and the Supreme Commander of Fujian Province, pleaded for lifting the ban on trading in Western Oceans and Eastern Oceans." The Maritime Trade Commission resumed its former work, being once again responsible for receiving foreign tribute vessels. Civilian merchants were allowed to depart from Yuegang in Zhangzhou to sail out for overseas trade.

Previously, the Ming government had allowed foreign merchants to trade in Guangdong as individuals, thus terminating the nearly 200-year history of the Ming Dynasty prohibiting overseas trade. The "tributary trade" lost its exclusive position, and private overseas trade was legalized eventually. The 200 years of practice of the "tributary trade" was overthrown in the Longqing period. The manifold reasons for this were as follows:

1. Lessons from the Wokou Rebellion in the Early Ming Period

Having failed to prevent people from going overseas for trade and to eliminate the disturbance caused by foreign enemies and *Wokou*, the prohibition policy of the early Ming Dynasty actually caused people along the coast to take up arms and smuggle. What is more, the Japanese pirates took advantage of the armed militias along the coast of China in order to extend their plunder. During the Jiajing period (1521–1566) in the reign of Emperor Shizong many people realized that "the Japanese peril" was related to the sea prohibition policy implemented by the Ming Court. It was already pointed out that "the Ming government imposed the ban on maritime trade, which made it impossible to carry out sea trade, so merchants had to turn to banditry to make their living."[25]

In 1564, Tan Lun, the Grand Coordinator and Supreme Commander of Fujian, listed the disadvantages of the ban on maritime trade in his letter to the Court and asked the Ming government to open overseas trade to

---

[25] (The Ming Dynasty) Chen Zilong. *Anthology of Statecraft Thought of the Ming Dynasty.* Vol. 270. Chinese Publishing House, 1962.

a moderate degree. He observed that "the Fujianese live by the sea, and banning them from going to sea is tantamount to wrecking their way of life. Since the prohibition in sea trade, fishermen in surrounding waters have been unable to make their living. As a result, theft is becoming more and more serious. Therefore, the government should moderately relax the ban on maritime trade."[26]

Some even explicitly suggested a prohibition on "tributary trade" instead, believing that it would stimulate non-governmental overseas trade. They claimed that "our loss in tributary trade needed to be complemented by the national treasures; what the maritime trade exchanged was civilian property with no influence on the national security. The tributary trade was more lost and less returned, while maritime trade was beneficial and harmless."[27]

In 1567, Emperor Muzong ascended to the throne, with his regnal period becoming known as "Longqing." Advocates for lifting the ban on overseas trade were to be heard everywhere. They outlined various disadvantages of the prohibition and the benefits of opening the sea trade, thereby pleading with the government for reopening private trade on the seas.

2. The Development of the Jiangnan Commodity Economy

With the development of social productivity, the Jiangnan commodity economy followed an unprecedented upward trend. The cultivation of cash crops for commodity exchange became widespread. For example, "cotton cultivation spread throughout the country. Regions in both the north and the south were suitable for planting this crop, and people, regardless of whether they were rich or poor could rely on it to make money."[28] Mulberry planting spread throughout China. In Huzhou, Zhejiang Province, for example, the acreage of rich households was very large and packed with mulberries. In the Jiangnan area, a number of commercial landlords emerged, supplying a variety of cash crops to the market. The commercialization of agricultural products provided sufficient raw materials for manufacturing production.

---

[26]Huang Zhangjian, *The Veritable Records of the Ming Dynasty*. Vol. 538. the Institute of History and Philology, Academia Sinica in Taiwan, 1962.

[27](The Ming Dynasty) Zhang Han. *Song Chuang Meng Yu.*

[28](The Ming Dynasty) Qiu Jun. *Daxue Yanyi Bu*. Vol. 22.

In the early Ming Dynasty, the government implemented an "artisan shift system" for common producers. That is to say, artisans were required to work together for the government without payment within a specified period each year. In 1529, this system was succeeded by a new one known as "artisan silver" (silver money paid to be exempt from corvee). This reform relaxed the relationship whereby artisans were rendered subordinate to the government. Craftsmen enjoyed more freedom, and their technology and products could flow onto the market with less hindrance.

With the expansion of commercialized agriculture and the reform of the corvee system by which craftsmen were bound, the private handicraft industry developed by leaps and bounds in the middle and late Ming Dynasties. Especially in textiles, porcelain and iron smelting industry, the production technology, scale and quality greatly exceeded those of the previous generations. For example, in the textile industry, in the late Ming period, the Jiangnan artificers exchanged their original manual machines for semi-mechanized "silk spinning machines." Advancement in production tools enhanced the productivity of labor, reducing production costs and increasing profits, thus stimulating more people to engage in specialized production. According to historical records, "in Wangjiangjing, Jiaxing, Zhejiang Province, there were more than 7,000 residents who made their living from the textile industry rather than farming land."[29]

In the late Ming Dynasty, there were several major centers of the handicraft industry in the Jiangnan area, whicih were divided according to their specialty. They had a sizeable scale of production, and included the cotton textile industry in Songjiang, the silk industry in Suzhou and Hangzhou, the dyeing industry in Wuhu, and the ceramic industry in Jingdezhen. Jingdezhen particularly became the center of China's ceramic industry in the mid-16th century. There were more than 900 kilns operated by ordinary subjects, and tens of thousands of people were engaged in the ceramic industry at that time. The porcelain produced there was sold "everywhere from east by the sea and west to Shu (present-day Sichuan)."

With the increase in the quantity of porcelain produced, there appeared quite a few endless innovations in new varieties. In the middle and later Ming Dynasties, porcelain, including five-colored porcelain and porcelain painted in "doucai" ("contrasting colors" or "contending colors"), were not only bright in color, but well-made and unique in

---

[29] Xiushui County Gazetteer in the Wanli Period. Vol. 1.

workmanship, becoming the top-quality products both at home and abroad. The white porcelain produced by the Dehua kiln in Fujian Province was very popular overseas and became a special export commodity. The unprecedented abundance of agricultural products and handicrafts provided sufficient supplies for domestic and foreign trade during the late Ming. In addition, because of the excess profits from overseas trade, Chinese coastal merchants strongly demanded that the ban on maritime trade be terminated.

3. Conciliatory Relations with Foreign Countries

Invasion by *Wokou* in the early Ming Dynasty was one of the reasons for the implementation of the overseas trade prohibition. This policy actually made the Japanese attacks increasingly acute. The year of 1552 turned out to be the year of unprecedented catastrophes, which was referred to in history books as the "Disaster of Yinzi (1552)." Aided by Chinese privateers, the *Wokou* plundered the southeast coast of China. "Hundreds of Japanese warships entered China's territory without permission. Those ships covered the ocean and coastline from the east and west of Zhejiang to the north and south of Jiangsu. Thousands of miles of coast were under threat at the same time."[30]

Lasting for 15 years until 1566, the disaster imperiled tens of thousands of miles, devastating Shandong, Jiangsu, Zhejiang, Fujian and Guangdong provinces, and damaging inland cities as well. Places such as "Huai'an, Yangzhou, Anhui, Taicang, Hangzhou, Jiaxing, Quzhou and Jinzhou, and even Nanjing were threatened, almost endangering half of the country."[31]

The armies of the Ming Dynasty and the inhabitants of the coastal areas organized armed attacks against the *Wokou*. In the last years of the Jiajing period (1521–1566), under the leadership of the patriotic General Yu Dayou and Qi Jiguang, the Chinese army and the residents of Fujian, Guangdong, Zhejiang and other places, defeated the *Wokou*. Thus, the turmoil was essentially over and the almost two-centuries harassment by the *Wokou* was finally put to an end.

The early reign of Emperor Wuzong saw Portuguese colonists encroaching upon China. They constantly harassed the coast of China. In

---

[30] *The History of Ming Dynasty*. Vol. 322.
[31] (The Ming Dynasty) Chen Zilong. *Anthology of Statecraft Thought of the Ming Dynasty*. Vol. 435. Chinese Publishing house, 1962.

1549, Zhu Wan, the Grand Coordinator and Supreme Commander of Zhejiang Province, commanded the Ming army to inflict heavy losses on those Portuguese invaders in Zoumaxi, Fujian Province. From then on, the Portuguese incursions upon the coasts of Fujian and Zhejiang were to some extent curtailed. In 1557, the Portuguese occupied the Chinese city of Macao by means of fraud and bribery, and were able to engage in lucrative triangular trade between Southeast Asia, China and Japan.

In summary, the objective environment at home and abroad in the late 16th century created a ripe condition for the lifting of the ban on foreign trade. However, the ruling class of the Ming Dynasty implemented the policy not out of a mindfulness of the significance of overseas trade to the economic development of the country. Rather it was just an expedient measure to minimize disaster and consolidate its domination. The rationale was that "in the repeal of the ban on Maritime Trade Policy, prohibition and control methods were implied." This meant that the purpose of partially opening-up was to consolidate government control over the people. Even Xu Guangqi, the grand scholar who had some knowledge of the western world, believed that "foreign trade would be beneficial to slaying the Japanese pirates, for foreign trade would enable the Chinese to gain more information about those outlaws, then control and murder them."[32] That is to say that repeal of the ban on maritime trade could help fight against the *Wokou*.

Therefore, although the ban on maritime trade was partially lifted in the late Ming Dynasty, it was still in effect a curb on overseas trade. Sea trading could only now be transacted via Zhangzhou,[33] which happened to be the most concentrated area for the smuggling trade in the early Ming Dynasty. The areas really suitable for foreign trade were not yet opened.

7.2.4 *Maritime Trade Development in the Late Ming Period*

1. Chinese Merchants Trade

In 1567, Yuegang Port in Zhangzhou, Fujian, a hot spot for smuggling, was opened to overseas trade. Merchants were allowed to obtain a "sailing

---

[32] *Ibid.*, Vol. 491.

[33] Zhangzhou in Fujian, being easily concealable, became an important port for private overseas trade and was called "little Suzhou Hangzhou" by smugglers.

pass" to transact trade. Thus, private overseas trade gained its legitimate legal status.

After Yuegang Port was opened, the private overseas trade was managed by the Coastal Defense Bureau (later changed to the Tariff Supervising Bureau). In the early Ming Dynasty, in order to implement the prohibition, a series of anti-smuggling agencies were set up in Yuegang Port, including the Jinghai Bureau and the Coastal Defense Bureau. In 1566 when Yuegang Port was reopened for overseas trade, the function of the Coastal Defense Bureau was changed to superintend private overseas trade. In 1593, the Coastal Defense Bureau was renamed the Tariff Supervising Bureau. Its main functions were as follows:

(i) Issuing a "Sailing Pass"

The pass was a permit for engaging in overseas trade. Before sailing overseas, merchants first of all had to apply for a pass from the Tariff Supervising Bureau. The application required the name of the merchant, the place of household registration, the type and quantity of the goods to be traded, the size of the ship, and the country to be visited. After the checking procedure, the merchant had to pay taxes, and then the Tariff Supervising Bureau's office would issue the pass. Only holders of a "Sailing Pass" were allowed to sail overseas. The number of passes was initially limited to 50 and increased to 88 in 1589. In 1597, when the overseas trade policy was further relaxed, the number of passes increased to 117. If the 20 spare passes for unexpected use were included, the total was 137.

(ii) The Collection of Import and Export Tax

Three kinds of import and export taxes were levied by the Tariff Supervising Bureau.

(a) Ship tax

The amount of tax levied was determined according to the beam head size of the vessel and the destinations to which it sailed. As for ships sailing to the Western Oceans, if the beam head of the ship measured over 1 cord (*zhang*) and 6 ells (*chi*) in width, taels of silver money per foot would be charged as water tax, and 5 *qian* would be added for each extra ell; as for ships sailing to *Eastern Oceans*, the tax rate would be 30% lower than that levied on ships sailing to the Western Oceans. Trade ships traveling to Jilong and Danshui in Taiwan also needed to pay taxes. The taxation standard was that every ell of extra width would be levied an extra 5 *qian* of silver money.

(b) Merchandise Tax

In order to prevent tax evasion, the Ming Court stipulated that when the merchant ship returned to the port, it was not allowed to unload without authorization. It should wait for the storekeepers (those who ran shops as domestic traders), who would board the ship to purchase the goods and pay the taxes. Then the ship was allowed to be unloaded. The taxation rate should be adjusted flexibly according to the type of goods and the resultant price.

(c) Additional Taxes

The object of this taxation was the merchant ships trading to Luzon (now the Philippines). At that time, a large number of Spanish colonists who occupied the Philippines carried out "vessel trade" between Luzon and Acapulco, Mexico. They shipped the merchandise of Chinese merchants from Luzon to Mexico to earn Mexican silver dollars. Therefore, Mexican silver dollars were loaded on the Chinese merchant ships when they returned from the Luzon, where there were few goods for international circulation. For this reason, the Ming Court stipulated that ships trading with Luzon must pay an extra 150 taels of silver money as "additional taxes" further to the water tax and land tax. In 1590 when merchants protested that the tax was too high, the "additional tax" was reduced to 120 taels of silver money.

The implementation of the *Xiangshui* tax system changed China's foreign trade tax from in-kind tax payment to a monetary tax. This indicated the advance of the commodity currency economy. In turn, it helped the commodity economy to proceed with dynamism. More importantly, it increased the financial revenue for the Ming government and military provisions as well.

iii The Supervision and Inspection of Import and Export Merchant Ships

Every early spring merchant ships would set out to the sea. The Tariff Supervising Bureau officials were responsible for inspecting each ocean-going vessel to see whether the type and quantity of the cargoes they carried were consistent with the application it had registered, and whether here were any prohibited articles onboard. In summer and autumn, when the merchant ships returned one after another, the Tariff Supervising Bureau would send officials to conduct an inspection tour in the southeastern coastal areas. The returning merchant ships were "escorted" to their destination. Ostensibly, this "escorting" served to prevent pirates from seizing goods. Actually, it was meant to prevent the merchants from illegally unloading goods and evading tax.

2. Guangzhou and Macao Open up to Foreign Trade

In the early Ming Dynasty, Chinese and foreign merchants resisted the policy of banning overseas trade. At the same time, the economic development of coastal areas also relied on overseas trade. Therefore, in 1509, coastal officials in Guangdong tried to open up foreign trade but were met with opposition from conservative bureaucrats. A cycle of first opening up and then banning overseas trade was thus initiated. This situation lasted until the middle and later Jiajing period (1522–1566). With the rise of Macao as a port, Chinese and foreign merchants often concentrated there. In the late Ming Dynasty, after Chinese merchants were allowed to sail for trade, Macao and Guangzhou were also open to foreign merchants under the management of the Maritime Trade Commission. Its main functions were as follows:

(i) The Tax Administration of Foreign Merchants in China

In the early Ming Dynasty, local officials in Guangdong and the Maritime Trade Commission were jointly responsible for the taxation of foreign merchants. The tax system was called the *choufen* (extraction), which was to collect a certain proportion of physical goods according to their quantity. In 1554, the Ming government set up a Maritime Trade Commission in Macao to collect import and export taxes and berthing taxes. Berthing tax was like the "Water Tax." It was collected according to the ships volume. The Import and Export Tax was actually the "Merchandise Tax, which was collected according to the *choufen* tax system, at a rate of 20%". In 1571, in order to prevent foreign merchants from concealing and under-reporting their goods, the *choufen* tax system was changed to the *zhangchou* tax system, that is, tax was collected according to the scale of the ship and paid in the form of currency.

(ii) Export Commodity Fairs in Guangzhou

In the late Ming Dynasty, export commodities fairs began to be held in Guangzhou almost every year. Initially, they were an annual event, but were held twice yearly from 1580. In the spring, as the southwest monsoon approached, foreign merchants in Guangzhou bought in goods and sailed to Southeast Asia and Europe. The summer season generally began in June. Before the approach of the northeast monsoon, foreign merchants bought in a large number of Chinese goods to be shipped to Japan. The Ming government stipulated that foreign merchant ships were prohibited from entering Guangzhou, but could dock on some nearby islands. Each country had a fixed berthing area designated by the Ming authorities. Foreign merchants required approval from the Ming government to purchase precious goods, while ordinary goods could be purchased freely. The Export Commodities Fair held in Guangzhou became an important channel for foreign merchants to buy Chinese goods.

(iii) The Supervision and Inspection of Foreign Trade
After the ships of foreign merchants entered port, they were first required to make a declaration to the local officials who then notified the Maritime Trade Commission and they examined the imported goods together. After confirming that there was no contraband, they would collect the tax accordingly.

The government still imposed various restrictions on overseas trade in the late Ming Dynasty. After all, non-governmental trade between China and foreign countries was no longer under absolute embargo. With the former ban lifted, overseas trade achieved unprecedented development. It was estimated that the revenue of the *Xiangshui* Tax totaled about 3,000 taels per year in the early years of the Longqing period (1567–1572). It surged to 29,000 taels some 20 years later during the Wanli period (1573–1620).

3. Maritime Smuggling after the Removal of Prohibition
After the embargo on the sea trade was lifted, maritime smuggling was still in operation. This was mainly due to the following reasons: First, the government enforced strict restrictions on overseas trade, and officials often used their power to extort money, seriously damaging the interests of merchants.

For instance, when examining ships before they departed the port, "customs officers greedy for money use customs inspection as one of their sources of revenue. Once a ship is to be inspected, every merchant who wants to trade out of the port will be subject to extortionate treatment to bribe relevant officials at different levels of governance.

The environment inside the port is very noisy with all the sounds of merchants being obstructed from leaving the harbor and having to contend with extortion and blackmail."[34]

When subordinates of the chief tax administrator saw ships return, all of them wanted to be allowed to make inquiries. Once they were appointed on any errand, they would winkle some money. They extorted and blackmailed merchants by inspecting, escorting and packing goods, which was originally free of tax. Those officials were actually the black sheep who extorted money from merchants."

"The local officials are even more shameless than the customs officers. When the number of goods is reported to them, they will claim to the government that the cargo was only half its actual amount. The rest will go directly into their chief's pockets. When reporting the number of cargoes which enter port, they will naturally conceal half, with the remainder also being given to the chief. When they are in a generous mood, they will only embezzle a little; if they feel dissatisfied, their blackmail would be ruthless. Those officials and subordinates are really abominable. They glean a fortune by concealing the taxes they stole, but they will report that everything is normal. That is why local governments are called a 'nest of poisonous bees' crippling the interests of merchants."

Secondly, although the Ming Dynasty officially forbade the sea merchants from trading in Japan, owing to the high profits available in trade between China and Japan, many merchants took risks and even formed a strong maritime smuggling clique.

Finally, the government only opened the port of Yuegang in Fujian for trade. This made life very inconvenient for merchants in Zhejiang and Guangdong. Their smuggling was therefore hard to police.

In a word, the overseas trade policy of the Ming Dynasty was quite different from that of the Song and Yuan Dynasties. In the 200 years before Emperor Muzong began to permit maritime trade, the embargo policy and the tributary trade policy were basically implemented, and private merchants were not allowed to go to sea, leading to the rise in smuggling. After Emperor Muzong sanctioned maritime trade, private merchants could go to sea for trade. However, due to shortcomings in government management, more and more ships became involved in smuggling activities.

---

[34](The Ming Dynasty) Zhang Xie. *On the Countries in the Eastern and Western Oceans.* Vol. 7.

7.3 The Evolution of the Maritime Trade System

Emerging in the Tang and developing in the Song and Yuan Dynasties, the Maritime Trade System as an apparatus of overseas trade management was inherited by the Ming Dynasty. In order to enforce the foreign trade policy of the Ming, great changes were implemented to the system in terms of institutional setup and function. In the late Ming Dynasty, with alterations in Sino-foreign trade relations, the role of the Maritime Trade Commission in superintending foreign trade weakened day by day.

7.3.1 *Setting up the Maritime Trade Commission in the Early Ming Period*

1. The Evolution of the Maritime Trade Commission
At the beginning of the Ming Dynasty, the Maritime Trade Commission was set up in Huangdu Town, Taicang, Jiangsu. It was located relatively close to Nanjing, the capital of the country, which may not have been conducive to national security. In view of this, Emperor Taizu revoked the Maritime Trade Commission there in 1370, and then fully implemented the Embargo Policy. The official tributary trade between China and foreign countries became the only legitimate means of foreign trade. In order to manage the tributary trade, the Ming government set up three Maritime Trade Commissions in Guangzhou, Quanzhou and Ningbo, respectively, which were frequented by tributary ships. Stipulations were made to determine the sea route from Ningbo port to Japan, from Quanzhou port to Ryukyu, and from Guangzhou port to Champa, Siam and western countries. In 1374, due to the serious harassment by the *Wokou*, the Ming Court ordered the disestablishment of the Maritime Trade Commissions in Zhejiang, Fujian and Guangdong.

In 1403, after Emperor Chengzu succeeded to the throne, he restored three Maritime Trade Commissions in Zhejiang, Fujian and Guangdong in order to resume the development of Sino-foreign relations and restore active tributary trade. In 1404, the Ming government built three courier hostels in Anyuan (in Zhejiang), Laiyuan (in Fujian) and Huaiyuan (in Guangdong) to receive envoys and their entourages. According to historical records, the courier hostel in Huaiyuan in Guangzhou alone contained

120 guest rooms, and received envoys from more than 10 countries every year.

In 1408, Emperor Chengzu set up two Maritime Trade Commissions in Cochin and Yunnan to receive ambassadors from countries on the Indochina Peninsula. However, those two commissions were abolished a bit later. In 1523, after the "two Japanese merchant groups battled for the right for tributary trade" in Zhejiang, the Ming Dynasty ordered the removal of the Maritime Trade Commissions in Zhejiang and Fujian, leaving only one commission in Guangdong. It was not until 1599 that Emperor Shenzong (r. 1572–1620) ordered the restoration of the Maritime Trade Commissions in Zhejiang and Fujian. It can be seen that during the whole reign of the Ming Dynasty, the number of Maritime Trade Commission was in decline compared with that of the Song and Yuan Dynasties. They were abolished and disestablished in turn, demonstrating an overall downward trend in their significance.

The Maritime Trade Commission was subordinate to the Provincial Administration Commission. It belonged to the fifth rank (in the Nine-Rank administration hierarchy in feudal China), its status being far inferior to what it had been in the Tang and Song Dynasties. Emperor Chengzu actively operated an overseas market and undertook tributary trade in a vigorous manner. As a maritime trade management organization, the Maritime Trade Commission was, to some extent, elevated to being an "important department" like the Salt Distribution Superintendency or the Horse Trading Office. Nevertheless, the relatively low position of the organ was left unchanged. According to the *History of Ming: Records of Officials*, the Maritime Trade Commission consisted of one supervisorate, a 5th-rank title, and two vice supervisors, a 6th-rank title. According to the actual situation, Maritime Trade Commissions in many places varied in numbers of personnel for the position of Supervisorate. This was probably due to the varying complexity of affairs in different regions.

Eunuchs played an important role in the management of ancient overseas trade. The trade management system was "government-oriented," and took shape in the Tang Dynasty. For example, the government set up the Maritime Trade Commissioners to supervise maritime trade affairs in Guangzhou. They operated independently from the local government. After the middle Tang Dynasty, eunuchs were ostensibly appointed as the Maritime Trade Commissioners, whose duty was actually practiced by Military Surveillance Officer. It was during the period of 1402–1424 that eunuchs became involved in foreign relations and foreign trade. The early Ming placed the specific affairs of tributary trade under the authority of the Maritime Trade Commission, which was subordinate to the local system.

In 1403, Emperor Chengzu sent the Maritime Trade Mid-year Officer (one of many generic terms for a eunuch) to the Guangzhou Maritime Trade Commission, which was superior in rank to the Maritime Trade Commissioner. There were many officials higher in rank than the Maritime Trade Commissioner, like the eunuchs, the Grand Defenders, the Grand Coordinator (Touring Pacifier), and the "Three Bureaus,"[35] who formed a multi-tiered leadership over the Commission. Eunuchs were permanently stationed in the local governments as envoys of the Emperor and often concurrently served as the governors of local military affairs, the salt administration, the coastal circuit, etc. They became so powerful as to be able to override the local government. This changed the trade management system of the early Ming and strengthened the Court's administration over tributary trade. Eunuchs managing maritime trade oversaw independent administrative bodies, namely the Maritime Trade Establishment, the Maritime Trade Institute, and the Superintendent of Maritime Trade Office, which were directly subordinate to the Palace Treasury.

2. The Maritime Trade Commission in the Early Ming Period

In the early Ming period, the government successively set up five Maritime Trade Commissions, with those in Zhejiang, Fujian and Guangdong being the more important ones. During the reign of Emperor Wuzong and Emperor Shizong (r. 1521–1566), the embargo influenced the transformation of foreign trade, and the Maritime Trade Commissions of Zhejiang and Fujian were closed down, with only the Maritime Trade Commission in Guangdong continuing to operate.[36]

(i) The Maritime Trade Commission in Taicang

Taicang lies at the estuary of the Loujiang River. During the reign of Kublai Khan (1264–1294) during the Yuan Dynasty, it was used to

---

[35] Provincial Administration Commission, Provincial Surveillance Commission and Regional Military Commission.

[36] Li Qingxin. *The Overseas Trade System of the Ming Dynasty* [M]. Beijing: Social Sciences Academic Press, 2007.

transport grain by sea. From then on, foreign ships gathered here. At that time, it was known as a "six-country wharf." Zhengxiao of the Ming Dynasty wrote that "in the early reign of the Hongwu period (1368–1398), the Maritime Trade Commission in Huangdu, Taicang was established. It was later celebrated as a 'six-country wharf.' It was closed down so as to expel barbarians from the capital for they were too duplicitous."[37] The Maritime Trade Commission in Taicang mainly managed foreign merchants who came to Zhejiang for trade. Its institutional system was probably similar to that in the Song and Yuan Dynasties, since it included a Supervisorate, two Vice Supervisors, and lower-ranked officers.

Although the Taicang Maritime Trade Commission did not exist for long, its management method determined the basic system for that in the early Ming Dynasty. Shen Defu of the Ming Dynasty observed that "when Emperor Taizu had just pacified the world, he set up a Maritime Trade Commission in Huangdu Town, Taicang Prefecture. There was one supervisor, two vice supervisors, and one courier aid in the commission. Later, the cunning barbarians cunning threatened the Metropolitan Area, so the Ming government shut down the Taicang commission. In 1375, the government established Maritime Trade Commissions in Ningbo and Guangzhou, with the same system as that in Taicang."[38]

(ii) The Maritime Trade Commission in Zhejiang

Zhejiang boasted traditional ports for trade with Japan. In the Song Dynasty, the Zhejiang Maritime Trade Commission was established in Yaojia Lane, in the northeast corner of Ningbo Prefecture.

In the Ming Dynasty, the commission was moved to the residence in the Marshal House of Fang Guozhen, leader of the peasant upring. The Maritime Trade Commission in Zhejiang set up four offices (*Yamen*), which respectively, suited in Weijia Lane, Xiaoliang Lane, Big Chitou and Yancang Gate, and were responsible for handling overseas trade affairs. The Commission had *Anyuan Yi* (Post Relay Station) under its management. Due to the frequent invasion of *Wokou* and pirates along the coast of Zhejiang Province, the coastal defense situation was quite tense. Therefore, as an institution for trade management, the Maritime Trade

---

[37] (The Ming Dynasty) Zheng Xiao. *Jin Yan*. Vol. 3. Commented by Li Zhizhong. Beijing: Zhonghua Book Company, 1984.

[38] (The Ming Dynasty) Shen Defu. *An Unofficial History of the Wanli Reign Period*. Vol. 12.

Commission fell into a state of virtual disuse for a long time. In 1522, the commission was abandoned after the incident where two Japanese battled for the right to develop the tributary trade with China. Later on, the then office of the Commission was taken as the headquarter of Surveillance Coastal Circuits Department.

(iii) The Maritime Trade Commission in Fujian

Fujian was an important trade area along the southeastern coast. In the Song and Yuan Dynasties, the Maritime Trade Commission was set up in Quanzhou. Later, it managed exclusively the tributary trade affairs of Ryukyu.

During the Jiajing period (1521–1566) of the Ming Dynasty, some people observed that "official posts, like supervisorate, were not always assigned in Fujian. Since Li Zhuang became the first supervisorate of the commission in 1151, the position was alternatively abolished and reinstated from time to time in different dynasties. Not until the Ming Dynasty was a supervisorate assigned to head the commission to handle foreign trade affairs who was exclusively responsible for dealing with the tributary trade of Ryukyu."[39]

Later, during the Chenghua period (1465–1487) in the reign of Emperor Xianzong, the Fujian Maritime Trade Commission moved from Quanzhou to Fuzhou owing to the following reasons:

Firstly, Fuzhou was the capital of Fujian Province, being more important than Quanzhou, having an advantageous geographic location, more cultural relics and stronger military defense capability. So it could perhaps earn more awe and respect from foreigners.

Secondly, the people of Ryukyu were loyal and obedient to China during the period 1368–1398, and the Ming government granted them "36 boatmen who were adept at steering, thus facilitating mutual exchanges." Most of the boatmen came from Hekou in Fuzhou, thus guiding the tribute envoys from Ryukyu to Fuzhou.

Thirdly, in the Ming Dynasty, the tribute envoys from Ryukyu were generally managed and received by the Provincial Administration Commission of Fujian. Relevant officials were all stationed in Fuzhou.

---

[39] (The Ming Dynasty) Gao Qi. *Chronicles of the Maritime Trade Supervisorates in Fujian.* Li Qingxin. *The Overseas Trade System of the Ming Dynasty* [M]. Beijing: Social Sciences Academic Press, 2007.

Receptions would be inconvenient to stage if the Maritime Trade Commission was still located in Quanzhou.

Fourth, the conditions in Fuzhou were indeed superior to those in Quanzhou. After the war at the end of the Yuan Dynasty, Quanzhou was no longer as prosperous as it had been before. Fuzhou as a port enjoyed greater convenience in transportation with official land routes for pack horses as well as rivers and lakes linking it to the sea. It was taken by Zheng He as the point of departure for his expeditions to the Western Oceans during the Yongle period (1402–1424).

(iv) The Maritime Trade Commission in Guangdong

The Maritime Trade Commission in Guangdong was originally located outside the Guide Gate of Guangzhou, but was later moved into the city. Its affiliated *Huaiyuan Yi* (Post Relay Station) housed 120 rooms of various types, being the largest among the three Post Relay Stations (the other two were the *Anyuan Station* and the *Laiyuan Station*). In the records contained in the *Chronicles of Guangdong Province* compiled in the Wanli period (1572–1620), the article "Yuan Guan" recorded that "during the Yongle period (1402–1424), foreign countries came to offer homage. The government sent eunuchs to work as supervisors with the Maritime Trade Commission in Guangzhou. Huaiyuan Station was built as the Post Relay Station in the southwest of the city, containing 120 rooms so as to supplement the military supply. At that time, ennuch officials sent from the Court took charge of the affairs of the commission, while the Supervisorate was reduced to being a puppet official. As for the foreign envoys, only the chief envoy could enter the city while their entourage waited and stayed at the station. They were allowed to enter the city when they were treated with a banquet, and left immediately afterwards. This continued to be the practice during the period 1465–1505. Foreign envoys dressed in a strange manner, with their hats adorned with golden beads and clothes in colors as bright as the sunrise. On their way to the banquet, local people, old and young, crowded over to watch them."

(v) The Maritime Trade Commission in Cochin

In 1406, the Ming government defeated the LêQuýLy regime in Annam, where 48 state prefectures (*zhou*) and subprefectures (*fu*) were set up afterward. In June 140, the Maritime Trade Commission in Cochin was set up by the Ming government and was stationed in Yuntun, which had been a very prosperous international trade port since the Southern Song. A man in the Jiajing period (1521–1566) recorded that "Yuntun was a coastal town, located in Yuntun Hill, Yuntun County, Xin'an Prefecture of Cochin. Foreign vessels usually gathered in Cochin. In the Yongle period (1402–1424), the Maritime Trade Commission was set up there."[40] Nevertheless, although the Ming set up commission officials in AnNam, its governance was unstable with frequent rebellions. In 1427, the Ming government ceded its control of Cochin, as did the Maritime Trade Commission there.

7.3.2 *Functions of the Maritime Trade Commission*

In the Ming Dynasty, the functions of the Maritime Trade Commission were closely related to the changes in its maritime trade policies. Distinct functional differences were found between the early Ming and the late Ming.

1. Functions of the Maritime Trade Commission in the Early Ming Period

In the Tang, Song and Yuan Dynasties, the Maritime Trade Commission took charge of maritime trade in an all-round manner. In the early Ming, the implementation of the embargo forbade Chinese merchants from trading overseas, and foreign merchants could only come to China in the name of tribute. That is, to say tributary trade was the only legal means of conducting foreign trade with China. In the early Ming Dynasty, relevant changes took place in the functions of the Maritime Trade Commission, so it became an organ the government relied on for the implementation of its embargo.

According to the *History of Ming: Records of Officials*, the duties of the Maritime Trade Commission included (a) taking charge of the maritime affairs concerning foreign tributes and exchanges; (b) verifying the envoys' identities, official documents and *Kanhe*; (c) prohibiting exchanges with foreign countries and collecting tax from civilian foreign trade; (d) maintaining equality in exchange." To be specific, after foreign ships entered the port, the commission together with local officials would inspect the *Kanhe* and verify its authenticity, and then seal the tribute to prevent it from being smuggled ashore. They then

---

[40](The Ming Dynasty) Chen Quanzhi. *Peng Chuang Ri Lu*. Vol. 2.

transported the tribute to the warehouse where the tributes were stored, took the envoys and their entourage to the Post Relay Station, and finally reported to the Court. After the Imperial Court granted permission, the Maritime Trade Commission together with the local officials escorted the tribute envoys as well as the tributes to the capital.

As for the commercial goods coming together with the tributes, the Maritime Trade Commission was responsible for inspecting whether there were any illegal or prohibited articles, and reported to the local government. Afterward, the commission practiced the *choufen* as tax from the foreign goods. After the *choufen* was done the remaining merchandise would be purchased by the government at a certain price, as a form of tax exemption. The trading of foreign goods as such was managed by the intermediary affiliated to the Maritime Trade Commission. The intermediaries were responsible for evaluation of the price of goods and introduction of Chinese merchants to trade with foreign merchants.

The Maritime Trade Commission had the responsibility of prohibiting Chinese merchants from carrying out trade activities overseas. For those merchants who traded at sea illegally, the commission had the right to arrest them. In order to combat the smuggling trade, the Maritime Trade Commission at one stage had the authority to mobilize the army.

In conclusion, there were three responsibilities that the commission had to fulfill in the early Ming: (a) managing the tributary trade; (b) inspecting and curbing the overseas trade of civilian merchants; (c) collecting taxes and managing the mutual market. Among them, the first was the major task.

2. Functions of the Maritime Trade Commission in the Late Ming Period

In 1567 and the years afterward, the Ming Dynasty partially opened non-governmental trade with foreign countries, allowing Chinese merchants to put to sea from Yuegang Port in Zhangzhou under the management of the Coastal Defense Bureau (later changed to the Tariff Supervising Bureau). It was stipulated that foreign merchants were allowed to sail to China, but could only dock at Guangzhou and Macao, under the supervision of the Maritime Trade Commission.

The responsibilities of the Maritime Trade Commission were to inspect import and export commodities, collect import and export taxes as well as berthing taxes. The intermediary (*Ya Hang*) was in charge of the exchanges and transactions between Chinese and foreign merchants. In the late Ming Dynasty, the intermediary was independent from the Maritime Trade Commission. With the increasing number of foreign merchants coming to China, the limitations of the intermediary system were gradually appeared. Therefore, during the late Ming Dynasty, the intermediary system was slowly replaced by Guangdong's 36 Factories, which were exclusively engaged in the import and export of goods. In this regard, one of the important functions of the maritime trade management system, namely operating and managing overseas trade, was completely lost. This maritime trade management system, having been implemented for nearly 1,000 years since the Tang Dynasty, was finally brought to an end.

7.4 Sino-Foreign Trade Relations

Prior to Europeans' coming to China in the 16th century, China still maintained its traditional foreign trade relations, mainly with Asian and African countries. After the 16th century, Europeans arrived in the East and established a few colonies in Southeast Asia and South Asia. Thereafter, the traditional trade relations between China and those regions were damaged whereas Sino-European trade relations were developed, and become increasingly dominant as far as China was concerned.

7.4.1 *China's Trade Relations with Asian and African Countries*

In the early Ming Dynasty, China's trade with Asian and African countries mainly consisted of the official tributary variety. As was mentioned previously, Zheng He's expeditions to the Western Oceans brought official Sino-foreign trade to its peak. At the same time, the civilian smuggling was rampant. Meanwhile, in late Ming times, with the decline of the tributary trade, civilian trade became the leading force in the development of China's trade relations with Asian and African countries.

1. East Asia
(i) Joseon
China had close political and economic ties with the Korean peninsula in the Ming Dynasty. In the early Ming Dynasty, the Lee Dynasty of Korea paid tribute to the Ming government and helped the Ming to crack down

on Chinese smugglers. According to historical records, in 1544, the Chinese Fujian merchant Li Wangqi and others smuggled in Joseon and were captured by North Korean soldiers. Thereafter, the soldiers of Joseon hunted down smugglers from China more than once and had them repatriated.

In view of Joseon's loyalty, the Ming government rewarded that country with a preferential policy in tributary trade. For example, with regard to the frequency of tribute, other countries were usually limited to once every three years, while Joseon could pay tribute twice or three times a year. As for the activities of envoys in Beijing, for instance, envoys of other countries were generally allowed to leave the *Huitong Guan Hostel* (where they were accommodated) once in every 5 days, while envoys of Joseon could go in and out at any time. In terms of traded commodities, the Ming Dynasty stipulated that sulfur and grains should not be exported, with North Korea being an exception.

During this period, China exported silk, porcelain, tea, medicine and books to Joseon, and imported horses, cattle, ramie fabric and folding fans from Joseon. The largest trade between them was the "silk–horse trade," with Joseon exchanging its horses for China's silk products. According to historical records, in 1393, Joseon "paid as tributes over 9,800 horses in exchange for over 16,700 items of silk yarn and satin."

In 1407 and 1423, Joseon envoys brought to China thousands of horses. In return, they received a large number of silk gifts from the Ming government.

(ii) Japan

The relationship between China and Japan in the Ming Dynasty was relatively complicated. In the early Ming Dynasty, due to the *Wokou* and the Hu Weiyong Rebellion, the Ming government implemented a very restrictive policy on Japan's tributes to China. The Ming government even stipulated that Japan was allowed to pay tribute to China only "once in a decade." Each time it paid tribute, its ships were limited to be no more than three and its personnel no more than 300. Nevertheless, this restriction did not fully work. Japan still paid tributes more frequently in the early Ming. During this period, a large number of Japanese swords were paid as tributes to China. Those swords were praised and welcomed by the Chinese people for their sharpness and fine quality.

Japan profited handsomely by paying swords as tributes to China. According to the *History of Cultural Exchange in Sino-Japan* (*Nikka bunka kōryūshi*), a blade was worth at most 1 tael in Japan. After it was traded with the Ming, each donor was paid as much as 5 taels. As a result, swords to China became the major component of Japanese tributes. In 1433, the Japanese brought 3,052 swords to China. In addition to swords, sulfur, copper, folding fans and gold-painted lacquerware were also important commodities shipped from Japan to China. Regarding China as a traditional big market, Japan had a great demand for Chinese raw silk and porcelain.

Regardless of the relatively strict restrictions on tributary trade, many Chinese and Japanese merchants took risks and engaged in black market trade between them. In the early Ming Dynasty, many Chinese merchants went to Japan. According to historical records, in 1557, 2,000–3,000 Chinese merchants gathered in Nagasaki, Japan. It was estimated that there were about 20,000–30,000 Chinese merchants in the Japanese archipelago at that time. In Hakata, Hirado, Goto-retto and Kagoshima, there were also "China towns" inhabited by Chinese residents.

After the opening of Yuegang Port in the late Ming Dynasty, the Ming government still prohibited Chinese merchants from trading in Japan, so the Sino-Japanese trade was mainly conducted on the black market. Some Chinese merchants applied for a "sailing pass" to trade in other countries. After they went abroad, they sailed southwestward first; having crossed the surveillance line of the Ming army, they then turned to the east heading for Japan.

During the reign of Tokugawa Ieyasu (1543–1616), the Japanese Emperor likewise took active measures to attract Chinese merchants to trade with Japan. In 1610, he issued a "red sealed order" to protect the trade between Guangzhou merchant ships sailing to and from Japan for trade. The "red sealed order" read that "any merchant ship of Guangdong coming to Japan could trade in any prefecture, county or island there. If Chinese merchants are accused of being met with Japanese villains who do them an injustice, the accused Japanese would be immediately executed. No Japanese were allowed to violate the order."[41]

By the end of the Ming Dynasty, Zheng Zhilong, a Fujian merchant, developed a mercantile clique through Sino-Japanese trade, particularly the trade with Taiwan and Japan. He opened a new route from Anping, Quanzhou directly to Nagasaki, Japan. Sino-Japanese trade reached its

---

[41](Japan) Yasuhiko Kimiya. *Nikka bunka kōryūshi*. Fuzanbō, 1955. Reprint 1977.

heyday. History recorded that "cargo ships were seen going to and from Japan every month without fail."[42]

(iii) Ryukyu

As early as in the Han Dynasty, the Ryukyu Islands and China started bilateral economic and trade exchanges. After the establishment of the Ming Dynasty, Emperor Taizu implemented a peaceful foreign policy. In 1372, the Ming sent emissaries to Ryukyu, which received the Ming's imperial canonization to be an important tribute country. The Ming also adopted a more favorable policy for tributary trade with Ryukyu, allowing the Japanese to pay tribute twice a year or three times a year, and chartering its merchant ships with tributes to dock at the Maritime Trade Commissions in Beijing and Fujian. There was no embargo for them to do trade with Chinese merchants.

In 1474, the Ming Court built the *Rouyuan Guan Hostel* in Fuzhou, to cater especially to envoys from Ryukyu. Ryukyu was backward in its economic development and did not produce spices and other bulk tribute products that China needed. The profitable tributary trade seduced the merchants of Ryukyu to sail abroad and purchase spices in Southeast Asia and ship them to China. At the same time, Ryukyu also re-exported silk, porcelain and copper coins they obtained from China to Southeast Asia, Japan and other places. Ryukyu made a huge profit from this transshipment trade, transforming it from being a tiny obscure place to a country of redoubt on the Maritime Silk Road.

In 1609, the Shimazu clan, the seignior of Kagoshima on Kyushu Island of Japan, invaded Ryukyu and issued the so-called "sanction" to Ryukyu. It stipulated that Ryukyu was not allowed to communicate with China or trade with other countries at will. The tributary trade between the Ming and Ryukyu go downhill afterward.

2. Southeast Asia

In the early Ming Dynasty, China's trade with Southeast Asian countries was also conducted in two ways: one was legal tributary trade, the other was private black market smuggling. By the late Ming, most Southeast Asian countries had been colonized by Europeans. Their official tributary relationship with China was interrupted, and private trade became the

---

[42] *The Comprehensive History of Taiwan.* Vol. 3.

only means. Moreover, such trade was not only the trade between China and Southeast Asia, but between China and Europe.

(i) The Indochina Peninsula

In the Ming Dynasty, the main countries on the Indochina Peninsula were AnNam (now northern Vietnam), Champa (now central and Southern Vietnam), Khmer (now Cambodia and Southern Vietnam), and Siam (now Thailand). Those countries and regions were traditional and longstanding trading partners of China. After the Ming Dynasty was founded, the two sides carried out tributary exchanges. Especially after the overseas expeditions by Zheng He to the Western Oceans, the tributary relations between the Indochina Peninsula countries and China became closer. At the same time, merchants from the southeast coast of China, ignoring the embargo, came to those countries from time to time to conduct trade activities. The countries of the Indochina Peninsula welcomed the arrival of Chinese merchant very cordially. In AnNam, "officers hosted feasts for the merchants. Signs were posted outside of the hostels Chinese merchants lived in to call people to trade with them."[43]

After the Ming Dynasty was established, it took the initiative to send envoys to make peace with Khmer. In 1370, Emperor Taizu sent his envoy Guo Zheng to Khmer to establish diplomatic relations. After Zheng He went to the Western Oceans, the friendly relations between China and Khmer developed to an unprecedented extent. According to statistics, from 1371 to 1452, Khmer paid tributes to China for a total of 21 times. The main articles in Khmer's tributes were elephants, ivory, rhinoceros horns, peacock feathers, gems, and various kinds of spices. The main gifts they gained from China were gold and silver, coins, silk fabrics, and porcelain.

The scale of tributary trade between the two sides was also considerable. For example, in 1387, Khmer paid as tributes 59 elephants and 60,000 catties of spices. In the next year, it contributed 28 elephants, 34 elephant trainers and 45 foreign slaves to China. The gifts returned from the Ming were even more generous. For example, in 1383, Khmer was given back 32 bolts (*pi*) of silk and 19,000 pieces of porcelain. Chinese goods were very popular in Khmer, where they were known as "the commodities of Tang." In Khmer,

---

[43] (The Ming Dynasty) Zhang Xie. *On the Countries in the Eastern and Western Oceans.* Vol. 1. The Commercial Press, 1936.

gold and silver were used for block trade, while "the commodities of Tang" were taken as transaction mediator in petty trade.

By the time the Ming Dynasty was founded, the Ayutthaya Kingdom of Thailand had unified Siam. In 1370, Emperor Taizu sent the emissary Lü Zongjun and his entourage to Siam and the two countries established friendly relations. During the Yongle period (1402–1424), the overseas expeditions by Zheng He further strengthened the relationship between the two sides. Subsequently, the envoys of the two countries paid exchange visits one after another, and Siam sent envoys to pay tributes to the Ming very frequently. According to records, during the Ming Dynasty, China sent diplomatic missions to Siam 19 times while Siam sent diplomatic missions to China 102 times. The scale of tributary trade was also sizable. For example, in 1387, Siam presented 10,000 catties of pepper; and in 1390, it contributed pepper and hematoxylon weighing 170,000 catties, together with 30 elephants.

Private trade between the two countries was terminated altogether by China's embargo. When Zheng He sailed to the Western Oceans, there were many overseas Chinese doing business in Siam. Siam welcomed Chinese merchants to trade. Moreover, its government provided convenient measures for Chinese merchants to trade within their borders. Chinese merchants "were allowed to enter Siam upon their arrival at the port without reporting to the superior." There were many Chinese merchants sailing to Siam. During the Jiajing period (1521–1566), "large ships built in Yuegang Port in Zhangzhou were seen to trade with the Siamese." Wang Zhi, a well-known armed smuggler "built ships to transport illegal goods, like nitrazine yellow and silk floss to Siam for the smuggling trade."

In the late Ming Dynasty, after the maritime trade ban was lifted at Yuegang Port, the Ming government stipulated that only four ships per year were allowed to sail to Siam, ranking first among foreign countries. Nevertheless, the actual number was much greater than that. According to western scholars, at that time, the Chinese from southern Fujian carried a large number of various kinds of local goods to Siam every year, and brought with them a large quantity of log wood, lead and other goods back to China.[44]

---

[44] G. William Skinner. "Ancient Overseas Chinese in Siam" in *Chinese Society in Thailand* 2010.

(ii) The Philippine Archipelago

As a close neighbor of China, the Philippines developed with the assistance of a long-standing trade relationship with China. In the Ming Dynasty, there were many states in the Philippine Islands, including Luzon in the north, Mindoro and Palawan in the middle, the Sultanate of Sulu, Cebu and Mindanao in the south, all of which maintained trade relations with China. In the early Ming Dynasty, the relationship between China and the Philippine Islands was mainly in the form of tributary trade. In 1405, Emperor Chengzu sent envoys to visit Luzon. Records had it that states of the Philippine Islands sent envoys to China frequently. Among them, Sulu developed the closest tributary relationship with China.

During the Yongle period, the King of the Sultanate of Sulu came to China many times with grandees to pay tributes. In 1417, the King led more than 300 dignitaries to China, and Emperor Chengzu of the Ming rewarded them with a large number of precious items with great courtesy. These included a band inlaid with gold and jade, 100 taels of gold, 2,000 taels of platinum, 200 bolts (*pi*) of tussores, 300 bolts of silk, 10,000 ingots of silver money, 3,000 *guan* of copper money, a gold-embroidered gown, and a gown embroidered with *qilin*[45] pattern. The officials in the entourage from the Philippines were given corresponding amounts of silk and money according to their respective rank. In addition, the King of ancient Malalang (now Mindanao in the Philippines) also led a delegation to China in 1421.

Due to the close proximity between the two locations, many Chinese merchants, especially from southern Fujian, traded in the Philippines. Chinese goods were popular among local residents there. According to the historical records, as soon as a Chinese merchant ship arrived in Sulu, local merchants would immediately "seize all the goods," and then "transport them to their own countries for sale, or sell them to other countries, and then repay their own goods to China." Local people often "used pearls to trade with Chinese merchants. Large transactions could earn as high as tenfold profits."

On account of the high profits from trading Chinese goods, Filipino merchants were eager for Chinese traders to come and trade with them. For this reason, Filipino merchants even took hostages. According to

---

[45] The Qilin is a mythical beast that symbolizes good luck and prosperity. It is believed that it would appear to signal the birth or death of a particularly benevolent ruler or sage scholar.

Volume 5 of *On the Countries in the Eastern and Western Oceans*, Filipino merchants were even worried that Chinese merchant ships would not return to the Philippines after they left for China. Therefore, whenever Chinese merchant ships returned to China, Filipino merchants would capture several Chinese merchants as hostages in order to force Chinese merchant ships to come trading there again.

In the early Ming Dynasty, tens of thousands of Fujianese merchants went to Luzon for trade activities, and many Chinese even settled there. After the embargo was lifted in 1567, the number of Chinese merchants sailing to the Philippine Islands further increased. In addition to southern Fujianese merchants, merchants from Jiangsu and Zhejiang also went to the Philippines in large numbers. With the increasing number of Chinese merchants traveling to the Philippines, more were apt to settle there. Thus, a Chinese community, known as "Jiannei," meaning "within the streams" was formed in Luzon.

In 1571, the Spanish occupied Luzon and then conquered other Philippine islands. Luzon's official tributary trade with China was suspended. Instead, it was superseded to a large extent by trade with the Spanish. The Spanish practiced a predatory approach to trade in order to maintain their colonial control there. They used Manila as a base for trade with China. On the one hand, the Spanish adopted the policy of encouraging Chinese merchants to trade with the Philippines; on the other hand, they monopolized the trade interests between China and the Philippines and squeezed overseas Chinese out in the Philippines. They stirred up persistent troubles and even massacred the Chinese in the Philippines. At that time, the Ming Dynasty lifted the embargo on developing overseas trade, yet eased the people's fight against the prohibition. Therefore, the traders who went out for overseas trade failed to gain protection from the Ming government. This made the Spanish treat the Chinese in an unscrupulous manner, seriously affecting the normal Sino-Philippine trade.

(iii) The Malay Peninsula and Archipelago

In the Ming Dynasty, many petty states were active on the Malay Peninsula and the Malay Archipelago. Some of the countries closely associated with the Ming Dynasty included Java Island (now parts of Java and Sumatra in Indonesia), Srivijaya (now Sumatra Port, destroyed by Java in 1397), Yavadvipa (now Java in Indonesia), Lamuri (present-day Banda Aceh, Sumatra), Burni (now Indonesia), Molucca (now the Maluku islands, Indonesia), and Melaka (now the Malacca Peninsula).

Java was a large country in the Malay Islands at that time. After the Ming Dynasty was established, Emperor Taizu sent envoys to Java, and the two sides established tributary trade relations and maintained constant contact. In 1381, Java even presented 300 black slaves to China. Java as the terminus of Zheng He's southward expeditions and the starting point of his westward expeditions was geographically important. Zheng He's expeditions greatly strengthened the ties between them. Thereafter, the bilateral relationship became closer, and official trade was seen to fully flourish for a while. In the first 100 years of the early Ming Dynasty, Java paid tributes to China more than 20 times.

Because Java was located at the intersection of the Eastern Oceans and the Western Oceans, it became a place where commodities from all countries were exchanged. Many merchants from Fujian and Guangdong went to Java privately and were welcomed by the Javanese people. According to the *On the Countries in the Eastern and Western Oceans,* "as soon as the Chinese merchant ships arrived in Java, local officials came to meet the ship's owner with a basket of oranges and two small umbrellas, and immediately sent someone to report to the King. The King arranged a messenger especially for each ship, and set up shops outside of the *Jiancheng* for them to trade." After Chinese traders shipped items like silk and porcelain to Java, they sold them and received local silver and lead money in exchange. Then they waited there. When foreign spices and other goods reached Java, they bought some overseas goods with the silver and lead money they earned.

In the late Ming Dynasty, Chinese merchants went to Java mainly to trade with European merchants, such as the Dutch and Portuguese. The trade was expanded to an unprecedented scale. It was recorded in Western accounts that "in 1609, the Chinese trading in Banten Province had never seen such a grand commerce as this in India. They came twice a year in their own Chinese sailing ships, bringing with them rare and expensive goods made in China."[46]

Burni also maintained a close official trade relationship with China in the early Ming Dynasty. In August 1408, the King of Burni led more than 150 delegates, including princesses, royal children and ministers, to visit China. Although Emperor Chengzu "treated them with great courtesy and rewards," the Burni King unfortunately died in China. Emperor Chengzu

---

[46]Iwao Seiichi. *The Prosperity and Decline of Chinatown in Banten, Southeast Asian Studies,* 1957 (4).

named his son as his successor and sent envoys to escort him back to Burni. Later on, the new king came to China many times in person to pay tributes. The relationship between China and Burni became ever closer.

Melaka was a country that rose in the late 14th century and had intimate trade relations with the Ming. During Zheng He's overseas expeditions, Malacca Strait was the place his fleet definitely passed through since it was a communications hub on the sea route between the East and the West. Melaka treated Zheng He's fleet in a friendly manner every time it arrived, and allowed Zheng He to set up a warehouse there as the transfer station for his fleet. The goods brought from China were stored there, classified according to the needs of different countries and then loaded onto ships sailing to different countries. All kinds of commodities from various countries were gathered here. When the southwest monsoon season began, they were packed, loaded and shipped back to China.

At the same time, envoys of Melaka also frequently paid tributes to China. According to *The Veritable Records of Ming Dynasty*, from 1405 to 1508, Melaka sent 26 envoys to China to pay tributes. In July 1411, King Paramesvara of Melaka led a group of more than 540 people, including his wife and ministers, to China. The Ming Court gave them a grand reception. Upon their return, Emperor Chengzu bestowed upon them a great quantity of gold, silver, banknotes, copper coins, various kinds of silk clothing and other things. In July 1419, the son of Paramesvara ascended to the throne and duly led his wife, son and subordinates to visit China. It became the custom that every new King of Melaka would pay tribute in person to China. Besides Zheng He, the Ming Dynasty also sent other envoys to Melaka many times.

In 1511, the Portuguese occupation of Melaka interrupted its tributary relationship with the Ming. But civilian trade continued to develop. Prior to the heyday of tributary trade, many Chinese maritime merchants sailed to Melaka without permission. During the early years of the 16th century, it was quite common for Chinese merchants to trade in Melaka. People at that time said that Chinese merchant ships "came in summer and went back in fall, and are familiar to people here."[47]

3. South Asia
The principal countries in South Asia at that time were mainly Bengala (now Bangladesh), Cail (in present-day southern India), Soli (the present-day

---

[47](The Ming Dynasty) Xie Zhaozhe. *Five Varied Groups*.

Corilon River estuary, Southern India), Calicut (now the west coast of India, Kozhikode), Cochin (now the west coast of India, Cochin), Quilon, Ceylon (now Sri Lanka), and the *Liushan* (now Maldives). Those places were all visited by Zheng He in the Ming Dynasty.

Stimulated by Zheng He's expeditions, South Asian countries sent envoys to China one after another. For example, the Maldives sent envoys to pay tributes four times in the Yongle period (1402–1424). Sri Lankan envoys came to China more often. The items presented to China, according to records, included pearls, coral, gemstones, crystal, Western cloth, frankincense, elecampane, sandalwood, myrrh, aloe, ebony, pepper, tame elephants, etc.

Zheng He's fleet made friendly exchanges in accordance with local customs throughout South Asia and so was welcomed by all countries. For example, "two leaders of Calicut (now Kozhikode) were rewarded by China. If Chinese treasure ships arrived there, they were responsible for the business." Cochin prepared its country's special products, such as gemstones, pearls and spices in advance, so that the Chinese treasure ship or foreign ship and guests could transact trade activities as soon as they arrived. The Ceylonese were very fond of Chinese musk, silk, colored silk, glazed porcelain dishes and bowls, copper and camphor, so they exchanged them for their own native gemstone and pearls. After Europeans came to the East in the 16th century, Malacca, the gullet for Chinese merchant ships to enter the Indian Ocean, fell under western control. Countries in South Asia were also successively fell into colonies of the west. The trade relations between China and South Asia declined gradually.

4. West Asia and Africa

Trade relations between China and West Asia and Africa continued to develop in the Ming Dynasty. During his fourth expedition to the West, Zheng He's fleet was seen to sail further into the Persian Gulf, the Arabian Sea and the Red Sea to make exchanges with countries along the Arabian Peninsula and East African coast. China's trade relations with those regions now reached their zenith.

Hormuz was a large Islamic country in the early 15th century. It was the main destination of Zheng He's fourth expeditions. After Zheng He arrived there, he gave great rewards to the King and his ministers. Following that, the King of Hormuz sent envoys to China many times.

The gifts he gave were horses, lions, giraffes, zebras, antelopes, pearls, gemstones, etc. Frequent trade was conducted between the two countries.

In 1416, the Kingdom of Adan (now Aden) sent envoys to China to offer local specialties. Emperor Chengzu ordered Zheng He to pay a return visit with gifts. In 1430, when Zheng He's fleet arrived in Adam, he was received with great warmth by King Dan. The King personally led all the civil and military officials to meet him. He informed the people of the whole country to take out their treasures and welcome Zheng He's fleet. During the years of Zheng He's expeditions, the Kingdom of Adan sent envoys to China five times.

Dhofar abounded with spices. In 1421, this country sent envoys to China. In the same year, the Ming government ordered Zheng He to pay Dhofar a return visit with credentials and various Chinese goods. In 1430, Zheng He's fleet visited Dhofar again and was received cordially by the local people. The King of Dhofar ordered his subjects to take out their products, such as frankincense, dragon's blood, aloe, benzoin, storesin oil, and cochinchinensis for exchange with Zheng He's fleet for Chinese silk, porcelain and other articles.

Mekka sent envoys to China more than 20 times in the early Ming Dynasty. The goods that the envoys brought to China included gemstones, camels, corals, woolen fabrics, various rare animals and valuable Arabian horses. Zheng He's fleet carried Chinese silk, musk, porcelain and other items to Mekka.

Every time Zheng He's fleet returned from the Arabian Peninsula, Arab envoys accompanied his ships back to China. These Arab envoys were mostly merchants, who often carried large quantities of smuggled goods to China for trade. The Ming government waived their taxes. In the late Ming Dynasty, some Arab merchants who did not fear the plunder of European colonists, still came across the Indian Ocean to trade with China. According to historical records, in those days, most Arab merchants formed a partnership and sailed to Macao for trade by merchant ships. Because Arab merchants were adept at evaluating treasures, they often bought precious goods at a very low price.[48]

---

[48] (The Ming Dynasty) Chen Renxi. *Records of Laws and Regulations of the Ming Dynasty.* Vol. 81.

Prior to Zheng He's arrival in Africa, envoys from East African countries had come to China. In 1412, Malindi sent envoys to China to present giraffes to the Ming government. In 1416, Malindi sailed to China to develop tributary trade with Brava, Mogadishu and other countries.

In that year, the Ming government ordered Zheng He to sail for the fourth time. His fleet crossed the Arabian Peninsula and paid East Africa a return visit with the African envoys coming to China. Zheng He gave as gifts Chinese silk, porcelain, iron wares, gold and silver coins and other items to the kings and ministers of East African countries. From there, Zheng He traveled on to many countries along the coast of East Africa, elevating the trade relationship between China and Africa to a new level, and established a regular official trade relationship.

Among them, the Ming Dynasty had the closest trade relations with Mogadishu, Brava, Jumbo, Somalia and Malindi. After Zheng He's visit to East Africa, these countries frequently sent envoys to China to pay tributes, and the commodities exchanged between them were rich in variety and quantity.

Among them, the goods that African countries transported to China included ivory and spices as well as animals unique to Africa, such as zebras, giraffes, African ostriches, leopards, muntjacs, lions and other precious items.

Chinese goods were also highly valued by Africans. Some of them became the currency there. For example, the currency in Mogadishu included gold and silver, colored satin, sandalwood, rice grain, porcelain and colored silk.

The currency used in Brava included gold and silver, colored satin, rice beans, porcelain, etc.

Jumbo also used earthen beads, colored satin, colored silk, gold and silver, porcelain, pepper, rice grain and other objects as currency. Among them, all kinds of silk and porcelain were obviously imported from China.

Many pieces of the Ming Dynasty's porcelain have been unearthed along the East African coast in modern times. They provide clear evidence of the development of trade relations between China and East Africa in this period. The Ming Dynasty also established trade relations with Egypt in North Africa. In latter-day archaeological excavations in Egypt, raw silk and silk fabrics of the early Ming Dynasty in China have been found. Historical records revealed that Mamluk Sultanate of Egypt sent envoys to China in 1441, and the Ming Dynasty presented dozens of bolts (*pi*) of exquisite silk to them.

7.4.2 *Trade Relations with European Countries*

China has a long history of trade with European countries. Long before the Silk Road was opened, Chinese goods had already entered Europe. The trade between China and *Daqin* in the Han Dynasty brought about further developments in trade between China and Europe. Nevertheless, owing to the limited level of productivity at that time, trade was conducted indirectly.

In the 15th century, capitalist relations of production gradually developed in Western Europe. In order to increase the primitive accumulation of capital, overseas exploration in the pursuit of material wealth won favor with Europeans. Ever since Marco Polo, the legend that the ancient and mysterious Orient was awash with gold and spices had always attracted Europeans. In the mid-15th century, the Byzantine Empire was destroyed by Ottoman Turkey. The Ottoman Empire occupied most of West Asia and North Africa, thus controlling the traditional trade routes to the Mediterranean through the Red Sea and the Persian Gulf. The Ottoman Empire arbitrarily imposed exorbitant taxes on the passing ships, which hindered the development of trade between the East and the West.

In 1492, Christopher Columbus, with the support of the Spanish royalty, sailed across the Atlantic Ocean to the Americas and set foot in the so-called "New World." In 1498, the Portuguese navigator Vasco da Gama opened a route from Europe to India by sailing across the Indian Ocean around the Cape of Good Hope in Africa, thus creating a sea passage from Europe to India.

From 1519 to 1522, Magellan's fleet sailed from Spain and successfully circumnavigated the world. The opening of the route to India and the discovery of the Americas were hailed as great geographical discoveries in human history. Those ships returned to Europe laden with gold, silver, precious stones, spices and other riches from the New World and the Orient. They roused a great sensation in Europe and set off a frenzy of overseas plundering and colonization. The vast areas of Asia, Africa and America became colonies of European powers.

The opening of the new route connected all regions of the world. Many countries in Asia, Europe, Africa and America were dragged into the whirlpool of the world economy. Traditional regional trade was superseded by global trade. This brought about great influence on China's traditional foreign trade.

From the early years of the 16th century, more and more Europeans arrived in China and altered the pattern of China's foreign trade dramatically. The increasing development of the trade relations between China and Western Europe gradually occupied the dominant position in China's foreign trade relations.

1. Portugal

Portugal was called "Farangi" in the *History of Ming*. In 1510, the Portuguese fleet sailed into the Indian Ocean, first occupied Goa on the west coast of India, and in 1511 occupied Melaka, the hub of maritime trade between the East and the West, and then actively sought the route to China.

In 1514, the Portuguese governor in Malacca sent an advance team headed by Alvarez to China. After the Portuguese arrived in Guangzhou, the Ming officials banned them from entering the city, only allowing them to sell their goods. It was said that "the Portuguese made a big profit and returned."

In 1518, the governor of Portugal sent Fernao Andrada and Thome Pires to China, accompanied by eight armed ships, to reach Tuen Mun, Guangdong Province, and demanded the establishment of a formal trade relationship with China. Local officials in Guangzhou believed that there was no tributary relationship between China and Portugal prior to the Ming Dynasty, and the development of bilateral trade should be reported to the Court for approval. Therefore, two Portuguese ships were allowed to enter Guangzhou and returned to their home country immediately after the transaction. But the Portuguese refused to obey this order and continued to reside at Tuen Mun. They not only smuggled along the southeast coast of China, but also killed, burned and looted in Tuen Mun, committing all kinds of atrocities.

In 1521, the Ming Court sent troops to expel the Portuguese who were occupying Tuen Mun. Then, the Portuguese fled to the coastal areas of Fujian and Zhejiang, colluded with the *Wokou*, and carried out armed robberies and smuggling activities. It was not until 1549 that they were driven out by Zhu Wan, Governor of Zhejiang Province.

In 1553, the Portuguese seized Macao by means of fraud and bribery. Macao, also known as Xiangshan'ao, was located at the southern tip of Xiangshan County (now Zhongshan City) in Guangdong Province. In 1535, the Maritime Trade Commission of Guangdong was moved to Macao, and the Portuguese seized the opportunity to enter Macao's trade market. In 1544, the Portuguese bribed Wang Bai, Commander of Coastal Defenses in Guangdong, to temporarily commandeer Macao beach to dry the goods under the pretext that his merchant ship was in a storm. Since then, the Portuguese built houses and lived in Macao for a long time. More and more Portuguese came to Macao and some Portuguese merchants even moved to Macao with their families.

Macao became a base for Portugal to conduct trade with China. After the Portuguese occupation of Macao, they organized for the Sino-Japanese fleet to engage in the entrepot trade between Southeast Asia, China and Japan. Macao gradually developed into a transfer center for international Oriental trade.

2. Spain

In the *History of Ming*, Spain was called "the Grand Luzon." In 1567, Spanish expeditionary forces arrived in the East and occupied Cebu, the Philippines. In 1571, the Spanish occupied Luzon, and then they actively sought to trade with China. In 1574, the Lin Feng clique, a band of Guangdong pirates, was defeated by the Ming army and fled to Luzon, where it was finally exterminated by the Spanish.

Since the Spanish had helped the Ming government to fight against the Lin Feng clique, they were congenially received by them when they came to China for trade in 1575. But their trade along the coast of Guangdong was blocked by the Portuguese. After that, the Spanish turned to Fujian, Zhejiang and Taiwan for trade activities, and asked the Ming Court to provide a refuge in which to live and trade. This was rejected by the Ming Court. In 1626, the Spaniards occupied the northern part of Taiwan by force as a base for trade with China. In 1641, they were expelled by the Dutch.

The Spanish-occupied Philippine Islands were relatively barren, with no spices, no gold or silver, and even some daily necessities were supplied from abroad. However, China was rich in materials and close to the Philippines. In order to maintain its colonial rule, at one time Spain encouraged Chinese merchants to come to trade. The lifting of the prohibitive maritime trade policies in the late Ming Dynasty saw a surge in Chinese merchants trading by sea. It was recorded that every year in the 1570s saw 12 to 15 Chinese merchant ships sailing to Manila; in the 1580s, the number was 20; in the 1590s, it grew to 30; and in the early years of the 17th century, it was 40–50 ships; sometimes it surged up to 60. The value of trade increased rapidly. According to Spanish records, from 1575 to 1583, the average annual trade volume reached 200,000 pesos; in 1598, it reached 1 million; from 1609 to 1610, it climbed to 2 million.

Various kinds of cargos were transported there by Chinese merchant ships, including: (a) articles for food and clothing, such as cattle, horses, mules, donkeys, chickens, ducks and other livestock and poultry; (b) raw silk, silk, cotton and linen fabrics and other textiles; (c) porcelain, iron, copper, tin, lead and other devices; (d) food, fruit and pepper, cinnamon, cloves, sugar, flour and other food supplies. Among them, the greatest bulk was raw silk and silk goods, accounting for about 90% of the total. After arriving at the port, the Chinese merchant ships first transported the goods to the Chinese shops in Jiancheng, and then the local Chinese sold the goods to the Filipinos and the Spaniards.

The Spanish met their survival needs in the Philippine islands by relying on goods shipped by Chinese merchants. They sold items brought there by Chinese merchant ships, like silk and porcelain, to American colonies, which spread Chinese silk and porcelain all over the world. At that time, Manila galleons (Spanish treasure ships) frequently traveled between Manila and the port of Acapulco in Mexico, selling Chinese silk, porcelain, lacquerware, etc. Because of the fine quality and low price of Chinese silk, it was very popular in all parts of the American continent. The Spaniards made huge profits from it. According to statistics, the profits that Spanish earned from shipping Chinese goods from Manila to the Americas must have been between 100% and 300%. This trade also played a major part in the prosperity of the Spanish colonies in the Americas.

The Spanish collected tariffs on Chinese goods in Mexico, enriching partially the Spanish royal treasury and plugging Manila's financial deficit. China's maritime trade in the Philippines made considerable profits, too. For example, shipping raw Huzhou silk to the Philippines could earn a profit margin of up to 100%. The Chinese sea merchants who went to the Philippines brought back a large amount of Latin American silver, which played a beneficial role in the development of commodity economy in the late Ming. However, a large number of Chinese goods, especially silk products, were sold in the Americas, which was a blow to Spain's textile industry. The silk industry guilds in Seville, Cadiz and Andalucía constantly wrote to the King of Spain requesting that he restrict the sales of Chinese silk in the Americas, so as to protect their domestic silk production. And so the Spanish king ordered embargoes to be placed on the trade of Chinese silk there. This met with resistance from the Spanish in Mexico and the Philippines, but to little effect.

From the 1620s, Portuguese in Macao began to traffic a large amount of Chinese silk and raw silk to the Philippines and Mexico. Chinese maritime merchants were therefore marginalized in the market. At the same time, the piracy of the Dutch who occupied Taiwan Province in China's coastal areas and Manila Bay also greatly reduced the number of Chinese merchant ships visiting the Philippines.

3. The Netherlands

In the *History of Ming*, the Dutch were referred to as "Red-haired Foreigners" At the end of the 16th century, the Netherlands won its independence from Spain and actively promoted the policy of developing overseas trade. By the 17th century, the navigational ability of the Dutch had surpassed that of Portugal and Spain. 80% of the world's shipping industry was controlled by the Dutch who were known as "the maritime coachman of the world." With their maritime superiority and commercial hegemony, the Netherlands occupied the vast colonies and defeated the Portuguese to capture most of their eastern territories.

In 1604, the Netherlands first sent warships to the coastal areas of Guangdong Province, to demand trade with China. Because the Dutch were blocked by the Portuguese, they finally failed to realize the purpose of trading in Guangdong. The Dutch then turned to Fujian and Taiwan. In 1624, they forcibly occupied the Penghu Islands and were soon expelled by the Ming army. The Dutch subsequently captured the southern part of Taiwan and drove the Spanish out of the northern part of the island in 1641, eventually monopolizing Taiwan.

Thereafter, the Dutch took Taiwan as a base for trade with China, and it was from here they carried out large-scale trade activities with Chinese merchants. In 1628, the Dutch chief executive in Taiwan concluded a three-year purchase contract with Zheng Zhilong, a maritime merchant. According to the contract, Zheng delivered 1,400 piculs (*dan*) of raw silk, 5,000 piculs of sugar and 5,000 bolts (*pi*) of silk to the Netherlands every year, for which the Dutch should pay 299,700 *yuan* of silver. At the same time, the Dutch East India Company, centered in Southeast Asia, earned high profits by trafficking in Chinese goods.

It was estimated that the Dutch East India Company made as much as 320% of profits on shipping Chinese grege to Europe. In order to obtain

Chinese silk, the Dutch also tried every means to induce Chinese traders to go to Batavia (now Jakarta), the base of the Dutch East India Company. In 1620, the Dutch East India Company instructed their Pattani quarter that "you must persuade the Chinese ships in Pattani, Songkhla, Phatthalung to bring a large amount of beautiful grege, silk and other Chinese goods to Batavia next year, and you should assure them that we do not lack cash, sandalwood and pepper. Moreover, they can come here without paying any taxes, and all taxes will be exempted."[49] From their base in Taiwan, the Dutch sold Chinese silk and porcelain products to Japan, Southeast Asia and Europe.

By the end of the Ming Dynasty, most of the Sino-Japanese trade was superintended by the Dutch. According to statistics, at the end of the Ming Dynasty, the quantity of Chinese silk and silk fabrics shipped to Japan by the Dutch almost exceeded that transported by Chinese maritime trade every year. In 1637, the volume of Dutch sea traffic was about 13 times that of the Chinese sea merchants.

4. Great Britain

In the 16th century, with the rapid development of the British economy, the House of Tudor carried out the policy of supporting overseas trade. In 1588, the British annihilated the Spanish Armada, and together with the Netherlands gained maritime hegemony. From the 17th century, on British industry, especially their textile industry, developed rapidly, and native capitalists strongly urged the exploration of overseas markets. In 1600, Great Britain set up the British East India Company to monopolize trade in the East.

In 1637, King Charles I authorized the "James Weddell fleet" of the Kraton Group to trade in China. In June of the same year, the Weddell fleet arrived in Macao and went to Guangzhou for trade without the permission of China.

The Ming officials tried to intervene, but the British side launched a flagrant attack on the Humen Battery, resulting in a serious incident in which Chinese merchant and naval vessels were sunk. Nevertheless, in the early years of the 17th century, the Dutch and Portuguese wielded power in China. They blocked other countries from trading with China, which led to the slow progress of the trade between Britain and the Ming.

---

[49] Femme S. Gaastra. *The Dutch East India Company: Expansion and Decline* [M]. Zutphen: Walburg Pers, 2003: 121.

7.5 Foreign Trade and Economic & Cultural Communication with Foreign Countries

In the early Ming Dynasty, the overseas expeditions by Zheng He established a long-distance transportation network between Asia and Africa, bringing the trade relations between Asian and African countries to a new level. After the 16th century, with the arrival of Europeans, China's international trade gradually developed. China's overseas trade increasingly broke through the traditional regions and was no longer limited to Asia and Africa. Chinese merchandise began to circulate all over Europe and America.

On the one hand, China's advanced material and spiritual civilization spread overseas with the commodities as the carriers and driven by the circulation of commodities; on the other hand, overseas civilizations, from more areas, penetrated into China. This promoted the economic development and cultural prosperity of both. Thus, the economic and cultural exchanges between China and foreign countries reached an unprecedented level and dimension.

7.5.1 *Economic Communication with Foreign Countries*

With the expansion of the trading area and the development of the social economy of various countries, the commodities of the Ming Dynasty were more abundant in variety. The foreign trade, in both scale and level, reached a new high.

1. Import and Export Commodities
(i) Export Commodities

Zheng He's fleet exported a large amount of Chinese merchandise overseas through rewarding, granting and trading channels. The bulk commodities recorded included porcelain, lacquerware, tea leaves, musk, camphor, umbrellas, raw silk, silk, silk floss, gold, silver, copper coins, iron, metal products, books, paper, grain, building materials, etc.

In the later period of the Ming Dynasty, with the development of private overseas trade, the types and quantities of Chinese merchandise exported to foreign countries were further increased. According to records, China exported more than 230 kinds of commodities including handicrafts, mineral products, aquatic products, agricultural and sideline products, cultural articles and pharmaceuticals. Among them, handicraft products, silk and porcelain, in particular, were still dominant exports.

(a) Silk Fabrics

Silk and silk fabrics were the largest export commodities of the Ming Dynasty. With the development of maritime transportation, Chinese silk fabrics spread all over the world. In the early Ming Dynasty, all the countries that maintained tributary relations with the Ming obtained large quantities of Chinese silk. By the late Ming Dynasty, China's silk market was open to more areas. In addition to the traditional Asian target countries and regions, with the influx of Europeans in the East, Chinese silk and silk products were also exported to Europe and the Americas.

(b) Porcelainware

In the Ming Dynasty, the second bulk export commodity was porcelain. Chinese porcelain began to be exported from ancient times. At that time, with progress in the porcelain manufacturing industry, especially the development of the private ceramic industry, the output and scale of ceramic production were significantly improved. The quantity of the porcelain exported to all parts of the world by way of tributary trade and merchants increased substantially.

In 1383, the Ming Dynasty presented 19,000 pieces of porcelain to Champa, Siam and Khmer. Zheng He's fleet carried a large number of blue and white porcelain (Qinghua porcelain) to the west. Zheng He's retainer, Ma Huan, noted in the *Overall Survey of the Ocean's Shores* that "Javanese like Chinese blue and white porcelain most." Fei Xin's *Overall Survey of the Star Raft* recorded that in Siam "Chinese blue and white porcelain was well used." In the early Ming Dynasty, Chinese porcelain was spread to Asia and Africa. In recent times, a large number of Chinese blue and white porcelain of the early Ming Dynasty has been unearthed in Southeast Asia and East Africa. Among them, Southeast Asia was where the largest number of porcelain items was excavated. It can be seen that Ming porcelain was part of the daily necessities of Southeast Asian people. In West Asia and East Africa, Chinese porcelain was also used for Islamic architectural decoration.

During the middle and late Ming Dynasties the export scale of porcelain was further expanded to many countries and regions in Asia, Africa,

Europe and the Americas. The Philippines, then controlled by the Spanish, was an important market for the export of Chinese porcelain during the Ming Dynasty. According to western documents, in addition to silk fabric, Chinese merchants "also brought some fine pottery, which was sold well on the market." Batavia in Java was another important export market for Chinese porcelain. Every year, the Dutch East India Company purchased from China a large amount of porcelain products and shipped them to Taiwan, where they were transported to Batavia.

According to western records, as many as 379,670 pieces of Chinese porcelain were transported to Batavia by the Dutch East India Company in 1636. The annual shipment of Chinese porcelain to Batavia by the Dutch East India Company was estimated to be over 150,000 pieces. The company traded at least 12 million pieces of Chinese porcelain at the end of the Ming Dynasty, most of which was resold to Europe in addition to Southeast Asia. In 1604, the Dutch East India Company auctioned Chinese porcelain in Amsterdam. The European royalty fought over the chance to purchase, setting off a buying spree for Chinese porcelain in Europe. Thereafter, traders from other European countries transported Chinese porcelain in a much-heralded manner.

At the end of the Ming Dynasty, in order to meet the needs of the export trade, customized export porcelain was also designed according to the requirements of foreign merchants in some civilian kilns of Jingdezhen, Jiangxi Province. For example, "Kraak porcelain" was a tailored product exclusively sold to Europe.[50]

(ii) Import Commodities

In the Ming Dynasty, Zheng He's fleet imported about 185 kinds of merchandise, including luxury merchandise and exotic animals, as well as handicraft products and daily necessities. There were 17 kinds of hardware, such as gold, silver and tin; 23 kinds of frankincense, wood fragrance, tree fragrance, cloves, sandalwood and aloe; 23 kinds of jewelry, such as crystal, agate, gems, coral and pearls; 21 kinds of animals, such as peacocks, lions, *qilin*, ostriches, chickens and leopards; 51 kinds of cloth such as white cotton cloth and western cloth; 22 kinds of medicine,

---

[50] The word was derived from the Portuguese carracks that transported cargo like ceramics that were specifically exported for the European market with their decoration typically divided into a number of panels within which motifs of tulips were painted

such as myrrh, nutmeg and hydnocarpus; 8 kinds of articles, such as iron knives, glass bottles, etc.; 8 kinds of pigments, such as azurite, densiflorum and Karpura; 3 kinds of food, such as foreign salt, icing and pepper; 3 kinds of hematoxylin, ebony and rosewood.

In the late Ming Dynasty, more than 100 kinds of imported commodities were recorded, including spices, jewelry, mineral products, raw materials, handicrafts articles, agricultural and sideline products, etc. Among them, spices, jewelry and other luxury merchandise were mainly from Southeast Asia, West Asia and Africa, and mineral products were mainly from Japan.

(a) Spices and Luxuries

From the Tang and Song Dynasties on spices played a dominant role in China's import trade. By the Ming Dynasty, the spice trade between China and Asian and African countries still flourished. In the early Ming Dynasty, pepper became a luxury in China due to the small scale of foreign trade and the scarcity of imported pepper. However, with more and more pepper being brought back on Zheng He's treasure ship, the domestic pepper market was nearly saturated. The price of pepper dropped from 20 taels of silver per 100 catties in the early Ming Dynasty to 5 taels of silver per 100 catties. During the reign of the Ming's Emperor Xuanzong (r. 1425–1435), officials had their salaries paid in pepper. Nevertheless, pepper from Southeast Asia and South Asia was still an important commodity for Chinese and foreign traders in the late Ming Dynasty.

According to the historical records, people in AnNam (now Vietnam) exchanged pepper for Chinese porcelain and paper. The hills around Brunei, in Borneo, were covered with pepper gardens and people there traded with China in large sailboats. According to western records, at the end of the 16th century, during the pepper harvest season, Chinese traders living in Java bought directly from farmers in the countryside. In February of the next year, a large number of Chinese merchant ships arrived in Java, and they carried pepper back to China. Other valuable spices in Southeast Asia, such as Phoebe, sandalwood, frankincense, eagle wood, etc., also entered China. In addition, spices from the Arabian Peninsula and the east coast of Africa continued to be shipped to China by European merchants. Apart from spices, African luxury merchandise, like ivory, were also imported into China as tributes and civilian trade commodities.

(b) Minerals

The mineral products imported to China in the Ming Dynasty mainly included gold, silver, copper, mercury, lead, tin, etc. Among them, gold, silver and copper were predominantly from Japan, which were mainly imported by Chinese and Japanese merchants by way of smuggling on a large scale. For example, in 1453, the amount of copper transported to China by ship reached 154,500 catties.

(c) Raw Materials and Handicrafts

The timber Zheng He's fleet imported from overseas enriched China's building materials. For example, during the Yongle period (1402–1424), the pillars of the Jinghai Temple[51] constructed in Nanjing were made of eaglewood that Zheng He's fleet brought back from Southeast Asia. Zheng He's fleet also gathered some raw materials for porcelain manufacturing. For example, the raw material employed in crafting blue and white porcelain in the Ming Dynasty "*sumali qing*," or the Samarra blue cobalt, which was brought back by Zheng He's fleet from their expedition to Samarra, a pottery center at that time around today's Iran. Another new type of porcelain in the Ming Dynasty, Jihong porcelain,[52] contained the powder of western rubies in its raw material. It was purported that the raw materials of the Xuande Furnace (Xuande Incense Burner) included wind-milled copper from Siam (today's Thailand), sal ammoniac from Arab, purple stone from Srivijaya, rouge stone from Burni, etc.

A considerable part of the imported raw materials and components used in Ming Dynasty handicrafts came from Japan. The most popular articles of merchandise were sulfur and Japanese swords. In the early Ming, Japan sent those articles by way of tributary trade to China in huge quantities, even exceeding the demand of the Ming. The Ming had to dissuade Japan from sending sulfur to China again. In the 14th century, Japan swords were well-known for their excellent forging and were deeply loved by the Chinese people, "so that the Chinese were crazy about

---

[51]Also known as Temple of the Calm Sea. It was built in 1416 to honor Zheng He, a eunuch and envoy of the Emperor who undertook a series of seven expeditions to India and as far west as the east coast of Africa.

[52]Also known as Blood Red Porcelain. It began to be produced for imperial sacrificial ceremonies in Jingdezhen during the Ming Dynasty.

them."[53] The later years of the Ming saw incessant warfare in various regions, so more military supplies were imported from Japan.

2. Exchanges of Plant Varieties with Foreign Countries

With the development from regional trade to global trade, Chinese and foreign spices could be exchanged worldwide. Some plant varieties from the Americas were brought to Southeast Asia by Europeans and then introduced to China. According to historical records, the new plant varieties introduced into China in the Ming Dynasty mainly included the following categories:

(i) Cash Crops

Overseas cash crops introduced to China in the Ming Dynasty principally included tobacco, groundnuts and melons. Tobacco was introduced to the Philippines from Latin America at the end of the 16th century, and later in the Wanli period (1572–1620) of the Ming Dynasty, Fujian merchants introduced it to China. After being introduced, it was promoted quickly because of its high profitability. Records state that "the yield of one *mu*[54] of tobacco could exceed that of ten *mu* of other planted crops, so that no farmland planted with tobacco fell barren."[55]

By 1622, tobacco had been "planted on both sides of the Yangtze River." The expanding scale of tobacco cultivation enabled the demand for local consumption to be satisfied. It was even exported overseas and sold back to the Philippines. The records have it that "more (tobacco) was exported to Luzon for sale despite this being the country of original export." With the prevalence of smoking, people came to know that tobacco was harmful to health. They realized that "tobacco was poisonous and could even cause death." Moreover, "Long-time smoking would cause great damage to the lungs." In 1639, an imperial edict was issued to prohibit the cultivation and sale of tobacco, but in vain. Tobacco finally became an omnipresent product in China.

Groundnuts were also introduced to China from Southeast Asia during the late Ming Dynasty. They were first planted in Fujian Province and

---

[53] (The Ming Dynasty) Zhang Xie. *On the Countries in the Eastern and Western Oceans.* Vol. 6. The Commercial Press, 1936.

[54] Unit of area equal to one-fifteenth of a hectare.

[55] (The Qing Dynasty) Yang Shicong. *Miscellaneous Notes of the Jade Hall (Hanlin Academy).*

then spread to Zhejiang Province in the Wanli period. Later, groundnuts gradually proliferated everywhere.

The Ming introduced many kinds of melons and fruits, including pumpkins. According to the *Haicheng County Gazetteer*, "pumpkins taste sweet and originate in Holland." It could be seen that pumpkins were also first introduced Southeast Asia by Europeans and then to China. Li Shizhen, a celebrated medical expert in the Ming Dynasty, said that "pumpkin could be used as medicine to tonify middle-*jiao*[56] and *qi* (nourishing the blood and tranquilization, to nourish liver and kidney to be specific)." Another introduction from foreign countries was balsam pear (bitter gourd). Li Shizhen wrote that balsam pear "came from countries to the south, and is now planted in Fujian and Guangzhou."[57]

(ii) Cereal Crops

The main cereal crops introduced in the Ming Dynasty were the sweet potato and maize. Sweet potatoes originate in the Americas. After the 16th century, they were introduced to Southeast Asia by Europeans and brought back to China by Fujianese merchants. He Qiaoyuan mentioned in the *Book of Fujian* that "many Fujianese merchants were trading in Luzon .... They picked some vines, saved them in a small box and brought them back. They have been growing in Fujian for over ten years now."

According to historical records, in 1593, Chen Zhenlong, a native of Changle, Fujian Province, who had long been a merchant in Luzon, mastered the technique of cultivating sweet potatoes in the Philippines, and later succeeded in the trial planting in his hometown of Nantou, Fujian Province. This high yield crop was promoted by the Governor of Fujian and planted widely in the southeast of the province, thereby solving the problem of food shortages in this area. It did not take long before the sweet potato spread from the coast to the mainland, becoming another new crop strain in China.

Maize was also native to the Americas and was introduced to Southeast Asia by Europeans in the 16th century before its being introduced to China.

---

[56]"*Zhong*" refers to "the middle *jiao*," the midsection of the body, including the spleen, stomach, gall bladder and liver organs.

[57](The Ming Dynasty) Li Shizhen. *Compendium of Materia Medica*. Vol. 28. People's Medical Publishing House, 2004.

Since both sweet potato and maize were tolerant of diverse natural conditions, they could be grown on arid hills, mountains and coastal dunes alike, thus greatly improving the utilization rate of the land, and increasing the food supply for the Chinese people. The land saved could be used to grow cash crops, which promoted the commercialization of agriculture. In addition to the introduction of new varieties, the Ming Dynasty obtained some higher quality seeds of existing crops during the development of Sino-foreign trade. For example, rice from Siam was introduced to the Jiangnan area, where it became known as "Siamese rice." At the same time, Chinese crop varieties, including tea bushes, citrus trees and cherries, were introduced to the Americas along the new route during the late Ming Dynasty.

3. Production Technology Communication

The development of Sino-foreign trade in the Ming Dynasty promoted the exchange of technology between China and foreign countries. In the early Ming Dynasty, exchanges were made mainly between Asian countries, while in the late Ming Dynasty, they were made predominantly with European countries.

The development of Sino-foreign trade witnessed an increase in the emigration of Chinese merchants and citizens overseas. China's advanced production tools and technologies were widely spread throughout Southeast Asia.

(i) Agricultural Tools

During this period, the main agricultural production tools introduced to Southeast Asia from China were the plow, waterwheels and water mills in China. In the 16th century, the Chinese plow was exported to the Philippines. According to the records made by British observers, the Filipino plow was of Chinese design with a handle, a plow head or a shaped iron coulter behind the plow head. The upper part of the plow head was flat, functioning by turning to one side while plowing. At the same time, the Chinese also transported horses and water buffaloes, the brawn for plow-pulling, to the Philippines.

(ii) Planting and Processing Technology of Farm Products

After the 16th century, China's intensive and meticulous farming technology gradually spread to Southeast Asia. In the Banten region of Indonesia, for example, pepper was widely cultivated before the 16th century, with yields limited by their backward technology. In the 16th century, Chinese immigrants adopted advanced planting technology, which increased the output by 100%. Westerners held that it was because the overseas Chinese implemented a superlative set of advanced cultivation techniques that Banten became as if by magic the largest pepper producer in the world. It improved its international trade status, thus becoming a center for world trade.

Prior to the 16th century, rice cultivation in Southeast Asia was relatively primitive in its methods. Sowing usually took place during rainy season with neither the addition of fertilizer nor weeding being carried out afterward. Thus, the yields were very low. Chinese immigrants introduced to Southeast Asia the technical expertise for planting seedlings, then transplanting, weeding and fertilizing. This greatly increased the yield per unit area. By the early 17th century, Chinese immigrants also brought Chinese sugarcane cultivation and processing techniques to places like Indonesia. Previously, the Indonesians were able to produce sucrose by indigenous methods, but the technology was backward and the output very low.

In the 17th century, when the Netherlands occupied Indonesia, Batavia developed rapidly into a prosperous international trade port. In 1637, Chinese immigrants set up the first sugarcane mill there and rented land to cultivate the raw crops. For about 200 years afterward, Indonesia's sugar industry was mainly operated by Chinese immigrants.

(iii) Measuring Outfits

Before the Ming Dynasty, owing to the relatively backward social economy in Southeast Asia, commodity exchange was also underdeveloped. After the Ming Dynasty, with the development of trade relations between China and Southeast Asia, China's measurement tools and currencies for commodity exchange were spread externally. At the request of the Dacheng Kingdom of Siam (now Thailand), the Ming government provided Chinese measuring instruments twice, in 1403 and 1404, respectively.

However, during the late Ming Dynasty, there were still no measuring instruments in many parts of Southeast Asia. When buying and selling merchandise, they were measured with a pair of hands. The Chinese immigrants brought the steelyard with them, which proved very popular with the local people. Even the Dutch colonists began to use it. History recorded that an agent of the Dutch East India Company in another country once asked the Batavia headquarters for a Chinese steelyard. He said that "the steelyard used by the Chinese could measure about two piculs of merchandise. We were badly in need of it, hoping the headquarters could deliver it right away, because we can't deal with the weight problem without it. What we had now was stone yards, so we had to do the conversion every day."

As early as in the Song Dynasty, Chinese copper coins had been introduced to Southeast Asia. However, owing to the limited level of productivity there, its currency economy was still backward in development. With the exception of Java, Palembang and Lambri, which used Chinese copper coins as their currency, most countries still used cowrie in trade transactions. During the Ming Dynasty, with the further development of trade relations and the increasing demand for money in Southeast Asian countries, the output of Chinese copper coins increased so they were used as cash in more regions.

At the same time, China's coin minting technology also spread to Southeast Asia. By the early Ming, Melaka used Chinese coinage technology to create their own currency called *jiashi*, which replaced the original "tin ingot" (a tin ingot weighing 1.8 kg).

By the late Ming Dynasty, Chinese currency was still in circulation in many parts of Southeast Asia. Westerners recorded that "when Dutch ships first came to Java in 1595, there was already a large amount of Chinese currency there and among its surrounding islands. It had been brought over by Chinese ships which were always loaded with pepper. Later, due to a dearth of minted coins, Chinese merchants traded in Banten with customized tin coins from China. They were forged by imitating Chinese copper cash coinage, so that coins were round and had square holes in their centers." The introduction of currency and coinage technology was conducive to the development of the commodity economy in Southeast Asia.

(iv) Architectural Technology
In the 15th century, the lifestyles of residents in many areas of Southeast Asia and South Asia were relatively backward. For example, the people of Cochin in South Asia mostly lived in caves or tree houses. Some lived in houses, but these were very cramped and low, "with eaves no more than three ells (*chi*) in height." The residents of the ancient Maldives also "lived in caves or tree houses." When Zheng He's fleet arrived in their country, his men taught them how to build houses. According to historical records, the usage of tiles in the houses of Melaka was also a legacy of Zheng He's fleet. His ships exported glazed tiles and high-end

Chinese building materials to Southeast Asia. They became widely used in royal palaces and Buddhist temples in Melaka, Siam and other countries.

(v) Silk-Weaving Techniques

Before Zheng He's expeditions, most people in the countries of the Indian Peninsula were not adept at weaving silk. For instance, in Calicut (now Kozhikode), locals could only weave five or six kinds of fine cloth. The craftsmen in Zheng He's fleet taught them Chinese silk weaving techniques.

In addition, the silk weaving technology of Bengalese was also learned from Zheng He's crew. Later, they gave the silk clothes they produced to Chinese officers and soldiers of the fleet to show their appreciation.

Sumatra had been cultivating mulberry trees introduced from China during the early Ming Dynasty, but they could only raise silkworms without knowing how to make silk from them. After Zheng He's expeditions, Sumatra and the Ming Dynasty developed increasingly close trade relations, and the Sumatra people gradually mastered the Chinese silk reeling and weaving technology.

Other production techniques introduced by Chinese merchants to Southeast Asia included those for ceramics and furniture, metal smelting, printing technology, etc. The dissemination of China's advanced technology accelerated the socio-economic development of Southeast Asia and played a beneficial role in promoting the region's connections with European capitalist market.

The most celebrated production technology introduced to China from Asian countries in the Ming Dynasty was glass manufacturing from Arabia. As was mentioned previously, western glass manufacturing technology was introduced to China in the period of the Wei, Jin, Northern and Southern Dynasties, though it was still underdeveloped then. In the Song and Yuan Dynasties, Chinese glass was very bright in color, but grainy in texture, with low temperature resistance. It was especially fragile and subject to fluctuations in cold and heat.

Foreign glass, though not as bright in color as Chinese glass, was so cold to the touch and durable that people found "no difference between it and porcelain or silver." After Zheng He's fleet arrived in the Arabian Peninsula, Zheng found craftsmen who mastered the advanced glass manufacturing technology and brought them back to China. During the Yongle period (1402–1424) of the Ming Dynasty, with the spread of western glass manufacturing technology in China, the level of domestic production caught up with the west. Exotic glass was not deemed precious.

During this period, China and Japan entered a stage of bilateral economic exchange. The golden folding fans from Japan enriched the variety of that accessory found in China, and the method of making them was gradually mastered by the Chinese. During the Jiajing period (1521–1566), China sent representatives to Japan to study specifically the manufacturing technology of gold-painting on lacquerware.

7.5.2 *Cultural Communication with Foreign Countries*

1. Cultural Communication with Asian Countries

The cultural exchanges between China and foreign countries in the early Ming Dynasty were mainly conducted among Asian countries. At the beginning of the Ming Dynasty, the residents of many areas in South Asia and Southeast Asia still subsisted in a primitive state. The import of Chinese commodities greatly promoted the progress of material and spiritual civilization in those areas. With the import of Chinese silk and clothing, the dress culture in some areas of South Asia and Southeast Asia gradually changed. The residents of the Maldives formerly "did not wear clothes, but covered their bodies with leaves." In the Nicobar Islands, "men and women were naked, like animals, with not an inch of their skin covered over." That situation changed soon after Zheng He's expeditions.

In the early Ming Dynasty, most Southeast Asian countries had no calendar. For example, in Champa, "people didn't understand what syzygy was. They regarded the rising of the moon as the beginning of a month, and the setting of the moon as the end of a month. They didn't have a leap moon. There were 10 *geng*[58] within a day and night."

The people of Timor-Leste "didn't even know the date and year." The introduction of the Chinese calendar by Zheng He's fleet helped people to organize their agricultural production according to the cycle of the year.

Spices were imported partly to meet the demand of the upper class for luxury items, but they were also treated as having curative properties, enriching the variety of Chinese medicine. What came together with the

---

[58] As in what was called as *shichen* (1 *shichen* was equal to 2 hours) in China.

spices was the Indian and Arabian medical knowledge, which contributed to the advance of Chinese medical science.

The influence of Chinese Confucianism on Japan, Korea and Southeast Asian countries was further expanded. For example, the *Analects of Confucius* was first published in Japan. Chinese poems and songs were so widespread there that they encouraged the emergence of "Gozan Literature," which specifically imitated Chinese poems in their writing style.

2. Cultural Communication with Western Countries
(i) Importing Western Science and Technology
The development of trade between China and the west during the late Ming Dynasty opened a path for the spread of western culture in China. With the support of Portugal, the Holy See sent missionaries to China one after another. European Catholicism began to spread in China, but met with resistance there in its early years.

To ensure that missionary activities proceeded smoothly, the Holy See sent to China a group of missionaries familiar with Chinese language and culture as well as possessing advanced western scientific knowledge. To adapt to the Chinese society, these missionaries paid attention to studying Chinese language and literature and tried to understand Chinese ways better. At the same time, they tried to weaken Chinese traditional ideas and social customs by means of spreading European science and culture, so as to propagate Catholicism. As a result, Catholicism gradually spread in China. Together with it came western science and technology. Meanwhile, Chinese culture was introduced to the western world.

In the 16th and 17th centuries, science and technology developed rapidly in Europe, with remarkable progress being made in astronomy, chemistry, physics and medicine. In the 16th century, Polish astronomer Nicolaus Copernicus proposed the theory of heliocentricity, "liberating natural science from theology." Western natural science began to enter a stage of modern development. In the late Ming Dynasty, foreign missionaries brought a large number of western classics into China and introduced western scientific knowledge to Chinese intellectuals. The main disciplines they introduced were astronomy, mathematics, geography and mechanical engineering.

The astronomical calendar could direct to ancient agriculture, which was highly valued by feudal dynasties in China. The Ming astronomical calendar had fallen behind that of the west with the "Datong Calendar" featuring considerable errors. At the end of the 16th century, Matteo Ricci, an Italian missionary from Europe, came to China. It was from him that some Chinese scholars, like Xu Guangqi and Li Zhizao, learned Western astronomy. In 1614, the first volume of the astronomical work the *Treatise on Geometry* was published in Beijing, co-authored by Matteo Ricci and Li Zhizao.

Western astronomy was gradually accepted by more and more people, and Chinese people appealed vociferously for reform of the traditional calendar. In 1629, Xu Guangqi, who was proficient in western astronomy, was appointed to be responsible for the revision of the calendar. He invited western missionaries to assist his research, including Nicolò Longobardo and Johann Adam Schall von Bell. Together they set about revising the calendar. After Xu Guangqi's death, Li Tianjing continued the work. In 1634, the new calendar was completed and was titled the *Chongzhen Calendar*, also known as the *New Western Calendar*. This book was much more accurate than the previous Chinese version, and it contained a great deal of western astronomy and mathematical knowledge, and positively assisted in the progress of the Chinese astronomical calendar.

The first western mathematical work introduced to China was *Euclid's Elements*. The first six volumes of this book were dictated by Matteo Ricci and set down by Xu Guangqi in 1607. In 1613, Matteo Ricci and Li Zhizao jointly translated and published *Tong wen suan zhi* (Arithmetic Guidance in the Common Language). The translation of those two books turned a new page in the introduction of European mathematics in China.

Matteo Ricci also brought western geography into China. In 1583, he arrived in Zhaoqing, Guangdong province, and introduced the world map to the Chinese people. Since then, it had been reprinted in many parts of China. The advent of the world map enriched geographical knowledge in China. For the first time, the Chinese were equipped with the concept of the tropical zone, the north–south temperate zone, the north–south cold zone and the five continents. Some of the names of places and countries, such as Asia, Europe, Rome, Canada, Cuba, the Atlantic Ocean and the Mediterranean, are still used today.

The hydrological science of mechanical engineering introduced to China was most valued after the introduction because it was closely related to the lifeblood of the feudal country, i.e. agriculture. In 1606, the Italian missionary Sabbathinus De Ursis came to China and translated many works of western hydraulics. In 1612, he compiled and published six volumes of European hydraulic engineering works, the *Hydraulic Machinery of the West*. This book described the manufacturing principle and function of hydraulic machinery in Europe and was illustrated with diagrams. Its publication made China initiate the application of western farmland irrigation technology.

Later on, Xu Guangqi wrote the *Encyclopedia of Agriculture*, which included almost all of the data on hydrological technology found in the *Hydraulic Machinery of the West*. This reflected the scale of influence of western hydrological technology in China. The systematic mechanical engineering was introduced to China by Deng Yuhan, a Swiss missionary. In 1627, Deng Yuhan translated and published the western mechanical engineering work the *Illustrations and Explanations of Wonderful Machines*, which was the first monograph on machinery in China. Later, Wang Zheng, a Chinese scholar, designed and invented many kinds of machines according to this book, such as the mechanical mill and bicycle.

(ii) Exporting Chinese Culture to the West

When European missionaries introduced European science and culture to China, they devoted themselves to the study of Chinese traditional culture and translated excellent Chinese classics into western languages and brought those back to their countries. In 1593, Matteo Ricci translated the *Four Books* into Latin and sent them back to Italy. He also compiled the *Chinese-Portuguese-Italian Dictionary* and the *Chinese Grammar* for Europeans to learn Chinese.

In his later years, Matteo Ricci wrote notes on his experiences in China. After his death, another missionary, Nicolas Trigault, arranged and published his notes under the title *Matteo Ricci's Diary*. The book elucidated China's politics, economy, culture and customs in detail, so that Europeans might "discover a new world and a new nation." Later, many Confucian classics, history, philosophy and works of prose were translated into western languages and introduced to Europe. Those books not only enhanced the European understanding of China, but advanced enlightenment as well.

Under the suppression of the feudal government, great progress failed to be made in the overseas trade of the Ming Dynasty. China thereby lost the opportunity to take advantage of the gradual formation of the global market and expand the wealth of foreign trade by virtue of the unique advantages of its own commodities. However, the official tributary trade and civilian smuggling trade in the early Ming Dynasty still promoted economic and cultural exchanges between China and foreign countries. The late Ming period saw the European colonists coming from the West. Civilian overseas trade was transacted privately without permission. This, to some extent, made the economic and cultural exchanges between China and foreign countries greatly surpass the previous dynasties in terms of regional scope and scale, playing a beneficial role in the progress of world civilization.

Chapter 8

Foreign Trade in the Early Period of the Qing Dynasty

In 1644, the Manchu army entered the Shanhai Pass, the key military fortification of defense against tribes from Manchuria, and established the Qing Dynasty, the last feudal regime in China. At the turn of the Ming and Qing Dynasties, western colonists from Portugal and Spain came to the southeast coast of China. Their lust for mercantilism and overseas expansion continuously impacted East Asia, Southeast Asia, South Asia and other regions. It destroyed the tributary trade of East Asia that had been dominated by China, and disrupted the original international trade pattern of the Asian continent. During this period, the balance of power within western colonial powers also changed rapidly, with the Netherlands and Britain catching up from behind. Tsarist Russia also advanced swiftly toward the east and began to occupy Chinese territory.

At the beginning of its establishment, the Qing Dynasty was faced with an unprecedentedly severe international situation and unprecedentedly strong opponents. In the early Qing period, since the productive forces of feudal Chinese society developed slowly, China gradually lost its leading position in the world economy. However, the Qing Dynasty still regarded itself as the "celestial Court and a magnificent country" on the Earth, despising all foreign civilizations and severing connections with them. More and more western merchants came to China during this period, which made the western countries' trade with China ascend in position to that of China's foreign trade. The Qing Dynasty always implemented rigid restrictions on foreign trade, and repeatedly strengthened this policy in the trade conflict with western countries. As a result, China found itself in a passive position in global commerce. Complacent and conservative, the country was doomed to be backward and beaten by others, especially when its autocratic regime was threatened by internal turmoil.

8.1 Socio-Economic Development

The Qing was the last feudal dynasty in Chinese history, and made marked achievements in both politics and economy. After the establishment of the Qing Dynasty, the border areas of Mongolia, Xinjiang, Tibet, Taiwan, Yunnan, Guizhou and the northeast were unified. Through management and development, the economic and cultural ties between the Central Plains and the border regions were greatly strengthened, and the central government established an effective system of political administration around its borders.

The Qing government strengthened national political unity and promoted social and economic progress. Thus, the early Qing period made great strides in areas such as grain production, commodity output in agriculture and the handicraft industry, and market integration, as well as the development and reform of the financial system, the leasing system, and the employment system. All of those greatly surpassed those of the previous generation. It was owing to such factors that the population increased so rapidly in the early Qing Dynasty and the "Kangxi-Yongzheng-Qianlong heyday" took shape. According to statistics, China's overall economy ranked first in the world, with its GDP accounting for 40% of the world total and its population 1/3 of the world total. However, due to massive military expenditure and the corruption of officials, the economy of the Qing Dynasty declined inexorably from this prosperity after the Jiaqing period (1796–1820).

8.1.1 *The Development of Agriculture and the Handicraft Industry*

1. Agriculture
The most outstanding aspect of grain production in the Qing Dynasty was the phenomenon of regional expansion. That is to say, the grain output per *mu* increased generally in many areas nationwide, leading to greater total grain output and higher average yields per *mu*. According to Professor

Guo Songyi's estimates, before the Opium Wars the national average out-put per *mu* was 239 catties, the total grain output was 274,509 million catties, and the per capita of grain was 653 catties. If the whole country were to be divided into two areas, with the north as the dry farming area and the south as the rice planting area, the average yield per *mu* in the north was 114 catties with a total yield of 60,123 million catties and 464 catties per capita; while the average yield per *mu* in the south was 344 catties with a total yield of 214,386 million catties and 737 catties per capita.

The level of agricultural production in the south was generally higher than that in the north with the exception of cash crops. The cultivation of cotton, sericulture, ramie, tobacco, sugarcane, tea, indigo plants, and pea-nuts developed, with especially remarkable progress being made in the cultivation of cotton, tobacco, sugarcane, and peanuts. It was estimated that the planted area of cash crops in the early Qing Dynasty accounted for about 1/10 of the total cultivated land. Taking Jiangnan as the advanced area in the Ming and Qing Dynasties, Professor Li Bozhong estimated that the labor productivity of peasant families increased during the early Qing period. Therefore, with the spread of advanced technology and production structure from the Jiangnan area, the growth in labor productivity of farm-ing families in the affected areas should be more significant. On the basis of the general increase in family labor productivity, a historical peak was reached in the total amount of agricultural production, handicrafts produc-tion, commodity production and self-sufficient production during the early Qing Dynasty.

There were many reasons for the development of grain production in the Qing Dynasty. In the first instance, this was due to the promotion of the multi-cropping system. Land utilization in the northern regions of the Ming Dynasty (1368–1644) was insufficient with quite a low multiple cropping index. In the Qing Dynasty (1636–1912), especially after the mid-18th century, "four crops in three years" or "three crops in two years" became the norm in many areas, gradually being per-fected in Shandong, Hebei, Guanzhong of Shaanxi and other regions, in addition to the areas in northern provinces with only "one crop in a year."

Secondly, high-yield crops, like rice, corn, and sweet potatoes, were promoted. The structure of grain crops was adjusted, too.

Thirdly, progress was made in the intensive and meticulous farming experience in crop variety improvement, cultivation management and fertilizer application, both officially and privately, especially by the immigrants, and was widely exchanged in various places. Especially in the field of irrigation and constructing water conservation systems, a large number of small and medium-sized irrigation projects were built in the Qing Dynasty, most of which were built according to local conditions and brought about favorable irrigation effects.

The development of agriculture in the Qing Dynasty was closely related to certain government-implemented systems. The Qing government took agriculture as a basis for long-term development. A series of measures were adopted to safeguard the development of farming, such as appealing for reclamation, tax relief or exemptions on disasters and agriculture taxes, regulating rivers and watercourses, and the development of diversified management. In the late reigning years of Emperor Kangxi (r. 1662–1722), the problem of a sprawling population and little land arose, and it became increasingly severe in the reign of Emperor Qianlong (r. 1735–1795). Great importance was attached to the development of agriculture under both these reigns. Emperor Qianlong put forward the idea of agriculture on a grand scale, calling for a diversified system of management. The land tax reduction policy (exemption system) was an important economic policy of the Qing government. In the book the *History of Qing Dynasty: Treatise on Food and Commodities*, it was regarded as "the first instance of benevolent governance in both ancient and modern times."

There were two systems of exemption: one was named the *en juan*, which was an exemption from land tax on occasions of national celebration or during military service; the other was the *zai juan*, which was an exemption from tax, postponement, relief, loans and all debts in the event of disaster. In the Qing Dynasty, the number of tax exemptions exceeded that of the previous dynasty. Especially in the reigns of Emperor Kangxi and Emperor Qianlong, taxes on money and food were exempted many times. The number of tax exemptions following disasters was countless. These policies to some extent relieved the burden on the people, helped to promote agricultural development, eased social contradictions, and also consolidated the regime.

Taxation determined by land area as well as corvee according to household size formed two long-term policies. All complicated feudal land taxes and various types of corvee practiced in the middle Ming were combined and levied in silver. The amount of tax was collected not based on the number of people in a household, but on the land area, thus opening up a channel to abolish the corvee and the poll tax, which, unfortunately, failed to be thoroughly implemented.

The Qing Dynasty continued the reform of the Ming Dynasty, that is, the Qing government continued to collect corvee silver, known as tax silver or the head tax, levied according to numbers of households. In 1713, the Qing government announced that it would take the number of people in the whole country in 1712 as the quota, and would not increase or decrease the tax any more. It would not levy poll tax on newborns. This was the so-called "population increased with no extra tax paid." Fixing the number of people and the amount of poll tax could create conditions conducive for the implementation of tax based on land policy. Tax based on land policy meant that poll tax was included in corvee silver, and incorporated poll tax into the land tax for collection.

During the reign of Emperor Yongzheng (1722–1735), reform was carried out in a comprehensive way throughout the country and was basically completed in the early reigning years of Emperor Qianlong. The two policies of never increasing taxes as well as tax collection based on land meant the tax system was now unified, simplified and quantified. After the implementation of tax based on land, poll tax was exempted from urban merchants, handicraft practitioners and non-landowners, all of which was amenable to the development of industry, commerce and the sharecropping economy. What is more, this policy simplified the bureaucratic process of taxation, thus reducing the opportunities for corrupt officials to line their pockets. On the whole, the agricultural policy of the Qing government was favorable to the development of the social economy. However, it should be clearly recognized that the governance, good or bad, was the key to the effective implementation of the imperial economic policy. From the end of the Qianlong period, the efficacy of the policy was greatly reduced because of increasing corruption in the official system. Other policies of the Qing concerning industry and commerce, met with almost the same fate.

2. The Handicraft Industry

The handicraft industry was the second most important production sector after agriculture. In the middle and late Ming periods (1368–1644), the development of the handicraft industry reached a very high level and in the early Qing came to surpass previous dynasties. During this period, the main sectors of the industry took on their embryonic form, with the scale of production expanding, the production of goods developing, and the market exchange growing. Especially in some economically developed areas, relatively centralized and large-scale handicraft production areas gradually took shape, and the specialized division of labor and cooperation emerged both inside and outside workshops.

The development of the handicraft industry in the Qing Dynasty was based on the prosperity of the whole social economy. First of all, there was a preexisting handicraft industry that had advanced through previous dynasties, especially the Ming Dynasty, reaching high levels in the production of tools and skills, and also accumulating rich production experience. In the late Ming Dynasty, the disintegration of the practice of registering craftsmen on a census register endowed artisans with personal freedom, mobilizing greatly the enthusiasm for production.

Secondly, the expansion of agricultural areas, especially those planted with cash crops, during the Qing Dynasty provided a more substantial material foundation for the development of the handicraft industry.

Thirdly, the population explosion during the Qing Dynasty led to heightened demand for handicraft products, including daily necessities as clothing, food, housing and production materials, as well as luxury consumer goods. In those regions where the handicraft industry was well-developed, the improvement of people's living standards also stimulated consumption. Social and economic development proceeded in a positive manner.

Fourthly, the early Qing Dynasty saw rapid development in domestic and foreign market conditions.

Since the middle period of the Ming Dynasty (1460–1552), the handicraft production was stimulated by the prosperity of commercial roads, the improvement of transportation conditions, and the active circulation of domestic markets and commodities. Meanwhile, the development of private overseas trade expanded the export of silk, tea, porcelain, sugar and other commodities. Both domestic and foreign markets provided a strong impetus for handicraft production. The development of the handicraft industry in the Jiangnan area and the Pearl River Delta was attributed to a combination of convenient transportation and markets, both domestic and foreign.

Fifthly, the policies implemented by the Qing government played a role in promoting the growth of the handicraft industry. The Qing government encouraged the textile industry. For example, some local governments funded the purchase of mulberry seedlings and gave them to farmers free of charge. They also hired skilled craftsmen from developed areas to replicate reeling and weaving tools. During the reign of Emperor Kangxi, the lifting of the embargo gradually relaxed the restrictions on the development of shipbuilding industry. In the Qianlong period, the Qing government lifted the ban on mining and allowed private extractive industry.[1]

According to scholars, the most important handicraft industries — cotton and silk — could boast a high level of productivity.[2] The principal tools for cotton textile making were spinning wheels and looms. In the Yuan and Ming Dynasties, the three-spindle spinning wheel appeared, but it did not gain widespread popularity because of the limitations of the small-scale peasant economy. The most common spinning wheel was the single-spindle hand reeling machine, which could spin about 4–8 taels of yarn per day. Cotton looms used during the Ming and Qing Dynasties were similar to those common during the Yuan Dynasty in terms of style and principle, and their production efficiency varied greatly due to the specifications of the cloth. The technique of cotton weaving was improved in the Ming and Qing Dynasties. The variety and designs of cotton were increased with better quality and were very suitable for ordinary people.

In the early days prior to the importing of western cloth, *tu bu (nankeen cloth)* was of good quality and low priced. This fabric was competitive and was even exported to foreign countries. It was estimated that at that time, the households engaged in cotton textile industry accounted for about 50% of the total rural population, and cotton production was about 600 million bolts (*pi*) per year, including 310 million bolts of commercial cloth.

The production tools used in the silk industry mainly consisted of looms, in addition to some special tools for auxiliary processes. During the Ming and Qing Dynasties, the performance of the loom improved greatly, and the process of silk weaving became more and more rigorous and specialized. It was estimated that there were about 80,000 looms in the Jiangnan area. During the reign of Emperor Xianfeng of the Qing (1851–1861), the silk weaving industry in Sichuan province produced 7 billion bolts a year. Supposing that every loom could produce 300 *pi* of silk per year, an output of 7 billion bolts ought to be feasible from about 2,000 looms.

---

[1]Fang Xing, Jing Junjian, Wei Jinyu. *A General History of the Chinese Economy.* Vol. 1. Beijing: The Economic Daily Press, 1999.
[2]*Ibid.*

Regarding the silk weaving technology, the level of traditional techniques was constantly improved. In the Ming and Qing Dynasties, silk fabrics came in various varieties, such as brocade, satin, yarn, silk, damask silk, silk fabric, velvet, etc., with sophisticated weaving techniques and gorgeous colors. It was estimated that during the early Qing Dynasty, the quantity of silk products in the Jiangnan area was 49,000 piculs, with a value of 14.55 million taels of silver. During the early Qing Dynasty, the silk industry was separated from agriculture, and workers specializing in it appeared in the Jiangnan area, Sichuan, Guangdong and other developed areas.

8.1.2 *The Development of Commerce*

The Qing Dynasty ruled an area unparalleled in its vastness with the domestic market seeing unprecedented expansion. Commerce developed to a previously unseen level of prosperity, which could be illustrated from the following perspectives: the basic conditions of commercial circulation, long-distance trafficking in the domestic market, town development, commercial cities and merchant organizations.

The first was concerned with the basic conditions for commercial circulation, such as transportation network, service facilities and financial institutions. To begin with, compared with the previous dynasties, the overland and sea route transportation in the Qing Dynasty was relatively impeded. The "official thoroughfare" which was managed and maintained by governments at all levels, together with the branch routes funded by the private gentry and local officials, formed a nationwide transportation network. Among them, the "official thoroughfare" was mainly a courier road, mostly overland, but with some submerged areas. During the early Qing period, the courier road, centered on the metropolitan area, stretching and leading to the capital of every province as well as important frontier cities, functioned like the main artery of the dynasty. It was also the main path of commodity circulation. Traders generally used this avenue because it was crisscrossed as a network as well as safe.

Secondly, during the early Qing period, various services facilitated the circulation of commodities, such as transportation, transfer, storage, safekeeping, board and lodging, tax-paying, safety guarding. Great improvements were made both in quantity and quality. Some of these facilities were set up by the government to meet existing needs; some were provided by ordinary people as a means of making a livelihood. Objectively, both kinds of lodging promoted the development of commercial circulation.

The Qing formulated many policies on the construction and management of government-established infrastructures, which were to be implemented by the authorities at all levels. The government laid out guarantees for ships, wagons and hotels and set up navigation signs, lifeboats, patrol boats, duty rooms to protect the safety of merchants and cargo. Facilities subsidized by civilians, such as hotels, warehouses and armed escorts, made up for the lack of official facilities and played an important role, too.

Thirdly, the financial sector grew rapidly during the Ming and Qing Dynasties. Local banks, private banks, money shops and exchange shops dealt with financial businesses ranging from simple exchange of silver to deposits, remittances and credit loans. This not only ensured the smooth circulation of commodities, but promoted the rapid realization of commercial transactions as well. In particular, the emergence of exchange shops greatly facilitated large-scale commercial activities and long-distance trade.

Lastly, there was long-distance commodity trafficking. The extension of the distance over which commodities could be circulated was one of the defining characteristics of the trafficking trade during the early Qing Dynasty. As the transportation route from the interior to the border was impeded to a great extent, inland merchants traded very actively in remote areas, such as Xinjiang, Qinghai, Tibet, Gansu, Yunnan, Guizhou, and so on.

Long-distance trafficking in the Central Plains was also very common. Trafficking might be undertaken within the confines of a single province or even extend as far as to other provinces. For example, merchants in Ningbo, Zhejiang Province, "left their homes to trade in so many places that they were seen all over the country." In the trafficking trade, there was a greater variety of commodities than ever before. More grain was to be seen traded in long-distance circulation. Transporting cotton to the south and cotton cloth to the north was as frequent as that during the Ming Dynasty.

In addition, commodities, such as silk, tea leaves, porcelain, ironware, dyestuff, writing brushes, ink sticks, paper, ink stones, tobacco, and wood, were also sold everywhere. Every place boasted well-known local specialty products which were sold all over the country. To take grain as an example, as a commodity sold during the early Qing Dynasty it was about 53.66 billion catties, accounting for 17.26% of the total grain output, among which the amount of grain transported as commodity over long distances accounted for 5.5% of the total grain output. The fact of the grain transported to be circulated in different areas was of great significance, since it showcased the remarkable social and economic development.

Next was the development of towns and cities. During the Qing Dynasty, towns and cities generally developed hierarchically from petty markets with such names as *shi*, bazaar, open air *chang*, and *xu* as well as military garrisons. The prosperity of towns and cities mobilized the development of petty markets, and promoted energetically the urban economy. Scholars classified the towns and cities of the early Qing Dynasty into five basic types, that is, the local supply market, and demand type market, the production and marketing type market, the commercial transshipment type market, the comprehensive type market in towns, and the military type market in towns.[3]

Towns characterized by local supply and demand were to be found in Changzhi County, Lu'an Prefecture, Shanxi Province. "Xihuo Town, located 90 *li* away from the county town proper, was densely populated with constant streams of merchants and vendors coming and going. It neighbored on three counties, i.e. Huguan, Gaoping and Lingchuan. There were several towns nearby, i.e. Yincheng, Sangzi, Qiaotou. All of the towns above were densely populated where merchants and commerce gathered."[4]

Shengze Town in Suzhou Prefecture was a settlement of the production-and-marketing type. It was located along the Grand Canal, flourished during the Ming Dynasty and continued to prosper until the Qing "when its population was one hundred times greater than that of the previous dynasties. Silk production was ten times what it had previously been. Merchants from nationwide came here with gold every day. The market began at boom. Ships docked in the harbor. People moved as crowds, cheek-by-jowl in the streets. The hustle and bustle made Shengze town the busiest among all the local towns."[5] "All the local silk products were to be seen in the town. Those products could meet the needs of the whole

---

[3] *Ibid.*
[4] *The Memorial to Emperor Qianlong of the Qing Dynasty* presented on August 1, 1764.
[5] *Wujiang County Gazetteer: Emperor Qianlong.* Vol. 4.

country."[6] It was the silk production center for the entire nation. "The development of the town depended on the yield of the farmland, particularly on the trade situation. That is to say, households produced silk products for silk shops, the business of which was dependent on customers' consumption and merchants' sales. Fewer consumers and merchants meant less profits, and then more complaints arose."[7]

The economic relationship between Shengze Town and surrounding villages was very closely developed, forming a complete mode of silk production and circulation. Towns of this type were highly distinctive and specialized in the handicraft industry.

The next type was the development of commercial cities. Cities in traditional society fell into two categories. One was the political and military cities where administrative centers or military centers at all levels were located; the other was the industrial and commercial cities with a developed handicraft industry and commerce. The latter could be subdivided into handicraft industry cities and commercial circulation cities.

During the Qing Dynasty, Suzhou, Hangzhou and Nanjing were famous for their developed handicrafts industry. Cities well-known as commercial circulation hubs included Linqing, Huai'an, Shanghai, Tianjin, Chongqing and Hankou. In addition, Guangzhou, Zhangjiakou and other cities were famous as trade ports.

The commercial cities in the Qing Dynasty flourished with the circulation of commodities. The transshipment trade, wholesale business, financial industry, transportation, hotel, catering and other industries serving the commercial circulation were relatively well developed. In a word, the commercial cities in the Qing Dynasty grew apace with the regional economy, which was closely related to the changes in the national economy and circulation.

Towns of the merchant organization type attracted fruitful research results. In short, merchants during the Qing Dynasty were to be found in every level of the society. The problem of "abandoning farming and sericulture but chasing after industry and commerce" in this era was even more acute than that during the Ming Dynasty, with more peasants engaging in commerce. In addition to the mercantile class dating back to the Ming Dynasty and found in Shanxi, Shaanxi, Huizhou, Fujian, Guangdong,

---

[6] *Ibid.*, Vol. 5.
[7] *Annals of Shengze Town: Emperor Qianlong* II.

Jiangxi, Dongting and Longyou, Qing era merchants appeared in Shandong, Ningguo in Anhui, and Ningbo in Zhejiang.

The guilds and offices set up by merchants from all over the country developed rapidly. The merchants in the Qing Dynasty possessed a great sum of commercial capital, and made innovations in the form of capital and profit distribution. Some new changes took shape in the mode of business operations, especially the separation of ownership and management rights. All those reflected the evolutionary trend from traditional stores to a system of enterprise. It could be seen that commercial development during the early Qing Dynasty reached an unprecedented level.

8.2 Overseas Trade Policy

In the 200 years from 1644 to 1840, sharp conflicts arose between the Manchu and the Han nationalities. Externally, western powers expanded their colonial dominion. In an effort to quell these internal and external situations, the Qing Dynasty inherited and further strengthened the strict policy of restricting foreign trade implemented during the Ming Dynasty. With changes in the external environment, China's foreign trade restriction policy of the Qing Dynasty underwent a transition from opening maritime trade to embargoing it, from opening the sea route to setting up trade barriers, and from multi-port trade to one-port trade.

8.2.1 *Overseas Trade Policy in the Early Reign of Emperor Shunzhi*

In the early reigning years of Emperor Shunzhi (1644–1661), the Qing Dynasty allowed merchants to engage in foreign trade, and at one time even encouraged them to become involved in importing copper.

In 1646, Emperor Shunzhi issued an edict that "merchants who carried their assets sailing to trade would be given license by the government as approval to trade in southeast, Japan and other islands. When they came back, the customs would buy their copper currency at the market price for official use."[8] The book *A Collection of Imperial Anecdotes*, mentioned that "it may be recalled that in 1649 and 1650, when there was no ban on

---

[8] (The Qing Dynasty) Song Wenwei, Zhang Shouyong. *A Collection of Imperial Anecdotes*. Vol. 19. Yangzhou: Jiangsu Guangling Ancient Book Engraving Press, 1987.

maritime trade, foreign products were seen in markets; foreign currency was used in civilian trade."

8.2.2 Overall Embargo on Maritime Trade and Partial Lifting of the Ban

This policy was implemented between 1656 and 1684. In view of the sharp ethnic contradictions between the Manchu and the Han, especially with Zheng Chenggong's resistance to the Qing government gradually growing stronger, the Qing Dynasty tried to block the connection between Zheng's group of Taiwan and the mainland. From 1655, a series of bans on maritime trade were promulgated by the Qing government to strictly prohibit merchants from conducting foreign trade and restrict foreign merchants from entering China.

In 1655, the Qing government approved the proposal made by Tuntai, the Governor General of Zhejiang and Fujian, that "among the coastal provinces, the ban on maritime trade should be promulgated and neither sails nor ships would be allowed to sail on the sea; violators should be punished severely." Furthermore, "this order was sent to Zhejiang, Jijian, Guangdong, Jiangnan, Shandong, and Tianjin ... From now on, all governors should admonish civil and military officials in the coastal areas and forbid merchants and ships from going to sea without permission. Once discovered by local officials or being delated by others, anyone who is found exchanging grains or products with traitors or intending to do so would be sentenced to death without delay, no matter whether he was an official or a civilian. The cargoes would be confiscated. The property of the prisoner would be given to the informant. Local officials, with no practice of their duty to cross-examine and arrest the violators, would be deposed and charged with severe crimes. Local *Baojia* (village heads or directors in the neighborhood) who covered up for the ban-breaker would be sentenced to death too."[9]

During the period when the ban was most strictly implemented, it was stipulated that "no ship would go to the sea and no boats or vessels would be allowed to enter China."

---

[9] *The Veritable Records of Emperor Shizu of the Qing Dynasty.* Vol. 102.

In order to effectively implement the embargo, from 1660 to 1678, the Qing government issued three decrees to force coastal residents to move inland. Under the threat of harsh punishments and draconian laws, the overseas trade of the Qing Dynasty basically drew to a standstill, thereby damaging greatly people's livelihoods in coastal areas.

In 1673, the Governor General of Fujian submitted his memorials to the throne and said that since moving inland, "the cottages, houses, farm-lands along the coastal areas have become ruins, while numerous seniors, women, and children have lost their homes. The rest lost their jobs with no way to earn a living, moving from place to place and becoming exhausted."[10]

When the overall embargo was implemented, the Qing government announced in 1680 the opening of Macao for trade, allowing Chinese and foreign merchants to conduct business there.

8.2.3 *Maritime Customs Establishment & Multiport Trade Development*

The policies of maritime customs and multiport trade were implemented from 1684 to 1757. After the Qing Dynasty pacified the three vassals' revolt and recaptured Taiwan, Emperor Kangxi, who issued the ban on maritime trade and coastal evacuation many times, immediately abolished that embargo and issued the order of sea trade in 1684, stating that "since China is reunited as one country with no wars, both the Manchu and the Han are allowed to trade in the sea so as to demonstrate the prosperity of China. The order should be implemented."[11]

The next year in 1685, Emperor Kangxi announced that Songjiang (now Shanghai) in Jiangsu, Ningbo in Zhejiang, Xiamen in Fujian and Guangzhou in Guangdong were to be made foreign trade ports, and set up the Jianghai Customs, the Zhejiang Customs, the Fujian Customs and the Guangdong Customs, respectively, to manage foreign trade in coastal areas of each province. This marked the birth of China's customs system as China's administration policy on foreign trade.

---

[10] Yang Tingzhang. *A Sequel to Records of Fujian*. Vol. 87.
[11] (The Qing Dynasty) Xi Lufu *et al. The Categorized History of China's Dynasties.* Vol. 117, 1982.

Emperor Kangxi's promulgating and implementation of the sea trade policy reflected the urgent demand from people of the southeast coast to have overseas trade develop during this period. It was also the result of an ideological struggle between factions in the administrative hierarchy who wished to open up maritime trade and those who wanted to ban maritime trade. The sea trade policy put forward by Emperor Kangxi aroused fierce debate in the Qing Court.

Emperor Kangxi criticized some officials who insisted on banning sea trade, saying that "people like to live in coastal areas, because they can conduct sea route trade and fish in the sea. We know this fact clearly. Why don't we allow people to trade in the sea?"

Xi Zhu, the Grand Secretary, asserted that "the embargo on maritime trade was enforced by the Ming Dynasty. The policy should be continued. No sea route trade should be allowed."

Emperor Kangxi explained that "the policy was made due to the invasion of the sea bandits in previous times. At present they pose no threat. What are we waiting for?"

Xi Zhu replied that "according to what the Governor General said, Taiwan, Kinmen, Xiamen are places we just conquered not long ago. Although officials are sent and soldiers are stationed for defense, one or two years' waiting should be needed for ripe moment to reopen the sea route trade."

Emperor Kangxi maintained that "ministers in the border areas seem to care about the national economy and people's livelihoods and strictly prohibit the maritime trade, but smuggling trade is seen continuing there. The main opponents to reopening foreign trade were governors, who cared simply about their own profits."

Xi Zhu replied: "Absolutely."[12]

Those in favor of repealing the ban on maritime trade eventually prevailed. They argued that "now the overseas environment is relatively stable. In Taiwan, Penghu, Zhili, Shandong, Jiangnan, Zhejiang, Fujian, and Guangdong provinces, the government sent officers and soldiers to be stationed there for defense. Thus, the previously stipulated system of punishment should be lifted as soon as possible."[13]

---

[12] *The Veritable Records of the Qing Emperors*. Vol. 116. Zhonghua Book Company, 1987.

[13] (The Qing Dynasty) Liu Jinzao. *Comprehensive Investigations based on Literature of the Qing Dynasty*. Vol. 33. Shanghai: Shanghai Ancient Books Press, 1988.

Emperor Kangxi further elaborated on the positive role of maritime trade, observing that "if an order was made to allow the opening of maritime trade, it would not only benefit the people of Fujian and Guangdong, but also the economic development of other provinces, for it would enable the circulation of goods and wealth between the two provinces. The government could levy taxes on rich merchants as military expenditure in Fujian and Guangdong to offset the transfer of labor from mainland provinces. Inland areas are rich in finance and food, and the country could provide a comfortable and secure life for civilians, so we should repeal the ban on maritime trade."[14]

It could be seen that Emperor Kangxi realized that overseas trade was conducive to improving the livelihoods of coastal people, increasing fiscal revenue and military pay.

However, when western merchants under the escort of their own warships sailed eastward and traded in the east, the Chinese were not really encouraged by their government to engage in overseas trade. The order to open up maritime trade issued by the Qing government had many restrictive provisions attached. Thereafter, a series of issued decrees imposed increasingly strict restrictions on Chinese merchants, merchant ships, and foreign merchants coming to China for trade and their vessels, as well as import and export commodities.

For example, the Qing stipulated that when coastal dwellers conducted maritime trade, they must "register their name at the local administrative department, apply for a license, and report the ship number before they sail to trade."[15]

Specifically, ships with a deadweight capacity of more than 500 piculs and ships with two masts were forbidden from sailing abroad. Nobody was allowed to sell ships to foreign merchants without permission. No ships built overseas were allowed to transport goods back to China. Merchants who traded abroad must return home within three years, otherwise they would never be allowed to return home. Foreign merchants must first come to Macao and then to Guangzhou after approval. No weapons, sulfur, gold, silver, copper, iron, ironware, grain, first-round silk etc. were allowed as commodities for exportation.

---

[14] Zhao Zhiheng *et al. Holy Teachings of Emperor Qianlong of the Grand Qing.* Vol. 21. Beijing: Yanshan Press, 1998.
[15] *Code of the Grand Qing.* Vol. 629.

In 1717, with the development of overseas trade, the number of emigrants increased. When the government found that "Jakarta and Luzon were where western ships moored, with many stowed away," a ban was issued to prohibit trade with Southeast Asia. It said that "except for the purpose of conducting trade with Japan, merchant ships were prohibited from going to Southeast Asia for trade activities. They would be intercepted in Macao, Guangdong and other places. The government ordered the navy to patrol the coastal waters of Guangdong and Fujian. Violators would be punished severely."[16] The order aroused strong opposition from merchants.

In the following year, Emperor Kangxi was forced to announce that he would no longer ban foreign trade between Macao and Southeast Asia, as well as the trade between the mainland and Vietnam. The reason why the Qing Government prohibited trade with Southeast Asia but not with the *Eastern Oceans* was that, on the one hand, it was worried that the anti-Qing forces would gather in Southeast Asia. On the other hand, it needed commercial ships to purchase "Japanese copper" from Japan.

In the early reigning years of Emperor Yongzheng, local officials along the southeast coast submitted numerous written statements to the government, pleading for the lifting of the ban on trade with Southeast Asia. However, it was not until 1727 and 1729 that the Qing government lifted the ban on trade between Fujian and Zhejiang and Southeast Asia. After that, the central government imposed some new restrictions on trading in Southeast Asia. One order stipulated that "from now on, the government would strictly check the shipowners, captains, bowmen, sailors and merchants of all ships going overseas. Outbound merchants should register their names and birthplaces to apply for a license as a sailing pass, which would be checked upon their return. As soon as the number of people returning was seen not to match the number of people who left, the crew would be punished harshly first, and then the families of those who didn't return would be maltreated as well."[17] At the same time, it also stated that "those who used to stay abroad were not allowed to return to China."

---

[16] *The Veritable Records of Emperor Kangxi of the Qing Dynasty*. Vol. 271.
[17] *Imperial Edict with Instructions and Comments made by Emperor Yongzheng of the Qing Dynasty*. Vol. 46.

It could be witnessed that Emperor Kangxi's marine foreign trade policy was still the continuation of the foreign trade policy based on restriction. The above restrictions made it impossible for Chinese merchants to take advantage of their absolute preponderance in the international market to obtain high profits. The restrictions on the size of ships and storing weapons on board prevented Chinese traders from carrying out oceangoing long-distance trade, and even removed their competitive edge in traditional trading regions, such as the western shores of the Indian Ocean and the Arabian Peninsula.

8.2.4 *One-Port Trade Development in Guangzhou*

With the development of foreign trade, the Qing Dynasty held misgivings about the European colonialists, which led to the escalation of the conflicts between China and foreign countries. During the Multi-Port Foreign Trade period, merchants from European countries mainly traded in Guangzhou. However, from the early 1750s, in order to open the wool market and be close to the sources of silk and tea, British merchants frequently traveled to Ningbo, Dinghai and other places. The Qing government became suspicious about the British ships' frequent northward movements. From the late reigning years of Emperor Kangxi, the Qing government mainly took preventive measures against foreign ships coming to China. In 1732, the Qing government moved the berthing places of foreign commercial ships to Macao from Huangpu to ensure the safety of Guangzhou.

In the spring of 1757, the Qing government issued an announcement stating that "of late, thieves and pirates have colluded with fisherfolk. More foreign vessels have been sighted in Ningbo. If foreign vessels stay too long, Ningbo will become another Macao in Guangdong Province. In view of the crucial coastal defense position of Ningbo and its local customs, the regulations were altered to take Guangdong province as a more important region. A proviso is hereby added that foreign vessels are not allowed to enter China if they bring no benefits to China."[18]

It could be seen that the Qing Court worried that the further development of Chinese and foreign trade would threaten coastal defenses and challenge traditional Chinese social customs and morals. Later, the Qing

---

[18] *The Veritable Records of Emperor Gaozong.* Vol. 533. Zhonghua Book Company, 1980.

government ordered the customs tariff rate at Zhejiang customs to be twice as much as that at Guangdong Customs, trying to "prohibit foreign business by taxing it heavily." However, this method failed to work. British merchants continued to proceed northward. At the end of 1757, the Qing government banned foreign merchants from trading in the three customs areas of Jiangsu, Zhejiang and Fujian, and opened up Guangzhou as the lone port for commercial trade.

When the One-Port Commercial Trade policy was implemented, the Qing government strictly managed the foreign merchant ships coming to Guangzhou, and successively promulgated a series of administrative trade regulations, including the *Regulations on the Prevention of Foreigners* (1759), the *Articles of Association of the Maritime Trade* (1809), the *Regulations on Banning the Export of Official Silver and the Import of Private Goods* (1830), the *Regulations on Banning Fine Silver Evasion and Opium Distribution* (1830), the *Eight Articles of the Constitution for the Prevention of Foreigners* (1831), the *Eight new Regulations on the Prevention of Foreign Affairs* (1835).

More stringent restrictions were imposed on foreign merchants. For instance, they were not allowed to ride in sedans, no documents were allowed to be delivered directly to the feudal government, no sightseeing was allowed at will, and no foreign women were allowed to enter Guangzhou City, and so on. The restrictions on foreign traders reached their peak during the Qing Dynasty.

8.3 Overseas Trade Management Policy

Overseas trade activities during the early Qing were mainly managed by the customs and the "Thirteen Factories." In 1685, the establishment of the four major customs offices in Jiangsu, Zhejiang, Fujian and Guangdong marked the establishment of the customs system in China and the end of the Maritime Trade Commission which had been in operation since the Tang Dynasty. Therefore, the management of China's overseas trade opened up a new world.

8.3.1 *The Customs System*

As mentioned above, in 1685, the Qing government established four major custom offices in Songjiang (now Shanghai), Ningbo in Zhejiang,

Xiamen in Fujian and Guangzhou in Guangdong. The four customs offices, as the general customs bureaus, managed the foreign trade of all the ports within the province where they were located. For example, the Guangzhou Customs had more than 50 subordinate customs ports, and the chief customs officer was called the supervisor.

As Guangzhou played an important role in national foreign trade, the Customs Supervisor was appointed directly by the Emperor. The position was generally taken by officials from the Imperial Household Department. Its status in the administrative hierarchy was next in line to the Governor, the Provincial Governor, and the Provincial Military Commander, but higher than the Provincial Administration Commission and the Surveillance Commissioner. As they were mostly trusted by the Emperor, they held high positions with greater power. In order to eliminate mal-practice, the Supervisor usually served only a single one-year term. Under the Supervisor was the Deputy Supervisor, the Defense Supervisor and other customs officers at every level. The Supervisors of Fujian, Zhejiang and Jiangsu were promoted from being local governors or the post was held concurrently by the Governor General.

The functions of the customs office were mainly divided into two aspects: (a) to supervise import and export merchants, the merchant vessels, and goods. During the Qing Dynasty, there were clear regulations on the size of the import and export vessels, the articles carried onboard, the procedures for merchants to leave the port, the types of import and export commodities, etc., and what the customs should supervise and administer in accordance with regulations; (b) to collect tariffs. During the early Qing Dynasty, the ports in China did not all share a uniform tariff system. Generally, there were three kinds of tariff levied by Customs: the ship tax, the cargo tax and the surtax. The ship tax was levied according to the volume of the cargo ship. The cargo tax was also known as a commercial tax or import and export tax. The Qing Dynasty customs divided cargoes into several grades, and tariffs were collected according to the weight of goods with some being collected according to price. Surtax, or the miscel-laneous tax, was also called regulated rites. It was a variety of incidental expenses other than the normal tax, and included regulated silver, the regulation of ships, head division, etc. Among them, the largest amount was regulated silver. In 1726, it was incorporated into the tariff rules. Foreign merchant ships entering the port needed to pay 1,125.96 taels of regulated silver per ship, and 533 taels of regulated silver upon departure.

The collection of miscellaneous levies was usually arbitrary with many disadvantages. The amount of miscellaneous tax collected was often several times more than the normal tax, becoming a major impediment to the development of import and export trade.

8.3.2 *The Thirteen-Factory System in Guangzhou*

The Thirteen Factories System was also called the Hong Merchants System. "Hong merchants" referred to the wholesaler getting the special approval of the Qing government) to operate overseas trade, and their commercial firms were called "foreign firms" or "foreign goods firms." They were collectively called the "Thirteen Factories."

1686 was the second year of the establishment of Guangzhou Customs. In order to enhance the management of overseas trade, the local government in Guangdong segregated merchants engaging in domestic trade from those in foreign trade, and divided the commercial firms into "golden silk firms" and "foreign goods firms." The former were mainly engaged in the domestic trade of domestic goods, while the latter were engaged in managing import goods and export goods. At the same time, the government also stipulated that those who acted as Hong merchants must be affluent personages. They should present their application first, and upon approval, they were required to pay a deposit and obtain a government-issued license before they could operate a trading company.

The Thirteen Factories did not refer to the precise number of foreign firms. Based on the business conditions, the number of foreign firms was variable, up to 26 companies at most and several at least. In addition to their owners, foreign firms also had compradors, interpreters, inspectors, etc. In 1720, the Hong merchants organized a guild group — the Gonghang. The Gonghang agreed on thirteen articles of trade regulations, such as jointly discussing and determining the price of goods, ensuring the quality of goods, and dividing the Hong merchants into three levels, each having different trade shares, so as to suppress competition. The Gonghang did not elect a legally empowered leader, nor did it possess uniform regulations, so their organization was slack and somewhat ineffectual. However, due to the expansion of its monopoly, it aroused strong complaints among foreign merchants.

According to the regulations of the Qing government, after arriving in Guangzhou, foreign merchants were not allowed to trade freely. They should stay in the business hotel set up by the Hong merchants. Merchants of all trades were residents in the hotel. That is why the trade of all Western merchants in Guangzhou was called the "business hotel trade." All their trade in Guangzhou was managed by their Hong merchants as agents, who also supervised and managed their activities. The Hong merchants performed certain functions and powers on behalf of the government, so they served a semiofficial function.

The main responsibilities of Hong merchants were as follows: (a) to underwrite rates. After the foreign merchant vessels entered the port, they should pay the import tax, which should be guaranteed by the Hong merchants to the customs and paid when the foreign ships returned to the port. Therefore, the Hong merchants were also called "security merchants." The export tax payable by foreign merchants ought to be paid by the merchants when purchasing goods for them; (b) to purchase and sell import and export commodities on behalf of others. When it came to foreign merchants in Guangzhou, a small number of handicrafts were allowed to be traded with ordinary merchants under the assurance of Hong merchants. Other bulk import and export goods must be superintended by the Hong merchants. In other words, the import goods brought by foreign merchants were underwritten by the Hong merchants, and the export goods needed by foreign merchants were purchased by the Hong merchants. After the Jiaqing period (1796–1820), the Hong merchants gradually relaxed their control over the import and export trade; (c) to handle all kinds of negotiation affairs on behalf of others. The Qing government officials did not have direct contact with the foreign merchants. All the negotiations between the foreign merchants and the Qing government were transmitted to or conveyed by Hong merchants on their behalf. That is to say, to deliver documents to the government on behalf of foreign merchants and to announce instructions to foreign merchants on behalf of the government; (d) to supervise and manage foreign merchants. The Hong merchants should be responsible for supervising and managing the activities of foreign merchants and sailors in Guangzhou in accordance with the *Regulations on the Prevention of Foreign Affairs*.

It could be observed that as a semi-official foreign trade monopoly organization chartered by the Qing government, Hong merchants became an intermediary between the national authorities and foreign merchants, as well as the bridge of communication between the Chinese market and the overseas market. This system restricted the free trade between Chinese and foreign merchants and became an important tool for the Qing government to strictly restrict overseas trade.

8.4 Foreign Trade Relations

8.4.1 *Trade Relations with East Asian and Southeast Asian Countries*

1. Joseon

Before the Opium Wars, the Qing Dynasty always maintained friendly trade relations with Joseon. During the reign of Emperor Shunzhi, all foreign envoys went to Beijing to trade in the guildhall on a scheduled date, while the Joseon envoys were not subject to this restriction.

When the ban on maritime trade was implemented during the reign of Emperor Kangxi, Joseon diplomatic envoys were still given preferential treatment. The Qing government banned the export of rice and grain, even after the opening of the maritime trade in 1685. However, in view of the fact that Joseon was stricken by disaster and suffering from food shortage, the Qing government relaxed its restrictions on trade with it.

2. Japan

Before the Opium Wars, especially during the reigns of Emperor Kangxi and Emperor Yongzheng, the Qing government attached great importance to Sino-Japanese trade. Since Emperor Kangxi lifted the ban on maritime trade, the number of Chinese merchant ships sailing to Japan increased.

Before the Opium Wars, Japan adopted the Lockdown Policy, prohibiting Japanese vessels from going overseas, with only Chinese and Dutch vessels being permitted to sail to Nagasaki for trade activities. It can be seen that "Sino-Japanese trade" at that time referred to the business transacted by Chinese merchant ships sailing to Japan, thus styled "Sino-Nagasaki Trade". Each year the number of Chinese vessels arriving in Japan ranged from dozens to hundreds. The exported goods to Japan increased in variety. Although China's exports to Japan were still dominated by traditional commodities, such as silk and porcelain, a large number of foods and fruit were added to the export inventory. Copper, gold and silver were the main commodities exported from Japan to China, with seafood being a new addition. This emphasized how the development of the Sino-Japan trade was no longer limited to luxury goods.

Faced with booming trade between China and Japan, the Japanese government became worried about the economic impact of an outflow of gold, silver and copper. Therefore, in 1685, the Japanese government began to promote the negative trade restriction policy. From that year onwards, Japan stipulated that the total annual trade volume of Chinese merchant ships to Japan should not exceed 60 million *guan*. In 1688, Japan again limited the number of Chinese merchant ships sanctioned to travel to Japan to 70,[19] and limited the date and place of their arrival. However, the above restrictions failed to achieve the anticipated effect. Chinese merchant ships that were ordered to return often wandered around Nagasaki and continued to smuggle a large amount of gold, silver and copper from Japan.

From 1662 to 1708, the weight of copper being brought from Japan was as high as 114,498,700 catties.[20] In view of this, in 1715, the Japanese government issued "the new order in the Zhengde period (1711–1716)." According to this edict, the number of Chinese merchant ships permitted to go to Japan was limited to 30 per year, with the trade volume still fixed at 60 million *guan*. The copper output was not allowed to exceed 3 million catties. Chinese merchant ships should apply for the "identification sign" used as the certificate for trade. In addition, the Japanese government used the opportunity of issuing the "identification sign" to extort money. Meanwhile, Japanese copper production was decreasing annually, which also caused the number of Chinese vessels sailing to Japan each year to shrink.

3. Siam

Before the Opium Wars, the trade between China and Siam was very active, via both official trade and the merchant shipping trade.

In 1652, Siam sent envoys to develop friendly relations with China. During the reign of Emperor Shunzhi, Siam generally sent a delegation to China once in three years, rising to almost every year during the reigns of Emperor Kangxi and Emperor Qianlong. In the Qing Dynasty, Siamese envoys to China were always treated with kindness. In the early years of

---

[19](Japan) Yasuhiko Kimiya. *Nikka bunka kōryūshi*. Fuzanbō, 1955. Reprint 1977.
[20]*Ibid.*

Kangxi, Siam was allowed to store and sell cargoes carried by her ships in Guangzhou. In 1684, after the lifting of the ban on maritime trade, it was stipulated that Siamese ships could trade on the spot after reporting their arrival in Humen, Dongguan.[21] Siamese ships carried a large number of local products of various varieties. The number of gifts given back by the Qing Dynasty was also considerable.

The merchant shipping trade between China and Siam was very frequent. According to statistics, since the lifting of the ban on maritime trade in 1689 there were 14 to 15 Chinese merchant ships sailing from China to Siam; in 1695, the number was 8; in 1698, 7; in 1699, 6; in 1702, more than 10.[22]

The Chinese merchant ships sailing to Siam mainly came from Guangzhou, Macao, Xiamen, Zhangzhou, Quanzhou, Ningbo and other ports. These arrived at Ayutthaya, Pattani, Songkhla, Ligor (now Nakhon Si Thammarat) in Siam.

The merchandise exported from China included silk, porcelain, iron, ironware, white copper, copperware, alum, mercury, nankeen cloth, paper, sugar, sweetmeats, dried fruit, etc. The most sizable import from Siam was rice. Siam was not only rich in rice, but also a major supplier of rice to its neighboring countries.

In order to solve the problem of food shortages, the Qing Dynasty encouraged the import of rice, offering the Siamese preferential tax relief on their rice. The great scale of the grain trade made Siam the largest trade partner of China in Southeast Asia during the early Qing Dynasty. In addition, China's imports from Siam included tin, lead, gemstones, rhinoceros' horns, ivory, pepper, sappan, areca, deerskin, cowhide, etc. Except for the period when trade with Southeast Asia was outlawed, the Qing government took a supportive and encouraging attitude toward business exchanges between Siam and China.

In addition to bilateral trade, China and Siam also carried out trilateral trade involving Japan. This played a positive role in promoting bilateral trade between the two countries. Since Japan adopted the Lockdown Policy in the mid-17th century, only Chinese and Dutch ships

---

[21] (The Qing Dynasty) Liu Jinzao. *Comprehensive Investigations based on literature of the Qing Dynasty*. Vol. 33. Shanghai: Shanghai Classics Publishing House, 1988.
[22] (Thailand) Sarasin Viraphol. *Tribute and Profit: Sino-Siamese Trade 1652–1853*. Cambridge, Mass: Harvard University Press, 1977.

were allowed to trade in Nagasaki. Thus, the King of Siam sent ships equipped with Chinese crews and Siamese officials to Japan for trade purposes. On their way to and from Japan, these ships often called at Chinese ports for repairment, avoiding wind, and more importantly, loading and unloading goods.

4. Myanmar

Prior to the Opium Wars, the Qing Dynasty further developed trade between China and Myanmar, with overland route trade as the main way. According to Hall James, "in the mid-17th century, China's silk and other goods were transported to Myanmar in large quantities by overland route. The trade caravan had as many as 300–400 carriages and up to 2,000 heads of pack hinnies."

"At that time, the Dutch manufacturers in Ava also established a close relationship with Chinese merchants."[23] According to Andersen, prior to 1765, one huge Chinese caravan was made up of 300–400 cattle and 2,000 horses. It walked in a great procession out of Yunnan conveying silk and other commodities to Bhamo, Myanmar. The variety of goods traded between China and Myanmar had also increased in number.

The commodities imported from China to Myanmar included raw silk, silk and satin, velvet for imperial clothes, Yunnan-grown tea leaves, gold, copper, steel, wine, ham, mercury, and a large number of needles and threads. Among them, cotton was the bulk commodity exported from Myanmar to China. By the early 19th century, the cotton of "at least two or three thousand *tuo* (camel) a year" was exported to China by the Yunnan caravans.[24] Records have it that the volume of Burmese cotton imported into China in the year 1862 reached 14 million pounds and was valued at 228,000 pounds.[25] The import of Myanmar cotton not only overrode the shortage of cotton in Yunnan, but promoted the development of the cotton textile industry there. Other Chinese imports from Myanmar included cubilose, salt, ivory, antlers, amber, lacquerwares and gemstones.[26]

---

[23] D. G. E. Hall. *Europe and Burma*. H. Milford: Oxford University Press, 1945.

[24] (The Qing Dynasty) Cun Kaitai. *Teng Yue Xiang Tu Zhi: Business Affairs*.

[25] John Leroy Christian. *Modern Burma*. University of California Press, 1942.

[26] G. E. Harvey. *History of Burma, from the Earliest Times to 10 March 1824, the Beginning of the English conquest*. Longmans, Green and Co., 1925.

8.4.2 *Trade Relations with European and American Countries*

1. Britain
(i) The Imbalanced Development of Sino-Britain Trade

By the early 18th century, Britain's trade volume with China had exceeded that of all countries, thus making it China's largest trading partner. According to statistics, from 1785 to 1833, the goods that Britain trafficked to China accounted for 80–90% of China's total import trade, and the goods exported from China accounted for 60–80% of the total export trade of the country. China was in obvious trade surplus. From 1710 to 1759, the trading volume of goods exported from Britain to China was only 9,248,306 pounds, valued as 26,833,614 pounds in silver money.

According to British statistics, during the seventy odd years from 1760 to 1833, China's exports to Britain increased by nine times, while its imports from the UK increased by 15 times. Those absolute figures highlighted that China's trade was in favorable surplus. In 1837–1839, prior to the Opium Wars, the annual average import of British goods into China was less than 0.91 million pounds, while the import of Chinese goods into Britain was 4.27 million pounds, so the annual average deficit of Britain was 3.3 million pounds. To afford the cost of importing Chinese tea leaves, Britain had to ship large quantities of silver to China as payment. At the end of the 17th century and the beginning of the 18th century, silver usually accounted for more than 90% of the cargo on the East India Company's merchant vessels to China. The unfavorable balance of trade resulted in the increasing amount of silver flowing into China. This ran counter to the British bourgeoisie's intention: to expand the British market, promote industrial products and generate more wealth.

The fundamental reason for the imbalanced state of Sino-Britain trade was China's feudal social and economic pattern. China's self-sufficient natural economy in which menfolk tilled and womenfolk wove had little reliance on markets and an especially weak demand for imported goods. This resulted in a stunted market for foreign goods in China.

The direct cause of the imbalance was the commodity structure of Sino-Britain trade. The major product that British merchants purchased from China was tea leaves as well as raw silk, *nankeen* cloth, rhubarb and other items.

In the late 18th century, tea leaves became a necessity for British people, so that the British Parliament ordered the East India Company to keep an inventory of each year's supply. From 1760 to 1764, Britain imported 42,065 piculs of Chinese tea annually; from 1780 to 1784, its import increased to 55,840 piculs annually; from 1800 to 1804, it was 221,027 piculs annually; in 1839, it was 300,000 piculs, valued at 40 million pounds. The East India Company earned mammoth profits, and the British government also received a large amount of revenue from taxes on tea leaf imports. Meanwhile, China lacked an effective demand for British goods. Before the 19th century, British imports to China were mainly woolen goods, which had no market because they were unsuitable and expensive. By the end of the 18th century and the beginning of the 19th century, Britain had realized its large-scale Industrial Revolution. The production of cotton textiles had been enhanced greatly, and a large number of them were exported to India, which destroyed almost completely India's hand-made cotton textile industry.

In 1786, the East India Company began to export cotton textiles to China. After checking the samples, the Hong Merchants determined that "none of them could be sold on the Chinese market, because the cost of Britain cotton cloth was too prohibitive, and Chinese could weave various cotton textiles themselves. Although domestic cloth was not very elegant, it was more suitable for local clothing." Two years later, the British East India Company tried again to export cotton cloth to China, but still met with failure. In 1819, the British East India Company sent a batch of imitated Chinese cotton cloth, which was "poorly imitated." According to the records of the British East India Company, "no one liked the striped cloth, and Chinese merchants couldn't feel the beauty of those fabrics at all."

China's foreign trade restriction policy was also an important factor hindering the development of Sino-Britain trade. The British in turn took this as the main reason. By the late 18th century, Britain's dominant trading ideology had transitioned from mercantilism to free trade.

In 1776, Adam Smith published *The Wealth of Nations* and put forward the theory of free trade. He believed that free trade could find market for domestic surplus products, so as to promote the division of labor, expand production, improve production and increase social wealth. Smith even specifically mentioned China, "... the home market of that country is of so great extent as to be alone sufficient to support very great manufactures, and to admit of very considerable subdivisions of labor. The home market of China is, perhaps, in extent, not much inferior to the market of all the different countries of Europe put together. A more extensive foreign trade, however, which to this great home market added the foreign market of all the rest of the world — especially if any considerable part of this trade was carried on in Chinese ships — could scarce fail to increase very much the manufactures of China, and to improve very much the productive powers of its manufacturing industry."[27]

Free trade theory became the guiding ideology of Britain foreign trade, which was in sharp contradiction to China's restrictive foreign trade system. Therefore, Britain took a series of measures to break down its counterparts' system.

2. The British Diplomatic Mission to China
(i) The Macartney Mission

In September 1792, claiming to pay tributes on the Emperor Qianlong's birthday, a British diplomatic mission led by Lord George Macartney came to China, funded by the British East India Company. The party were accompanied by several gunboats with such presents as a celestial globe, a tellurian, a self-propelled gun, and a telescope. The Qing government initially regarded the British missions as barbarians who admired Chinese civilization and had come to pay tribute. Hence, they treated them with great courtesy and were unimpressed by the technology and production techniques embodied in their gifts. When the generals of Qing were invited to inspect the drill of the British mission guards demonstrating firearms, the officials unexpectedly showed no interest.

In September 1793, Emperor Qianlong received the British mission at the Rehe Palace in the northern part of Hebei Province. Macartney put forward five demands, namely that (a) China opens Zhoushan, Ningbo and Tianjin ports; (b) China delimits small islands near Zhoushan for British merchants to stock and live in; (c) China allows Britain to set up a business center and sends people to Beijing for trade; (d) China exempts Britain from commercial tax; (e) China allows British merchants to stay freely in Guangzhou and other places.

Claims of this sort, with their strong colonial overtones, clearly reflected the British demand for a climate of free trade. This fiercely contravened China's conservative foreign trade ethos. Emperor Qianlong was incensed at the British request. In his reply to the British King, he asserted that "our Celestial Empire possesses all things in prolific abundance and lacks no product within its own borders. Therefore there was no need to

---

[27] Adam Smith and Edwin Cannan. *An Inquiry Into the Nature and Causes of the Wealth of Nations: Book 4*. University of Chicago Press, 1977, p. 906.

import the manufactures of outside barbarians in exchange for our own produce. But as the tea, silk and porcelain which the Celestial Empire produces are absolute necessities to European nations and to yourselves, we have permitted, as a signal mark of favor, that foreign *hongs* (groups of merchants) should be established at Macao, so that your wants might be supplied and your country thus might participate in our beneficence... What your emissaries required is infeasible."[28]

Meanwhile, Emperor Qianlong warned that "... your Ambassador has now put forward new requests that ... your merchants may reside and goods be warehoused ... a flagrant infringement of the usage of my Empire that cannot possibly be entertained."[29] In other words, the Emperor did not deem foreign trade as beneficial to China. The limited foreign trade to be made at China's permission was a unilateral favor to foreigners. The requirement of the British was not in line with China's feudal political and economic system, so it was not feasible. Although the Macartney delegation failed to fulfill its expressed diplomatic mission, it collected a lot of information about China's products, geographical environment, military strength and other aspects on its way to Guangzhou. This bolstered early preparations for the wars Britain later launched against China.

(ii) William Pitt Amherst's Mission
In 1816, Britain sent the Amherst mission to visit China again. In August of that year, the British party arrived in Tongzhou and failed to enter Beijing because of the "Rites controversy." In 1833, Britain abolished the privileges of the East India Company and adopted a free trade policy. More British merchants poured into the East. The conflict between China and Britain further intensified.

(iii) The Opium Trade
As early as the Tang Dynasty, Arab merchants introduced the knowledge of opium cultivation and its functions into China. Since then, Chinese medical books had recorded the medicinal properties of opium. From the 16th century onwards, with the extensive development of trade between China and Europe, Portuguese and Dutch merchants had trafficked opium

---

[28] *The Veritable Records of Emperor Gaozong*. Vol. 1435. Chinese Publishing House, 1987.
[29] *Letter to George III*.

from Turkey to China. Prior to the 18th century opium was, instead of as a drug, used as a narcotic, with limited amount imported.

In 1757, after Britain occupied Bangladesh, the center of opium production, British merchants became the biggest opium traffickers. In 1773, in order to reverse the trade deficit with China, Britain granted the East India Company the patent right of opium trafficking, which established the British policy of opium trade with China. The East India Company auctioned the rights to individual British merchants, who became the operators of the opium trade. Thereafter, Britain's opium trade with China expanded rapidly.

As early as 1729, the Qing government decreed a ban on opium smoking. However, the import of opium and the increase in the number of opium smokers in China formed a vicious circle. With the growth of opium imports, there more and more opium smokers in China. In 1796, the Qing government ordered the cessation of opium tax and forbade the import of the drug. The opium trade was made illegal thereafter. However, the opium merchants flouted the ban, continued to organize smuggling and secret trafficking by bribing officials of the Qing government. The quantity of opium exported to China increased year on year after the beginning of the 19th century. According to statistics, during the 45 years (1794–1839) prior to the Opium Wars, a total of 420,000 crates of opium were imported into China, becoming the main commodity exported by Britain and the United States to China in the 18th and 19th centuries. In the early 19th century, opium accounted for about 50% of China's total imports, 90% of which were operated by British merchants.

The large-scale contraband in opium reversed the balance of trade between China and Britain, with the Chinese side shifting from surplus to deficit in foreign trade (while the trade of other commodities was still in surplus). Britain not only reversed its trade deficit with China, but earned a lot of silver from its opium trade. The revenue made from the opium trade accounted for 1/7 of its total revenue. Opium merchants also made huge profits. It was estimated that the profit margin of opium business was as high as 600%. Statistics showed that in the 40 years before the Opium War, British merchants earned more than 200 million silver money by smuggling opium to China. Therefore they thought that opium trade was "the safest and gentlest business of speculation." However, China's trade surplus shifted to deficit. From 1827, China's balance of payments also showed a deficit. Silver began to gush out of China.

Secondly, China's social productivity shrank seriously. By 1835, there were millions of opium smokers in China, covering more than ten provinces, including people in all walks of life, "such as officials, gentry, merchants, women, monks, nuns and Taoists." Opium smoking made people depressed and lethargic, which directly damaged the social economy.

Thirdly, opium smoking hindered the development of the economy. Chinese spent a great deal of wealth on opium consumption, which led to social poverty, and the decline of purchasing power. This hindered the growth of agriculture, industry and commerce, resulting in a sluggish market.

Finally, opium smoking brought about financial crisis for the Qing government. The outflow of silver resulted in the increase of silver in price, currency devaluation, tax evasion, thus further generating the financial panic, especially the financial crisis of the Qing government.

In 1839, Emperor Daoguang (r. 1821–1851) ordered that Lin Zexu eradicate opium smoking in Guangdong. On June 3, Lin Zexu destroyed the confiscated opium by burning it at the East Tiger Gate, thus triggering directly the Opium Wars between Britain and China. This brought about the end of independent feudal society in China.

3. France

At the end of the Ming Dynasty and the beginning of Qing, Louis XIV, (1638–1715) King of France, actively supported missionaries to come to China to promote trade with China. In 1660, King Louis XIV organized a "Chinese company" to monopolize the Sino-French trade, and sent merchant ships to China for the first time, but it failed because of the maritime accident halfway. In 1664, France reorganized the French East India Company, which enjoyed the patent rights of navigation and trade in India and the East, successively established trading institutions and several commercial bases in the west of India and on the east coast of India. All this was in active preparation to begin to trade with China. In 1698, King Louis XIV sent several Navy officers and a group of Jesuit missionaries to China on the ship *L'Amphifrite*, this being the first time that French merchant vessels came to China. In addition to extending a warm reception and tariff exemption, the Qing government also allowed the French to set up the trading institution in Guangzhou. From then on, French merchant ships kept coming to Guangzhou for trade.

After the return of the French *L'Amphifrite*, a second "Chinese company" in France was established in 1700. In 1705, the company was reorganized into the "Royal China Trading Company" and obtained the patent right for trade with China. By 1712, France had established a new "Royal China Trading Company" and secured the patent right for 50 years. The company had sent successively three vessels to China for trade. However, due to the French trade protectionism policy, the company's trade activities were difficult to conduct, and the company was merged into the East India Company in 1719. From then on, France continued to trade with China in various ways, but little progress had been made.

From 1716 to 1833, only one or two French vessels came to China annually in half of the period. Some years saw more vessels coming, but the number of which was no more than seven or eight. As for the foreign trade between France and Guangzhou, taking the year 1792 as an example, France mainly exported feather with a value of 40,000 taels, and cloth, with a value of 3,540, and tin with a value of 3,195.

France mainly imported black tea with a value of 210,880 taels of silver, and nankeen cloth with a value of 114,000 taels, and rock candy with a value of 10,060 taels.

In that year, Guangzhou's import value from France was 49,120 taels of silver, accounting for only 0.97% of the total of 5,069,653 taels of silver of Guangzhou's import value from Europe and America; Guangzhou's export value to France was 361,925 taels of silver, accounting for only 4.83% of the total of 7,490,524 taels of silver of Guangzhou's export value to Europe and America.[30] It can be observed that before the Opium Wars, France's trade with China progressed slowly.

4. The United States

As early as the 1770s, with the British East India Company as the intermediary, North America conducted indirect trade with China. After the American War of Independence, China and the United States established direct trade relations. In 1784, the voyage of the American merchant vessel *Empress of China* to Guangzhou marked the first journey of a US ship to China. From then on, the major ports of the United States had direct trade contacts with Guangzhou, and the trade between the United States and China grew apace. From 1784 to 1833, 997 US merchant vessels sailed to Guangzhou, making an average of nearly 20 per year. From 1833 to 1840, there were 246, making an average of more than 35 per

[30] Yao Xianhao. *Historical Materials of Modern Chinese Foreign Trade*. Vol. 1. Beijing: Zhonghua Book Company, 1962.

year.[31] Compared with the countries of Europe, direct trade between the United States and China began relatively late. Even so, its speed of development was very rapid so that the United States surpassed France, the Netherlands, Denmark and Portugal, becoming second only to the United Kingdom among China's western trading partners.

In the early Qing Dynasty, Sino-US trade was mainly operated by the Perkins Company and the Archer Company of Boston, the Jones Oakford Company of Philadelphia, and the Thomas Smith Company of New York.

Cotton was the bulk commodity exported by the United States to China, and the mainstay of Sino-US trade. For example, in 1792, the value of cotton exported by the United States to Guangzhou reached 54,120 taels, accounting for 49.74% of the total value (108,816 taels) of commodities exported by the United States to Guangzhou in that year. In the early 19th century, American cotton exports increased continuously. From 1804 to 1805, Guangzhou imported 4,219 piculs of American cotton; from 1819 to 1820, the import volume increased to 19,354 piculs.

The second largest commodity was fur. American merchants mainly sold in Guangzhou American Indians' otter skin and seal skin from South Pacific Islands. From 1804 to 1805, 269,756 pelts were imported to Guangzhou by American merchants. From 1804/1805 to 1828/1829, the amount of fur imported varied, with the highest quantity being 477,300 pelts in 1821–1822. Other goods shipped to China and trafficked by American merchants included American ginseng, mercury, sandalwood, silver currency, and opium.

The commodities that the Americans exported from Guangzhou included tea leaves, silk and satin, silk thread, raw silk, porcelain, nankeen cloth, mercury, cinnamon and sugar. Among them, tea leaves were a bulk commodity, the demand for which grew rapidly. For example, in 1784–1785, the export volume of Chinese tea to the United States was only 880,100 pounds; in 1795–1796, it rose to 2,819,600 pounds; while in 1805–1806, it further climbed to 9,830,480 pounds; in 1818–1819, it reached 12,035,280 pounds; during 1836–1837, it achieved a figure of 16,942,122 pounds. In the 53 years from 1784 to 1837, the volume of tea multiplied by more than 18 times, accounting for about half of the total export value of the United States from Guangzhou.

The second most popular export was of silk and satin, which accounted for only 29,385 bolts (*pi*) in 1804–1805, growing to 291,396

---

[31] *Ibid.*

bolts in 1818–1819, and further increasing to 421,136 bolts in 1827–1828, accounting for about 20% of China's total exports to the United States during that period.

During this period, the US trade with China was actually operated trilaterally. In the first instance, American merchant ships carried their domestic products to Europe for sale, taking the Spanish silver dollars they earned back to America. Then they brought this currency to Guangzhou to buy the Chinese goods they needed. In the second instance, American merchant ships carried out transshipment trade among various European ports, and then sailed to Guangzhou after having made enough Spanish silver dollars. Once Chinese tea leaves, silk, *nankeen* cloth and other goods from Guangzhou had been purchased, they set out to return home.

American imports from China were not just obtained to meet domestic demands. Most of the cargoes were transferred to other countries. For example, Chinese tea leaves imported by the United States were often transported to the Netherlands, Germany, France, Brazil and elsewhere.

In this period, China always maintained a balance of surplus in Sino-US trade. In order to make up for the trade deficit, American merchant ships often carried a large amount of silver to China. During the 25 years from 1804 to 1829, American silver inundated China almost every year, with the peak amount of 7,369,000 *yuan* being reached in 1818–1819. In 1824, the largest trader in New York exported 1,311,057 *yuan* to China, of which 900,000 *yuan* were silver, accounting for 68.64% of the total.[32]

After 1826, on the one hand, the United States began to transship British cotton; on the other hand, they followed the United Kingdom to smuggle opium to China on a large scale. Subsequently, the total amount of US silver reaching China decreased significantly. According to statistics, from 1805 to 1829, 3,757 piculs of opium were smuggled into Guangzhou by the United States, of which 1,256 piculs were smuggled in 1828–1829 alone.[33]

Opium smuggling to China greatly improved the US trade deficit with China. Thomas Pushkin, a Boston merchant, once said the "although our imports of Chinese products with silk and *nankeen* cloth as bulk

---

[32] Yao Xianhao. *Historical Materials of Modern Chinese Foreign Trade*. Vol. 1. Beijing: Zhonghua Book Company, 1962.

[33] *Ibid.*

commodities for several years had averaged over 1 million *yuan* per year, we did not ship a single Spanish silver dollar to China in the past few years. Our fund came from Turkish-exported opium, and British-made commodities ..."[34]

American merchants made huge profits through trade with China, which constituted an important portion of the primitive capital accumulation in the early period of the United States.

5. Russia

As early as the years before the 17th century, China and Russia developed indirect trade through the Central Asian caravan. After the 17th century, with the expansion of Russia, Russia and China became neighbors, which made the direct trade between the two sides grow in scale. In 1656, Russia sent the Baikoff mission to discuss trade affairs with the Chinese. The Qing government integrated Russia into the tributary trade system and allowed it to trade with China by land route.

In 1689, China and Russia signed *the Treaty of Nerchinsk*, which stipulated that "all people of the two countries who hold passports could cross the border and be allowed to exchange and trade with each other." Since then, Russia sent official caravans to China for trade. In order to monopolize trade interests, the Russian government prohibited private merchants from coming to China. The mode of trade between the two sides was practiced mainly in the manner of bartering. The chief goods sent by Russia were fur and a small number of printed products. The goods China sent to Russia included porcelain, silk, rhubarb, etc. In addition to the trade caravans to Beijing, Chinese and Russian merchants also traded in border areas, like Kulun and Qiqihar.

Due to the continuous territorial expansion of Russia, Sino-Russian trade was constantly affected by the border conflicts between the two countries. In 1727, China and Russia signed *the Treaty of Kiakhtu*, which clearly specified the border (mid-section) between the two countries, as well as the mutual relationship in terms of politics, economy, religion and other aspects. On this basis, Russia had obtained the right of free trade in Beijing and Kiakhtu. In 1762, Russia canceled the monopoly on fur and did not send caravans to Beijing. The Kiakhtu trade between China and Russia became the main form of trade. With Russia advancing toward industrialization, the proportion of fur exported inevitably declined, and

---

[34] *Ibid.*

industrial products, such as cotton cloth and woolen goods, began to increase. As tea drinking was very popular in Russia grew, the amount of tea leaves imported from China increased constantly.

In addition, the trade between China and the Netherlands, Denmark, and Sweden also persisted on a certain scale during the early Qing Dynasty.

8.5 Major Import & Export Commodities and Silver Circulation

With the expansion of trade scale between China and western countries, the composition of import and export commodities in the early Qing Dynasty also changed significantly. Before the mid-18th century, imports to China were still mainly luxury items, while the greatest exports were tea leaves, raw silk and other local products. From the mid-18th century on with the increased competitiveness of western industrial products and the contraband trading of opium into China, the composition of China's imports altered. Cotton, *nankeen* cloth and opium were now the bulk commodities. Exports were still dominated by tea leaves and silk. The export of nankeen cloth rose markedly, too. With the reversal of China's foreign trade balance, China experienced a process from importing silver to exporting silver.

8.5.1 *Major Import Commodities*

1. Woolen Fabrics
Woolen fabrics were the main commodity imported from Britain at the inception of Sino-Britain trade. However, due to its high price and poor practicability, it was difficult to find the market in China. For example, from 1775 to 1779, the average annual value of woolen fabrics imported into China by British East India Company was only 277,000 taels. After that, the British East India Company tried its best to expand the sale volumes of woolen fabrics in China by various promotional measures, even reducing price. From 1790 to 1794, the volume of traded woolen products increased to more than 1.5 million taels per year. From 1820 to 1824, the volume rose to in excess of 2 million taels per year.[35] But on the eve of

---

[35] Yan Zhongping *et al. Selected Statistical Data of Modern Economic History in China.* Beijing: Science Press, 1955.

the Opium Wars, with progress being made in the British cotton textile industry, the import of wool fabrics fell gradually, so that it now ranked third behind cotton (including cotton cloth) and yarn.

2. Cotton

Cotton was a new commodity imported in the Qing Dynasty before the Opium Wars. In order to meet the demands of China's *nankeen* cloth industry, as early as 1768, Indian cotton began to flow into China. During the first quarter of the 19th century, the annual average import volume of cotton from British and American merchant vessels to Guangzhou was nearly 240,000 piculs. From 1825 to 1833, the annual average import volume of cotton increased to 440,000 piculs.[36] During the two or three decades before the Opium War, cotton shot up to being the premier import commodity to China. Due to the huge scale of cotton production in India, Britain exerted its colonial prerogative to buy cotton at a predatory low price and then sold it to China for greater profits. This partially eliminated its trade deficit with China. In addition to the British East India Company, individual British and Indian merchants in Guangzhou as well as American merchants were also engaged in the import of Chinese cotton.

3. Cotton Cloth and Cotton Yarn

Cotton cloth and cotton yarn were also newly-imported commodities before the Opium Wars. Both were mainly imported from the United Kingdom and the United States. The imports from UK mainly consisted of cotton yarn, calico and natural colored foreign cloth; while those from the United States were mainly coarse cloth, damask, and natural colored foreign cloth. Before the Opium Wars, the import of cotton cloth and cotton yarn reached over 2 million taels per year,[37] ranking second only to raw cotton.

4. Narcotic Drugs — Opium

In order to reverse the trade deficit with China and seize huge profits, Britain and the United States initiated a crazy large-scale opium smuggling trade with China in the late 18th century. The amount of opium exported to

---

[36] *Ibid.*

[37] Yao Xianhao. *Historical Materials of Modern Chinese Foreign Trade.* Vol. 1. Beijing: Zhonghua Book Company, 1962.

China by western merchants multiplied. According to statistics, from 1795 to 1798, 1,814 crates of opium were exported to China by Western merchants; from 1798 to 1800, there were 4,113 crates; from 1800 to 1811, there were 4,016 crates per year; from 1811 to 1821, there were 4,494 crates per year; from 1821 to 1828, there were 8,708 crates per year; from 1835 to 1839, there were 35,445 crates per year. In the 44 years from 1795 to 1839, 358,763 crates of opium were imported into China, with an astonishing average of 8,153 crates each year.[38]

Among western countries, Britain ranked as China's main supplier of opium, and gained huge profits. According to statistics, from 1773 to 1839, the revenue of the British government from opium followed a constant upward trend. From 1773 to 1774, the revenue was only 77,894 taels; from 1825 to 1829, it grew to 5,744,286 taels annually. If the annual average index of 1815–1819 was 100, the annual average index of 1825–1829 would rocket to 244.3. From 1809 to 1828, the proportion of income from opium among Bangladesh's total revenue also expanded year by year. From 1809 to 1810, this accounted for 8% of the total revenue; from 1827 to 1828, it had increased to 12%.[39] Therefore, the British maintained that "this export business was too profitable for our Indian colonies to give up easily."[40]

The volume of illicit opium smuggled by the United States was second only to that of the United Kingdom. By 1805, the United States had already sold Turkish opium to China. In 1817, American merchants sold Persian opium to China. By 1821, the United States was involved in the trade of Indian opium. According to incomplete statistics, from 1805 to 1837, the United States smuggled 9,644 crates of opium into China.[41] In fact, this data was underestimated, though, being far from the actual amount.

---

[38] *Ibid.* From 1795 to 1838, China's opium import was estimated to be 451,260 crates, with an average annual average of more than 10,494 crates, according *to the Selected Statistical Data of China's Modern Economic History. Also see* Yan Zhongping *et al. Selected statistical data of Modern Economic History in China.* Beijing: Science Press, 1955.

[39] Yan Zhongping *et al. Selected statistical data of Modern Economic History in China.* Beijing: Science Press, 1955.

[40] (U.K.) John Elliot Bingham. *Narrative of the Expedition to China, from the Commencement of the War to Its Termination in 1842* [M]. London: Henry Colburn Publisher, 2004.

[41] (U.S.) Hosea Ballou Morse. *The Chronicles of the East India Company Trading to China 1635–1834* [M]. Oxford: The Clarendon Press, 1926.

As a later American scholar remarked, "at that time, the relationship between Americans and the opium trade was much deeper than any statistics indicated. Opium sales were increasing, so Americans, like the British and other foreigners, paid their return cargo by bill of exchange from opium trade instead of cash or silver. Where the opium trade was concerned, Americans merchants earned more profits than any others... The opium trade, like slaves and wineries, became the basis of many of America's great assets."[42] Most of the American firms in Guangzhou sold opium as business. Among them, the main ones were Perkins & Co and Russell & Co.

8.5.2 *Major Export Commodities*

1. Tea Leaves
Before the Opium Wars, tea leaves were one of the main export commodities, ranking first in export trade. As early as the mid-16th century, the Portuguese had shipped Chinese tea to Europe. At the end of the 16th century, the Dutch also bought tea from Southeast Asian Chinese merchants. By the mid-17th century, Chinese tea was directly imported into Britain, which led to the rise of tea drinking there. Before the Opium Wars, the export volume of tea leaves ranked first among the traded commodities in Guangzhou.

In 1817, the export value of tea leaves reached 10,707,017 silver dollars, accounting for 55% of the total export value; in 1825, the export value of tea leaves was 13,572,892, equaling 51% of the total export value; in 1832, the number was 15,241,712, accounting for 58% of the total.[43]

According to the statistics, the volume of Chinese tea leaves exported by the East India Company grew exponentially. From 1760 to 1764, the annual average export volume was 42,065 piculs; from 1785 to 1789, it rose to 138,417 piculs; from 1800 to 1804, the annual average export volume expanded to 221,027 piculs; from 1825 to 1829, it increased to 244,704 piculs. If the annual average index from 1780 to

---

[42](U.S.) Tyler Dennett. *Americans in Eastern Asia* [M]. New York: The Macmillan Company, 1941.

[43]Yao Xianhao. *Historical Materials of Modern Chinese Foreign Trade*. Vol. 1. Beijing: Chinese Publishing House, 1962.

1784 was 100, the annual average index of 1800–1804 would be 397.6, and 440.2 from 1825 to 1829.[44] From the 1760s to the 1820s, the proportion of tea leaves in the total output value of British East India Company from China increased from 73.7% to 94.1%.

It could be seen that before the Opium Wars, the major export from China to Britain was Chinese tea leaves, from which the British East India Company gained high profits. The British government obtained huge financial revenue from the collection of import taxes.

2. Raw Silk and Silks & Satins
Silk fabrics were a traditional export commodity of China. Before the Opium Wars, they were still the main export commodity to East Asia, Southeast Asia and Europe. At that time, the British East India Company began to trade raw silk in China. From 1760 to 1764, the annual average trade value was 3,749 taels, accounting for only 0.4% of the company's total export value from China.

In 1764, the Qing government relaxed the restrictions on raw silk exports, causing the expansion of trade of Chinese raw silk run by the British East India Company. From 1770 to 1774, the annual trade value increased to 358,242 taels of silver, accounting for 25.3% of the company's total imports from China; from 1775 to 1779, it climbed to 455,376 taels of silver, accounting for 37.7%; from 1780 to 1784, the annual trade value was 376,964 taels, accounting for 23.1%. From 1785 to 1789, the annual trade value of raw silk grew to over 500,000 taels of silver, but the proportion of raw silk in the company's total exports from China declined to only 11.7%, due to the growth of the tea leaves trade.[45]

3. *Nankeen* Cloth
The export of *nankeen* cloth began in the 1730s. In 1736, China's *nankeen* cloth began to be exported to Britain, with its export value increasing year by year. From 1760 to 1764, the annual average export value was only 204 taels of silver, taking up 0.1% of the total export value of the British East India Company from China; from 1785 to 1789, it multiplied to 19,533 taels of silver, taking up 0.4%; from 1817 to 1819, it expanded to

---

[44] Yan Zhongping *et al. Selected Statistical Data of Modern Economic History in China.* Beijing: Science Press, 1955.
[45] *Ibid.*

121,466 taels of silver, accounting for 2.4%.[46] After 1825, British cotton cloth began to be exported to China, so the East India Company exported less and less *nankeen* cloth and even stopped the trade. Before the Opium Wars, Chinese *nankeen* cloth was not only exported to Britain, but to Denmark, Sweden, Netherlands, France and other European countries, as well as the United States.

8.5.3 *The Influx and Outflow of Silver*

Over the 18th century, China continued to enjoy a healthy long-term surplus in its trade with western countries. At that time, all countries needed to carry a large amount of silver to trade in China. According to statistics, during the entirety of the 18th century, Britain exported 208.9 million silver dollars into China to obtain Chinese goods.[47] During the 51 years from 1700 to 1751, the amount of silver directed from western European countries to China totaled 68,073,182 *yuan*, with an annual average of 1,334,768 *yuan*.[48] In the early 19th century, western silver continued to flow into China from 1800 to 1827, with the exceptions being the periods 1809–1810 and 1818–1819. During the 25 years from 1804 to 1829, the net inflow of silver amounted to 49,513,297 taels of silver, or about 68,328,349 *yuan*, with an annual average of 273,134 *yuan*.[49]

Before the Opium Wars, China always kept a surplus in the legal trade. With the surge of opium imports, China's foreign trade gradually shifted from surplus to deficit. From 1827, China's balance of payments slipped into deficit, and its silver began to bleed out. In 1833–1834, the net outflow value of silver reached 4,340,589 taels — about 5,990,012 silver dollars — or 4.49 times of the annual average value of 1,334,768 silver dollars Western European countries imported into China in the first half of the 18th century. The outflow of silver

---

[46]Yan Zhongping *et al. Selected Data of Modern Economic History in China.* Beijing: Science Press, 1955.

[47]Qian Jiaju. *The Dissolution of the East India Company and the Opium Wars*. Journal of Tsinghua University. Vol. 37.

[48]Yu Jieqiong. *An Estimate of China's Silver Exports and Imports from 1700 to 1937*. Beijing: The Commercial Press, 1940.

[49]Yan Zhongping *et al. Selected Data of Modern Economic History in China.* Beijing: Science Press, 1955.

aggravated the social crisis of the Qing Dynasty, causing a series of conflicts, and further deteriorating the developmental environment of China's foreign trade.

8.6 Foreign Trade and Economic & Cultural Communication with Foreign Countries

During the early Qing Dynasty, with the development of trade between China and western countries, global trade expanded. Sino-foreign economic and cultural exchanges were operated across more extensive regions in a more diversified manner and with more substantial content.

8.6.1 *Exporting China's Handicraft Technology*

As was mentioned previously, during this period, China's bulk exports were predominantly raw silk, tea and porcelain, and the country occupied a position of monopoly in their international market. With the development of trade, the production technology of these commodities spread all over the world in various ways.

From the 17th century on with extensive trade between China and Europe, exquisite Chinese porcelain found favor in Europe and was exported there in considerable quantities. "During the eighty years within the 17th century, the Dutch East India Company alone transported 16 million pieces of Chinese porcelain from Jingdezhen and other places. From 1729 to 1794, the Dutch East India Company alone shipped 43 million pieces of porcelain from Jingdezhen and other places in China. From 1750 to 1755, the Swedish East India Company with ordinary national power in Europe imported 11 million pieces of China porcelain."[50] The popularity of Chinese porcelain had aroused competition among European countries which wished to imitate it. However, owing to the lack of systematic understanding of Chinese porcelain-manufacturing technology, Europe was unable to produce sufficiently hard porcelain for a long time.

In the early 18th century, Francois Xavier d'Entrecolles, one of the first French Jesuits to China, came to Jiangxi to preach. Besides preaching, Francois Xavier d'Entrecolles also worked for the French Science

---

[50]Liu Changbing. *Jingdezhen Porcelain Industry under the Influence of Overseas Porcelain Trade*. Cultural Relics in Southern China, 2005 (3).

Academy, studying Chinese science and technology. He visited porcelain workshops, consulted porcelain makers and found other ways to further investigate the porcelain-manufacturing techniques in Jingdezhen. "Besides what I myself have seen, I have learned a great many particulars from my neophytes, several of whom work in porcelain, while others do a great trade in it. I also confirmed the truth of the information given me through studying the Chinese books on the subject, so that I believe I have obtained a pretty exact knowledge of all that concerns this beautiful art, so that I can talk about it with some confidence."[51]

In 1712, Francois Xavier d'Entrecolles brought Jingdezhen's porcelain-making skills, like mold-making, glazing and firing techniques, back to Europe by means of his letter. In addition, he also posted *baibuzi*, the raw materials used in Jingdezhen in porcelain-making, and soil samples in Gaoling to Europe.[52] In this way, Europe mastered the systematic and comprehensive porcelain-manufacturing technology of China, and developed it creatively on this basis. By the late 18th century, the porcelain products of Germany, France, Britain and other countries gradually showed their own characteristics and artistic styles, and also surpassed the quality of Chinese porcelain, which began to be marginalized in the European market.

In 1792, Guangzhou exported a total of 7,490,524 taels of goods, of which the value of the porcelain was 44,230 taels, accounting for only 0.59% of the total.[53] According to the business records of the East India Company, the British East India Company stopped importing Chinese porcelain entirely in 1801 due to the sharp drop in profits from those wares.[54]

At the same time, the export of Chinese porcelain to America also stimulated the development of the local porcelain industry. By the 18th century, Mexico had opened dozens of porcelain kilns employing Chinese craftsmen.

---

[51] Lettres édifiantes et curieuses. *écrites des missions étrangères, Mémoires de la Chine.* Elephant Publishing House, 2001.

[52] Hong Xiuming. How China's Gaoling Became Famed and What Contributions Francois Xavier d'Entrecolles has Made [J] Chinese Ceramics, 2006 (1).

[53] Hosea Ballou Morse. *The Chronicles of the East India Company Trading to China: 1635–1834*, Trans. Qu Zonghua. Sun Yat-sen University Press, 1991.

[54] *Ibid.*

In addition, Chinese tea leaves, citrus, cherry, and other spices were introduced to the Americas through European merchants.

8.6.2 *Importing Western Natural Science and Production Technology*

The change in China's dynasties which did nothing to curtail the spread of Western learning by missionaries begun in the late Ming Dynasty. At the beginning of the Qing Dynasty, the Jesuit Johann Adam Schall von Bell was appointed as an official in the Imperial Board of Astronomy. In 1645, the Qing Court promulgated the *Shi xian li* (calendar) compiled by him. During the reign of Emperor Kangxi, western astronomy was further disseminated in China, and the Chinese calendar was being constantly revised and improved on the basis of absorbing western astronomy.

During the reign of Emperor Kangxi, importance was attached to western mathematics due to the Emperor's support. The Qing Court set up a department bureau, a place within the imperial palace designated for the study of this subject. Under the auspices of Emperor Kangxi, an encyclopedia of western mathematics, the *Essence of Mathematics*, was compiled through joint efforts of Chinese and foreign scholars.

During the early Qing Dynasty, western geographical wisdom continued to spread to the East. The introduction of western works on geography into China enhanced the native understanding of the world. Meanwhile, the western method of mapmaking improved traditional cartography. In 1718, Chinese and foreign scholars participated in the drawing of the national map of the Great Qing Dynasty — *Emperor Kangxi's Nationwide Map*.

As Europe continuously imitated China's porcelain, the Chinese upper classes developed a strong demand for new items imported from Europe, such as the European striking clock, and frosted glassware. Guangzhou kept pace with this fad, opening a number of workshops which imitated western artifacts. The European striking clock, with its exquisite designs and sumptuous decorations, was imported to China as early as the Ming Dynasty. In the early Qing era, Guangzhou, Suzhou, Beijing were replete with Chinese craftsmen producing their own imitation striking clocks.

In 1749, Emperor Qianlong issued a decree to the Governor of Guangdong and Guangxi that "clocks and foreign that were presented previously to the imperial palace were imitations. When more clocks, foreign lacquerware, gold and silver wire forging, carpets, etc., were to be imported, only foreign-made ones were allowed."[55] This indicated that the imitations at that time still seemed inferior to the originals from Europe. In 1696, Emperor Kangxi ordered a glass foundry to be set up in the Hall of Mental Cultivation. Cheng Xianggui, Zhou Jun and other craftsmen from the glass workshops in "Thirteen Factories" were summoned to the palace to engage in this work. They produced a new type of glassware, combining the European ground glass technique together with Chinese aesthetics.

During the early Qing Dynasty, under the policy of stringent restriction, foreign trade was limited to Guangzhou and other southeastern coastal areas, and its development was greatly curtailed. However, in the global trade tide dominated by European and American countries, China became passively involved in a deeper and wider international trade market. The development of trade inevitably promoted the economic and cultural exchanges between China and foreign countries. Natural science assisted the development of the agricultural economy; western utensils met the need for luxury among the upper class in society, and manufacturing technology found favor among the feudal rulers.

However, as the authorities were blinkered in their mindset and felt that the Chinese society was self-sufficient, the introduction of western natural science and production technologies was felt in only a few fields and spread to an extremely limited area. As such their arrival yielded neither large-scale, influential industries, nor played a role in the progress of the macro-economy.

In conclusion, from the 16th century, with the breakthrough of regional trade, China further developed its economic exchanges with Europe and the Americas. Prior to the Opium Wars, the trade between China and Europe was in its preliminary stage of development, and the European trade with China bore the complexion of colonial plunder. From a global perspective, trade activities with the Pacific Coast and the Atlantic Coast were developed. With European countries as their

---

[55] The First Historical Archives of China, Art Museum of the Chinese University of Hong Kong. *Archives of the Imperial Workshops of the Imperial Household Department of the Qing Dynasty*. Vol. 17. People's Publishing House, 2005.

intermediary, communications were initiated between Asia and the Americas, facilitating trade between the eastern and western hemispheres on a global scale. Meanwhile, conflicts between countries having different cultures and different economic forms were aggravated continuously, making China's independent feudal foreign trade begin to turn precarious.

Index